The Management and Control of Quality

The Management and Control of Quality

JAMES R. EVANS
University of Cincinnati

WILLIAM M. LINDSAY
Northern Kentucky University

WEST PUBLISHING COMPANY
Minneapolis/St. Paul   New York   Los Angeles   San Francisco

Copyediting: Lorretta Palagi
Text Design: LightSource Images
Artwork: Miyake Illustration
Composition: The Clarinda Company
Indexing: Schroeder Indexing Services

WEST'S COMMITMENT TO THE ENVIRONMENT

In 1906, West Publishing Company began recycling materials left over from the production of books. This began a tradition of efficient and responsible use of resources. Today, up to 95 percent of our legal books and 70 percent of our college texts are printed on recycled, acid-free stock. West also recycles nearly 22 million pounds of scrap paper annually—the equivalent of 181,717 trees. Since the 1960s, West has devised ways to capture and recycle waste inks, solvents, oils, and vapors created in the printing process. We also recycle plastics of all kinds, wood, glass, corrugated cardboard, and batteries, and have eliminated the use of styrofoam book packaging. We at West are proud of the longevity and the scope of our commitment to our environment.

Production, Prepress, Printing and Binding by West Publishing Company.

Library of Congress Cataloging-in-Publication Data

Evans, James R. (James Robert), 1950–
    The management and control of quality/James R. Evans,
William M. Lindsay.—2nd ed.
      p. cm.
    Includes bibliographical references and index.
    ISBN 0-314-00864-0 (hard)
    1. Production management—Quality control—Statistical methods.
2. Quality assurance.   I. Lindsay, William M.   II. Title.
TS156.E93   1993
658.5′62—dc20   92-16910
                             ∞   CIP

To Our Families

Contents in Brief

Contents

ix

Preface to the Second Edition

The changes in the quality profession over the last several years have been phenomenal. As we were completing the first edition of this book, the Malcolm Baldrige National Quality Award was only being signed into legislation; the first winners had not yet been announced by the time the book appeared in print. Terms such as "quality function deployment," "policy deployment," "kaizen," and "Taguchi's loss function" were not part of the vocabularies of most quality professionals. The last few years have witnessed a remarkable resurgence in interest in quality that has permeated business, the government, and educational institutions. We are fortunate and proud to have had the foresight to write a comprehensive textbook focused primarily on teaching quality within schools of business.

Today, the need to teach quality and integrate it into curricula is crucial to the survival of the modern business school. This edition represents a substantial revision and expansion of our first edition to reflect the unprecedented growth of knowledge in the quality profession. While the basic structure of the book remains the same, the changes are too numerous to describe in detail. In essence, the book has been completely rewritten. Among the highlights of this edition are:

- Focus is expanded on managerial philosophies and techniques.

- New chapters are included on the quality management philosophies of Deming, Juran, and Crosby; total quality management (TQM), including an extensive discussion of the Malcolm Baldrige National Quality Award; quality improvement and problem solving, with practical examples of quality problem-solving tools; human resource management with a TQM focus; and sampling techniques.

- Extensive revisions have been made to every other chapter to reflect new concepts and practices. New topics include the expanded role of quality in the service sector, the Taguchi loss function, activity-based costing, benchmarking, quality function deployment, policy deployment, materials control and just-in-time, quality audits, the Deming cycle and Juran's breakthrough sequence, statistical distribution assumption testing, ISO 9000 inspection standards, measurement repeatability and reproducibility studies, design for manufacturability, the Taguchi philosophy in product and process design, design for services, ASQC charts for statistical process control, detailed interpretation of control charts, sampling procedures in service applications, and many more.

- New Quality in Practice cases are provided, and all QIPs have been moved to the end of chapters with added discussion questions.

- New end-of-chapter summaries of key points, many new questions and problems, and selected answers to problems are provided.

- Minicases at the end of most chapters allow for more extensive analysis and problem solving.

- A Baldrige Award examiner training case has been included in the Instructor's Manual for student project work. The complete solution and suggested teaching approaches for this case are also included.

ORGANIZATION

The book is divided into five parts. Part 1, The Quality System, deals with the fundamental nature of quality, its strategic importance in business and industry, and the economic impacts of quality. In Part 2, The Management System, we develop the foundation of modern quality practices through the philosophies of Deming, Juran, and Crosby; total quality management and the Baldrige Award; planning for customer satisfaction; organization; control; quality improvement and problem solving; human resource management; and employee involvement. The remaining chapters deal with the technical system. In Part 3, The Technical System: Quality Measurement, we review fundamental statistical principles and techniques necessary for the analysis and interpretation of quality data and discuss the role of inspection and measurement. Part 4, The Technical System: Quality of Design and Performance, deals with issues in product and process design for manufacturability as well as reliability of products and processes. Part 5, The Technical System: Quality of Conformance, provides a solid foundation in the development and use of control charts and sampling techniques in quality control.

Because the material is comprehensive, it cannot be covered in one semester or quarter. The book is designed to serve two audiences, both of which we have taught while writing it: technically oriented undergraduate students in industrial and operations management and managerially oriented MBA students. We believe that undergraduate majors in industrial and operations management are best served by developing hands-on knowledge that they will be able to use in their entry-level jobs. Thus, a typical course for these students should probably be slanted toward the technical material, Chapters 11 through 17, with a solid introduction of selected material from Chapters 1 through 10, especially Chapters 1, 4, 7, and 8. For MBAs, a focused managerial course is more appropriate, with more emphasis placed on Chapters 1 through 10 and appropriate selections from the remaining chapters, especially Chapters 12, 13, and 15. The Baldrige case is a highly appropriate exercise for this audience. Thus, the instructor has virtually unlimited flexibility in using the book.

SOFTWARE SUPPLEMENT

A new stand-alone package, *The Quality Management Analyst,* is available for use with this edition. The disk and manual are provided in the Instructor's Manual. Adopters of this text have permission to copy and distribute the software and manual to their students during the terms the book is used. The software includes modules for

- statistical analysis
- probability computations
- linear regression and scatter diagrams
- process capability analysis
- reliability computations
- control charts
- acceptance sampling
- pareto analysis.

In addition, *The Quality Management Analyst SPC Simulation* is included in the package to allow instructors to generate data sets for control chart analysis having specified characteristics. This is very useful for classroom illustrations and student projects.

INSTRUCTOR'S SUPPORT MATERIAL

An expanded Instructor's Manual has been developed for this edition. In addition to answers to questions and problems, we provide the Baldrige Award case and solution and *The Quality Management Analyst* software manual and disk. The test bank was prepared by Henry S. Maddux III.

ACKNOWLEDGMENTS

We are extremely grateful to the following reviewers who provided excellent feedback and suggestions for both the first and second editions:

David Lewis, University of Lowell

Russell Heikes, Georgia Institute of Technology

Brooke Saladin, Wake Forest University

Joseph Nachlas, Virginia Polytechnical Institution

Dan Bullard, Idaho State University

Maling Ebrahimpour, University of Rhode Island

Kathryn Plum, DeAnza College

Jeffrey Heyl, University of Colorado—Denver

It would be impossible to name all of the quality managers, students, colleagues, editors, and family members who have contributed to this book by sharing their information, criticism, guidance, and support. Suffice it to say that we owe a great debt to dozens of people who have influenced our thoughts. A special thanks goes to our editors at West: Richard Fenton, Esther Craig, and Brad Smith for their support and encouragement.

To paraphrase Tom Cruise in the movie *Risky Business:* "Quality—There Is No Substitute." We hope that you find this book a useful source of inspiration to improve all aspects of society and mankind.

James R. Evans
William M. Lindsay

PART ONE
The Quality System

EVER HEARD OF Globe Metallurgical? It's a small company, employing 210 people at plants in Beverly, Ohio, and Selma, Alabama. The company produces about 100,000 tons of ferroalloys and silicon metal for more than 300 customers. With the decline of the automobile and steel industries in the early 1980s, and a glut of low-priced imported material from Brazil, Argentina, and Canada, Globe lost millions of dollars annually. At Beverly, only two of the five furnaces were operating and more than a third of the work force was laid off. In 1985, 44 customer complaints resulted in the return of 49,000 pounds of product. By 1987, however, customer complaints had decreased by 91%, to just 4, and no product was returned. The employee accident rate decreased while the industry average increased. Absenteeism dropped; in 1987 one plant reported only four days of absenteeism for 135 employees. Annual sales were projected to increase by 30% during 1988. How did they do it? By aiming their sights at becoming the lowest cost, highest quality producer in the world. Just about every professional in the quality field knows about Globe by now. In 1988, they were one of the first winners of the United States' highest quality award—the Malcolm Baldrige National Quality Award.

On June 8, 1987, the same year as Globe began to reap the benefits of its success, *Business Week* began a special report with the following statement:

> Quality. Remember it? American manufacturing has slumped a long way from the glory days of the 1950s and '60s when "Made in the U.S.A." proudly stood for the best that industry could turn out. . . . While the Japanese were developing remarkably higher standards for a whole host of products, from consumer electronics to cars and machine tools, many U.S. managers were smugly dozing at the switch. Now, aside from aerospace and agriculture, there are few

markets left where the U.S. carries its own weight in international trade. For American industry, the message is simple: Get better or get beat.[1]

Globe Metallurgical is one of only a handful of companies who proactively focused on quality improvement during the 1980s. Unfortunately, many others did not, as evidenced by the statements in *Business Week*. During the 1980s, the United States received a rude awakening on the importance of quality. Since then, the publicity surrounding quality improvements by Japanese manufacturers has made quality a subject of vital national importance. Quality has captured the attention of consumers, industrialists, and government officials alike. The quest for quality continues. A special issue of *Business Week* in October 1991 called quality "a global revolution affecting every facet of business. . . . For the 1990s and far beyond, quality must remain the priority for business."[2]

This section of the text introduces basic concepts of quality. Chapter 1 deals with the history, definition, and importance of quality in manufacturing and service organizations and lays the foundation for the organization of the book. Chapter 2 discusses the role of quality in manufacturing and service systems. Chapter 3 focuses on the economics of quality and the significant impact that quality has on profitability. These issues drive both management and technical decisions involving quality that we discuss throughout the remainder of the book.

---

[1]"The Push for Quality," *Business Week*, June 8, 1987, p. 131.
[2]"The Quality Imperative," *Business Week*, October 25, 1991, p. 7.

CHAPTER 1

Introduction to Quality

Managers of manufacturing and service organizations deal with a very critical issue: profitability. Productivity (the amount of output achieved per unit of input), the cost of operations, and the quality of the goods and services that are produced all contribute to profitability. Of these three determinants of profitability—productivity, cost, and quality—quality can be the most significant factor in determining the long-run success or failure of any organization. High quality of goods and services can give an organization a competitive edge; good quality reduces costs due to returns, rework, and scrap and increases productivity, profits, and other measures of success. Most importantly, good quality generates satisfied customers, who reward the organization with continued patronage and favorable word-of-mouth advertising. Quality has even become a focal point for industry-union cooperation. In working with Chrysler Corporation to improve quality, a UAW vice president succinctly stated the importance of quality: No quality, no sales. No sales, no profit. No profit, no jobs.

In this chapter we introduce the concept of quality. We discuss the history and importance of quality in business and ways in which quality is defined. Finally, we present a total quality system model that provides the organizational structure of this book.

THE HISTORY AND IMPORTANCE OF QUALITY

In a broad sense, **quality assurance** refers to any action directed toward providing consumers with products (goods and services) of appropriate quality. Quality assurance has been an important aspect of production operations throughout history.[1] Egyptian wall paintings from around 1450 B.C. show evidence of inspection and measurement activity. Stones in the pyramids were cut so precisely that it is impossible to put a knife blade between the blocks. The Egyptians' success was due

---

[1] Early history is reported in Delmer C. Dague, "Quality—Historical Perspective," *Quality Control in Manufacturing* (Warrendale, PA: Society of Automotive Engineers, February 1981); and L. P. Provost and C. L. Norman, "Variation Through the Ages," *Quality Progress,* December 1990, pp. 39–44; recent events are discussed in Nancy Karabatsos, "Quality in Transition, Part One: Account of the '80s," *Quality Progress,* December 1989, pp. 22–26.

to uniform methods and procedures and precise measuring devices. The Egyptians also entertained the idea of interchangeable bows and arrows. Since variation in materials, craftspeople, and tools existed, some method of quality control was necessary.

During the Middle Ages in Europe, the skilled craftsperson served both as manufacturer and inspector. Since the "manufacturer" dealt directly with the customer, considerable pride in workmanship existed. Craft guilds, consisting of masters, journeymen, and apprentices, emerged to ensure that craftspeople were adequately trained. Every effort was made to ensure that quality was built into the final product. These themes are important foundations of modern quality assurance efforts.

During the middle of the eighteenth century, a French gunsmith, Honore Le Blanc, developed a system for manufacturing muskets to a standard pattern using interchangeable parts. Thomas Jefferson brought the idea to America, and in 1798 the government awarded Eli Whitney a contract to supply 10,000 muskets to the government in two years. The use of interchangeable parts necessitated careful control of quality. While a customized product built by a craftsperson can be tweaked and hammered to fit and work correctly, random matching of mating parts provides no such assurance. The parts must be produced according to a carefully designed standard. Whitney designed special machine tools and trained unskilled workmen to make parts to a fixed design that were measured and compared to a model. However, Whitney underestimated the effect of variation in production processes (the *same* obstacle that continues to plague American managers to this day). Because of the resulting problems, it took more than 10 years to complete the project. However, the concept of interchangeable parts eventually led to the industrial revolution, and made quality assurance a critical component of the production process.

In the early 1900s, the work of Frederick W. Taylor, the Father of Scientific Management, led to a new philosophy of production. By decomposing a job into individual work tasks, inspection tasks were separated from production tasks, which led to the creation of a separate quality department in production organizations.

The Bell Telephone System was the leader in the early modern history of quality control.[2] An inspection department was created in the Western Electric Company in the early 1900s to support the Bell Operating Companies. Quality assurance was applied to design, manufacturing, and installation.

In the 1920s, employees of the inspection department of Western Electric were transferred to Bell Telephone Laboratories. The duties of this group included the development of new theories and methods of inspection to improve and maintain quality. The early pioneers of quality assurance—Walter Shewhart, Harold Dodge, George Edwards, and others—were members of this group. It was here that the term "quality assurance" was coined. The development of control charts by Shewhart, sampling techniques by Dodge, and economic analysis techniques for quality problem solving laid the foundation for modern quality assurance.

During World War II, the U.S. military began using statistical sampling procedures and imposing strict standards on suppliers. Thus, statistical quality control became widely known and gradually adopted by other industries. Sampling tables labeled "MIL-STD" for "military standard" were developed and are still widely used

---

[2]M. D. Fagan, ed., *A History of Engineering and Science in the Bell System, the Early Years (1875–1925)* (New York: Bell Telephone Laboratories, 1974).

today. In 1944, *Industrial Quality Control* was first published, and professional societies, notably the American Society for Quality Control, were founded soon after.

During the 1950s two noted American consultants, Drs. Joseph Juran and W. Edwards Deming, introduced statistical quality control techniques to the Japanese during Japan's rebuilding period. Improvements in Japanese quality did not occur overnight; some 20 years passed before the quality of Japanese products exceeded that of Western manufacturers. While the Japanese were improving quality and their methods of quality assurance, quality levels in the West remained stagnant. During the 1970s, Japanese companies made significant penetration into Western markets, primarily due to the higher quality levels of their products.

The decade of the 1980s was a period of remarkable change and awareness of quality by consumers, industry, and government. Consumers began to notice a difference in quality between Japanese and American-made products. One of the more startling facts was reported in 1980 by Hewlett-Packard. After testing 300,000 16K RAM chips from three U.S. and three Japanese manufacturers, Hewlett-Packard found that the Japanese chips had an incoming failure rate of zero compared to rates of 11 and 19 failures per 1,000 for the U.S. chips. After 1,000 hours of use, the failure rate of the U.S. chips was up to 27 times higher. In a few short years, the Japanese had penetrated a major market that had been dominated by American companies.

Extensive product recalls mandated by the Consumer Product Safety Commission in the early 1980s and the *Challenger* space shuttle disaster in 1986 increased awareness of our quality gap with the Japanese. In 1980 NBC aired a white paper entitled "If Japan Can . . . Why Can't We?" Because this program revealed his key role in the development of Japanese quality, the name of W. Edwards Deming became a household word among corporate executives. He then led U.S. companies, such as Ford Motor Company, in a concerted effort to revolutionize their approach to quality.

In 1985, NASA announced an Excellence Award for Quality and Productivity. The goal of total quality excellence has been identified by top managers and promoted throughout industry as one of the keys to worldwide competitiveness.[3] Most major companies embarked on extensive quality improvement campaigns. In 1984, the U.S. government designated October as National Quality Month. In 1987, the Malcolm Baldrige National Quality Award, a statement of our national intent to provide quality leadership, was established by an act of Congress. By the end of the decade, Florida Power and Light became the first overseas company to win Japan's coveted Deming Prize for quality. The emphasis on quality has shifted from a purely technical methodology of inspection, sampling, and control to a managerial obsession that affects every employee.

However, not every company has developed an obsession with quality, and the implications for competitiveness are startling. A recent study by Ernst and Young and the American Quality Foundation found that while 55% of U.S. firms use quality information to evaluate business performance monthly or more frequently, 70% of Japanese firms do.[4] Eighteen percent of U.S. businesses look at the business consequences of quality performance less than once each year; the comparable figure in Japan is 2%, and in Germany, 9%. Financial and sales reviews occur much more frequently in the United States. Quality must be integrated with traditional

[3]"Manufacturing Tops List of Concerns Among Executives," *Industrial Engineering,* June 1990, p. 8.
[4]*International Quality Study: Top Line Findings,* American Quality Foundation and Ernst & Young, 1991.

management practices if any business is to be competitive in today's global marketplace.

Quality Awareness

On examining the historical developments in quality, we can point to four significant influences that affect attitudes on quality: consumer awareness, improvements in technology—especially in electronics, inadequate managerial philosophies and practices, and the economic impact on national competitiveness.

Quality begins with the consumer. During the 1950s and 1960s when "made in Japan" was associated with inferior products, consumers purchased domestic goods and accepted their quality without question. During the 1970s, however, the increase in foreign competition and the development of higher quality foreign products led consumers to examine more carefully their purchasing decisions. Consumers began to expect and demand high quality and reliability in goods and services at a fair price. They began to demand that products function properly and not break or fail under reasonable use, and courts of law supported this view. This increased focus on consumerism, strengthened by the activities of Ralph Nader and various consumer interest groups, has affected the operations of nearly every manufacturing and service organization. Consumers are more apt now than ever before to compare, evaluate, and choose products critically for total value—quality, price, and serviceability. Magazines such as *Consumer Reports* and newspaper reviews make this task much easier.

This growth in consumer quality awareness has put a greater strain on business. The more technologically complex a product, the more likely something will go wrong. Government safety regulations, product recalls, and the rapid increase in product liability judgments have changed society's attitude from "let the buyer beware" to "let the producer beware." Industry has realized that increased attentiveness to quality is vital to survival. Even nonprofit institutions such as hospitals and schools are looking more closely at quality. Liability issues involving medical and professional malpractice have caused considerable concern in nonprofit organizations.

Consumer demands and dynamic technological changes have opened up new and highly competitive markets. The quality of goods and services can no longer be taken for granted. Even industries that previously enjoyed a monopoly over domestic demand now must deal with foreign competition. The quality of goods produced worldwide has dramatically improved, particularly in Japan and Germany. For example, Garvin closely studied the production of room air conditioners in the United States and Japan.[5] Among his findings were the statistics that showed 63.5 assembly line defects per 100 units in the United States versus 0.95 in Japan, and 10.5 service calls per 100 units during the first year of warranty in the United States versus only 0.6 in Japan.

The automobile industry is another, more publicized, example. The June 8, 1987, *Business Week* special report on quality noted that the number of problems reported per 100 cars in the first 60 to 90 days of ownership of 1987 domestic models averaged

---

[5]David A. Garvin, "Quality on the Line," *Harvard Business Review,* September/October 1983, pp. 66–75. Copyright © 1983 by the President and Fellows of Harvard College; all rights reserved.

between 162 and 180. Comparable figures for Japanese and German automobiles were 129 and 152, respectively. Japan's efforts at improving its quality over several decades have resulted in Japanese automotive products gaining a significant share of the U.S. market. Only recently have domestic automakers taken a fresh look at quality. Efforts by Chrysler, General Motors, and Ford at retooling their manufacturing operations, developing new designs, and devising new promotional campaigns have all been focused around quality. Traditional manufacturing approaches to quality control were recognized to be inadequate and are now being replaced by improved managerial tools and techniques. In 1991, the industry average had dropped to 125 with domestic models averaging 136. Nevertheless, Japanese automobiles averaged only 105, and held seven of the top ten spots in the J.D. Power and Associates Survey. Ironically, the two key U.S. consultants, Deming and Juran, who helped educate the Japanese in quality management, finally won the respect of U.S. managers.

The rapid growth of the service sector has also introduced new perspectives for quality management. Institutions such as the government, banks, and hospitals do not produce tangible goods. The interaction between employees and customers is much more critical in such organizations. As a result, the skills, attitudes, and training of service personnel affect the quality of the service delivered.

Information processing represents a large component of the work done by service organizations and poses special quality considerations. Errors in computer billing or airline and hotel reservations are the result of poor quality control of computer software and data input systems. We shall see throughout the book that many of the same quality management and control techniques that apply to manufacturing can be used in service applications.

Finally, quality and productivity have become important issues at the national level. The economic health of a nation is dependent on the ability to produce high-quality products at a low cost. In recent years, the United States has lagged behind countries such as Japan and West Germany in productivity growth. For example, in the period from 1967 to 1974, Japan increased its productivity by 99.6%, West Germany by 43.3%, and the United States by only 29.25%. In 1984, productivity in the United States advanced only 1.6% and did not improve at all in 1985.[6] Increased productivity is a natural benefit of and is often associated with quality improvement.

Governments have begun to realize that quality is essential to international trade and the national economy.[7] For example, in July 1982, the British Department of Trade presented to Parliament a white paper entitled "Standards, Quality, and International Competitiveness." The paper formed the basis for Britain's National Quality Campaign and established an action plan to make the national standards system a more effective instrument to help improve quality and thus competitiveness. The government developed procedures for assisting firms to install quality assurance systems. A register of more than 5,000 manufacturers throughout the United Kingdom was published. This register provides potential buyers with a list of companies whose quality systems have been assessed to conform to British Standards Institute (BSI) criteria.

---

[6]*Business Week*, February 10, 1986, p. 22.

[7]Adapted from "Britain's National Campaign for Quality" by John Butcher, *Quality Progress,* Vol. 16, No. 11, November 1983, pp. 39–41.

Public purchasing authorities have been instructed to buy goods that conform to quality standards. The government also offers free consulting on quality assurance systems to factories with up to 1,000 employees, subsidies of up to 25% of the cost of implementing consulting recommendations for companies with 500 or fewer employees, and financial support for research aimed at improving BSI measurement and test specification standards. In summarizing the importance of quality to the British economic system, Margaret Thatcher is quoted as follows:

> Quality of design, production and marketing wins markets. Only satisfied customers will repeat orders and make British goods and services their first choice.
>
> Responsibility for achieving competitive quality rests squarely with top management. But everyone involved in industry must recognize that quality is their business too.
>
> The National Quality Campaign makes quality a national objective. The Government is contributing to this by offering practical help to firms, developing training and encouraging certification. The Government will also promote quality through its own purchasing decisions.
>
> I believe the drive for quality will appeal to the good sense of the British people. Pride in quality must become the hallmark of British enterprise. I hope the National Quality Campaign will receive the most enthusiastic and widespread support.

Recently, the European Economic Community has collectively established a common set of quality standards known as ISO 9000, which are described in a later chapter. The United States has also taken a serious view of the issue of quality. In 1983, the White House Conference on Productivity was held in Washington, D.C. Some 66 recommendations to improve quality and productivity were developed. Among them are the following:

- Target product and service quality as a principal objective of the organization. Integrate quality into the production and services processes rather than treating it as a separate management or inspection system.

- Make "doing it right the first time" a principle of management and learn how it improves productivity and profitability in the organization.

- Make certain that all employees (including managers) know that quality output will be the standard for evaluation and not just volume throughput.

- Measure and reward quality improvement at all levels of the organization.

- Develop strategies to guide and direct policies and procedures for quality improvement.

- Work with educational institutions to reestablish the concept and importance of quality and productivity among students who will be America's future employees and employers.

In 1984, the American Society for Quality Control (ASQC) designated October as the first Quality Month. This was followed by a Senate resolution designating it as National Quality Month. This has become an annual event, and publicity grows each year. Canada has also proclaimed October as National Quality Month. The most important commitment to quality that the U.S. government has made is the establishment of the Malcolm Baldrige National Quality Award. This will be discussed further in Chapter 5.

WHAT IS QUALITY?

Webster's New World Dictionary (Second College Edition) defines quality as "that which makes something what it is; characteristic element; basic nature, kind; the degree of excellence of a thing; excellence, superiority." This is not a practical definition, since it does not fully describe the many uses and understandings of quality in business and industry.

Official definitions of quality terminology were standardized in 1978 by the American National Standards Institute (ANSI) and ASQC.[8] Quality is defined as "the totality of features and characteristics of a product or service that bears on its ability to satisfy given needs." This definition implies that we must be able to identify the features and characteristics of products and services that relate to quality and form the basis for measurement and control. The "ability to satisfy given needs" reflects the value of the product or service to the customer, including the economic value as well as safety, reliability, and maintainability.

The automobile industry serves as a good example of applying this definition. In designing the Lexus automobile, Toyota bought several competitors' cars, including Mercedes, Jaguar, and BMW, and put them through grueling test-track runs, then took them apart.[9] The chief engineer decided that he could match Mercedes on performance and reliability, as well as on luxury and status features. He developed 11 performance goals. The final design had a drag coefficient smaller than any other luxury car, lighter weight, a more fuel-efficient engine, and a lower noise level. Sturdier materials were used for seat edges to maintain their appearance longer. The engine was designed with more torque than German models to give the car the quick start that Americans prefer. The instrument cluster was called "a work of art" by Ford's director of North American interior design.

Although the ANSI/ASQC definition is operationally useful, it does not completely describe the various viewpoints of quality that are commonly used. Garvin[10] discusses five different approaches to defining quality. One common notion of quality, often used by laypeople, is that it is synonymous with superiority or innate excellence. Garvin calls this the *transcendent definition,* which the ANSI/ASQC A3 standard defines as *relative quality.* In this sense, quality is absolute and universally recognizable. It is often loosely related to a comparison of features and characteristics of products. For example, high-priced German automobiles are often thought of as being of higher quality than the lower priced production models of other manufacturers. If one accepts this view, true quality cannot be precisely defined but

---

[8]ANSI/ASQC A3–1978, *Quality Systems Terminology* (Milwaukee, WI: American Society for Quality Control, 1978).

[9]"A New Era for Auto Quality," *Business Week,* October 22, 1990, pp. 84–96.

[10]Reprinted from "What Does 'Product Quality' Really Mean?", by David A. Garvin, *Sloan Management Review.* Vol. 26, No. 1 (1984), pp. 25–43. By permission of the publisher. Copyright © 1984 by the Sloan Management Review Association. All rights reserved.

can be recognized only through experience. This is not a useful operational definition, since quality cannot be measured, compared, or analyzed.

A second, *product-based definition* is that quality is a precise and measurable variable and that differences in quality reflect differences in *quantity* of some product attribute, for example, the number of stitches per inch on a shirt or the number of cylinders in an engine. As a result, quality is often mistakenly related to cost: the higher the cost, the higher the quality. However, a product—a term used in this text to refer to either a manufactured good or a service—need not be expensive to be considered a quality one. Sears, Roebuck & Co. has not become one of the world's largest retailers by selling the most expensive items, but it has gained a reputation for selling quality products. Likewise the food and service at many inexpensive restaurants would be considered quality by many people.

A third definition is based on the presumption that quality is determined by what a customer wants and what he or she is willing to pay for. Individuals have different wants and needs and hence different quality standards. This leads to a *user-based definition:* Quality is defined as "fitness for intended use," or how well the product performs its intended function. Both a BMW and a Jeep are fit for use; they simply serve different needs and groups of customers. To determine fitness for intended use, one must consider issues such as the product's intended use, frequency of use, cost, performance, reliability, and serviceability requirements.

Nissan is an example of applying the fitness-for-use concept.[11] Nissan tested the U.S. market for Datsun in 1960. While the car was economical, it was slow, hard to drive, low powered, and not very comfortable. In essence, it lacked most of the qualities that American drivers expected. The U.S. representative, Mr. Katayama, kept asking questions and sending answers back to Tokyo. For some time, the company refused to believe that American tastes were different from their own. After many years of nagging, Mr. Katayama finally got a product that Americans liked—the 240Z. Eventually, the name Datsun was changed to Nissan to remove the old quality image and suggest movement to a higher level.

A second, but negative, example is an American appliance company whose stoves and refrigerators were admired by Japanese buyers. Unfortunately, the small living quarters of the typical Japanese home did not have enough space for the American models. Some could not even pass through the narrow doors of Japanese kitchens. While the performance characteristics were high, the products were simply not fit for use.

The fitness-for-use definition is driven by *customer satisfaction,* and has become the principal definition of quality from a managerial perspective. By the end of the 1980s, a related, though fundamentally different definition, emerged: Quality is *meeting or exceeding customer expectations.* To understand this definition, we must understand the meaning of "customer." Most employees think of a customer as the ultimate purchaser of a product or service; for instance, the person who buys an automobile or the guest who registers in a hotel. These customers are **external customers.** Clearly, meeting the expectations of external customers is the ultimate goal of any business. However, every employee in a company also has **internal customers**—the individual or department, who performs the next operation. Failure

[11]Gregory M. Seal, "1990s—Years of Promise, Years of Peril for U.S. Manufacturers," *Industrial Engineering,* January 1990, pp. 18–21.

to meet the needs and expectations of internal customers can result in a poor quality product. For example, a poor design for a computerized hotel reservation system makes it difficult for the reservation clerk to do his or her job, and consequently affects the customer who stays in the hotel. Understanding who your customers are and what their expectations are is fundamental in achieving customer satisfaction. Who are the customers of your university, your instructor, and you, the student?

The quality concept of customer satisfaction has been fundamental to Japanese success. The International Quality Study Top Line Findings[12] showed that the percentage of businesses which stated that they develop new products and services based on customer expectations always or almost always was 58% for Japanese firms, 40% for German firms, and only 22% for U.S. firms.

A fourth definition of quality is a *manufacturing-based definition:* Quality is an outcome of engineering and manufacturing practice, or "conformance to specifications." Specifications are targets and tolerances determined by designers of products and services. Targets are the ideal values for which production should strive; tolerances are specified because designers recognize that in manufacturing it is impossible to meet the targets all of the time. For example, a part dimension might be specified as 0.236 ± 0.003 cm. The target, or ideal value, is 0.236 cm, but the allowable variation is 0.003 cm above or below the target. Thus, any dimension in the range from 0.233 to 0.239 cm is deemed acceptable, or said to conform to specifications. Likewise, in services, "on-time arrival" for an airplane might be specified as within 15 minutes of the scheduled arrival time. The target is the scheduled time, and the tolerance is specified to be 15 minutes. This is a key definition of quality and will be used extensively throughout this book in the context of technical aspects of quality control.

Finally, the *value-based definition* states that quality is defined in terms of costs and prices: a quality product is one that provides performance at an acceptable price or conformance at an acceptable cost. Thus, one might purchase a computer "clone" rather than a name brand since it provides the same performance at a lower cost. Although the Yugo automobile was introduced with great hype and a base price of under $4,000, it bombed in the U.S. market because the quality of conformance was not good despite its low cost. This definition is difficult to apply in practice, however, since it incorporates two distinct concepts—quality and value.

As an illustration of how these different views can apply to a single product, consider the services provided by a hospital. The transcendent definition of quality is characterized by an image of excellence as perceived by the competency of the medical staff, the availability of treatments for rare or complicated disorders, or the availability of advanced medical technology. These judgments are made by patients and third-party organizations. Auditing of hospital efficiency and measurement of treatment consistency and resource consumption views quality along the product-based dimension. This view is predominant among government and healthcare accrediting agencies.

The patient's (external customer's) perception of care is focused on the user-based definition. Expectations have increased because of improvements in medical care and advances in therapeutic drug treatments and innovative surgery. This increases the pressure on hospitals to provide services to meet these expectations. As the demand for flawless service increases, the medical staff and ancillary services

---

[12]*Op. cit.*

FIGURE 1.1 The Production-Distribution Cycle

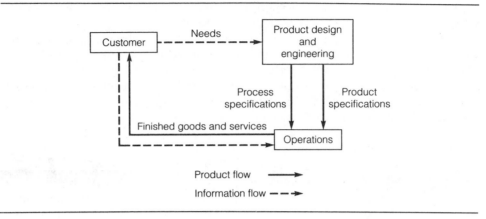

(internal customers) must turn their attention to quality to a manufacturing-based definition. Accrediting agencies and the medical profession mandate conformance to various practices and determine licensing requirements for practice.

Finally, the value-based definition has received the greatest attention in recent years because of the increase in medical care costs. All constituencies—consumers, the government, and the medical profession—are involved in this controversy. This example shows that quality in a single organization can and need be viewed from several different perspectives.

In considering these definitions of quality, we see that the meaning of quality depends on one's position in the organization; that is, whether one is the designer, customer, manufacturer, or distributor. To understand this more clearly, let us consider the production-distribution cycle for a manufactured good as illustrated in Figure 1.1. The customer is the driving force behind the production of goods. Goods are produced to meet the customer's needs; indeed, business organizations exist for this very purpose. The needs of the customer are related to product performance, reliability (freedom from failure over a specified period of time), length of serviceable life, and price. It is the role of the marketing function to assess these needs. A product that meets the needs of the customer, both in performance and price, can rightly be described as "quality." Hence, the user-based definition of quality applies here.

The manufacturer must translate customer requirements into detailed product and process specifications. This is the role of research and development, product design, and engineering. Product specifications might consist of such attributes as size, form, finish, taste, dimensions, tolerances, materials, operational characteristics, and safety features. Process specifications include the types of equipment, tools, and facilities used in production. Product designers must balance performance and cost; thus, the value-based definition of quality is most useful at this stage.

A lot can happen during manufacturing operations. Machine settings can fall out of adjustment; operators and assemblers can make mistakes; materials can be defective. Even under the most closely controlled process, variations in product output are inevitable and cannot be predicted except in an aggregate sense. The responsibility of the manufacturer is to guarantee that design specifications are adhered to during production and that the final product performs as intended. From the viewpoint of production personnel, quality follows the manufacturing-based definition of conformance to specifications. That is, quality is *defined* by product specifications and is *achieved* by manufacturing.

The completion of the product manufacturing cycle is the distribution of the product from the plant, perhaps through wholesale and retail outlets to the customer. However, this does not end the customer's relationship with the manufacturer. The customer may have a need for various services such as installation, user information, and special training. Such services are part of the product and cannot be ignored in quality management.

The quality of customer service is a key factor to the success of a business. This has been noted by Peters and Waterman in their best-selling book in which they observe that the excellent companies "provide unparalleled quality, service and reliability—things that work and last."[13] Service is the rule, not the exception. The success of IBM shows the value of good service. IBM's success in computers was a result of its strategy in the punched-card business. IBM knew the needs of data processing users. While other companies focused on hardware, IBM focused on software and service. From this perspective, the transcendent definition of quality—a perception of excellence—is perhaps most applicable.

The need for different definitions of quality is now clear. Perspectives change at different points in an organization. Reliance on a single definition is frequently a source of problems. One needs to shift one's perspective of quality as products move from design to market. All views are necessary—and must be embodied in an overall company philosophy—in order to result in a quality product. The diversity of these definitions can also be explained by examining eight principal quality dimensions listed by Garvin[14]:

1. *Performance:* a product's primary operating characteristics.

2. *Features:* the "bells and whistles" of a product.

3. *Reliability:* the probability of a product's surviving over a specified period of time under stated conditions of use.

4. *Conformance:* the degree to which physical and performance characteristics of a product match preestablished standards.

5. *Durability:* the amount of use one gets from a product before it physically deteriorates or until replacement is preferable.

6. *Serviceability:* the speed, courtesy, and competence of repair.

7. *Aesthetics:* how a product looks, feels, sounds, tastes, or smells.

8. *Perceived quality:* subjective assessment resulting from image, advertising, or brand names.

To illustrate these quality dimensions, consider an automobile. Performance includes acceleration, braking distance, steering, and handling; features include power options, a tape or CD deck, antilock brakes, leather seats; reliability includes its ability to start

---

[13]Thomas J. Peters and Robert H. Waterman, Jr., *In Search of Excellence: Lessons from America's Best-Run Companies* (New York: Harper & Row, 1982), p. 14.
[14]David A. Garvin, "Product Quality," pp. 29–30.

on cold days and the frequency of failures; conformance refers to fit and finish, and freedom from noises; durability includes corrosion resistance and the wear of seat cover material; serviceability includes access to spare parts, number of miles between major maintenance service, and expense of service; aesthetic features are color, instrument panel design, control placement, and "feel of the road"; and perceived quality includes the brand image, quality, and repair history as reported by consumer magazines, and ranking in enthusiasts' magazines.

Because each of the five basic definitions focuses on different quality dimensions, conflicts are inevitable. The most applicable definitions are *fitness for use* (the design perspective) and *conformance to specifications* (the manufacturing perspective). Both are necessary for customer satisfaction. These are the definitions that will be most useful throughout this book. A further definition, based on the economic consequences of poor quality, will be introduced in the next chapter.

THE TOTAL QUALITY SYSTEM

A General Electric task force studied what customers thought of various GE product lines.[15] Those with relatively poor images in the marketplace downgraded the customer's viewpoint, made quality synonymous with tight tolerance and conformance to specifications, tied quality objectives to manufacturing flow, expressed quality objectives as the number of defects per unit, and formalized quality control systems only in manufacturing. In contrast, product lines that received customer praise emphasized customer expectations, established customer needs through market research, used customer-based quality performance measures, and formalized quality control systems for all business functions, not solely manufacturing. The lesson here is that quality must not be viewed solely from a technical point of view; a significant emphasis must be placed on managerial activities.

In this book, we view the total quality system as composed of two related systems—the **management system** and the **technical system** (see Figure 1.2). The management system is concerned with planning, organizing, controlling, and human resources management processes relating to quality assurance programs. Growing out of human resources management are structures for employee involvement and team approaches to decision making, quality improvement, and problem solving.

The important terms in this global view of quality are *system, process, structure,* and *technique.* A system, as we use it here, is the interrelated set of plans, policies, processes, procedures, people, and technology required to meet the objectives of an organization. A process consists of policies, procedures, steps, technology, and personnel needed to carry out a significant segment of operations within an organization. Usually, a process will cross several organizational boundaries within an operating unit and require coordination across those boundaries. A structure is a formal or informal organizational entity that is developed to perform a certain process or set of tasks. A technique is a systematic approach, procedure, and associated technology required to carry out a task.

---

[15]Lawrence Utzig, "Quality Reputation—a Precious Asset," *ASQC Technical Conference Transactions,* Atlanta, 1980, pp. 145–154.

FIGURE 1.2 The Total Quality System Model

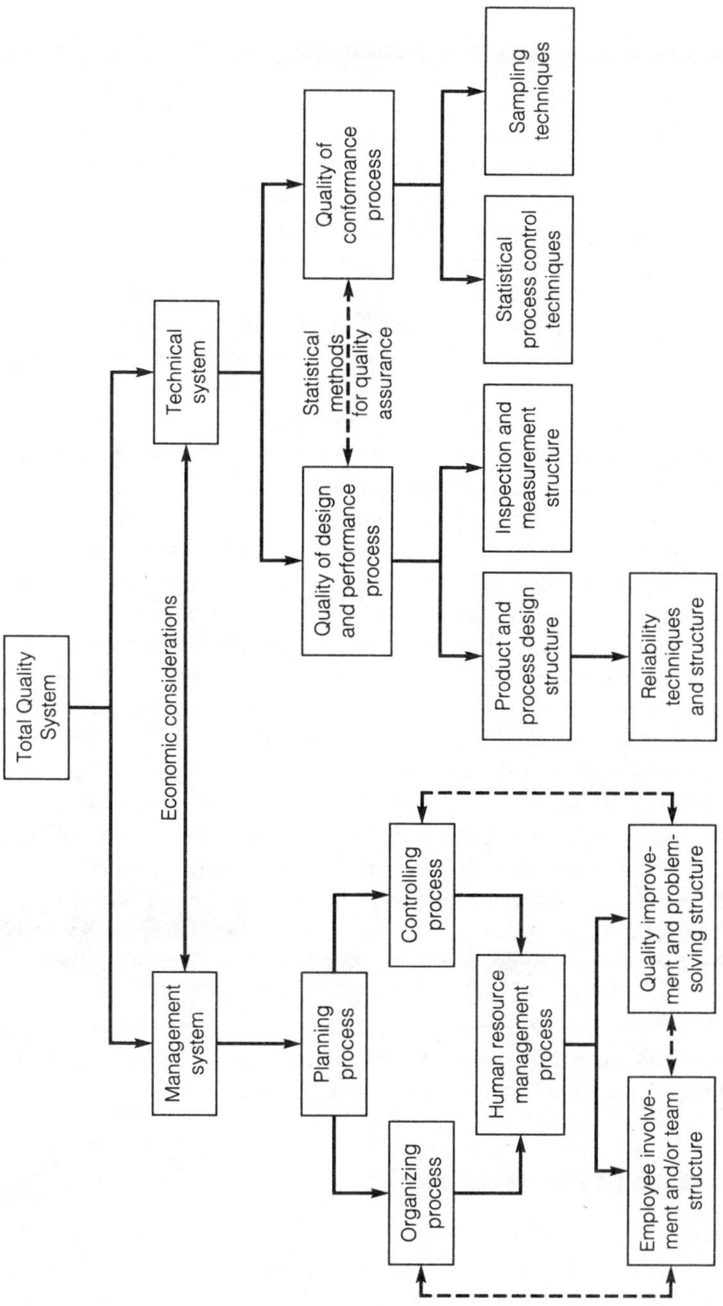

Management must be aware of customer needs, the capability of the company's production processes, and the financial implications of any decision; in short, management must know how all the components in the organization tie together.

Quality is the responsibility of everyone in the organization, from the operators on the production floor to the chief executive officer. People such as machine operators, assembly line workers, ticket agents, nurses, and waitresses are the craftspeople who build quality into products and services. First-line supervisors must provide the motivating climate for employees, direct them in proper procedures, work together with them to locate problems, and assist in eliminating sources of error. Middle management must plan, coordinate, execute, and monitor quality policy. Finally, top management must commit the resources and provide the leadership necessary to set the tone and carry out the requirements of an ongoing, dynamic quality policy.

The technical system involves the assurance of quality in product design, the planning and design of manufacturing or service-producing processes, and the control of incoming materials, intermediate production and finished goods. These are included in the "Quality of Design and Performance Process" block of Figure 1.2. To ensure *conformance* to the requirements of the process or service, the "Quality of Conformance Process" must be developed. Statistical process control techniques and sampling techniques are usually employed in each of these areas for the identification of quality problems and for controlling the quality of production processes. Both the design and performance process and the conformance process must be coordinated and work together. Information transfer between the two systems is necessary for effective problem solving and quality improvement.

Economic considerations and total quality management play a crucial role in tying together the management and technical systems. New technologies such as on-line process control, automatic gaging, and new analytical tools also present new opportunities to both management and technical personnel for quality assurance.

The structure of the management system, the technical system, and the interaction between them form the plan of this book. Our primary objective is to examine the integration of management and technology for effective quality assurance systems. This is reflected in Procter & Gamble's definition of total quality; *the unyielding and continually improving effort by everyone in an organization to understand, meet, and exceed the expectations of customers.* It is our aim to provide the understanding necessary to achieve total quality.

THE NEW QUALITY DYNAMIC

In the late 1980s, as the first edition of this book was being completed, it became clear that the only thing in the quality area that was constant was change. Tom Peters, author of several best-selling management books, wrote a book entitled *Thriving on Chaos* that captured the essence of the quality revolution. In a related article,[16] he outlined how business functions, processes, and concepts change, have been changing, and will be changing to meet the demands of a dynamic environment. Peters listed 10 specific areas of change, gave characteristics of old versus new approaches to managing these areas, and specified companies that were exemplars of the new

---

[16]Tom Peters, "A World Turned Upside Down," *The Academy of Management Executive,* Vol. 1, No. 3, 1987, pp. 233–243.

approach in each area. The 10 areas were manufacturing, marketing, sales and service, international, innovation, people, organization, MIS (management information systems), financial management and control, and leadership. We will address each of these areas at various points throughout this text. Although his table is too large to reproduce here, a couple of Peters' examples will be sufficient to show how these rapid changes are affecting the area of quality management.

In the manufacturing area, Peters pointed out that the *old* mindset was to focus on volume, low cost, and efficiency to the detriment of quality, responsiveness, and people. Now, not only is there a *new* shift to flexibility, but quality, responsiveness, and people have become more important than capital *per se*. Manufacturing is being used as a primary *marketing tool*. Customers are being invited into plants for inspection tours and team meetings. Exchange visits between plant personnel and customers have been arranged so that operating conditions in the customers' organizations may be better understood. Exemplars of this approach are such familiar names as 3M, Hewlett-Packard, Harley-Davidson, IBM, Chaparral Steel Co., Motorola, and Worthington Industries. Companies working to develop the new approach included Ford, GE, Xerox, Chrysler, and Westinghouse.

In the people area, Peters described the *old* approach as focusing on capital rather than people, tight control, close supervision, adversarial union relations, money as the only motivator, and training only when needed, because turnover was an unsolvable problem. With the *new* focus on quality, service, and responsiveness, emphasis is increasing on the importance of people to the organization's success. This has brought on the development of individual and team participation programs, elimination of one or more layers of supervision, and more people involvement in budgeting, inventory management, day-to-day problem solving, and quality monitoring. Exemplary companies in this area are Lincoln Electric, Apple Computer, Johnsonville Sausage, W. L. Gore, North American Tool and Die, DEC, Wal-Mart, Walt Disney, and several of the companies listed previously.

Finally, in the leadership area, the *old* approach was the detached, analytic "manager as leader." Strategic planning was centralized, with corporate decision making dominated by central corporate and group staffs. Today, the *new* approach is decentralized, with values (such as quality) set from the top, but staff functions— planning, purchasing, personnel, MIS, etc.—decentralized. Top managers and lean staff are in touch with customers and operations, generally in the field, with the leader acting as dramatist, tone setter, and visionary. Exemplars in this area include Federal Express, Nordstrom, North American Tool and Die, Stew Leonard's Dairy, and The Limited as well as several other companies.

Quality is an exciting and rapidly changing field. Opportunities for individuals with a quality focus in business and engineering are endless. The quality revolution has moved from manufacturing into services, governmental operations, and educational institutions; indeed, into every aspect of modern life. As you embark on the study of this discipline, keep in mind the broad range of applications in all aspects of your life.

QUALITY IN PRACTICE

At the end of each chapter, we present several "Quality in Practice" case studies that describe applications of quality concepts in manufacturing and service organizations. Our first case is a description of steps taken to improve quality at Cadillac, a 1990 winner of the Malcolm Baldrige National Quality Award.

The Cadillac Quality Story[17]

Cadillac Motor Car Company is the flagship division of General Motors' North American Automotive Operations. Founded in 1902 by Henry Martin Leland, Cadillac was built on a legacy of superior craftsmanship and unsurpassed quality, which gave it recognition as "the standard of the world." Cadillac's first official quality recognition came in 1908 when it was awarded the Dewar Trophy, a prize sponsored annually by the Royal Automobile Club of England to encourage technical progress. Cadillac won the trophy for its demonstration of the complete interchangeability of parts. This was the first time an American company had won this prestigious honor. Cadillac won the Dewar Trophy again in 1915 for the first application of the electric self-starter.

Cadillac's quality leadership went unchallenged for decades. Then the early 1980s ushered in an era of progressively stringent emissions standards and fuel economy requirements. Cadillac responded with new powertrain components and, ultimately, new exterior designs that did not completely meet customer expectations. By the mid-1980s, Cadillac's prestigious image was in jeopardy.

Since 1985, a turnaround has occurred. Cadillac has demonstrated continuous improvement in both quality and customer satisfaction. The story of Cadillac's transformation—the people, systems, processes, and products responsible for the improvement—earned Cadillac the 1990 Malcolm Baldrige National Quality Award, the first American automobile company so honored.

Three strategies are behind the transformation:

- a cultural change

- a constant focus on the customer

- a disciplined approach to planning.

These three strategies support one another and are totally integrated. Together, they reflect Cadillac's total quality process.

Teamwork and employee involvement are at the

heart of Cadillac's cultural change. Four initiatives that are primarily responsible for increasing teamwork and employee involvement are simultaneous engineering, supplier partnerships, the UAW-GM Quality Network, and Cadillac's People Strategy.

Simultaneous engineering is a process in which appropriate disciplines are committed to work interactively to conceive, approve, develop, and implement product programs that meet predetermined objectives. Simultaneous engineering teams involving 700 employees including suppliers and dealers are responsible for defining, engineering, marketing, and continuously improving all Cadillac vehicles. In 1985, Cadillac began redefining its supplier relationships by asking suppliers to take on additional product development responsibilities. This effort led to a reduction in the supply base and a closer, more focused relationship.

Since 1973, GM and the United Auto Workers (UAW) have worked together to improve product quality and the quality of work life. In 1987 corporate management and the UAW recognized that a consistent, joint quality improvement process was needed to improve competitiveness. The UAW-GM Quality Network comprises joint union and management quality councils at the corporate, group, division, and plant levels of the organization. These councils oversee all quality improvement efforts and assist in the implementation of the business plan.

The success of teamwork and employee involvement depends on people. At Cadillac, people are considered their greatest strength and the true differentiators of successful organizations. Cadillac's People Strategy is designed to meet the needs of Cadillac employees while achieving business objectives. Selection processes are developed to place or reallocate people in concert with the needs of the business. Efforts are then made to develop employees, involve them in decision making, communicate to them in ways that ensure their understanding, and create an environment in which they can work effectively. These efforts are reinforced with recognition and reward systems that support the behaviors necessary to achieve the business plan.

At Cadillac, customer satisfaction is the master

[17]Adapted from "Cadillac, The Quality Story," Cadillac Motor Car Division, Detroit, MI.

(continued)

plan. Cadillac's cultural change broke down the walls between functions and allowed them to focus on the customer—both internal and external. Each Cadillac employee is committed to providing the customer with products or services that exceed expectations. An example of their focus on internal customers is the Assembly Line Effectiveness Center, a simulated manufacturing environment used to evaluate the "buildability" of future models. In this environment, design teams hear and can understand the "voice of the assembler" much earlier than ever before.

The Cadillac Market Assurance Process integrates the needs of customers at every phase of product development. Cadillac uses extensive market research to collect information about its external customers. Much research is also conducted after the sale to collect data on Cadillac's target market and the performance of their vehicles and to monitor customer satisfaction. Several customer service programs include Cadillac Roadside Service and Cadillac Consumer Relations Center, which are designed to respond to emergencies, questions, and concerns of its customers and potential customers. Cadillac was the first domestic manufacturer to offer a four-year 50,000-mile warranty without a deductible payment, reflecting Cadillac's confidence in the quality of their cars.

Cadillac's approach to business planning is focused on continuously improving the quality of Cadillac products, processes, and services. The business planning process has four objectives:

1. To involve every employee in the running of the business.

2. To reinforce continually Cadillac's mission and

long-term strategic objectives throughout the organization.

3. To align the short-term business objectives with the goals and action plans developed by every plant and functional staff.

4. To institutionalize continuous improvement of products and services.

Each staff and plant develops a quality plan that aligns with the overall Cadillac business plan. The business plan is distributed to all employees to make them aware of the organization's major objectives and acts as a guide to ensure that all employees are moving in the same direction.

These strategies have resulted in continuous improvement in quality, productivity, and customer satisfaction measures. Since 1986 (through 1990), warranty-related costs have dropped nearly 30%. Productivity at the Detroit-Hamtramck Assembly Center has increased by 58%. Lead time for a completely new model has been cut by 40 weeks. Also, Cadillac has led domestic makes on J. D. Power and Associates' Customer Satisfaction Index and Sales Satisfaction Index.

Key Issues for Discussion

1. Discuss the elements of the Cadillac quality story that relate to concepts presented in this chapter, for example, the definition of quality, the reasons for quality awareness, role of customers, and so on.

2. Explain why all three strategies behind the Cadillac quality transformation were necessary. What do you think might have happened if one of these were deemphasized?

Summary of Key Points

■ Quality assurance refers to any action directed toward providing consumers with goods and services of appropriate quality.

■ Modern techniques of quality assurance were developed at Bell Telephone Laboratories during the 1920s and 1930s and found widespread use during World War II.

- W. Edwards Deming and Joseph Juran taught techniques of quality control and management to the Japanese in the 1950s. Over the next 20 years, Japan made massive improvements in quality.

- Four significant influences contributed to the awareness of quality in the 1980s: consumer awareness, improvements in technology, inadequate managerial thinking, and economic impact on national competitiveness. Quality reached a level of unprecedented importance in the United States during this time.

- The official definition of quality is "the totality of features and characteristics of a product or service that bears on its ability to satisfy given needs." However, many viewpoints of quality exist; among these are relative quality, product-based quality, fitness for use, conformance to specifications, and the value-based approach.

- Eight principal dimensions of quality were proposed by David Garvin: performance, features, reliability, conformance, durability, serviceability, aesthetics, and perceived quality.

- In this book, the total quality system is viewed as two interacting systems: the management system and the technical system.

Questions for Review and Discussion

1. Briefly discuss the history of quality before and after the industrial revolution. Why was the industrial revolution a key turning point? Do you feel that the "Japanese revolution" will be viewed as a similar turning point?

2. What factors have contributed to the increased awareness of quality in modern business?

3. Discuss the importance of quality in the national interest.

4. What steps has Great Britain taken to revitalize a national campaign for quality?

5. Discuss the various definitions of quality. Can a single definition suffice?

6. Choose a product or service (such as the hospital example in the text) to illustrate how several of Garvin's definitions of quality can apply simultaneously.

7. Choose a product *and* a service. Develop a list of appropriate fitness-for-use criteria.

8. Select a service activity with which you are familiar. If you were the manager of this activity, what "conformance to specifications" criteria would you use to monitor this activity?

9. Describe the elements of quality of design and quality of conformance.

10. Select three different manufactured goods and three service organizations. Discuss how Garvin's eight dimensions of quality apply to each.

11. Discuss the changes that Tom Peters has recognized in the manufacturing, people, and leadership areas of organizations.

Bibliography

Freund, Richard A. "Definitions and Basic Quality Concepts," *Journal of Quality Technology,* January 1985.

Garvin, David A. *Managing Quality,* New York: The Free Press, 1988.

Hayes, Glenn E. "Quality: Quandary and Quest," *Quality,* Vol. 22, No. 7, July 1983, p. 18.

Page, Harold S. "A Quality Strategy for the '80s," *Quality Progress,* Vol. 16, No. 11, November 1983, pp. 16–21.

Van Gigch, John P. "Quality—Producer and Consumer Views," *Quality Progress,* Vol. 10, No. 4, April 1977, pp. 30–33.

Wachniak, Ray. "World Class Quality: An American Response to the Challenge," *Quest for Quality: Managing the Total System,* M. Sepehri, ed. Norcross, GA: Institute of Industrial Engineers, 1987.

CHAPTER 2

Quality in Production and Service Systems

s we saw in Chapter 1, the origins of quality began in manufacturing operations, and many of the tools for quality analysis and improvement were developed for manufacturing problems. Through the 1980s, this manufacturing emphasis dominated the profession. In the late 1980s and into the 1990s, business began to recognize the importance of quality service in achieving customer satisfaction and competing in the global marketplace. In a very important sense, this recognition has expanded the definition and concept of quality to include nearly *any* organizational improvement such as the reduction of manufacturing cycle time and improved worker skills. Ancillary services in manufacturing companies as well as "stand-alone" service organizations such as hospitals and banks are beginning to realize the benefits of a focus on quality.

In this chapter we explore the role of quality in both production and service systems. We also examine the relationship between quality and productivity and introduce the concept of total quality management.

QUALITY IN PRODUCTION SYSTEMS

Obviously, quality affects every aspect of an organization. Thus, for a product to be successful, the assurance of quality requires a comprehensive systems approach. This section discusses quality within a functional business organization.

Production is the process of converting the resources available to an organization into products—goods and services. The collection of all interrelated activities and operations involved in producing goods and services is called a **production system.** Production systems are typically thought of in the context of manufacturing, although it is important to note that service organizations are also production systems. For the present discussion, we shall focus primarily on manufacturing; service organizations are addressed in a separate section.

Three major areas of quality are critical to any production system: product development, the production process, and product use. Product development and product use are customer-oriented activities. The quality effort in these activities should focus on determining customer needs and service requirements and on translating these needs and requirements into product designs that meet fitness-for-use criteria. The production process includes the physical facilities and information and control systems that are required to convert resources into products or services. The production process is largely under the control of the business organization. Quality efforts here are oriented toward ensuring that the product conforms to specifications. Note, however, that for service organizations, the production process and the beginning of product use occur at the same point in time. Thus, services require different quality perspectives.

Components of the Production System

Figure 2.1 illustrates a typical production system for manufactured goods. If quality assurance is to be effective, it must include all components of the production system. The role of quality in each component of this system is described in the following paragraphs.

Marketing and Sales. Marketing and sales personnel are responsible for determining the product needs and expectations of customers. This includes the functional requirements and the price customers are willing to pay for the product meeting those requirements. This information is necessary to define products that are fit for use and capable of being produced within the technological and budgetary constraints of the organization. Effective market research and solicitation of customer feedback are necessary for developing quality products.

Product Design and Process Engineering. These activities are responsible for developing technical specifications for products and production processes that meet the requirements determined by marketing. Products that are overengineered,

FIGURE 2.1 The Production System

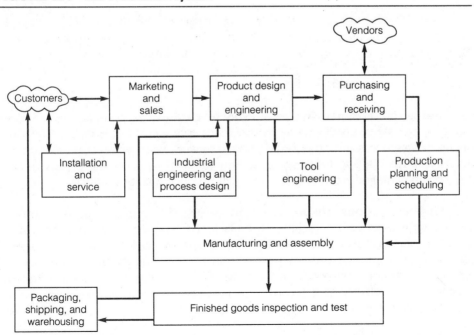

that is, exceed the customer requirements, result in inefficient use of a firm's resources and lower profits. They can also create a complacency that leads to poor quality. Underengineered products as well as poor process designs also often result in poor quality. Quality in product design and process engineering are considered further in Chapter 14.

Purchasing and Receiving. Purchasing is usually thought of only in regard to price and delivery criteria, although its role in quality assurance is crucial. The purchasing department must ensure that purchased parts meet the quality requirements specified by product design and engineering. Thus, its responsibility includes the selection of quality-conscious vendors. Purchasing must maintain good communication with vendors as quality requirements and design changes occur. Receiving must ensure that the purchased items actually delivered are of the quality that was contracted for by purchasing and that defective parts are not received.

Production Planning and Scheduling. The correct materials, tools, and equipment must be available at the proper time and in the proper places to maintain a smooth flow of production. Poor quality often results from time pressures due to poor planning and scheduling. Recently, new concepts in production planning and scheduling such as "just-in-time" have been shown to lead to quality improvements. This is addressed briefly in Chapter 8.

Manufacturing and Assembly. The first rule of quality assurance is that quality must be *built* into a product; it cannot be *inspected* into it. Proper control of labor, materials, and equipment is necessary to achieve high quality. The interaction of first-line supervisors with production workers, engineers, production control staff, and others is one of the most important aspects of effective quality assurance.

Tool Engineering. This is a supporting activity that is responsible for designing and maintaining the tools used in manufacturing and inspection. Worn manufacturing tools result in defective parts, and inspection gages not properly calibrated may give misleading information to management and can result in poorer quality than would otherwise be possible.

Industrial Engineering and Process Design. A manufacturing process must be capable of producing items that repeatedly meet specifications. The job of industrial engineers and process designers is to work with product design engineers to develop realistic specifications. In addition, they must select appropriate technology, equipment, and work methods that will produce quality products.

Finished Goods Inspection and Test. The purpose of final product inspection is to judge the quality of manufacturing, to uncover and help resolve the problems that may arise, and to ensure that no defective items reach the customer. If quality is built into the product properly, such inspection should be unnecessary, except for auditing purposes and functional testing. Electronic components, for example, are subjected to extensive "burn-in" tests to check proper operation and eliminate short-life items.

Packaging, Shipping, and Warehousing. Even good quality items that leave the plant floor can be damaged in transit or incorrectly labeled. Packaging, shipping, and warehousing—often termed *logistics* activities—are the functions that protect quality after goods are produced.

Installation and Service. Products must be used correctly to be beneficial to the customer. Users must understand the product and have adequate instructions for proper installation and operation. Should any problem occur, customer satisfaction is dependent on good after-the-sale service.

Business Support Systems

The preceding functions are directly related to the product itself. In addition to these, other supporting activities in a business organization are necessary for achieving quality. Among them are the following:

Finance and Accounting. Finance must ensure that sufficient budgets are authorized for quality programs, and accounting provides quality cost information to management for decision making.

Human Resources Management. Employees must be properly trained and motivated to do quality work. Education on the importance of quality is essential. More and more training in statistical problem solving, communications, and interpersonal skills is being given to managers and to technical and operative level employees.

Legal Services. A firm's legal department must guarantee that laws and regulations regarding such functions as product labeling, performance, safety, packaging, and transportation are adhered to; that warranties are properly designed and worded; that contractual requirements are met; and that proper procedures and documentation are available in the event of liability claims. The rapid increase in liability suits has made legal services an important aspect of quality assurance.

Since each of the preceding activities has a definite impact on quality, **quality assurance** is defined as *the total effort involved in planning, organizing, directing, and controlling quality in a production system with the objective of providing the consumer with products of appropriate quality*. It is simply making sure that quality is what it should be.

QUALITY IN SERVICE ORGANIZATIONS

Service is a "social act which takes place in direct contact between the customer and representatives of the service company."[1] Services include all nonmanufacturing organizations except industries such as agriculture, mining, and construction. The U.S. government's Standard Industrial Classification system describes service organizations as those "primarily engaged in providing a wide variety of services for individuals, business and government establishments, and other organizations. Hotels and other lodging places, establishments providing personal, business, repair, and amusement services; health, legal, engineering, and other professional services; educational

---

[1]Richard Norman, *Service Management: Strategy and Leadership* (New York: John Wiley & Sons, 1984).

institutions, membership organizations, and other miscellaneous services are included." We also usually include in this category real estate, financial services, retailers, transportation, and public utilities.

In many organizations, the production of goods and services go hand in hand. For instance, a fast-food restaurant produces tangible goods in the form of burgers and sandwiches. However, the distinguishing feature is the speed and quality of customer service. We tend to classify such organizations as services rather than as manufacturing organizations since they compete primarily on the basis of service rather than product. It is also important to realize that for many manufacturing companies, service is a key element. For instance, a computer equipment manufacturer such as IBM may provide extensive maintenance and consulting services.

In recent years, the service sector has grown rapidly. In 1945, 22.9 million people were employed by service-producing industries and 18.5 million people were employed by goods-producing industries. However, by 1985, the number of people employed in services grew to 72.5 million while only 25.0 million people were employed in goods-producing industries. Much of this growth occurred in the 1970s.

Modern methods of quality assurance were developed and refined in manufacturing industries. The introduction and adoption of quality assurance programs in services has lagged behind manufacturing, perhaps by as much as a decade. Managers of service organizations had usually assumed that their service was acceptable if the customers did not complain frequently. Only rather recently have they realized that the quality of service can be managed as a competitive weapon. A hospital in Detroit, for example, promises to see its emergency room patients in 20 minutes or less, or the care will be free.[2] Like many other urban hospitals, the 101-bed hospital was suffering financially and was searching for ways to boost revenues.

Differences between Manufacturing and Service

The production of services differs from manufacturing in many ways. The output of service systems is generally intangible, while manufacturing produces tangible and visible products. Service organizations usually handle a large volume of transactions. For example, on any given day, the Royal Bank of Canada handles more than 5.5 million transactions for 7.5 million customers through 1,600 branches and more than 3,500 banking machines, and Federal Express handles 1.5 million shipments at 1,650 sites in 127 countries. Such large volumes increase the opportunity for error. Services are consumed as they are created and cannot be inventoried as can manufactured goods. This eliminates the opportunity for inspection as a means of quality control. Services are generally more labor intensive, whereas manufacturing is more capital intensive. For example, patient care in hospitals depends heavily on the performance of nurses, doctors, and other medical staff. Hence, the behavioral aspects of management, such as motivation, are critical in the service sector. In recent years, the growth of information technology has reduced the labor intensiveness of some service operations. Automatic teller machines and banking by mail, for instance, have removed some service workers from the picture. While automation reduces the labor intensity, it can have an adverse effect on quality. Some would argue that customer satisfaction is decreased because of the lack of personal interaction.

---

[2]"Mich. Hospital Promises to Deliver," *The Cincinnati Enquirer,* July 17, 1991, p. A-2.

The service delivery system is often very time sensitive; customer needs and performance standards are often difficult to identify. The customer and the service worker often must interact for delivery of the service to be complete. Customers in a fast-food restaurant place orders, carry their food to the table, and even clear the table when finished.

Finally, the production of services usually requires a higher degree of customization than that of manufactured goods. A doctor, lawyer, insurance salesman, and even a food-service employee must tailor the service provided to the individual customer.

These differences have important implications for quality assurance. Quality depends on the individual who provides the service, the equipment used, the data available, and the decisions made. As with manufactured goods, quality of service is determined from customer requirements and must be designed into the production of the service. Consider a metropolitan transit agency, for example. The regional planning function is responsible for determining the ridership needs of the community. These needs are translated into "product specifications," that is, specific transit routes and schedules for buses or rapid transit systems. These specifications *define* the quality of service. Vehicles, equipment, maintenance policies, personnel, and adherence to schedules actually *achieve* the quality of the service.

The importance of quality in services cannot be underestimated. A company called Technical Assistance Research Programs, Inc., has conducted studies that reveal the following:

- The average company never hears from 96% of its unhappy customers. For every complaint received, the company has 26 customers with problems, 6 of which are serious.

- Of the customers who make a complaint, more than half will do business again with that organization if their complaint is resolved. If the customer feels that the complaint was resolved quickly, this figure jumps to 95%.

- The average customer who has had a problem will tell 9 or 10 others about it. Customers who have had complaints resolved satisfactorily will only tell about 5 others.[3]

The definitions of quality that apply to manufacturing apply equally to services. The very nature of service implies that it must respond to the needs of the customer, that is, the service must be "fit for use." In services, standards for conformance must be developed for the service product in a way that is similar to manufacturing. Thus, conformance to requirements relates to how well the service is actually delivered when compared to how it should have been delivered. It is important to match standards of conformance with fitness for use. For example, in a fast-food restaurant, lunch would be expected to be served within 5 minutes. In an elegant restaurant, however, one would expect to have 10 to 15 minutes between courses.

In services, the distinguishing features that determine quality differ from manufacturing. The most important dimensions of service quality include:

- *Time:* How much time must a customer wait?

---

[3]Karl Albrecht and Ronald E. Zemke, *Service America* (Homewood, IL: Dow Jones-Irwin, 1985).

- *Timeliness:* Will a package be delivered by 10:30 the next morning?

- *Completeness:* Are all items in the order included?

- *Courtesy:* Do front-line employees greet every customer?

- *Consistency:* Are services delivered in the same fashion for every customer?

- *Accessibility and convenience:* Is the service easy to obtain?

- *Accuracy:* Is the service performed right the first time?

- *Responsiveness:* Can service personnel react quickly to unexpected problems?

Many service organizations such as airlines, banks, and hotels have well-developed quality assurance systems. Most of them, however, are generally based on industrial system analogies and tend to be more product oriented than service oriented. For instance, a typical hotel's quality assurance system is focused on technical standards such as properly made up rooms. However, service organizations have special requirements that manufacturing systems cannot fulfill. Service systems must go beyond product orientation and include customer service transaction and employee performance and behavior. King suggests several points that service organizations should consider when instituting quality assurance systems[4]:

- The quality characteristics that should be controlled may not be the obvious ones. Customer perceptions are critical, and it may be difficult to define what the customer wants. For example, speed of service is an important quality characteristic, yet perceptions of speed may differ significantly among different service organizations, such as restaurants.

- Behavior is a quality characteristic. The quality of human interaction is a vital factor in every service transaction that involves human contact. For example, banks have found that the friendliness of tellers is a factor in retaining depositors.

- Image is a quality characteristic. Image is a major factor in shaping customer expectations of a service and in setting standards by which customers evaluate that service. A breakdown in image can be as harmful as a breakdown in delivery of the service itself.

- Setting service levels may be difficult. Many quality characteristics cannot be easily measured. Often standards must be set judgmentally and tested for satisfactory levels.

- Measures of system efficiency are different. The efficiency of manufacturing systems is often measured in terms of output per time period and the amount of scrap and rework generated. Service systems often cannot be measured in terms of such hard data; one must consider, for example, customer attitudes and employee competence.

- Quality control activity may be required at times or in places where supervision and control personnel are not present. Work must often be

---

[4]Carol A. King, "Service Quality Assurance Is Different," *Quality Progress,* Vol. 18, No. 6, June 1985, pp. 14–18.

performed at the convenience of the customer. Hence, more training of employees and "self-management" are necessary.

These differences among service organizations create distinct challenges for quality assurance. Thus, quality assurance demands an understanding of the behavioral sciences as well as the technical sciences. Firms noted for service excellence such as Walt Disney, Marriott Hotels, and Holiday Inn have recognized this need and routinely apply behavioral sciences. Throughout this book we will discuss the special role of quality in service organizations.

QUALITY AND PRODUCTIVITY

The relationship between quality and productivity is often very confusing to managers. Traditionally, quality and productivity have been seen as conflicting. This is because production efficiency has been the major force driving manufacturing decisions. Many managers will state that quality cannot be improved without significant losses in production efficiency and increased costs. The modern view is that improved quality leads to improved productivity and vice versa. In this section we discuss these relationships.

Productivity—a measure of how well the resources of a firm are being used—has been an important concern to U.S. manufacturers in recent years, particularly since American productivity growth has fallen behind other countries, such as Japan and Germany. In its general form,

$$\text{productivity} = \frac{\text{output}}{\text{input}}$$

Input usually includes labor, capital, material, and energy or some subset of these. As output increases for a constant level of input, or as input decreases for a constant level of output, productivity increases. The U.S. Government Bureau of Labor Statistics uses the productivity measure "total economic output/total worker-hours expended" in computing measures of national productivity. Other examples of productivity measures are labor productivity—units of output per labor hour; machine productivity—units of output per machine-hour; capital productivity—units of output per dollar input; and energy productivity—units of output per unit of energy consumed.

To illustrate a productivity measure, suppose that a company produces 400 printed circuit boards per eight-hour day using 50 employees. The labor productivity is computed as

$$\frac{400 \text{ boards}}{(50 \text{ persons})(8 \text{ hours})} = 1 \text{ board per labor hour}$$

If the company increases its production to 600 circuit boards per day by hiring 25 additional employees, the labor productivity is

$$\frac{600 \text{ boards}}{(75 \text{ persons})(8 \text{ hours})} = 1 \text{ board per labor hour}$$

Even though production has increased, productivity has remained the same, since the labor input increased proportionately.

In this example, we have not taken quality into account. It takes just as many resources to make a bad product as it does to make a good one. More labor spent on reworking poor quality increases the denominator of this measure; the production of more scrap decreases the numerator. Thus, productivity can increase dramatically if a product is made right the first time. However, high productivity does not necessarily imply good quality. Many managers can report good productivity measures by playing numbers games. Reporting total output rather than only *good* output can mask quality problems.

We often use the term **hidden factory** to refer to the portion of plant capacity that exists to rework unsatisfactory parts, to replace products recalled from the field, or to retest and reinspect rejected units. The hidden factory can account for 15 to 40% of a plant's capacity. Clearly, eliminating such unnecessary operations will increase productivity significantly.

Productivity measures provide managers with an indication of how to improve productivity: either increase the numerator, decrease the denominator, or both. This can be accomplished in the following ways:

- *Improve efficiency* by lowering total operating costs, generating savings in machine time, and reducing waste.

- *Improve effectiveness* by better decision making and communication.

- *Achieve higher performance* by increasing quality, reducing accidents and lost time, and minimizing equipment breakdowns.

- *Develop better organizational health* by improving morale, satisfaction, and cooperation.

Productivity improvement is usually associated with improvements in technology such as automation and specialization; however, it has been recognized that they are not panaceas for productivity problems. Quality improvement is often overlooked as a potential means of increasing productivity by reducing defective output and necessary effort spent on rework. In fact, a study by Shetty of 171 of the 1,300 largest U.S. companies during 1983–84 found that quality improvement ranked *sixth* behind cost reduction, employee participation, productivity incentives, goal setting, and increased automation as a productivity improvement tool.[5] Managers are only beginning to recognize the potential of quality as a productivity improvement tool.

Many business decisions have a positive influence on both productivity and quality. For instance, a simple and easy-to-make product design should reduce defects and increase productivity at the same time. Streamlining production processes has a similar effect: Chances for errors are eliminated, and the removal of unnecessary operations improves productivity. We will examine several examples when we discuss product and process design in a later chapter. Improved equipment, worker training, and preventive maintenance also contribute to improved productivity and quality.

When productivity measurement is viewed from a narrow perspective, it may seem as if quality improvements lead to lower levels of productivity. For example, consider a financial services employee who transcribes applications into a computer database. A typical productivity measure for such an operation might be "number of

---

[5]Y. K. Shetty, "Corporate Response to Productivity Challenges," *National Productivity Review,* Winter 1984–85, pp. 7–14.

applications per hour." If quality is measured as the rate of errors in transcription, it is clear that an inverse relationship will exist between speed and error rate. Efforts to improve quality by reducing time pressures for output or adding some self-checking activities will clearly decrease productivity as it is measured. However, managers who focus solely on such an analysis are missing the big picture. Increased errors will cause decreased customer satisfaction, more rework, increased inspection, and low employee morale. Eventually the costs associated with these activities will outweigh the costs of a lower productivity level. (We discuss these aspects further in Chapter 3.) Thus, managers must view productivity measurement, not in isolation, but in the global context of quality, cost, and customer satisfaction. This is especially important in labor-intensive activities such as service operations. Leonard and Sasser provide some examples for which quality improvements have led to increased productivity:[6]

- One company's installation of a new "clean room" reduced contaminants on printed circuit boards and boosted output by almost 35%.

- Elimination of rework stations at one television factory forced assembly workers to find and solve their own quality mistakes. These adjustments resulted in an increased production rate per hour of direct labor and in the elimination of thousands of dollars of rework costs.

- One company using precision assembly equipment designed components that would not fit together unless they were "right." This arrangement raised production rates as well as distribution efficiencies. It also improved the productivity of the sales force, who no longer had to spend time collecting, boxing, and replacing returned components.

TOTAL QUALITY MANAGEMENT

An internal quality survey conducted at Polaroid identified seven major areas of concern within the corporation[7]:

1. Quality was too often entered downstream, that is, at final assembly, rather than in the design and development stages.

2. Customer needs and satisfaction were not well understood.

3. Quality was not an important issue until it became a problem.

4. Management seemed willing to sacrifice quality when costs or scheduling conflicted.

5. Operators were not sufficiently trained in their jobs and in quality issues.

6. Quality problems were observed with vendors.

7. Quality costs were determined to be high.

---

[6]Frank S. Leonard and W. Earl Sasser, "The Incline of Quality," *Harvard Business Review,* Vol. 60, No. 5, September/October 1982, pp. 163–171. Copyright © 1982 by the President and Fellows of Harvard College; all rights reserved.

[7]Harold S. Page, "A Quality Strategy for the '80s," *Quality Progress,* Vol. 16, No. 11, November 1983, pp. 16–21.

These issues involve *people, technology, information,* and *management.* Polaroid's response to them was a comprehensive and integrated quality strategy.

Polaroid's experience is not unique. In every organization, effective quality management must be a total, company-wide effort that is aimed at the avoidance of problems through the planning and engineering of products, processes, and methods, the identification of problems that inevitably will arise, correction of these problems, and continuous improvement of quality performance. The term **total quality control** was coined by A. V. Feigenbaum to denote this managerial effort.[8] To accomplish these goals, manufacturing and service organizations require strong management and leadership, technical skills for problem identification, and problem-solving methodologies for improvement of quality.

The Japanese adopted Feigenbaum's concept and renamed it **company-wide quality control.** They are using the concept very successfully to compete in world markets. This has led many American managers to investigate how this concept might improve their quality and competitiveness. Reiker lists five aspects of total quality control practiced in Japan.[9]

1. Quality emphasis extends through market analysis, design, and customer service rather than only the production stages of making a product.

2. Quality emphasis is directed toward operations in every department from executives to clerical personnel.

3. Quality is the responsibility of the individual and the work group, not some *other* group, such as inspection.

4. There are two types of quality characteristics as viewed by customers: those that satisfy and those that motivate. Only the latter are strongly related to repeat sales and a "quality" image.

5. The first customer for a part or piece of information is usually the next department in the production process.

Reiker emphasizes that total quality control involves achieving objectives more efficiently at every level of the company from daily work to managing the entire enterprise.

According to Juran, the key factors in Japan's success were that (1) upper managers personally took charge of leading the quality revolution, (2) all levels of employees and functions underwent training in managing for quality, and (3) quality improvement was undertaken at a continuing, rapid pace.[10]

Today, the term **total quality management** (TQM) is becoming more popular. The principles of TQM are embodied in the following:

1. Business success can only be achieved by understanding and fulfilling the needs of customers.

2. Leadership in quality is the responsibility of top management.

---

[8] A. V. Feigenbaum, *Total Quality Control,* 3rd ed. (New York: McGraw-Hill, 1983).

[9] Wayne S. Reiker, "Integrating the Pieces for Total Quality Control," *The Quality Circles Journal* (now *The Journal for Quality and Participation*), Vol. 6, No. 4, December 1983, pp. 14–20.

[10] J. M. Juran, "Managing for Quality," *Journal for Quality and Participation,* Vol. 11, No. 1, Jan./Feb. 1988, pp. 8–12.

3. Statistical reasoning with factual data is the basis for problem solving and continuous improvement.

4. All functions at all levels of an organization must focus on continuous improvement to achieve corporate goals.

5. Problem solving and process improvement are best performed by multifunctional work teams.

6. Continuous learning, training, and education is the responsibility of everyone in the organization.

TQM implies that quality is not solely a control, or technical, issue, but that quality must be addressed from the perspective of strategic management. Strategic planning involves the long-range determination of business policy and usually includes product and market planning, financial planning, and facility and equipment planning. Each of these strategic planning areas has a bearing on quality; in fact, quality is perhaps the most important issue in strategic planning. A strategic orientation toward quality will generate growth, provide a competitive advantage, and contribute to a firm's profitability.

In Chapter 1 we presented the eight principal quality dimensions proposed by Garvin. He notes that companies can create a niche in the marketplace by focusing on only a few of these dimensions, the ones competitors ignore.[11] For example, Japanese automobiles initially emphasized reliability and conformance ("fit and finish") over other quality dimensions in which they may not have been superior. Their success suggests that the quality dimensions they chose to emphasize were indeed important dimensions from a fitness-for-use perspective. Another example contrasts the Steinway & Sons piano company to a new competitor, Yamaha. For a long time, Steinway has been the quality leader due to quality characteristics such as even voicing, durability, and distinctive tone. Each piano is built by hand and is unique in sound and style. Yamaha has achieved a significant market share by emphasizing reliability and conformance, two dimensions that are low on Steinway's list.

A U.S. Government General Accounting Office (GAO) study of 20 companies that were among the highest scoring applicants in the 1988 and 1989 Malcolm Baldrige National Quality Award competition indicated that companies that adopted quality management practices experienced an overall improvement in corporate performance.[12] In nearly all cases, companies that used total quality management practices achieved better employee relations, higher productivity, greater customer satisfaction, increased market share, and improved profitability.

Table 2.1 lists some of the major benefits that can be obtained by strategic quality planning. Since profit equals revenue less cost, any improvement that will increase sales or decrease costs will improve profitability. Likewise, the consequences of poor quality planning can be devastating. For example, when Coleco released its personal computer, Adam, with much hype and many marketing promises in late 1983, the first batch had many problems. As many as 30% of those sold were being returned.

---

[11]David A. Garvin, "Competing on the Eight Dimensions of Quality," *Harvard Business Review,* November/December 1987, pp. 101–109. Copyright © 1987 by the President and Fellows of Harvard College; all rights reserved.

[12]*Management Practices: U.S. Companies Improve Performance Through Quality Efforts,* United States General Accounting Office, GAO/NSIAD-91-190, May 1991.

TABLE 2.1 Benefits of Strategic Quality Planning

Product Quality
Improved product design
Reduced liability risk
Smoother new product introduction
Improved reaction to competition
Enhanced reputation
Improved after-the-sale service
Better advertising strategies

Production Quality
Reduction of rework and other operating losses
Decreased labor and material costs
Improved managerial control of operations
Better employee morale
Smoother production flow
Improved reliability

Business Performance
Improved delivery times
Reduced order processing times
Reduced cycle times for new product introduction
Improved return on investment
Smaller inventory turnover
Lower costs
Higher market share
Customer retention

Obviously, a serious quality problem existed, and some chain stores stopped carrying the machine. By the time Coleco fixed the technical problems and reduced the computer's price, the damage had already been done; soon after, Coleco let Adam die a natural death.[13]

However, achieving quality results takes time. It typically takes two to five years for the benefits of a TQM approach to become clear. TQM is not a short-term, quick-fix solution; it involves continuous leadership and hard work. A. V. Feigenbaum, a quality consultant who advised the GAO on its study, estimated that fewer than one-third of all companies had implemented formal quality improvement programs as of mid-1991. He projected that the country's gross national product (GNP) would increase 7% within five years if every business reorganized its operations around the TQM concept.

---

[13]"Coleco's Adam Bomb Case Study in Disaster," *The Cincinnati Enquirer,* February 10, 1985.

QUALITY IN PRACTICE

The Spare Parts Quality System at DEC[14]

Digital Equipment Corporation (DEC) is one of the world's largest computer manufacturers. The reputation of DEC's Field Service Organization depends mostly on the quality of the spare parts provided to customers. At DEC, spare parts are referred to as "field replaceable units" or FRUs. To prevent problems from occurring or to correct those that do occur, DEC created a field service logistics quality assurance group, which was responsible for providing the field with functional and reliable FRUs. The group consists of five functional units within the organization; these units and their responsibilities are listed in Table 2.2.

Maintaining a high level of service requires continual planning and revision through all the stages of a product's life. DEC can see how well it has performed each task by using measurements that include the mean time to repair, the mean time between failures, and defective FRU percentage. Predictive measurements are also available from internal sources. For example, manufacturing provides quality measures that indicate their contribution to any problem that may arise.

Because design problems are the most difficult and expensive to correct, DEC emphasizes FRU development early in a product's design. To provide high-quality FRUs, DEC uses several different tools and techniques, including quality contracts, FRU manufacturing certifications, and detailed information about activities to be completed before FRUs are ready to be shipped. The emphasis is on prevention rather than detection and correction. The company also employs statistical tools to track FRU performance in the field—to spot trends, signify differences, forecast future activity, and show geographic differences in FRU usage.

An application of this spare parts quality system is in DEC's family of personal computers. The maintenance strategy formulated during product design and development took into account that customers were expected to install and maintain the new products. Therefore, it was necessary to incorporate the needs and the level of computer sophistication of this new customer base into a maintenance strategy and into quality and reliability requirements for FRUs.

Design engineers were given certain constraints. The system had to be able to self-diagnose faults down to the FRU level and to communicate this information to the user. The user then had to be able to remove the defective part and install the replacement without worrying about compatibility or the need for adjustments.

Manufacturing had to be able to mass produce this design at very high-quality levels. DEC knows that it has more to lose when a customer finds a defective spare part than when a field service engineer encounters a problem with a FRU. The quality of spare parts can become a competitive edge, and the manufacturing process must reflect this fact in such areas as process control, test capability, and length of burn-in.

TABLE 2.2 Management Responsibilities for Spare Parts Quality Assurance at DEC

Group	Responsibility
Marketing	Define end-user needs and abilities
Engineering	Understand end-user application
	Component selection
	Assembly layout
	Repairability
	Maintainability
Manufacturing	Process quality
	Process control
	Test coverage
	Infancy failures removed
Logistics	Packaging
	Handling
	Storage
	Revision control
Field service	Training
	Handling
	Storage
	Adjustments
	Diagnosing

[14]Adapted from "Spare Part Quality Assurance" by Robert Rosenthal, *Quality Progress,* Vol. 16, No. 5, May 1983, pp. 24–27.

(continued)

The packaging, storage, and distribution of replacement parts for personal computers become increasingly important as more and more customers perform their own maintenance. To ensure that spare parts are available to customers, the parts are stocked at many more locations. This procedure increases transportation and handling by individuals unfamiliar with electronics components and thus increases the potential for damage to such components.

The personal computer market makes spare parts performance reporting more complex, but it also necessitates that reports be timely. Each location with parts stocked has information about how customers currently perceive FRU performance. A summary of that information is available at DEC corporate headquarters, allowing the company to react rapidly to trends so that it can isolate problems, determine causes, and implement solutions.

Key Issues for Discussion

1. Discuss how the management responsibilities for the various functional groups at DEC support a total quality management concept.

2. Describe how this discussion of the DEC field service organization relates to the various issues of quality in service organizations as discussed in the chapter.

QUALITY IN PRACTICE

Productivity and Quality at Westinghouse[15]

"Wherever you find you have a problem with productivity, it usually translates into a dimension of quality," says L. Jerry Hudspeth, Vice President of Productivity and Quality at Westinghouse Electric Corporation. The Westinghouse Productivity and Quality Center gives the company a way to integrate its efforts at improving quality and increasing productivity. It serves as a central clearinghouse for quality-enhancement and productivity-improvement concepts and technologies. The mission of the center's 300 employees is first to locate and develop technology and techniques and then to help the various Westinghouse divisions use these ideas to improve profitability by increasing productivity and improving quality.

The center was formed in 1980 as a result of Westinghouse management's grappling with the problem of productivity, which was widely discussed throughout the United States in the 1970s. Westinghouse management has reported that the original focus was on productivity, stressing the important roles of both people and technology in increasing productivity. The quality connection was actually developed and reinforced later.

The center provides consulting and operational services in five broad disciplines:

1. *Value and operations analysis* looks at user values, such as reasonable price, reliability, and quality, and at such producer concerns as reasonable cost and serviceability. The purpose of this function is to assist Westinghouse divisions in the design of profitable products that will best meet a customer's requirements. It also conducts productivity surveys of facilities or entire divisions with the aim of improving white-collar productivity.

2. *Manufacturing technology* develops advanced manufacturing processes using state-of-the-art techniques in machining, metals joining, materials processing and handling, electronics manufacture, computer-aided work measurement, and materials and inventory management.

3. *Automation systems* seek out existing technologies to solve specific manufacturing problems

[15]Adapted from "The Productivity/Quality Connection—Plugging in at Westinghouse Electric" by John Ryan, *Quality Progress,* Vol. 16, No. 12, December 1983, pp. 26–29.

(continued)

and create innovative manufacturing equipment to perform jobs that available equipment cannot handle.

4. *Systems integration* develops and puts into place information systems for computer-aided design and manufacture, telecommunications, material planning systems, shop floor control, office systems, and computer-based business systems.

5. *Quality improvement* acts as a resource for quality enhancement concepts and technologies. It provides training and consultation on quality-related matters.

Ralph Barra, Director of Corporate Quality, states, "It's a misconception that quality and productivity are somehow at odds, that you have to sacrifice quality to increase productivity. We're seeing a change in attitude, organizationally, at Westinghouse. We believe in stressing quality *first*—quality of products and processes, quality of performance, and quality of workers' life—and the attitude that things *can* be done right the first time. Quality precedes productivity."

Based on experiences in the company, the center has also uncovered some interesting figures on the cost of quality and the benefits of quality improvement. It has found that eliminating one dollar of waste results in a four-dollar increase in operating margin. The potential is great, considering that failure costs typically have amounted to 10 to 20% of sales.

The integration of people, technology, information, and management at Westinghouse can be summarized by the company's Conditions of Excellence for Quality:

Strategic Plan: The business unit strategic plan includes key quality issues and improvement programs with measurable goals. Quality is used to maintain a competitive advantage with a superior product reputation.

Quality Program Plan: A division-wide, written prevention-oriented quality program plan is supported by functional departmental procedures and updated in accordance with changing requirements.

Customers' Perception: Customers' perception of quality is understood, regularly monitored and measured, and used for performance improvement.

Design Assurance: Designers accurately understand customer needs and work to approved, proven procedures and methods. Designs are adequately verified, and requirements are clearly and completely communicated.

Purchased Materials: Suppliers always meet fitness-for-use requirements with rejection rates in the magnitude of parts per million.

Participative Management: The environment continually encourages and provides the means for all employees to contribute to improved performance.

Training: Ongoing training develops a quality enhancement dedication and competence throughout the organization.

Advanced Technology: A continuous upgrading program uses optimized state-of-the-art equipment and processes.

Performance Measurement: Reports exist that accurately identify all quality costs, indicate performance trends, and pinpoint improvement opportunities.

Recognition: Employee contributions to improvements are encouraged by timely and appropriate recognition.

Key Issues for Discussion

1. How does the Westinghouse Productivity and Quality Center relate to the total quality system framework in Figure 1.2 of Chapter 1?

2. Explain how the Conditions of Excellence for Quality can enhance both quality and productivity.

Summary of Key Points

- Quality plays an important role in each component of the production and business support systems in a manufacturing firm.

- The role of quality in service organizations has become a key aspect of competitive advantage. The differences between services and manufacturing require different approaches in designing and implementing quality assurance programs.

- Improvements in quality generally lead to improvements in productivity.

- Total quality control (company-wide quality control) involves a comprehensive effort toward improving quality involving every individual in an organization. The term *total quality management* is used today to signify that managerial activities must guide a total quality effort.

Questions for Review and Discussion

1. Discuss the role of quality within each major component of a manufacturing system.

2. Discuss the differences between manufacturing and service organizations. What implications are there for quality assurance?

3. What do we mean by the term *hidden factory?*

4. How do the Japanese practice the total quality control concept? What competitive advantages does this give them in world markets?

5. Discuss the relationship between productivity and quality.

6. What are some benefits of strategic planning for quality?

7. Consider the following scenarios:[16]

   a. An organization inspects incoming resources on receipt, inspects at key partial product completion states, and final inspects. Unacceptable output at each stage is rejected and dealt with accordingly or appropriately. Rework is possible, and those defects identified as correctable are taken care of.

   b. A group of five spray painters on an assembly line operates with basic job training but with little feedback as to the actual outcomes resulting from their efforts. Inspectors down the line, isolated from the direct line personnel, evaluate the output from the painting department based on specific quality attributes (runs, too wide or narrow shading, stripes, etc.). These quality attributes are clear to the inspectors but virtually unknown to the actual painters themselves. Painters never talk to the inspectors for a variety of reasons (job classifications, physical location, no time).

---

[16]Adapted from "Productivity and Quality: What Is the Connection?", by D. Scott Sink and J. Bert Keats, 1982 Fall Industrial Engineering Conference Proceedings (Norcross, GA: Institute of Industrial Engineers), pp. 277–283.

c. A firm is committed to achieving high quality in the goods and services it produces. The quality control department has convinced management that to accomplish this, all goods and services produced must be inspected. A significant amount of effort and other resources has been devoted to building and developing a large quality organization that emphasizes inspection, correction, and zero defects.

Discuss the productivity/quality interaction in these situations and suggest steps that management might take to improve each situation.

8. For the production system shown on page 40, discuss possible quality measurements and analyses that might be taken at each stage and that might be useful in improving productivity and quality.

Case Problem

Deere & Company is a world leader in the supply and manufacture of agricultural, industrial, and lawn and grounds care equipment. Because of the company's close ties to the agricultural industry, corporate performance in both sales and profits suffered during the period between 1984 and 1987. During this time, the company made adjustments in its product mix and manufacturing processes to enable it to compete in a global environment. Deere's objective was to become the low-cost producer of products for the markets they serve.

In this chapter, we noted that the 1980s represented an era of increased quality awareness for American industry. Below are listed some quotations from Deere's annual reports. From this information, prepare a brief report discussing how quality is viewed by the company, and how its definition or approach has changed over time. Relate your discussion to appropriate issues that are discussed in this chapter. You may also wish to study some recent annual reports to see how the company has progressed through the 1990s.

1984

In spite of the industry environment of low demand, the challenge is to do what we do better. Provide more value per dollar of purchase price. To accomplish this will require cost effectiveness in all facets of our business which includes being more flexible and more aggressive in adopting the most modern design and manufacturing technologies.

Product design is being systematically reviewed to provide improved performance and quality at a lower cost.

New manufacturing technologies such as robot welding have enabled Deere employees to become more efficient while producing parts of higher and more consistent quality.

Underlying most changes in the forestry equipment line was a special emphasis on increased reliability.

1986 (The farm economy was in poor condition.)

Lower production volumes are forcing U.S. manufacturers to consider sourcing of parts and components. OEMs [original equipment manufacturers] are recognizing John Deere's technological advantage and are giving their accounts to John Deere, resulting in increased production volume.

As we improve our existing operations and expand into new but related businesses we are guided by the same principles we have followed throughout our history—those that express excellent value for our customers and fair dealing with all who come into contact with our company.

New products that offer features and quality of particular value to the customer, coupled with competitive pricing and excellent dealer service, have enhanced the company's position in the consumer products market.

The use of leveraged engineering has resulted in new products that meet the current needs of the market, do so promptly and uphold the John Deere reputation for quality without compromise.

1987

John Deere is determined to be the lowest cost producer in our industries and to sustain a competitive advantage on a global basis. However, we all must perpetuate the company's reputation for providing the best quality and value to our customers. While we're making structural changes in our operations we must continue to adhere to these business principles.

John Deere leadership in the agricultural equipment business is based on a line of products that has earned a reputation for excellent quality and reliability, on the skills and services we have to support the product line and on our strong network of independent dealers.

In our continuing effort to improve the quality and performance of John Deere agricultural equipment, we have traditionally invested a higher percent of sales in product R&D than any of our major competitors.

The industrial equipment improvement reflects our strong product line and dedicated organization, and our employees' determination to reduce costs, improve quality, and to deliver the best value to the customer.

The total value of John Deere equipment is quality, reliability, dealer support, finance plans, resale value, and the company that stands behind it all.

1988

The company's productivity, whether measured in terms of production, sales, or net income per employee, has improved dramatically. Our products and manufacturing facilities are frequently cited as examples of industrial excellence.

This ongoing commitment to product excellence through large research and development expenditures has contributed to the recognition of John Deere products as the finest in the market.

These new products represent new standards of performance and quality consistent with the company's primary principle to give the customer greater value.

John Deere's advancements in engineering and manufacturing technology help hold the line against cost and allow the company to focus more primarily on what the customer wants.

1989

Many of the principles guiding this company are as old as the company itself—principles like integrity, the quality and value of our products and services, and the esteem in which the company holds its customers, dealers, and employees. Other principles that guide us have emerged more recently; we learned in the trials of the 1980s that cost reduction is not just a competitive necessity. It must become a way of life in all aspects of our business.

We must continue to ensure that John Deere products offer the customer the best value in all respects—in quality, reliability, features, resale price, and especially in the value added by an independent network of well-placed, full-servicing dealers people can rely on.

We must further improve manufacturing efficiencies, through both technology and the participation of wage and salaried employees.

FIGURE 2.1   The Production System

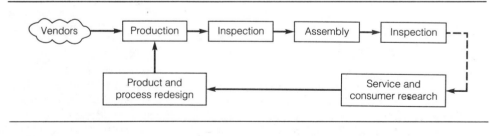

Bibliography

Berry, Leonard L.; Zeithaml, Valarie A.; and Parasuraman, A. "Five Imperatives for Improving Service Quality," *Sloan Management Review,* Summer 1990, pp. 29–38.

Chowdhury, A. R. "The Basics of Productivity Analysis," *Quality Progress,* October 1986, pp. 68–70.

Freund, Richard A. "The Role of Quality Technology," *Quality Assurance: Methods, Management, and Motivation,* H. J. Bajaria, ed. Dearborn, MI: Society of Manufacturing Engineers, 1981, pp. 10–13.

Garvin, David A. *Managing Quality,* New York: The Free Press, 1988.

Haywood-Farmer, John, "A Conceptual Model of Service Quality," *International Journal of Operations and Production Management,* Vol. 8, No. 6, 1988, pp. 19–29.

Lewis, Barbara R. "Quality in the Service Sector: A Review," *International Journal of Bank Marketing,* Vol. 7, No. 5, 1989, pp. 4–12.

Midas, Michael T., Jr. "The Quality/Productivity Connection," *Quality,* Vol. 21, No. 2, February 1982, pp. 22–23.

Murray, David J. "Quality Assurance and Other Departments," *Quality Assurance: Methods, Management, and Motivation,* H. J. Bajaria, ed. Dearborn, MI: Society of Manufacturing Engineers, 1981, pp. 41–46.

Rosander, A. C. "Service Industry QC—Is the Challenge Being Met?" *Quality Progress,* Vol. 13, No. 9, September 1980, p. 34.

Scanlon, Frank, and Hagan, John T. "Quality Management for the Service Industries—Part I," *Quality Progress,* Vol. 16, No. 5, May 1983, pp. 18–23.

Shetty, Y. K., and Ross, Joel E. "Quality and Its Management in Service Businesses," *Industrial Management,* November/December 1985.

Sink, D. Scott, and Keats, J. Bert. "Productivity and Quality: What Is the Connection?" *1982 Fall Industrial Engineering Conference Proceedings.* Norcross, GA: Institute of Industrial Engineers, pp. 277–283.

Thompson, Phillip; DeSouza, Glenn; and Gale, Bradley T. "The Strategic Management of Service Quality," *Quality Progress,* Vol. 18, No. 6, June 1985, pp. 20–25.

Williams, Roy H., and Zigli, Ronald M. "Ambiguity Impedes Quality in the Service Industries," *Quality Progress,* July 1987, pp. 14–17.

CHAPTER 3

The Economics of Quality

conomic considerations play an important role in quality. Quality can have a significant effect on profitability. Each time work must be redone, such as remanufacturing a defective item or retesting an electronic assembly, costs increase. Consider, for instance, the costs associated with quality problems in the automobile industry. American Motors figured that it spent about $3 million to correct pollution control systems on 270,000 of its 1976 cars, including close to $40,000 just for the postage to notify owners. For Firestone, the cost of replacing 7.5 million tires in a recall case in 1976 was more than $135 million after taxes, more than the company's net income in the fiscal year.[1]

Quality not only has an effect on direct costs, but also on indirect costs resulting from lost customers. For example, credit card companies spend an average of $51 to recruit a customer and set up a new account.[2] For the first year, the typical profit generated by a customer is $30. Thus, if the customer leaves after the first year, the company takes a $21 loss. More importantly, profits of service firms typically rise for each year a customer stays with the firm. For one auto-service company, the expected profit from a fourth-year customer is more than triple the profit that same customer generates in the first year. However, most companies do not know how much it costs to lose a customer.

Experts estimate[3] that the cost due to poor quality can range as high as 40% of total sales with the industry average running close to 25%. Many feel that it should be only about one-tenth of this amount, or about 2.5%. This is clearly an area where substantial savings can be achieved. Yet a survey conducted by Grant Thornton, a major accounting and consulting firm, reported that while 83% of companies surveyed said that quality is a top priority, less than one-third have calculated costs associated with quality. More and more organizations are beginning to recognize the importance of quality costs and have installed systems for managing, measuring, and controlling them. Quality cost data are used in several ways. Two of the most important applications of quality cost data are in tracking the effectiveness of the

---

[1]Robert N. Reece, "Quality Control as an Inflation Fighter," *Quality Progress,* August 1980, pp. 24–25.

[2]Frederick F. Reichheld and W. Earl Sasser, Jr. "Zero Defections: Quality Comes to Services," *Harvard Business Review,* September–October 1990, pp. 105–111. Copyright © 1990 by the President and Fellows of Harvard College; all rights reserved.

[3]J. William Semich, "The Costs of Quality," *Purchasing,* Vol. 103, No. 8, November 5, 1987, p. 61.

quality assurance program and in identifying quality problems and improvement opportunities. In addition, quality costs are being used in strategic planning, budgeting, and capital investment decisions, much in the traditional manner that production and marketing costs have been used.

The attention paid to quality costs is reflected in military specifications for government contracts. MIL-Q-9858A, "Quality Program Requirements," requires contractors to maintain and use quality cost data as a management element of the quality program.[4] A more recent military standard, MIL-STD-1520B, specifies actual categories of costs that must be collected and summarized by Air Force contractors and subcontractors who have MIL-Q-9858A requirements in their contract, with the objective of providing "current and trend data to be used for contractor and government management review and appropriate action."[5]

Quality cost programs should not have to be forced on an organization. Their value lies in their ability to contribute to customer satisfaction and to profits. This fact needs to be recognized by top management. Traditionally, capital investments in new facilities and equipment have been financially analyzed by estimating their savings in direct labor and material costs. Alternatives that do not appear to be attractive by these criteria alone may indeed yield a significant return when quality costs are taken into account. Thus, quality costs are an important part of total financial performance. This chapter introduces concepts relating to quality costs that will be fundamental throughout the book.

QUALITY AND PROFITABILITY

Profitability is driven by quality. To understand this, let us first examine the fundamental economic relationships that determine profit:

profit = revenue − cost

revenue = price × quantity sold

To increase profit, we need to either increase revenue or decrease cost. To increase revenue, we must increase price (keeping quantity sold constant) or increase the quantity sold or market share (maintaining a fixed price). Quality is closely related to each of these terms: price, market share, and cost.[6]

Quality and Price

The relationship between quality and price is subject to much debate. One theory suggests that higher quality can only be produced at a higher cost, and if costs and prices are positively related as economic theory suggests, then quality and price will be positively related. Thus, according to this theory, higher prices imply higher

---

[4]Department of Defense, MIL-Q-9858A, *Quality Program Requirements,* December 16, 1963.

[5]Department of Defense, MIL-STD-1520B, *Corrective Action and Disposition System for Nonconforming Material,* July 3, 1980.

[6]David A. Garvin, "What Does 'Product Quality' Really Mean?" *Sloan Management Review,* Fall 1984, pp. 34–52; J. M. Juran, "Quality and Income," *Juran's Quality Control Handbook,* 4th ed. (New York: McGraw-Hill, 1988).

quality. This theory assumes, however, that consumers have enough information on which to evaluate product quality. Most consumers possess only limited technological literacy and lack objective information on product quality. Therefore, they generally rely on other factors to make a quality assessment. Research studies have found that when other factors such as brand name, store image, product features, or country of manufacture influence consumer perception, quality assessment is not as heavily influenced by price. Also, if managers observe that consumer perceptions of quality and purchasing decisions are positively related to price, they may command higher prices without actually increasing quality. Such behavior breaks down this price-quality theory. As a result, price often bears a positive relationship to perceived quality rather than to actual quality. High prices may actually reflect inefficiencies in production, high fixed costs, and poor quality.

Quality improvements can allow a company to command higher prices. Juran relates an example of a power tool manufacturer who improved the reliability of the tools.[7] The marketing manager resisted increasing prices on the grounds that market share would be lost. A field study disclosed that the high-reliability tools greatly reduced the costs of maintenance and downtime for the industrial users. This information became the means of convincing the customers to accept a price increase.

On the other hand, price premiums leave a firm open to competitive threats. For example, Japanese luxury car divisions such as Lexus and Infiniti claim to have equaled the quality of German luxury automobiles at significantly lower prices and thus have made a significant penetration into this market.

Quality and Market Share

The relationship between quality and market share often depends on how quality is defined. If the product-based definition applies, that is, if high quality is related to superior performance or quantity of features, the product will generally be more expensive and will sell in smaller quantities. However, if the fitness-for-use definition applies, high quality need not be accompanied by premium prices. In this case, quality and market share will be positively related. Many Japanese products have gained significant market share in the United States on this basis.

Many research studies have verified that quality and market share are closely related. One study found that businesses that improved quality during the 1970s increased their market share five to six times faster than those whose quality declined, and three times as fast as those whose quality remained unchanged.

Quality and Cost

As with price, different views regarding quality and cost have been debated. One camp argues that improved quality requires more expensive materials, additional labor, more precise machines, and so forth, which results in higher costs. A second viewpoint sees improved quality as decreasing costs through savings in rework, scrap, and warranty expenses. Both views are justified, depending on the frame of reference.

---

[7] J. M. Juran, *Quality Control Handbook*, p. 311.

Improved quality of design clearly requires higher costs in terms of materials and processes. In his book *Quality Is Free,*[8] Philip Crosby argues that building quality into a product does *not* cost the company more because of the savings in rework, scrap, and servicing the product after the sale, in addition to the benefits of customer satisfaction and repeat sales. Even if additional features are added that require a premium price, these features can improve fitness for use and actually lower the cost of the product over its lifetime. As Crosby states[9]:

> Quality is not only free, it is an honest-to-everything profit maker. Every penny you don't spend on doing things wrong, over, or instead of, becomes half a penny right on the bottom line. In these days of "who knows what is going to happen to our business tomorrow," there aren't many ways left to make a profit improvement. If you concentrate on making quality certain, you can probably increase your profit by an amount equal to 5% to 10% of your sales. That is a lot of money for free.

Cost savings result from improved quality of conformance. The real issue that can be overlooked is the net effect on profitability.

These relationships are summarized in Figure 3.1, which shows the effect of improved quality on profitability. The value of a product in the marketplace is determined by the quality of design. Improvements in such aspects as performance, features, and reliability will improve a firm's quality reputation and the perceived value of the product, resulting in the company's ability to command higher prices and achieve an increased market share. This in turn leads to increased revenues. These revenues will cover the added costs of improved design, thus defeating the argument that quality increases costs. Improved conformance leads to lower manufacturing and service costs. The net effect of improved quality of design and conformance is increased profits.

---

[8]Philip Crosby, *Quality Is Free* (New York: McGraw-Hill, 1979).
[9]Philip Crosby, *Quality Is Free,* p. 1.

FIGURE 3.1   **Quality and Profitability**

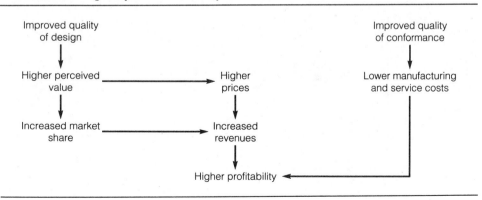

ECONOMIC MODELS FOR QUALITY OF CONFORMANCE

For years, many books and articles have presented an economic model for the "optimum" level of quality of conformance. Because this model has serious flaws and can be dangerously misleading, it is important to discuss it here.

Traditional Economic Model

Quality costs are incurred by each activity devoted toward assuring conformance to specifications in a production system. For example, purchasing must monitor quality costs in relation to the price paid; receiving must guarantee that incoming materials meet quality standards; tool engineering must maintain tools and gages in proper condition; industrial engineering and process design personnel must spend time selecting equipment and work methods that will produce conforming parts; expenses are incurred for inspection and testing of work in process and finished goods; and logistics activities must ensure that no damage occurs in transit. These costs are generally referred to as the **costs of quality assurance.** On the other hand, failure to conform to specifications will result in losses due to poor quality such as scrap, rework, and warranty adjustments. These costs are called **costs due to nonconformance.**

Figure 3.2 illustrates the classic relationship between the costs of quality assurance and the costs due to nonconformance. As the quality of conformance (which can be measured by the percentage of defective products manufactured) increases as a result of improved quality assurance, the quality assurance costs increase and the costs due to nonconformance decrease. From a strict economic viewpoint, one seeks the optimal level of conformance that minimizes the total costs to the organization. This is shown as the point that minimizes the total cost curve in Figure 3.2. To the left of the optimum point, there is significant opportunity to improve quality through increased control. To the right, however, the cost of control outweighs the savings that are generated.

FIGURE 3.2   **Classic Economic Model of Quality of Conformance**

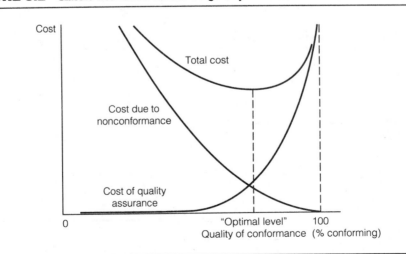

Modern Viewpoints

The model shown in Figure 3.2 has been used to justify operating at a level of quality conformance *less* than 100%. Many Japanese firms, however, seemingly ignore the economic trade-offs in an attempt to drive defects to zero. In reality, they are depending on increases in market share and consumer acceptance to offset the cost of "excess" quality control. This strategic decision tends to work best in expanding markets and less well in shrinking markets. To this end, Hsiang and Lee[10] have argued that the traditional quality cost model illustrated in Figure 3.2 ignores several important realities. This model assumes that sales of the product are constant. There is evidence, however, that quality improvement or degradation can significantly alter the demand for the product. Dissatisfied customers are less likely to be repeat purchasers than are satisfied customers. Word-of-mouth reputation can be significant in maintaining market share. Under the assumption that the firm seeks to maximize revenue, Hsiang and Lee show mathematically that the optimal level of conformance should be *higher* than that shown in Figure 3.2 when the revenue effect is considered (see problem 10).

As prevention of poor quality becomes a focus, the inherent failure rates of materials and products have been reduced through new technologies, and improvements in automation have reduced human error during production and appraisal. Thus, we now have the ability to achieve perfection in quality at a finite cost, and the cost of assuring quality does not extend to infinity as 100% conformance is reached. This causes the total quality cost curve to reach its minimum at 100% conformance, justifying the philosophy of continuous improvement from an economic viewpoint. This new economic model is shown in Figure 3.3.

---

[10]T. C. Hsiang and L. Lee, "Zero Defects: A Quality Costs Approach," *Communications in Statistics—Theory and Methods,* Vol. 14, No. 11, 1985, pp. 2641–2655.

FIGURE 3.3 Modern Economic Model of Quality of Conformance

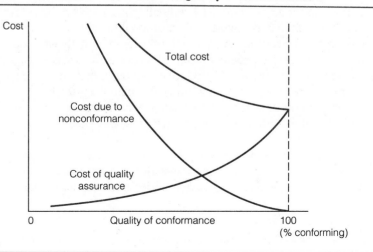

We note that this model does not necessarily apply in every situation, such as when automation cannot be justified or used. It is, however, a long-term goal. The traditional model does help in assessing a firm's current position and in identifying quality improvement strategies. For example, if nonconformance costs greatly exceed quality assurance costs (to the left of the optimum), then it is sensible to identify specific improvement projects to improve the quality of conformance and reduce the costs of poor quality. To the right of the optimum, the costs of quality assurance are high relative to the costs of nonconformance. In such situations, it may be possible to reduce the costs of quality assurance without sacrificing the level of conformance. This might be done by improving technology, reducing inspection through more appropriate control mechanisms, or relaxing unnecessarily tight quality standards relative to fitness-for-use criteria. The net effect of these activities is a continued shift of the "optimum" point to the right.

THE TAGUCHI LOSS FUNCTION

Dr. Genichi Taguchi has proposed a significantly different approach to viewing quality based on the economic implications of poor quality. Taguchi defines quality as the (avoidance of) "loss a product causes to society after being shipped, other than any losses caused by its intrinsic functions."[11] The loss to society includes costs incurred by the product's *failure to meet customer expectations,* the *failure to meet performance characteristics,* and *harmful side effects* caused by the product.

When a product fails to meet customer expectations, numerous direct and indirect losses occur. For example, many years ago one of the authors purchased an automobile that was praised for its features, performance, and quality. (The car carried a two-year warranty when most other cars had only a one-year warranty, and it had even won a prestigious "car of the year" award.) Unfortunately, the automobile required frequent repair for numerous problems. Many of these occurred during the warranty period, which resulted in costs to the manufacturer and considerable inconvenience to the customer. Problems continued out of warranty, resulting in more cost and inconvenience. The dealer acknowledged that this particular model year had a poor quality record, but that quality had improved considerably (and even suggested a trade-in for a new model!). Eventually the car was replaced (by a different make) much sooner than anticipated, with additional losses due to high depreciation. The manufacturer lost a repeat buyer, and the dealer eventually went out of business.

Failure to meet performance characteristics results in similar losses. If a product does not perform correctly when purchased, service costs must be borne by the dealer or manufacturer and the reputation of the manufacturer is hurt. Finally, poor quality may result in other societal losses, such as pollution or noise, that eventually lead to medical claims, workmen's compensation, and other costs that eventually affect society in general.

Taguchi measures loss in monetary units and relates it to quantifiable product characteristics. In this way, he makes the translation from the language of the engineer to the language of the manager. To better understand Taguchi's philosophy, let us

---

[11]Genichi Taguchi, *Introduction to Quality Engineering* (Tokyo: Asian Productivity Organization, 1986) p. 1.

reconsider the manufacturing-based definition of quality as "conformance to specifications." Suppose that a specification for some quality characteristic is 0.500 ± 0.020. Using this definition, it makes no difference whether the actual value of the quality characteristic is 0.480, 0.496, 0.500, or 0.520. This approach assumes that the customer, either the consumer or the next department in the production process, would be equally satisfied with any value between 0.480 and 0.520, but not satisfied outside of this tolerance range. Also, this approach assumes that costs do not depend on the actual value of the quality characteristic as long as it is within the tolerance specified (see Figure 3.4). This is often referred to as the "goalpost mentality."

But what is the real difference between 0.479 and 0.481? The former would be considered as "out of specification" and either reworked or scrapped while the latter would be acceptable. In reality, however, the impact of either on the performance characteristic of the product would be about the same. Neither is close to the nominal specification of 0.500. The nominal specification set by the designer is considered an ideal target value for the critical quality characteristic. Taguchi's approach is based on the assumption that the smaller the variation about the target value, the better the quality. The loss increases (as a quadratic function) the further one moves from the target, as illustrated in Figure 3.5. When nominal specifications are met, products are more consistent and total societal costs will be lower.

An example was published in the Japanese newspaper *Ashai* comparing the cost and quality of Sony televisions at two plants in Japan and San Diego.[12] The color density of all the units produced at the San Diego plant was within specifications, while some of those shipped from the Japanese plant were not (see Figure 3.6). However, the average loss per unit of the San Diego plant was $0.89 greater than that of the Japanese plant. This resulted from the fact that units out of specification at the San Diego plant were adjusted within the plant, adding cost to the process. Furthermore, a unit that was adjusted to just within specifications was more likely to generate customer complaints than a unit that was closer to the original target value, therefore incurring higher field service costs. From Figure 3.6 it is clear that fewer U.S.-produced sets met the target value for color density. The distribution of quality in the Japanese plant was more uniform around the target value, and even though some units were out of specification, the total cost was less. Thus, any variation from the

[12]*Ashai,* April 17, 1979; cited in L. P. Sullivan, "Reducing Variability: A New Approach to Quality," *Quality Progress,* Vol. 17, No. 7, July 1984, pp. 15–21.

FIGURE 3.4   **Traditional Conformance-to-Specification Loss Function**

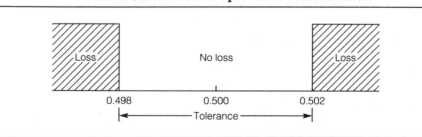

FIGURE 3.5 Taguchi Loss Function

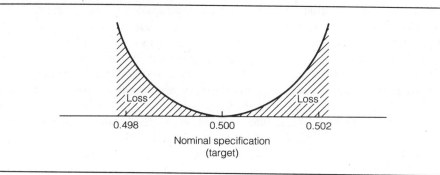

target value causes a loss to the customer. Generally, the larger the deviation, the larger the loss. Akio Morita, the chairman of Sony, explained the difference this way:

> When we tell one of our Japanese employees that the measurement of a certain part must be within a tolerance of plus or minus five, for example, he will automatically strive to get that part as close to zero tolerance as possible. When we started our plant in the United States, we found that the workers would follow instructions perfectly. But if we said make it between plus or minus five, they would get it somewhere near plus or minus five all right, but rarely as close to zero as the Japanese workers did.

Computations Using the Taguchi Loss Function[13]

It would be difficult to determine the exact nature of the loss function for every quality characteristic. Taguchi assumes that the losses can be approximated by a quadratic function so that larger deviations from target cause increasingly larger losses. For the case in which a specific target value is best and quality deteriorates as the value moves

---

[13]This section may be skipped without loss of continuity.

FIGURE 3.6 Color Density of TV Sets

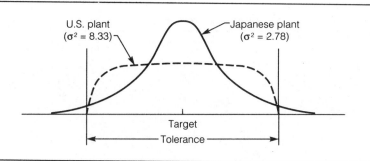

FIGURE 3.7   Nominal-Is-Best Loss Function

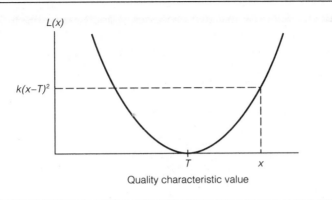

from the target on either side (called "nominal is best"), the loss function is represented by

$$L(x) = k(x - T)^2$$

where x is any value of the quality characteristic, T is the target value, and k is some constant. This is illustrated in Figure 3.7.

The constant k can be estimated by determining the cost of repair or replacement if a certain deviation from the target occurs, as the following example illustrates.

EXAMPLE 1   Estimating the Taguchi Loss Function.   Let us assume that we have a quality characteristic having a specification 0.500 ± 0.020. Suppose that if the value of the quality characteristic exceeds the target of 0.500 by the tolerance of 0.020 on either side, the product will be likely to fail during the warranty period and cost $50 for repair. Such values can be determined through the analysis of company records. Then,

$$50 = k(0.020)^2$$
$$k = 50/0.0004 = 125,000$$

Therefore, the loss function is

$$L(x) = 125,000(x - T)^2$$

Thus, if the deviation is only 0.010, the loss is estimated to be

$$L(0.010) = 125,000(0.010)^2 = \$12.50$$

If the distribution of the variation about the target value is known, the average loss per unit can be computed by statistically averaging the loss associated with possible values of the quality characteristic. In statistical terminology, this is simply the expected value of the loss. (You may wish to review first some basic concepts in probability and statistics in Chapter 12.) To keep the mathematics simple, consider Example 2.

EXAMPLE 2 Computing Expected Loss with the Taguchi Loss Function. Suppose that two processes, A and B, have the following distributions of a quality characteristic with specification 0.50 ± 0.02. For example, in process A, the process produces output having values from 0.48 to 0.52, all of which are equally likely. For process B, 60% of the output is expected to have a value of 0.50, 15% has a value of 0.49, and so on.

Value	Process A Probability	Process B Probability
0.47	0	0.02
0.48	0.20	0.03
0.49	0.20	0.15
0.50	0.20	0.60
0.51	0.20	0.15
0.52	0.20	0.03
0.53	0	0.02

Notice that the output from process A is equally spread over the range from 0.48 to 0.52 and lies entirely within specifications, while that for process B is concentrated near the target value, but does not entirely lie within specifications. Using the loss function

$$L(x) = 125,000(x - 0.50)^2$$

we compute the expected loss for each process as follows:

Value, x	Loss	Process A Probability	Weighted Loss	Process B Probability	Weighted Loss
0.47	112.5	0.00	0	0.02	2.25
0.48	50.0	0.20	10	0.03	1.50
0.49	12.5	0.20	2.5	0.15	1.875
0.50	0.0	0.20	0	0.60	0
0.51	12.5	0.20	2.5	0.15	1.875
0.52	50.0	0.20	10	0.03	1.50
0.53	112.5	0.00	0	0.02	2.25
		Expected loss	25.0		11.25

Clearly process B incurs a smaller total expected loss despite the fact that not all output falls within specifications.

The expected loss can be computed using a simple formula that involves the variance of the quality characteristic, σ^2, and the square of the deviation of the mean value from the target $D^2 = (\bar{x} - T)^2$. The expected loss is

$$EL(x) = k(\sigma^2 + D^2)$$

For instance, in process A, it is easy to show that the variance of the quality characteristic is 0.0002 and that $D^2 = 0$ since the mean value is equal to the target. Thus,

$$EL(x) = 125,000(0.0002 + 0) = 25.$$

A similar computation can be used to compute the expected loss for process B.

In the Sony television example, k was determined to be 0.16. Since the mean of both distributions of color density was on the target value, $D^2 = 0$ for both the U.S. and the Japanese plant. However, the variance of the distributions differed. For the San Diego plant, $\sigma^2 = 8.33$ while for the Japanese plant, $\sigma^2 = 2.78$. Thus the average loss per unit was computed to be:

San Diego plant: $0.16(8.33) = \$1.33$

Japanese plant: $0.16(2.78) = \$0.44$

This was a difference of $0.89 per unit.

The expected loss provides a measure of variation that is independent of specification limits. This helps managers to focus on continuous improvement and not accept the status quo simply because a product "conforms to specifications."

Not all quality characteristics have nominal targets with tolerances on either side. In some cases, such as impurities in a chemical process or fuel consumption, "smaller is better." In other cases, "larger is better" as with breaking strength or product life. The loss function for the smaller-is-better case is

$$L(x) = kx^2$$

and for the larger-is-better case is

$$L(x) = k(1/x^2).$$

These can be applied in a manner similar to the previous examples. In Chapter 14 we will see how the Taguchi loss function can be used in setting tolerances for product design.

THE COST OF QUALITY

Cost accounting has traditionally been an important function in business. All organizations measure and report costs as a basis for control and improvement. The concept of the cost of quality emerged in the 1950s. Traditionally, the reporting of quality-related costs had been limited to inspection and testing; other costs were accumulated in overhead accounts. As managers began to define and isolate the full range of quality-related costs, a number of surprising facts emerged.[14] First, quality-related costs were much larger than had been traditionally reported, generally in the range of 20 to 40% of sales. Second, quality-related costs were not only related to manufacturing operations, but to ancillary services such as purchasing and customer service departments as well. Third, most of the costs were the result of poor quality and were avoidable. Finally, while the costs of poor quality were avoidable, there was no clear responsibility for action to reduce them nor was there any structured approach to do so. As a result, many companies began to develop **cost of quality** programs. By "cost of quality" we mean specifically the cost of *poor* quality—those costs associated with avoiding poor quality, or that are incurred as a

---

[14]Frank M. Gryna, "Quality Costs," *Juran's Quality Control Handbook,* 4th ed. (New York: McGraw-Hill, 1988).

result of poor quality. The concept of quality costs was popularized by Philip Crosby as we noted earlier in this chapter.

Quality cost programs have numerous objectives. Perhaps the most important is the fact that quality problems are translated into the language to which upper management can easily relate—the language of money. Juran makes special note that workers and supervisors speak in the "language of things"—units, defects, and so forth. Quality problems expressed as the number of defects have little impact on top managers since they are generally concerned with financial performance. But if the magnitude of quality problems can be translated into monetary terms, such as "How much would it cost us to run this business if there were no quality problems?," the eyes of upper management are opened. Dollars can be added meaningfully across departments or products and compared to other dollar measures. Middle managers, who must deal with both workers and supervisors as well as top management, must have the ability to speak in both languages. We will discuss other aspects of the "language of quality" in later chapters.

Quality cost information serves a variety of other purposes. It helps management evaluate the relative importance of quality problems and thus identify major opportunities for cost reduction. It can aid in budgeting and cost control activities. Finally, it can serve as a scoreboard to evaluate the organization's success in achieving quality objectives.

To establish a cost of quality program, one must *identify* the activities that generate cost, *measure* them, *report* them in a way that is meaningful to managers, and *analyze* them to identify areas for improvement. The following sections discuss these activities in more detail.

QUALITY COST CLASSIFICATION

Quality costs can be organized into four major categories: prevention costs, appraisal costs, internal failure costs, and external failure costs. **Prevention costs** are those expended in an effort to keep nonconforming products from occurring and reaching the customer. **Appraisal costs** are those expended on maintaining quality levels through measurement and analysis of data in order to detect and correct problems. Failure costs are a result of nonconformance: **internal failure costs** result from unsatisfactory quality that is found before the delivery of a product to the customer; **external failure costs** are those that occur after poor quality products reach the customer. The specific sources of these costs are discussed below.

Prevention Costs

Quality planning costs are those costs associated with the time spent planning the quality system. They include salaries and development costs for the establishment of manufacturing controls, procedures, and instructions for testing and inspection; reliability studies; and new equipment design. **Process control costs** include costs spent on the analysis of production processes to improve capability and the implementation of process control plans. **Information systems costs** involve salaries expended to develop data requirements and quality measurements. **Training costs** are those associated with developing and operating formal training programs or attending seminars on quality assurance. **General management costs** include those for clerical staff, supplies, and communications related to quality efforts.

Appraisal Costs

Test and inspection costs are those associated with testing and inspecting incoming materials, work-in-process, and finished goods and includes salaries for inspectors, supervisors, and other personnel as well as the cost of equipment. **Costs of maintaining instruments** include such costs as those associated with calibration of gages and test equipment, and repair of such instruments. **Process control costs** involve the cost of time spent by operators in gathering and analyzing quality measurements.

Internal Failure Costs

Scrap and rework costs include material, labor, and overhead associated with production losses. **Costs of corrective action** arise from time spent determining the causes of failure and correcting production problems. **Downgrading costs** include lost revenue as a result of selling a product at a lower price because it does not meet specifications but is still usable.

External Failure Costs

Costs of customer complaints and returns include the cost of investigating complaints and taking corrective action. **Product recall costs** are those of administration and direct production costs of making adjustments. **Warranty claims costs** include the cost of repair or replacement of products under warranty. **Product liability costs** of legal action and settlements are a major source of external failure costs.

It is often estimated that 60 to 90% of total quality costs are the result of internal and external failure and are not easily controllable by management. In the past, the typical managerial reaction to high failure costs has been increased inspection. This, however, leads to higher appraisal costs. While external failures may be reduced, the costs of internal failures will rise. The overall result is little, if any, improvement in quality or profitability.

The key to improving quality and profitability is *prevention*. A fundamental assumption of total quality assurance—and it has proven to be true in practice—is that an increase in prevention expenditures will generate a larger savings in all other cost categories. Better prevention of poor quality will clearly reduce internal failure costs, since fewer defective items will be made. External failure costs will also be reduced. In addition, less appraisal will be required, since the products will be made correctly the first time. Since production is usually viewed in the short run, it is difficult to establish such a strategic orientation. This is another reason that quality efforts must be well planned and quality costs must be understood. Quality costs are both a management responsibility and a technical responsibility.

One of the more interesting opportunities available to prevent quality problems is to work with suppliers of purchased material on improving *their* quality. Japanese manufacturers have been very successful in following this approach. Japanese manufacturers often provide free assistance to suppliers in developing quality assurance programs or solving quality problems. The reason is quite simple. If a manufacturer knows that its suppliers are producing quality products, it will spend less on verifying the quality of incoming material and reworking or scrapping defective products that may be found in later stages of production. U.S. automakers are now working more closely with suppliers and are beginning to insist on sound quality practice in their businesses.

Another very popular and increasingly important type of prevention effort is that devoted to employee involvement teams. This training is being extended both to the operating level and to white-collar employees. Employee involvement and team approaches to problem solving are discussed in more depth in Chapter 11.

QUALITY COST MEASUREMENT AND REPORTING

The purpose of quality cost measurement and reporting is to determine the cost of maintaining a certain level of quality. Such activity is necessary to provide feedback to management on the performance of quality assurance and to assist management in identifying opportunities for quality improvement and cost reduction. Quality costs are often reported by product line, department, work center, operator, or defect classification.

Quality costs can be used in several ways for decision making. They can be used as a measurement tool for performance reporting in a strict accounting sense, for planning and budgeting, or for evaluating strategic goals. However, the most important application of quality cost data is to identify quality problems and to use the results to convince management that changes are needed and justified.

Data Collection

The problem with attempting to collect and measure quality costs is that many costs involve different departments or functions within an organization and are difficult to measure. Many quality cost data are available from an organization's accounting system. Items such as time sheets, expense reports, and purchase orders are typical data sources. Standard accounting systems are generally able to provide quality cost data for direct labor; overhead; scrap (vendor and production); warranty expenses; product liability costs; and maintenance, repair, and calibration efforts on test equipment.

Despite the increasing importance of accounting for quality costs, most accounting systems are poorly designed to handle the task of accounting for such costs.[15] Johnson and Kaplan note that "Today's management information, driven by the procedures and cycle of the organization's financial reporting system is too late, too aggregated and too distorted to be relevant for managers' planning and control decisions." They summarized the consequences as follows:

- Accounting information provides little help for reducing costs and improving productivity and quality. Indeed, the information might even be harmful.

- The systems do not produce accurate product costs for pricing, sourcing, product mix, and responses to competition.

---

[15]Thomas S. Johnson and Robert S. Kaplan, *Relevance Lost* (Cambridge, MA: Harvard Business School Press, 1987); quoted in Joel E. Ross and David E. Wegman. "Quality Management and the Role of the Accountant," *Industrial Management,* July/August 1990, pp. 21–23.

■ The system encourages managers to contract to the short-term cycle of the monthly profit-and-loss statement.

Costs such as service effort, remedial engineering effort, rework, in-process inspection effort, and engineering change losses must usually be estimated or collected through special forms and procedures. For example, the effort spent specifically on quality activities during product design is generally not readily available. Work sampling procedures can be used to estimate the time spent on such activities. Also, determining the cost of scrap or rework and allocating it to individual departments usually requires special data collection forms.

Some costs due to external failure such as customer dissatisfaction and future lost revenues are impossible to estimate accurately. While prevention costs are the most important, it is usually easiest to collect appraisal costs, internal failure, external failure, and prevention costs in that order. New data processing techniques, such as database management systems, are helping to overcome such problems.

Behavioral considerations are also important in quality cost data collection. It is difficult to discover the *source* of costs. If the "discovering" department is charged, they will stop reporting bad quality. It is also hard to get one department to "tattle" on another. Thus poor quality often goes unreported. One solution is to organize by product or program instead of by functions as is predominant in the United States.

A convenient way of reporting quality costs is by a breakdown by organizational function as shown in Figure 3.8. This matrix serves several purposes. First, it allows all departments to recognize their contributions to the cost of quality and participate in a cost of quality program. Second, it helps to pinpoint areas of high quality cost and helps focus improvement efforts.

FIGURE 3.8   Cost of Quality Matrix

	Design engineering	Purchasing	Production	. . .	Finance	. . .	Accounting	Totals

Prevention costs
  Quality planning
  Training
  . . .								

Appraisal costs
  Test and inspection
  Instruments
  . . .								

Internal failure costs
  Scrap
  Rework
  . . .								

External failure costs
  Returns
  Recall costs
  . . .								

Totals								

Measuring Quality Costs

This section focuses on ways to measure quality costs that can be meaningfully interpreted. **Index numbers** are often used in a variety of applications to measure prices, costs, or other numerical quantities and to aid managers in understanding how conditions in one period compare with those in other periods. A simple type of index is called a **relative index.** Such an index is computed by dividing a current value by a base period value. Sometimes the result is multiplied by 100 to express it as a percentage. As an example, consider the following direct labor costs per quarter for a manufactured product:

Quarter	Cost ($)
1	1500
2	1800
3	1700
4	1750

If the first quarter is the base period, the cost relative indexes expressed as percentages are computed as

$$\text{cost index in quarter } t = \frac{\text{cost in quarter } t}{\text{base period cost}} \times 100$$

Thus we have

Quarter	Cost Relative Index
1	(1500/1500)(100) = 100
2	(1800/1500)(100) = 120
3	(1700/1500)(100) = 113.33
4	(1750/1500)(100) = 116.67

Costs and prices are often sensitive to changes in the firm. For example, if the number of units produced in each quarter differs, comparisons of direct labor costs are meaningless. However, a measure such as cost per unit would provide useful information to managers.

Index numbers are often used to analyze quality cost data. Quality costs themselves provide little information, since they may vary due to such factors as production volume or seasonality. Generally, a measurement base is chosen that is sensitive to change. Typical measurement bases are labor, manufacturing cost, sales, and units of product. Several examples are given in the following paragraphs.

Labor Base Index.   A typical quality cost index that is easily understood by managers is **quality cost per direct labor hour.** Direct labor data are easily obtained from accounting departments. Either total labor hours or standard labor hours are used. Standard hours often provide a better measure than total labor hours, since they represent planned rather than actual production. Because labor-based indexes are drastically influenced by automation and other changes in technology, one must be careful in using them over long periods of time. Often quality cost per direct labor *dollar* is used to eliminate the effects of inflation.

Cost Base Index. **Quality cost per manufacturing cost dollar** is a common index in this category. Manufacturing cost includes direct labor, material, and overhead costs that are usually available from accounting departments. Cost-based indexes are more stable than labor-based indexes, since they are not affected by price fluctuations or by changes in the level of automation.

Sales Base Index. **Quality cost per sales dollar** is a popular index that appeals to top management. However, this measure is rather poor for short-term analysis, since sales usually lag behind production and are subject to seasonal variations. In addition, this index is affected by changes in the selling price.

Unit Base Index. A common measure in this category is **quality costs per unit of production.** This simple index is acceptable if the output of production lines is similar; however, it is a poor measure if many different kinds of products are made. In such a case, an alternative index of quality costs per *equivalent* unit of output is often used. To obtain this index, different product lines are weighted to approximate a "standard" or "average" product that is used as a common base.

All of these indexes, while extensively used in practice, have a fundamental problem. A change in the denominator can appear to be a change in the level of quality assurance or productivity alone. For instance, if direct labor is decreased through managerial improvements, the direct labor-based index will increase even if there is no change in quality. Also, the inclusion of overhead in manufacturing cost, which is commonly used, is certain to distort results. Nevertheless, use of such indexes is common and useful for comparing quality costs over time. Generally, sales bases are the most popular, followed by cost, labor, and unit bases.[16]

Quality Cost Reporting

Quality cost data can be broken down by product line, process, department, work center, time, or cost category. This makes data analysis much more convenient and useful to management. The following example illustrates some of these concepts.

EXAMPLE 3 **Quality Cost Analysis.** Digital Time Corporation (DTC) produces a high volume of inexpensive quartz watches and finer desk clocks. DTC is primarily an assembly operation, with quartz crystals imported from Japan and other materials from domestic suppliers. The desk clocks are made from oak that is cut and stained in the plant. The process used is labor-intensive; therefore, a measurement base of direct labor cost has been chosen. DTC recently implemented a quality cost program. The first year's results in dollars is presented in Table 3.1, which gives an accounting report of quality costs by quarter for each product and cost category. Using direct labor as the base, the quality cost indexes are computed as follows:

$$\text{quality cost index} = \frac{\text{total quality costs}}{\text{direct labor costs}}(100)$$

---

[16]Edward Sullivan and Debra A. Owens, "Catching a Glimpse of Quality Costs Today," *Quality Progress,* Vol. 16, No. 12, December 1983, pp. 21–24.

TABLE 3.1   **Quality Cost Data and Index Calculations for DTC (in thousands of dollars)**

	Quarter							
	1		2		3		4	
	Watch	Clock	Watch	Clock	Watch	Clock	Watch	Clock
Prevention	2	4	2	4	2	4	2	4
Appraisal	10	20	13	31	16	22	9	24
Internal failure	19	106	16	107	23	194	17	195
External failure	23	16	21	14	34	14	30	12
Total quality costs	54	146	52	156	75	234	58	235
Standard direct labor costs	35	90	28	86	40	94	30	93
Index	154.3	162.2	185.7	181.4	187.5	248.9	193.3	252.7

Multiplication by 100 expresses the result as a percentage. For example, the index for watches in the first quarter is 54/35(100) = 154.3.

A cursory inspection of the indexes in Table 3.1 reveals that the total quality cost index for watches is relatively stable after a slight increase in the second quarter. However, for clocks, a significant increase occurs in the third and fourth quarters. This method of reporting does not provide managers with useful information for problem diagnosis and decision making. Better information can be obtained by computing cost indexes by product for each quality cost category. Table 3.2 provides such data for the DTC example. For instance, the index for prevention costs for watches in the first quarter is computed by dividing the cost in Table 3.1 by the direct labor costs, or 2/35 × 100 = 5.7.

Good visual aids are important communication tools. Graphs are particularly useful in presenting comparative results to management. Time-to-time comparisons can be used when absolute dollars are related to total manufacturing activity. Figures 3.9 and 3.10 show graphs of each product cost category over time. This is called *trend analysis* and illustrates the changes in cost over time. Trend analysis can be used with different measurement bases, by departments and work centers, and in many other ways.

TABLE 3.2   **Quality Indexes by Cost Category**

	Product: Watches Quarter			
	1	2	3	4
Prevention	5.7	7.1	5.0	6.7
Appraisal	28.6	46.4	40.0	30.0
Internal failure	54.3	57.1	57.5	56.7
External failure	65.7	75.0	85.0	100.0

	Product: Clocks Quarter			
	1	2	3	4
Prevention	4.4	4.7	4.3	4.3
Appraisal	22.2	36.0	23.4	25.8
Internal failure	117.8	124.4	206.4	209.7
External failure	17.8	16.3	14.9	12.9

FIGURE 3.9 Trend Analysis of Quality Costs: Watches

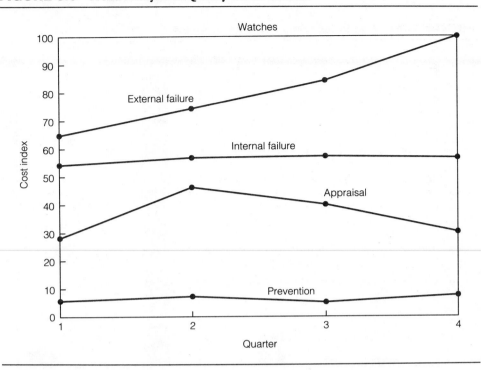

FIGURE 3.10 Trend Analysis of Quality Costs: Clocks

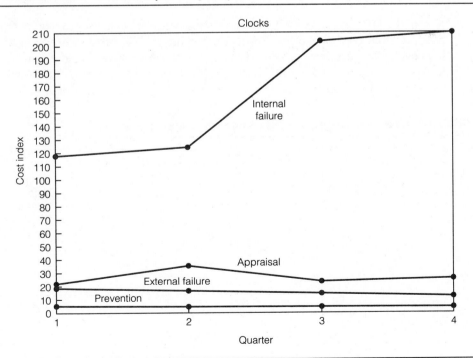

FIGURE 3.11 **Cost Index Comparisons by Product**

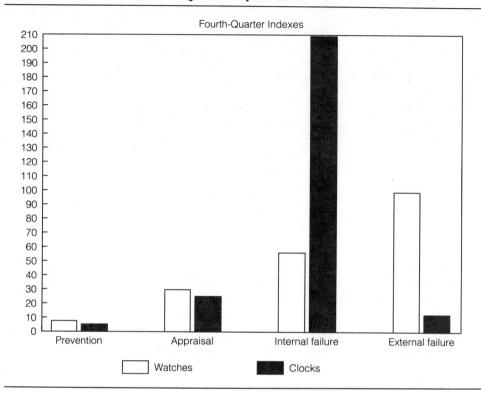

In the DTC example, we have simply shown trends by quarter for each of the major quality cost categories. Thus, for watches, we see that prevention and internal failure costs have remained steady over the four quarters. Appraisal costs initially rose during the second quarter, possibly because of startup of the quality program, and have since steadily declined. A major problem, however, appears to

FIGURE 3.12 **Percentage Cost Distribution by Category: Watches**

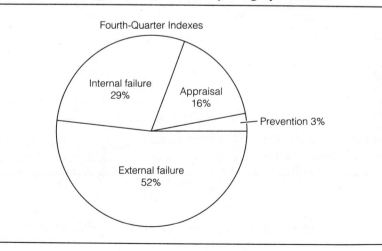

FIGURE 3.13 Percentage Cost Distribution by Category: Clocks

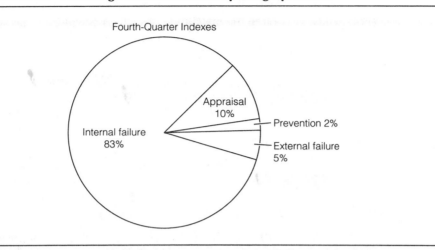

be growing with regard to external failure costs. For clocks, all costs except internal failure have remained relatively constant. Figure 3.10 shows that internal failure costs have taken a significant jump between the second and third quarters. This frequently occurs when quality costs first begin to be monitored. In general, as efforts to control quality increase, prevention costs should increase substantially, appraisal costs should level off, and failure costs should decline.

The graphs in Figures 3.11 through 3.13 provide some additional comparisons of quality cost indexes for the most recent (fourth) quarter. Figure 3.11 shows significant differences between products in the failure categories. Figures 3.12 and 3.13 illustrate some interesting statistics for each product. For watches, 52% of all quality costs are accounted for by external failure, and for clocks, internal failure costs make up 83% of the total. Such information enables managers to direct their attention to problem areas that will yield the greatest improvement per dollar expended. For example, a 10% improvement in internal failure costs for watches will improve total costs by only 2.9%, while the same percentage improvement in external failure costs will result in a 5.2% overall reduction.

Establishing Cost of Quality Reporting System[17]

The National Association of Accountants recommends a 12-step process to establish a quality cost reporting system. This process is summarized below.

   1. *Obtain management commitment and support:* The idea of establishing a quality cost system might be initiated by top management; in such cases, the commitment is clear. In other cases, the idea might arise from accounting or

[17]For further discussion, see Wayne J. Morse, Harold P. Roth, and Kay M. Poston, *Measuring, Planning, and Controlling Quality Costs* (Montvale, NJ: National Association of Accountants, 1987, Now Institute of Management Accountants).

quality assurance personnel. Often, management must be convinced of its necessity. This can be easily accomplished by developing an estimate of the cost of quality. Very often the magnitude of such costs will gain management support immediately. Without management support, any initiatives are likely to fail and should not be pursued.

2. *Establish an installation team:* The quality cost team should include individuals from throughout the organization, including product managers, engineers, line workers, customer service representatives, and others who can identify specific quality cost elements. Users of the information also should participate actively.

3. *Select an organizational segment as a prototype:* As with any new program, it is best to start small and expand after experience has been gained. The initial segment might be a specific product, department, or plant. It should be one that is believed to have high, measurable quality costs.

4. *Obtain cooperation and support of users and suppliers of information:* Both users and suppliers of information should be part of the installation team. Uncooperative suppliers can force delays in reporting information and render the system useless. Unused reports are of no benefit. Open communication is the key to obtaining cooperation. All must understand the nature of quality costs and how they will be used—as a tool for improvement, not punishment.

5. *Define quality costs and quality cost categories:* The idea of quality costs is new to most individuals. While the classifications of prevention, appraisal, internal failure, and external failure are typical, other suggestions should be considered. To avoid misunderstandings, operational definitions of each cost category should be written and distributed to all users and suppliers of quality cost information.

6. *Identify quality costs within each category:* A starting point is to ask users and suppliers of information to identify specific costs incurred because of poor quality. Defining and classifying specific quality costs often involves considerable debate. Often, several iterations are necessary before consensus is reached.

7. *Determine the sources of quality cost information:* Data may not be readily available in existing accounting systems. If the information is to be useful, quality costs must be visible and not buried within other accounts. Because some data may not be available, the team must determine if the extra effort necessary to collect them is warranted or if estimates will suffice.

8. *Design quality cost reports and graphs:* Reports and visual aids must meet the needs of the users of the information. Lower organizational levels generally require more detailed information than upper levels. Appropriate stratification of the information by product line, department, or plant, for example, must be developed to aid in analysis. Also, the form of quality cost indexes must be determined.

9. *Establish procedures to collect quality cost information:* Specific tasks must be assigned to individuals, and they must understand what they are to do and

how to do it. Forms should be designed to make the task as simple as possible, and computer system personnel need to be consulted as necessary.

10. *Collect data, prepare, and distribute reports:* If the preceding steps have been carefully performed, this step should become routine.

11. *Eliminate bugs from the system:* In early trials, data may prove to be unreliable or not available, employees may feel uncomfortable in collecting the data or interpreting the results, computer system problems may arise, and so on.

12. *Expand the system:* After the initial project has succeeded, plans should be developed to expand the system to other segments of the organization. Membership on the quality cost team should be rotated to broaden the base of persons who understand the system operation. Also, the system should be reviewed periodically and modified as necessary.

Quality Costs in Service Organizations

The nature of quality costs differs between service and manufacturing organizations. In manufacturing, quality costs are primarily product oriented; for services, however, they are generally labor dependent. Since quality in service organizations depends on employee-customer interaction, appraisal costs tend to account for a higher percentage of total quality costs than they do in manufacturing. In addition, internal failure costs tend to be much lower for service organizations, since there is little opportunity to correct an error before it reaches the customer. By that time, the error becomes an external failure.

Since a far greater proportion of operating cost is attributed to people, a reduction in total quality costs often means a reduction in time worked and hence in personnel. This is particularly true if a large proportion of time is built into the system for rework and other failure activities. Unless a positive strategy is developed to make alternative use of human talents, the threat of job losses will surely result in the lack of cooperation in developing and using a quality cost program.

External failure costs can become an extremely significant out-of-pocket expense to consumers of services. Consider the costs of interrupted service, such as telephone, electricity, or other utilities; delays in waiting to obtain service or excessive time in performing the service; errors made in billing, delivery, or installation; or unnecessary service. For example, a family moving from one city to another may have to pay additional costs for lodging and meals because the moving van does not arrive on the day promised; a doctor's prescription needs to be changed because of faulty diagnosis and the patient pays for unnecessary drugs; or a computer billing error requires several phone calls, letters, and copies of cancelled checks to correct.

Work measurement and sampling techniques are often used extensively to gather quality costs in service organizations. For example, work measurement can be used to determine how much time an employee spends on various quality-related activities. The proportion of time spent multiplied by the individual's salary represents an estimate of the quality cost for that activity. Consumer surveys and other means of customer feedback are also used to determine quality costs for services. In general, however, the intangible nature of the output makes quality cost accounting for services very difficult.

USING QUALITY COSTS FOR PRODUCTIVITY IMPROVEMENT

Statistical information summarized in tables and graphs tells managers only *where* the potential for cost reduction and quality cost improvement lies; it does not tell them *what* the problems are. It is up to the managers and engineers to uncover the sources of problems and determine appropriate corrective action. For instance, in the DTC example, the steady rise in internal failure costs and decline in appraisal costs for watches might indicate that there is a problem in assembly, a problem with the maintenance of testing equipment, or a lack of proper inspection of purchased materials. For clocks, the high external failure costs will probably be viewed closely by top management, since this might adversely affect the company's reputation. Since the appraisal and prevention costs are low, the trend analysis might suggest that a different supplier was used during the last two quarters and that poor materials were not discovered. The fact that prevention costs are very low for both products indicates that perhaps the quality assurance function was not well planned.

For most companies embarking on a quality cost program, it is typical to find that the highest costs occur in the external failure category, followed by internal failure, appraisal, and prevention in that order. Clearly, the order should be reversed; that is, the bulk of quality costs should be found in prevention, some in appraisal, perhaps a little in internal failure, and virtually none in external failure. Thus, companies should first attempt to drive external failure costs to zero by investing in appraisal activities to discover the sources of failure and take corrective action. As quality improves, failure costs will decrease, and the amount of appraisal can be reduced while shifting the emphasis to prevention activities.

Pareto Analysis

A very useful tool for quality cost analysis is *Pareto analysis*. The term *Pareto analysis* was coined by Joseph Juran in the 1950s after observing that a vast majority of quality problems generally results from only a few causes. Juran named this technique after Vilfredo Pareto (1848–1923), an Italian economist who determined that 85% of wealth in Milan was owned by only 15% of the people. This concept, which will be studied further in Chapter 9, can easily be applied to quality costs.

Quality losses are rarely uniformly distributed. In the DTC example, we saw that a large proportion of quality cost was accounted for by only one cost category for each product. The same is usually true within a category. For example, chances are that 70 or 80% of all internal failures are due to only one or two manufacturing problems. Identifying these "vital few" as they are called, and ignoring the "trivial many" will assure that corrective action will have a high return for a low dollar input.

ACTIVITY-BASED COSTING[18]

The importance of quality has had a major impact on the role of accounting systems in business. As we have noted earlier in this chapter, most accounting systems are not structured to capture important cost-of-quality information. They traditionally have

---

[18]For a thorough treatment of this topic, the reader is referred to Robin Cooper and Robert S. Kaplan *The Design of Cost Management Systems: Text, Cases, and Readings* (New York: Prentice-Hall, 1991).

been focused on promoting the efficiency of mass production, particularly where few standard products and high direct labor exist. Traditional cost systems can measure accurately the resources that are consumed in proportion to the number of units produced of individual products. Today's products are characterized by much lower direct labor, and many activities that consume resources are unrelated to the volume of units produced. Due to automation, direct labor is typically only 15% of manufacturing cost and can be as low as 5% in high-tech industries. Meanwhile, overhead costs have grown to 55% or more and are spread across all products using the same formula. Traditional cost systems can present an inadequate picture of manufacturing efficiency and effectiveness, and do a poor job of allocating the expenses of these support resources to individual products. Moreover, they attach no value to such elements as rework or bottlenecks that impede processing. Since these costs are hidden, there is little incentive to reduce them.

A new approach to management accounting is based on a concept called *activity-based information*. This information is about the work (or activity) that consumes resources and delivers value in a business. People consuming resources in work ultimately cause the value for which customers pay. Examples of activities might be moving, inspecting, receiving, shipping, and order processing. To oversee these activities, cross-functional teams of workers, managers, and even secretaries map each step of every business process (see the discussion of flowcharts in Chapter 9). These flowcharts pinpoint the operations that add value and reveal the ones that do not.

Activity-based costing allocates overhead costs to the products and services that use them. Knowing the costs of activities supports efforts to improve processes. Once activities can be traced to individual products or services, additional strategic information becomes available. The effects of delays and inefficiencies become readily apparent. The company can then focus on reducing these hidden costs.

The differences between traditional and activity-based cost accounting systems are reflected in Figures 3.14 and 3.15. In Figure 3.14, overhead costs are assigned to

FIGURE 3.14 Two-Stage Allocation Process: Traditional Cost System

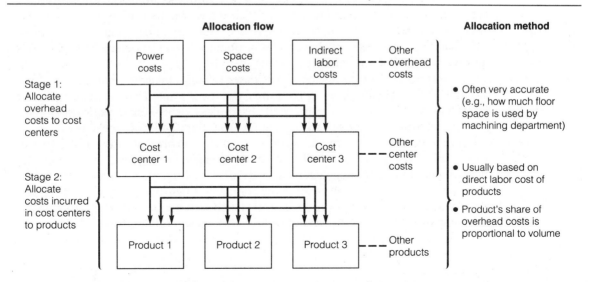

SOURCE: Robert S. Cooper and Robert S. Kaplan, *The Design of Cost Management Systems: Text and Readings* © 1991, p. 269. Reprinted by permission of Prentice-Hall, Englewood Cliffs, NJ.

FIGURE 3.15 Two-Stage Assignment Process: Activity-Based Cost System

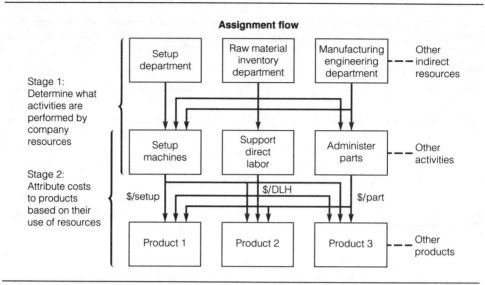

SOURCE: Robert S. Cooper and Robert S. Kaplan, *The Design of Cost Management Systems: Text and Readings* © 1991, p. 270. Reprinted by permission of Prentice-Hall, Englewood Cliffs, NJ.

cost centers, and then the accumulated costs are allocated to products proportional to elements such as direct labor or machine hours. In Figure 3.15, the expenses of support departments are assigned to the activities performed, such as machine setup, direct labor support, and parts administration. The expenses of each activity are then assigned to products based on the products' demand for the activities.

The new information provided by activity-based costing helps managers make better decisions about product designs, process improvements, pricing, and product mix. Other benefits include the facilitation of continuous improvement activities to reduce overhead costs, and the ease in which relevant costs can be determined. For instance, Caterpillar, Inc., used activity-based costing to determine the value of intangibles such as better quality and faster time-to-market to persuade the board to approve a $2 billion modernization effort in 1987.

An example of the power of activity-based costing involves Tektronix, Inc.,[19] In late 1987, Gene Hendrickson, a plant manager of a printed circuit board plant in Forest Grove, Oregon, was concerned that unless profit-center performance improved, Tektronix would sell the operation. The plant had only recently adopted a just-in-time inventory system and rigorous quality controls that drastically improved reject rates. Using an activity-based cost management system, he found that high-volume, low-technology circuit boards produced mainly for internal consumption drew on so many resources that they generated negative profit margins of 46% and stole profits from other products. The system also uncovered other hidden costs stemming from delays in processing orders. With these findings, he got the company

---

[19]"A Bean-Counter's Best Friend," *Business Week/Quality 1991,* October 25, 1991, p. 42.

to install new systems, such as an electronic link to let customers place orders directly with the plant's production scheduling computer. Factory operating margins improved to about four times the industry's average. Hendrickson observed that once activity-based costing showed them their true costs, all their quality efforts came together.

This method can easily be adopted by service organizations. One of the major differences between service organizations and manufacturing is that in manufacturing demands for support resources arise from product volumes and mix. In services, many expenses are caused by the demands of individual customers. Large variations occur in the demands that different customers place on the organization even when they are using the same basic product. Thus, customers' behavior must be modeled when analyzing the source of demands for service functions.

The activity-based costing approach is gaining increased popularity as inexpensive computer software is made available to support it. Executives of the "Big Six" accounting firms believe that cost management is headed for sweeping reform based on this approach.

Quality Cost Reporting at NAP Consumer Electronics Corporation[20]

North American Philips Consumer Electronics Corporation (NAPCEC) is a division of North American Philips Corporation, which ranks among the 100 largest industrial corporations in the United States. NAPCEC manufactures and sells a full line of

[20]Adapted from Morse *et al., op. cit.,* Chapter 6.

consumer electronics products including televisions, tape players, VCRs, video cameras, and other types of audio systems. Because of the importance of quality in consumer electronics products, NAPCEC uses a wide variety of activities, including the measurement and reporting of quality costs, in its quality function. These activities are a part of North

FIGURE 3.16 Quality Cost Accounts

Account Number	Account Title
100	**Prevention:**
100	Analysis and Planning for Quality and Reliability
120	Process Control
130	Specification Design and Development of Quality Information Equipment
140	Quality Training and Manpower Development
150	Product Design Verification
160	Systems Development and Management
170	Other Prevention Costs
180	Cost of Specific Plans and Actions Aimed at Preventing Administrative Errors and Management Systems Failures
200	**Appraisal:**
210	Test and Inspection of Purchased Direct Materials
220	Laboratory Testing of Purchased Materials
230	Laboratory or Other Measurement Services
240	Test and Inspection
250	Test and Inspection Equipment and Material
260	Quality and Quality System Audits
270	Outside Endorsements
280	Field Testing
290	Cost of Auditing and Inspection for Administrative Errors and Management System Failures Including Carrying out the Physical Inventories
300	**Internal Failure:**
310	Scrap
320	Repair
330	Rework
340	Scrap and Rework—Suppliers Fault
350	Salvage
360	Revisions and Corrective Actions
370	Down time Costs Due to Quality Reasons
380	Cost of Administrative Errors and Systems Failures
400	**External Failure:**
410	Complaints in Warranty
420	Complaints Out of Warranty
430	Product Liability Costs
440	Product Service
450	Traffic Damage
460	External Administrative Errors or Systems Failures Cost

(continued)

FIGURE 3.17 Internal Failure Costs of Administrative Errors and Systems Failures

Account Number	Account Title
381	Wasted Effort Due to Aborted Product Plans
382	Cancellation Due to Aborted Product Plans
383	Cost of Moving or Dumping Product that Did not Sell According to Plan
384	Cost of Missed Schedules
385	Cost of Redundant Staffing to "Crutch" Administrative Errors and Systems Failures
386	Cost of Net Losses Found in Physical Inventories
387	Cost of Corrective Actions for Account 380

American Philips Corporation's Quality Improvement System, which represents an ongoing commitment to quality at every level of the organization.

NAPCEC began its quality cost system in 1976. The Quality Assurance Group was responsible for the development and implementation of the system and today continues to be responsible for its operations. Quality cost data are collected by plant, product, and quality cost category. The financial accounting system is used to collect and develop quality cost data by determining which quality costs are recorded in the accounting system and identifying the specific accounts where they are recorded. Other quality costs that cannot be identified specifically in the accounts are developed through an estimation and allocation procedure, which consists of having department heads estimate the percentage of time spent on quality activities and then multiplying the departmental costs by this percentage. An example of the quality cost accounts used by one of the plants is shown in Figure 3.16. Each of these major accounts may be further divided into more detailed accounts as shown in Figure 3.17.

The quality cost reports are usually in statement format. Graphs are used on occasion. In these reports, costs are broken down by quality cost

TABLE 3.3 Quality Cost Summary for the Month of September

				% of Manufacturing Standard		
				Current Year		Prior Year
	Plan	Actual	Variance	Plan	Actual	Actual
Prevention						
Appraisal						
Internal failure						
External failure						

TABLE 3.4 Direct Labor Quality Cost Report

		Appraisal		Failure	
Category	Total Cost	Cost	%/Total	Cost	%/Total
Monochrome TV					
Color portable					
Color console					
Audio					
Odyssey					
VLP					
OEM					
Miscellaneous					
Plant total					

(continued)

category and by product. Appraisal and internal failure costs are also reported as a percentage of direct labor and standard product cost. The format of the summary report, which is distributed to plant management and to higher levels of management, is shown in Table 3.3. Actual quality costs are compared to planned quality costs over each year, and a variance between planned and actual quality costs is computed. Quality costs as a percentage of standard manufacturing costs are shown for actual and planned costs for the current year and actual costs for the preceding year.

Table 3.4 shows an example of a direct labor quality cost report. Direct labor costs associated with appraisal and internal failure are reported by product. These reports are prepared for each operation, with the costs presented in dollar amounts and as a percentage of the total.

NAPCEC uses the data in the quality cost reports for budgeting activities, control activities, quality-related decisions, and trend analyses. A quality cost budget, which includes overhead costs, is developed from the manufacturing plan for the upcoming year. The budget for warranty and testing and repairs also makes extensive use of the data contained in the reports. Although the primary control feature is in the area of controlling service and warranty costs, appraisal and internal failure costs have been reduced significantly as a result of the quality cost program.

Key Issues for Discussion

1. Explain the various reports used by NAPCEC in their Quality Improvement System.

2. How do you believe that quality cost data are used in preparing the budget for warranty, testing, and repairs as suggested here?

QUALITY IN PRACTICE

Quality Cost Analysis with Color Computer Graphics[21]

Travenol Laboratories, Inc., began a new quality cost program at one of its northern Illinois manufacturing facilities in 1981. The program was designed to incorporate quality cost concepts and decision support systems to assist managers to discover significant improvement opportunities. Fundamental to the program is a plant quality cost steering committee consisting of the plant manager, the production manager, the quality control manager, the engineering manager, and the controller. The committee meets once a month to identify areas of opportunity for improving quality and reducing costs. Once the committee has found an area of opportunity, it assigns a diagnostic team consisting of technical and operations staff to investigate the problem. The diagnostic team seeks to discover causes and remedies, evaluates the quality and economic impact of various alternatives, and recommends courses of action to the steering committee.

To identify areas for diagnostic teams to tackle, the steering committee requires quality cost data to be

presented in a variety of ways that are difficult to define in advance. Data may be expressed in dollars, adjusted for production volume or value of production, or expressed in some other terms. To isolate a particular area for investigation, the committee must first take a broad view, then consider alternative views, and finally examine selectively narrower perspectives. For instance, it may look at quality cost categories, then cost elements, and then cost subelements. The committee may look plant-wide or at a specific department or product line. Additionally, it is desirable to observe performance over time in order to identify trends and track improvement. Top management felt that it was important for the line managers themselves to conduct these analyses, since they have the proper perspective to identify areas for improvement.

To allow the steering committee to perform the analyses, a decision support system (DSS) was designed. The system was hierarchical, interactive, and menu-driven with a color graphic screen and copy output. Hierarchical data provided the ability to go quickly from summaries to specifics. Interactive menus allowed quick designation of the output.

[21]Adapted from Joseph J. Tsiakals, "Management Team Seeks Quality Improvement from Quality Costs," *Quality Progress,* Vol. 16, No. 4, April 1983, pp. 26–27.

(continued)

Graphic displays allowed managers to spot trends and disparities immediately. The color feature—at first thought to be unnecessary—turned out to be an important attribute of the system. Much more data could be analyzed and displayed in terms of trends when each line was a different color than when all lines were the same.

All data from the DSS is presented in trend chart fashion. A legend on the chart defines each line. Users may select monthly or year-to-date data, dollars, dollars divided by the value of production, or dollars divided by machine-hour as performance measures. Machine-hour is a good measure of the level of production when operations are automated and machine dominant. In labor-intensive environments, Travenol prefers to measure production in earned labor hours. Users may also select their own performance measures such as prevention/internal failure, product A/product B, and prevention + appraisal divided by internal failure + external failure.

A typical analysis might proceed as follows. A first graph shows the dollar amounts in each of the four quality cost categories. The user notes that internal failure costs have increased and calls up quality cost totals in terms of dollars per machine hour. This graph reveals that production has increased and that internal failure costs have actually fallen, rather than risen, when corrected for the increased production.

The graph also shows an upward trend for appraisal costs—a trend that was not apparent on the first graph. By calling up a third graph showing dollars per machine-hour for each element of the appraisal cost category, the user discovers that in-process inspection costs are rising. The user then selects a fourth graph—dollars per machine-hour for in-process inspection, broken down by department—and finds that in-process inspection costs are going up in Department B.

At this point, the manager might point out that a major new product has been introduced into Department B and that higher-than-normal shakedown inspections are planned. The manager might look into this analysis further with additional graphs or assign a diagnostic team to evaluate it more thoroughly. The diagnosis might include a comparison of specific cost categories and elements for the new product, use of technical data, action plans, and a recommendation of new performance goals.

Key Issues for Discussion

1. Explain how Travenol's quality cost system operates.

2. What advantages did the use of color graphics have for management analyses?

Summary of Key Points

- Quality is closely related to price, market share, and cost. Improvements in both the quality of design and the quality of conformance can lead to increased revenues, lower costs, and hence higher profits.

- Traditional economic models which suggest an optimum level of quality are flawed. Modern viewpoints suggest that a focus toward ever-improving quality will result in lower costs.

- Genichi Taguchi defines quality as the loss a product causes to society after being shipped. The Taguchi loss function is a way of quantifying the costs due to variation from a target specification. This function has been used to demonstrate the economic value of meeting nominal specifications rather than simply staying within tolerances.

- Quality cost programs allow quality problems to be translated into the language of upper management—money. Quality cost information allows management to identify opportunities for quality improvement, aids in budgeting and cost control, and serves as a scoreboard to evaluate an organization's success.

■ Quality costs generally are broken down into prevention, appraisal, internal failure, and external failure costs. These costs are often expressed as indexes using labor, manufacturing cost, sales, or unit measurement bases. Graphs and charts help to explain the data in a fashion that is easy for managers to understand.

■ Pareto analysis is a useful tool to identify those quality problems that account for a large percentage of costs and, if solved, will result in high returns on investment.

■ Activity-based costing is a new accounting approach that allocates overhead cost on the products and services that use them. This provides more useful information for quality improvement than traditional cost accounting systems.

Questions for Review and Discussion

1. Discuss the relationship between quality and price. How does theory differ from practice?

2. Since quality is closely related to market share, many companies use quality extensively in advertising. Using several examples of printed advertisements, discuss the role that quality plays in marketing efforts.

3. What does the phrase "quality is free" mean?

4. Explain the difference between the traditional and modern views of the economic trade-offs in quality of conformance.

5. Define the two categories of costs associated with quality of conformance. Where in the production system do these costs arise?

6. Explain the trade-offs between costs of quality assurance and costs due to nonconformance. Why have the Japanese seemed to ignore such trade-offs?

7. How does Taguchi define quality? How is quality measured according to his definition?

8. Explain how the Taguchi loss function differs from the traditional loss function assumed from specifications and tolerances.

9. Why are quality cost programs valuable to managers?

10. List and explain the four major categories of quality costs, giving examples of each.

11. How are quality costs measured and collected in an organization?

12. Discuss how index numbers are often used to analyze quality cost data.

13. If you are familiar with microcomputers and spreadsheet software, discuss how such programs can be used by managers to analyze quality cost data. Design a spreadsheet that would be appropriate for this task.

14. How do quality costs differ between service and manufacturing organizations? What collection techniques are more applicable to services?

15. Discuss the importance of each of the 12 steps suggested by the National Association of Accountants for implementing quality cost reporting systems.

16. What is Pareto analysis and how is it used in analyzing quality cost data?

17. The percentage of total quality costs in a firm are distributed as follows:

    Prevention 11%
    Appraisal 29%
    Internal failure 38%
    External failure 22%

    What conclusions can you reach from this data?

18. What conclusions can be drawn from the following data:

Cost Category	Amount
Equipment design	20,000
Scrap	300,000
Reinspection and retest	360,000
Loss	90,000
Vendor quality surveys	8,000
Repair	80,000

19. Explain the concept of activity-based costing. How does it differ from traditional cost accounting? What role does it play in quality?

Problems

1. A steel company produces long thin sheets of steel called coils that weigh 10 to 15 tons. The slitting operation involves cutting these large coils into smaller widths. An average of 5,000 tons per month is sold. The scrap rate from this operation is 3%. Material costs are $600 per ton. It takes 0.75 hours of labor to produce one ton sold at a rate of $20 per hour.

    a. How many tons per month must be produced to meet the sales demand?
    b. What is the annual savings that would result from decreasing the scrap rate from 3 to 2%?

2. A blueprint specification for the thickness of an automotive part is 0.120 ± 0.009 inch. It costs $3 to scrap a part that is outside of the specifications. What is the Taguchi loss function for this situation?

3. An electronic component has an output voltage specification of 75 ± 5 millivolts. Scrapping the component results in a $300 loss.

    a. What is the value of k in the Taguchi loss function?
    b. If the process is centered on the target specification with a standard deviation of 2 millivolts, what is the expected loss per unit?

4. A computer chip is designed so that the distance between two adjacent pins has a specification of 2.000 ± 0.002 mm. The loss due to a defective chip is $4. A

sample of 25 chips was drawn from the production process and the results are shown below.

2.001	2.000	2.001	1.998	1.999
2.000	2.000	2.002	1.999	2.000
1.998	1.999	2.001	2.000	2.000
2.000	1.999	2.001	2.001	2.000
2.000	2.002	2.000	2.000	2.001

a. Compute the value of k in the Taguchi loss function.

b. What is the expected loss from this process based on the sample data?

5. Analyze the following cost data. What implications do these data suggest to management?

	Product		
	A	B	C
Total sales	$537,280	$233,600	$397,120
External failure	42%	20%	20%
Internal failure	45%	25%	45%
Appraisal	12%	52%	30%
Prevention	1%	3%	5%
(figures represent percentages of quality costs by product)			

6. Compute a sales dollar index base to analyze the following quality cost information and prepare a memo to management:

	Quarter			
	1	2	3	4
Total sales	$4,120	$4,206	$4,454	$4,106
External failure	40.8	42.2	42.8	28.6
Internal failure	168.2	172.4	184.4	66.4
Appraisal	64.2	67.0	74.4	166.2
Prevention	28.4	29.2	30.2	40.2

7. Prepare a graph or chart showing the different quality cost categories and percentages for a printing company:

Cost Element	Amount
Proofreading	710,000
Quality planning	10,000
Press downtime	405,000
Bindery waste	75,000
Checking and inspection	60,000
Customer complaint remakes	40,000
Printing plate revisions	40,000
Quality improvement projects	20,000
Other waste	55,000
Correction of typographical errors	300,000

8. Given the following cost elements, determine the total percentage in each of the four major quality cost categories.

Cost Element	Amount	Cost Element	Amount
Incoming test and inspection	7,500	Rework	70,000
Scrap	35,000	Quality problem solving by	
Quality training	0	product engineers	11,250
Inspection	25,000	Inspection equipment	
Test	5,000	calibration	2,500
Adjustment cost of complaints	21,250	Writing procedures and	
Quality audits	2,500	instructions	2,500
Maintenance of tools and dies	9,200	Laboratory services	2,500
Quality control administration	5,000	Rework due to vendor faults	17,500
Laboratory testing	1,250	Correcting imperfections	6,250
Design of quality assurance		Setup for test and inspection	10,750
equipment	1,250	Formal complaints to vendors	10,000
Material testing and			
inspection	1,250		

9. Use Pareto analysis to investigate the following quality losses in a paper mill. What conclusions do you reach?

Category	Annual Loss
Downtime	38,000
Testing costs	20,000
Rejected paper	560,000
Odd lot	79,000
Excess inspection	28,000
Customer complaints	125,000
High material costs	67,000

10. Let $C(q)$ represent the total cost as a function of q, the quality of conformance, in Figure 3.2. Also, define p = unit price of the product, m = manufacturing cost (exclusive of quality-related costs) per unit of product (assumed constant with respect to volume), I = net income, and $D(q)$ = demand as a function of q. If $I = [p - C(q) - m]D(q)$, show that the value of q that maximizes I must be larger than the one that minimizes $C(q)$. (This is a rather difficult question that requires calculus.)

Case Problem[22]

Table 3.5 (on page 78) presents a quality cost report for the installment loan function in a bank. Prepare a report analyzing these data. What suggestions would you make to management?

[22]Adapted from Charles A. Aubrey, "Effective Use of Quality Cost Applied to Service," *American Society for Quality Control 42nd Annual Quality Congress Transactions,* May 1988, Dallas, Texas.

TABLE 3.5 Quality Cost Report for Installment Loans

Operation	Prevention	Appraisal	Internal Failure	External Failure	Total
Making a Loan					
2. Run a credit check	0	0	26.13	0	$26.13
8. Prepare and put thru GL tickets and I/L input sheets	0	0	248.19	0	$248.19
9. Review documents	0	3,013.78	7.84	0	$3,021.62
10. Make document corrections, gather additional documents or information	0	0	1,013.65	0	$1,013.65
11. Prepare tickler file, review and follow up on titles, insurance, second meetings, and UCC's	0	156.75	0	0	$156.75
12. Review all output	0	2,244.14	0	0	$2,244.14
13. Correct rejects and incorrect output	0	0	425.84	0	$425.84
15. Work associated with the incomplete collateral report	0	0	0	78.38	$78.38
16. Work associated with dealer calls dealing with any problems and the time to research and communicate	0	0	0	2,481.88	$2,481.88
17. I/L system downtime	0	0	519.89	0	$519.89
18. Time spent training or being trained on I/L	1,366.34	0	0	0	$1,366.34
Loan Payment					
1. Receive and process payments from all sources	0	261.25	783.75	0	$1,045.00
2. Respond to inquiries when no coupon is presented with payments	0	0	783.75	0	$783.75
Loan Payoff					
2. Receive and process payoff and release document	0	0	13.06	0	$13.06
4. Research payoff problems	0	0	13.06	0	$13.06

Bibliography

Asher, J. M. "Cost of Quality in Service Industries," *International Journal of Quality and Reliability Management,* Vol. 5, No. 5, 1988, pp. 38–46.

Blank, Lee, and Solorzano, Jorge. "Using Quality Cost Analysis for Management Improvement," *Industrial Engineering,* Vol. 10, No. 2, February 1978, pp. 46–51.

Campanella, Jack, and Corcoran, Frank J. "Principles of Quality Costs," *Quality Progress,* Vol. 16, No. 4, April 1983, pp. 16–22.

Cooper, Robin, and Kaplan, Robert S. *The Design of Cost Management Systems: Text, Cases, and Readings.* New York: Prentice-Hall, 1991.

Gale, Bradley T., and Klavans, Richard. "Formulating a Quality Improvement Strategy," *Journal of Business Strategy,* Vol 5., No. 3, Winter 1985, pp. 21–32.

Hill, Robert R., and Anthony, Ted. "Economics of Product Liability: Caveat for Producers," *Quality Progress,* Vol. 12. No. 2, February 1979, pp. 34–35.

Johnson, H. Thomas. "Activity-Based Information: A Blueprint for World-Class Management Accounting," *Management Accounting,* June 1988, pp. 23–30.

Kaplan, Robert S. "Yesterday's Accounting Undermines Production," *Harvard Business Review,* July–August 1984.

Rosander, A. C. *Applications of Quality Control in the Service Industries.* New York: Marcel-Dekker, Inc., 1985.

Ross, Philip J. *Taguchi Techniques for Quality Engineering.* New York: McGraw-Hill, 1988.

Roth, Harold P., and Morse, Wayne J. "Let's Help Measure and Report Quality Costs," *Management Accounting,* August 1983.

Sullivan, Edward. "Quality Costs: Current Ideas," *Quality Progress,* Vol. 16, No. 4, April 1983, pp. 24–25.

Taguchi, G., Elsayed, E. A., and Hsiang, T.C. *Quality Engineering in Production Systems.* New York: McGraw-Hill, 1989.

PART TWO

The Management System

IN CHAPTER 1 we discussed the *total quality system*—the integration of management philosophy and skills with technical expertise in order to achieve high quality. The best technology, whether automated equipment or statistical tools and procedures, cannot be effective without the managers who plan, design, and develop the quality system and the employees who operate it. Total quality can be achieved only through proper management and with the commitment of all employees in the organization.

Managers are concerned with planning, organizing, controlling, and improving productive operations in order to meet the objectives of the organization. *Planning* provides the basis for all future managerial activities by establishing the guidelines and actions that must be taken to meet stated objectives as well as establishing the timing of these actions. *Organizing* is the process of bringing together the resources—personnel, materials, equipment, and capital—necessary to perform planned activities. *Controlling* includes the evaluation of performance and the application of corrective measures as necessary. *Improvement* is necessary in order to maintain a competitive edge and meet the increasing needs and demands of customers.

In this section of the book we focus on managerial issues in quality. Chapter 4 sets the foundation by describing the leading thoughts in management philosophy as expounded by the international leaders in quality, W. Edwards Deming, Joseph Juran, and Philip Crosby. Chapter 5 provides a discussion of total quality management, a global philosophy that provides the basis for achieving quality excellence throughout an organization. Chapters 6 through 9 focus on the four basic managerial functions described above: planning, organizing, controlling, and improvement. In Chapters 10 and 11, we deal with issues of human resource management and employee involvement in the quality function.

CHAPTER 4

Quality Management Philosophies

Three individuals, W. Edwards Deming, Joseph Juran, and Philip Crosby, have emerged as major international "philosophers" in the quality revolution. They have developed distinct philosophies on how to measure, manage, and improve quality. Two other individuals, Armand V. Feigenbaum and the late Kaoru Ishikawa, have also had a significant impact on the development of the international quality movement, although in a different way than Deming, Juran, and Crosby. Their major contribution has been in disseminating the quality philosophies of others, although they have made several notable contributions of their own.

Because of their unique personalities, Deming, Juran, and Crosby have been likened to a fire-and-brimstone preacher, a theologist, and an evangelist, respectively. Deming's gruff demeanor strikes fear into most corporate executives who attend his seminars; Juran's *Quality Control Handbook* is often called the "bible" of quality; and Crosby has been recognized for his inspiring and motivational speaking. In this chapter we present their philosophies in an integrated fashion, focusing on the commonalities and differences. In later chapters we will describe further aspects of their philosophies and focus specifically on implementation details.

THE DEMING PHILOSOPHY

W. Edwards Deming was originally trained as a statistician, and much of his philosophy can be traced to these roots. He worked for Western Electric during its pioneering era of statistical quality control development in the 1920s and 1930s. During World War II he taught quality control courses as part of the national defense effort. Deming began teaching statistical quality control in Japan shortly after World War II and is credited with having been an important contributor to the Japanese quality improvement programs. In fact, the highest award for quality improvement in Japan is called the Deming Prize. While Japan embraced his methods for 30 years, he was virtually unknown in the United States until 1980.

Deming focuses on the improvement of product and service conformance to specifications by reducing uncertainty and variability in the design and manufacturing process. In Deming's view, variation is the chief culprit of poor quality. In mechanical assemblies, for example, variations from specifications for part dimensions lead to inconsistent performance and premature wear and failure. Likewise, inconsistencies in service frustrate customers and hurt the reputation of the company. To achieve

82

reduction of variation, he advocates a never-ending cycle of product design, manufacture, test, and sales, followed by market surveys, then redesign, and so forth. Deming claims that higher quality leads to higher productivity, which in turn leads to long-term competitive strength. The Deming "chain reaction" (Figure 4.1) theory summarizes this view. The theory states that improvements in quality lead to lower costs because of less rework, fewer mistakes, fewer delays and snags, and better use of time and materials. Lower costs, in turn, lead to productivity improvements. With better quality and lower prices, the firm can achieve a higher market share and thus stay in business, providing more and more jobs. Deming stresses that top management has the overriding responsibility for quality improvement.

To aid in developing useful measures of quality, Deming advocates the extensive use of statistics, particularly control charts. We will discuss control charts in detail in later chapters. He proposes that *every* employee in the firm be familiar with statistical techniques and other problem-solving tools. In this way, statistics becomes a common language that every employee—from top executives to line workers—can use to communicate with one another. Statistics are objective; there is no room for ambiguity or misunderstanding.

Deming identifies two sources of improvement in any process: reducing the "common causes" of variation inherent in the production system, and eliminating isolated "special causes" identifiable with a specific individual, machine, or batch of materials. Common causes are a result of the design of the system—as management has designed it. For instance, suppose that a piece of wood is to be cut to a precise length of 25.35 inches. If the worker is provided with only a hand saw, table, and a yardstick, it will be virtually impossible to cut consistently lengths of such precision. Improvements in conformance can only be achieved if management provides more accurate equipment and training in the correct work methods. On the other hand,

FIGURE 4.1 **The Deming Chain Reaction**

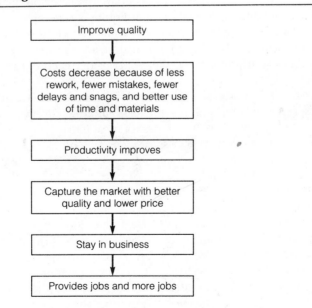

TABLE 4.1 Deming's 14 Points for Management

1. Create and publish to all employees a statement of the aims and purposes of the company or other organization. The management must demonstrate constantly their commitment to this statement.
2. Learn the new philosophy, top management and everybody.
3. Understand the purpose of inspection, for improvement of processes and reduction of cost.
4. End the practice of awarding business on the basis of price tag alone.
5. Improve constantly and forever the system of production and service.
6. Institute training.
7. Teach and institute leadership.
8. Drive out fear. Create trust. Create a climate for innovation.
9. Optimize toward the aims and purposes of the company the efforts of teams, groups, staff areas.
10. Eliminate exhortations for the work force.
11. (a) Eliminate numerical quotas for production. Instead, learn and institute methods for improvement.
    (b) Eliminate M. B. O. Instead, learn the capabilities of processes, and how to improve them.
12. Remove barriers that rob people of pride of workmanship.
13. Encourage education and self-improvement for everyone.
14. Take action to accomplish the transformation.

SOURCE: Reprinted from *Out of the Crisis* by W. Edwards Deming, by permission of M.I.T. and W. Edwards Deming. Published by M.I.T., Center for Advanced Engineering Study, Cambridge MA 02139. Copyright 1986 by W. Edwards Deming. (Revised by Dr. Deming, 10 January, 1990.)

suppose that an accurate measurement instrument, a fixture for holding the wood, and an electric saw are available. Clearly, the output from this system will have smaller variability and more consistent quality. If the saw blade is worn or chipped however, the quality will deteriorate. Such special causes can be identified by the worker and corrected. Statistical methods provide a means for identifying special causes and understanding common causes. We will discuss these concepts further in later chapters.

Statistical thinking is only a portion of the modern Deming philosophy. Deming emphatically states that managerial practices are in need of a radical overhaul. His "14 Points" constitutes the core of his program for achieving quality excellence. Table 4.1 lists these 14 Points. Some of these are quite controversial and often misunderstood. The Deming philosophy is an all-or-nothing proposition. According to Deming, none of the 14 Points can be viewed in isolation, and companies cannot be selective in the ones they wish to implement. We will consider each in turn.

Point 1. Create a Vision and Demonstrate Commitment. This is the foundation of Deming's philosophy: a commitment to never-ending improvement in quality. Businesses face two types of problems: the problems of today and the problems of tomorrow. Problems of today are short term and involve maintenance of quality, efficiency, profits, and sales; problems of tomorrow are long term and involve improvement and innovation.

The emphasis on short-term profits has eroded American industry. American management is driven by quarterly dividends, annual performance appraisals, and monthly sales quotas. Deming states that job-hopping, where personal career advancement is placed ahead of the welfare of the firm, is one of the major diseases of American industry. The costs due to lost knowledge and experience as well as hiring and training are staggering. This is very evident in American sports. How many teams can build a dynasty with free agency? Many players go to the highest bidder with little team loyalty. In business, short-term thinking is fed by the fear of hostile takeovers and the emphasis on quarterly dividends. Consequently, managers work only for their department or individual performance measurements, and not for the company's future.

Deming believes that business must adopt a long-term perspective and take responsibility for providing jobs and improving a firm's competitive position. Japanese companies, for example, spend considerably more on research and development than those in the United States. They are willing to give up short-term profits knowing that they will achieve a high market share several years in the future because of improved design quality. Investments in innovation, training, and research must be made for the future.

Top management has the responsibility of keeping the company alive and providing jobs for their employees. Only they can develop a vision since they set the policies and mission of the organization. They must then act on the policies and show commitment.

Point 2. Learn the New Philosophy. The world has changed in the last few decades. Many industries in America have lost their competitiveness in world markets; foreign goods now dominate markets. Old methods of management, such as numbers-driven production, work measurement-based quotas, a bottom-line mentality, and adversarial work relationships will not work in today's global business environment. The current system creates mistrust, fear, and anxiety, with a focus on "satisficing" rather than on "optimizing." We must develop a quality consciousness and a new attitude that "good enough" just isn't. This can only be done with a never-ending cycle of improvement and changes in managerial and worker attitudes.

We have built waste and rework into our processes, accepting poor quality as a way of life. Several years ago one of the authors purchased a new dining room set, delivered directly from the factory. One of the doors was missing a brass knob. The company was very prompt in sending the missing knob. In fact, a package containing about six of them arrived the following week. Later, another package of six arrived. A few weeks later a *third* package came. Imagine the cost to the company of administrative time as well as the items themselves!

The new focus of management must be on customer-driven quality. Companies cannot survive if their customers are dissatisfied because of poor quality of conformance or poor fitness for use. We are still trying to catch up with the Japanese in quality of conformance while their emphasis is shifting to better quality of design. In 1990, Chrysler CEO Lee Iacocca stated that "Our cars are every bit as good as the Japanese [cars]." In terms of defect levels, U.S. automakers have made significant strides in closing the gap. However, Mazda chairman Kenichi Yamamoto noted that defect-free quality is "taken for granted." It is the finer design touches that impress consumers.[1] Everyone, from the boardroom to the stockroom, must learn the new philosophy.

Point 3. Understand Inspection. Routine inspection acknowledges that defects are present, but does not add value to the product. Rather, it encourages the production of defective products by letting someone else catch and fix the problem, it is rarely accurate, and the rework and disposition of defective material decreases

---

[1]"A New Era for Auto Quality," *Business Week,* October 22, 1990, pp. 84–96.

productivity and increases costs. In services, rework cannot be performed; external failures are the most damaging to business.

Workers must take responsibility for their work, rather than leave the problems for someone else down the production line. Managers need to understand the concept of variation and how it affects their processes and seek to reduce the common causes of variation. Simple statistical tools can be used to help control processes and eliminate mass inspection as the principal tool for quality control. Inspection should be used as an information-gathering tool for improvement.

Point 4. Stop Making Decisions Purely on the Basis of Cost. Purchasing departments have long been driven by cost minimization without regard for quality. In 1931 Walter Shewhart noted that price has no meaning without quality.[2] Yet the purchasing manager's performance traditionally has been evaluated by cost. What is the true cost of purchasing less-than-standard materials? The direct costs that can arise during production or during warranty periods resulting from poor quality materials, not to mention the loss of customer goodwill, can far exceed the cost "savings" perceived by purchasing. Purchasing must understand its new role as a supplier to production. This point causes individuals to rethink what is meant by an "organizational boundary." It is not simply the four walls around the production floor. The supplier and manufacturer must be considered as a "macro organization."

Deming has stressed building long-term relationships with vendors and moving toward a single supplier for any one component. Management has always justified multiple vendors for reasons such as providing protection against strikes or natural disasters but has ignored "hidden" costs such as increased travel to visit suppliers, loss of volume discounts, increased setup charges resulting in higher unit costs, and increased inventory and administrative expense. Most importantly, constantly changing vendors solely on the basis of price increases the variation in the material supplied to production, since each supplier's process is different.

In contrast, a reduced supply base decreases the variation coming into the customer's process, thus reducing scrap, rework, and the need for adjustment to accommodate this variation. A long-term relationship strengthens the bond between the supplier and the customer and allows the supplier to produce in greater quantity, fosters improved communication with the customer, and therefore enhances opportunities for process improvement. The supplier knows that to stay in business, only quality goods are acceptable. Statistical methods provide a common language for communication between customers and suppliers.

Point 5. Improve Constantly and Forever. Quality improvement will be discussed extensively in Chapter 9. Western management traditionally has viewed improvement in the context of large, expensive innovations such as robotics and computer-integrated manufacturing, yet the success of Japanese manufacturers is due primarily to continuous, small, incremental improvements. In Japan, improvement is a way of life.

Quality improvement in both *design* and *conformance* must be a never-ending process. Design quality can only be improved through the constant gathering of customers' attitudes and needs. Thus, Deming stresses continual market surveys,

---

[2]Walter A. Shewhart, *Economic Control of Quality of Manufactured Product* (New York: Van Nostrand, 1931).

redesign, and customer feedback. To improve the quality of conformance, one must attack the causes of variation. Improvement in conformance should be made not only in production, but also in every activity of the firm. This includes transportation, engineering, maintenance, sales, service, and administration. When quality improves, productivity improves and costs decrease.

Improvement means reducing variation by eliminating special causes and reducing the effects of common causes. Confusion about special and common causes of variation leads to frustration by both managers and workers. Management blames workers for problems beyond their control—the common causes. Workers who may be trying their best cannot understand why they cannot do a better job. Eliminating special causes of variation provides a stable and predictable process. Using statistical methods, workers can identify special causes when they occur and take corrective action, which is their responsibility, but common causes of variation are due to the system that management designs. Deming states that 85 to 95% of variation is due to the system. Statistical methods can be used by managers to understand common causes and lead to their reduction.

Point 6. Institute Training. For continuous improvement, employees—both management and workers—require the proper tools and knowledge. People are an organization's most valuable resource and want to do a good job, but often do not know how. It is management's responsibility to help them. Deming notes that in Japan entry-level managers spend 4 to 12 years on the factory floor and in other activities to learn the problems of production. All employees should be trained in statistical tools for quality problem solving. Not only does training result in improvements in quality and productivity, but it adds to workers' morale, showing them that the company is dedicated to helping them and investing in their future. In addition, training reduces barriers between workers and supervisors, giving both more incentive to improve further. At Honda of America in Marysville, Ohio, all employees start out on the production floor, regardless of their job classification!

Point 7. Institute Leadership. As Deming states, the job of management is leadership, not supervision. Supervision is simply overseeing and directing work; leadership is providing guidance to help employees do their jobs better with less effort. In many companies, supervisors know little about the job itself because the position is often used as an entry-level job for college graduates. The supervisors have never worked in the department and cannot train the workers, so their principal responsibility is to get the product out the door.

Supervision should provide the link between management and the work force. Supervisors should not be policemen or paper-pushers, but rather coaches, helping workers to do a better job and develop their skills. Leadership can help to eliminate the element of fear from the job and encourage teamwork.

Point 8. Drive Out Fear. Driving out fear underlies many of Deming's 14 Points. Fear is manifested in many ways: fear of reprisal, fear of failure, fear of the unknown, fear of relinquishing control, and fear of change. No system can work without the mutual respect of managers and workers. Workers are often afraid to report quality problems because they might not meet their quotas, their incentive pay might be reduced, or they might be blamed for problems in the system. Managers are afraid to cooperate with other departments because the other managers might receive higher performance ratings and bonuses, or because they fear takeovers or reorganizations. Fear encourages short-term thinking.

Managers fear losing power. One example is presented by Bushe.[3] After a statistical quality control program was implemented in an automotive plant, worker groups were sometimes able to offer better advice about system improvements than the corporate engineering staff. This ran counter to the plant's well-established culture. Middle managers were no longer the "experts." Their fear diminished their support for the program, which was eventually eliminated.

Point 9. Optimize the Efforts of Teams.   Teamwork helps to break down barriers between departments and individuals. Barriers between functional areas arise from fear when managers feel they might lose power. Internal competition exists for raises and performance ratings. The lack of cooperation leads to poor quality because other departments cannot understand what their "customers" want and do not get what they need from their "suppliers." In Japan, emphasis is placed on the fact that your customer is the next department or individual in the production process, and you are trained to manage such customer relationships.

Perhaps the biggest barrier to team efforts in the United States is between union and management. With some notable exceptions, the history of management-labor relations in U.S. firms has been largely adversarial. Lack of sensitivity to worker needs, exploitation of workers, and poor management practices and policies have frequently resulted in strained relations between managers and their subordinates. Labor leaders also must bear their share of the blame. They have had a tendency to resist any management effort to reduce rigid, rule-based tasks, preferring to adhere to the structured approaches that have their roots in Frederick W. Taylor's historical principles of scientific management.[4]

An example of how adversarial relations can affect labor and management in the workplace is presented in Figure 4.2 which shows actual comments of hourly maintenance employees of a transit company. Both columns of descriptive adjectives were provided by hourly employees to the director of maintenance education and development. The director, who was later successful in developing an employee

---

[3]Gervase R. Bushe, "Cultural Contradictions of Statistical Process Control in American Manufacturing Organizations," *Journal of Management,* Vol. 14, May 1988, pp. 19–31.

[4]"Detroit vs. the UAW: At Odds Over Teamwork," *Business Week,* August 24, 1987, pp. 54–55.

FIGURE 4.2 Perceived Labor Versus Management Attitudes

Hourly Employee Perceptions (Related to company and management)	Management Perceptions (Related to hourly employees)
Unionization	Labor agreement
Grievance procedures	Excuse makers
Job duties and assignments	Untrustworthy
Poor basic skill development	Ignorant
Poor training	Lazy
Poor working conditions	Stepchildren
Low morale	No team players
Untrained leadership	No goals
Suspicious (of management)	"Bus driver" orientation
No information (from management)	No sound basis for improvement

involvement program to reverse the attitudes, confirmed that the employees' perceptions of how hourly employees regarded management and how management regarded them were generally accurate. The contrast between the conditions viewed by the workers and the same conditions seen through the eyes of the managers is quite revealing. For example, managers frequently thought of the workers as ignorant (unable to learn) or lazy, while the workers merely viewed themselves as having poor basic skills (math, reading, etc.) and poor training. When management realized that there was some truth in the workers' perceptions and instituted courses in basic skill development, job-related skills, and participative problem solving, attitudes quickly became more positive.[5] This illustration shows that training and employee involvement are important means of removing such barriers. We will discuss the subject of employee involvement further in Chapter 11.

Point 10. Eliminate Exhortations. Posters, slogans, and motivational programs calling for "Zero Defects," "Do It Right the First Time," or "Improve Productivity and Quality," etc., are directed at the wrong people. These motivational programs assume that all quality problems are behavioral in nature, and that workers can improve simply through motivational methods. Workers become frustrated when they cannot improve or are penalized for defects.

Motivational approaches overlook the fact that most of the problems stem from the system, that is, are a result of the common causes of variation. This is management's problem, not the workers'. If anything, workers' attempts to fix problems only increase the variation. Improvement occurs by understanding the nature of special and common causes. Thus, statistical thinking and training, not slogans, can improve quality. Motivation can be better achieved from trust and leadership than from slogans and goals.

Point 11. Eliminate Numerical Quotas and M.B.O. (Management by Objective). Measurement has been, and often still is, used punitively. Standards and quotas are born of short-term perspectives and create fear. They do not encourage improvement, particularly if rewards or performance appraisals are tied to meeting quotas. Workers may short-cut quality to reach the goal. If you reach the standard, there is no incentive to continue production or to improve quality. Workers will do no more than they are asked to do.

Management also is driven by goal-setting. Arbitrary goals such as increasing sales by 5% next year or decreasing costs next quarter by 10% have no meaning without a method to achieve them. Deming states that goals are useful, but numerical goals set for others without a method to reach the goal generate frustration and resentment. Further, variation in the system makes year-to-year or quarter-to-quarter comparisons meaningless. A 5% increase or a 6% decrease may occur simply due to the variation within the system. Management must understand the system and continually try to improve it, rather than focus on short-term goals.

Point 12. Remove Barriers to Pride in Workmanship. People on the factory floor and even in management have become, in Deming's words, "a commodity." Factory workers are given monotonous tasks, provided with inferior

---

[5]William M. Lindsay, Kent Curtis, and Ralph C. Hennie, "Houston Metropolitan Transit Authority: Where Cooperative Team Efforts Produce Measureable Results," Presented at the *IAQC Fall Conference,* Orlando, FL, 1986.

machines, tools, or materials, told to run defective items to meet sales pressures, and report to supervisors who know nothing about the job. Salaried employees are expected to work evenings and weekends to make up for cost-cutting measures that resulted in layoffs of their colleagues. Many are given the title of "management" so that overtime need not be paid. As a recent study demonstrated, even employees in the quality profession are not immune.[6] An inspection technician stated "This profession always seems to end up being called the troublemakers." A quality engineer stated "The managers over me now give little direction, are very resistant to change, and do little to advance their people." A quality supervisor said "Someone less qualified could perform my job . . . for less money." How can these individuals take pride in their work? Many cannot be certain they will have a job next year.

Deming believes that one of the biggest barriers to pride in workmanship is performance appraisal. Performance appraisal destroys teamwork by promoting competition for limited resources; fosters mediocrity since objectives typically are driven by numbers and what the boss wants, not by quality; focuses on the short term and discourages risk-taking; and confounds the "people resources" with other resources. If all individuals are working within the system, then they should not be ranked on an individual basis. Some people *have* to be "below average." This can only result in frustration if those individuals are working within the confines of the system. Deming suggests that there are only three categories of performance: the majority that work within the system, those that are outside the system on the superior side, and those that are outside the system on the inferior side. Statistical methods provide the means of making this classification. Superior performers should be compensated specially; inferior performers need extra training or replacement.

Pride in workmanship can be achieved through teamwork and continuous improvement strategies. Workers must not be viewed as objects or commodities; they must be considered as valuable resources.

Point 13. Encourage Education and Self-Improvement.   The difference between this point and Point 6 is subtle. Point 6 refers to training in specific job skills; Point 13 refers to continuing, broad education for self-development. Organizations must invest in their people at all levels for the long term. A fundamental mission of business is to provide jobs as stated in Point 1, but business and society also have the responsibility to improve the value of the individual. Developing the worth of the individual is a powerful motivation method.

Point 14. Take Action.   The transformation must begin with top management and include everyone. Applying the Deming philosophy represents a major cultural change that many firms find difficult, particularly since many of the traditional management practices that Deming feels must be eliminated have been ingrained in the organization's culture for decades. Ford Motor Company is one firm that has embraced the Deming philosophy totally. Their experience is discussed in the Quality in Practice section later in this chapter.

In addition to the 14 Points, Deming proposes "Seven Deadly Diseases" that obstruct the quest for quality:

---

[6]Brad Stratton, "The Price Is Right: ASQC Annual Salary Survey," *Quality Progress,* Vol. 21, No. 9, September 1988, pp. 24–29.

1. *Lack of constancy of purpose:* This is the antithesis of the first of his 14 Points. Many companies have only short-term quality programs. They do not look toward the long term and ingrain the philosophy into the corporate culture. When the quality champion leaves or retires, the quality focus begins to crumble.

2. *Emphasis on short-term profits:* Quality is undermined when firms seek only to increase the quarterly dividend. Japanese firms invest significantly more in research and development, forsaking short-term profits with the goal of capturing market share 5 to 10 years later. Short-term thinking is fed by fear of unfriendly takeovers and leveraged buy-outs.

3. *Evaluation of performance, merit rating, or annual review of performance:* This is clearly spelled out in his 14 Points. Such activity destroys teamwork, builds fear, and encourages defection from management. Deming calls this "management by fear."

4. *Mobility of management:* Managers who continually job-hop never understand the companies for which they work, focus on the short term, and can never implement the long-term changes necessary for lasting quality improvement.

5. *Running a company on visible figures alone:* The most important figures are unknown and often unknowable, such as the effect of a satisfied customer.

6. *Excessive medical costs for employee health care that increase the final costs of goods and services:* These have been increasing at a phenomenal rate over the years. The long-term effect is a deterioration in competitiveness.

7. *Excessive costs of warranty, fueled by lawyers who work on the basis of contingency fees:* Consider the amount of malpractice insurance that medical professionals must now pay due to a proliferation of lawsuits and multimillion dollar judgments. The fear built into the system is driving many doctors, such as obstetricians, to abandon their practices.

THE JURAN PHILOSOPHY

Joseph Juran joined Western Electric in the 1920s during its pioneering days in the development of statistical methods for quality and spent much of his time as a corporate industrial engineer. In 1951, the *Quality Control Handbook* was written, edited, and published to a large extent by Juran himself. This book, often regarded as the "bible" of quality, has been revised several times and continues to be a popular reference.

Juran taught quality principles to the Japanese in the 1950s just after Deming and was a principal force in their quality reorganization. Like Deming, he concludes that we face a major crisis in quality due to the loss of sales to foreign competition and the huge costs of poor quality. To solve this crisis, new thinking about quality that includes all levels of the managerial hierarchy is required. Upper management in particular requires training and experience in managing for quality.

As opposed to Deming, however, Juran did not propose a major cultural change in the organization, but rather sought to improve quality by working within the system to which American managers are accustomed. Thus, his programs are designed to fit into a company's current strategic business planning with minimal risk of rejection. Juran contends that employees at different levels of an organization speak in different "languages." (Deming, on the other hand, believes statistics should be the common language.) Top management speaks in the language of dollars, workers speak in the language of things, and middle management must be able to speak both languages and translate between dollars and things. Thus, to get top management's attention, quality issues must be cast in the language they understand—dollars. Hence, Juran advocates the use of quality cost accounting and Pareto analysis to focus attention on quality problems. At the operational level, Juran's focus is on increasing conformance to specifications through elimination of defects, supported extensively by statistical tools for analysis. Thus, his philosophy fits well into existing management systems.

Juran defines quality as "fitness for use." (Deming advocates no specific definition.) This is broken down into four categories: quality of design, quality of conformance, availability, and field service. Quality of design focuses on market research, the product concept, and design specifications. Quality of conformance includes technology, manpower, and management. Availability focuses on reliability, maintainability, and logistical support. Field service quality comprises promptness, competence, and integrity.

The pursuit of quality is viewed on two levels: (1) The mission of the firm as a whole is to achieve high product quality and (2) the mission of each individual department in the firm is to achieve high production quality. Like Deming, Juran advocates a never-ending spiral of activities that includes market research, product development, design, planning for manufacture, purchasing, production process control, inspection and testing, and sales, followed by customer feedback. Because of the interdependency of these functions, the need for competent company-wide quality management is important. Senior management must play an active and enthusiastic leadership role in the quality management process.

Juran's prescriptions focus on three major quality processes, called the *quality trilogy:* quality planning—the process for preparing to meet quality goals; quality control—the process for meeting quality goals during operations; and quality improvement—the process for breaking through to unprecedented levels of performance.

Quality planning begins with identifying customers, both external and internal, determining their needs, and developing product features that respond to customer needs. Thus, like Deming, Juran wants employees to know who uses their products, whether in the next department or in another organization. Quality goals are then established that meet the needs of customers and suppliers alike, and do so at a minimum combined cost. The process that can produce the product that meets customers' needs *and* quality goals under operating conditions must be designed. Strategic planning for quality should be similar to the firm's financial planning process. The process should determine short-term and long-term goals, set priorities, compare results with previous plans, and mesh the plans with other corporate strategic objectives. These planning issues will be discussed in Chapter 6.

Paralleling Deming's emphasis on identifying and reducing sources of variation, Juran states that quality control involves determining what to control, establishing units of measurement so that data may be objectively evaluated, establishing standards of performance, measuring actual performance, interpreting the difference between actual performance and the standard, and taking action on the difference. Chapter 8 will focus on control in more detail.

Unlike Deming, Juran specifies a detailed program for quality improvement. Such a program involves proving the need for improvement, identifying specific projects for improvement, organizing guidance for the projects, diagnosing the causes, providing remedies for the causes, proving that the remedies are effective under operating conditions, and providing control to maintain improvements. At every point in time, hundreds or even thousands of quality improvement projects should be under way in every area of the firm. In Chapter 9, we shall discuss the specifics of Juran's quality improvement approach.

Juran's assessment of most companies is that quality control is *the* top priority among the trilogy and most companies feel they are strong in this category. Quality planning and quality improvement, however, are not important priorities and are significantly weaker in most organizations. He feels that more effort needs to be placed on quality planning and even more on quality improvement.

Juran supports these conclusions with several case examples in which Japanese firms using technology, materials, and processes identical to those of American firms had much higher levels of quality and productivity. His explanation is that, since the 1950s, the Japanese have implemented quality improvement projects at a far greater pace than their Western counterparts. The result is that sometime in the 1970s, Japanese product quality exceeded Western quality and continues to improve at a greater pace (see Figure 4.3).

Japanese efforts at quality improvement were supported by massive training programs and top management leadership. Training in managerial quality-oriented concepts as well as training in the tools for quality improvement, cost reduction, data collection, and analysis is one of the most important components of Juran's philosophy. Juran maintains that the Japanese experience leaves little doubt as to the significance of the return to quality training in competitive advantage, reduced failure costs, higher productivity, smaller inventories, and better delivery performance. The Juran Institute, founded by Dr. Juran, provides substantial training in the form of seminars, videotapes, and other materials.

Many aspects of the Juran philosophy are similar to that of Deming. The focus on top management commitment, the need for improvement, the use of quality control

FIGURE 4.3 Quality Improvements in Japan and the West

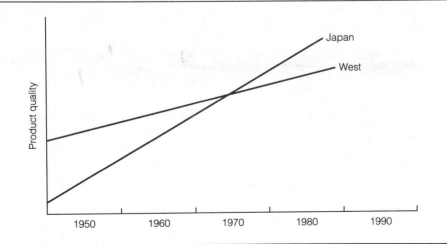

SOURCE: J. M. Juran, "Product Quality—A Prescription for the West," *Management Review*, June/July 1981.

techniques, and the importance of training are fundamental to both philosophies. However, Juran does not agree with all that Deming says. For instance, Juran believes that Deming is wrong to tell management to drive out fear; "fear can bring out the best in people," states Juran.[7]

THE CROSBY PHILOSOPHY

Philip B. Crosby was corporate vice president for quality at International Telephone and Telegraph (ITT) for 14 years after working his way up from line inspector. After leaving ITT, he established Philip Crosby Associates in 1979 to develop and offer training programs. He is also the author of several popular books. His first book, *Quality is Free,* sold about one million copies.

The essence of Crosby's quality philosophy is embodied in what he calls the "Absolutes of Quality Management" and the "Basic Elements of Improvement." Crosby's Absolutes of Quality Management are described below.

- *Quality means conformance to requirements, not elegance.* Crosby quickly dispels the myth that quality follows the transcendent definition discussed in Chapter 1. Requirements must be clearly stated so that they cannot be misunderstood. Requirements are communication devices and are ironclad. Once this is done, then one can take measurements to determine conformance to those requirements. The nonconformance detected is the absence of quality. Quality problems become nonconformance problems, that is, variation in output. Setting requirements is the responsibility of management.

- *There is no such thing as a quality problem.* Problems must be identified by those individuals or departments that cause them. Thus, there are accounting problems, manufacturing problems, design problems, front-desk problems, and so on. This implies that quality originates in functional departments, not in the quality department, and that the burden of responsibility for such problems falls in these functional departments. The quality department should measure conformance, report results, and lead the drive to develop a positive attitude toward quality improvement. This is similar to Deming's third point.

- *There is no such thing as the economics of quality; it is always cheaper to do the job right the first time.* In Chapter 2 we discussed several flawed economic models for the "optimum" level of quality. Crosby supports the premise that "economics of quality" has no meaning. Quality is free. What costs money are all actions that involve not doing jobs right the first time. The Deming chain reaction sends a similar message.

- *The only performance measurement is the cost of quality.* The cost of quality is the expense of nonconformance. Crosby notes that most companies spend 15 to 20% of their sales dollars on quality costs. A company with a well-run quality management program can achieve a cost of quality that is less than 2.5% of sales, primarily in the prevention and appraisal categories. Crosby's program calls for measuring and publicizing the cost of poor quality. Quality cost data are useful to call problems to management's attention, to select opportunities

---

[7]Jeremy Main, "Under the Spell of the Quality Gurus," *Fortune,* August 18, 1986, pp. 30–34.

for corrective action, and to track quality improvement over time. Such data provide visible proof of improvement and recognition of achievement. Juran also supports this approach.

■ *The only performance standard is "Zero Defects."* Crosby feels that the Zero Defects (ZD) concept is widely misunderstood and resisted. Zero Defects is not a motivational program. It is described as follows:

> Zero Defects is a performance standard. It is the standard of the craftsperson regardless of his or her assignment. . . . The theme of ZD is *do it right the first time.* That means concentrating on preventing defects rather than just finding and fixing them.
>
> People are conditioned to believe that error is inevitable; thus they not only accept error, they anticipate it. It does not bother us to make a few errors in our work . . . to err is human. We all have our own standards in business or academic life—our own points at which errors begin to bother us. It is good to get an A in school, but it may be OK to pass with a C.
>
> We do not maintain these standards, however, when it comes to our personal life. If we did, we should expect to be shortchanged every now and then when we cash our paycheck; we should expect hospital nurses to drop a constant percentage of newborn babies. . . . We as individuals do not tolerate these things. We have a dual standard: one for ourselves and one for our work.
>
> Most human error is caused by lack of attention rather than lack of knowledge. Lack of attention is created when we assume that error is inevitable. If we consider this condition carefully, and pledge ourselves to make a constant conscious effort to do our jobs right the first time, we will take a giant step toward eliminating the waste of rework, scrap, and repair that increases cost and reduces individual opportunity.[8]

Juran and Deming, on the other hand, would argue that it is pointless, if not hypocritical, to exhort a line worker to produce perfection since the overwhelming majority of imperfections are due to poorly designed manufacturing systems beyond the workers' control.

Crosby's Basic Elements of Improvement include *determination, education,* and *implementation.* By determination, Crosby means that top management must be serious about quality improvement. The Absolutes should be understood by everyone; this can be accomplished only through education. Finally, every member of the management team must understand the implementation process. In Chapter 9 we discuss the details of his approach to quality improvement.

Unlike Juran and Deming, Crosby's program is primarily behavioral. He places more emphasis on management and organizational processes for changing corporate culture and attitudes than on the use of statistical techniques. Like Juran and unlike Deming, his approach fits well within existing organizational structures.

Crosby's approach, however, provides relatively few details about how firms should address the finer points of quality management. The focus is on managerial thinking rather than on organizational systems. By allowing managers to determine the best methods to apply in their own firm's situations, his approach tends to avoid

---

[8]Philip B. Crosby, *Quality Is Free* (New York: McGraw-Hill, 1979), pp. 200–201.

some of the implementation problems experienced by firms that have adopted the Deming philosophy.

Crosby's philosophy has not earned the respect of his rivals.[9] While they agree that he is an entertaining speaker and a great motivator, they say he lacks substance in the methods of achieving quality improvement. Nevertheless, hundreds of thousands have taken his courses in-house or at his Quality College in Winter Park, Florida.

We see that while Deming, Juran, and Crosby all view quality as imperative for the future competitiveness of Western industry, they have significantly different approaches to implementing organizational change. In each philosophy, it should be clear that quality requires a total commitment from everyone in an organization. Any organizational activity can be viewed in three different ways, depending on the intensity of commitment to the activity:

1. *Function:* a task or group of tasks to be performed that contribute to the mission or purpose of an organization.

2. *Process:* a set of steps, procedures, or policies that define how a function is to be performed and what results are expected.

3. *Ideology:* a set of values or beliefs that guide an organization in the establishment of its mission, processes, and functions.

Managers may view the activity of quality assurance in any of the above three ways. Many managers view quality as a set of tasks to be performed by specialists in quality control. Other managers have a broader perspective and see quality as a process in which many people at the operating level from a number of functional areas of the organization are involved. The broadest viewpoint is that quality is an ideology or philosophy that must pervade the organization: Everyone must believe in it and support it.

Business firms tend to be highly individualized. Because of this, it is difficult to apply one specific philosophy as advocated by either Deming, Juran, or Crosby. Although each of these philosophies can be highly effective, a firm must first understand the nature and differences of the philosophies and then develop a quality management approach that is tailored to its individual organization. Any approach should include goals and objectives, allocation of responsibilities, a measurement system and description of tools to be employed, an outline of the management style that will be used, and a strategy for implementation. Once this is done, it is up to the management team to lead the organization through successful execution.

OTHER QUALITY PHILOSOPHERS

A. V. Feigenbaum and Kaoru Ishikawa were both awarded the title of Honorary Members of the American Society for Quality Control in 1986.[10] At that time there were only four living honorary members, two of whom were W. Edwards Deming and Joseph M. Juran. Obviously, the title of "Honorary Member" is not given lightly by the ASQC, and it serves to validate the premise that Feigenbaum and Ishikawa are among the world-class leaders of the quality movement. In this section we briefly review the accomplishments that have made them part of this elite group.

---

[9]Main, "Quality Gurus," pp. 30–34.

[10]Facts in this section were obtained from "Profile: the ASQC Honorary Members A. V. Feigenbaum and Kaoru Ishikawa," *Quality Progress,* Vol. 19, No. 8, August 1986, pp. 43–45.

A. V. Feigenbaum

A. V. Feigenbaum's career in quality began more than 40 years ago. For 10 years, he was the manager of worldwide manufacturing and quality control at General Electric. As of 1992 he was president of General Systems Company of Pittsfield, Massachusetts.

Feigenbaum is known for three primary contributions to quality—his international promotion of the quality ethic, his development of the concept of total quality control, and his development of the quality cost classification discussed in the previous chapter.

The first contribution has been a constant theme of Feigenbaum's as he has traveled and spoken to various audiences and groups around the world over the years. It resulted in his being elected as the founding chairman of the board of the International Academy of Quality, which has attracted active participation from the European Organization for Quality Control, the Union of Japanese Scientists and Engineers (JUSE), as well as the American Society for Quality Control.

The second and third concepts were presented in his book *Total Quality Control,* which was first published in 1951 under the title *Quality Control: Principles, Practice and Administration.* The concept of "total quality control" was picked up by the Japanese and became the foundation for their practice of CWQC—company-wide quality control, which began in the 1960s. Of course, the four categories of quality costs have become the standard for analysis around the world.

Kaoru Ishikawa

It may be safely said that without the leadership of Kaoru Ishikawa, the Japanese quality movement would not have enjoyed the worldwide acclaim and success that it has today. Dr. Ishikawa was a professor of engineering at Tokyo University for many years. Ishikawa was instrumental in the development of the broad outlines of Japanese quality strategy, the concept of CWQC, the audit process used for determining whether a company will be selected to receive the Deming Award, the quality control circle, and cause-effect diagrams—a principal tool for quality improvement.

As a member of the editorial review board for the Japanese journal *Quality Control for Foremen,* founded in 1962, and later as the chief executive director of the QC Circle Headquarters at JUSE, Dr. Ishikawa had a substantial influence on the development of a participative, bottom-up view of quality that became the trademark of the Japanese approach to quality management. However, Ishikawa was also able to get the attention of top management and to persuade them that a *company-wide* approach to quality control was necessary for total success.

Cause and effect diagrams, which will be described in Chapter 9, are the only truly Japanese technique being used by quality circles in either Japan or the United States. They were invented by Dr. Ishikawa in 1950.[11] This simple and powerful technique has been taught to workers in more than 50 countries. In summary, Kaoru Ishikawa had a profound effect on the course of quality development, not only in his own country, but in the United States and around the world.

---

[11]Robert Amsden, Jeff Beardsley, and Virgil Rehg. "QC Circle Workshop: Cause and Effect Diagrams, A Most Useful Tool," *1976 ASQC Technical Conference Transactions,* Toronto, p. 244; reprinted in David M. Amsden, and Robert T. Amsden, eds. *QC Circles: Applications, Tools and Theory* (Milwaukee, WI: ASQC, 1976), p. 85.

Ford Becomes a "Deming Company"

Ford Motor Company has been one of the leaders in adopting the Deming philosophy. Dr. Deming came to Ford in 1981 to meet with President Donald Petersen and other company officials, who were stimulated by NBC's program "If Japan Can, Why Can't We?" Actually, as the story goes, Deming was first approached by one of Ford's vice presidents. Deming's response was that he would not come unless invited by the CEO as an indication of top management commitment.

Deming began by giving seminars for top executives and meeting with various employees, suggesting changes corresponding to his 14 Points. Ford managers visited Nashua Corporation to learn how statistical methods were used. Chief executives from many of Ford's major suppliers visited Japan. Petersen himself took a course on statistical methods. The 14 Points became the basis for a transformation of Ford's philosophy. Their commitment is evident in statements made in various annual reports:

> Last year [1982] we pledged our efforts to continuous improvement . . . We renew that pledge. In product, this means unqualified commitment to customer-responsive excellence world-wide . . . we made quality our No. 1 objective several years ago. We have achieved steady and substantial quality improvement in the United States, where Ford now leads its major domestic competition. . . . Ford's quality goals also include leadership in customer service. . . . Our key to continued success in the quest for product quality is establishing an effective long-term relationship with our suppliers. . . . Ford is involving suppliers far earlier in the design process. . . . This helps reduce engineering and production costs and ensures uninterrupted improvement in quality. Ford has instituted a system that makes quality considerations a critical factor in every supplier-selection decision and establishes formal quality ratings for every supplier. The Q1 Preferred Quality Award recognizes suppliers who achieve and maintain a consistently high level of quality and prove their commitment to continuing improvement. (Ford Motor Company 1983 Annual Report)

Company Mission and Guiding Principles

Mission Ford Motor Company is a worldwide leader in automotive and automotive-related products and services as well as in newer industries such as aerospace, communications and financial services. Our mission is to improve continually our products and services to meet our customers' needs, allowing us to prosper as a business and to provide a reasonable return for our stockholders, the owners of our business.

Values How we accomplish our mission is as important as the mission itself. Fundamental to success for the company are these basic values:

- *People.* Our people are the source of our strength. They provide our corporate intelligence and determine our reputation and vitality. Involvement and teamwork are our core human values.

- *Products.* Our products are the end result of our efforts, and they should be the best in serving customers worldwide. As our products are viewed, so are we viewed.

- *Profits.* Profits are the ultimate measure of how efficiently we provide customers with the best products for their needs. Profits are required to survive and grow.

Guiding Principles

- *Quality comes first.* To achieve customer satisfaction, the quality of our products and services must be our number one priority.

- *Customers are the focus of everything we do.* Our work must be done with customers in mind, providing better

(continued)

products and services than our competition.

- *Continuous improvement is essential to our success.* We must strive for excellence in everything we do: in our products, in their safety and value—and in our services, our human relations, our competitiveness and our profitability.

- *Employee involvement is our way of life.* We are a team. We must treat each other with trust and respect.

- *Dealers and suppliers are our partners.* The Company must maintain mutually beneficial relationships with dealers, suppliers and our other business associates.

- *Integrity is never compromised.* The conduct of our Company worldwide must be pursued in a manner that is socially responsible and commands respect for its integrity and for its positive contributions to society. Our doors are open to men and women alike without discrimination and without regard to ethnic origin or personal beliefs.

(Ford Motor Company 1984 Annual Report)

After the industry-wide crisis at the turn of the decade, Ford embarked on an intensive quality improvement process. Results have been dramatic. Customer research shows that the quality of our 1986 cars and trucks is more than 50 percent better than that of our 1980 models. . . . We have explored new approaches to accelerate the rate of improvement. This led us to focus on strategic issues related to our quality effort. The strategy that evolved was to concentrate on developing and implementing fundamental changes in the overall quality/customer satisfaction process. . . . Quality includes every aspect of the vehicle that determines customer satisfaction and provides fundamental value. This means how well the vehicle is made, how well it performs, how well it lasts, and how well the customer is treated by both the Company and the dealer. There will be no

compromise in our quest for quality. (Ford Motor Company 1985 Annual Report)

Ford's 1987 earnings were the highest for any company in automotive history, despite a seven percent drop in U.S. car and truck industry sales, higher capital spending, and increased marketing costs. (Ford Motor Company 1987 Annual Report)

Ford has developed a policy of Total Quality Excellence that emphasizes the importance of quality in every action, operation, and product associated with Ford Motor Company. The fundamental precepts of this policy are:

- Quality is defined by the customer; the customer wants products and services that, throughout their life, meet his or her needs and expectations at a cost that represents value.

- Quality excellence can best be achieved by presenting problems rather than by detecting and correcting them after they occur.

- All work that is done by Company employees, suppliers, and dealers is part of a process that creates a product or service for a customer. Each person can influence some part of that process and, therefore, affects the quality of its output and the ultimate customer's satisfaction with our products and services.

- Sustained quality excellence requires continuous process improvement. This means, regardless of how good present performance may be, it can become even better.

- People provide the intelligence and generate the actions that are necessary to realize these improvements.

- Each employee is a customer for work done by other employees or suppliers, with a right to expect good work from others and an obligation to contribute work of high caliber to those who, in turn, are his or her customers.

The goal of Ford Total Quality Excellence is to achieve superior external and internal customer satisfaction levels. Each employee's commitment to the precepts of Ford Total Quality Excellence and management's further commitment to implementation of supporting managerial and operating systems is essential to realizing that goal.

(continued)

Donald Petersen has stated:

The work of Dr. Deming has definitely helped change Ford's corporate leadership. It is management's responsibility to create the environment in which everyone can contribute to continuous improvement in processes and systems. We're making good progress along these lines with employee involvement and participative management. Real gains of the new management system are shared with employees through job security, recognition of contribution, and compensation.

While employees have benefited, so has the company and our customers. For example, we are running well over 60 percent better levels of quality in our products today. I dare say we would not have predicted that much improvement in that short a time. Dr. Deming has influenced my thinking in a variety of ways. What stands out is that he helped me crystallize my ideas concerning the value of teamwork, process improvement and the pervasive power of the concept of continuous improvement.[12]

Key Issues for Discussion

1. Discuss specific themes in the Deming philosophy that are evident in statements made in Ford's annual reports.

2. Which definition of quality (see Chapter 1) is used in the 1985 Annual Report? Which of Garvin's eight dimensions of quality are stressed?

[12]Donald R. Katz, "Coming Home," *Business Month*, October 1988, p. 58.

Summary of Key Points

- W. Edwards Deming, Joseph Juran, and Philip Crosby are recognized as the top three international leaders of modern quality. A. V. Feigenbaum and Kaoru Ishikawa have also made significant contributions.

- Deming's philosophy is based on improving products and services by reducing uncertainty and variation. Statistical thinking is the foundation of his philosophy. He advocates a radical cultural change in organizations that is embodied in his "14 Points."

- The Deming chain reaction states that quality improvement reduces cost, increases productivity, increases market share, and allows firms to stay in business and provide jobs.

- Joseph Juran's philosophy seeks to provide change within the current American management system. Quality is defined as fitness for use, and the quality trilogy—planning, control, and improvement—provides a program for quality assurance in organizations.

- Philip Crosby's approach to quality is summarized in his Absolutes of Quality Management. He places more emphasis on behavioral change rather than on the use of statistical techniques as advocated by Deming and Juran.

- A. V. Feigenbaum coined the term "total quality control" and was responsible for developing cost of quality approaches.

- Kaoru Ishikawa was instrumental in the Japanese quality movement, particularly in advocating a company-wide quality control approach, the use of quality circles, and problem-solving tools such as cause and effect diagrams.

Questions for Review and Discussion

1. Explain the interrelationships among Deming's 14 Points. How do they support each other? Why must they be viewed as a whole rather than separately?

2. The following themes form the basis for Deming's philosophy. Classify the 14 Points into these categories and discuss the commonalties within each category.

   a. Organizational purpose and mission
   b. Quantitative goals
   c. Revolution of management philosophy
   d. Elimination of seat-of-the-pants decisions
   e. Build cooperation
   f. Improve manager-worker relations.

3. Which of Deming's 14 Points are most controversial to current managers in the United States? Why?

4. Discuss how Deming's 14 Points can apply to an academic environment. How can learning and classroom performance be improved by applying Deming's philosophy?

5. If Dr. Deming were to define quality explicitly, how do you think he would do it?

6. Explain Juran's "quality trilogy."

7. Discuss Crosby's Absolutes of Quality Management.

8. What are Crosby's Basic Elements of Improvement?

9. What were the contributions of A. V. Feigenbaum and Kaoru Ishikawa? Considering their international outlook and contributions, would you say that *any* firm today could have an effective quality process if they ignored the international changes occurring in the quality arena? Why or why not?

10. Study the annual reports of some major companies over a period of several years. Using liberal quotations, discuss the role of quality in these companies. How have their perspectives on quality changed over the years? Do you see any evidence of implementation of the quality philosophies discussed in this chapter?

Bibliography

Deming, W. E. *Out of the Crisis,* Cambridge, MA: MIT Center for Advanced Engineering Study, 1982.

Duncan, W. Jack, and Van Matre, Joseph G. "The Gospel According to Deming: Is It Really New?" *Business Horizons,* July–August 1990, pp. 3–9.

Juran, J. M. "Product Quality—A Prescription for the West," *Management Review,* June/July 1981.

Juran, J. M. "The Quality Trilogy," *Quality Progress,* Vol. 19, August 1986, pp. 19–24.

Ohio Quality and Productivity Forum Roundtable, "Deming's Point Four: A Study," *Quality Progress,* December 1988, pp. 31–35.

Raturi A., and McCutcheon, D. "An Epistemological Framework for Quality Management," Working Paper, Cincinnati, OH: Department of Quantitative Analysis and Information Systems, University of Cincinnati, March 1990.

CHAPTER 5

Total Quality Management

The philosophies of the quality leaders discussed in the previous chapter all share one important premise: Quality must be a total effort involving all employees of the organization, as well as suppliers and customers. **Total quality management,** or **TQM,** is the term that has become popular to describe a comprehensive view of quality assurance.

Companies who subscribe to and succeed in total quality management have been honored by two prestigious awards, the Deming Prize and the Malcolm Baldrige National Quality Award. Since 1951, the Japanese Union of Scientists and Engineers has sponsored the Deming Prize, an award given to individuals and companies who meet stringent criteria in the pursuit of quality. In 1989 Florida Power and Light was the first non-Japanese company to win this coveted award. The Baldrige Award was instituted in 1987 by an act of Congress to recognize high-quality businesses in the United States and to provide an incentive for all companies in the nation to improve quality. The European community established a similar award in 1991.

There are probably as many different TQM programs as there are business firms. While no one program is ideal, successful programs share many common attributes. In this chapter we discuss the principles of total quality management and strategies for successful implementation of TQM programs. Also, we will discuss the Deming Prize and Baldrige Award, and profile several companies that have won these awards to show how successful TQM programs are designed and implemented.

PRINCIPLES OF TOTAL QUALITY MANAGEMENT

Total quality management is an integrative management concept for continuously improving the quality of goods and services delivered through the participation of all levels and functions of the organization. TQM is simply the process of building quality into goods and services from the beginning, and making quality everyone's concern and responsibility. The success of TQM depends on the genuine commitment to quality of every member of the organization. The benefits of TQM include:

- improving customer satisfaction

- enhancing the quality of goods and services

- reducing waste and inventory, thus reducing costs

- improving productivity

- reducing product development time

- increasing flexibility in meeting market demands

- reducing work in process

- improving customer service and delivery times

- better utilizing human resources.

TQM incorporates several dimensions: the *design* of products that meet customers' needs, *control of processes* to ensure their ability to meet design requirements, and *quality improvement* for the continued enhancement of quality.

The customer is the driving force behind quality of design. Customer satisfaction is based on their subjective comparisons between expectations and the actual quality received. All too often, management tends to focus exclusively on the product, instead of the customer. While sales of the product clearly generate the hard dollars, we must also recognize that customer satisfaction is derived from ancillary services associated with the product and the sensitivity and timeliness with which problems are handled. Thus, a sound behaviorally based quality system must parallel the traditional technical system. To develop such a system, management must research customer preferences, train employees to be sensitive to customer needs, and reward employees for making customer satisfaction a primary objective.

The ability to control a process to meet design specifications is essential to ensuring customer satisfaction. In fact, the term **total quality control,** coined by A. V. Feigenbaum, was a forerunner to TQM. The language of statistics provides a common basis from which we can understand total quality control. While TQM does not require that everyone obtain advanced degrees in statistics, it does require that the basic vocabulary of statistics and process control be understood by everyone. In addition to controlling processes and systems, TQM must also include *internal* self-control by people.

Finally, TQM is based on the premise that any product or service can be improved and that a successful organization must consciously seek out and exploit improvement. The essence of TQM is continuous improvement through collaborative efforts across functional boundaries and between organizational levels with the ultimate goal of providing customer satisfaction.

A. V. Feigenbaum defined four characteristics of the "engineered total quality system":

1. It represents a *point of view* for thinking about the way quality really works in a modern business company or governmental agency and how quality decisions can best be made.

2. It represents the basis for the deeply thought-through *documentation* . . . of the key, enduring quality activities and the integrated people-machine-information relationships which make a particular activity viable and communicable throughout the firm.

3. It is the *foundation* for making the broader scope quality activities of the company *manageable* because it permits the management and employees of the plant and company to get their arms firmly around their customer-requirements-to-customer-satisfaction quality activities.

4. It is the basis for systematic *engineering of order-of-magnitude* improvements throughout the major quality activities of the company.

Feigenbaum states that the quality of products and services is directly influenced by what he terms the "9 M's": markets, money, management, men and women, motivation, materials, machines and mechanization, modern information methods, and mounting product requirements. Although he takes an obvious engineering focus, he is strongly customer oriented as well.

The principles of total quality management are embodied in the strategies and leadership philosophies of nearly every major company. For example, the total quality philosophy at Procter & Gamble focuses on delivering superior consumer satisfaction and boils down to four principles:

- *Really know our customers and consumers:* Know those who resell our products and those who finally use them—and then meet and exceed their expectations.

- *Do right things right:* This requires hard data and sound statistical analysis to select the "right things" and to direct continual improvement in how well we do those things.

- *Concentrate on improving systems:* In order to achieve superior customer and consumer satisfaction and leadership financial goals, we must continually analyze and improve the capability of our basic business systems and sub-systems.

- *Empower people:* This means removing barriers and providing a climate in which everyone in the enterprise is encouraged and trained to make his or her maximum contribution to our business objectives.[1]

The *P&G Statement of Purpose* captures the "what," "how," and expected "results" of their quality efforts:

We will provide products of superior quality and value that best fill the needs of the world's consumers.

We will achieve that purpose through an organization and a working environment which attracts the finest people; fully develops and challenges our individual talents; encourages our free and spirited collaboration to drive the business ahead; and maintains the Company's historic principles of integrity, and doing the right thing.

Through the successful pursuit of our commitment, we expect our brands to achieve leadership share and profit positions and that, as a result, our business, our people, our shareholders, and the communities in which we live and work, will prosper.

A similar philosophy is described by the *American Express Quality Leadership* approach. The fundamental beliefs about quality that provide the philosophical underpinnings and guide decision making at American Express are:

- *Quality* is the foundation of our continued success.

- *Quality* is a journey of continuous improvement and innovation.

---

[1]"Total Quality at Procter & Gamble," The Total Quality Forum, Cincinnati, Ohio, August 6–8, 1991.

- *Quality* provides a very high return, but requires the investment of time and resources.

- *Quality* requires committed leadership.

- *Quality* begins by meeting or exceeding the expectations of our people.

- *Quality* requires teamwork and learning at all levels.

- *Quality* comes from the energy of a diverse community of motivated and skilled people who are given and take responsibility.

The General Accounting Office (GAO) has developed a general framework[2] for describing total quality management, shown in Figure 5.1. The solid line shows the direction of the total quality processes to improve competitiveness. This begins with a leadership dedicated to improving products and services as well as the quality systems. Improvements in these areas lead to customer satisfaction and benefits to the

---

[2]U.S. General Accounting Office, "Management Practices: U.S. Companies Improve Performance Through Quality Efforts," GA/NSIAD-91-190, May 1991.

FIGURE 5.1 **Total Quality Management Model**

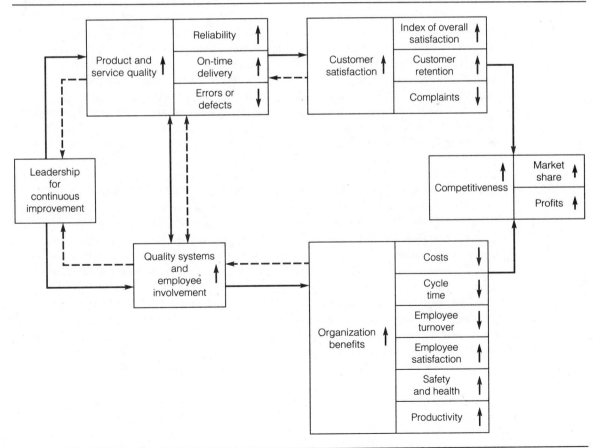

organization, both of which improve competitiveness. The dotted lines show the information feedback necessary for continuous improvement. The arrows in the boxes show the expected direction of the performance indicators.

The Language of Total Quality Management

New languages exist in the world of TQM. William Wiggenhorn, corporate vice-president for training and education at Motorola, discussed the new "language of quality" in a *Harvard Business Review* article.[3] He discussed the need to teach basic concepts of statistics such as "bell curves, probabilities, and standard deviations expressed in multiples of the Greek letter sigma" to all 102,000 employees in his company. Deming, as we have noted in the last chapter, promotes similar education in statistical thinking. In addition to the language of statistics, "new" dialects have been developed by marketing and customer service experts, organizational behavior specialists, industrial and mechanical engineers, cost accountants, participative (employee involvement) team coordinators, and others. Meeting the needs of customers requires new tools and a vocabulary to gather, analyze, interpret, and act. The "voice of the customer," "counterpart characteristics," and "quality function deployment" are representative of this new dialect.

Organization behavior specialists apply their theories to help solve leadership and motivation problems in dynamic, fast-moving organizations. Their language and tools are now being learned by managers and TQM workers. Some of these concepts include attention to the details of the *task* in the design of jobs so as to build-in purposefully the motivation and interest that will enhance "quality of worklife," and develop "team approaches to problem solving." Managers and first-line employees are challenged through training and work-related projects to be "self-managed," which requires creativity, problem-solving skills, and a constant effort and desire to increase their knowledge, skills, and value to the organization.

Technical advancements have required that industrial and mechanical engineers assume the role of "on-the-spot" troubleshooters, rather than aloof "gurus" of technology. Even design engineers are being forced to coordinate and interact with process engineers, sales people, and customers to design a better product that will meet customer needs. In addition, industrial engineers have developed tools over the years that are now being adapted for use as group problem-solving techniques.

Cost accountants have historically been in charge of controlling costs, but are now being asked to provide explicit numbers, analysis, and guidance on reducing quality costs. Frequently, they find themselves being called on to provide figures to update line workers and managers on the competitive position of the company. They are also being asked to provide information and expertise to assist problem-solving teams with their projects.

Last, but not least, employee involvement team coordinators are helping to develop, train, and evaluate the results of teams. These specialists may be drawn from any of the above areas, but are required to have a thorough grounding in both the technical and human resources areas. The teams that they coordinate (or *facilitate,* as they like to call it) are using structured problem-solving techniques to make

---

[3]William Wiggenhorn, "Motorola U: When Training Becomes Education," *Harvard Business Review,* July–August 1990, p. 74.

significant improvements in quality improvement, cost reduction, and process simplification.

You may already have learned the basics of many of these dialects in your earlier studies. However, it is important to use the universal language of quality to sharpen the focus on what may otherwise simply be interesting theories. By focusing on quality *applications,* the theories developed in marketing, accounting, operations management, information systems, and organizational behavior courses, seminars, and texts can take on new meaning. The person who learns to adapt his or her vocabulary and expertise to the requirements of TQM is bound to be in demand.

IMPLEMENTING TOTAL QUALITY MANAGEMENT PROGRAMS

Successful implementation of TQM depends on several key concepts[4]: a long-term perspective, customer focus, top management commitment, systems thinking, training and tools, participation, measurement and reporting systems, communications, and leadership. We will discuss each briefly now; however, many of these topics will be addressed more fully in subsequent chapters.

Long-term Perspective. Improvements do not happen overnight. The planning and organizing of improvement activities take time and require major commitments from everybody in the organization. While time is necessary, it can work against the organization. First, the longer an organization takes to implement TQM, the further ahead its competitors will be. Second, unless steps are taken to ensure that TQM remains a priority, the organization risks losing the commitment of its employees.

An example of taking a long-term perspective, coupled with swift implementation of quality improvement concepts, is the case of Scandinavian Airlines System (SAS) in Sweden[5]. When President and CEO Jan Carlzon took over SAS in 1980, the company was suffering from the effects of an oil shock, two years of financial losses, and high labor costs. These factors prevented the company from competing on price alone with U.S. and Asian airlines. Carlzon set about creating a quality image by instituting low standby fares for passengers under age 27; reconfiguring airplanes to give more comfort and amenities to business-class passengers; training and empowering employees to handle problems swiftly, competently, and without excessive "red tape"; and improving ground service. In the latter category, changes included providing better express check-in service, new business facilities such as computers and fax machines, and automatic delivery of luggage to hotels owned by or linked to SAS's full-service travel agency. To attain their quality objectives, Carlzon stressed the need to have behavioral change take place at the "moment of truth" where the employee comes into contact with the customer during the process of delivering the company's service.

---

[4]Loren D. Pfau, "Total Quality Management Gives Companies a Way to Enhance Position in Global Marketplace," *Industrial Engineering,* Vol. 21, No. 4, April 1989, pp. 17–21; U.S. General Accounting Office, "Management Practices." The Budd, GM, and Rockwell examples are found in Brad Stratton, "The Refined Focus of Automotive Quality," *Quality Progress,* October 1989, pp. 47–50.

[5]Kenneth Labich, "An Airline that Soars on Service," *Fortune,* December 31, 1990, pp. 94–96.

Customer Focus. An essential attribute of TQM is the understanding that the customer is the final arbiter of quality. TQM is based on the premise that quality is driven by and defined by the customer. Product and service attributes that create a perception of quality will increase customer satisfaction and, ultimately, customer demand. Various means, such as customer opinion surveys and focus groups, are used to understand customer requirements and values. New techniques must be adopted to obtain customer feedback. For example, many companies established toll-free telephone numbers. Several companies require their sales and marketing executives to meet with random groups of key customers on a regular basis. Other companies bring customers and suppliers into internal product design and development meetings.

A firm also must recognize that internal customers—the next department in a manufacturing process or the order-picker who receives instructions from an order entry clerk—are as important in assuring quality as are external customers who purchase the product. Employees must view themselves as both customers of and suppliers to other employees. This process can help to identify and eliminate many useless activities.

Top Management Commitment. If commitment to quality is not a priority, any initiative is doomed to failure. Lip service to quality improvement is the kiss of death. The CEO of Motorola, one of the first Baldrige winners, had quality as the first agenda item at every board meeting. He frequently left after quality was discussed, sending the message that once quality was taken care of, financial and other matters would take care of themselves. Another example is The Budd Company, a major automobile body component supplier, which has a Corporate Quality Council made up of top executives and managers. The council sets quality policy and reviews performance goals within the company. Quality should be a major factor in strategic planning and competitive analysis processes as will be pointed out in the next chapter.

Systems Thinking. TQM is only effective when all employees are a part of TQM implementation. Traditionally, organizations are integrated vertically by linking all the levels of management in a hierarchical fashion. TQM requires horizontal coordination between organizational units. Poor quality can often be traced to breakdowns in responsibility that occur when an organization focuses solely on vertical structures and fails to recognize the horizontal interactions. A process focus, by which inputs are transformed into outputs, provides better insights into how the organization actually operates.

General Motors is moving toward more of a process focus. Their new approach is very people oriented and involves teamwork and cooperation among all of the people who are associated with the company and its products. An internal reorganization is taking the company from the old functional focus to a new product focus. Historically, people have worked in areas such as engineering, manufacturing, or finance. The organization is now focused on car and truck groups. Teams center all their efforts on the product: market research, product design, styling, purchasing parts, manufacturing, and interfacing with customers.

Training and Tools. Every employee, from entry-level workers to the CEO, requires training in TQM philosophies and techniques. This is evident in the philosophies of Deming, Juran, and Crosby. Training is necessary to reach a common understanding of goals and objectives and the means to attain them. Training usually begins with awareness in quality management principles and is followed by particular skills in quality improvement. Training must be viewed as a continuous effort, not a one-time project. This requires the commitment of significant resources, and many firms are reluctant to make this move.

Participation. Everyone must participate in the improvement efforts. The person in any organization that best understands his or her job and how it can be improved is the one performing it. Employees must be empowered to make decisions that affect quality and develop and implement new and better systems. This often represents a profound shift in the philosophy of senior management, because the traditional philosophy is that the work force should be "managed" to conform to existing business systems. Participation can be encouraged by recognizing team and individual accomplishments, sharing success stories throughout the organization, encouraging risk-taking by removing the fear of failure, encouraging the formation of employee involvement teams, implementing suggestion systems that act rapidly, provide feedback, and reward implemented suggestions, and providing financial and technical support to employees to develop their ideas.

Mariott and American Express[6] are two examples of companies that exemplify the ideal of empowering and rewarding their employees for service quality. At Marriott, customer service representatives are called "associates," are given wide discretion to call on any part of the company in order to help customers, and earn lush bonuses for extraordinary work. At American Express, cash awards of up to $1,000 have been given to "Great Performers" such as Barbara Weber, who in 1986 cut through miles of State Department and Treasury Department red tape to refund $980 worth of stolen traveler's checks to a customer stranded in Cuba.

General Motors is trying to eliminate the practice of competing internally in order to promote the concept of teamwork. (One manager had characterized GM as one of the most fiercely internally competitive companies that ever existed.) GM developed a system called the Quality Network. Not only is this system common across all of General Motors, but it is a joint process between management and the United Auto Workers union. The heart of the Quality Network is a variation of the Ishikawa model that is focused on customer satisfaction (see Figure 5.2). This approach encourages teamwork and cooperation. The topic of teamwork will be developed more fully in a future chapter on employee involvement teams.

Measurement and Reporting Systems. Measures based on facts must be established to assess quality improvement. Reporting of information must be timely and accurate, and a systematic process to measure and evaluate quality continuously is necessary. Traditional information systems focus on cost and financial accounting, sales, marketing, purchasing, and scheduling. Quality measures must become part of the reports that are regularly provided to middle and upper management. Line workers and supervisors also require quality reports so that problems can be identified, analyzed, and solved.

Communication. TQM requires improved communications to support improvement. Traditional lines of communication are slow and sometimes inaccurate. People need to communicate across organizational levels, functions, product lines,

---

[6]Bro Uttal, "Companies that Serve You Best," *Fortune,* December 7, 1987, p. 101.

FIGURE 5.2 The General Motors Quality Network Process Model

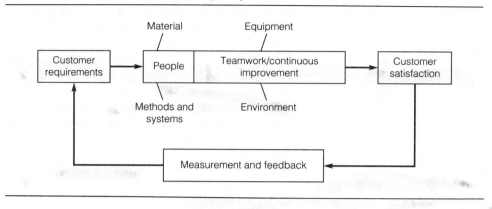

and locations to solve problems and implement change. Rockwell International Automotive Operations discovered that the human resources people had the same goals as the quality people, but they took different approaches. While the quality people were concentrating on tools and techniques, the human resources people were concentrating on clarity, communication, and effective organization flow. By communicating with one another, they found "a marriage that's made in heaven." More on communication between quality and human resources activities will be found in Chapter 10.

Strong Leadership.   Many of the management principles and practices that are required in a TQM environment may be contrary to a company's long-standing practices. Top managers, ideally starting with the CEO, must become the organization's TQM leaders. He or she must be the focal point that provides broad perspectives and vision, encouragement, and recognition. The leader must be determined to establish TQM initiatives and committed to sustaining its activities through daily actions. This is necessary to overcome the inevitable resistance to change. Various aspects of leadership will also be developed in the human resources chapter.

Pitfalls in Implementing TQM

Implementing TQM is like a marriage; the first year can be trying and crises inevitably arise.[7] Xerox described its pursuit of quality as three steps forward and one step back. The initial period is focused on quality awareness, infrastructure, measurement systems, and new skills. After about a year, the quality message is no longer new and has lost some of its excitement. As measurement improves, companies begin to see problems more clearly. The realization that things are not going as well as expected causes disappointment, anxiety, and sometimes panic. We tend to look for quick

---

[7]Barry Sheehy, "Hitting the Wall: How to Survive Your Quality Program's First Crisis," *National Productivity Review,* Vol. 9, No. 3, Summer 1990, pp. 329–335.

results, rather than at long-term improvement. First-year objectives typically are not achieved until the third or fourth years.

Perceived crises in implementing TQM programs arise from two sources. The first is change. TQM requires significant changes of an organization—changes in its methods, processes, attitudes, and behavior. It takes time for this realization to set in, and sometimes change is painful. Line workers receive more responsibility and authority and become more accountable for their own work. Supervisors who were experts and order-givers are now forced to become facilitators and coaches. Middle managers who maintained processes are now forced to become problem solvers. Top managers are forced to think differently, to become more aware of and interact with customers. The second cause of a quality crisis is rising expectations. As people become more knowledgeable about what a quality organization should look like, they become more sensitive to problems within the organization and in their own behavior. This creates anxiety.

Such situations can be avoided through proper planning. At the beginning of the process, expectations should be kept simple. Everyone needs to recognize that setbacks will occur as a normal evolution. Managers should be trained to use interpersonal skills so that they can manage the human issues associated with change. The first year's projects should be simple and have a high probability of success. All improvements, no matter how small, should be documented and publicized. Progress should be reviewed periodically, and goals revised accordingly.

The Role of Union/Management Relations

A major stumbling block in the United States in implementing TQM has been the traditional adversarial relationship between unions and management.[8] For example, in 1986 General Motors introduced a team concept for quality improvement in Van Nuys, California. Only 53% of the union membership supported the concept. Since then, the union members opposed to the team concept have actively resisted it. In many cases, management must share the responsibility in working with unions as equal partners. Both union and management have important roles in TQM.

Labor's role is first to recognize the need to change its relationship with management and then to educate its members as to how cooperation will affect the organization. This includes what its members can expect and how working conditions and job security might change. Labor must carefully select members for such a program and have a positive attitude. TQM programs must be separated from collective bargaining processes.

Management must realize that it needs the skills and knowledge of all employees to improve quality and meet competitive challenges. Management must be willing to develop a closer working relationship with labor and ready to address union concerns and cultivate trust. Both sides should receive training in communication and problem-solving skills. Union and management should have equal representation in committees and have total trust and commitment. External consultants can play an important role as facilitators and mediators in such efforts.

---

[8]John Persico, Jr., Betty L. Bednarczyk, and David P. Negus, "Three Routes to the Same Destination: TQM, Part 1," *Quality Progress,* January 1990, pp. 29–33.

THE DEMING PRIZE, MALCOLM BALDRIGE NATIONAL QUALITY AWARD, AND EUROPEAN QUALITY AWARD

Successful TQM efforts have been recognized in Japan since Deming's initial visits in the early 1950s. The Deming Prize was established to honor Dr. Deming, who was designated a "National Treasure" in Japan. It was awarded to Japanese companies that best exemplified quality. It was not until the decade of quality awareness—the 1980s—that the United States established a similar award. Winning U.S. companies serve as national examples of the gains that can be realized from TQM. They also tend to be the leaders in their industries and are among the most successful in competitive markets. In this section we discuss the Deming Prize and the Malcolm Baldrige National Quality Award, as well as efforts by the European community to recognize quality.

The Deming Prize

The Deming Application Prize was instituted in 1951 by the Union of Japanese Scientists and Engineers (JUSE) in recognition and appreciation of W. Edwards Deming's achievements in statistical quality control. The purpose of the Deming Prize is to "award prizes to those companies which are recognized as having successfully applied CWQC (Company-Wide Quality Control) based on statistical quality control and which are likely to keep up with it in the future." The Deming Prize has several categories, including prizes for individuals, factories, and divisions or small companies. The judging criteria consist of a checklist of 10 major categories: policy and objectives, organization and its operation, education and its extension, assembling and disseminating information, analysis, standardization, control, quality assurance, effects, and future plans. Each major category is broken down into subcategories. For example, the policy category includes:

1. policies pursued for management, quality, and quality control
2. method of establishing policies
3. justifiability and consistency of policies
4. utilization of statistical methods
5. transmission and diffusion of policies
6. review of policies and the results achieved
7. relationship between policies and long- and short-term planning.

Hundreds of companies apply for the award each year. After an initial application is accepted as eligible for the process, the company must submit a detailed description of its quality practices. This is an extraordinary effort in itself. Based on review of the written descriptions, only a few companies believed to be successful in CWQC are selected for a site visit. The site visit consists of a company presentation, in-depth questioning by the examiners, and an executive session with top managers. Examiners visit plants and are free to ask any worker any question. For example, at Florida Power and Light, the first non-Japanese company to win the Deming Prize, examiners asked questions of specific individuals such as What are your main accountabilities? What are the important priority issues for the corporation? What indicators do you have for your performance? For your target? How are you doing today compared to your target? They request examples where performance has not been adequate. Documentation must be made available immediately. The preparation, as can be imagined, is extensive and sometimes frustrating.

The Deming Prize is awarded to those companies that meet a standard. All applicants that meet the standard are recognized, although the fact that there are only a small number of awards given each year is an indication of the difficulty of achieving the standard. The objectives are to ensure that a company has so thoroughly deployed a quality process that it will continue to improve long after a prize is awarded. There are no "losers." For those that do not qualify, the examination process is automatically extended up to two times over three years.

Some winners of the Deming Prize include Toyota Motor Company, Ltd., NEC IC/Microcomputer Systems, Shimizu Construction Company, Ltd., and the Kansai Electric Power Company. Toyota has captured nearly 10% of the world automotive market and is likely to increase in market share. NEC has earned a reputation for exceptional quality in a diverse set of electronics areas and is pioneering practical integration of computers and communication systems. Shimizu Construction is one of the top five construction firms in Japan and has entered the U.S. market by developing golf courses and condominium communities. They are exceptionally adept at managing properties after development is complete. Kansai Electric helped to bring recognition of total quality management into the service sector. Kansai offers electric service at consistently low rates and has managed to shorten service interruptions significantly in comparison to other Japanese electric utilities.

The Deming Prize was opened to overseas companies in 1984 and Florida Power and Light won the award in 1989. Kansai Electric was the major "benchmark" firm to whom FP&L looked when it began to consider seriously making a bid for the prize. The FP&L story is profiled in the Quality in Practice case at the end of this chapter.

The Malcolm Baldrige National Quality Award

Recognizing that American productivity was declining, President Reagan signed legislation mandating a national study/conference on productivity in October 1982. The American Productivity and Quality Center (formerly the American Productivity Center) sponsored seven computer networking conferences in 1983 to prepare for an upcoming White House conference on productivity. The final report on these conferences recommended that "a National Quality Award, similar to the Deming Prize in Japan, [should] be awarded annually to those firms that successfully challenge and meet the award requirements. These requirements and the accompanying examination process should be very similar to the Deming Prize system to be effective." The Baldrige Award, named after Secretary of Commerce Malcolm Baldrige, who was killed in an accident shortly before the Senate acted on the legislation, was signed into law on August 20, 1987. Its purposes were to:

- Help stimulate American companies to improve quality and productivity for the pride of recognition while obtaining a competitive edge through increased profits.

- Recognize the achievements of those companies that improve the quality of their goods and services and provide an example to others.

- Establish guidelines and criteria that can be used by business, industrial, governmental, and other enterprises in evaluating their own quality improvement efforts.

- Provide specific guidance for other American enterprises that wish to learn how to manage for high quality by making available detailed information on how winning enterprises were able to change their cultures and achieve eminence.

The award examination is based on criteria designed to provide a standard of quality excellence for organizations seeking to reach the highest levels of overall quality performance and competitiveness. The examination addresses all key requirements to achieve quality excellence as well as the important interrelationships among these key requirements. The examination is built on a number of key concepts that underlie all requirements in the examination items:

- Quality is defined by the customer.

- The senior leadership of businesses needs to create clear quality values and build the values into the way the company operates.

- Quality excellence derives from well-designed and well-executed systems and processes.

- Continuous improvement must be part of the management of all systems and processes.

- Companies need to develop goals, as well as strategic and operational plans to achieve quality leadership.

- Shortening the response time of all operations and processes of the company needs to be part of the quality improvement effort.

- Operations and decisions of the company need to be based on facts and data.

- All employees must be suitably trained and developed and involved in quality activities.

- Design quality and defect and error prevention should be major elements of the quality system.

- Companies need to communicate quality requirements to suppliers and work to elevate supplier quality performance.

The award criteria include planning, implementation, measurement, and feedback processes related to quality. Companies must excel in the following seven areas.

Leadership. The leadership category examines how senior executives create and sustain clear and visible quality values along with a management system to guide all activities of the company toward quality excellence. Upper management should set goals and plans for integrating quality principles and practices into their organization. They must be committed to involving all employees in improving the organization by training them properly and rewarding them for their efforts in quality improvement. Management must ensure that everyone in the organization has a clear understanding of their competitive environment. Leadership requires communicating quality values throughout the organization and establishing a measurement system to determine how well these quality values are adopted.

The organization also has a responsibility to share its quality effort with the public, including the community, business, trade, school, and government organizations. Quality leadership must include business ethics, public health and safety, environmental protection, waste management, and other regulatory requirements.

Information and Analysis. This category examines the scope, validity, use, and management of the data and information that support the company's overall quality management system. The criteria for the selection of data used to support quality programs must be sound. Also examined is the adequacy of the data, information, and analysis to support a responsive, prevention-based approach to quality and customer satisfaction built on "management by fact." Processes must be in place to ensure the consistency, standardization, review, update, and timely access of data.

Strategic Quality Planning. This category examines the company's planning process for achieving or retaining quality leadership and how the company integrates quality improvement planning into overall business planning. The planning process defines how the plan will be implemented, and how resources will be committed to key elements of the plan. Competitive benchmark measures must be defined so that the organization can accurately assess its position compared to the industry as a whole and its competitors in particular. A plan must exist to improve these benchmarks. The company's short- and long-term plans to achieve and/or sustain a quality leadership position are also examined. This includes measures to determine if suppliers can meet quality requirements and the impact that quality requirements will have on the organization.

Human Resource Utilization. The areas examined in this category are the effectiveness of the company's efforts to develop and realize the full potential of the work force, including management, and to maintain an environment conducive to full participation, quality leadership, and personal and organizational growth. The organization must encourage employee involvement, empowerment, teamwork, and innovation. A quality education and training program is necessary, and the effectiveness of such programs must be measured. A performance measurement system must be in place for employees. Employees need to be recognized for their achievements and involved in the formation of performance measures by which they are evaluated. The company must be able to evaluate whether the performance measures are obtaining the desired results.

Employee well-being and morale are important to quality. Health, safety, satisfaction, and ergonomics are fundamental to working conditions that are conducive to quality. Counseling, assistance, recreation, cultural, and other special programs to help employees are important ingredients of well-being. Finally, the organization must determine the level of employee satisfaction and use this information to achieve improvements in quality.

Quality Assurance of Products and Services. This category examines the systematic approaches used by the company for assuring quality of goods and services based primarily on process design and control, including control of procured materials, parts, and services. Customer needs must be converted into appropriate product and process requirements. The organization must create methods for designing, developing, and validating the products, processes, and services in a timely manner. Also examined is the integration of process control with continuous quality improvement. When a product, process, or service does not meet specifications, the root causes of the problem must be determined and corrected to prevent future problems. Process control methods should be used for continuous improvement.

Documentation to support the quality system must be maintained and shared throughout the organization. In addition, the quality of support services must be assured, assessed, and improved. This includes external suppliers as well as internal support.

Quality Results. The quality results category examines quality levels and quality improvement based on objective measures derived from analysis of customer requirements and expectations and from analysis of business operations. Also examined are current quality levels in relation to those of competing firms.

Customer Satisfaction. The final category examines the company's knowledge of the customer, overall customer service systems, responsiveness, and its ability to meet requirements and expectations. Customer problems must be resolved. The scope of complaints must be analyzed to determine the effect on the customer base and used to improve the organization's products and services. Commitment is exemplified through product and service guarantees and warranties. Also examined are current levels and trends in customer satisfaction. The organization must measure where it stands compared to competitors to determine if customers have been lost or gained and if market share has changed.

Each major category is assigned a maximum number of points that can be earned during the evaluation process. These points are distributed among several subcategories, as shown in Table 5.1. A scoring system for examination items is based on three evaluation dimensions: approach, deployment, and results. *Approach* refers to the methods the company uses to achieve the purposes addressed in each category. *Deployment* refers to the extent to which the approaches are applied to all relevant areas and activities addressed and implied in each category. *Results* refers to the outcomes and effects in achieving the purposes addressed and implied in the criteria. Table 5.2 shows the scoring guidelines that are used.

An application guidelines booklet is published each year and describes in detail the information that must be documented. Like quality itself, the specific award criteria are being continually improved each year to better reflect the changing process of TQM. The applications guidelines booklet can be obtained by writing to the location referenced below.[9]

According to the award guidelines, up to two companies can win a Baldrige award in each category of manufacturing, small business, and service. Table 5.3 shows the winners through 1991. Out of 24 possible awards, only 12 have been won. Motorola, winner in the first year of the award, and Federal Express are profiled in Quality in Practice sections at the end of this chapter.

---

[9]Copies of the current year application guidelines can be obtained by writing to the Malcolm Baldrige National Quality Award, National Institute of Standards and Technology, Route 270 and Quince Orchard Road, Administration Building Room A537, Gaithersburg, MD 20899.

TABLE 5.1 1991 Examination Categories and Items for the Malcolm Baldrige National Quality Award

1991 Examination Categories/Items	Maximum Points
1.0 Leadership	100
1.1 Senior Executive Leadership 40	
1.2 Quality Values 15	
1.3 Management for Quality 25	
1.4 Public Responsibility 20	
2.0 Information and Analysis	70
2.1 Scope and Management of Quality Data and Information 20	
2.2 Competitive Comparisons and Benchmarks 30	
2.3 Analysis of Quality Data and Information 20	
3.0 Strategic Quality Planning	60
3.1 Strategic Quality Planning Process 35	
3.2 Quality Goals and Plans 25	
4.0 Human Resource Utilization	150
4.1 Human Resource Management 20	
4.2 Employee Involvement 40	
4.3 Quality Education and Training 40	
4.4 Employee Recognition and Performance Measurement 25	
4.5 Employee Well-Being and Morale 25	
5.0 Quality Assurance of Products and Services	140
5.1 Design and Introduction of Quality Products and Services . 35	
5.2 Process Quality Control 20	
5.3 Continuous Improvement of Processes 20	
5.4 Quality Assessment 15	
5.5 Documentation 10	
5.6 Business Process and Support Service Quality 20	
5.7 Supplier Quality 20	
6.0 Quality Results	180
6.1 Product and Service Quality Results 90	
6.2 Business Process, Operational, and Support Service Quality Results ... 50	
6.3 Supplier Quality Results 40	
7.0 Customer Satisfaction	300
7.1 Determining Customer Requirements and Expectations 30	
7.2 Customer Relationship Management 50	
7.3 Customer Service Standards 20	
7.4 Commitment to Customers 15	
7.5 Complaint Resolution for Quality Improvement 25	
7.6 Determining Customer Satisfaction 20	
7.7 Customer Satisfaction Results 70	
7.8 Customer Satisfaction Comparison 70	
TOTAL POINTS	1000

Baldrige Award winners have made stunning achievements within a few years.[10] With respect to quality, customer service response time has been reduced by an order of magnitude; defect levels have been reduced by an order of magnitude; productivity has been doubled; and costs have been halved. Improvements have taken place throughout the entire spectrum of the organizations: customer satisfaction, field

[10]J. M. Juran, "Strategies for World-Class Quality," *Quality Progress,* March 1991, pp. 81–85.

TABLE 5.2 Scoring Guidelines

Score	Approach	Deployment	Results
0%	■ Anecdotal, no system evident	■ Anecdotal	■ Anecdotal
10–40%	■ Beginnings of systematic prevention basis	■ Some to many major areas of business	■ Some positive trends in the areas deployed
50%	■ Sound, systematic prevention basis that includes evaluation/ improvement cycles ■ Some evidence of integration	■ Most major areas of business ■ Some support areas	■ Positive trends in most major areas ■ Some evidence that results are caused by approach
60–90%	■ Sound, systematic prevention basis with evidence of refinement through evaluation/ improvement cycles ■ Good integration	■ Major areas of business ■ From some to many support areas	■ Good to excellent in major areas ■ Positive trends—from some to many support areas ■ Evidence that results are caused by approach
100%	■ Sound, systematic prevention basis refined through evaluation/- improvement cycles ■ Excellent integration	■ Major areas and support areas ■ All operations	■ Excellent (world-class) results in major areas ■ Good to excellent in support areas ■ Sustained results ■ Results clearly caused by approach

performance of products, quality of the manufacturing processes, supplier quality, timeliness of customer service, quality of the business processes, and employee safety. Most important, the employees became experienced at, and got into the habit of, making improvements.

The Baldrige Award criteria form a blueprint for quality improvement in any organization. Hundreds of thousands of copies of the award guidelines are distributed each year, yet only a handful of completed applications is received. For example, in 1991, 250,000 copies were mailed, but only 106 applications were received. Many companies are using the award criteria to evaluate their own quality programs, set up and implement TQM programs, communicate better with suppliers and partners, and for education and training. Using the award criteria as a self-assessment tool provides an objective framework, sets a high standard, and helps compare units that have different systems or organizations. It is also being used as a basis for giving awards within companies and at the local, state, and federal levels.

TABLE 5.3 Malcolm Baldrige Award Winners

Year	Manufacturing	Small Business	Service
1988	Motorola, Inc. Westinghouse Commercial Nuclear Fuel Division	Globe Metallurgical, Inc.	
1989	Xerox Corporation Business Products and Systems Milliken & Company		
1990	Cadillac Motor Car Div. IBM Rochester	Wallace Co., Inc.	Federal Express
1991	Solectron Corporation Zytec Corporation	Marlow Industries	

As we have seen, many different philosophies and quality improvement programs exist. Organizations just getting started in quality improvement often have problems defining the quality system and setting objectives. The Baldrige Award addresses the full range of quality issues and can help those setting up new systems to obtain a complete picture of TQM.

The award criteria assist companies with internal communications, communications with suppliers, and communications with other companies seeking to share information. The criteria provide a focus on what to communicate and a framework for comparing strategies, methods, progress, and benchmarks. Finally, the award examination is being used for training and education, particularly for management. It represents a summary of major issues that managers must understand. It helps to draw distinctions between excellence and mediocrity.

The European Quality Award

In October 1991, the European Foundation for Quality Management (EFQM) in partnership with the European Commission and the European Organization for Quality announced the creation of the European Quality Award. The award will be given to the company that is best able to demonstrate that its approach to TQM has made a significant contribution toward satisfying the expectations of customers, employees, and others with an interest in the company. The award process will be similar to the Deming Prize and Baldrige Award. The assessment will be based on customer satisfaction, business results, processes, leadership, people satisfaction, resources, people management, policy and strategy, and impact on society.

The award was designed to increase awareness throughout the European Community, and businesses in particular, of the growing importance of quality to their competitiveness in the increasing global market and to their standards of life. It is also hoped that the award will influence development of quality concepts in educational institutions. The first winner was to be announced in October 1992.

LESSONS FROM QUALITY AWARD WINNERS

What differentiates winners of the Deming Prize and Baldrige Award from other businesses? A study by Labovitz and Chang[11] suggests that Deming Prize winners have obtained a sharp focus on quality through planning, emphasizing the role of top management, integrating customer satisfaction across functions, and providing for employee participation and training. Similar observations have been made about the Baldrige winners.[12]

To meet the Deming Prize requirements, the winning companies have developed detailed, well-communicated total quality improvement plans and reinforced them by visual aids posted throughout the company rather than by using volumes of documentation. These plans have firm time horizons, usually three to five years, with specific annual objectives such as reliability improvement, strengthening of vendor relations, and cycle time reduction. Most plans are reviewed and adjusted at least once each year. Further focus is provided through the designation of a limited number of

---

[11]George H. Labovitz and Yu Sang Chang, "Learn from the Best," *Quality Progress,* May 1990, pp. 81–85.

[12]J. M. Juran, "World-Class Quality"; U.S. General Accounting Office, "Management Practices."

quality improvement projects to be completed each year. Finally, award winners tend to designate defensive and offensive quality improvement goals. Defensive goals are similar to traditional goals in the West: reducing defects or costs. Offensive goals are more aggressive and directed toward improving an organization's competitive position and building market share. For example, most construction firms pay attention to the durability and conformity of bricks used (a defensive goal). A builder who wishes to stand apart might use only bricks that weather in an aesthetically pleasing way (recall Garvin's eight quality dimensions). Over the years, it will enhance customer satisfaction and differentiate that firm from its competitors.

The role of top management is often significantly different. Executives must be personally involved and are required to seek out middle managers and solicit their input on quality improvement opportunities. This also helps to gain commitment from the middle managers. An annual schedule of 30 or more field visits for each senior executive is not uncommon. Information is gathered before each field visit so that it can be expanded on, challenged, and clarified during the visit. Within a week after the visit, the executive writes a commentary to document the performance of each plant for the chairperson and the quality department.

The need for a customer satisfaction focus is widely recognized and is integrated across functions. Customer satisfaction drives the quality effort. Specific tasks and responsibilities are assigned to nearly all departments and sections. Any customer satisfaction breakthroughs are replicated throughout the company. Many companies, such as Toyota, use quality function deployment in this effort, which is discussed in the next chapter.

Employee participation is high, especially among Deming Prize winners in Japan. Sixty-five percent or more of employees are active in total quality efforts within leading Japanese firms, while in the United States, only about 25% are involved. Implementation plans clearly spell out provisions for employee involvement activity. Plans specifically call on even the most junior line managers to lead quality improvement teams. Suggestion systems have much greater importance than in the West. In 1986, 95% of Toyota's employees submitted suggestions (nearly 50 per employee), totaling more than 2.6 million for the company. Ninety-six percent of the suggestions were implemented.

The Baldrige winners likewise use employee involvement to an unprecedented degree. They provide employees the opportunity to participate in quality planning and quality improvement. Self-supervising work teams seem to be an emerging trend.

Extensive training is the final area that is common to all award winners. Training is steady and continuous and includes everyone in the company. New employees receive quality training within a few days of joining the company. At Xerox, training started at the top and cascaded down the organization. Milliken spent $1,900 per employee for training during 1989. Motorola provides 40 hours of training to *each* employee every year.

These studies of award-winning companies suggest that TQM requires, first and foremost, a plan. The plan should put the burden of TQM on management and be used to unite the diverse functions within the company toward customer satisfaction. Most companies have found that the process of applying for one of these awards is incentive itself for improving quality. At Florida Power and Light, for example, peer pressure to excel spread throughout the company. The preparations for the Deming Prize process were so demanding that no one wanted to endure yet another year of work if FPL did not receive the Prize and decided to apply again the next year. The cultural change and the increased level of confidence that resulted have become nearly irreversible.

Implementation of TQM requires an organized effort—an infrastructure. A high-level quality council is needed to direct and coordinate the effort. A process is needed for choosing which projects to tackle. Teams need to be taught how to operate as teams, and a review process is needed to monitor progress and help teams that get stuck. This requires a lot of work for all participating personnel, including upper management. Ten percent has been estimated as the bare minimum amount of additional time that is required. Upper managers must personally lead the TQM effort. In the winning companies, upper managers virtually took charge of quality by accepting personal responsibility for critical decisions and actions; these could not be delegated.

Overall, the concept of quality must be viewed in a broader framework. "Product" applies to services as well as goods. "Process" applies to business functions as well as manufacturing. "Customer" applies internally as well as externally. Quality goals must be incorporated into the business plan; this is rather new for U.S. industry, but is likely to be the dominant form of ensuring that quality improvement will continue.

The 1991 General Accounting Office study[13] found that there were four key measurable areas of a company's operations that could demonstrate the impact of TQM practices on corporate performance: employee relations, operating procedures, customer satisfaction, and financial performance. In the first area, employee relations, significant improvements were realized in employee satisfaction, attendance, turn-over, safety and health, and suggestions received. In the second area, operating procedures, favorable results were realized in reliability, timeliness of delivery, order-processing times, errors and defects, product lead time, inventory turnover, cost of quality, and overall cost savings. In the third area, overall customer satisfaction improved, customer complaints fell, and customer retention rose. Finally, in the financial performance area, market share, sales per employee, return on assets, and return on sales all showed positive improvement for most companies.

In concluding his observations on the Baldrige Award winners, Dr. Juran stated in 1990:

> I have become optimistic for the first time since the quality crisis descended on the United States. I now believe that, during the 1990s, the number of U.S. companies that have achieved stunning results will increase by orders of magnitude. I also believe that, during the 1990s, the United States will make great strides toward making "Made in the USA" a symbol of world class quality.

TQM IN THE GOVERNMENT

The federal government has a surprisingly long history of quality improvement activities. Quality circle programs were developed in the late 1970s at several Department of Defense installations such as the Norfolk Naval Shipyard and the Cherry Point Naval Air Station. NASA began its efforts in the early 1980s, both internally

---

[13]U.S. General Accounting Office, "Management Practices."

and with its suppliers.[14] However, only recently have senior elected officials and top civil servants begun to develop a total quality management focus. The TQM process has caught the attention of a number of agencies and managers within the federal government within the past three years, due to the dissemination of requirements for productivity and quality improvement mandated by Executive Order[15] 12637, "Productivity Improvement Program for the Federal Government," signed by President Reagan on April 27, 1988.

Although quality improvement with a participative management focus is by no means a new concept in some federal agencies, in a number of other agencies, managers are just now becoming aware of the requirements set forth in Section 3 of the executive order. Senior managers are now required to:

- Inform agency managers and employees that they are expected to be responsible for improvements in the *quality,* timeliness, and efficiency of services.

- Include productivity and *quality* improvement goals in the performance appraisals of managers and supervisors.

- Encourage *employee participation* in the productivity program *through employee training, employee involvement in work-related decisions, incentives, recognition, and rewards* and by taking actions to minimize negative impacts that may occur as a result of the productivity program. [emphasis added]

To aid various agencies in learning about TQM and implementing their own programs, the Federal Quality Institute was established in Washington to be the "primary source of leadership, information and consulting services on quality management in the federal government." The institute provides such products and services as seminars, start-up assistance, national and regional conferences, support of quality awards, a listing of private sector consultants, an information network and research and publications. The institute's logo, reproduced in Figure 5.3, shows in graphic form that their TQM concept does not appear to differ substantially from that of the private sector of business.

Federal Quality Awards

The Presidential Quality Award and the Quality Improvement Prototype Awards given each year are the federal government's equivalent of the Malcolm Baldrige National Quality Award. The federal government awards are administered by the Office of Management and Budget, whereas the Baldrige Award is administered by the Department of Commerce. Figure 5.4 shows the concept for the award and lists the winners from 1988–1990. The story of the Cincinnati Service Center of the IRS, a 1990 award winner, will be presented in a Quality in Practice Case in Chapter 7.

---

[14]Ned Hamson, "The FQI Story: Today and Tomorrow," *The Journal for Quality and Participation,* July/August 1990, pp. 46–49.

[15]Executive Order No. 12637, *Volume 7 United States Code Congressional and Administrative News,* 100th Congress–Second Session. (St. Paul, MN: West Publishing Company, 1988), pp. B21–B23.

FIGURE 5.3 Federal Quality Institute Logo

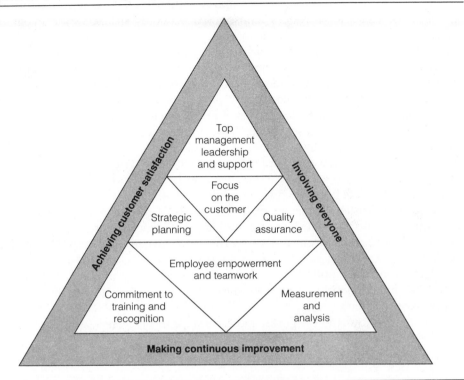

FIGURE 5.4 The 1988–1990 Quality Improvement Prototype Award Winners

The President's Productivity Improvement Program: Quality Improvement Prototype Awards

"A prototype organization demonstrates an extraordinary commitment to quality improvement, focuses attention on satisfying its customers and establishes high standards of quality, timeliness and efficiency. This kind of organization also serves as a model for the rest of government—showing how a commitment to quality leads to better and more efficient services and products for its customers."—*James C. Miller III: Director of the Office of Management and Budget, 1988.*

1988	**1989**	**1990**
Equal Employment Opportunity Commission	Internal Revenue Service: Ogden Service Center	Defense Logistics Agency: Defense Industrial Supply Center
Naval Aviation Depot: Cherry Point, North Carolina	Internal Revenue Service; Fresno Service Center	Internal Revenue Service; Cincinnati Service Center
Internal Revenue Service; Federal Tax Deposit System	Naval Sea Systems Command: Norfolk Naval Shipyard	NASA: Johnson Space Center
Internal Revenue Service: One Stop Account Service	Naval Supply Systems Command: Naval Publications and Forms Center	
	NASA: Lewis Research Center	
	Department of Veteran Affairs: Medical Center, Kansas City, Missouri	

SOURCE: Ned Hamson, "The FQI Story."

Some of the improvements of the 1990 winners provide examples of what a concerted emphasis on TQM can accomplish within the federal government's vast agencies. For example, at NASA's Johnson Space Center, managers are integrating continuous improvement concepts throughout the center by means of strategic planning, culture surveys, and team excellence projects. Improvements have been implemented in both administrative and technical operations. Some of the results include the following: The time required for processing small purchases was reduced by 25%; supply returns were cut 75%; a new inspection device was developed to enable recovery of thrusters at a savings of $1 million each; and implementation of a resources management and scheduling system reduced laboratory labor costs by an estimated $200,000 annually.

At the Defense Industrial Supply Center (DISC) at Wright Patterson Air Force Base, a quality "turnaround" was undertaken after problems in supply availability and increased backorders became apparent. Although a quality circle program had been successfully established, managers realized that a TQM commitment was lacking. The turnaround results were evident in the improvements reported, including the reduction of backorders from 273,000 to 263,000, between fiscal year (FY) 1988 and FY 1989; an increase in supply availability (the percentage of time the customers' orders are filled the first time through the system) to 87.6%, the highest it has been since 1984; and the development of an "introspection program" to identify, eliminate, and prevent problems.

Figure 5.5 shows the categories and criteria for those agencies that apply for the President's Award.

FIGURE 5.5 Categories and Criteria for the President's Award

Categories and Criteria for the President's Award for Quality and Productivity Improvement

1. *Top Management Leadership and Support (20 points)* This category examines how all levels of senior management create and sustain a clear and visible quality value system along with a supporting management system to guide all activities of the organization.

2. *Strategic Planning (15 points)* This category examines the extent to which quality considerations are taken into account in the planning process.

3. *Focus on the Customer (40 points)* This category examines the organization's overall customer service systems, knowledge of the customer, responsiveness and ability to meet requirements and expectations.

4. Employee Training and

Recognition (15 points) This category examines the organization's efforts to develop and utilize the full potential of the workforce for quality improvement and personal and organizational growth, as well as its efforts to use rewards and incentives to recognize employees who improve quality and productivity.

5. *Employee Empowerment and Teamwork (15 points)* This category examines the effectiveness and thoroughness of employee involvement in TQM.

6. *Measurement and Analysis (15 points)* This category examines the scope, validity, use, and management of data and information that underlie the organization's TQM system

and how the data are used to improve processes, products and services.

7. *Quality Assurance (30 points)* This category examines the systematic approaches used by the organization for total quality control of products and services, and the integration of quality control with continuous quality improvement.

8. *Quality and Productivity Improvement Results (50 points)* This category examines the measurable and verifiable results of the organization's TQM practices. Data tables and graphs summarizing trends and achievement should be utilized as much as possible.

SOURCE: Ned Hamson, "The FQI Story."

TQM in City and State Government

City governments have also recognized the potential of total quality management. Joseph Sensenbrenner, mayor of Madison, Wisconsin, from 1983 to 1989, was one of the leaders in bringing TQM to city government.[16] After a 1983 audit disclosing problems at the city garage such as long delays in repair and equipment unavailability, but offering no explanations as to the root causes of the problems, Sensenbrenner attended a seminar by W. Edwards Deming. While he found himself in agreement with the Deming philosophy, Sensenbrenner also recognized the ingrained bureaucratic culture of government.

He began at the city garage, where the manager and mechanics were surprised to see "top management" personally visible and committed to their problems. Sensenbrenner obtained the cooperation of the union president, and formed a team to gather data from individual mechanics and the repair process itself. They found that many delays resulted from insufficient stocking of repair parts. This was the result of having more than 440 different types, makes, models, and years of equipment—all obtained by purchasing from the lowest bidder. It became a classic case of passing the buck. The parts purchaser said that central purchasing would not let him stock fewer parts from fewer reliable suppliers; central purchasing said the comptroller would not let them do it; the comptroller said the city attorney would never approve it. The city attorney said "Why, of course you can do that. All you need to do is write the specifications so they include the warranty, the ease of maintenance, the availability of parts, and the resale value over time. . . . I assumed you were doing it all along." As Deming stated, the problem was not with the workers; it was with the system.

Solving the problem required teamwork and breaking down barriers between departments. The concept of an internal customer was virtually unknown. Finding a solution meant introducing front-line employees to problem solving. When they changed their purchasing policy, reducing 24 steps to 3, employees were stunned and delighted that someone was listening to them. They began to study the potential of a preventive maintenance program and discovered, for example, that city departments did not use truck-bed linings when hauling corrosive materials such as salt. Mechanics rode along on police patrols and learned that squad cars spent more time idling. This information was used to tune engines properly. Other departments helped gather data. As a result, the average vehicle turnaround time was reduced from nine days to three with a net annual savings of about $700,000.

The lessons learned in the city garage were expanded to other departments from painting to health. Although employee morale improved, considerable resistance was created by middle management. At one point, all team members in one set of projects resigned, feeling that their managers—who should have been giving them guidance and support—were instead setting them up for failure and blame. Direct involvement by the mayor along with improved planning and communication solved the problem.

By the time Sensenbrenner left office in 1989, Madison's city departments were running between 20 and 30 quality improvement projects at a time, five agencies were focusing on long-term commitment to new management practices (including

[16]Joseph Sensenbrenner, "Quality Comes to City Hall," *Harvard Business Review,* March–April 1991, pp. 64–75. Copyright © 1991 by the President and Fellows of Harvard College; all rights reserved.

continuous quality improvement skills and data-gathering techniques), the city was providing training in quality to every employee, joint efforts were under way with several state agencies eager to follow their approach, and city workers throughout were continuing to invent service improvements for internal and external customers.

Many state governments are now developing TQM programs. Massachusetts, for example, has formed a Quality Improvement Council to oversee and facilitate a broad TQM program. Governor Fife Symington of Arizona introduced TQM into state management processes as part of his Strategic Long-Term Improvement Management project. In North Carolina, pilot projects for improvement in the quality of services are underway in the Department of Administration and the Division of Motor Vehicles. New York announced a "Quality through Participation" program in August 1991 to improve service delivery in state operations. Many firms such as Corning, IBM, Kodak, and Xerox are cooperating in this effort. Many other states are investigating TQM and working with corporate partners in developing programs.

QUALITY IN PRACTICE

In this chapter, the Quality in Practice cases will be devoted exclusively to highlighting winners of the Deming Prize and the Baldrige Award. Specifically, we will profile Florida Power and Light, Motorola, and Federal Express as examples of some of the best American companies in manufacturing and service.

Florida Power and Light[17]

Florida Power and Light (FPL) is one of the largest electric utilities in the United States. Its territory covers 27,650 square miles, about half of Florida, and services a population of 5.7 million people. FPL has about 15,000 employees, operates 13 plants, 397 substations, and more than 53,000 miles of transmission and distribution lines.

During the 1970s, the company was forced to increase utility rates repeatedly because of increasing costs, slower sales growth, and stricter federal and state regulations. The company had become bureaucratic and inflexible. In 1981, Marshall McDonald, then chairman of the board, realized that the company had been concerned with keeping defects under control rather than improving quality. Due to his concern for quality, FPL introduced quality improvement teams. Management knew this was a step in the right direction, but such teams alone would not bring about the change needed for the company to survive. McDonald tried to convince other executives that a total quality improvement process was needed, but all the experts that FPL talked to were in manufacturing, while FPL was primarily a service company. In 1983, while in Japan, McDonald met the president of Kansai Electric Power Company, a Deming Prize winner, who told him about their total quality efforts. Company officials began to visit Kansai regularly, and with their help, FPL began its Quality Improvement Program (QIP) in 1983.

"Policy deployment" was the driving force behind the QIP program. Policy deployment is a method that takes corporate vision and determines priority issues that will make the vision a reality. For FPL, the issues involved improving reliability, customer satisfaction, and employee safety while keeping costs in control. Each department was then responsible for developing plans to help improve these areas. Once plans were determined, their status was checked regularly to make sure they were on schedule. Each

department was limited to working on no more than three items that had the most influence on their department's performance, but the work on these was expected to be done in great detail.

"Quality in daily work" (QIDW) is the expression that FPL used for another concept for improving business systems quality. It involves standardizing work routines, removing waste from them, promoting the concept of internal customers, and enabling better practice to be replicated from one location to another. QIDW control systems consist of flowcharts, process and quality indicators, procedure standards, and computer systems. By examining and analyzing work over and over again, employees in every area contribute to simplifying their work and improving processes. They discover opportunities for computer systems to free line employees from repetitive tasks.

One illustration of how QIDW was used was to develop a computer system for processing customer trouble calls. In the system, the computer first checks to find out if the customer has been disconnected for nonpayment, then begins to locate places and devices that may be malfunctioning, and routes the call through a dispatcher to a troubleshooter. A repairman heading to the scene may have a diagnosis before arrival. The information is stored in a database to be used for future improvement planning.

FPL revamped a centralized suggestion system it had been using for many years. Only about 600 suggestions had been submitted annually and it usually took six months for evaluation. A new decentralized system was proposed with simplified procedures to improve the response time. Employees would participate in the implementation of their own suggestions. In 1988, 9,000 suggestions were submitted; in 1989 this increased to 25,000 suggestions.

Training played an important role in FPL's quality transformation. They found that training enhanced enthusiasm and participation. Supervisors were expected to train their employees and play a more active role as coaches and cheerleaders. As line employees become more skilled in diagnosing and solving problems, issues that once required manage-

[17]Brad Stratton, "A Beacon for the World," *Quality Progress,* May 1990, pp. 60–65; Al Henderson and *Target* Staff, "For Florida Power and Light After the Deming Prize: The "Music" Builds . . . And Builds . . . And Builds," *Target,* Summer 1990, pp. 10–21.

(continued)

ment attention are now handled by line employees. Problems are dealt with on a factual basis, not with intuition. All employees developed a much broader view of the company and more flexibility in dealing with customers.

The management system also changed. Customer satisfaction became the focus of attention rather than cost control. Management reviews checked on improvement progress monthly. Goals are now long term, but progress checks are frequent. Managers review progress with better statistical insight, recognizing that variation will exist, but seeking to rid the system of common causes. Cross-functional teams are used to carry out large-scale improvement projects. Finally, the budget is integrated with quality improvement.

The influence of total quality control at FPL can be seen in Figure 5.6. The average length of service

FIGURE 5.6 Some of Florida Power & Light's Accomplishments

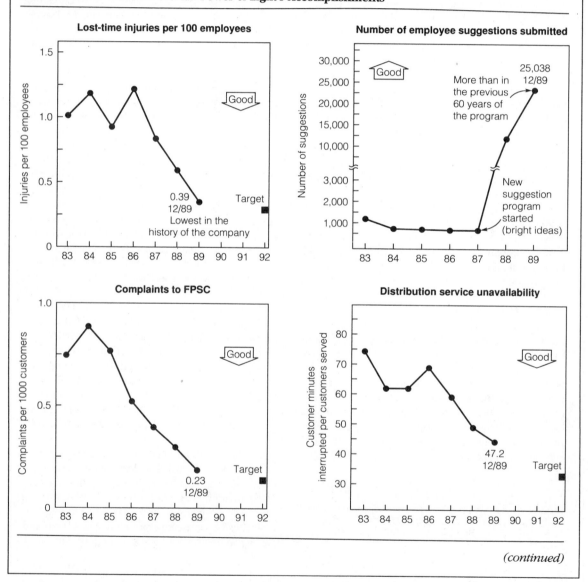

(continued)

interruptions dropped from about 75 minutes in 1983 to about 47 minutes in 1989; the number of complaints per 1,000 customers fell to one-third of the 1983 level; safety has improved; and the price of electricity has stabilized.

Key Issues for Discussion

1. What makes FPL unique in the types of quality problems that it encounters? How is its product

similar to and different from oil being processed in a refinery? From water being delivered by a city water department?

2. How did FPL use policy deployment to improve quality?

3. What was the role of QIP teams at FPL in developing quality to the point of being able to win the Deming Prize?

QUALITY IN PRACTICE

Motorola, Inc.[18]

In 1988, 66 companies applied for the Baldrige Award. Motorola and the Commercial Nuclear Fuel Division of Westinghouse were selected from among 45 manufacturing entries as the first recipients in that category. Motorola employs over 100,000 workers at more than 50 facilities across the world and is among America's 150 largest industrial corporations. Its principal product lines include communication systems and semiconductors. Products are distributed through direct sales and service operations.

Motorola is an engineering-oriented company. Historically, Motorola created new markets with innovative products, essentially telling customers what they wanted. As customers became more sophisticated and as competition increased, Motorola recognized the need to change its objectives from a product focus to a customer focus. Over the years, the customer focus evolved from simply meeting customer expectations, to exceeding them, and finally to anticipating customer needs. In 1979, the company set its fundamental objective as *total customer satisfaction*. Customer satisfaction, in Motorola's view, is achieved when the product is delivered when promised with no defects, the product does not experience any early life failures, and the product does not fail excessively in service.

Two key beliefs guide the culture of the firm: respect for people and uncompromising integrity. Motorola is a union-free company. Employees with 10 or more years of service are not let go for economic reasons; if any do have to be let go, the decision must have the personal approval of the CEO. Many of the breakthroughs in quality were developed by employees who were more than 50 years of age. Motorola's goals are to increase global market share and to become the best in class in all aspects—people, marketing, technology, product, manufacturing, and service. For example, being best in class in terms of people means that Motorola wants to be one of the top three firms for which anyone worldwide would want to work.

Prior to Motorola's total quality transformation, the unstated philosophy was to "make the product right eventually." This meant 20 percent of employees doing testing, and countless hours spent servicing failures in the field. The new target is to reach "Six Sigma" (described below). Beyond that, the new quality goal is simply stated: "Zero defects in everything we do."

Initially, Motorola focused on eliminating manufacturing defects. Two incidents early in the process opened their eyes toward new perspectives. One engineer called up the CEO and told him point blank that they were taking the wrong approach in not concentrating on latent defects, defects hidden by design flaws that manifested themselves by early life failures in the field. He was invited to meet with the CEO the next day. The CEO and a group of vice presidents listened and took the engineer's advice,

[18]Ed Pena, "Motorola's Secret to Total Quality Control," *Quality Progress,* October 1990, pp. 43–45; "Reagan Lauds First Baldrige Award Winners," *Quality Progress,* January 1989, pp. 25–27; A. William Wiggenhorn, "Stalking Quality at Motorola," presentation at the 1990 Council of Logistics Management Conference.

(continued)

resulting in a fundamental change of emphasis in the quality program. That engineer was one of three individuals awarded a prestigious corporate-wide quality award.

A second incident involved a $7,000 per day Japanese quality consultant who was brought in to tell the company "how to do it." He said: "Buy a stack of 3 x 5 cards and write on them 'May I see your Pareto chart?'. Give these to executives and send them out to the factories to hand out cards to the workers. The next week, write on other cards 'May I see your Ishikawa diagram?' and repeat this." The consultant had no more to say. One vice president asked him what he wanted to do the rest of the day, and his response was "to play some golf." The VP said that, after word got out that the consultant had been paid $7,000, he (the VP) would probably have to begin looking for a new job. The consultant replied that he missed the point of what he was trying to say. "You were training people to seek new answers by asking old questions. You must ask new questions to get new answers."

Motorola concentrates on several key themes. Foremost among these is Six Sigma Quality, a term used to denote a maximum of 3.4 nonconformances per million opportunities—the corporate goal by 1992. The Six Sigma program applies to all products and services within the company, from computer chips to invoices. In manufacturing, the Six Sigma principle requires designs that accommodate reasonable variation in component parts but production processes that yield consistently uniform final products. Motorola employees record the defects found in every function of the business, and statistical techniques are increasingly made part of each and every employee's job. To Motorola, this is part of learning the new "language of quality" referred to previously.

Another key aspect of Motorola's quality program is reducing total cycle time. Cycle time was formerly viewed only in the context of manufacturing. It took nine months to agree on a definition for cycle time: It is the time that begins when a customer expresses a need and ends when the customer happily pays the company. In Motorola's eyes, cycle time reduction applies to all processes in the company. This includes design, order entry, manufacturing, marketing, and administrative functions such as auditing. Products that used to take weeks to produce are completed in less than an hour; the time to fill an order for portable radios was reduced from 55 days to 15; the financial closing of the books, which used to take one month, was reduced to four days; and the time to write and file a patent claim was cut from two or three years to two months.

Benchmarking is an important function in each of Motorola's six major product groups. Xerox, another Baldrige winner, worked with Motorola in their benchmarking efforts. Motorola has measured the products and processes of about 125 companies against its own standards to verify its position versus the best in class. For example, they found that they were spending upwards of 10% on warranties while the best were spending less than 1%. All aspects of competitors' products—manufacturability, reliability, manufacturing cost, and performance—are analyzed to determine improvements. (Benchmarking is discussed more in Chapter 6.)

Quality leadership is demonstrated in various ways; by means of top-level meetings to review quality programs and pass the results on through the entire organization; by workers at lower ranks who contribute through the Participative Management Program (PMP); and by PMP teams that meet to assess progress toward meeting quality goals, identify new initiatives, and work on problems. Savings resulting from projects are shared, and PMP bonuses have averaged about 3% of Motorola's payroll.

Motorola has set up its own training center and spent more than $170 million on worker education between 1983 and 1987. About 40% of the training is devoted to quality issues. For example, between 1986 and 1988, more than 10,000 technical personnel were trained in statistical process control and design for manufacturing techniques. More on the quality focus in training will be presented in Chapter 10.

Motorola seeks to reduce the number of suppliers by an average of 50% each year, and only those suppliers who meet its quality expectations will be retained. In fact, after winning the Baldrige award, Motorola told 3600 of its larger suppliers that they must prepare to compete for the award or be dropped. Two hundred suppliers who balked were quickly dropped.

Motorola has made significant strides in reaching its Six Sigma goal. By 1990, most operations in the company were at a five sigma level, up from a three sigma level in the early 1980s, which represented an improvement of thousands of defects per million.

(continued)

Key Issues for Discussion

1. Why did Motorola find it necessary to switch from a product focus to a customer focus in the early 1980s?

2. What were the components of Motorola's quality improvement process that enabled it to get from a three sigma level and to approach a six sigma level in a little over ten years?

QUALITY IN PRACTICE

Federal Express Corporation[19]

In the third year of the Baldrige Award program, Federal Express became the first winner in the service category. Federal Express began operations in 1973 with a fleet of eight airplanes. By 1990, some 89,000 employees processed 1.3 million shipments daily. Within 10 years of its founding, annual revenues reached $1 billion.

According to CEO Frederick W. Smith, "Our number one managerial task is to improve the quality of our services. Therefore, not to compete for the Malcolm Baldrige National Quality Award would have been to relegate our quality focus to a secondary status." Smith stated five criteria for improving quality:

1. Establish clear quality goals.

2. Measure accurately what is done.

3. Identify critical points in the value chain, such as final sort points, and manage flawlessly.

4. Demonstrate discipline in operations.

5. Provide immediate and accurate feedback to employees.

The Federal Express management philosophy emphasizes people, service, and profit—in that order. The company has a well-developed and thoroughly deployed management evaluation system called SFA (survey/feedback/action) that involves a survey of employees, analysis of each work group's results by the work group's manager, and a discussion between the manager and the work group to develop written action plans for the manager to improve and become more effective.

---

[19]Brad Stratton, "Four to Receive 1990 Baldrige Awards," *Quality Progress,* December 1990, pp. 19–21; Federal Express Corporation Information Book, Malcolm Baldrige National Quality Award.

Data from the SFA process are aggregated at all levels of the organization for use in policy-making.

Training of front-line personnel is a responsibility of managers and "recurrency training" is a widely used instrument for improvement. Teams regularly assess training needs and a worldwide staff of training professionals devises programs to address those needs. To aid in these efforts, Federal Express has developed an interactive video system for employee instruction.

Federal Express has a "no layoff" philosophy and a "guaranteed fair treatment procedure" for handling grievances. Front-line employees can participate in a program to qualify them for management positions. In addition, the company has a well-developed recognition program for team and individual contributions to company performance.

The goal of Federal Express is 100% customer satisfaction. This means delivering each shipment on schedule 100% of the time and maintaining 100% accuracy of all information about each item. To approach this goal, Federal Express replaced its old measure of quality performance—percent of on-time deliveries—with a 12-component index that comprehensively describes how its performance is viewed by customers. Each item in the Service Quality Indicator (SQI) is weighted to reflect how significantly it affects overall customer satisfaction. SQI measurements are directly linked to the corporate planning process and form the basis on which corporate executives are evaluated. Individual performance objectives are established and evaluated. Executive bonuses rest on the performance of the whole corporation. In the annual employee survey, if employees do not rate management leadership at least as high as they rated them the year before, no executive receives a year-end bonus.

Technology plays an important role in the Federal Express service process. The "SuperTracker" is

(continued)

a hand-held computer used for scanning a shipment's bar code every time a package changes hands between pickup and delivery. Not only does the SuperTracker keep tabs on individual packages, but information from the device is sent to a corporate data base that allows daily, weekly, and monthly analysis of operations. This information helps quality action teams locate root causes of problems. The digitally assisted dispatch system keeps 26,000 couriers in touch with customers' latest needs through video screens located in company vans. The system allows for quick response to pickup and delivery dispatches and allows couriers to better manage their time and routes.

Since 1987, overall customer satisfaction with domestic service has averaged better than 95%, and in an independently conducted survey of air-express industry customers, 53% gave Federal Express a perfect score, as compared with 39% for the next-best competitor.

Key Issues for Discussion

1. Why do you think that it took three years for a service organization to win the Baldrige Award?

2. In what ways does the quality philosophy at Federal Express differ from Motorola?

3. How is customer satisfaction viewed at Federal Express? Can their approach be applied to other service organizations? Provide an example.

Summary of Key Points

- Total quality management (TQM) is an integrative management concept for continuously improving the quality of goods and services delivered through the participation of all levels and functions of the organization.

- TQM incorporates design, control, and quality improvement, with the customer as the driving force behind the process.

- TQM requires that new "languages" be spoken throughout an organization, with full participation by employees in every area.

- Successful implementation of TQM depends on a long-term perspective, top management commitment, systems thinking, training and tools, participation, measurement and reporting systems, communications, and leadership. Change and rising expectations can cause setbacks and anxiety, which can be avoided through proper planning.

- Unions must separate TQM from collective bargaining and recognize its importance for the future of the firm. Likewise, management must recognize the skills and knowledge of employees and develop a closer working relationship with labor.

- The Deming Prize was developed in Japan to recognize companies that have successfully applied company-wide quality control and the Deming philosophy. The Malcolm Baldrige National Quality Award was instituted over three decades later to recognize companies in the United States for achievements in improving quality.

- Winners of the Deming Prize and Baldrige Award are found to have a sharp focus on quality through planning, top management involvement, an integrated focus on customer satisfaction, and extensive employee participation and training.

- TQM has gone beyond the private sector and has become an important aspect of government operations. Awards similar to the Baldrige Award are given to federal agencies that provide a role model for quality improvement.

Questions for Review and Discussion

1. Define total quality management. What benefits does TQM provide to organizations?

2. What new "languages" have developed around TQM? Why are they important?

3. Explain the key success factors for implementation of total quality management.

4. Discuss some of the pitfalls to implementing TQM. How can they be avoided?

5. What are the respective roles of union and management relations in promoting and developing TQM within a firm?

6. Compare the Deming Prize and Baldrige Award. What common themes do both awards share? Can you point to any differences?

7. Discuss the award criteria for the Baldrige Award. Can you think of anything that might be added?

8. Rank the Baldrige examination categories by maximum point totals. Discuss why the Baldrige developers have chosen these particular ratings. Would you change this? Why or why not?

9. Research information on companies that have won the Baldrige Award since the publication of this book. Write a "Quality in Practice" summary on one of these companies.

10. What factors appear to differentiate quality award winning companies from others?

11. Study the financial and market performance of Baldrige Award winning companies prior to and after winning the award. What changes are evident? Do you believe that a causal effect exists with quality?

12. What is the role of the Federal Quality Institute?

13. Compare the President's Award for Quality criteria with the Baldrige Award criteria. Discuss any differences in categories and weights assigned to each category.

14. What *long-term* benefits may be obtained from governmental initiatives such as Executive Order 12637, establishment of the Federal Quality Institute, and development of the President's Award for Quality and Productivity Improvement?

15. With all of the success that the example companies in this chapter have attained, do you think that the pace of quality improvement in the United States is increasing fast enough to keep up with worldwide competition? Why or why not? Relate your answer to the TQM process.

Bibliography

Application Guidelines, Malcolm Baldrige National Quality Award, U.S. Department of Commerce, National Institute of Standards and Technology, 1991.

Bush, David and Dooley, Kevin. "The Deming Prize and Baldrige Award: How They Compare," *Quality Progress,* January 1989, pp. 28–30.

Coopers & Lybrand Cincinnati Management Consulting Services, "Manufacturing Insights: The Malcolm Baldrige National Quality Award Criteria," December 1990.

DeCarly, Neil J., and Sterett, W. Kent. "History of the Malcolm Baldrige Award," *Quality Progress,* March 1990, pp. 21–27.

Main, Jeremy, "How to Win the Baldrige Award," *Fortune,* April 23, 1990, pp. 101–116.

"Reagan Lauds First Baldrige Award Winners," *Quality Progress,* January 1, 1989, pp. 25–27.

Reimann, Curt W. "The Baldrige Award: Leading the Way in Quality Initiatives," *Quality Progress,* July 1989, pp. 35–39.

CHAPTER 6

Planning for Quality Assurance

Planning forms the basis for all managerial activities: organizing, directing, and controlling. It is the process by which goals and objectives are determined and actions are selected in order to achieve desired results. Planning is the starting point for ensuring that a total quality concept—quality of design and quality of conformance of the manufactured good or service—is developed. In today's complex business and industrial environment, the future is highly variable and unpredictable. Effective planning is necessary to anticipate and take advantage of future opportunities and to recognize and avoid potential problems that may occur. Juran, for example, has done extensive studies concerning quality problems to determine the proportion that were operator controllable versus those that were management controllable.

> The box score on defects in most controllability studies indicates that over 80 percent are management-controllable and 20 percent are operator-controllable. This ratio does not appear to vary greatly from one industry to another, but it does vary considerably from one process to another. Obviously, no one needs to accept such figures as applying to his or her own company. Any particular situation can be clarified by making a controllability study.[1]

Despite the caveats, it is certainly evident that a high proportion of quality problems can be prevented through proper managerial planning. Good planning, when it permeates all levels of the organization, can set the stage for efficient and successful performance in every critical area of quality assurance. This chapter discusses the important role that planning plays in quality assurance.

GENERAL CONCEPTS OF MANAGERIAL PLANNING

Many definitions of planning have been proposed. Peter Drucker, a noted management consultant, defines planning as follows:

> . . . the continuous process of making present entrepreneurial (risk-taking) decisions systematically and with the greatest knowledge of their futurity;

---

[1] In J. M. Juran and Frank M. Gryna, Jr., *Quality Planning and Analysis,* 2d ed. (New York: McGraw-Hill, 1980), p. 107.

organizing systematically the efforts needed to carry out these decisions; and measuring the results of these decisions against expectations through organized, systematic feedback.[2]

A more descriptive and straightforward definition is given by Koontz and O'Donnell:

Deciding in advance what to do, how to do it, when to do it, and who is to do it.[3]

These fundamental questions—what, how, when, and who—must be addressed in any effective planning effort. Addressing these questions adequately often makes planning a costly and time-consuming process, and one that many ineffective managers shun. Planning requires careful analysis, imagination, foresight, and creativity—the characteristics of effective managers. Thus, we see that planning is not a trivial task.

A variety of facts, data, and information is required for planning. *What* refers to the activities that must be accomplished to achieve a desired goal. This might include a description of the technology necessary to carry out the activities. *How* specifies the manner in which the tasks are to be accomplished as well as the sequence in which they must be performed. *When* is concerned with the timing of activities. Any successful plan should have a definite beginning and an end. This must also be true for each of the individual activities identified in the plan. Finally, the answer to the *who* question establishes duties and responsibilities for the personnel who will implement the plan. Proper assignment of tasks to individuals' skills and abilities is important to meet the goals and objectives of the organizations. Authority and resources must be given to those to whom responsibility is assigned.

To illustrate these components of planning, consider a small electronic components firm that has an objective of providing documented evidence of quality to its customers in order to comply with contract specifications. Although the firm produces high-quality products, it has no organized quality reporting system. *What* must be accomplished includes defining the quality characteristics that must be measured and the format in which they must be reported. *How* includes determining, among other things, the statistical techniques and procedures that will be employed to gather, analyze, and report the data; the possible selection of computer software; and training of personnel in the proper techniques. *When* specifies the deadline by which these tasks must be accomplished, perhaps within the next three months. *Who* might consist of a university consultant to oversee the project, a production manager to have internal responsibility, and a president of the firm to assure that the project is completed on time.

The Importance of Planning

Planning is important for many reasons. Clearly, it is better to decide what is to be done and to evaluate the consequences of alternative plans before actually implementing such plans. Without planning, a manager's job becomes one of continuous firefighting and can result in disastrous consequences. Planning estab-

---

[2]Peter F. Drucker, *Management: Tasks, Responsibilities, Practices* (New York: Harper and Row, 1974).

[3]Harold Koontz and Cyril O'Donnell, *Management: A Systems and Contingency Analysis of Managerial Functions* (New York: McGraw-Hill, 1976).

lishes a sense of purpose to decision making and enables the manager to meet goals and objectives more easily. Planning reveals what resources are needed to achieve a goal (organizing) and establishes a strategy for implementation of the plan (directing) and a means for assuring conformance to the plan (controlling).

The process of planning itself creates better managers. By putting the relevant facts and information down on paper, a manager obtains a better handle on the overall situation and the potential decisions that can be made. Planning reduces duplication of effort, minimizes costs of achieving objectives, creates consistency and a coordination mechanism for future activities, and establishes a basis for control.

Nevertheless, planning has some limitations and disadvantages. Plans are never perfect, since the information used to develop them is never accurate or reliable. Planning can take considerable time, cost, and discipline to be effective. Also, it can create psychological barriers to making the best decisions if strict reliance on the plan—rather than reaction to new opportunities—becomes the norm. However, the advantages of planning far outweigh the disadvantages.

The terms *planning* and *decision making* are often confused. Planning and decision making go hand in hand, but they are not synonymous. Decision making is the choice of a course of action to follow, the "what" of the planning activity. Decisions can be made without any planning. Planning, however, is the activity of developing courses of action, their timing, their sequence, and their implementation.

THE HIERARCHICAL NATURE OF PLANNING

The management of any organization is generally divided into three levels: (1) top management, (2) middle management, and (3) supervisory management. Managers at each level must plan, organize, direct, and control, although the emphasis on each activity differs from level to level.

Top management is responsible for setting the broad goals of the organization, such as achieving profit, growth, competitive position, or good public relations. Clearly, quality is an important aspect of each of these goals. Without full support of top management through its plans, policies, actions, and attitudes, a company will never develop a reputation for having a quality product. Successful quality programs depend on top management commitment; those without such commitment inevitably fail.

Plans made by top management specify the goals that middle managers, such as production managers and directors of quality assurance, must accomplish. Middle managers concentrate on the design of products and systems that will allow the organization to meet its technical objectives. Middle managers are responsible, for example, for the development of inventory, quality, and labor reporting systems. Planning at the middle management level is made over a shorter time frame, and more direction is required, because a larger number of subordinates frequently report to middle managers.

At the supervisory, or first-line, management level, the emphasis is on achieving the short-range goals of the organization. Much of a line manager's time is spent directing machine operators, clerks, and other personnel. Thus, the line manager's primary effort is devoted to controlling operations according to the directives given by middle management. First-line supervisors and workers have responsibilities that involve reporting and data entry to various systems as well as the responsibilities of

FIGURE 6.1 **Managerial Planning Activities**

Level of management	Managerial activity			
	Planning	Organizing	Directing	Controlling
Top	High	Low	Low	Moderate
Middle	Moderate	High	Moderate	Moderate
Supervisory	Low	Low	High	High

performing the productive work of providing services or making manufactured goods. As operating technologies become more complex, first-line supervisors and line workers become more and more involved in operations planning. Workers and supervisors in many firms plan, set goals, and solve problems relating to quality, productivity, procedures, training, safety, and housekeeping under guidelines provided by such participative management programs as quality circles and quality of worklife (QWL).

Figure 6.1 summarizes the relative emphasis of managerial activities at the different management levels. In general, we see that top management is concerned with long-range plans and decisions, middle management with intermediate-range plans and decisions, and supervisory management with short-range plans and decisions. This leads us to categorize planning using a *hierarchical classification.* Planning activities can be placed into one of three categories: (1) strategic, (2) tactical, and (3) operational. This framework was first proposed by Robert N. Anthony in 1965.[4]

These three categories are hierarchical in nature. That is, strategic plans made at the top levels of an organization are fed downward and provide the boundaries within which tactical plans and decisions are made. These, in turn, are fed downward and provide boundaries for operational plans. As broadly conceived plans are fed downward through the organization, they become more detailed in scope.

The purpose of developing this hierarchy is to ensure that managerial and operational planning supports rather than hinders the overall direction and strategy of the organization. A well-integrated planning structure is the backbone of a total quality assurance system. Hierarchical planning puts specific quality decisions in the hands of the proper managers, who know what they are responsible for and what results are expected. Lines of authority become clearer, and deadlines are easier to manage.

Hierarchical Planning for Quality Assurance

Figure 6.2 presents a hierarchical classification of quality planning and control activities. This model shows that broad product-quality decisions are made at the top management level, objectives and systems to support strategic goals are developed at

---

[4]Robert N. Anthony, "Planning and Control Systems: A Framework for Analysis," Graduate School of Business Administration, Harvard University, Boston (1965).

FIGURE 6.2 Hierarchical Structure of Quality Planning and Control

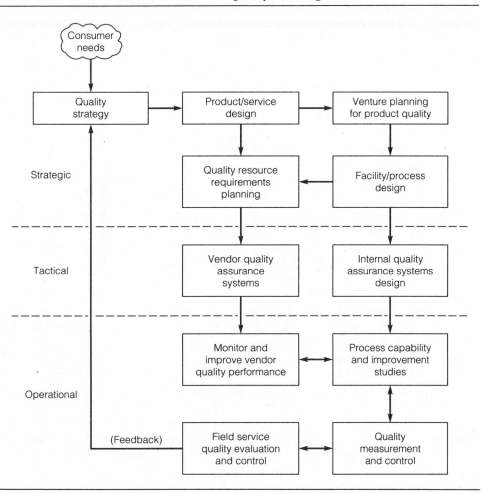

the middle management level, and detailed procedures for operating control are developed and carried out at the first-line management level. At the strategic or top-management level, the paramount concern is to meet consumer needs by developing products that are functional, aesthetically pleasing, and generally fit for their intended use. In the initial design of a product, management is concerned with defining markets and choosing a quality strategy. A typical question asked at this point is: Will our product be aimed at the top-of-the-line buyer, the average buyer, or the economy-minded purchaser? Regardless of which market segment is chosen, all products must be designed and produced to ensure fitness for their intended use.

Since the planning responsibilities for management tend to increase as a function of the level at which the managers are found, it follows that a large part of the responsibility for overall planning for quality will fall on top and middle management. In an article about the impact of strategic planning and profit performance, Schoeffler and others reported that improved quality had a significant bottom line impact on profitability and tended to be closely related to high market share.[5] Therefore, careful attention to quality planning should be one of the fundamental responsibilities of top managers. Once fundamental marketing and quality decisions are made, product (or service) design is initiated. (Details of the product design process are discussed in Chapter 14.)

Venture planning for a new or improved product frequently requires new investment in plant, equipment, or process design and is usually accompanied by an analysis of the projected return on investment and by other financial indicators. A favorable result from the venture analysis triggers the need for facility design and quality resource requirements planning. Both of these stages ensure that facilities, personnel, materials, and equipment will be in place when the new or improved product or service is launched.

At the tactical planning level, the emphasis is on the design of systems to support product quality and meet strategic goals and objectives. Vendor quality assurance systems—those that monitor the quality of purchased parts and materials—have become crucial to overall quality in recent years. Automotive manufacturers have become extremely vocal on the subject, to the point of pressuring their vendors to adopt methods of proving their quality capabilities or risk losing their business. In fact, in 1982, a GM vice president stated that half of the parts suppliers serving their assembly plants would be eliminated.[6] Internal quality assurance systems must also be developed to monitor and improve quality levels within the firm.

At the operating level, control and monitoring becomes the central activity. Monitoring and improving vendor quality conformance requires developing a working relationship with vendors, setting mutual goals, and cooperating to find solutions to quality problems as they arise. Process capability and improvement studies must be performed to determine the ability of a process to meet required quality levels and to determine potential quality improvements. These activities require that cooperative efforts of quality, production, engineering, and service personnel be focused on identifying, isolating, and solving quality problems. Planned change must take place, and the causes that contribute to defective products must be eliminated.

To ensure that the standards defining quality are continually met, a quality measurement and control activity must also be established. This function monitors current quality levels and helps to fine tune quality at the operating level of the organization. Additionally, field service quality evaluation and control are also required if there is to be long-term commitment to the product. Many times the customer's perception of the product is vitally affected by the way the supplier services the product after it is sold. Quality criteria must be established and monitored if "fitness for use" is to have any real meaning. This requires gathering data, analyzing it, and taking corrective action to meet problems of reliability, maintainability, and customer service in the field. Feedback on consumer needs, which can result in the design of new and improved products, is often the dividend that accrues from good field coverage of quality characteristics. Subsequent chapters detail various aspects of

---

[5]Sidney Schoeffler, Robert D. Buzzell, and Donald F. Heany, "Impact of Strategic Planning on Profit Performance," *Harvard Business Review,* March–April 1974, pp. 137–145. Copyright © 1974 by the President and Fellows of Harvard College; all rights reserved.

[6]"GM Spreads the Misery," *Newsweek,* April 15, 1982, pp. 54–55.

organization and control relating to each of these levels and quality functions in the process.

THE QUALITY PLANNING PROCESS

Although methods of planning vary greatly among individuals and companies, planning is generally characterized by several common elements. Figure 6.3 illustrates the steps involved in most planning efforts.

"Vision" refers to guiding values, principles, and the direction of expected growth of an organization or some segment of it. The vision is generally developed by key managers and others who are responsible for planning and carrying out that vision. Today, it is common for vision statements to be developed at many levels within the organizational hierarchy. This is a very worthwhile activity, as long as the statements are coordinated so as to fit with those of the next higher level and the overall organization's vision.

"Purpose" refers to the *raison d'être* of the organization—their reason for existence. In the past, the purpose of the organization was frequently stated in terms of products or services produced, or profitability to stockholders. TQM-focused firms are now stating their purpose in terms of customer satisfaction and commitment to strive for higher levels of quality. Deming's philosophy clearly defines the purpose of quality-driven firms: to stay in business and provide jobs. The vision and purpose of an organization together lead to the organization's *mission*.

FIGURE 6.3 Elements of the Planning Process

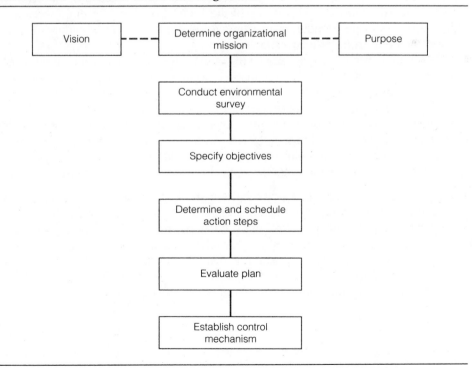

The mission of an organization is a broad, general statement of the direction in which the organization intends to move. It addresses the question of what the organization should plan for. The mission of a firm is often stated in terms of the key products that the company intends to produce or the markets that it intends to serve. The mission statement also often provides an indication of the quality commitment of the organization. Some of the questions addressed in a mission statement are: What is the purpose of planning? What are the strategic goals? How do they relate to one another?

In ensuring that quality is not neglected in defining the mission of the organization, Juran suggests that the following questions be addressed:[7]

- What should be the quality mission of the company?

- What are the key qualities as seen by the clients?

- As to the key qualities, what is the company's state of competitiveness?

- What opportunities does the company have for quality improvement and reduction of quality-related costs?

- What can the company do to make better use of its human resources?

- What threats are coming over the horizon?

An example of a corporate mission statement is that of Hughes Aircraft:

> Our mission is to creatively apply electronics-based technology to products and services for the defense, space, and commercial markets. In accomplishing this mission, it is essential that our customers receive exceptional value in terms of cost-effective products and services of the highest quality, our employees and business associates benefit from our success, and our shareholders receive superior value from their investment.
>
> We are committed to advancing the state of the art in electronics and related technologies and to developing market opportunities that are built on our unique technical capabilities. We will extend our leadership position in our core defense electronics and space businesses. In addition we will expand our business in the areas of communications, large-scale integrated systems and training systems, and will form alliances within the GM family for the purpose of developing new products and services that strengthen GM.
>
> Our goal is to be the recognized world leader in electronic systems.

It is important that all areas of an organization participate in determining the quality goals of the organization. For example, engineering might establish a goal of eliminating potential quality problems in production; production control's goal might be to eliminate material shortages and establish realistic production schedules; purchasing's goal might be to guarantee that all purchased parts meet quality standards; finance might set a goal of supplying necessary funds to meet quality objectives. For quality planning, a key component of a mission statement is the

---

[7] J. M. Juran, "Product Quality . . . A Prescription for the West." Reprinted with permission from *Quality*, April 1982, pp. 16–22. A publication of Hitchcock Publishing, a Capital Cities/ABC, Inc., Company.

consideration of the quality image that the organization wishes to present to its customers. When all elements of an organization are involved, the task of developing a quality image becomes easier. Specific goals such as those listed above will be translated into detailed objectives that ultimately define the quality level of products.

The purpose of an *environmental survey* is to gather knowledge about those internal and external activities that will affect the mission of the organization. Such activities might include customer demand, competitive conditions, and resource constraints. A significant amount of data collection and retrospective analysis of past decisions and consequences is essential in order to gather usable information. This information must be carefully examined and evaluated before establishing goals and objectives. The key to achieving successfully a superior quality image is to determine what characteristics the customer considers to be critical for the product.

The next step in the planning process is to develop *specific, measurable objectives.* They must agree with overall corporate goals. If they are not compatible, revisions must be made. As discussed earlier, objectives set at one level of an organization provide boundaries for objectives and actions made at lower levels. Thus, coordination between managerial levels must be taken into account during the planning process.

The major purpose of planning is to decide what *action steps* to take in order to meet objectives, and to schedule such actions. In developing the details of a plan, one must consider the assumptions made regarding the future and the boundaries or restrictions that limit the choice of actions. Several means to attain certain objectives may be available, and creativity is required to develop different alternatives to be considered. In selecting a specific set of actions, questions such as the following must be taken into account: Is the plan simple or complex? Is it flexible? What resources are required? A time schedule and detailed instructions for implementation must also be developed.

The *evaluation* of a proposed plan must be done in light of financial constraints. Adjustments to budgets and possible revisions to objective statements may be required. Hence, planning is not necessarily a serial process; often one must repeat previous steps in the process to develop an effective plan.

Finally, a *control mechanism* must be established. Methods for measuring results in light of objectives need to be devised. Records and reports for doing this must be designed. Management must consider possible avenues of corrective action or revisions to the original plan.

Quality audits are popular ways of monitoring a quality program. Auditing is a flexible technique and can be applied in a variety of settings, although the best-known audits are probably financial in nature. A quality assurance audit is a periodic and systematic external review and evaluation of the documented requirements of a quality assurance program. Its purpose is to generate information on the status of quality assurance in an organization, reveal any inadequacies, and define the scope of improvement. Quality audits will be discussed further in Chapter 8.

Benchmarking

The development of objectives is often aided through a process known as **benchmarking.** Benchmarking is defined as "measuring your performance against that of best-in-class companies, determining how the best-in-class achieve those performance levels, and using the information as a basis for your own company's targets, strategies, and implementation."[8] Benchmarking helps a company to learn its strengths and weaknesses and those of other industrial leaders and to incorporate the best practices into its own operations. Benchmarking was initiated by Xerox, an eventual winner of the Malcolm Baldrige National Quality Award. Xerox was losing market share and profitability during the late 1970s, and the company authorized a study of the quality, features, and unit costs of the competition's machines compared to Xerox machines. They were shocked by the initial results. Xerox's unit manufacturing cost equaled the Japanese selling price in the United States; the number of Xerox's production suppliers was nine times that of the best companies; assembly line rejects were ten times higher; product lead times were two times longer; and defects per hundred machines were seven times higher. Although Xerox executives could not believe the results, new benchmarking studies confirmed the data. The benchmarking process led to a meeting in 1983 by the top 25 managers in the company to plan a quality strategy. The benchmarking results helped them understand the amount of change that would be required, and set realistic targets to guide their planning efforts.

The benchmarking process can be illustrated with the six-step process used by Alcoa:[9]

1. *Decide what to benchmark.* Questions such as the following are asked to guide the activities of the benchmarking team: Is the topic important to the customers? Is the topic consistent with Alcoa's mission, values, and milestones? Does the topic reflect an important business need? Is the topic significant in terms of costs or key nonfinancial indicators? Is the topic an area where additional information could influence plans and actions? Answers lead to the development of a purpose statement that describes the topic to be benchmarked and guides subsequent activities.

2. *Plan the benchmarking project.* A team leader is chosen who is responsible for seeing that the project is successfully completed. The leader should have the authority to make changes in processes, products, and services based on the benchmarking information. A team is then created, based on the range of skills needed for the project. The team's first task is to refine the purpose statement by considering questions such as: Who are the customers of the study? What is the scope of the study? What characteristics will be measured? What information is readily available?

3. *Understand current performance.* The team examines the factors that influence performance to learn which characteristics are most important and which are least important. They learn what data relate to the important characteristics and how to collect and measure those data. The collected performance data create the baseline and structure for benchmarking comparisons.

4. *Study others.* The team identifies benchmarking candidates, narrows the list down to a few candidates, prepares general and specific questions, decides the best way to get the questions answered, and performs the study.

---

[8]Lawrence S. Pryor, "Benchmarking: A Self-Improvement Strategy," *The Journal of Business Strategy,* November/December 1989, pp. 28–32.

[9]Karen Bemowski, "The Benchmarking Bandwagon," *Quality Progress,* January 1991, pp. 19–24.

5. *Learn from the data.* The team analyzes the data collected, quantifies performance gaps, and identifies which pieces of information might be particularly useful for improving performance.

6. *Use the findings.* The team works with the project sponsor to determine how the benchmarking findings can best be used and what other organizations in the company can benefit from its work.

Benchmarking is a multidimensional, multifunctional approach toward determining planning objectives and improving quality. To be effective, it must be applied to all facets of a business. For example, Motorola encourages everyone in the organization to ask "Who is the best person in my own field and how might I use some of their techniques and characteristics to improve my own performance in order to be the best (executive, machine operator, chef, purchasing agent, etc.) in my 'class'?"

Some of the benefits realized through benchmarking include:[10]

- The best practices from any industry may be creatively incorporated into a company's operations. For example, the warehousing and distribution practices of L. L. Bean were adapted by Xerox. Thus, benchmarking should not be aimed solely at direct competitors and, in fact, it would be a mistake to do so.

- Benchmarking is motivating. It provides targets that have been achieved by others.

- Resistance to change may be lessened if ideas for improvement come from other industries.

- Technical breakthroughs from other industries that may be useful can be identified early.

- Benchmarking broadens peoples' experience base and increases knowledge.

Benchmarking can be used to develop superiority in an industry. However, if a company simply benchmarks within its own industry, it may be competitive and have an edge in those areas in which it is the industry leader. However, if benchmarks are adopted from outside the industry, a company may learn of new applicable ideas and processes that allow it to surpass easily the best within its own industry and achieve distinctive superiority.

Benchmarking provides more than just targets to guide the planning process. It becomes a tool for continuous improvement. Xerox, for instance, has used benchmarking to institutionalize continuous improvement throughout its organization. Benchmarking is used to identify activities that are necessary to satisfy customer requirements and eliminate those that are not.

Influence of the Baldrige Award on Quality Planning

The criteria developed by the Malcolm Baldrige National Quality Award committee as standards against which to measure award applicants are also having an impact on the planning processes of many organizations. As pointed out in Chapter 5 on TQM, the

[10]Robert C. Camp, *Benchmarking: The Search for Industry Best Practices That Lead to Superior Performance* (Milwaukee, WI: ASQC Quality Press and UNIPUB/Quality Resources, 1989).

section in the award criteria on strategic quality planning examines: (1) the company's planning process for achieving or retaining quality leadership, (2) how the company integrates quality improvement planning into overall business planning, and (3) the company's short- and long-term plans to achieve and/or sustain a quality leadership position. The impact of these requirements is fourfold and incorporates the elements of the planning process presented in Figure 6.3. Strategic thinking must be performed on: (1) the *mission, vision, and purpose,* represented by goals for quality leadership that must be set by the organization; (2) the level of competition in the *environment,* and how to exceed the quality levels of competitors in order to be a "world class" producer; (3) how to *take action steps* to develop data, information, and analysis *(control systems)* for *evaluating* customer requirements, process capabilities, competitor and benchmark data, and supplier capability to meet *objectives* contained in goal-based plans; and (4) how to evaluate and improve both goal-setting and strategic planning processes.

The Baldrige Award criteria do not substitute a new requirement for quality planning or act as a replacement for a systematic approach to quality. Instead, they make it clear that planning for quality requires a systematic and sustained effort to integrate customer-focused quality goals, deploy them throughout the organization, maintain awareness of the "best in class" benchmarks in the competitive environment, and incorporate continuous improvement as a constant focus in the planning process and organization as a whole.

An Example of a Quality Planning Statement

To illustrate an integrated set of quality policies and objectives, consider a computer firm interested in being a leader in home computer development. The mission of the firm might be defined as follows:

> To produce home computers of sufficiently high quality to appeal to adults and older youth, be competitive with similar medium-priced products, and be capable of being upgraded to a more sophisticated unit.

This mission statement is the starting point for the planning process outlined in Figure 6.3. It also suggests that the firm has done its homework by taking an environmental survey. The firm has identified its mission as producing a quality computer product that will not be primarily in the "game" category. It has identified its competition as those companies producing similar medium-priced products. Presumably, it knows its competitors' quality characteristics by using such techniques as "reverse engineering" (taking apart competitors' products to assess their quality and production capabilities). The company has also found that the capability to upgrade the computer is a characteristic of major interest to its customers as well as a potential area for product improvement and development.

To meet the broad goals set by the mission statement, quality objectives must be specified, some of which might include the following:

- Reduce the average outgoing quality level from two defects per unit to 0.5 defect per unit in two years.

- Develop a team approach to quality improvement projects within the next year to include representation from engineering, quality assurance, and line units (both salaried and hourly employees). At least three teams to be in operation by year-end.

These statements are more concrete than the mission statement and are designed to be operational rather than inspirational goals. They contain specific, measurable targets and a time frame within which they should be accomplished.

At the tactical level, the firm must determine and schedule the action steps to support the defined mission and objectives, including the following:

- Form the steering committee for development of quality improvement teams by January 31.

- Schedule training of engineers, quality assurance personnel, and line supervisors on quality improvement processes and techniques from February 15 to April 1.

- Carry out training listed above and plan for training of hourly employees to be completed by September 1.

- Pilot test team approach to quality improvement, with first results to be presented by November 1.

- Evaluate plan (steering committee) by November 15.

- Given favorable results, establish three teams and begin work on projects by December 1.

Note that this training and development plan contains the action steps and evaluation and control mechanisms necessary to carry out the complete process. Outcomes from such a study team might result in a specific procedure, such as the following:

Each assembled unit will be given the normal tests for operation and functioning at each work station. At the completion of the last assembly operation, each unit will be taken to the final test area and "burned in" for 10 hours on the automatic test unit. An extended test of another 30 hours will be given to five percent of the units, chosen in a random fashion. Every test instrument used by the quality control department must be sent out for calibration according to a schedule to be set up and monitored by the quality control manager.

PLANNING FOR CUSTOMER SATISFACTION

The focus on the traditional planning elements is being modified in companies that have moved to a TQM philosophy. Planning is the first step in Juran's quality trilogy. Juran has had a major influence on how U.S. and Japanese managers plan and implement quality concepts and systems. He believes that the process of operationalizing quality planning involves two principal activities: planning products that meet customers' needs and planning the system to produce those products.

Customer Needs and Expectations

All quality assurance activities must be customer-driven; that is, both the planning of products and the planning of the system must be focused on fulfilling the needs and expectations of the customer to make the product "fit for use." Customer-driven

FIGURE 6.4   Customer-driven Quality Cycle

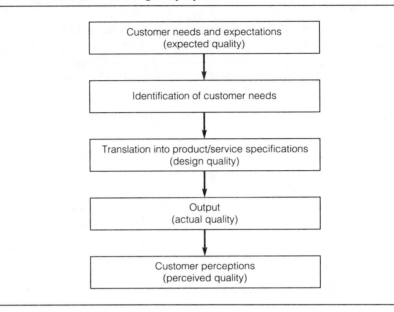

quality is the cornerstone for many firms. Figure 6.4 provides a view of how customer needs and expectations can be affected during the production process.

The process begins with customer needs and expectations (expected quality) and ends with what the customer sees and believes the quality of the product to be (perceived quality). Expected quality is what the customer assumes will be received from the product as a reflection of the customer's needs. Perceived quality is the customer's measure of satisfaction in the product, the "feel" for its quality. Between these two extremes, the product is in the hands of the producer.

The first task of the producer is to identify customer needs and expectations. As we saw in Chapter 1, there are many dimensions to quality, and it is difficult to satisfy all of them simultaneously. Table 6.1 gives some examples of the different quality dimensions for both a manufactured product and a service product. The firm must focus on the key dimensions that are reflected in specific customer needs. If these expectations are not identified correctly or are misinterpreted, then the final product will not be perceived to be of high quality by customers. Considerable marketing efforts are needed to ensure that the needs are correctly identified.

In addition to the technical quality characteristics of a product, customers have other needs and expectations throughout the life cycle of product purchase and use.[11] Before the sale, for instance, customers must have clear and unambiguous specifications. They must relate to the application for which the product is intended. It must be clear that the product will function correctly in the environment for which the customer intends it. Delivery information must be reliable. After delivery, the

---

[11]A. Richard Shores, *A TQM Approach to Achieving Manufacturing Excellence* (Milwaukee, WI: ASQC Quality Press, 1990), p. 99.

TABLE 6.1 Examples of Quality Characteristics

Quality Dimension	Manufactured Product (Stereo Amplifier)	Service Product (Checking Account)
Performance	Signal-to-noise ratio; power	Time to process customer requests
Features	Remote control	Automatic bill paying
Conformance	Workmanship	Accuracy
Reliability	Mean time to failure	Variability of time to process requests
Durability	Useful life	Keeping pace with industry trends
Serviceability	Ease of repair	Resolution of errors
Aesthetics	Oak cabinet	Appearance of bank lobby

SOURCE: Adapted from Paul E. Pisek, "Defining Quality at the Marketing/Development Interface," *Quality Progress,* June 1987, pp. 28–36.

product should be received when promised and the shipment should contain everything expected and needed to use the product. Operating and setup instructions must be clear and complete. The product should function as expected without defects and be easy to learn to use. During use, not only should the product continually meet specifications, but it should be easy to verify that it does. As the product ages, preventive maintenance should be easy and economical. Factory and service center repairs should be handled promptly. Finally, spare parts should be available at reasonable cost and over the life of the product.

A Japanese professor, Noriaki Kano, suggested that three classes of customer needs exist:

1. *Dissatisfiers,* which are those needs that are *expected* in a product or service. In an automobile, a radio, heater, and required safety features are examples. These generally are not stated by customers but assumed as given. If they are not present, the customer is dissatisfied.

2. *Satisfiers,* which are needs that customers say they want. Air-conditioning or a compact disc player would be examples for an automobile. Fulfilling these needs creates satisfaction.

3. *Exciters/delighters,* which are new or innovative features that customers do not expect. Antilock brakes, air bags, or collision avoidance systems would be examples. The presence of such unexpected features leads to high perceptions of quality.

The importance of this classification is that while satisfiers are relatively easy to determine through routine marketing research, it takes special effort to elicit customer perceptions about dissatisfiers and exciters/delighters. Over time, exciters/delighters become satisfiers as customers become used to them, and eventually satisfiers become dissatisfiers. Thus, companies must continually innovate and study customer perceptions to ensure that needs are being met.

Customer needs next must be translated into technical specifications. Technical specifications determine the design quality of the product. Engineering perceptions of customers' needs can often be different from their actual needs. For instance, one need of the "average" customer might be that a product should be able to withstand stressful use. An engineering decision might be made to specify a plastic component instead of a metal component to save weight or cost, thus causing the product to fail prematurely under normal use. If engineers and designers never have an opportunity to interact with customers, the probability that they will lose or misinterpret the expected quality is greatly increased.

Next, product designs are transferred to manufacturing or service delivery, the group responsible for producing the good or delivering the service. The output results in the actual quality, that is, the true level of quality provided by the production system. Poor attention to customer needs here also can affect the perceived quality. For example, if the system is not designed to assure conformance to the technical specifications, then the actual quality produced may not be the same as the design quality.

A fundamental equation that relates these different levels of quality is:

perceived quality = actual quality − expected quality

Any differences between the expected quality and actual quality can cause either unexpected satisfaction by the customer (if actual quality is higher than expected quality) or dissatisfaction (if actual quality is lower than expected quality). Therefore, producers must take great care to ensure that customer needs are met (or exceeded, in some cases) both by the design and production process.

Quality Function Deployment

A major problem with the process illustrated in Figure 6.4 is that customers and engineers speak different languages. A customer might say that he or she wants a car that is easy to start. The translation of this requirement into technical language might be "car will start within 10 seconds of continuous cranking." Or, a requirement that "soap leaves my skin feeling soft" must be translated into pH or hardness specifications for the bar of soap. Much can be lost in the translation and subsequent interpretation by production personnel.

The Japanese have developed the concept of *quality function deployment (QFD)* to ensure that customers' requirements are met throughout the design process and also in the design of production systems. QFD is basically a philosophy and a set of planning and communication tools that focuses on customer requirements in coordinating the design, manufacturing, and marketing of goods.

QFD originated in 1972 at Mitsubishi's Kobe shipyard site. Toyota began to develop the concept shortly thereafter, and it has been used since 1977. The results have been impressive. Between January 1977 and October 1979, Toyota realized a 20% reduction in start-up costs on the launch of a new van. By 1982, start-up costs had fallen 38% from the 1977 baseline, and by 1984, were reduced by 61%. In addition, development time fell by one-third and quality had improved. Today, QFD is successfully used by manufacturers of electronics, appliances, clothing, construction equipment, and by firms such as General Motors, Ford, Mazda, Motorola, Xerox, Kodak, IBM, Procter & Gamble, Hewlett-Packard, and AT&T. The 1992 model Cadillac was planned and designed entirely with QFD. The concept has been publicized and developed in the United States by two organizations, the American Supplier Institute, Inc., a nonprofit organization, and GOAL/QPC, a consulting firm.

At the strategic level, QFD presents the challenge and opportunity for top management to break out of the traditional narrow focus on "results," which can only be measured after the fact, and to begin to focus on the broader *process* of how the results are obtained. Lawrence P. Sullivan, Chairman and CEO of the American Supplier Institute, stated:[12]

> Policy management, on the other hand, is structured as a method to achieve company business or policy objectives. Here top management must do the work—delineate objectives and relate the activities or *means* for deployment through contact, inspection, and adjusting. This method *effectively changes the top management role in results-oriented companies.* The *means* to achieve become the primary focus and *results* measure only how well policy management was carried out. *Results, therefore, are indicative of the management system and not so much the basis for individual success or failure.* [Emphasis added.]

At the tactical and operational levels, QFD represents a departure from the traditional product planning process in which product concepts are originated by design teams or research and development groups, tested and refined, produced, and marketed. Traditionally, as more information on customer perceptions, use, and problems is gathered, the product is redesigned, the production system is modified, and the improved product is released to the market. There are two problems with this approach. First, customers whose expectations and needs are not met by the original product are not likely to continue buying the product, and serious problems will tarnish the image of the firm. Second, a considerable amount of wasted effort and time is spent on redesigning the product and production systems until the product that meets customer needs is eventually produced. If customer needs can be identified properly in the first place, then such wasteful effort is eliminated. This is the focus of QFD.

A major benefit of QFD is improved communication and teamwork between all constituencies in the production process, such as between marketing and design, between design and manufacturing, and between purchasing and suppliers. Product objectives are not misunderstood or misinterpreted during the production process. QFD helps to determine the causes of customer dissatisfaction, and it is a useful tool for competitive analysis of product quality by top management. Productivity as well as quality improvements are the result, and, most significantly, the time for new product development is reduced. QFD allows companies to simulate the effects of new design ideas and concepts. This allows companies to bring new products into the market sooner and gain a competitive advantage. Details of the QFD process and its use are presented in the next section.

THE QUALITY FUNCTION DEPLOYMENT PROCESS

The term quality function deployment represents the overall concept that provides a means of translating customer requirements into the appropriate technical requirements for each stage of product development and production. The customers' requirements—expressed in their own terms—is called appropriately, the ***voice of the customer.*** These requirements are the collection of customer needs, including all satisfiers, exciters/delighters, and dissatisfiers. For example, a consumer might state

---

[12]Lawrence P. Sullivan. "Policy Management Through Quality Function Deployment," *Quality Progress,* June 1988, p. 20.

that a dishwashing liquid should be "long lasting" and "clean effectively," or that a portable stereo should have "good sound quality." Sometimes these requirements are referred to as *customer attributes.* Under QFD, all operations of a company are driven by the voice of the customer, rather than by edicts of top management or the opinions or desires of design engineers.

Technical features, sometimes called *counterpart characteristics,* are the translation of the voice of the customer into technical language. For example, a dishwashing detergent loosens grease and soil from dishes. The soil becomes trapped in the suds so dishes can be removed from the water without picking up grease. Eventually the suds become saturated with soil and break down. Thus, a design characteristic of a dishwashing liquid would be the weight of greasy soil that the suds generated by a fixed amount of dishwashing liquid can absorb before breaking down. Another might be the size of the soap bubble (which, incidentally, has been found to be an important attribute of customers' perceptions of cleaning effectiveness and only discovered by listening to the voice of the customer!). Technical descriptors of a stereo system that affect sound quality include the frequency response, flutter (the wavering in pitch), and the speed accuracy (a cassette tape player should have a speed of 1-7/8 inch/second—inconsistency affects the pitch and tempo of the sound).

A set of matrices is used to relate the voice of the customer to counterpart characteristics when they are expressed as technical specifications and process control requirements. There are four principal planning documents:

1. *Customer requirement planning matrix:* This translates the voice of the customer into counterpart characteristics of the final product.

2. *Product characteristic deployment matrix:* This translates counterpart characteristics of the final product into critical component characteristics.

3. *Process plan and quality control charts:* This document identifies critical process and product parameters and control points for each.

4. *Operating instructions:* This identifies operations to be performed by plant personnel to assure that important parameters are achieved.

The customer requirement planning matrix is the basis for the QFD concept. Because of its structure, shown in Figure 6.5, it is often referred to as the *House of Quality.* The House of Quality relates customer attributes to the counterpart characteristics to ensure that any engineering decision has a basis in meeting a customer need. In the next section we shall describe the features of the House of Quality in more detail and illustrate its development through an example.

Building the House of Quality

Building the House of Quality consists of six basic steps:

1. Identify customer attributes.

2. Identify counterpart characteristics.

3. Relate the customer attributes to the counterpart characteristics.

4. Conduct an evaluation of competing products.

5. Evaluate counterpart characteristics and develop targets.

FIGURE 6.5 The House of Quality

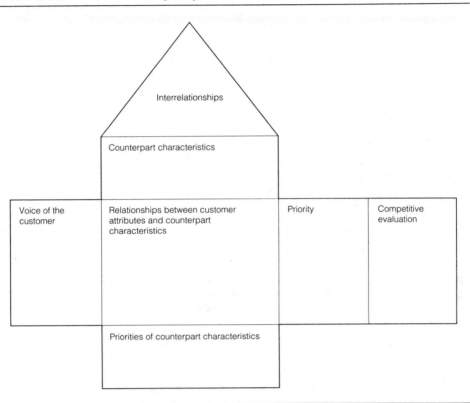

6. Determine which counterpart characteristics to deploy in the remainder of the production process.

Step 1: Identify Customer Attributes. Customer attributes are the product requirements in customer's terms. There are many ways to gather valid customer information. Market research plays an important role in determining what features are important to customers. Market research involves the direct survey of buyers as to their needs, satisfaction, and reasons for purchasing products. Questions such as "What does the customer expect from the product?" and "Why does he or she buy the product?" are important means of identifying customer attributes.

Information on customer needs comes from other sources besides market research. Salespeople have first-hand knowledge of customers' needs, desires, and comments about products. Technicians who repair products understand the reasons for product failure and hear the comments of customers. Designers and engineers can learn much by spending time in sales and repair. Other techniques such as focus groups can be used to learn about customer needs.[13] For example, Nissan has hired anthropologists to help understand what makes people buy cars. They study how a car

---

[13]"A New Era for Auto Quality," *Business Week,* October 22, 1990, pp. 84–96.

fits into consumers' lives by going into homes, videotaping interviews, and observing living conditions. These studies have translated into subtle new features such as an easy closing trunk designed "with women juggling groceries and children in mind." The chief engineer at Lexus spent weeks interviewing U.S. consumers, often at their homes, chatting about hobbies and values. Each Lexus employee must contact at least one owner each week. At Mazda, focus groups discuss everything from food to fashion. Engineers monitor the heart and breathing rates of drivers who narrate their feelings into a microphone as they travel along at different speeds. This helps to determine settings such as steering wheel angle and suspension stiffness so that each model has a "personality" geared to its market.

To illustrate the development of the House of Quality and the QFD process, we shall use the design and development of a new textbook, such as an operations management or quality management text. In designing a textbook, two primary customer attributes might be "meets instructional needs" and "enhances student ability to learn." Such descriptions are not technical specifications; they represent the voice of the customer, the professor who adopts the book and the student who uses it.

An important question to ask is: Are these attributes the *real* needs of the customer, or were they developed from the opinions of editors and authors? It is vitally important to talk to real customers, and not to rely on "second-hand" opinions in determining customer needs. Textbook publishers use a number of techniques to gather information from customers. Since their primary customer is the professor teaching the course, they use manuscript reviews, discussions with sales representatives, discussion with convention representatives, and feedback cards in examination copies.

The most critical and most difficult step of the process is to capture the essence of the customer's comments. It is important to keep the customer's own words so as to prevent misinterpretation by designers and engineers.

Not all customers are end-users. For a manufacturer, customers might include government regulators, wholesalers, and retailers. In writing a textbook, authors must consider the needs of both instructors and students. While much is done to solicit input directly from professors, relatively little information is gathered from students, who are the end-users of texts. This is not unlike the situation that happened in hospitals a few years ago when doctors, not patients, were considered the primary customers of hospitals.

Customer attributes normally are expanded into secondary and tertiary requirements. For a textbook, the primary attribute "meets instructional needs" might be expanded into secondary attributes of "good topical coverage," "appropriate level for the course," and "good exercises." "Good exercises" might be further expanded into "sufficient quantity" and "range of difficulty." These are the customer attributes that are used as inputs to the QFD process. Figure 6.6 shows the voice of the customer in the House of Quality.

Step 2: List the Product Characteristics that Should Be Assured to Meet the Customer Requirements. These "counterpart characteristics" are design attributes expressed in the language of the designer and engineer and represent the technical characteristics that must be deployed throughout the design, manufacturing, and service processes. They must be measurable, since the output will be controlled and compared to objective targets.

FIGURE 6.6   Voice of the Customer

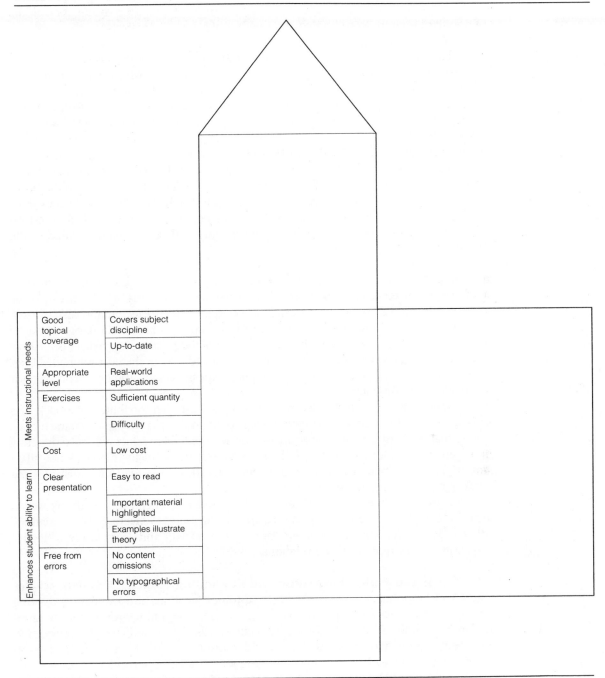

The author and publisher of a textbook have a variety of technical characteristics to consider. These might include the amount of research literature to cite, the amount of popular literature to reference, the number of numerical exercises, the number of open-ended exercises, the design and purpose of software ancillaries, the use of figures and tables, color, correctness of grammar, and size of the book.

The roof of the House of Quality shows the interrelationships between any pair of counterpart characteristics. Various symbols are used to denote these relationships. A typical scheme is to use the symbol ⊙ to denote a very strong relationship, ○ for a strong relationship, and △ to denote a weak relationship. These relationships help in answering questions such as "How does one change of product characteristics affect others?" and in assessing trade-offs between characteristics. For example, increasing one textbook characteristic such as the amount of popular literature coverage might help to improve the number of discussion questions that can be included in the book. However, it will probably increase the size of the book. Thus, strong relationships exist among these characteristics. This process enables features to be focused on collectively rather than individually. Figure 6.7 shows this information added to the House of Quality.

Step 3: Develop a Relationship Matrix Between the Customer Attributes and the Counterpart Characteristics. Customer attributes are listed down the left column; counterpart characteristics are written across the top. In the matrix itself, we use symbols to indicate the degree of relationship in a manner similar to that used in the roof of the House of Quality. The purpose of the relationship matrix is to show whether the final counterpart characteristics adequately cover the customer attributes. This assessment is often based on expert experience, customer responses, or controlled experiments.

Counterpart characteristics can affect several customer attributes. The lack of a strong relationship between a customer attribute and any counterpart characteristic shows that the attributes are not addressed or that the final product will have difficulty in meeting customer needs. Similarly, if a counterpart characteristic does not affect any customer attribute, it may be redundant or the designers may have missed some important customer attribute.

For example, the amount of research literature referenced in a textbook would bear a strong relationship to the customer attributes "covers subject matter," "up-to-date," "omissions in content," "applications focus," and "easy to read." Figure 6.8 shows an example of these relationships.

Step 4: Add Market Evaluation and Key Selling Points. This step includes identifying importance ratings for each customer attribute and evaluating existing products for each of the attributes. Customer importance ratings represent the areas of greatest interest and highest expectations as expressed by the customer. Competitive evaluation helps to highlight the absolute strengths and weaknesses in competing products. This step enables designers to seek opportunities for improvement. It also links QFD to a company's strategic vision and allows priorities to be set in the design process. For example, if an attribute receives a low evaluation on all competitors' products, then focusing on this attribute can help to gain a competitive advantage. Such attributes become key selling points and help to establish promotion strategies.

FIGURE 6.7 **Counterpart Characteristics**

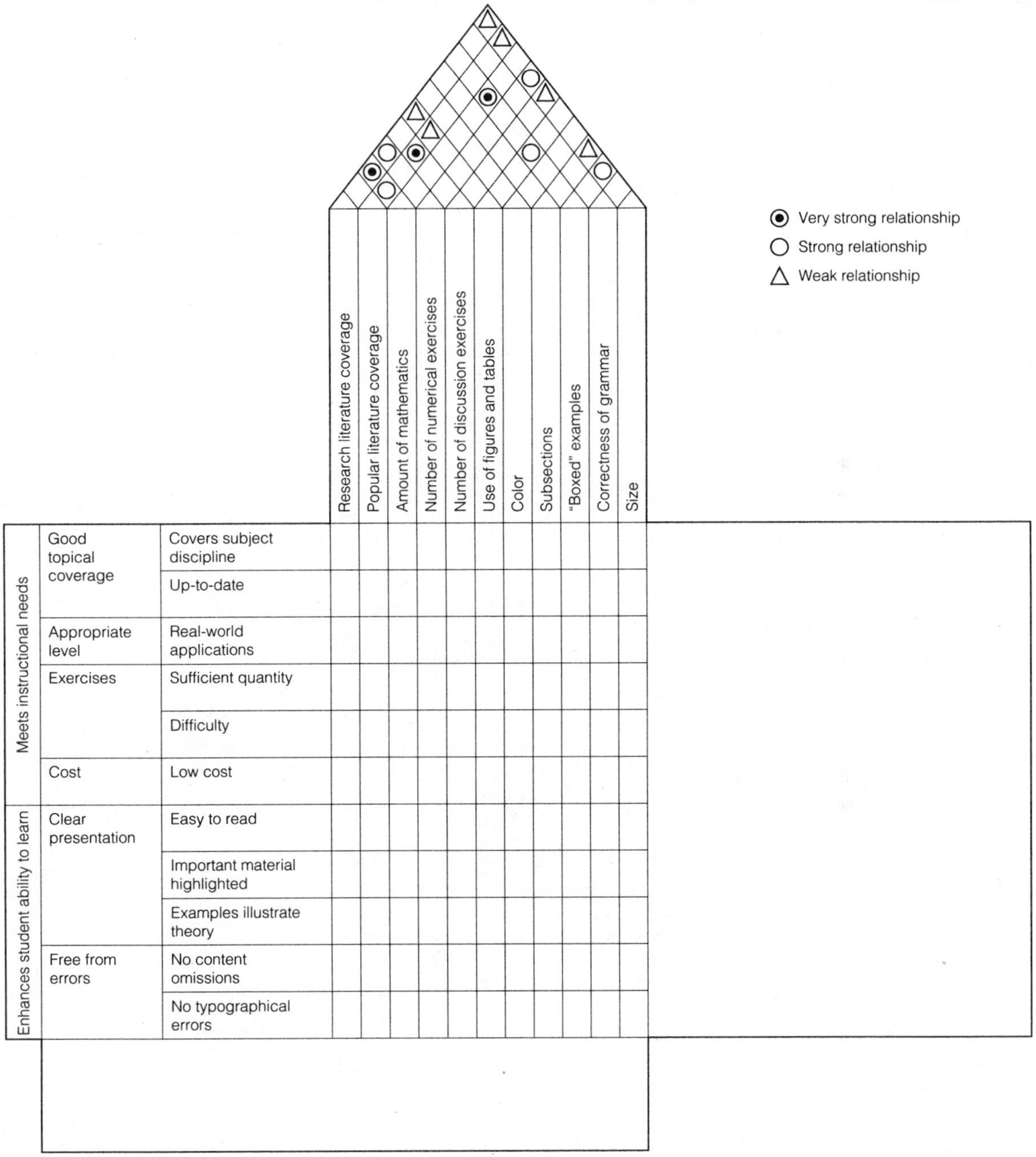

FIGURE 6.8 **Relationship Matrix**

Legend:
- ⊙ Very strong relationship
- ○ Strong relationship
- △ Weak relationship

			Research literature coverage	Popular literature coverage	Amount of mathematics	Number of numerical exercises	Number of discussion exercises	Use of figures and tables	Color	Subsections	"Boxed" examples	Correctness of grammar	Size
Meets instructional needs	Good topical coverage	Covers subject discipline	⊙	⊙							△		○
		Up-to-date	⊙	⊙									○
	Appropriate level	Real-world applications		⊙			○						
	Exercises	Sufficient quantity				⊙	⊙						△
		Difficulty			⊙	○	○						
	Cost	Low cost	○	○	○			△	⊙	○	○		⊙
Enhances student ability to learn	Clear presentation	Easy to read	⊙	△	⊙			△	△	○	○	⊙	
		Important material highlighted						⊙	○	△	⊙		
		Examples illustrate theory	△	△							⊙		
	Free from errors	No content omissions	⊙	⊙									
		No typographical errors			○			○					⊙

In designing a textbook, the author and publisher might find that two major competing textbooks, A and B, are weak in applications, whereas customer surveys of instructors reveal that this is a highly desirable attribute. By focusing on this attribute and using it as a key selling point, a competitive advantage can be gained, as demonstrated in Figure 6.9.

Step 5. Evaluate Counterpart Characteristics of Competitive Products and Develop Targets. This is usually accomplished through in-house testing and then translated into measurable terms. These evaluations are compared with the competitive evaluation of customer attributes to determine inconsistency between customer evaluations and technical evaluations. For example, if a competing product is found to best satisfy a customer attribute but the evaluation of the related counterpart characteristics indicates otherwise, then either the measures used are faulty or else the product has an image difference (either positive toward the competitor or negative toward our product) that is affecting customer perceptions. On the basis of customer importance ratings and existing product strengths and weaknesses, targets for each counterpart characteristic are set. This is shown in Figure 6.10.

For example, suppose that a number of instructors say that extensive research literature coverage is an important attribute. An evaluation of a competitor's text determines that it is *extremely easy* for undergraduates to read and comprehend. These findings seem to be counterintuitive. The answer may be due to one of several possible reasons: (1) The text does not contain the level of research content that the adopting instructors *think* it does; or (2) the research literature is being presented in an extremely novel and readable way that could be adapted and/or improved on; or (3) the writer of the competing textbook is a known guru in the field and has an image as *the expert* whose text should be the primary one to be considered.

Step 6. Select Counterpart Characteristics to Be Deployed in the Remainder of the Process. This means identifying the characteristics that have a strong relationship to customer needs, have poor competitive performance, or are strong selling points. These characteristics will need to be "deployed" or translated into the language of each function in the design and production process so that proper actions and controls are taken to ensure that the voice of the customer is maintained. Those characteristics that are not identified as critical do not need such rigorous attention.

For example, if "important material stands out" is an important customer attribute in a textbook, then particular attention must be paid to the counterpart characteristics relating to chapter layout—the use of figures and tables, subsections, and color. If in addition, high importance is given to the attributes of "covers subject matter" and "up-to-date," then the size of the book is of little concern. This is also given in Figure 6.10.

Using the House of Quality

The House of Quality provides marketing with an important tool to understand customer needs and it gives top management strategic direction. However, it is only the first step in the QFD process. The voice of the customer must be carried throughout the production process. Three other "houses of quality" are used to

FIGURE 6.9 Competitive Evaluation

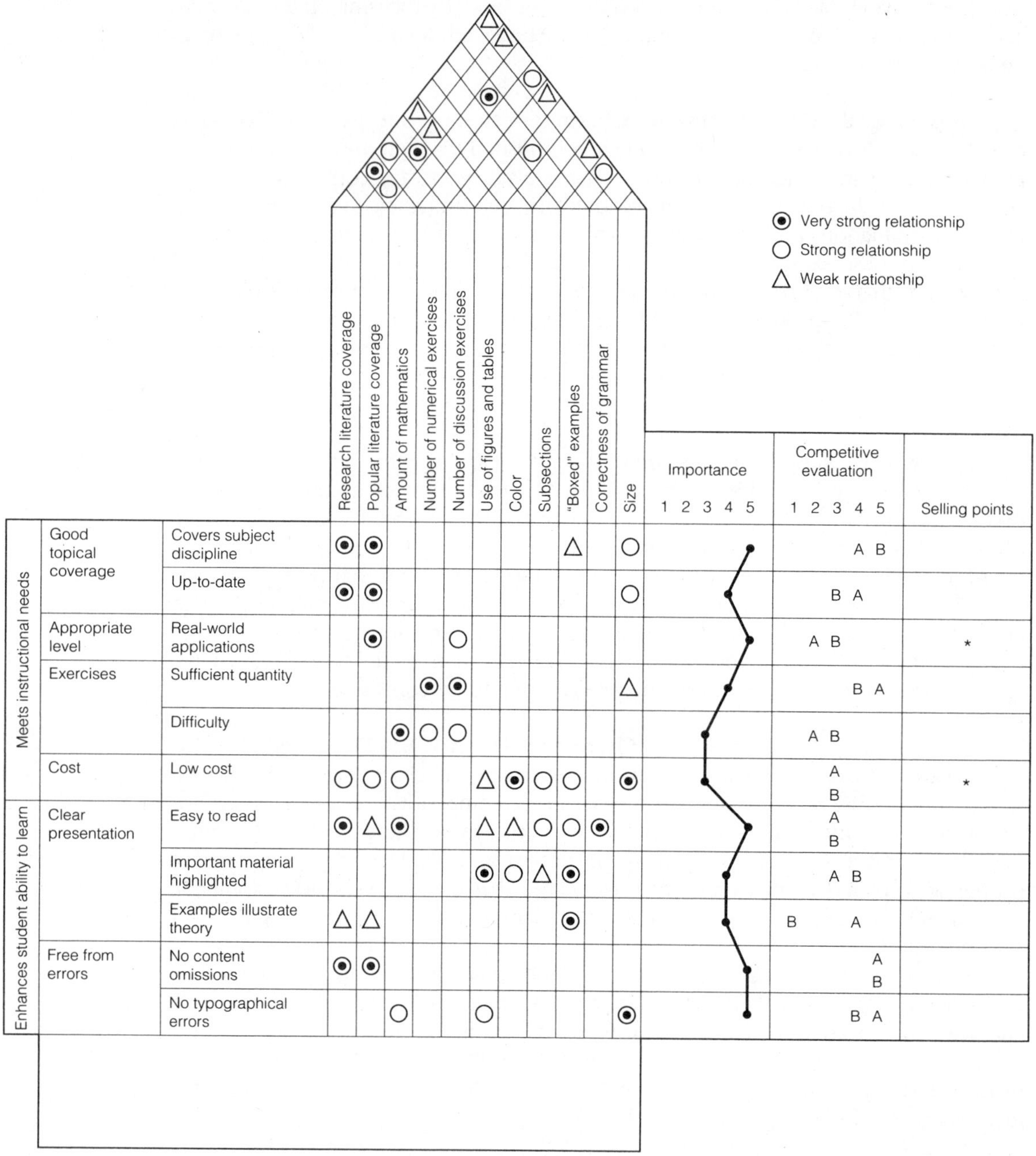

FIGURE 6.10 Completed House of Quality

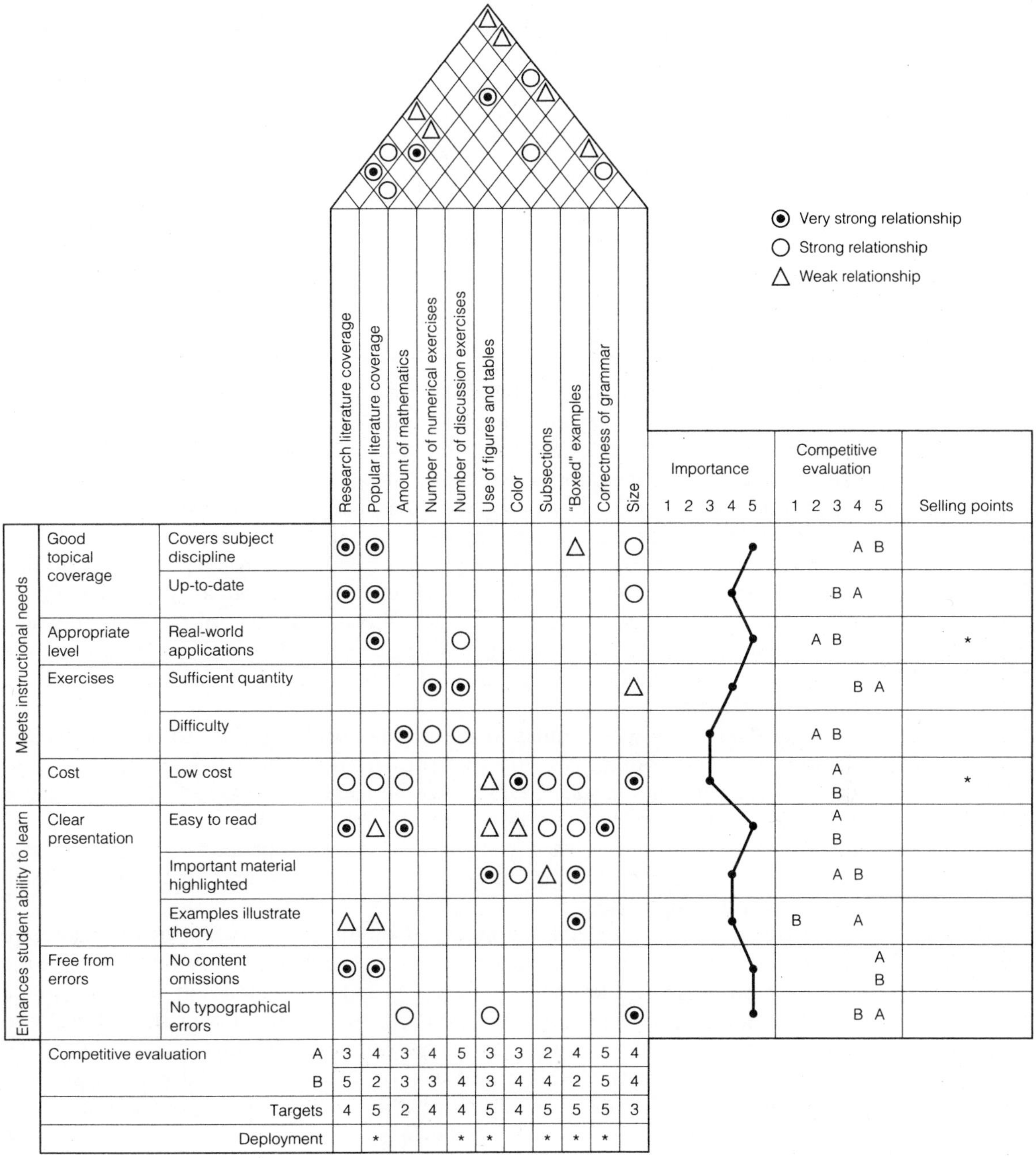

Legend:
- ◉ Very strong relationship
- ○ Strong relationship
- △ Weak relationship

		Research literature coverage	Popular literature coverage	Amount of mathematics	Number of numerical exercises	Number of discussion exercises	Use of figures and tables	Color	Subsections	"Boxed" examples	Correctness of grammar	Size	Importance (1 2 3 4 5)	Competitive evaluation (1 2 3 4 5)	Selling points
Meets instructional needs — Good topical coverage	Covers subject discipline	◉	◉						△			○		A B	
	Up-to-date	◉	◉									○		B A	
Appropriate level	Real-world applications		◉		○									A B	★
Exercises	Sufficient quantity				◉	◉						△		B A	
	Difficulty			◉	○	○								A B	
Cost	Low cost	○	○	○			△	◉	○	○		◉		A / B	★
Enhances student ability to learn — Clear presentation	Easy to read	◉	△	◉			△	△	○	○	◉			A / B	
	Important material highlighted						◉	○	△	◉				A B	
	Examples illustrate theory	△	△							◉				B A	
Free from errors	No content omissions	◉	◉											A / B	
	No typographical errors			○			○					◉		B A	

		Research literature coverage	Popular literature coverage	Amount of mathematics	Number of numerical exercises	Number of discussion exercises	Use of figures and tables	Color	Subsections	"Boxed" examples	Correctness of grammar	Size
Competitive evaluation	A	3	4	3	4	5	3	3	2	4	5	4
	B	5	2	3	3	4	3	4	4	2	5	4
Targets		4	5	2	4	4	5	4	5	5	5	3
Deployment			★		★	★			★	★	★	

deploy the voice of the customer to component parts characteristics, process planning, and production planning. We shall continue with the textbook development example to illustrate these concepts.

The textbook production process can be described in the following fashion:[14]

Stage	Functions
Acquisition	Proposal
	Review
	Contracting
Development	Writing
	Editing
Preproduction	Galleys
	Proofs
	Page makeup
	Cover design
Production	Printing

The textbook production process begins with a proposal, with perhaps a draft chapter or two that the author(s) sends to the publisher. After simultaneous reviews by professors who teach in that field, the idea is approved and the author(s) proceed with the writing stage. After further reviews and editing, the text goes into the preproduction stages of galleys, proofs, page makeup, and cover design. Galleys are used to check to ensure that wording, citations, and other details are correct. Proofs provide a check on the final typesetting process; page makeup involves adding pictures, figures, and complex tables; and cover design, of course, involves design of the cover. Then begins the relatively long and complex stage of production, which includes such processes as printing, cutting the pages, binding, and packaging the texts. The concept of QFD is to ensure that the voice of the customer is carried through each stage.

The second house is similar to the first house but applies to subsystems and components. The counterpart characteristics from the first house are related to detailed characteristics of subsystems and components (see Figure 6.11). At this stage, target values representing the best values for fit, function, and appearance are determined. For example, each chapter in a textbook could be considered as a component of the complete product and will have some unique characteristics in terms of writing and style.

Most of the QFD activities represented by the first two houses of quality are performed by product development and engineering functions. At the next stage, the planning activities begin to involve supervisors and production line operators. In the next house, the process plan is developed relating the component characteristics to key process operations. It represents the transition from planning to execution. If a product component parameter is critical and is created or affected during the process, it becomes a control point. This tells us what to monitor and inspect and forms the basis for a quality control plan for achieving those critical characteristics that are crucial to achieving customer satisfaction.

In our textbook example, for instance, we might find that the characteristic "free from typographical errors" relates to a component characteristic "correctness of

---

[14]H. Richard Priesmeyer, "Integrating Educational Software and Textbook Development," *Academic Computing,* September 1988, pp. 32–33, 50–51.

FIGURE 6.11 **The Four Houses of Quality**

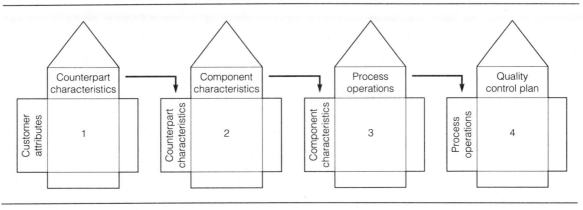

numerical computations." A key process operation might be to have an external individual check all numerical computations directly from the galley proofs, during the preproduction stage.

Finally, the last house relates the control points to specific requirements for quality control. This includes specifying control methods, sample sizes, and so on to achieve the appropriate level of quality. This might involve final page makeup checking in the preproduction stage and statistical process control steps taken by the printer and binder to ensure that a quality product is produced.

The vast majority of applications of QFD in the United States concentrate on the first and, to a lesser extent, the second house of quality. Lawrence Sullivan, who brought QFD to the West, suggests that the third and fourth houses of quality offer far more significant benefits, especially in the United States.[15] In Japan, managers, engineers, and workers are more naturally cross-functional and tend to promote group effort and consensus thinking. In the United States, we are more vertically oriented and tend to suboptimize for individual and/or departmental achievements. The United States tends to promote breakthrough achievements, which often inhibits cross-functional interaction. If U.S. companies can maintain the breakthrough culture with emphasis on continuous improvement through more effective cross-functional interactions as supported by QFD, it can establish a competitive advantage over foreign competitors. The third and fourth houses of quality utilize the knowledge of about 80% of a company's employees—supervisors and operators; if they are not used, this potential is wasted.

PLANNING FOR QUALITY IN SERVICE ORGANIZATIONS

Many aspects of services are identical to manufacturing. Thus, the quality planning process for services is often the same as for manufacturing. The major goals of service quality planning are to produce services that satisfy customer needs and expectations,

---

[15]L. P. Sullivan, "Quality Function Deployment: The Latent Potential of Phases III and IV," in A. Richard Shores, "A TQM Approach," pp. 265–279.

to produce the required services efficiently, and to plan for quality control and quality improvement under operating conditions.[16]

However, some aspects of services are quite different from manufacturing and require special attention. Managers in service organizations do not have as well defined products as do manufacturing firms. For example, even though all banks offer similar tangible goods such as checking, loans, automatic tellers, and so forth, the real differentiating factor among banks is the service provided. Thus, to plan for quality in services, one must carefully define criteria that determine fitness for use and customer satisfaction. To do this, managers must talk with and listen to customers. Most service processes involve a greater interaction with the customer, often making it easier to identify needs and expectations. On the other hand, customers often cannot define their needs for service until after they have some point of reference or comparison. Also, needs are dynamic and frequently change. These factors can make identification of needs difficult.

The second major planning activity is developing procedures to produce the service efficiently. This includes doing things right the first time, minimizing process complexities, and making the process immune to inadvertent human errors, particularly when interacting with customers. A complicating factor is that service processes often involve both internal and external activities. For example, in a bank, poor service can result from the way that tellers treat customers and also from poor quality of computers and communications equipment beyond the control of the tellers. Internal activities must primarily be concerned with efficiency (quality of conformance), while external activities—with direct customer interaction—must focus on effectiveness (quality of design). All too often, those involved in internal operations do not understand how their work affects the customer who they do not see. It is just as important for those involved in internal activities to understand how they add value to the customer.

It is quite easy to deal with symptoms of errors in internal operations and to introduce extra inspection steps rather than to seek the root cause of errors and correct them. This leads to inefficiencies and unnecessary costs. To prevent errors in external activities, one must plan by designing work so that tasks cannot be performed unless the person doing it devotes complete attention to the work. This requires keen insight into the work process. This is often gained through suggestions from the people that do the work.

Because service organizations are primarily labor-intensive, developing measurable quality characteristics is difficult. For example, a "clear picture" on a television set can be precisely defined and measured. However, the quality characteristic "courtesy" of the TV repairperson is much more ambiguous and difficult to measure. In some cases, it may be sufficient to develop a checklist of activities that must be performed. For instance, a hotel receptionist might be required to greet the customer in a friendly fashion, use the customer's name, provide an overview of hotel services, give instructions on how to find the elevator, and state that if anything else is needed to please call.

As we have noted in earlier chapters, time, completeness, and consistency are vital quality characteristics of service activities. In planning for quality in services, Zimmerman and Enell suggest some questions that should be considered:[17]

---

[16]Raghn N. Kacker, "Quality Planning for Service Industries," *Quality Progress,* August 1988, pp. 39–42.

[17]Charles D. Zimmerman III and John W. Enell, "Service Industries," Sec. 33 in J. M. Juran, ed., *Juran's Quality Control Handbook,* 4th ed. (New York: McGraw-Hill, 1988).

- What service standards are already in place?

- Which of these standards have been clearly communicated to all service personnel? Have these been communicated to the public?

- Which of these require refinement?

- What is the final result of the service provided? What should it ideally be?

With regard to time, some important questions include the following:

- What is the maximum access time that a patron will tolerate without feeling inconvenienced?

- How long should it take to perform the service itself?

- What is the maximum time for completion of service before the customer's view of the service is negatively affected?

- When do we consider that the service begins and what is used as an indicator of completion of the service?

- How many different people must deal with the consumer in completing the service?

Concerning completeness and consistency, a service organization should ask:

- What components of the service are essential? Desirable? Superfluous?

- What components or aspects of service *must* be controlled to deliver a service encounter of equal quality each time it occurs?

- Which components can differ from encounter to encounter while still leading to a total service encounter that meets standards?

- What products that affect its service performance does a service organization obtain from other sources?

Answers to such questions, while difficult to develop, provide important information for quality planning. Techniques such as quality function deployment can be used in service quality planning.

Finally, service industries also must pay attention to auxiliary and unobligatory services. Auxiliary and unobligatory services are those extra services that are provided in connection with a primary service or product.[18] These include:

- no breaks in service

- safety

- information to reduce the customer's anxiety and inconvenience

- clearly explained instructions

- extra services at no extra cost

- services that make the customer feel important.

---

[18]Kacker, "Quality Planning."

Auxiliary services often are "dissatisfiers"; failure to provide them results in dissatisfaction. Unobligatory services are the "exciters/delighters" that customers often do not expect.

PLANNING FOR IMPLEMENTATION: POLICY DEPLOYMENT

Top management requires a method to ensure that their plans and strategies are successfully executed within the organization. The Japanese deploy strategy through a process known as *hoshin planning,* or *policy deployment.* Hoshin means "policy" or "policy deployment." Policy deployment is a planning and implementation methodology that ties improvement activities to the long-term strategies of the organization. Policy deployment is driven by data and supported by documentation. It emphasizes organization-wide planning and setting of priorities for improvement.

Policy deployment is based on the following principles:[19]

- Top management is responsible for developing and communicating a vision, then building organization-wide commitment to its achievement.

- The vision is deployed through the development and execution of annual policy statements (plans).

- All levels of employees actively participate in generating a strategy and action plans to attain the vision.

- At each level, progressively more detailed and concrete means to accomplish the annual plans are determined. The plans are hierarchical, cascading downward from top management's plans. There should be a clear link to common goals in activities throughout the organizational hierarchy.

- Each organizational level sets priorities to focus on areas needing significant improvement, and to concentrate on activities that are the most highly related to the vision.

- Implementation responsibilities, timetables, and progress measures are determined.

- Frequent evaluation and modification based on feedback from regularly scheduled audits of the process are provided.

- Plans and actions are developed based on analysis of the root causes of a problem, rather than only on the symptoms.

- Planning has a high degree of detail, including the anticipation of possible problems during implementation.

- Emphasis is on the improvement of the process, as opposed to a results-only orientation.

Policy deployment is a hierarchical system that starts with the CEO of the company. The CEO states a few critical hoshins, which include an objective statement, a goal or target, a strategy, a measure, and the person who is accountable for

---

[19]The Ernst & Young Quality Improvement Consulting Group, *Total Quality: An Executive's Guide for the 1990s* (Homewood, IL: Dow Jones-Irwin, 1990).

achievement of the strategy. These hoshins represent the organization's high-level objectives that support the long-term vision. An example of an objective might be "to improve delivery," which supports the long-term vision of "to be the industry leader in customer satisfaction." Goals specify numerically the degree of change that is expected. These should be challenging, but people should feel that they are attainable. Strategies specify the means to achieve the goals. They include more specific actions to be taken. Measures are specific checkpoints to ensure the effectiveness of individual elements of the strategy. At the next level of the organization, managers develop their own hoshins, goals, strategies, and measures, and the process is repeated throughout the business until the plans are complete for every operation.

An example of policy deployment is provided by Imai:[20]

> To illustrate the need for policy deployment, let us consider the following case: The president of an airline company proclaims that he believes in safety and that his corporate goal is to make sure that safety is maintained throughout the company. This proclamation is prominently featured in the company's quarterly report and its advertising. Let us further suppose that the department managers also swear a firm belief in safety. The catering manager says he believes in safety. The pilots say they believe in safety. The flight crews say they believe in safety. Everyone in the company practices safety. True? Or might everyone simply be paying lip service to the idea of safety?
>
> On the other hand, if the president states that safety is company policy and works with his division managers to develop a plan for safety that defines their responsibilities, everyone will have a very specific subject to discuss. Safety will become a real concern. For the manager in charge of catering services, safety might mean maintaining the quality of food to avoid customer dissatisfaction or illness.
>
> In that case, how does he ensure that the food is of top quality? What sorts of control points and check points does he establish? How does he ensure that there is no deterioration in food quality in-flight? Who checks the temperature of the refrigerators or the condition of the oven while the plane is in the air?
>
> Only when safety is translated into specific actions with specific control and check points established for each employee's job may safety be said to have been truly deployed as a policy. Policy deployment calls for everyone to interpret policy in light of his own responsibilities and for everyone to work out criteria to check his success in carrying out the policy.

While policy deployment bears some similarity to management by objectives (MBO), an approach that is condemned by Deming, there are some important differences. First, MBO focuses on the performance of individual employees rather than on improvement of the organization as a whole. Attainment of objectives is closely tied to performance evaluation and rewards. Second, in MBO, objectives generally are not supportive of the company's vision but are set independently. Third, the focus of MBO is primarily a means of management control; in practice, most subordinates succumb to their supervisor's wishes. Finally, in MBO, objectives usually are not used in daily work, but are only resurrected during performance reviews. Policy deployment, in contrast, focuses more on the process of planning how objectives will be met and what actions individual managers and employees will take.

---

[20]M. Imai, *Kaizen: The Key to Japan's Competitive Success* (New York: McGraw-Hill, 1986), pp. 144–145.

Quality Function Deployment at Digital Equipment Corporation[21]

Digital Equipment Corporation (DEC) was interested in developing direct access to an automated purchasing system for noncomputer-literate consumers. The system was to be made available in public places with accompanying telecommunications and terminal system development. DEC needed the right combination of features, pricing,

distribution, and promotion for the system so that it could be used frequently and also be profitable. QFD was applied by taking the four houses of quality and changing their names so that software engineers would have a better understanding of the concepts. This is shown in Figure 6.12.

They began the process by brainstorming ideas of what the service should achieve. (The individuals involved were typical consumers of the targeted service.) Examples were:

- I want to see a high-quality photo of every product.

[21]Adapted from George Van Treeck and Ray Thackeray, "Quality Function Deployment at Digital Equipment Corporation," *Concurrent Engineering,* Vol. 1, No. 1, January/February 1991, pp. 14–20.

FIGURE 6.12 **Adaptation of the Houses of Quality to Software Development**

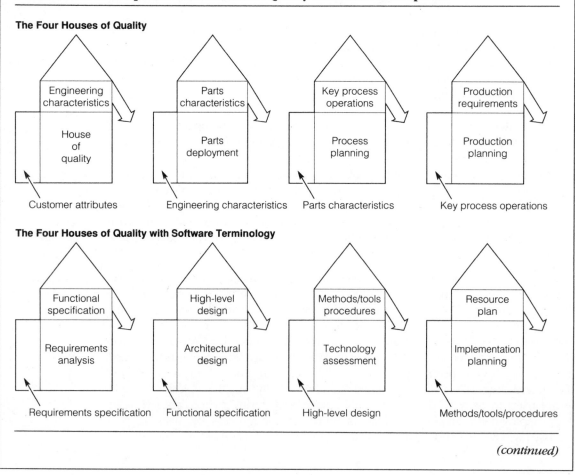

(continued)

- I want my phone number, address, and other information kept secure.

- I want to be able to access the system day or night.

- I want a simple method of payment.

More than 100 requirements were created. Potential customers were then queried for their inputs and a few minor features were added.

The next step was to create functional specifications. For example, a security function had to exist to meet the requirement that personal information be kept confidential. This was then broken down into more detailed functions. Another example is that a person who has never used a computer before must be able to use this service within 30 seconds without having to read any manuals or refer to on-line help.

At this point, they departed from the conventional QFD process and did not conduct any weighting exercise because observations have shown that weighting can delay the process, be difficult for customers to do if they cannot see a working prototype, and inhibit engineers' creativity. Figure 6.13 shows a high-level view of the matrix that was developed.

The developers discovered that the functional specifications became the basis for a test plan. Tests could be written immediately from the first house of quality, independent of design implementation, which increases the amount of concurrency in the development process and leads to a faster time-to-market.

The second house of quality consisted of determining high-level design elements for each functional specification. They would continually think that certain problems had not been considered, but find out that they had already addressed the problem 99% of the time by looking at the matrix. The design was more than just a software design; it included distribution channels, pricing, and selling the service as well as the hardware terminals, telecommunications, and billing systems required.

QFD enabled DEC to evaluate and make choices between critical design alternatives. For example, consider the following requirements:

- It must be easy for the noncomputer customer to use.

- It must perform well no matter how many people are using the system.

- It must be inexpensive to order products through this service.

Some of the functional specifications might be:

- Noncomputer-literate customers must be able to use the system within 30 seconds with no manuals or on-line help.

- It must always respond to any user input within one second.

- The cost of use must be less than $15 per access.

Some of the design decisions to meet the ease-of-use requirement might be to:

- Use a very simple keyboard or no keyboard at all in order to eliminate confusion and computer phobia.

- Have the customer point at the desired option rather than use a keyboard or keyboard commands.

- Use a bit-mapped display with 3-D buttons on the screens for intuitive pressing to pick options, an approach with which most customers are already familiar.

However, bit-mapped displays cost more money, which affects the low cost of manufacture and capital equipment investment criteria. They also affect performance if each display is miles away from the central data base because it takes a long time to download bit maps through phone lines. In addition, bit-mapped graphics require a lot of computer resources, which increases the capital equipment investment. At this point, numbers can be put into the cells of the matrix to see the effect of one design feature on other design features and requirements.

The third house of quality was used to resolve design alternative issues. Design features were mapped to the technology, procedures, and methods used to create the product. They looked at various pointing technologies to meet the ease-of-use criteria (cursor keys, mice, finger pads, touch screens). They also took into account such factors as an angry person yanking a mouse or smashing a fist

(continued)

FIGURE 6.13 QFD Requirements Analysis Matrix

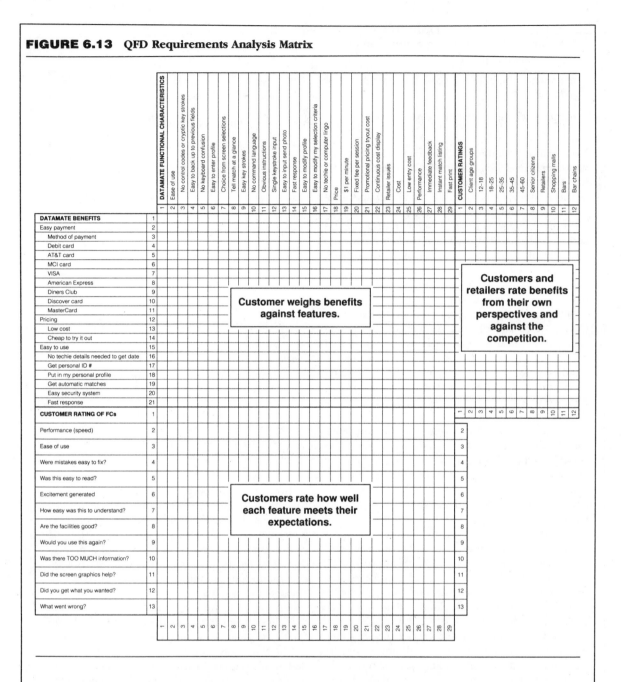

on the keyboard, or someone spilling a drink on the keyboard. This provided a clear record of the trade-offs to be made.

The final house of quality matches the technology, methods, and procedures with people, time, equipment, building facilities, and money. It can be very costly to misjudge the resources and time required if the requirements and the design are not complete and accurate. To reduce this risk, DEC created a prototype and test-marketed it, which

(continued)

allowed them to refine the first three houses before completing the fourth house. Building a prototype would require little rework if the initial requirements were close to being complete and accurate. With the prototype, they could then ask customers to rate the service against the competition which would provide competitive weights in the first house of quality. At this point, the engineers could determine the importance of design features and make better trade-offs.

DEC found that one of the benefits of QFD was that the first house of quality provided information to use in sales literature and advertisements, eliminating the need for this to be done by the marketing department. Engineers are now doing their own marketing, and breaking down traditional barriers between marketing and engineering. They are performing traditional marketing functions, including surveys, prototype testing, and developing key items for advertising.

Key Issues for Discussion

1. Explain the relationships and analogies between the original four houses of quality and DEC's implementation. How are they similar? How are they different?

2. DEC has suggested that marketing's role has been essentially eliminated. Can this be done in other industries? Does this present any limitations? What implications does this have for business organizations?

Summary of Key Points

- Planning is the process by which goals and objectives are determined and actions are selected in order to achieve desired results. Fundamental questions that must be addressed are what, how, when, and who?

- Planning is hierarchical in nature. Plans made by top management specify the goals for middle management, which must be achieved at the supervisory level. Planning at these three levels is called strategic, tactical, and operational, respectively.

- The bulk of the responsibility for quality planning falls to top and middle management employees.

- The planning process begins by determining an organization's vision and purpose, which define its mission. This is followed by a fact-finding environmental survey; the development of specific, measurable objectives; determination of action steps to meet objectives; evaluation of the plan; and the establishment of a control mechanism.

- Benchmarking is the process of searching for the best practices in any industry that lead to superior performance, determining how best-in-class organizations achieve those performance levels, and using the information to improve a company's targets, strategies, and implementation.

- All quality planning must be customer-driven. Customer needs must be identified, translated into product specifications, and realized through the production process. How well this process maintains the character of customer needs will affect final customer perceptions.

- Customer needs include dissatisfiers that are expected in a product, satisfiers that customers expressly state they want, and exciters/delighters that are not expected.

Special market research efforts are needed to elicit information on dissatisfiers and exciters/delighters.

■ Customers and engineers/designers speak different languages. Quality function deployment (QFD) is a technique to ensure that the voice of the customer is carried through the design and production process.

■ The major planning document in QFD is called the House of Quality and provides a planning structure for relating customers' needs to technical specifications and ensuring that key specifications are identified and deployed throughout the subsequent production process.

■ Service organizations present special problems for quality planning. The development of measurable quality characteristics is difficult, and both internal and external activities affect the quality of the service.

■ Policy deployment, or hoshin planning, is a methodology for setting objectives, targets, strategies, and measurements at every level of an organization to ensure that the long-term objectives of the organization are achieved. Active participation by every employee with a focus toward continuous improvement differentiates policy deployment from management by objectives, which is focused primarily on performance appraisal.

Questions for Review and Discussion

1. Define planning in the context of quality management. Why is planning important?

2. Explain the what, how, when, and who classifications of quality planning. Give examples.

3. Discuss the hierarchical nature of planning. What types of planning activities are carried out at each level?

4. How does the hierarchical approach to planning relate to quality? Specifically, what quality activities are appropriate to each level.

5. Explain what is meant by *vision* and *purpose* of an organization.

6. Discuss the steps in the planning process. Choose a manufacturing firm or a service organization and outline how these steps might be carried out.

7. Why is it important that the mission statement of any organization make reference to the anticpated quality of the firm's product? Find the mission statement for a university, a hospital, a manufacturer, or a service firm. What emphasis, if any, is placed on quality in the mission statement?

8. Explain how quality plans should be made more focused and specific down the organizational hierarchy through the use of the mission statements, objectives, policies, procedures, and rules. What coordination is required to ensure that such plans are carried out effectively?

9. Explain the concept of benchmarking. How might this process be used to improve classroom instruction in a business school?

10. How is the importance of planning reflected in the Baldrige Award criteria?

11. Choose a firm or industry noted for its high quality. Through library research or personal interviews, determine how it makes its quality plans operational. Were there any surprises in your findings?

12. Discuss how real customer needs and expectations can change during the production process.

13. Define Kano's classification of customer needs and its significance.

14. Explain the basic principles of quality function deployment. What is required to implement them in an organization?

15. What are the principal benefits of QFD?

16. Outline the process of building the House of Quality. What types of personnel (e.g., marketing, engineering, manufacturing, etc.) should be involved in each step of the process?

17. In what ways did Juran's focus on quality planning anticipate those of QFD and the Baldrige Award? Do you see any gaps in his concept of planning versus QFD and the Baldrige criteria? Explain.

18. What special problems do service organizations have with regard to quality planning?

19. Explain the methodology of policy deployment. How does it differ from MBO?

Problems

1. Using whatever "market research" techniques that you feel are appropriate, define a set of customer attributes for

   a. an "excellent cup of coffee"
   b. a picnic cooler
   c. your college registration process.

   For each case, determine a set of counterpart characteristics and construct the relationship matrix for the House of Quality.

2. *PC Week,* a computer periodical, conducts reviews of software products. Readers are surveyed and asked to rate the importance of six or more attributes for each product set (i.e., a description of the type of product; not the actual product names) and are invited to list other attributes they believe are important. The five attributes that rank highest in importance to respondents are communicated to product reviewers who score each product in the set against each of the five criteria on a scale of 0 to 10. A "scoreboard" is prepared that lists the five attributes in order of importance along with a weighting factor based on respondents' evaluations and the actual scores assigned by reviewers for each of the attributes.

   Figure 6.14 shows such a scoreboard for six project management packages that offer resource leveling, can handle at least 500 tasks with as many as 500 resources, and cost less than $700.

  a. What information is contained in this scoreboard that applies to the quality function deployment process?

  b. Try to develop a House of Quality matrix using this information. What further information do you need?

  c. If you were considering developing a competing product, how would you use this information?

3. Most children (and college students) like to assemble and fly balsa wood gliders. From your own experiences (or from interviews with other students), define a set of customer attributes that would make a good glider. (Even better, buy one and test it to determine these attributes yourself.) If you were to design and manufacture such a product, how would you define a set of counterpart characteristics for the design? Using your results, construct a relationship matrix for a House of Quality.

4. Review the Hughes Aircraft mission statement presented in this chapter. The mission statement includes a set of goals for the firm and actions that the firm can take. Thinking of the goals as "customer attributes" and the actions as "counterpart characteristics," build a relationship matrix similar to the House of Quality. How

FIGURE 6.14 **Project Management Scoreboard**

	Computer Associates International Inc. Super-Project Expert 1.1	InstaPlan Corp. InstaPlan 2.0 (with tracking option)	Microsoft Corp. Project 4.0	William H. Roetzheim & Assoc. Structured Project Manager's Toolbox 2.0	Scitor Corp. Project Scheduler 4 2.0	Symantec Corp. Time Line 3.0
1. Ease of use (1.09)	8	7	7	7	10	8
2. Ease of report generation (1.04)	6	6	7	6	6	7
3. Quality of documentation (1.01)	8	7	6	3	8	8
4. Quality of critical path method task-analysis support (0.96)	7	6	6	9	9	8
5. Number of resources automatically leveled (0.91)	4	2	6	10	10	6
Weighted Score	6.7	5.7	6.4	6.9	8.6	7.4

1. Based on quality of command interface, logical command sequences, and on-line and context-sensitive help. 2. Based on the ease of selecting standard reports, number of options available, and the capacity to develop customized reports. 3. Based on clarity and organization of the documentation, including table of contents, index, section tabs, and page headers or footers. 4. Based on different dependencies, required start and end dates, number of successors and predecessors, number of tasks and number of resources per task. 5. Based on number and quality of automatic resource leveling and use of float and task priorities.

would you assess the strength of relationships among the various factors? How could this be used to prioritize company actions in an action plan? Can you think of other innovative uses of the House of Quality structure for planning?

Case Problem

A large national consumer products corporation has recently acquired a regional chain of fast food restaurants, BurgerMate. Plans are under way to expand this chain nationally. As a result, they are looking seriously at developing improved products and services. Based on consumer surveys, the company has determined that it is vital to improve their basic burger in order to capture a significant share of market from other competitors. They have decided to approach this using quality function deployment.

Using focus groups and other market research methods, they have found that consumers have four primary expectations for a hamburger. It should be tasty (moist and flavorful), healthy (nutritious), visually appealing (thick and "beefy"), and have good value for the money. Based on this research, the company has found that the highest importance is placed on nutrition and value, followed by visual appeal and flavor. Moistness was only casually noted as an important attribute in the surveys.

BurgerMate faces three major competitors in this market: Grabby's, Queenburger, and Sandy's. Studies of their products have yielded the information shown in Exhibit 1. Results of the consumer panel ratings for each of these competitors are shown in Exhibit 2 (a 1 to 5 scale with 5 being the best):

EXHIBIT 2

Attribute	Grabby's	Queenburger	Sandy's
Moistness	4	4	5
Flavor	4	5	3
Nutrition	4	2	3
Visual appeal	3	5	4
Value	5	3	4

Using this information, construct a completed House of Quality and develop a deployment plan for a new burger. On what attributes should the company focus its marketing efforts?

EXHIBIT 1

	Price	Size (oz.)	Calories	Sodium (mg.)	Fat (%)
Grabby's	$1.45	5.5	492	576	15
Queenburger	$1.85	9.0	663	1081	16
Sandy's	$1.55	7.25	547	886	23

Bibliography

Akao, Yoji (ed.) *Quality Function Deployment.* Cambridge, MA: Productivity Press, 1990.

Cohen, L. "QFD: An Application Perspective from DEC," *National Productivity Review,* Vol. 7, No. 3, 1988, pp. 197–208.

Conti, Tito. "Process Management and Quality Function Deployment," *Quality Progress,* December 1989, pp. 45–48.

Eureka, William E., and Ryan, Nancy E. *The Customer-Driven Company.* Dearborn, MI: American Supplier Institute, 1988.

Fortuna, R. "Beyond Quality: Taking SPC Upstream," *Quality Progress,* June 1988, pp. 23–28.

Johnson, George. "Benchmarking to Success," *APICS—The Performance Advantage,* July 1991, pp. 12–13.

King, R. "Listening to the Voice of the Customer," *National Productivity Review,* Vol. 6, No. 3, 1987, pp. 277–281.

Newcomb, John E. "Management by Policy Deployment," *Quality,* January 1989, pp. 28–30.

Reid, R., and Hermann, M. "QFD . . . The Voice of the Customer," *Journal for Quality and Participation,* December 1989, pp. 44–46.

Sullivan, L. "Quality Function Deployment," *Quality Progress,* June 1986, pp. 39–50.

CHAPTER 7

Organizing for Quality

The previous chapter discussed the planning process and its implications in quality assurance. Organization links planning with doing. An integral part of the planning process is to decide *what* tasks must be performed and *who* will carry them out; this defines the organization.

What tasks must be carried out requires a detailed and thoughtful analysis of an organization's quality objectives. *Who* will carry out the plans implies that managers and workers must be found with the right skills and characteristics to get the job done. Every employee in the organization must have a clear task assignment that is challenging and interesting. This requires careful selection, training, supervision, and recognition of employees. Hence, task design is an important component of organization. An effective organization also depends on providing the right policies, procedures, tools, and support to get the tasks done, along with adequate communication and cooperation between workers and managers.

The formal link between the *what* and the *who* of organizing consists of assigning authority, responsibility, reporting lines, and performance standards to individuals at each level of the organization. The informal link, which usually makes the difference between a mediocre organization and an excellent one, is called the *corporate culture.*

The major steps in organizing are (1) to identify the tasks that must be performed, (2) to assign responsibility for these tasks, and (3) to assign work to individuals to accomplish these tasks. Following a brief introduction to the scope of organizing, the remainder of the chapter addresses these three steps in detail.

THE SCOPE OF ORGANIZING

Organization to achieve certain purposes and objectives has been taking place since the human race came into existence. The basic organizational unit in all societies is the family. People in families learned to cooperate on various tasks and activities at a very early time to survive and prosper. Typical tasks of these early "organizations" included the following.

- Obtaining basic resources such as food and materials for clothing.

- Processing materials; for example, cooking, making clothes, creating weapons.

- Developing human resources; for example, teaching children to do the two preceding tasks.

- Trading processed products for basic resources.

- Defending against attacks by animals or hostile humans.

Generally, each individual performed all of these tasks at one time or another. Quality control was automatic, and lack of quality was potentially deadly; anyone who did not do the task properly was subject to starvation, injury, or calamity.

In the early days of manufacturing, work was performed by skilled craftsmen who were responsible for most manufacturing tasks such as procurement, production, inspection, and sales. With the industrial revolution, organizations grew and became more complex. Different individuals assumed responsibility for different tasks; and they organized themselves into work groups, departments, and different functional units. Since the quality assurance function involves people throughout the entire organization, it is essential that it be organized effectively.

We define **organizing** as the process of assigning work and responsibility to functions and individuals along with the appropriate delegation of authority. The three principal reasons for organizing are as follows:

1. To establish lines of authority.

2. To improve efficiency and quality of work through synergism.

3. To improve communication.

These reasons for organizing would be unnecessary if there were no common objectives toward which people in organizations were working. The purpose of any organization is to carry out the planned activities necessary to meet organizational objectives. Therefore, the organizational structure should be designed to support the established direction in which the organization is moving, and it should be modified whenever there is a significant change in direction. Often, managers are hesitant to make needed organizational changes as the organization grows, even when their need becomes obvious.

Quality must be an integral part of the production system, from product development all the way through the product use stage. Organizational factors have a definite influence on quality and must be properly addressed for effective quality assurance. Organizing for quality is an organization-wide task affecting all functional areas from design, engineering, and production to marketing, finance, and field service.

Several factors affect the organizational structure of a company and, consequently, the quality organization.[1] These include:

- *Company operational and organizational guidelines:* Standard practices that have developed over the firm's history often dictate how a company organizes and operates.

- *Management style:* This refers to the way the management team operates. Management style might be formal or informal, or democratic or autocratic.

---

[1]Kermit F. Wasmuth, "Organization and Planning," in Loren Walsh, Ralph Wurster, and Raymond J. Kimber (eds.), *Quality Management Handbook* (Wheaton, IL: Hitchcock Publishing Company, 1986), pp. 9–34.

- *Customer influences:* Specifications or administrative controls may be required by customers, particularly governmental agencies.

- *Company size:* This influences the ability to maintain formal systems and records.

- *Diversity and complexity of product line:* An organization suitable for the manufacture of a small number of highly sophisticated products may differ from an organization required to produce a high volume of standard products.

- *Stability of the product line:* Frequent changes in products make necessary more control and changes to the quality system.

- *Financial stability:* Quality managers need to recognize that their programs must fit within the overall budget of the firm.

- *Availability of personnel:* The lack of certain skills may require other personnel, such as supervisors, to assume duties they ordinarily would not be assigned.

These factors, while sometimes ignored by organizational theorists, are real issues that must be addressed in any organizing effort. Flexibility and the ability to change must be built into the organization to deal with such issues.

In building an effective quality system, the authority and responsibility of individuals leading the quality effort must be defined clearly. Authority is the right to command resources of people, money, and materials to carry out an assigned task. Responsibility implies the need to be accountable to a superior for the outcomes of decisions made by the person with the authority to make such decisions. Authority must be granted to match responsibility if a unit of an organization is to be effective. Excellent quality does not just happen; it must be *made* to happen. One does not have to be a manager to have authority or to bear responsibility for decisions. A lathe operator in a machine shop may have the authority to work on materials worth thousands of dollars. The operator also bears the responsibility to produce the highest quality parts possible and not to damage raw materials through neglect or bad judgment.

Many situations arise, however, in which it is difficult to develop or maintain the ideal balance of authority and responsibility. The degree to which this can be successfully accomplished depends on such variables as the corporate culture, type of organization structure used, level of a person or department within the organization, and even interpersonal dynamics. A number of these issues are addressed in this chapter and in Chapters 10 and 11.

Organization and Corporate Culture

Corporate culture can be simply described as "This is the way we do things at XYZ Company." Measurement of corporate culture, however, is much more difficult. Peters and Waterman[2] pointed to a number of companies, such as Procter & Gamble, Digital

---

[2]Abstract from pp. 13–15 of *In Search of Excellence,* by Thomas J. Peters and Robert H. Waterman. Copyright© 1982 by Thomas J. Peters and Robert H. Waterman. Reprinted by permission of Harper & Row, Publishers, Inc.

Equipment, and Walt Disney Productions, that have developed a unique corporate culture that contributes to their overall excellence. Corporate culture, excellence, and a total quality philosophy go hand in hand. Peters and Waterman give eight points, or prescriptions, by which excellence was attained by these firms and presumably could be attained by others willing to apply such techniques to their own organization:

1. A bias for action.

2. Staying close to the customer.

3. Autonomy and entrepreneurship.

4. Productivity through people.

5. Hands-on, value-driven operation.

6. Sticking to knitting (translation: focus on doing what you do best).

7. Simple form, lean staff.

8. Simultaneous loose-tight controls.

All of these can contribute to overall quality in various ways. For example, a "bias for action" implies that a proactive approach toward quality will be taken. Instead of talking about quality improvement, people will *move* to make things happen to improve quality. By "staying close to the customer," suggestions for quality improvements by customers will be heeded and followed up. Even "simultaneous loose-tight controls" can be applied to quality where it is advantageous. For instance, receiving inspections on vendors who provide consistently high-quality products to a firm can often be eliminated. This saves the customer money and encourages the vendor to continue to maintain high quality levels. Vendors who don't have consistently high quality will be tightly controlled and eliminated if they do not improve.

Philip Crosby points out the importance of a cultural revolution in establishing a total quality concept in a firm. He states, "One of the reasons I cheerfully share these (quality improvement) programs with other companies is that I know that many will probably not be able to use them. Not because they are not capable, but because they do not have a top management willing to be patient while the program is ground out four yards at a time. It took five to seven years of unrelenting effort to achieve the cultural revolution at ITT and I seriously doubt if it will ever be eliminated there."[3] The corporate culture plays a crucial role in quality assurance organization. Proper organization can create the type of corporate culture that will enable total quality to be achieved.

The importance of organization to quality can be illustrated by an example involving the First National Bank of Chicago.[4] Since 1971 the required return on equity of the banking industry has declined. Research showed that quality is the key buying determinant in noncredit services. First Chicago was determined to become the best in the noncredit services business. The bank began its quality transformation by altering its organizational framework. Separate strategic business units were

---

[3]Philip Crosby, *Quality Is Free* (New York: McGraw-Hill, 1979), p. 17.
[4]"Banking on Quality," *Incentive,* September 1988, pp. 62–75.

created, each based on an individual product family. The strategic business unit manager suddenly became an entrepreneur. The manager was vested with the power to control not only expenses, but also product features, pricing, promotion, and quality. This framework brought the managers closer to the customer and made them more directly accountable for the quality of the products. Each business unit has its own customer service representatives to handle inquiries and problems. Because the customer service function and production area are in the same location, the representatives can respond more efficiently to problems.

The Three Levels of Quality in Organizations[5]

The traditional vertical definition of organization structuring is oriented primarily toward ensuring that the organization is effective, that is, doing the right things. An equally important requirement is that the organization must set up a horizontal structure to ensure that it is efficient, that is, doing things right. Quality requires a simultaneous focus on both dimensions. This approach to system definition is based on the following premises:

- Organizations are systems that employ various processes to convert inputs into outputs.

- Organizational systems adapt to feedback from both internal and external sources.

- Work gets done (or fails to get done) horizontally or cross-functionally, not hierarchically.

- The greatest opportunities to improve organizational performance often lie in the organizational interfaces (the white space between the boxes on an organization chart).

- Functions already have managers; persons who manage a wide variety of functions add value only through managing the white spaces.

An organization committed to quality must examine quality at three levels: the organizational level, the process level, and the performer/job (sometimes called the job or task design) level.

At the *organizational level,* quality involves meeting customer requirements. As discussed in the last chapter, an organization must seek customer input on a regular basis. Questions such as the following help to define quality at the organizational level: Which products and services meet your expectations? Which do not? What products or services do you need, but are not receiving? Are you receiving products or services that you do not need? Customer-driven performance standards should be used as the basis for goal setting, problem solving, performance appraisal, incentive compensation, nonfinancial rewards, and resource allocation.

At the *process level,* organizational units are classified as functions or departments, such as marketing, design, product development, operations, finance,

---

[5]Adapted from Alan P. Brache and Geary A. Rummler, "The Three Levels of Quality," *Quality Progress,* October 1988, pp. 46–51.

purchasing, billing, and so on. Since most processes are cross-functional, the danger exists that managers will try to optimize the activities under their own control, which may suboptimize activities for the organization as a whole. At this level, managers must ask questions such as: What products or services are most important to the customer? What processes produce those products and services? What are the key inputs to the process? Which processes have the most significant effect on the organization's customer-driven performance standards?

At the *performer level,* standards for output must be based on quality and customer service requirements that originate at the organizational and process levels. Such standards may include requirements for accuracy, completeness, innovation, timeliness, cost, etc. For each output of an individual's job, one must ask: What is required by the customer? How can the requirements be measured? What is the specific standard for each measure? These questions lead to the development of effective control systems, which we will discuss in the next chapter.

You may also observe the relationship between this organizational framework and quality function deployment (QFD). QFD begins with customer needs and expectations and carries these needs down to the process and performer levels through the house of quality linkages. Thus, QFD provides the basis for implementing an effective organizational structure.

QUALITY TASK IDENTIFICATION

The components of quality organization often follow the stages of product development and production, especially in those organizations that produce a tangible product. These stages include the following:

- *New design control*—quality assurance effort while marketing and manufacturing quality characteristics are being specified. This includes the determination of customer needs, product and process design, and reliability engineering.

- *Incoming material control*—the process of accepting materials, parts, or components purchased from other companies or operating units or departments of the same company. This includes inspection and testing of raw materials and purchased parts and quality certification of suppliers.

- *Manufacturing quality assurance*—the control of production at the source to detect deviations from specifications and to correct them before defective products are produced. This includes in-process measurement and control and final inspection of the finished product.

- *Special process studies*—product and process improvement to improve quality characteristics and reduce costs. This includes process capability studies and various statistically designed experiments.

- *General management*—the planning and monitoring of all quality assurance activities. This includes planning the quality system, quality cost collection and analysis, customer feedback analysis, and initiating corrective action and improvements.

New Design Control

At one time or another, every organization has developed a new product or service to meet the demands of certain customers or clients in the marketplace. Some of these products have been new inventions, and others have merely been improvements on a previous product. Some recent examples of these are the desktop microcomputer, the disposable diaper, the digital watch, and the variable interest rate mortgage.

The landscape of business is littered with good or great design ideas that never made it to the marketplace or did not succeed because of design or quality problems. Some examples of these were pointed out by Putnam:[6]

> An electronics manufacturer assigned 600 engineers and two consulting companies to solve critical problems in order to hold to a new product deadline. The product then has heavy service and replacement demands for 12 additional months.
>
> A computer manufacturer works its engineering crew seven days a week for six months to meet the next show but only half of the "box" is ready.
>
> Manufacturing, Engineering and Service are in a state of confusion, and there are high costs of finishing and maintaining the product for two more years. (Over 500 parts are scrapped or reworked.)
>
> A textile machine manufacturer playing catch-up with foreign competition releases a new product without model test and eventually withdraws the product after shipping 50–100 units in the first two years.
>
> A jet engine model is bought by the Air Force based on the performance of the prototype (as most military products are), with the assumption that the tolerances are held to print in the model. When made with manufacturing tooling, many parts are rejected, requiring Material Review Board action, many delays and many changes. Little consideration is given to whether the Production model could meet the output requirements as readily as the Engineering model. Further examination reveals that the Engineering model does not match the print tolerances.

All of these examples show the importance of the design stage in the process of organization. They also demonstrate the difficulty of "getting it right the first time" and the need to build extra planning and lead time into the design phase of any product development process. In addition, quality must be an integral part of the design of manufacturing processes. These issues are discussed in Chapter 14. Related issues of reliability are discussed in Chapter 15.

Incoming Material Control

Incoming material control has always been an important part of the quality function. As with other quality assurance activities, such control would not be necessary if materials were of high quality at all times. As a practical matter, costs must be incurred to test and inspect incoming materials, maintain equipment or laboratories, and visit

---

[6]Arnold O. Putnam, "Three Quality Issues Management Still Avoids," *Quality Progress,* December 1983, p. 12.

vendors to audit their quality methods and systems. Many companies are now beginning to require that their suppliers provide proof that their processes are under statistical control, and to provide preferential treatment for those who can maintain high levels of quality performance over time.

Quality of incoming materials and parts is becoming more and more critical as automation increases. Many U.S. firms are investigating or attempting to put into effect the Japanese management concept of just-in-time scheduling, which we will discuss in the next chapter. Naturally, materials managers would like to gain the benefits of having on hand only enough inventory to produce the products that must be completed today. Production managers would be pleased to be able to automate their processes so that materials could be transferred from one machine to the next without time-wasting delays and inventory buildups between machines or processes. Such desires of inventory and production managers will be only dreams until high-quality production allows incoming materials control to be reduced to the barest minimum. The Japanese have been successful in doing this for many of their products.

An example of the quality consciousness of Japanese manufacturers is related in a story told in one of the authors' classes by an American plant manager who was supplying stock to a Japanese firm that used the materials to make semiconductor devices for electronics applications. The American manager was justifiably proud of having the best quality material of this type available from any American supplier. That was why his company had been chosen as a supplier to the Japanese firm. However, when the Japanese firm tested the first shipment of 9,000,000 parts, it was quite upset over the lack of quality and informed the American firm that it would have to do better or face being replaced by a Japanese supplier. The incoming inspection had detected *five* bad parts in the total shipment!

Concepts of inspection and measurement are discussed in Chapter 13. Chapters 8 and 18 discuss acceptance sampling techniques that are often applied to incoming material control.

Manufacturing Quality Assurance

Manufacturing quality assurance is at the heart of the quality management process. It is at the point where a good or service is produced that quality is "built-in." Unless all parts of the organization agree on a quality philosophy, it does no good to have the finest inspection department in the industry. At the same time, it is necessary to build in operating checks and balances to ensure that conformance to quality standards is maintained at a high level. Quality managers at this level must ensure that measurement, control, and improvement activities are carried out in timely and cost-effective ways. Specifically, the appraisal activity must be addressed in the areas of inspection, testing, development of procedures, training of operators and inspectors, maintenance of test equipment, and reporting of quality levels and results. Statistical quality control, discussed in Chapters 16 and 17, is the major technique used for in-process quality assurance.

Special Process Studies

Every quality manager has a responsibility to study and improve the quality of the operating process for which he or she is responsible. Process capability—that is, the ability of a process to meet design specifications—is largely unknown for most manufacturing processes in the United States. Putnam states, "Less than 10–20% of American operations have determined process capability. We don't really know the statistical limits of variability of the operation or process."[7] Thus, the most critical type of special process study is to determine the capability of all—or at least the most important—processes that are currently in operation in a location or firm. From an organizational standpoint, this may require full-time assignment of a quality engineer or technician to the project of performing such a study if it has never been done in that location before. This topic is also addressed in Chapter 13.

The improvement study is another class of special process studies that often requires a team approach. Kukla lists some indicators that may signal the need for starting an improvement process.[8] He included unfavorable trends or information based on the following:

- employee feedback

- internal nonconformance

- external failures

- quality auditing feedback

- customer feedback.

If these indicators or trends are unfavorable, problem-finding and problem-solving approaches should be used (see Chapter 9).

Several aspects of organizing for quality control do not fit neatly into one of the four categories of new design control, incoming materials control, manufacturing quality assurance, or special process studies. They include external relations with groups such as vendors and customers, internal relations with functions and departments upon whom quality managers and technicians are often dependent for success, and modifications in quality organizations that have to be made to accommodate for differences between large and small organizations or manufacturing versus service organizations. However, the organizational structure chosen by a firm will have an impact on all these aspects.

General Management

General management, in which we include finance and marketing groups, has the overall responsibility for planning and executing the quality assurance program. Cost collection and analysis, as discussed in Chapter 3, is a principal responsibility. In addition, general management must obtain customer feedback, analyze complaints, and initiate corrective action when necessary.

Figure 7.1 summarizes the relationships between quality responsibilities and various organizational functions. Such a chart is useful for analyzing, identifying, and establishing an effective quality organization.

---

[7]Putnam, "Three Quality Issues."
[8]R. E. Kukla, "Organizing a Manufacturing Improvement Program," *Quality Progress,* November 1983, p. 28.

FIGURE 7.1 Quality Assurance Relationship Chart

Code: (R) = Responsible
C = Must contribute
M = May contribute
I = Is informed

Areas of Responsibility	General Manager	Finance	Marketing	Engineering	Manager Manufacturing	Manufacturing Engineering	Quality Control	Materials	Shop Operations
Determine needs of customer			(R)						
Establish quality level for business	(R)		C	C	C				
Establish product design specs				(R)					
Establish manufacturing process design				C	M	(R)	M	M	C
Produce products to design specs			M	C	C	C	C	C	(R)
Determine process capabilities					I	C	(R)	M	C
Qualify suppliers on quality							C	(R)	
Plan the quality system	(R)		C	C	C	C	(R)	C	C
Plan inspection and test procedures						C	(R)	C	C
Design test and inspection equipment						C	(R)		M
Feed back quality information			C	C	I	M	(R)	C	C
Gather complaint data			(R)						
Analyze complaint data			M	M			(R)		
Obtain corrective action			M	C	C	C	(R)	C	C
Compile quality costs		(R)	C	C	C				
Analyze quality costs		M					(R)		
In-process quality measurements							(R)		C
In-process quality audit				C		C	(R)		
Final product inspection			C	C	M	C	(R)		

SOURCE: A. V. Feigenbaum, *Total Quality Control*, 3rd ed. (New York: McGraw-Hill, 1983), p. 161.

ORGANIZATION STRUCTURE

Organization structure describes the reporting relationships, responsibility, and authority to carry out the tasks that meet organizational objectives. A complete description of organization structure includes the following:

- The organization chart—the skeleton of the organization.
- Job descriptions—tasks for certain job classifications, such as inspector or quality manager.
- Position descriptions—definitions of authority, responsibility, and reporting relationships for specific positions, in addition to the more general tasks outlined in the job description.

- Policies—guidelines for management action, written in accordance with organizational objectives and plans.

- Procedures—detailed instructions for performing specified tasks so as to carry out the policies and objectives of the organization.

- Committees—coordinating groups that do not make decisions.

- Facilities—places where organizational work is carried out and the established systems needed to communicate with others in the organization, such as telephones, mail, or transportation, can be found.

The Organization Chart

The organization chart shows the structure of the formal organization. Although thousands of different organization structures exist, all are variations or combinations of three basic types: (1) the line organization, (2) the line and staff organization, and (3) the matrix organization.

The line organization is a functional form, having departments that are responsible for marketing, finance, and operations. In this type of organization, quality planning and assurance usually are part of the responsibility of each operating manager and employee at every level. In all likelihood, in a pure line organization, the quality function would be "invisible" when the organization chart was drawn up, since no one would have a full-time job of quality manager. In theory, this organizational form could exist in a fairly large organization if all employees were thoroughly indoctrinated in the philosophy of quality and could be counted on to place quality as the top priority in all aspects of their daily work. In practice, this organization structure is not generally successful except when used in small firms.

The line and staff organization is the most prevalent type of organization structure for medium-sized to large firms. In such organizations, line departments carry out the functions of marketing, finance, and production for the organization. Staff personnel, including quality managers and technical specialists, assist the line managers in carrying out their jobs by providing technical assistance and advice. Variations on the basic line and staff organization can include geographic or customer organizations. In this traditional form of organization structure, quality managers and inspectors may take on the role of guardians of quality instead of technical experts who assist line managers and workers in attaining quality. This also happens when the quality assurance function is placed too low in the organization; there is a tendency to receive pressure from higher levels of the organization to ease up on quality so that more products can be shipped. The major cause of this problem is too much responsibility with insufficient authority.

The matrix type of organization is a relatively new form that was developed for use in situations where large, complex projects are designed and carried out, such as defense weapons systems or large construction projects. Firms that do such work have a basic need to develop an organization structure that will permit the efficient use of human resources while maintaining control over the many facets of the project being developed. In a matrix-type organization, each project has a project manager and each department that is providing personnel to work on various projects has a technical or administrative manager. Thus, a quality assurance technician might be assigned to the quality assurance department for technical and administrative activities but would be attached to Project A for day-to-day job assignments. The technician would report to the project manager of Project A and to his or her "technical boss" in the quality assurance department. When Project A is completed, the technician might be reassigned to Project B under a new project manager. He or she would still be reporting to the "technical boss" in quality assurance, however.

The matrix type of organization for project work has a number of advantages. It does help to improve coordination in complex project work as well as to improve the efficiency of personnel use. It has a major drawback in requiring split loyalty for people who report to two supervisors. This can be especially troublesome—or even dangerous—in a quality assurance area. For example, in a nuclear power plant project, a project manager who is under pressure to complete a project by a certain deadline might try to influence QA inspectors to take shortcuts in completing the inspection phase of the project. The QA manager, who might be hundreds of miles away from the site, would often not have the influence over the inspectors that the project manager would have.

The chart in Figure 7.2 shows a "typical" quality control organization based on a line and staff organizational form. The term *typical* is used not to convey an idea of perfection but to illustrate some good principles applicable to quality assurance functions within any type of organization. Organization charts will differ considerably among organizations, depending on size, degree of automation, product line, and so on.

The chart in Figure 7.2 represents quality assurance within a manufacturing type of organization. It shows how personnel in the staff function of quality assurance report to a manager for control of day-to-day projects, assignments, and work activities. This is the *formal* organizational relationship. However, the *semiformal* advisory relationship can often be crucial to a successful quality program. In a way, the subordinate may be the *superior* (in a technical sense) of a manager in operations, marketing, or even his or her own department. Because of superior technical expertise about how to run a certain quality test or develop a quality circle solution, the subordinate gains the *expert* label that provides power to have a suggestion accepted.

Feigenbaum suggests three important considerations in structuring the quality control component of an organization, to which we have added a fourth criterion (illustrated in the organization chart):[9]

1. Keep "layers" of supervision to a minimum so that lines of communication can be kept as short as possible.

2. Keep "spans" of supervision as broad as possible. (This follows if "layers" are to be kept at a minimum.) The "span" is the number of persons reporting directly to a supervisor or manager. The lower in the organization one goes, the greater the spans should become, because the work of the reporting positions usually becomes more uniform in nature.

3. Place similar portions of work into a similar work package that can be handled by a person in the position considered.

---

[9]A. V. Feigenbaum, *Total Quality Control,* 3rd ed. (New York: McGraw-Hill, 1983), p. 182.

FIGURE 7.2 An "Ideal" Quality Organization Chart

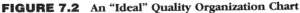

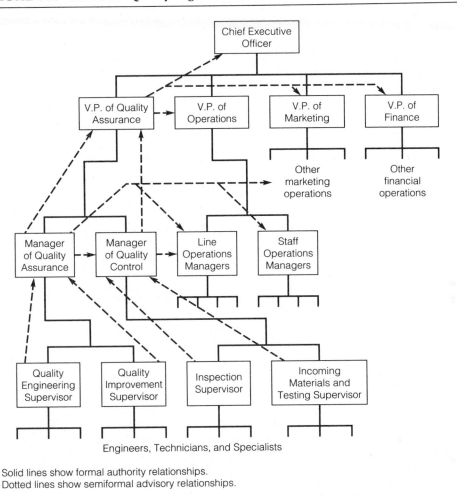

Engineers, Technicians, and Specialists

Solid lines show formal authority relationships.
Dotted lines show semiformal advisory relationships.

4. Ensure that the top reporting level of the quality organization is sufficiently high to indicate the importance of the quality function and to ensure ready access to the key decision makers in the organization.

Job and Position Descriptions

In well-organized firms, job and position descriptions aid managers in assigning responsibilities for certain tasks and in assessing the capabilities of people who will be promoted or recruited to fill the positions.

The job description details tasks that are to be performed by anyone having the same title regardless of where that person is assigned in the organization. For example, an inspection supervisor may have a job description such as the one in

FIGURE 7.3   Job Description for Inspection Supervisor

I. Title and Department: Inspection Supervisor, Quality Assurance Department

II. Function: To manage all activities pertaining to inspection of incoming, in-process, and outgoing materials and products to ensure adherence to quality standards and specifications.

III. Scope
  A. Internal. Interacts with other members of the department above and below his/her level for routine reporting and problem solving, process and system improvement, and policy-making.
  B. External (within company). Interacts with line plant supervisors and staff managers to provide QA information and technical advice needed to detect, analyze, and solve QA conditions and problems.
  C. External (outside company). Interacts with vendors to coordinate and improve quality of incoming parts and materials. Interacts with customers to provide information and data on quality processes and levels to assist in the solution of quality problems.

IV. Responsibilities
  A. Ensure that the necessary complement of trained inspectors and lab technicians is available to perform incoming, in-process, and outgoing quality checks as specified in local and company procedures.
  B. Prepare reports, disseminate information and keep records assigned by the QA manager.
  C. Supervise inspectors and technicians according to the provisions of appropriate personnel policies and procedures.
  D. Ensure that all inspection gages, tools, and equipment are maintained and calibrated according to standard procedures.
  E. Immediately report quality problems or conditions that require management attention to designated managers.

V. Reporting Relationships
  A. Reports to Quality Assurance Manager
  B. Supervisory relationship: Supervises inspectors and materials laboratory technicians.

VI. Equipment, Materials, Machinery
  A. Equipment. Meters, gages, precision measuring machines, lab equipment, calculators, microcomputers.
  B. Responsibility. Maintenance, calibration, safekeeping, training in proper use.

VII. Physical Conditions or Hazards
  A. Conditions. Work in office, in lab, and on shop floor.
  B. Hazards. Exposure to typical shop hazards in a metal machining environment is likely. Normal precautions must be observed.

VIII. Other
  Other duties as assigned.

Figure 7.3. As in the case of the previous organization chart, this description cannot be considered as ideal but merely suggests the types of duties that may be assigned to a first-line supervisor.

Position descriptions are unique to a specific part of the organization, such as quality manager of the Cincinnati plant of the XYZ Corporation. The position description details the authority, responsibility, and reporting relationships of the person who is holding, or will hold, that exact position. It will also include any special qualifications that the individual may need to carry out the responsibilities for that position. An example of the position description for a quality manager is given in Figure 7.4.

Policies and Procedures

Policies and procedures were described in Chapter 6 in the discussion of the hierarchical approach to planning. They are important in organization because they provide the direction in which the organizing effort must flow. Policies are the broad guidelines for action, and procedures are the specifications by which the policies are to be carried out. For example, a company may have a policy of using only the highest quality components in an electronic device. Procedures would then have to be developed to ensure that only qualified vendors would be allowed to supply the components and that the components accepted from those vendors would meet the required quality specifications.

FIGURE 7.4 Position Description for a Quality Manager

Position Description for Quality Manager

I. Title and Location:
   Quality Assurance Manager, Centralville Plant

II. Education and Training
   A. Education. Should have at least a bachelor's degree, preferably in a technical area such as mathematics, science, or engineering.
   B. Experience. Must have at least two years of managerial experience in a metal-cutting industrial environment. If no college degree is held, up to two years of college may be waived by substituting two years of quality assurance experience for each year of college waived.
   C. Skills. must be proficient in problem analysis and solution techniques, familiar with machine-tool capabilities, blueprint reading, tolerancing, gaging, control charting, and process specifications. Should have a basic understanding of the human and technical aspects of total quality control, including participative management approaches and statistical process control. Must be able to manage a small staff of technical supervisors.

III. Behavioral Characteristics
   A. Must be a proactive individual with initiative and drive to start, sustain, and complete improvement projects, often in the face of resistance to change.
   B. Must have interpersonal skills necessary to work effectively with line and staff personnel several levels above and below his/her position.

IV. Reporting Liaison, and Management
   A. The QA manager reports directly to the division vice president for quality assurance in matters of technical authority and responsibility, detailed in the job description.
   B. The QA manager provides staff advice to the plant manager, purchasing manager, material control manager, manufacturing engineering manager, and shop superintendent. He/she will ensure that incoming and outgoing quality are maintained and/or improved on by using direct and indirect authority provided for in the job description.
   C. The QA manager manages the inspection, testing, laboratory, and quality circle activities in the plant according to provisions of the job description.

Committees

Complex tasks of design, operations, and quality assurance require coordination between individuals with a variety of interests and specialized talents. Multidisciplinary approaches to solving problems and coordinating efforts are the rule rather than the exception in most organizations today. Committees, by their nature, can benefit or hinder the coordination process. When well managed, committees can be used to transmit information, gather opinions, and gain support for decisions. If misused, they can block progress, foster dissension, and diffuse responsibility to the point of meaninglessness. It should be noted that power to make decisions cannot reside within a committee. Committees have the power only to recommend what decision should be made in any situation. Two of the many examples of where committees can be used in QA include material review boards and employee involvement program steering committees.

According to Juran and Gryna, material review boards were originally conceived for the specific purpose of expediting decisions on nonconforming lots of material for defense contracts.[10] There, board membership consisted of a military representative, a quality control specialist, and the component's designer. If the product was to be shipped, the board was required to examine the nonconformity to product specifications and to make a unanimous decision that the product's defect would not materially affect the product's proper functioning or fitness for use.

The purpose of the material review board in many other companies has been broadened to include recommending the disposition of raw materials or semifinished

---

[10]J. M. Juran and Frank M. Gryna, Jr., *Quality Planning and Analysis,* 2d ed. (New York: McGraw-Hill, 1980), p. 371.

or finished products that are nonconforming to standards. The committee may recommend that the products in question be returned to the vendor, reworked, scrapped, or sold as seconds. The committee might be made up of process engineers, QA personnel, and line supervisors. Once it has made its recommendation on a particular problem, it is up to a high-level line manager to make the final decision concerning disposition of the material.

Employee involvement (EI) teams are small groups of employees from the same, or related, work areas who meet regularly to solve quality, productivity, and other problems affecting their daily work activities. EI program steering committees are charged with the responsibility of ensuring that the process, approaches, projects, and progress of an EI program are on track. In the early stages of implementing such a program, members of the steering committee recommend the selection of a program coordinator, or facilitator. This person ensures that training is provided and monitors the progress of the program. The committee is typically composed of line, staff, and operating-level workers who have an interest in the program. Some of the representatives might include the QA manager, the personnel and human resources manager, representatives of line management, and a union representative such as the shop steward. Once again, the line manager is responsible for the implementation of the program and must decide how to put steering committee recommendations into effect. More details about the organization and operation of EI programs are contained in Chapter 11.

Facilities

Facilities are an important part of the organizing process because they provide the *where* that the organization needs to carry out its work. QA departments need offices, laboratories, and inspection equipment to carry out their jobs. In many cases, inspection functions that could be performed only in a laboratory several years ago can now be done on the shop floor using sophisticated measuring instruments that have been designed to withstand the rigors of operating under conditions found in the shop environment. Such equipment is not always cheap or simple to use. It often requires a significant amount of time and money to be effectively integrated into the production process.

Planning the Organization Structure

Feigenbaum suggests six steps for planning a quality control organization:[11]

1. Define the company quality purposes.

2. Establish the objectives that the organization must achieve if it is to implement these purposes.

3. Determine the basic work activities that must be accomplished in meeting the organization objectives. Classify these work activities into an appropriate number of basic functions.

---

[11]A. V. Feigenbaum, *Total Quality Control,* pp. 163, 167.

4. Combine these basic functions into job packages that pass the screen of seven acid-test questions:

   a. Does the position comprise a logical, separate field of responsibility?

   b. Is the position clear-cut and definite as to scope, purpose, objectives, and results to be achieved?

   c. Can a single individual be held responsible and know the measuring sticks by which he or she is being judged?

   d. Are the functions of the position closely related and do they "belong together"?

   e. Does the position have authority commensurate with its responsibility?

   f. Does the position have easy, workable relationships with other positions in the organization?

   g. Can the number of people reporting to the holder of the position be genuinely supervised?

5. Consolidate the job packages into an organization component or components best suited to specific company requirements, recognizing the particular character of the organization component that has been created.

6. With this in mind, locate the component in that segment of the larger company organization where it can do its job and achieve its objectives with maximum effectiveness and economy and a minimum of friction. Establish the relationships with other organization components that are necessary to the organization objectives.

Many other issues need to be addressed, such as centralization versus decentralization and special problems of international organizations. These six steps are only guidelines.

TASK DESIGN

The final step in organizing is to assign work to individuals in order to accomplish the tasks required. A **task** is defined as a group of routine or nonroutine activities that make up a basic unit of work. Griffin defines **task design** as "the formal and informal specification of an employee's task-related activities, including both structural and interpersonal aspects of the job, with considerations for the needs and requirements of both the organization and the individual."[12]

From the standpoint of the organization, the major goal of task design is to ensure that tasks are performed efficiently and effectively. This means that employees must follow standard methods and practices, both formal, such as job descriptions, and informal, such as filling in for a fellow worker who is ill. From the point of view of the individual performing a task, the major goal of task design is to have a job that contributes to a sense of meaning, self-worth, and accomplishment and helps the

---

[12]Ricky Griffin, *Task Design: An Integrative Approach* (Glenview, IL: Scott, Foresman Publishing Co., 1982).

organization meet its economic goals. The individual worker would like to avoid having "just another job" or a meaningless task.

Since most jobs in modern organizations are not performed in isolation, the concept of the work group must be included when considering task design. The next few paragraphs outline three approaches that have been used to develop frameworks for analysis of task design in organizations: the *classical,* the *behavioral,* and the *sociotechnical* approaches.

The Classical Approach

The classical task design approach has its roots in Frederick W. Taylor's "scientific management" philosophy, developed in the early 1900s. Taylor, cited as the father of both modern management and industrial engineering, approached task design primarily from the viewpoint of efficiency and cost to the firm. His four major tenets are still present in industrial engineering approaches to job design today. In his writings, he gave detailed instructions to managers as to how they should install a scientific management system in their organizations, including the following:

1. Develop a science for each element of work, replacing the old rule-of-thumb method.

2. Scientifically select and then train, teach, and develop the workers. (Previously, workers chose their own work and trained themselves as best they could.)

3. Heartily cooperate with the workers so as to ensure that all of the work is being done in accordance with the principles of the science that has been developed.

4. Assure an almost equal division of the work and the responsibility between the management and the workers. Management takes over all the work for which it is better fitted than the workers. (Previously, almost all of the work and the greater part of the responsibility were thrown upon the workers.)

Taylor has been criticized by modern behavioral scientists for ignoring motivational considerations in his prescriptions for task design and efficient management. This criticism has not been entirely justified. First, his concept of providing incentive pay for increased productivity was revolutionary for the times and was motivationally sound. It is still used quite effectively today in the form of commissions for salespeople, merit pay for college professors, and incentive piece rates for production workers in the garment industry. Second, Taylor argued evangelistically for a complete "mental revolution" by those who were being asked to adopt his scientific management approach. As we shall see in Chapter 10, expectations of success and accompanying rewards are critical to the motivation of individuals who are required to accomplish tasks for the organization.

Although there are questions of job satisfaction and intangible costs associated with using a "pure" classical management or industrial engineering approach to job design today, many firms are still successful in applying this basic concept. In highly competitive mass-production industries, the use of detailed job descriptions, operation sheets, methods studies, time standards, and production incentive systems works well in obtaining optimum levels of efficiency, quality, and costs. Such approaches are often applied to routine inspection tasks in the quality function of high-volume industries.

Organizational Behavior Approaches

The first systematic studies of individual and group behavior in an industrial setting were the Hawthorne studies performed by a team of Harvard professors at the Hawthorne Works of Western Electric in the 1920s and 1930s. Developmental work on individual motivation and group interaction progressed until the 1950s and 1960s, when experiments on three different approaches to task design began. These approaches were called job enlargement, job rotation, and job enrichment.

IBM was apparently the first user of *job enlargement,* in which workers' jobs were expanded to include several tasks rather than one single, low-level task. This approach reduced fragmentation of jobs and generally resulted in lower production costs, greater worker satisfaction, and higher quality, but it required higher wage rates and the purchase of more inspection equipment.

Job rotation is a technique wherein individual workers learn several tasks by rotating from one to another. The purpose of job rotation is to renew interest or motivation of the individual and to increase his or her complement of skills. Griffin mentions several firms that have used job rotation, including American Cyanimid, Baker International, Bethlehem Steel, Ford Motor Company, Prudential Insurance Company, TRW Systems, and Western Electric.[13] He cites several studies to show that the main benefit was to increase workers' skills but that little, if any, motivational benefit could be expected.

Finally, *job enrichment* was developed by Frederick Herzberg as a strategy for implementing his two-factor theory of motivation (see Chapter 10 on motivation). Job enrichment involves "vertical job loading" in which workers are given more authority, responsibility, and autonomy rather than simply more or different work to do. Job enrichment has been used successfully in a number of firms, notably AT&T, which experienced better employee attitudes and performance, as well as Texas Instruments, IBM, and General Foods.

In the early 1970s, Hackman and Oldham developed a more sophisticated approach to job design, called *job characteristics theory,* to integrate various components of motivation and job design theories.[14] Since the theory is one of the major approaches to task design and motivation today, a thorough discussion of the model is included in Chapter 10. A comprehensive field test of the job characteristics theory to redesign jobs of clerical employees showed a number of positive results.[15] Those who were in the experimental group had their jobs redesigned, while those in a control group did not. Members of the experimental group showed lower levels of absenteeism and turnover, higher job satisfaction, and the perception of more scope to their jobs. The employees did not exhibit any higher levels of work performance, however.

---

[13]Ibid., p. 25.

[14]J. R. Hackman and G. R. Oldham, "Motivation Through the Design of Work: Test of a Theory," *Organizational Behavior and Human Performance,* Vol. 16, 1976, pp. 250–279.

[15]C. Orpen, "The Effects of Job Enrichment on Employee Satisfaction, Motivation, Involvement and Performance: A Field Study," *Human Relations,* Vol. 32, 1979, pp. 189–217.

Sociotechnical Approaches

Sociotechnical approaches to job design grew out of the work of several groups of industrial sociologists, including Trist and Bamford, Burns and Stalker, Emery and Trist, and Woodward in the 1950s and early 1960s (see the bibliography at the end of this chapter). At approximately the same time, a pioneering study by Harvard professors Lawrence and Lorsch was being carried out in the United States to develop insights into the impact of technology on task design.

Several characteristics have made the sociotechnical approach to job design unique:

- Consideration of technology and the task environment.

- Teams or groups of people working together.

- Job redesign emphasizing self-direction or autonomy of the work teams.

- A comprehensive "systems" frame of reference, as opposed to a narrow motivational or task focus.

Employee involvement approaches may be seen as an outgrowth of this approach to job design. The team approach to problem solving emphasizes the development of technical skills and human interaction skills in order to allow employees to participate successfully in making improvements in the technology (methods, equipment, and processes) of the task environment in which the employees work. Chapter 11 details the application of EI and other participative management approaches as an integrating mechanism in the attainment of total quality.

Modern Viewpoints of Task Design for Quality

One of the more difficult concepts for managers and academicians to grasp is the *holistic* nature of quality management in general, and task design in particular. In the past, tasks for workers to perform were often specified by an industrial engineer, personnel manager, or some line manager. These individuals were given this responsibility because they were thought to have superior knowledge about the job and its requirements. Today, this responsibility is being spread to all employees. Management is beginning to recognize that all workers have considerable knowledge and experience about their jobs and fully understand the specialized techniques often needed to perform or improve the task.

After reviewing the classical, organizational behavior, and sociotechnical approaches to task design, it has been suggested that organizational structure is shifting to a new paradigm that goes beyond any of the limits of the above types of structures.[16] This new perspective on quality goes beyond viewing it simply as conformance to specifications, fitness for use, or customer satisfaction; instead, quality is viewed from a holistic perspective. Quality can be viewed as a "state of mind" and an entity that puts "meaning into work."

---

[16]Phil Alexander, Michael Biro, Everett G. Garry, Dale Seamon, Tom Slaughter, and Duane Valerio. "New Organizational Structures and New Quality Systems," in Jill P. Kern, John J. Riley, and Louis N. Jones (eds.), *Human Resources Management, Quality and Reliability Series, Sponsored by the ASQC Human Resources Division* (New York: Marcel Dekker, Inc., and Milwaukee: ASQC Quality Press, 1987). Reprinted with the permission of ASQC.

The implications for an organizational structure that will support such a holistic gested that a highly structured, technically proficient, statistical process control department or quality assurance branch *inside* the organization might have sufficed as a quality management organization. But as the perspective of quality broadened from the narrow conformance-to-specifications view to customer satisfaction, *teamwork* has been recognized as necessary to integrate the various functional perspectives to provide a customer-oriented product or service. Thus, a more flexible, organic approach to organization that integrates techniques such as quality function deployment and employee involvement teams must be used.

What kind of structure is required for the organization that has a holistic philosophy? The answer is challenging, but elusive. Alexander et al.[17] have stated:

> From the perspective of the new paradigm, quality, as we think of it related to goods and services, is an expression of the lives of those who create those goods and services. Thus, quality of work life, as a particular subset of the quality of life in general, is not an interesting parallel phenomenon to product or service quality; it is the underlying fabric on which the design of product or service quality is expressed. Nor is quality of work life simply a collection of techniques or training programs, such as quality circles, important as these are. Rather it is a way of understanding individuals in their work environments such that these individuals on their own volition, individually and collectively, will create an environment commensurate with the best they know and will choose to further develop themselves in ways that will enhance their own skills, abilities, and well-being as well as society in general and the company in particular. In short, people can be trusted to create quality goods and quality services. They do not have to be coerced or exceptionally rewarded for their efforts. However, they must see themselves as being able to make creative contributions—to make real differences in the world.

Thus, future organizational structures that support quality are likely to have a high degree of self-management and innovation and be subject to rapid change to meet current needs. Beyond this, it is difficult to determine the specifics or to speculate on exact forms of organizational structure. In succeeding chapters, we will deal with the technical, human, and administrative issues that will all have ties to organizational structure.

---

[17]Ibid.

Digital Equipment Corporation's Enfield, Connecticut, Plant[18]

Digital Equipment Corporation's manufacturing facility in Enfield, Connecticut, assembles printed board modules for computer storage systems. Though its 180 employees represent only a tiny fraction of the 85,000 people employed by this $5 billion electronics giant, this small manufacturing plant has received an unusual amount of nationwide attention from management personnel and publications because it represents an innovative deviation from contemporary organizational practice. The Enfield plant's basic purpose, like that of any other manufacturing facility, is to build a quality product at the lowest possible cost and deliver it on time to achieve maximum customer satisfaction. This purpose is in keeping with the corporate philosophy, which states that "growth is not our principal goal. Our goal is to be a quality organization and do a quality job, which means we will be proud of our work and our products for years to come. As we achieve quality, growth comes as a result." The specific strategy developed by Enfield to achieve this goal is a sociotechnical design experiment, known as the "high-performance work system," which recreates the manufacturing environment from the ground up, integrating such concepts as "team management," "participative management," and "job enrichment" into a truly creative organizational structure.

Much of the vision for Enfield's present structure came from Plant Manager Bruce Dillingham. "It's just the stuff I believe in," he says now. Dillingham recalls that when Digital asked him in 1980 to head the new plant being planned for Enfield, "I knew where I wanted to go, but I didn't know how to get there. So I hooked up with some people in organization design." Together they developed the values and norms that would govern the plant. The

[18]Adapted from a case by Michael Biro discussed in Phil Alexander, Michael Biro, Everett G. Garry, Dale Seamon, Tom Slaughter, and Duane Valerio. "New Organizational Structures and New Quality Systems," in Jill P. Kern, John J. Riley, and Louis N. Jones (eds.), *Human Resources Management, Quality and Reliability Series, Sponsored by the ASQC Human Resources Division* (New York: Marcel Dekker, Inc. and Milwaukee: ASQC Quality Press, 1987). Reprinted with the permission of ASQC.

design period involved the participation of a cross-section of the plant's entire work force, as well as the usual architectural and engineering specialists. About 15 workers began the design process, and more were gradually added until the plant became fully operational in April 1983. The 77,000-square-foot physical plant, though modern in appearance, was structured in a fairly conventional manner; the simplicity and efficiency of the building alone saved $500,000 in normal setup costs for the plant.

The guiding principles of the Enfield operation are expressed not in a simple "mission statement," but in a rather lengthy, multipart document, which fully states the dual commitment to producing a quality product while emphasizing recognition of the work force as not just a production resource, but also as a human resource worthy of recognition and growth. Dillingham states, "We wanted to hire people with positive attitudes, minimize red tape, develop a strong commitment to community within the plant, pay above-average salaries, and expect above-average performance. We wanted never to increase costs, and to maintain a strong commitment to training and developing people." This dual emphasis on the product and the people producing it has already shown bottom-line results. The Enfield plant reaches its break-even point at 60% of capacity. Compared to other Digital facilities, overhead has been reduced by 40%, and there has been 40% reduction in the amount of time required to produce a module. Scrap is half the amount common to the industry, and the "yield"—modules that work perfectly the first time—is two to three times higher than that of other plants within Digital.

The crucial area of concern regarding the employee/product synthesis is the manufacturing operation itself. Plant Manager Dillingham oversees two support and three (manufacturing) product-line groups. The product-line groups consist of four teams of approximately 18 members each. The teams are totally responsible for the product they manufacture, from the receiving of raw materials, to assembly, testing, packaging, and shipping. Workers set their own hours, plan their own schedules, check their own work, and take team responsibility for

(continued)

each module. Team members take on responsibility normally reserved for management in that they select personnel, train themselves, do budgeting and costing, evaluate performance, and allocate benefits. There are no time clocks at Enfield, nor are there security guards or quality-control personnel, and each employee has a key to the building. Corporate information about how the organization functions and how an employee can influence the organization's direction is made explicit to everyone. "This is a high-trust society," says Dillingham. His goal is to have an atmosphere that is informal, relaxed, and trusting, where people are self-motivated, creative, and flexible.

In making Enfield a highly advanced manufacturing system, full advantage was taken of all of Digital's resources, thus avoiding the "not-invented-here" syndrome. A "just-in-time" production system has been implemented; there are no incoming inspection, stockrooms, or buffers in work-in-process. Teams have learned to balance the production flow of their lines, and individual workers contact vendors for daily supplies of materials. With JIT, there is a necessary emphasis on vendor quality. In its first year of operation, Enfield had 15 inventory turns, compared to the traditional one or two. The comprehensive training and responsibility taken on by the production teams make the entire operation very fluid and adaptable to change, allowing more creative possibilities for engineering.

The two support groups also operate on the team concept and provide critical information, support systems, and material, thus enabling the production teams to meet their daily schedule. The group managers themselves operate as an informal team and are responsible for allocating resources, leading the decision-making process, and managing the integration between teams. They act in a consulting role, managing the boundaries between teams, shifts, and support groups, while implementing and facilitating changes in the organizational design and evolution.

Training and development is a very serious concern at Enfield. Because each team member is expected to perform each of the 26 functions involved in making a module, three months of "off-line" training is required before a new team member is fully certified to make the total product. Workers also receive training in group interaction skills, such as communication, conflict management, problem solving, and interviewing. There is an emphasis on the whole person that can be seen in measures taken for employee recreation. The plant is surrounded by 50 acres of undeveloped Digital land, which contains an outdoor running path, a softball field, and a volleyball net. Aerobic exercise is taught year-round in a special area on the shop floor, and there is within the building a weight room complete with men's and women's locker rooms. The fitness program is designed to reduce stress and promote well-being among the employees. Through the training and development process, new workers become fully assimilated into the Enfield culture, learning not only the manufacturing process, but behavioral norms as well.

The emphasis of the Enfield culture is in working together to teach one another, and in sharing the knowledge and responsibilities inherent in the entire operation. Dillingham explains that "it's the level of responsibility that you put on people that's different here. Some people don't want to have that kind of responsibility. They want to go to work, do their thing, and then go home and not worry about it. Technical engineers and other professionals have to see that their value is to teach other people—to share their knowledge—not to act as an authority figure. It takes a certain kind of engineer who would want to work in this plant."

To speak of the role of the quality professional at Enfield is, to a great extent, to discuss just one of the many important responsibilities each worker assumes. The inspection, testing, documentation, and analysis functions are performed by the team members themselves, not by a separate quality function. The theme of "ownership" emerges often in the literature describing the Enfield operation. Because of the broadly based training and assembly skills utilized by the worker in assembling each module, the workers take on a feeling of ownership of the product, a pride of craftsmanship that gives each module a human face, a hallmark, so to speak, of the person who made it. Thus, quality emerges quite naturally in the inherent nature of a product built by people who, through feelings of ownership, have internalized the concern for functional fitness and customer satisfaction.

There does exist within the technical support group a number of individuals with backgrounds in the quality sciences, several of whom have ASQC affiliation and quality-engineer certifications. These

(continued)

people are not assigned strictly to the performance of traditional quality functions, but rather view themselves as a quality-support function, using their skills, knowledge, and experience to act as in-house consultants in facilitating and implementing quality-related activities. They assist in the design and process-related activities and also provide the interface with corporate quality personnel.

It is important to realize that what has been created at Enfield is not just a new type of manufacturing system, but a very special cultural environment as well. The culture-building social skills are developed first at Enfield, followed by the technical skills. It is the high level of group dynamics, coupled with feelings of responsibility and ownership, that allows Enfield to operate as an efficient and productive manufacturing facility, not just an interesting example of social experimentation. The difficulties involved in creating a new culture are not to be overlooked. The commitment by senior management to carrying through such an endeavor is crucial to its success, as is a willingness to take risks in order to see the vision through to completion. The Enfield operation had the advantage of having been developed—quite literally—from the ground up. Other organizations with conventional management structures may find it more difficult to implement major changes in their way of doing things. The team management approach may be perceived as a threat to the role of middle management, as it involves a considerable transfer of power and responsibility. Thus, the transition within many facilities will be a gradual one, as the new forms of organization are implemented on a trial basis, prove themselves, and then slowly gain acceptance. Bruce Dillingham has often stated that it takes a certain, special kind of person to work at Enfield, one who sees his or her duties not as defined by a job title and description, but rather developed through strong interaction within the team framework. He describes this "management technology" as a total-system approach, one in which everyone in the organization takes on the responsibility to develop and diffuse the new technology, as knowledge and perspectives widen through horizontal growth and development. The new organizational structure at Enfield is a constantly evolving one which has already proven its effectiveness, as it stands as yet another significant development in the evolution of organizational design.

Key Issues for Discussion

1. What unique opportunities were available to Plant Manager Bruce Dillingham when he was asked to head up the new plant being planned for Enfield? How did he take advantage of this "window of opportunity"?

2. Analyze the characteristics of the organization along the dimensions of (a) organization structure, (b) task design, (c) leadership style, (d) innovation, (e) communications, (f) quality management and control, and (g) *fun* (as in, "Would it be *fun* to work there?).

3. Which of the characteristics in question 2 build on the legacy of classical organization theory, behavioral theories, and sociotechnical systems theory?

4. On what factors would duplication of Enfield's success in another company depend?

QUALITY IN PRACTICE

Quality Organization at the IRS[19]

Like Rodney Dangerfield, the Internal Revenue Service (IRS) frequently "gets no respect." Very few people *enjoy* paying their taxes! Yet, from the

[19]Adapted from Martha Curry. "Application Package Quality Improvement Prototype," Cincinnati Service Center, September 1989. The CSC won the Federal OMB Award in 1990. Appreciation is expressed to Martha Curry, QIP Coordinator, who assisted in editing this case.

viewpoint of a production system, one finds that conformance to specifications is high within the IRS. Also, from the standpoint of at least *one* of its customers, the U.S. Congress, it is achieving fitness for use. The IRS estimates a "compliance rate" of more than 90%; that is, more than 90% of all the taxes owed are paid.

(continued)

The importance of quality at the IRS can be seen by examining the Quality Improvement Prototype initiative that was undertaken at the Cincinnati Service Center (CSC) in Covington, Kentucky. This initiative resulted in the center being designated as a "Quality Prototype" facility in 1990 by the Office of Management and Budget (OMB), which oversees the operations of all federal agencies.

The Cincinnati Service Center is one of 10 tax return processing centers within the United States. It conducts operations at seven sites in the immediate area using almost 600,000 square feet of office space and employing up to 6,000 people at peak periods. It processes approximately 22 million returns per year from the states of Indiana, Kentucky, Michigan, Ohio, and West Virginia, and also handles taxpayer correspondence, correction, updating, compliance, storage, warehousing, and forms distribution responsibilities for the region. The CSC considers its external and internal customers to be taxpayers and tax practitioners in five states, six IRS district offices, and employees located in seven separate buildings.

The mission of CSC has been clearly articulated by center managers and is derived from the overall mission statement of the IRS:

> The goal of the Cincinnati Service Center is to do a superior job of meeting customers' needs and expectations with products and services of the highest quality and value.

The CSC formally began its quest for quality in 1981 when quality circles, an early type of EI program discussed in Chapter 11, were begun at the center. While as many as 15 such groups were created, this program did not represent a comprehensive approach to quality. In 1987, the active quality circle teams were integrated into a broader framework called the Quality Improvement Program (QIP). This new program was initiated in the top echelons of the IRS as a comprehensive, customer-driven adaptation of the Juran approach to quality. One particularly successful employee involvement team of clerical employees redesigned a tax forms cart to assist them in carrying and filing tax forms on shelves in a large storage facility.[20]

An extensive effort to publicize the program throughout the seven off-site CSC facilities began in

[20]"IRS Team Designs New Tax Form Cart," *IAQC Circle Reporter,* May–June 1987.

1988. Some of the types of publicity included a special QIP edition of the center's newsletter, and development of problem identification forms and volunteer signup sheets that were made available in all parts of the organization. To heighten interest and add a little humor, a mascot, "Captain Q," was designed and cloned. Fashioned of plywood, painted in bright colors, and clothed in jeans and a captain's hat, Captain Q called attention to the QIP boxes placed around the center's main and off-site buildings.

The center develops an annual business plan that includes quality targets and projects personnel and training requirements for the fiscal year, based on quality and productivity estimates. Some quality goals for the 1990 fiscal year included:

- Improving the timeliness and quality of correspondence to taxpayers.

- Improving the quality of the Underreporter Program, which involves center correspondence with taxpayers.

- Continuing innovations in the Electronic Filing Program (ELF).

- Emphasizing product quality throughout pipeline processing.

- Continuing the Performance Indicator Program as a weekly monitoring tool.

Internal goals included:

- Expanding the child-care center to include kindergarten and, if demand justifies, expanding care to nonprime shifts.

- Expanding an existing Employee Assistance Program to address the needs of employees faced with the care of elderly family members.

- Providing additional health-related programs and referrals to professional programs, such as health and exercise-programs; referrals to substance, drug abuse, and smoking cessation programs; stress reduction, and financial assistance programs.

- Adding at least 12 QIP teams during the year.

The CSC is organized in a typical line-and-staff form. The center is headed by a director, who is responsible for accomplishing the mission and

(continued)

carrying out the programs related to tax collection. In his office is the assistant director, who acts as the center's chief operating officer, overseeing the day-to-day operations of the CSC. Six major program areas are managed by division chiefs, with responsibilities subdivided into branches, sections, and units within each of the program areas. On a separate reporting path to the director is a Problem Resolution Unit whose staff serves as an ombudsman for the center's external taxpayer customers. The QIP coordinator is responsible for purchasing training materials, promotional items and team awards, professional association memberships for coordinators, and planning of the annual QIP Recognition day.

An innovative structure, having mixed IRS/National Treasury Employee's Union (NTEU) representation, was developed to guide the QIP at each level in CSC. At the top management level, a Quality Council was established, consisting of the director, assistant director, NTEU president and vice president, members of the director's staff of division chiefs, and the QIP coordinator. Quality subcouncils, consisting of a mix of managers and bargaining unit employees, were selected from a list of volunteers. They have the responsibility for creating and appointing QIP teams and monitoring their progress. As of the end of 1990, there were 45 trained QIP teams.

Extensive efforts are made to communicate with employees on various levels. Reports on progress, problems, and results of the QIP originate at the top of the local IRS organization. Center managers meet regularly for an update on CSC activities. The vision is constantly communicated and reinforced by the center's director and his management team. A cascade system is used to transmit information downward to division, branch, section, and unit levels. In addition to the director's and managers' attendance at project presentation and award ceremonies, articles on quality and participation are written for the employee publication, and such symbols as QIP-imprinted pens, notepads, quality logos, and the director's announcements over the public address system are constant reminders of the stress on quality.

The center now has a different focus on quality as contrasted with pre-QIP years, with an emphasis on "productivity, not *production.*" Consequently, the Quality Assurance Branch has been charged with the responsibility of devising a system that will generate data to measure quality and assist in identifying root causes of problems in each operation. This is done through a variety of systems, reports, process reviews, and demonstration projects. Communications via such information sheets as "Quality Alerts" and "The Daily Wire" as well as individual and group reports help to keep employees and managers informed of where "hot spots" in a process or program are trending incorrectly.

We will highlight other aspects of the IRS QIP program that relate to human resource management and employee involvement in Chapters 10 and 11.

Key Issues for Discussion

1. How is the total quality management concept integrated throughout the CSC?

2. What inferences can you make about the effects of the organization structure on the QIP process? How could a structure such as is found in the IRS help or hinder a total quality management philosophy?

Summary of Key Points

- Organizing is the process of assigning work and responsibility to functions and individuals along with the appropriate delegation of authority. Organizing establishes lines of authority, improves efficiency and quality of work, and improves communication.

- The corporate culture, and hence the ability to achieve total quality, is influenced by the organizational structure.

■ The major steps of organizing are to identify the tasks that must be performed, assign responsibility for these tasks, and assign work to individuals to accomplish these tasks.

■ Quality must be viewed at the organization level, the process level, and at the individual performer level. Like quality function deployment, the organizational structure must support the achievement of customer needs at all levels.

■ Major components of quality organization are new design control, incoming material control, manufacturing quality assurance, special process studies, and general management.

■ A complete description of the organization structure includes the organization chart, job descriptions, position descriptions, policies, procedures, committees, and facilities.

■ The goal of task design is to ensure that tasks are performed efficiently and effectively. Theories developed over the years have important implications in quality.

■ Future organizational structures are likely to have a high degree of self-management and innovation, and will be subject to rapid change to support a holistic quality philosophy.

Questions for Review and Discussion

1. What is the purpose of organizing?

2. Define the term *organizing*.

3. What are three reasons for organizing? How does the process of organizing relate to the process of planning?

4. What factors affect organizational structure? How can these affect the quality organization?

5. Discuss the concepts of authority and responsibility. What are the differences between them?

6. What is *corporate culture,* and why is it important for an effective quality control organization?

7. Describe the "three levels of quality." How can this framework be used to improve the quality organization?

8. Identify the major tasks that must be performed for quality assurance.

9. What must be included in describing the structure of an organization?

10. Describe the basic types of organization structure commonly used. What advantages or disadvantages does each have?

11. Matrix organization forms have become popular in recent years. Discuss the advantages and drawbacks in adopting the matrix organizational form. Find an organization that uses the matrix and interview a project manager for new insights on this question.

12. Is it worth the effort to draw up detailed job and position descriptions for each job in an organization? Why or why not?

13. An old management cliche is "A camel is a horse designed by a committee." What are the problems and advantages of using committees for quality assurance? How can such problems be overcome?

14. What can one tell about an organization if one has access to organization charts, job and position descriptions, policy manuals, written procedures, committee minutes, and facility floor plans? Is there anything that cannot be determined about the organization from these documents?

15. What general principles should be followed in structuring a quality assurance organization?

16. Why is task design important in defining the quality assurance organization?

17. Describe the three major approaches to task design. What advantages or disadvantages does each have?

18. How do modern viewpoints of organization for task design differ from traditional views? What implications does this have for future organizational structures?

Bibliography

Burns, T., and Stalker, G. M. *The Management of Innovation.* London: Tavistock, 1961.

Coud, Dana M. "The Function of Organizational Principles and Process," in *Quality Control and Reliability Management,* ASQC Education and Training Institute. Milwaukee: ASQC, 1969, pp. 6-1 to 6-3.

Emery, F. E., Trist, E. L., and Woodward, J. *Management and Technology.* London: Her Majesty's Stationery Office, 1958.

Hackman, J. R., and Oldham, G. R. "Motivation Through the Design of Work: Test of a Theory," *Organizational Behavior and Human Performance,* Vol. 16, 1976, pp. 250–279.

Kukla, R. E. "Organizing a Manufacturing Improvement Program," *Quality Progress,* November 1983, p. 28.

Lawrence, P. R., and Lorsch, J. W. *Organization and Environment.* Boston: Harvard University, Division of Research, Graduate School of Business Administration, 1967.

Orpen, C. "The Effects of Job Enrichment on Employee Satisfaction, Motivation, Involvement, and Performance: A Field Study," *Human Relations,* Vol. 32, 1979, pp. 189–217.

Rue, L. W., and Byars, L. *Management Theory and Application,* 4th ed. Homewood, IL: Richard D. Irwin, 1986.

Sinha, Madhav N., and Willborn, Walter W. O. *The Management of Quality Assurance.* New York: John Wiley & Sons, 1985.

Taylor, F. W. *The Principles of Scientific Management.* New York: Harper and Row, 1911.

Trist, E. L., and Bamford, K. W. "Some Social and Psychological Consequences of the Long-Wall Method of Coal Getting," *Human Relations,* Vol. 4, 1951, pp. 3–38.

CHAPTER 8

Controlling for Quality

I n the last two chapters we have discussed planning and organizing for quality assurance. *Control* is the third principal managerial function that is vital to an effective quality assurance system. Control is the continuing process of evaluating performance, comparing our performance to goals or standards that we seek to attain, and taking corrective action when necessary.

In this chapter we discuss various aspects of control for quality assurance. We will discuss variation and the need for control, a framework for viewing control systems, general approaches to product and process control, control through prevention, and quality audits.

VARIATION AND THE NEED FOR CONTROL

Just as no two snowflakes are exactly alike, no two outputs from any production process are exactly alike. The measurements of several items may be the same, but this is due to a lack of true precision in any measurement instrument. A more precise instrument will always reveal slight differences. The goal of production is to produce output of consistent quality that meets technical specifications. When quality is consistent, both the producer and the consumer benefit. The producer benefits by having less need for inspection, less scrap and rework, and higher productivity. The consumer is assured that all products have similar quality characteristics; this is especially important when the consumer is another firm using large quantities of the product in its own manufacturing or service operations.

A production process contains many sources of variation. Among them are variations in the inputs, the conversion process, and measurement of the outputs (Figure 8.1). Different lots of material will vary in strength, thickness, or moisture content, for example. Cutting tools will also have inherent variation in strength and composition. During the conversion process, tools will experience wear, machine vibrations will cause changes in settings, and electrical fluctuations will cause variations in power. Environmental factors such as temperature and humidity will also affect materials and processes. Operators using only visual guides cannot position parts on fixtures precisely. Compounding the problem, their physical and emotional states may have an effect on their work. Finally, measurement gages and human inspection capability are not always uniform. Because of these variations, design

FIGURE 8.1 Factors Affecting Variation in Process Output

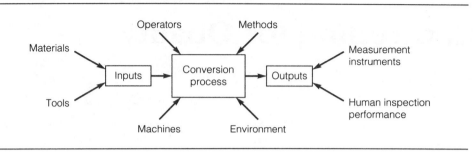

specifications can be expressed not as single values but rather with acceptable tolerances.

The complex interaction of such minor variations in materials, tools, machines, operators, and the environment frequently cannot be understood. Such variations occur at random, and although any one of them results only in a very small amount of variation, their combined effect can yield a substantial amount of variation. These factors that are always present as a natural part of the process are called **common causes** of variation. Although one cannot predict common causes individually, the combined effects of common causes can be stable and can be described rather accurately using probability distributions. It is important to recognize that common causes exist and that not every part produced will be the same. The only way to reduce the negative effects from the system of common causes is to change the technology or process design, that is, alter at least one of the 5 Ms—men and women, machines, materials, methods, or measurements. Putting pressure on operators to perform at higher quality levels cannot accomplish this and may be counterproductive.

Common causes generally account for about 85% of the observed variation in a production process. The remaining 15% are a result of **special causes,** often called **assignable causes,** of variation. Special causes arise from external sources that are not inherent to the process. Factors such as material purchased from different suppliers, differences among operators, tool wear, and miscalibration of equipment are examples of special causes. They may cause the output of a process to be nonconforming with specifications and disrupt the random pattern of common causes. Any one special cause may result in a substantial amount of variation. Hence, special causes are generally easy to detect, and it usually is economical to remove them.

Walter Shewhart is credited with recognizing the distinction between common and special causes of variation in the 1920s at Bell Laboratories. A process governed only by common causes is stable and remains essentially constant over time. The variation is predictable within established statistical limits. Prediction was the key idea in Shewhart's definition of control:[1]

> A phenomenon will be said to be controlled when, through the use of past experience, we can predict, at least within limits, how the phenomenon may be expected to vary in the future.

---

[1]Walter A. Shewhart, *Economic Control of Quality of Manufactured Product* (New York: Van Nostrand, 1931).

Controlling a process, therefore, is tantamount to identifying and removing special causes of variation.

If the output of a production process is governed only by common causes, we say that the process is *in statistical control* (or simply *in control*), and no changes or adjustments are necessary. When special causes are present, the process is said to be *out of control* and needs to be corrected. Production personnel need to be able to determine when a process is in or out of control in order to maintain adequate levels of productivity and quality. Quality control charts are tools to do this and are studied in Chapters 16 and 17.

Controlling for quality extends beyond the actual production process. Variation exists in purchased materials, human performance, and in the quality assurance system itself. In this chapter, therefore, we also discuss the role of control in these areas.

The Concept of Control

Any control system has three components: (1) a standard or goal, (2) a means of measurement of accomplishment, and (3) comparison of actual results with the standard along with feedback to form the basis for corrective action. Goals and standards are defined during planning and design processes. They establish what is supposed to be accomplished. These goals and standards are reflected by measurable *quality characteristics,* such as dimensions of machined parts, number of defectives, waiting times, and so on. We require methods of measuring these quality characteristics; these may be automated or performed manually by the work force. The measurements tell us what has actually been accomplished. Workers, supervisors, or managers must assess whether or not the actual results meet the goals and standards. If not, then remedial action must be taken. Remedial action might be short term, such as adjusting a machine setting, or it may be long term, such as changing the technology of the process. Short-term remedial action often can be taken by workers on the shop floor. Long-term remedial action is the responsibility of management.

Quality control often is separated into two categories: *on-line* quality control and *off-line* quality control. On-line quality control consists of all control activities that are conducted during the production cycle of a product. These activities typically are called *process control.* On-line methods include a feedback loop for immediate corrective action. Examples of on-line quality control include the use of control charts (Chapter 16) by production operators to identify and remove special causes of variation, and automated devices for controlling manufacturing operations through the use of sensors, vision systems, and so forth. Off-line methods are those conducted externally to the production process, for example, activities to improve product design, control of incoming materials, and other special process studies. These topics will be addressed in subsequent chapters.

An example of a quality control process is the "10-Step Monitoring and Evaluation Process" set forth by the Joint Commission on Accrediting Health Care Organizations. This process, shown in Figure 8.2, provides a detailed sequence of activities for monitoring and evaluating the quality of health care in an effort to identify problems and improve care. We see that standards and goals are defined in steps 2 through 5; measurement is accomplished in step 6; and comparison and feedback is performed in the remaining steps.

FIGURE 8.2 **10-Step Monitoring and Evaluation Process for Health Care Organizations**

- *Step 1: Assign Responsibility.* The emergency department director (or chairman) is responsible for, and actively participates in, monitoring and evaluation. The director assigns responsibility for the specific duties related to monitoring and evaluation.

- *Step 2: Delineate Scope of Care.* The department considers the scope of care provided within emergency services to establish a basis for identifying important aspects of care to monitor and evaluate. The scope of care is a complete inventory of what the emergency department does.

- *Step 3: Identify Important Aspects of Care.* Important aspects of care are those that are high-risk, high-volume, and/or problem-prone. Staff identify important aspects of care so that monitoring and evaluation focuses on emergency department activities with the greatest impact on patient care.

- *Step 4: Identify Indicators.* Indicators of quality are identified for each important aspect of care. An indicator is a measurable variable related to a structure, process, or outcome of care. Examples of possible indicators (all of which would need to be further defined) include insufficient staffing for sudden surges in patient volume (structure), delays in physicians reporting to the emergency room (process), and transfusion errors (outcome).

- *Step 5: Establish Thresholds for Evaluation.* A threshold for evaluation is the level or point at which intensive evaluation of care is triggered. A threshold may be 0% or 100% or any other appropriate level. Emergency department staff should establish a threshold for each indicator.

- *Step 6: Collect and Organize Data.* Appropriate emergency department staff should collect data pertaining to the indicators. Data are organized to facilitate comparison with the thresholds for evaluation.

- *Step 7: Evaluate Care.* When the cumulative data related to an indicator reach the threshold for evaluation, appropriate emergency department staff evaluate the care provided to determine whether a problem exists. This evaluation, which in many cases will take the form of peer review, should focus on possible trends and performance patterns. The evaluation is designed to identify causes of any problems or methods by which care or performance may be improved.

- *Step 8: Take Actions to Solve Problems.* When problems are identified, action plans are developed, approved at appropriate levels, and enacted to solve the problem or take the opportunity to improve care.

- *Step 9: Assess Actions and Document Improvement.* The effectiveness of any actions taken is assessed and documented. Further actions necessary to solve a problem are taken and their effectiveness is assessed.

- *Step 10: Communicate Relevant Information to the Organization-wide Quality Assurance Program.* Findings from and conclusions of monitoring and evaluation, including actions taken to solve problems and improve care, are documented and reported monthly through the hospital's established channels of communication.

SOURCE: "Medical Staff Monitoring and Evaluation—Departmental Review," Chicago. Copyright by the Joint Commission on Accreditation of Health Care Organizations, Oakbrook Terrace, IL. Reprinted with permission (undated).

CONTROL SYSTEMS FOR QUALITY

Terry and Franklin[2] have provided a useful conceptualization of control by dividing it into three stages: preliminary control, concurrent control, and feedback control. This is illustrated within the structure of the general control system model in Figure 8.3.

The purpose of *preliminary control* is to ensure that everyone knows how outcomes will be measured and standards evaluated. Thus control needs to be built

---

[2]George R. Terry and Stephen G. Franklin, *Principles of Management,* 8th ed. (Homewood, IL: Richard D. Irwin, 1982), pp. 426–428.

FIGURE 8.3 **Control System Structure**

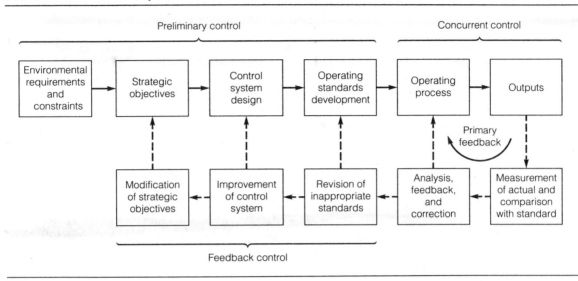

into the system at the planning stage. For example, if a firm's mission is to produce good-quality inexpensive integrated circuits for household appliances, it must design a control system with appropriate policies and procedures to accomplish that mission. Environmental requirements and constraints need to be taken into account in establishing strategic objectives for the control system design. Preliminary control should include systems for discovering potential quality problems prior to manufacturing operations. We will discuss some of these techniques in later chapters on product design and reliability.

In the second stage of control, feedback must occur immediately, often in real time, so that errors can be corrected as they happen. This feedback process is called *concurrent control*. Typically, the output from an operating process is measured and compared to a standard. As problems are diagnosed, the process is adjusted appropriately. In recent years, as electronic technology has become more and more sophisticated, concurrent control in manufacturing has become less difficult. Much of the required industrial process control is being performed through automation. For example, in the production of plastic sheet stock, thickness is dependent on temperature. Sensors can monitor the sheet thickness, and if it begins to go out of tolerance, the feedback loop in the system can send a signal that will cause a change in temperature in order to change the thickness.

For a vast majority of companies, concurrent process control is still performed manually by the work force. A typical control function is called *setup verification*. At the start of a new process or setup, the worker checks the first few parts to determine if they conform to specifications. If they do not, an adjustment to the setup must be made. During production, control is performed by inspecting samples of parts periodically. If an indication exists that the process has gone out of control, corrective action is taken. Control charts, which will be introduced briefly in the next chapter, and discussed thoroughly in Chapters 16 and 17, are useful tools for helping workers make these assessments. Many Japanese companies use very short production runs (in a just-in-time environment) to produce customized parts for special applications. Often they will simply inspect the first and last pieces of these runs; if these pieces are acceptable, it is assumed that the entire run conforms to specifications.

Finally, the control system itself must often be modified as standards become obsolete or objectives change. This is called **feedback control.** In machining of metal parts, for instance, it is not uncommon to have parts designed by engineers who are not familiar with the capability of machine tools in the plant. The engineer will often specify dimensions to a degree of accuracy that cannot be produced. If the plant has good feedback control, the engineer will be informed of the difficulty, and machining specialists will meet with the engineer to reach an agreement on whether to relax the tolerance on the required dimension, purchase a new precision machine to meet the tolerance, or continue to incur the cost of screening inspections and inevitable waste caused by the mismatch of requirements and capabilities. At the very least, the engineer and plant personnel will have discussed the problems, and both will have a better understanding of capabilities, limitations, and conflicting viewpoints. Thus, feedback control becomes a necessity from both a human and technical point of view. If no system of feedback control exists, the engineer will never become aware of the problem and will continue to make similar mistakes in the future. This bears out the need for additional efforts to develop team approaches to both innovation and quality improvement efforts.

Feedback control takes many forms. At lower levels of the organization, reports on product quality and process performance are used for short-term corrective action and as a basis to propose long-term improvements. Such reports are typically generated on a daily or weekly basis. At higher levels, quality results are typically translated into cost of quality reports for upper managers on a less frequent basis. Information on long-term trends, or comparative performance of plants, divisions, and departments is used for strategic decision making.

Figure 8.4 relates the type of control to the level of management. We see that top managers are most concerned with preliminary control and the performance aspects of feedback control. Middle managers have more balanced interests in all areas of control but are charged with the responsibility of developing control systems and maintaining standards for concurrent control purposes. First-line managers have high concern for immediate feedback and correction through concurrent control. They are less concerned about establishing the overall mission in preliminary control or the analysis of results in feedback control except where these affect day-to-day control factors.

Figure 8.5 illustrates a generic quality control system in production. Control of inputs, operating processes, and outputs are important elements of the system. The feedback loops unify these elements. Chapters 13 through 17 discuss specific quantitative techniques used in these quality control systems.

PRODUCT AND PROCESS CONTROL

Inspection and measurement, which will be discussed fully in Chapter 13, form the basis for both product and process control. As illustrated in the generic process control model of Figure 8.5, inspection for quality occurs at three major points in the production system: at the receipt of incoming materials and purchased parts, during production, and at the finished product stage. If we look back at the cost of quality

FIGURE 8.4 Management Control Emphasis

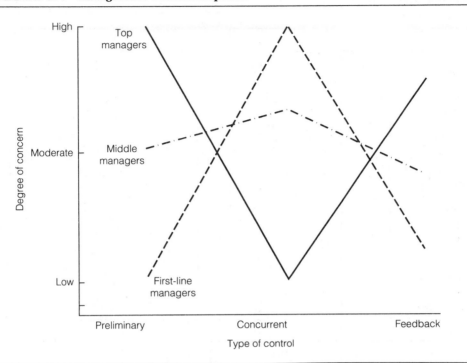

SOURCE: George R. Terry and Stephen G. Franklin, *Principles of Management,* 8th ed. (Homewood, IL: Irwin, 1982), p. 430.

discussion from Chapter 3, we see that inspection is a major contributor to appraisal costs. Historically, quality control was built around inspection. Today, the trend is to eliminate inspection, particularly for product control, through better prevention and concurrent process control. Many Japanese and U.S. manufacturers work closely with suppliers to solve quality problems and establish programs for statistical quality control. Often, however, manufacturers will perform additional inspections of incoming goods and final products to ensure compliance to quality specifications.

Acceptance Inspection

Historically, the control of incoming materials is performed by means of an *acceptance inspection.* The purpose of acceptance inspection is to make decisions on whether to accept or reject a group of items (formally called a *lot*) based on specified quality characteristics. Several different types of acceptance inspection methods are used in industry. The most common are spot checks, 100% inspection, and acceptance sampling.

Spot-check procedures select a fixed percentage of a lot for inspection. This might typically be 10% of the lot, or periodic removal of every tenth, twentieth, etc., box of items that are delivered. The problem with spot checking is its lack of scientific basis. Spot checking is not based on statistical principles and hence does not give an assessment of the risks of making an incorrect decision. In fact, a fixed percentage

FIGURE 8.5 Generic Process Quality Control System

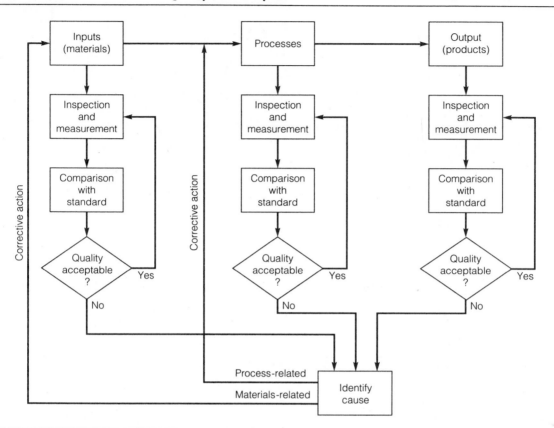

method gives different levels of risk for different lot sizes. Spot checking is more useful as a quantity-verification tool to reconcile billing invoices than as a decision tool for quality verification.

One hundred percent inspection is essentially a sorting method and theoretically will eliminate all nonconforming items from a lot. However, it is usually very costly and impractical for large lot sizes or when destructive tests are used. One hundred percent inspection may even give false results, because the monotony and repetition associated with the task can create boredom and fatigue in inspectors. Situations exist where 100% inspection is necessary, however. They include inspection of products with critical safety requirements or those with high internal or external failure costs.

Recent technological advances in automated inspection are making 100% inspection increasingly feasible in some industries. Such technology, when integrated with manufacturing tools, can eliminate the need for manual control-charting techniques. However, this technology is still in its infancy and is not available on a widespread basis, especially to small manufacturers.

The third method, often the most desirable, is **acceptance sampling.** This method is based on taking a statistically determined random sample and using a

FIGURE 8.6 Acceptance Sampling Procedure

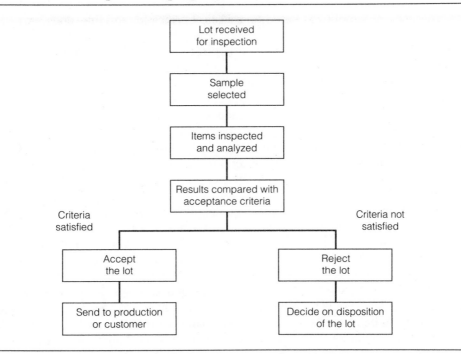

decision rule to determine acceptance or rejection of the lot based on the observed number of nonconforming items. This is the only feasible method to test quality when destructive testing is used or when 100% inspection is not feasible or is too time-consuming.

The general acceptance sampling procedure is shown in Figure 8.6. A lot is received from a vendor or from final assembly. Items from the lot are inspected for quality characteristics, and the results are compared with acceptance criteria. If these criteria are satisfied, the lot is accepted and sent to production or shipped to the customers; otherwise, the lot is rejected. Determination of whether to accept or reject a lot is often called **lot sentencing.** We emphasize that this is the true purpose of acceptance sampling; it is not appropriate for estimation of the quality of lots. That is, acceptance sampling techniques should not be used to attempt to determine the fraction nonconforming or average value of a quality characteristic. Other statistical sampling schemes are appropriate.

The rejection of a lot brings up the questions of the lot's disposition, remedial action to be taken, rework time, difficulty in meeting delivery schedules, and additional financial burdens on the supplier. The most common alternatives are (1) to keep the lot (often at a reduced price to compensate the buyer for lower quality) and remove nonconforming items during production or (2) to return the rejected lot to the supplier. The first alternative is not a good one, although if no other sources of product are available, it may be preferable to a production stoppage. With the second alternative, the supplier must pay the shipping cost, and the rejected lot will be screened, defective units will be reworked or replaced, and the lot will be resubmitted by the supplier. The extra burden placed on the supplier often provides good motivation to improve quality!

Acceptance sampling is based on statistical principles and thus does provide an assessment of risk in the decision. In addition, it has other advantages. Acceptance sampling is relatively inexpensive and particularly well suited to destructive testing situations. It takes less time than 100% inspection, thus reducing the workload of inspectors. It also requires less handling and therefore decreases the chance of damage. Finally, acceptance sampling generally does not lead to inspector fatigue as does 100% inspection. Acceptance sampling is also a very flexible method; the amount of inspection can be varied depending on the quality history. Since entire lots are rejected, there is economic and psychological pressure on vendors to improve quality rather than simply to replace the nonconforming items.

Despite its widespread use, acceptance sampling has been condemned as a traditional approach to inspection because it does not involve the philosophy of prevention and improvement. Acceptance sampling is based on a policy of *detection,* that is, after-the-fact product inspection by quality control personnel not associated with production. The problem with this approach is that a large quantity of nonconforming products might have already been made and unnecessary costs will have to be incurred to correct any mistakes. Additionally, the quality control inspector would not know whether nonconformance was caused by special causes or whether the controlled process is simply not capable of producing to specifications. This can easily result in behavioral problems among manufacturing, engineering, purchasing, and quality personnel; low employee morale; and customer dissatisfaction. An alternative is to maintain ongoing control over the process by the person who knows it best—the operator.

Line employees should be trained to recognize when out-of-control conditions arise. Their responsibility is to call attention to the problem and help propose solutions. In most cases, they do not have the expertise or authority to determine process capability, revise specification limits, or make major improvements in processes. These are all actions that management must take if quality is to be improved with these activities.

This approach of *process,* rather than *product,* inspection is a prevention-oriented strategy and allows an organization to reduce the variation in its production output. It is simply good management to try to reduce the variation of any quality characteristic. Low variation means greater uniformity of product, higher productivity due to reduction of scrap and rework, and improved competitive position. This last point is worthy of note from the viewpoint of business strategy. If two companies produce the same product, the one that can demonstrate more consistent uniformity and quality is likely to receive more business. In the automotive industry today, for example, suppliers are *required* to provide evidence of statistical process control to their customers. The survivors in this competitive market will be those with demonstrated quality.

As a temporary measure for quality control, however, acceptance sampling can serve a critical role.[3] A key factor is whether or not the process from which the product is manufactured is in statistical control. In a process that is in statistical control, the only changes in the process are caused by random variation—common

---

[3]Dan K. Fitzsimmons, "Gaining Acceptance for Acceptance Sampling," *Quality Progress,* April 1989, pp. 46–48.

causes. Since the only difference between "good" lots and "bad" lots is random variation, the likelihood of another bad lot occurring after one bad lot is no greater than a bad lot occurring after a good one. Thus, there is nothing to gain by accepting or rejecting lots that are, in reality, statistically indistinguishable. This is one of Deming's principal criticisms of acceptance inspection.

If a process is not in statistical control, variation in lots is due to an assignable cause outside of the system of common causes. In this case, the likelihood that a bad lot will occur after one bad lot is much greater than after a good one. It is reasonable to inspect the lot more carefully as well as subsequent lots. Sampling inspection only makes sense if there is something to be learned from it.

Motorola, one of the first recipients of the Malcolm Baldrige National Quality Award, uses sampling inspection as a temporary means of quality control until permanent corrective actions can be implemented.[4] Statistical sampling plans are used to inspect each lot as each operation is finished. Historical data on defects per million are used to select a sampling plan that has a high confidence level of rejecting lots that do not meet requirements. Each operator can decide to either scrap or to 100% inspect the product in question before sending it to the next operation. The result is that each operation receives only product that is known to be good and can therefore concentrate on process control and avoiding defects. While no sampling plan or 100% inspection can guarantee that all defects are eliminated, the combination of these techniques makes near-perfection possible.

An Economic Model for Inspection Decisions

In deciding whether or not to use acceptance sampling, one must first ask: What would be the result of allowing a nonconforming item to continue through production or on to the consumer? If the result might be a safety hazard, costly repairs or correction, or some other intolerable condition, the conclusion would probably be to use 100% inspection. If the sampling plan is properly chosen and implemented, lots of good quality will be accepted more often than rejected, and lots of poor quality will be rejected more often than accepted. Remember, however, that with sampling, there is always a risk that a small percentage of nonconforming items will be passed.

Unless there is destructive testing (in which case, sampling is necessary) or there are critical safety concerns (in which case, 100% inspection is warranted), the choice among the three options (no inspection, 100% inspection, and sampling) is basically an economic issue. In fact, we can easily show that on a strict economic basis, the choice is to have either no inspection or 100% inspection. This viewpoint is strongly advocated by Deming.

Let C_1 = cost of inspection and removal of a nonconforming item, C_2 = cost of repair if a nonconforming item is allowed to continue to the next point in the production process, and p = true fraction of nonconforming items in the lot. The expected cost per item for 100% inspection is clearly C_1; the expected cost per item for no inspection is pC_2. Setting these equal to each other yields the break-even value for p:

$$pC_2 = C_1$$
$$p = C_1/C_2$$

---

[4]Ed Pena, "Motorola's Secret to Total Quality Control," *Quality Progress,* October 1990, pp. 43–45.

Thus, if $p > C_1/C_2$, the best decision is to use 100% inspection; if $p < C_1/C_2$, it is more economical to do nothing at all.

In practice, however, both the costs C_1 and C_2 and the true fraction nonconforming p are difficult to determine accurately. The value of C_1 includes the capital cost of equipment used in the inspection process, depreciation, and residual value, and operating costs including labor, rent, utilities, maintenance, and replacement parts. Included in C_2 are the costs of disassembly and repair, sorting products to find the nonconformances, warranty repair costs if the products are shipped, and cost of lost sales. Many of these costs change over time. In addition, finding p requires sampling inspection in the first place. A useful rule of thumb is that if p is known to be much greater than C_1/C_2, use 100% inspection; if p is much less than this ratio, do not inspect. If p is close to C_1/C_2 or is highly variable, use sampling for protection and auditing purposes. In any case, sampling can actually increase costs if performed indiscriminately.

The choice of an acceptance inspection method should be based on the quality history of the supplier. If the quality history is very good—as evidenced by good statistical control of the supplier's processes and a low process average—there should be no need for inspection. If, on the other hand, quality history is poor or there is evidence of lack of statistical control, some form of acceptance sampling should be used.

Control through Prevention

As we have seen, acceptance inspection serves only as a control mechanism for attempting to prevent poor-quality products from being delivered to customers. Because it is a sampling technique, a risk always exists that some nonconforming products will pass through the acceptance inspection process. On-line methods of process control are better alternatives since they allow corrective action to be taken at the source of production to reduce the defect rate. Typical sources of defects in production are omitted processing, processing errors, setup errors, missing parts, wrong parts, and adjustment errors. The most effective approach to controlling quality is a simple one: *Prevent* defects from occurring at all. The Japanese call this a **Zero** (defect) **Quality Control (ZQC)** system.[5] ZQC consists of the following processes:

1. *Source inspection:* Checking for factors that cause errors, not the resulting defect.

2. *100% inspection:* Using inexpensive *poka-yoke* (mistake-proofing) devices to inspect automatically for errors or defective operating conditions.

3. *Immediate action:* Operations are stopped instantly when a mistake is made and not resumed until it is corrected.

ZQC is based on the fact that human beings tend to make mistakes inadvertently. Mistakes can result from forgetfulness, misunderstanding, errors in identification, lack of skill, absentmindedness, lack of standards, or equipment malfunctions. Blaming workers not only discourages them and lowers morale, but does not solve the problem. **Poka-yoke** is a technique for avoiding simple human error at work. It was

[5]From *Poka-yoke: Improving Product Quality by Preventing Defects.* Edited by NKS/Factory Magazine, English translation copyright © 1988 by Productivity Press, Inc. P.O. Box 3007, Cambridge, MA 02140, (800) 394-6868. Reprinted by permission.

FIGURE 8.7 A Poka-yoke Example of Screw Redesign

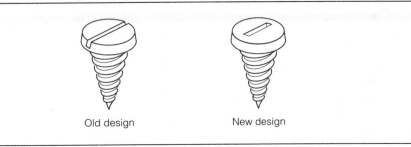

Old design   New design

problem. **Poka-yoke** is a technique for avoiding simple human error at work. It was developed and refined by the late Shigeo Shingo, a Japanese manufacturing engineer who developed the Toyota production system. The idea is to take over repetitive tasks or actions that depend on vigilance or memory so as to free workers' time and minds to pursue more creative and value-adding activities.

Poka-yoke is focussed on prediction—recognizing that a defect is about to occur—and detection—recognizing that a defect has occurred. Many applications of poka-yoke are deceptively simple, yet very creative. One example might be color-coding a wiring template to assist the worker. Another is installing a device on a drill to count the number of holes drilled in a workpiece; a buzzer sounds if the workpiece is removed before the correct number of holes has been drilled. A third example involves cassette covers that were frequently scratched when the screwdriver slipped out of the screw slot and slid against the plastic covers. The screw design was changed as shown in Figure 8.7 to prevent the screwdriver from slipping. A fourth example involved a metal roller used to laminate two surfaces bonded with hot melted glue. The glue tended to stick to the roller and cause defects in the laminate surface. An investigation showed that if the roller were dampened the glue would not stick. A secondary roller was added to dampen the steel roller during the process, preventing the glue from sticking. As a final example, one production step at Motorola involves putting alphabetic characters on a keyboard, then checking to make sure each key is placed correctly. A group of workers designed a clear template with the letters positioned slightly off center. By holding the template over the keyboard, assemblers can quickly spot mistakes. In the next chapter we shall discuss various methods for creatively generating ideas to solve problems.

MATERIALS CONTROL

Control of incoming materials depends heavily on purchasing practices and supplier involvement in total quality. One of Deming's 14 Points suggests establishing long-term relationships and moving toward single sourcing of purchased materials. By establishing long-term relationships, companies can work more closely with suppliers to improve the incoming quality of purchased materials.

The role of the purchasing department involves assuring that specifications are clear and precise, that the vendor understands these instructions, that purchasing has good information on vendor performance, and that vendor selections be made based on quality considerations, not solely on price. Close cooperation between purchasing departments and vendors frequently benefits both suppliers and customers.

One example of such cooperation involves the Swingline Company, a manufacturer of staplers.[6] A case involved a part called a "follow block" that pushes the staples forward. The tolerances on the part used to be very tight and the part had to be assembled by hand. A supplier suggested that the tolerances could be opened. After review, the tolerances were loosened and the part could be assembled automatically, improving productivity while retaining quality.

Many different approaches are used to ensure supplier quality. A drill bit manufacturer in Texas conducts quality evaluations at suppliers' plants. The inspections are always on short notice and are designed to see if the supplier is following appropriate quality control procedures. The Delco Moraine Division, a manufacturer of automotive brake controls, uses a vendor awareness program that includes a videotape presentation that is shown at supplier plants. The tape focuses on quality, and the company has found that supplier employees are better able to relate their work to Delco. At Bell Helicopter Textron, "quality alerts" are sent to subcontractors telling them of quality problems that have surfaced. They state the problem, outline corrective action, and require receipt to be acknowledged.

Formal programs typically are established to rate and certify vendors who provide quality materials in a cost-effective and timely manner. A survey by *Purchasing* magazine reported that almost two-thirds of major manufacturing firms in the United States have supplier rating programs.[7] The reasons reported for rating suppliers were

- to improve quality: 91%
- to reduce costs: 56%
- to end inspections: 56%
- to reduce suppliers: 45%
- to award/reward suppliers: 39%
- to improve delivery: 15%

The Pharmaceutical Manufacturers Association defines a certified supplier to be one that, after extensive investigation, is found to supply material of such quality that it is not necessary to perform routine testing on each lot received. Customers rely on sound in-process inspection, effective process controls, and inspection data generated by the supplier. Certification provides recognition for high-quality suppliers, which motivates them to improve continuously and attract more business.

Florida Power and Light has a three-tier vendor certification program.[8] Suppliers can be certified as a "Quality Vendor," "Certified Vendor," and "Excellent Vendor." To become a Quality Vendor, a supplier's products or services must meet basic requirements of quality, cost, delivery, and safety. In addition, the supplier must have a quality improvement process in place and must demonstrate that they have achieved

---

[6]"Quality Rests on an Active Supplier," *Purchasing,* January 28, 1982.

[7]Tom Stundza, "Suppliers on the Hot Seat," *Purchasing,* January 17, 1991, pp. 92–98.

[8]John J. Hudiburg, *Winning With Quality: The FPL Story* (White Plains, NY: Quality Resources, 1991).

significant improvements. They must also have an audit system to certify the process and the results. To become a Certified Vendor, the supplier must also have demonstrated the use of statistical process control and prove that their processes can meet FPL's specification requirements. They must also be able to document their capability and have a plan for continuous quality improvement. To achieve Excellent Vendor status, suppliers must demonstrate the ability to exceed FPL's specification requirements, employ reliability assurance techniques, and show that quality improvement is a central part of their management system.

Successful suppliers have a culture that shares in customers' goals, commitments, and risks to promote a long-term relationship (recall one of Deming's 14 Points about supplier relationships—not purchasing solely on the basis of price). At the Gillette Company, for example, the supplier certification program begins with Gillette identifying those suppliers that have a proven ability to meet its specifications.[9] Once a supplier is selected to participate, Gillette looks for them to establish a preproduction planning system to assess the capability of their process to meet Gillette's specifications. Feedback is provided in the form of recommended changes that will improve quality, reduce cost, or facilitate ease of manufacture. The responsibilities of Gillette's certified suppliers are:

1. To control production processes during manufacture to prevent nonconformities.

2. To control product and measure conformance against acceptance criteria to ensure that the product shipped will meet Gillette's requirements.

3. To provide suitable quantitative and/or qualitative inspection data with each lot.

4. To maintain the integrity of the production lot and ensure traceability of inspection data to a specific lot.

5. To develop internal and external feedback systems to provide prompt and effective corrective actions when required.

The American Society for Quality Control's Customer-Supplier Technical Committee developed specific criteria for supplier certification.[10] A certified supplier should:

■ Have virtually no product-related lot rejections for a significant time period, usually for 12 months, or in some cases two years.

■ Have no nonproduct-related rejections for a stated period of time. By nonproduct-related, we mean mismarkings on a container, for example. Nonproduct-related problems require different types of corrective action than product-related problems. Typically, it is easier and faster to correct nonproduct-related problems.

■ Have no production-related negative incidents for a stated period of time, usually six months. While incoming inspections determine conformance to

---

[9]Mike Lovitt, "Responsive Suppliers Are Smart Suppliers," *Quality Progress,* June 1989, pp. 50–53.

[10]Richard A. Maass, "Supplier Certification—A Positive Response to Just-In-Time," *Quality Progress,* Vol. 21, No. 9, September 1988, pp. 75–80.

specifications, specifications cannot possibly define every aspect of a product. Production-related problems are not always detectable by inspection and can result in latent defects that only become apparent later in the product's life.

- Have successfully passed a recent on-site quality system evaluation (audit), usually within the past year.

- Have an agreed-on specification. Documentation should not contain ambiguous phrases such as "free of flash" or "no characteristic odor."

- Have a fully documented process and quality system. This should include the use of statistical process control and a program for continuous improvement.

- Have the ability to furnish timely copies of certificates of analysis, inspection data, and test results.

The details of supplier certification programs vary by company, and such programs are time-consuming and expensive to administer. Nevertheless, they are an important means of controlling incoming materials, particularly in a "just-in-time" environment, which we discuss next.

Just-in-Time as a Quality Control Method

Inventory is any idle good that is held for future use. Inventory is a major contributor to poor quality because it hides quality problems; if a part is bad, there is always a backup. Large lot sizes that may have been produced hours, days, or even months ago do not provide proper feedback for identifying and correcting quality problems. With automation, in particular, high-quality materials are essential. In addition, inventory causes excessive material handling, which contributes to cost and does not add value to the product. The Japanese consider inventory simply as *waste*.

George Stalk, Jr., vice president of the Boston Consulting Group, pointed out that many companies are finding that traditional methods of forecasting, production scheduling, and control do not work in a dynamic, competitive environment.[11] He states that excessive delays in receiving and acting on information from the marketplace distorts the production system and creates disruption, waste, and inefficiency. To alleviate these problems, he advocates correcting manufacturing techniques, sales and distribution, and innovation processes. The correction of manufacturing techniques involves the adoption of a variety of material management techniques that fall under the label of "time-based" innovations. Time-based techniques revolve around cutting delays in generating and processing paperwork, reducing costs, and improving customer service. It also involves decentralized design, use of cross-functional teams, simultaneous engineering where several groups work on various components of the product simultaneously, and introduction of small increments of improvement frequently, rather than large increments infrequently. All this becomes focused in the "just-in-time" philosophy at the operating level.

Just-in-time (JIT)[12] is the Japanese approach to material management and control. JIT is more than a new way of handling material management; it represents a

---

[11]George Stalk, Jr., "Time—The Next Source of Competitive Advantage," *Harvard Business Review,* July/August 1988. Copyright © 1988 by the President and Fellows of Harvard College; all rights reserved. Reprinted in *Quality Progress,* June 1989, pp. 61–68.

[12]Portions of this section were adapted from James R. Evans et al., *Applied Production and Operations Management,* 3rd ed. (St. Paul, MN: West Publishing Co., 1991), pp. 706–714.

philosophy whose objective is to eliminate all sources of waste, including unnecessary inventory and scrap in production. Richard J. Schonberger describes JIT as a "quality and scrap control tool, as a streamlined plant configuration that raises process yield, as a production line balancing approach, and as an employee involvement and motivational mechanism."[13] The basic philosophy is to reduce inventories to as close to zero as possible by producing only enough units to keep the next work station in a production process in operation. For example, grocery stores routinely receive only enough merchandise to keep their shelves stocked. There is very little inventory kept in the stockroom. Consequently, delivery trucks bring in milk and bread each day. Other trucks deliver canned goods every two or three days. In manufacturing operations, Japanese auto manufacturers in both Japan and the United States routinely encourage their suppliers to locate plants as close as possible to their factories so that frequent deliveries of small lots of parts can be made to the assembly lines.

JIT cannot function properly if production has a high rate of defective items. Implementation of JIT requires painstakingly careful attention to quality both in purchasing and in production. Since lot sizes are small and there is no safety stock to back up nonconforming items, any quality problem disrupts the flow of materials through the plant. Conversely, a TQM philosophy can be strengthened by the immediate feedback on quality that is a natural result of having a JIT system in place. A joint TQM/JIT philosophy focuses on the fact that there must be continuous, intensive effort to coordinate closely all production activities into a single integrated system. Quality is the bonding force that holds the system together.

Coopers & Lybrand, a prominent consulting firm, outlines requirements for linking suppliers, JIT, and a TQM philosophy.[14] They prescribe a 10-step approach:

1. Reduce the number of active suppliers to reduce travel and administrative costs. To choose the best suppliers, use a supplier rating system based on past or potential performance on dimensions of quality, schedule, and cost.

2. Hold a meeting between top management and quality and purchasing representatives of supplier and customer firms to obtain commitment to a supplier certification process.

3. Conduct a supplier audit (detailed later in this chapter) to determine the supplier's capability to produce a quality product.

4. Consider the supplier preliminarily qualified. Since the initial audit may require follow-up on certain items, preliminary qualification indicates that the supplier meets "entrance" requirements, subject to certain restrictions and follow-up activities.

5. Form a supplier/customer team consisting of manufacturing, engineering, quality, and purchasing representatives who will review technical requirements and processing methods so as to deliver a conforming product every time.

---

[13]Richard J. Schonberger, *Japanese Manufacturing Techniques,* (New York: The Free Press, 1982), pp. 17–18.

[14]Adapted from "Supplier Participation in Total Quality Control and Just-in-Time," *Manufacturing Insights,* newsletter of Coopers & Lybrand, Cincinnati, OH, Management Consulting Services.

6. During the requirements review, the team will identify, agree to, and document the following:

   a. specific product and process specifications

   b. product characteristics that can impact the reliability and manufacturability of the finished product

   c. preventive methods to ensure conformance and reduce variation.

7. Use statistical methods to project the amount of variation that is permissible in the qualified product. Consider variations in raw materials, machines, gages, fixtures, and processes that may affect the product.

8. During the validation process, the team has the responsibility for determining root causes of any problems and deciding whether immediate quick fixes or permanent fixes are warranted. They will recommend a move to the final phase of certification if:

   a. variation in product, process, and equipment is stable

   b. the supplier and customer agree that the product will meet the requirements on a continuing basis.

9. To further the objectives of a just-in-time system, companies should strive for elimination of incoming inspection of goods from suppliers. One of the following three procedures for certification will advance that goal:

   a. For new local suppliers or a product with a history of nonconformance, conduct an on-site inspection at the supplier's facility while the product is being made for a series of 5 to 20 lots or shipments. Review control charts, inspection and process data that documents conformance to requirements, and actual inspection procedures to determine adequate methods and training.

   b. For out-of-town suppliers or products with a history of nonconformance, the company should perform acceptance sampling of initial lots from the supplier in the company's facility. Perform sampling inspections of the first 5 to 10 lots received. If they pass inspection, then sample inspect every other lot for the next 10 to 20 lots. If all lots conform, end incoming inspection. If any lot fails, determine root causes, take corrective action, and restart the qualification process based on judgment of the problem and the probable effectiveness of the corrective action taken.

   c. For suppliers who have a very good history, use historical inspection results to end incoming inspection. Be sure, however, that new products are similar enough to old ones to provide a valid comparison before taking steps to end such inspections.

10. Perform re-audits on a quarterly, semiannual, or annual schedule to determine if steps are needed to correct current problems or prevent future ones. Ask questions about the need for equipment overhaul, tool replacement, and process and quality improvement plans and activities.

CONTROL OF HUMAN PERFORMANCE

The control of the quality of human performance is as important as the control of manufactured output. Clearly this is an important function in service organizations. Many managers believe that control can be accomplished through performance appraisal systems. One of Deming's 14 Points criticizes the use of such systems because they do not recognize the nature of variation properly. The contribution of one individual is often impossible to separate from that of the system. Performance appraisal destroys teamwork if people are rated only on meeting individual goals. Variability actually increases as people try to emulate others who receive high ratings. Furthermore, it is not practical for managers to rank individual performance when it is affected by complex interactions within the work system. The result degenerates to a lottery. Managers, therefore, need to understand the concept of variation and its implications for control.

Some quality problems are management-controllable while others are operator-controllable. To be operator-controllable, three conditions must be met: (1) The operators must have the means of knowing what is expected of them through clear instructions and specifications, (2) they must have the means of determining their actual performance, typically through inspection and measurement, and (3) they must have a means of making corrections if they discover a variance between what is expected of them and their actual performance. If any of these criteria is not met, then the quality problem must be management-controllable, not operator-controllable.

Both Juran and Deming make this important distinction. One of the major problems that has confronted American industry is the inability to distinguish between these two types of controllability. If operators are held accountable for or expected to act on problems that are beyond their control, the result is only frustration and eventual game-playing with management. Juran and Deming state that the vast majority of quality problems are management controllable; they are the result of common cause variation. For the smaller proportion of operator-controllable problems resulting from special causes, operators must be given the tools to identify them, and the authority to take action. It is this philosophy that has shifted the burden of quality from inspection departments and quality control personnel to workers on the line. Operator-controllable quality problems can be identified using control charts. Management-controllable problems require more creative approaches. In the next chapter on quality improvement, we address some of these.

One of the vital links in a control system is the statistical reporting of quality. The use of statistical quality reports can help managers to determine quality at every level. Top managers need to be assured that "Our quality is as good as or better than our competitors' and is improving." Middle managers need feedback that tells them "Our system is working properly to correct errors in a timely fashion, and our managers are quality oriented." First-line managers need feedback that tells them "Here are yesterday's quality problems that were corrected, and here are today's problems that must still be corrected."

Recently, with increasing competition, the need for improvements in quality, productivity, and effectiveness, and the accelerated pace of technological change, managers have begun to realize that historical concepts of control of human resources no longer work very well. The old concept was based on the premises that (1) people were part of the process, (2) the process needed to be controlled to be productive, and (3) managers thus had to control carefully what people did. Today there has been a shift in that thinking to (1) people design and redesign the process; (2) the process must be controlled by people to be productive; and (3) managers thus must obtain the commitment of people to design, redesign, and control processes so that they can remain productive. There are benefits, costs, and long-range strategic issues that must be addressed if the movement from a "control philosophy" to a "commitment philosophy" is to continue.

A study of the benefits versus costs of moving from a control to a commitment model suggests the following.[15] Benefits include higher in-plant quality, lower warranty costs, less waste, higher machine utilization, increased capacity with the same plant and equipment, reduced operating and support personnel, reduced turnover and absenteeism, faster implementation of change, and the development of human skills and individual self-esteem. The costs to managers include investment in extra effort, development of new skills and relationships, coping with higher levels of ambiguity and uncertainty, pain and discomfort associated with changing habits and attitudes, and obsolete skills and careers that are casualties of change. The costs to workers and unions include the discomfort over changes in attitudes and skills and the uncertainty associated with increased responsibility.

To obtain long-term worker commitment, significant organizational changes must occur: Unions must be convinced to support the changes, provisions must be made for job security, compensation must be adequate for the increased responsibilities, the effects of changing technology must be monitored carefully, and the role of supervisors must change. Motivation and leadership theories can play a central role in moving from a state of control to one of commitment. Additional impacts of quality on human resource management will be discussed in a later chapter.

CONTROL OF THE QUALITY SYSTEM

Most business people think of an audit as related to an examination of financial records. Such audits are routinely performed and often required by law. Managers must also think of audits of the quality system. A **quality audit** is a systematic and independent examination and evaluation to determine whether quality activities and results comply with planned arrangements and whether these arrangements are implemented effectively and are suitable to achieve objectives.[16] As such, quality audits provide a means of control over the quality system itself. Quality audits are necessary for several reasons:[17] (1) Audits provide benchmarks for determining whether or not a quality system is complete; (2) periodic audits make everyone aware that the organization is serious about continually improving quality; (3) audits often reveal activities that are innovative or performed in an exceptional fashion and can be highlighted and shared throughout the organization; (4) audits can reveal areas that are inadequate or need improvement; (5) audits become a permanent record of the progress in achieving the goals of the quality system; and (6) audits have become an important part of supplier quality certification systems.

---

[15]Richard E. Walton, "From Control to Commitment in the Workplace," *Harvard Business Review,* Vol. 63, No. 2, March/April 1985, pp. 77–84. Copyright © 1985 by the President and Fellows of Harvard College; all rights reserved.

[16]ANSI/ASQC A3-1987, "Quality Systems Terminology" (Milwaukee, WI: ASQC, 1987).

[17]Joseph R. Tunner, *A Quality Technology Primer for Managers* (Milwaukee, WI: ASQC Quality Press, 1990).

A typical quality audit focuses on a variety of issues, including:

- *Management involvement and leadership:* Are all levels of management involved? To what extent are they involved?

- *Product and process design:* Do products meet customer needs? Are products designed for easy manufacturability?

- *Product control:* Is a strong product control system in place? Does the system concentrate on defect *prevention,* before the fact, rather than defect *removal* after the product is made?

- *Customer and supplier communications:* Does everyone understand who the customer is? To what extent do customers and suppliers communicate with each other?

- *Quality improvement programs:* Is there a quality improvement plan? What results have been achieved?

- *Employee participation:* Are all employees actively involved in quality improvement?

- *Education and training:* What is done to ensure that everyone understands his or her job and has the necessary skills? Are employees trained in quality improvement techniques?

- *Quality information:* How is feedback on quality results collected and used?

The Baldrige Award criteria can provide a convenient checklist for a quality audit.

Quality audits, performed in a timely fashion and in a positive spirit, can be invaluable in achieving quality excellence. Care must be taken not to allow audits to become a trivial exercise, but to provide valuable information to managers.

The Ford Q1 Award[18]

"A plant designated as Q1 is recognized as having achieved a level of excellence, and as having in place processes/systems for continuous improvement in meeting the customers' needs and expectations." This is Ford Motor Company's description of its Q1 Award for suppliers, the basis for their vendor certification program. The Q1 program was initiated in 1981 and expanded in 1984 to include Ford manufacturing plants worldwide.

Figure 8.8 illustrates the qualification process. It begins with a plant conducting a complete self-evaluation, using a set of criteria, assessment factors, and scoring guidelines. The purpose of the self-evaluation is to identify the areas in which a plant's quality system may be deficient so that corrections and improvement may be made and evaluated prior to petitioning for Q1 consideration. Ford's Safety Office and Corporate Quality Office then conduct in-plant reviews of safety compliance and process capability. Once the plant has completed its self-evaluation, made improvements, and had the in-plant reviews conducted, the plant can initiate a formal petition.

The criteria used to determine if a plant is qualified for the Q1 Award is based on five categories:

1. *Adequacy of the quality system:* This includes indicators on how the plant manages change, employs teamwork and statistical methods, reviews incoming material, and rewards employees.

2. *Process capability review:* This is a check of selected process parameters and product characteristics to determine stability and capability.

3. *Internal quality indicators:* These are measured by quality audits.

4. *Customer satisfaction.*

5. *Management commitment:* This includes an evaluation of support and training.

[18]Adapted from *Q1 for Assembly Plants,* Copyright Ford Motor Company, 1989. Used with permission.

Specific items that are evaluated for the adequacy of the quality system include:

- advanced quality planning
- training for change
- organizational preparedness
- quality objectives during change periods
- change control procedures
- production responsibility for quality
- implementation of the team approach
- implementation support
- preliminary statistical studies
- measurement system variation studies
- statistical process control planning
- statistical control and capability implementation
- continuous improvement
- problem solving
- incoming material quality
- written procedures
- quality instructions
- gages and test equipment
- repair procedures
- reward system.

A scoring system is used to assess each of these criteria. For example, one of the items evaluated is "change control procedures." This is concerned with written procedures developed by the plant to maintain and improve quality during change. Questions considered are as follows: Are there written procedures describing responsibilities and actions during change? Are they current? Are they readily accessible to all affected personnel? The plant must show how this procedure was implemented during recent changes. Examples of how points are awarded are described below. Each plant may use

(continued)

FIGURE 8.8 **Ford's Q1 Qualification Process**

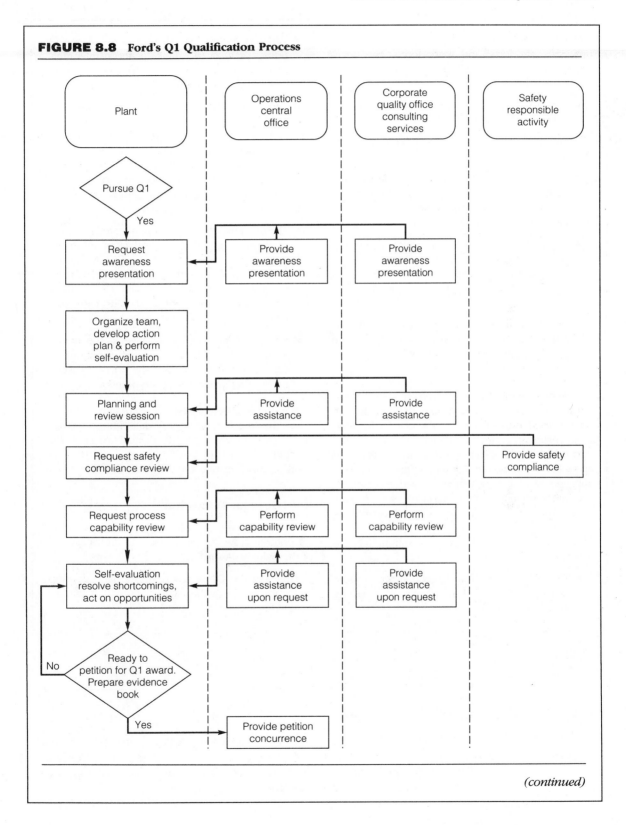

(continued)

varying approaches based on the nature of their processes, products, and work force. Any documented evidence that speaks to the intent of the questions will be considered.

- The plant has no procedure of any sort for managing change (0 points).

- The plant uses verbal procedures only for managing change (1 point).

- The plant has a written procedure on managing change, but there are major (2–4 points) or minor (5–6 points) shortcomings of a specific nature that should be resolved.

- The plant has an adequate written procedure on managing change. There is some evidence (7 points) or comprehensive evidence (8 points) that the procedure is implemented as written.

- The plant's change management procedure is innovative and disseminated throughout the plant's organization (9–10 points).

A second example is "measurement system variation studies." This question deals with the evaluation of and reaction to variation in the plant's measurement process. A Q1 plant will have statistical information on all of its major measurement systems and will have implemented improvement actions as appropriate. Questions that are considered include: Are measurement systems variation studies conducted on new and carryover devices, instruments, and systems for which the variation is not known? The scoring in this category is summarized as follows:

- There have been no studies conducted to assess variation on some of the plant's key measurement systems (0 points).

- Variation studies have been run on several (1 point) or most (4 points) of the plant's measurement systems, but no verification of process stability has taken place.

- Variation studies incorporating assessments or stability have been conducted on some (up to 30%–5 points) or most (31% to 90%–6 points) of the plant's measurement processes. Some of these studies have shown instability. Corrective actions have either not been incorporated or have not been in effect long enough to provide verification of effectiveness.

- The plant has effectively implemented measurement systems variation studies of all major measurement processes and will have implemented improvement actions on several (1 to 4 processes–7 points) or many (5 or more processes–8 points) of its measurement processes.

- The plant has been innovative in the understanding of measurement system variation and has advanced the state of the art of measurement of its processes (9–10 points).

A minimum weighted score is required for Q1 status. The focus of the overall qualification process is the *self-evaluation* by the plant. Ford provides consulting service to clarify, interpret, or provide additional information and assistance in the process.

Key Issues for Discussion

1. How would you describe the overall thrust of the Q1 criteria? How does it compare to the categories of the Baldrige Award?

2. How can the Q1 program help a plant develop and improve its quality system, even if it fails to qualify for the award?

Summary of Key Points

- Variation exists in all processes. Common causes of variation are the result of interactions of minor variations in all the elements of a process that can only be described in an aggregate sense. Special, or assignable causes of variation, arise from external sources and can be identified and corrected.

- A process is in statistical control if it is governed only by common causes. A process is out of control if special causes are present.

- Control is the continuing process of evaluating performance, comparing outputs to goals or standards, and taking corrective action when necessary.

- A control system has three components: (1) a standard or goal, (2) a means of measurement of accomplishment, and (3) comparison of actual results with the standard along with feedback to form the basis for corrective action.

- On-line quality control consists of control activities conducted during the production process itself; off-line quality control consists of control activities external to the production process.

- A useful conceptualization of control is a division into three stages: preliminary control, concurrent control, and feedback control. Top managers are most involved in preliminary control; first-line managers in concurrent control; and middle managers coordinate all categories.

- Acceptance inspection is making decisions on whether to accept or reject a lot based on specified quality characteristics. Since it is based principally on detection, it is a poor quality control method.

- An effective quality control method is prevention. The Japanese have developed a zero defects approach based on mistake-proofing or "poka-yoke."

- Purchasing departments play an important role in materials control. Vendor certification programs can help to eliminate receiving inspection and assure good quality of incoming materials.

- Just-in-time, while principally a method of material and inventory control, can support a TQM philosophy and provide a means of controlling quality.

- The majority of quality problems are management-controllable. Management must work closely with the work force and change antiquated approaches to the control of human performance.

- A quality audit is a systematic and independent examination and evaluation to determine whether quality activities and results comply with the planned goals of an organization.

Questions for Review and Discussion

1. Explain the difference between common and special causes of variation.

2. Provide examples of common causes and special causes of variation in the following:
   a. taking a college examination
   b. grilling a hamburger
   c. meeting a scheduled appointment.

3. Define the concept of statistical control in terms of common and special causes. How does this relate to Shewhart's definition of control?

4. Discuss the three components of any control system.

5. What is the difference between on-line and off-line quality control? Provide some examples.

6. Explain the concepts of preliminary control, concurrent control, and feedback control. How are these related to one another? Which of these is more important to which levels of management?

7. What is the purpose of acceptance inspection? Why is it not a good approach to quality control?

8. Describe different types of acceptance inspection methods. Under what conditions would each have advantages over the others?

9. Explain the economic model for choosing between no and 100% inspection? Why is this model difficult to apply in practice?

10. Describe the Japanese concept of Zero (defect) Quality Control.

11. What is *poka-yoke?* Provide some examples in your own activities at school or work.

12. What is the role of purchasing departments in quality control?

13. Explain why vendor certification programs are useful.

14. What is the relationship between quality control and just-in-time production methods?

15. How does the Coopers & Lybrand approach to JIT support a TQM philosophy?

16. What do we mean by "operator-controllable"? What implications does this have for management?

17. What is a quality audit? What issues typically are addressed during a quality audit?

18. Consider the following descriptions of two manufacturing facilities resulting from a quality audit:[19]

    Company A. In the PC board department, there is no in-process inspection, no agitation in the plating tanks, uncalibrated timing devices, improper stacking, inadequate temperature control of drying oven, no solder analysis, no pin gages for operators, poor lighting for final 100% inspection, and many rejects. General housekeeping was very poor with dust and corroded chemicals on shelves to contaminate the printed circuit boards placed on them.

    Company B. Complete in-line QC program with quality data sheets that stay with the lot from start to finish. Plating operations appear to be well instrumented. Enforced safety regulations. Neatly kept records. All workers seemed to be quality-minded. Every inspector is equipped with necessary gages, and all gages and instruments seem calibrated. Housekeeping of the entire plant was excellent. Workers in critical areas wear white coats and gloves to reduce contamination.

    Discuss the differences in control strategies between these two firms. What recommendations would you make to the manager of company A?

---

[19]Edward A. Reynolds, "The Science (Art?) of Quality Audit and Evaluation," *Quality Progress,* July 1990, pp. 55–56.

Problems

1. A radio manufacturer using 100% inspection was finding an average of two nonconforming items out of lots of 10,000 purchased electronic components. It is estimated that the cost of inspecting the component is $0.25, while the cost of replacing a nonconforming component after it has been assembled is about $25. What is the best economic inspection decision? How much is the manufacturer saving or losing per radio by his current inspection practice if each radio contains 60 of these components?

2. The cost to inspect a credit card statement in a bank is 25 cents, while correction of a mistake later amounts to $500. What is the break-even point in errors per thousand transactions for which 100% inspection is no more economical than no inspection?

Case Problem[20]

You are an internal auditor at Circle H Company, a producer of snack foods. The company has lost three major customer accounts in the last six months, at a cost of $3.5 million in annual sales. Preliminary investigation has revealed that, when these customers were asked to list five main reasons why they no longer buy your product, their responses were as listed:

Survey of Customer Responses

We no longer buy Circle H products because:

The product is stale or soggy.	0.9%
The flavor is poor.	3.9%
The product is too expensive.	16.0%
The packaging is inconvenient.	24.5%
Delivery and restocking are too slow.	21.3%
Preferred items aren't always available.	20.0%
Incorrect quantities are often delivered.	9.7%
Billing errors are often made.	2.9%
Other reasons.	0.8%

The president of Circle H has assigned you to perform a complete investigation to determine the causes of these quality problems and to recommend appropriate corrective action. You have authority to talk to any other person within the company.

[20]Adapted from ASQC Quality Auditor Certification Brochure, July 1989.

The early stages of your investigation reveal that the three reasons most often cited by customers as reasons why they are no longer buying the product are symptomatic of some major quality problems in the company's operations. In proceeding with the audit, you decide that it is necessary to review available data, which may yield indications of the root causes of these problems.

Further investigation reveals that, over a four-month period of time in the recent past, a procedural change was made in the order approval process. You wish to find out whether this change caused a significant difference in the amount of time required to process an order from field sales through shipping, and therefore decide to investigate this particular situation.

On completion of your investigation into the problems with order processing, you determine that the change in procedures for order approval have led to an increase in the amount of time required to restock your goods in the customers' stores. You want to recommend corrective action for this problem, but you first do additional investigation as to why the change was made. You learn that, because of large losses on delinquent accounts receivable, the change was made to require approval of restock orders by the credit manager. This change added an average of three hours of internal processing time to the amount of time to process a restock order.

On review of your report, the president of Circle H notes that there were administrative problems whose existence he had never suspected. To assure that corrective action will be effective and sustained, the president assigns you to take charge of the corrective action program.

Questions

1. What types of data would be most useful to review for clues as to why the three major customer complaints occurred?

2. How would you investigate whether the change in the order approval process had a significant effect on order processing time?

3. Given your knowledge that there are problems with both order processing and accounts receivable, what should you do?

Bibliography

Milligan, Glenn W. "Is Sampling Really Dead?," *Quality Progress,* Vol. 24, No. 4, April 1991, pp. 77–81.

Nikkan Kogyo Shimbun, Ltd./Factory Magazine. *Poka-yoke: Improving Product Quality by Preventing Defects,* Cambridge, MA: Productivity Press, 1988.

Shingo, Shigeo. *Zero Quality Control: Source Inspection and the Poka-yoke System,* (English translation), Cambridge, MA: Productivity Press, 1989.

Tunner, Joseph R. *A Quality Technology Primer for Mangers,* Milwaukee, WI: ASQC Quality Press, 1990.

Vardeman, Stephen B. "The Legitimate Role of Inspection in Modern SQC," *The American Statistician,* Vol. 40, No. 4, November 1986, pp. 325–328.

CHAPTER 9

Quality Improvement and Problem Solving

I n the last three chapters, we examined some of the important managerial and organizational issues in designing systems for assuring quality in organizations. Many managers believe that once a commitment to quality has been obtained and steps are taken to design and implement a quality assurance system, their quality problems are over. In fact, their problems may have just begun! Generally, when a new quality assurance system becomes operational, problems that have been covered up for a long time are discovered. Even after months and years of operation, a good quality assurance program will continue to reveal areas for improvement. Indeed, every manager's true goal should be the continual improvement of quality.

One of the key differences between managerial attitudes in Japan and the United States is encompassed in the old cliche "If it ain't broke, don't fix it." In other words, much of Western management is focused primarily on *maintaining* technical and operating functions. Japan, on the other hand, has a distinctive focus toward *improving* them. The improvement of quality should be a *proactive* task of management, not simply a reaction to problems and competitive threats.

In this chapter we focus on quality improvement, the improvement process, approaches to problem solving, and simple tools for quality improvement that assist in the problem-solving effort.

KAIZEN

The Japanese have a term for improvement—**kaizen** (ky'zen).[1] Kaizen is a philosophy, a way of life, that subsumes all business activities. Kaizen strategy has been called "the single most important concept in Japanese management—the key to Japanese competitive success." Often in the West, quality improvement is viewed simply as improvements in *product* quality. In the kaizen philosophy, improvement in all areas of business such as cost, meeting delivery schedules, employee safety and skill development, supplier relations, new product development, or productivity all enhance the *quality of the firm*. Thus, any activity directed toward improvement falls under the kaizen umbrella. Activities such as establishing traditional quality control systems, installing robotics and advanced technology, instituting employee suggestion

---

[1]Imai Masaaki, *KAIZEN—The Key to Japan's Competitive Success* (New York: McGraw-Hill, 1986).

systems, maintaining equipment, and implementing just-in-time production systems all lead to improvement.

Kaizen is different from innovation. Innovation, which generally represents the focus of Western management, results in large, short-term, and radical changes in products or processes. Often innovation is the result of substantial investment in equipment or technology with major rebuilding of entire plants. Innovation is dramatic and often championed by a few proponents. Formal economic analyses shown large returns on investment. Major innovations such as material requirements planning (MRP) or flexible manufacturing systems (FMS) grab the attention of top managers. The American automotive industry, for example, believed that it could cure its quality and competitive problems in the 1970s by the introduction of robots and other types of automated equipment. They learned that innovative technologies are not the magic cure.

Kaizen, on the other hand, is focused on small, frequent, and gradual improvements over a long term. Financial investment is minimal. Everyone, not just top management, is involved in the process; many improvements result from the know-how and experience of workers. People, not technologies, are the principal focus. Kaizen is a process-oriented way of thinking rather than a results-oriented approach, which is so characteristic of Western management thought. At Nissan Motor, for instance, any suggestion that saves at least 0.6 seconds in a production process is seriously considered by management. The concept of kaizen is so deeply ingrained in the minds of both managers and workers that they often do not even realize they are thinking in terms of improvement. Innovation is recognized to be an important aspect of kaizen; however, it is emphasized far less in Japan than in the West.

Quality improvement in the kaizen philosophy is first and foremost concerned with the quality of people. If quality of people is improved, then the quality of products will follow. By instilling kaizen into people and training them in basic quality improvement tools, workers can build this philosophy into their work and continually seek improvement in their jobs. This is the process-oriented approach to improvement and encourages constant communication among workers and managers.

How can everyone be involved in improvement activities? Top management, for example, can focus on improvement as an important component of corporate strategy, provide support to improvement activities by allocating resources effectively, and build systems, procedures, and reward structures that are conducive to improvement. Middle management can implement top management improvement goals by establishing, upgrading, and maintaining operating standards that reflect those goals; by improving cooperation between departments; and by making employees conscious of their responsibility toward improvement and developing their problem-solving skills through training. Supervisors can direct more of their attention to improvement rather than "supervision," provide better guidance for workers, and improve communication. Finally, workers can engage in improvement through suggestion systems and small group activities, self-development programs for problem solving, and enhanced job performance skills.

The foundation for quality improvement in the kaizen philosophy is the use of statistically-based tools for problem solving; we introduce these tools later in this chapter. The use of statistical tools ensures that problems are addressed objectively using hard data—not opinions or gut feelings. Thus, training is a critical aspect of kaizen. Training is conducted regularly for all levels of management and workers. Quality control and engineering knowledge is made available to shop floor personnel so that they can solve their own problems better. Employee involvement teams (see

Chapter 11) and other activities such as suggestion systems are also fundamental to kaizen.

The essence of kaizen is simple and just plain common sense. Much more can be said about kaizen, and we encourage readers to consult Imai's book. His thoughts are closely related to the philosophies of other leaders in quality, such as Deming, Juran, and Crosby. In the next section we discuss problem solving from a general perspective to provide the foundation for problem-solving methodologies for quality improvement.

THE NATURE OF PROBLEM SOLVING

For many years, problem solving and decision making have been the subjects of close scrutiny by scientists, management theorists, managers, and others. More than 20 years ago, Charles Kepner and Benjamin Tregoe wrote a classic book on problem solving and decision making.[2] In it, they define a **problem** as follows:

> A problem is a deviation between what should be happening and what actually is happening that is important enough to make someone think the deviation ought to be corrected. An unanticipated change produces this unwanted effect in place of the desired and expected effect. Before this often unknown change occurred, things were going as expected; afterwards, they are out of kilter, off plan, and out of control. Decision making will choose the action necessary to bring things back into line.

Three conditions characterize a problem. First, there must be several alternative courses of action available from which to choose. Second, the choice of a course of action can have a significant impact in the future. Third, there is some doubt as to which one to select. The selection of a course of action from several alternatives is called **decision making. Problem solving** is the activity associated with changing the state of what is actually happening to what should be happening.

Most problems usually can be categorized in one of three ways: structured, semistructured, or ill-structured. This classification is determined by the amount of information available about the "gap" between the present and desired states of affairs. For structured problems we have complete information about the problem — what is actually happening, what should be happening, and how to get there. Ill-structured problems, on the other hand, are characterized by a high degree of fuzziness or vagueness about this information. Semistructured problems fall somewhere in between. The usefulness of these classifications is that structured problems generally can be solved using routine, programmed decision-making techniques. Ill-structured problems require more creative solutions.

An example of a structured problem situation would be the case in which it is determined, perhaps using a control chart, that the diameter of a machined hole is larger than the desired specification. The operator might be instructed to check the cutting tool for wear and replace it when necessary.

An example of a semistructured problem might be the case of determining what quality control actions to take when a new production setup on the shop floor has been initiated. This is certainly less routine and well-defined as the previous case. A

---

[2]Charles H. Kepner and Benjamin B. Tregoe, *The Rational Manager* (New York: McGraw-Hill, 1965). Copyright © Kepner-Tregoe, Inc., 1965. All rights reserved. Reprinted with permission.

solution to this problem might be to employ the following rules: Run the first five parts after the setup and compute the average dimension. If it is within one standard deviation of the target, continue production. If it is between one and two standard deviations of the target, take another sample. If it is beyond two standard deviations, stop and adjust the setup. Such problems can generally be solved using routine decision aids, although it may take more creative effort to develop an acceptable solution.

Finally, an example of an ill-structured problem would be the situation in which it is determined that 35% of final assemblies do not meet performance requirements. There is considerably more ambiguity about the problem and how to go about solving it than in either of the two previous cases. Simple, programmed decision rules cannot be developed. Such problems must be addressed individually using structured problem-solving methodologies.

Problem solving is at the heart of quality improvement. The following example shows how Hewlett-Packard dealt with a problem involving one of its suppliers.

EXAMPLE 1 Solving a Supplier Reject Problem.[3] A supplier to Hewlett-Packard's Computer Division, in Cupertino, California, provided a unique assembly at a reasonable price but could not deliver the part without a high number of rejects. Management's first reaction was to consider a new supplier. However, the supplier had been difficult to find, and the decision was made to help the supplier do a better job.

A project team, headed by the procurement engineer and aided by the buyer and incoming inspection supervisor, was formed. Its goals were to eliminate incoming inspection and establish direct shipment of the supplier's assemblies into stock. The project team developed a three-stage plan to achieve these goals: investigation of why rejects occur, elimination of causes to gain quality confidence, and implementation of a plan to eliminate incoming inspection. Investigation was initiated by analyzing the vendor's production and quality assurance capabilities. HP had to make sure that the supplier had correct information on the product specifications required. It was found that the vendor's interpretation of the specification did not agree with HP's expectations for the part specified. The specification was therefore modified to better meet the objectives of both the supplier and HP.

Next, it was necessary to assure that the vendor's production process was capable of meeting HP's requirements. The vendor outlined the production process and noted several improvements that could be made to improve quality. HP and its supplier established the same quality-measuring methods, materials, and equipment at the vendor's facility that were used at the HP plant. HP also videotaped the supplier's process for better communication and as a reference for future audits, and performed on-site inspections on production runs prior to shipment.

To gain confidence, a close monitoring of HP data and vendor data was performed to ensure that the quality methods, materials, and equipment

---

[3]Adapted from John Flores and Constantine Pavsidis, "Help Your Supplier." Reprinted with permission from *Quality,* Vol. 23, September 1984, pp. 42–43, a publication of Hitchcock Publishing, a Capital Cities/ABC, Inc., Company.

established earlier were being used. The vendor was given positive feedback as encouragement to make corrections to its production processes. Communications were improved and control charts were used to verify that the processes were producing at an acceptable quality level.

Two of the major problems that were uncovered involved a disparity in specifications and measurement. The brightness specification for computer monitors was 47 foot lamberts (F.L.). For customers other than HP, the supplier's average brightness level was 38.25 F.L., with a minimum of 35 F.L. The supplier apparently misread or misunderstood HP's specification of 47. Also, a check revealed that measuring equipment and the adjustment instructions in the supplier's assembly stations were incompatible. The problems were corrected.

Eventually, routine incoming inspection was stopped. Product quality was monitored by using control charts and by making yearly visits to the vendor. When the charts indicated a quality problem, special inspections were made and corrective measures were taken. The benefits of this planning and action were that supplier appraisal costs and average lead times were reduced and 100% inspection and rework returns were eliminated.

How would you classify the problem faced by Hewlett-Packard? It probably falls into the ill-structured category due to its complexity and lack of clear information. This is characteristic of many important problems in quality assurance.

The HP case reveals some important aspects of problem solving. First, the number-of-rejects problem was not specific enough to be solved; it was a symptom of other problems, but not the problem in itself. We often call such a situation a *mess*. HP and the supplier first had to identify specific problems, such as the misinterpretation of specifications, in order to correct the situation. Second, the "gaining confidence" phase of the project relied on a significant amount of data collection and analysis. This enabled the problem solvers to generate ideas for possible solutions. The third step was to implement the solutions that were developed. The following section discusses these aspects of problem solving in more detail.

PROBLEM-SOLVING METHODOLOGY FOR QUALITY IMPROVEMENT

Problem solving is a highly creative effort. There are four major components of any problem-solving process:[4]

1. Redefining and analyzing the problem.

2. Generating ideas.

3. Evaluating and selecting ideas.

4. Implementing ideas.

---

[4]A. VanGundy, "Comparing 'Little Known' Creative Problem Solving Techniques," in *Creativity Week III, 1980 Proceedings* (Greensboro, NC: Center for Creative Leadership, 1981). The reader is also referred to James R. Evans, *Creative Thinking in the Decision and Management Sciences* (Cincinnati, OH: South-Western Publishing Co., 1991) for a thorough treatment of creative problem solving.

In redefining and analyzing a problem, information is collected and organized, the data and underlying assumptions are analyzed, and the problem is reexamined for new perspectives. At this stage, the goal of the problem solver is to collect facts and achieve a workable problem definition. The purpose of generating ideas is to develop potential solutions. The two most important considerations in this step are to defer all judgment about the ideas and to use many different techniques to generate them. After ideas have been generated, they are evaluated and the best ones are identified and selected. When problem solving is done in a group, as is most often the case with ill-structured problems, conflicts can easily develop. Thus, it is important at this stage to have a good leader and facilitator to reach a consensus. Finally, implementing ideas involves putting the solution to work. A great deal of psychology in selling ideas and solutions and gaining acceptance often is necessary. All these components were evident in the Hewlett-Packard example.

A variety of structured problem-solving processes that refine these general activities have been proposed. One process that we suggest for quality improvement (and for any problem-solving activity, for that matter) is adapted from creative problem-solving concepts advocated by Osborn[5] and Parnes.[6] This strategy consists of the following steps:

1. Understanding the "mess."

2. Finding facts.

3. Identifying specific problems.

4. Generating ideas.

5. Developing solutions.

6. Implementation.

Let us examine how these steps can be applied to quality improvement.

Mess Finding

Russell Ackoff, a noted authority on problem solving, defines a **mess** as a "system of external conditions that produces dissatisfaction."[7] Ackoff is careful to distinguish problems from messes. Managers in any organization generally deal with messes; problems must be identified and extracted from the "mess."

The mess in quality assurance is the true state of quality within an organization. Only if this is determined can specific problems be identified. Messes arise from several sources:

- A lack of knowledge about how a process works. This is particularly important if the process is performed by different people. Such lack of knowledge results in inconsistency and increased variation in outputs.

- A lack of knowledge about how a process *should* work. This includes understanding customer expectations and the goal of the process.

---

[5]A. Osborn, *Applied Imagination,* 3rd ed. (New York: Scribners, 1963).

[6]S. J. Parnes, R. B. Noller, and A. M. Biondi (eds.), *Guide to Creative Action* (New York: Scribners, 1977).

[7]Russell Ackoff, "Beyond Problem Solving," presented at the Fifth Annual Meeting of the American Institute for Decision Sciences, Boston, November 16, 1973.

- Errors in performing the steps involved in the process. In most cases, errors are inadvertent. The worker does not want to make errors and is unaware of having made them. Inadvertent errors occur randomly and occur because of lack of attention. In some cases, errors are willful. Often these are the result of poor management practices.

- Waste and complexity. Waste and complexity manifest themselves in many ways, such as unnecessary steps in a process, excess inventories, and so on.

- Excess variation. Reducing variation is the foundation of the philosophies of Deming and Juran.

Contributors to poor quality are often faults of the production system itself. They include hasty design and production of parts and assemblies; poor design specifications; inadequate testing of incoming materials and prototypes; failure to understand process capability; failure to provide production workers with statistical signals of control; inadequate training of production workers; lack of instrument calibration and false reporting from tests; and poor environmental characteristics such as light, temperature, and noise.

To understand messes, we must first determine how a process works and what it is supposed to do. By clearly defining a process, all involved reach a common understanding and will not waste time by collecting irrelevant data. Variation can be eliminated by eliminating inconsistencies in the process. Understanding how a process works also enables one to pinpoint obvious problems, error-proof the process, and streamline it by eliminating unnecessary steps.

Opportunities for improvement often can be found simply by walking around a work area and making observations. For example, the following are indicators of messes:[8]

- Lots of work-in-process materials. Many shelves in the work area to hold material.

- Many people walking from place to place, standing in a line waiting for something, or standing idle.

- Work areas that are in disarray. Dusty boxes on the floors, bookcases full of dusty binders, and desks and walls covered with little scraps of paper serving as reminder notes.

- People who can give only a brief, vague explanation of what they are working on and why it is important.

- Humorous signs taped to the walls that say things like "You want it when? Ha! Ha!" or "A clean desk is a sign of a sick mind."

- In office areas, piles of processed and unprocessed documents stored in the work area.

- Supervisors and managers pacing around trying to find out what's going on, ascertain who made a critical mistake, and expedite late orders.

---

[8]Adapted from F. Timothy Fuller, "Eliminating Complexity from Work: Improving Productivity by Enhancing Quality," *National Productivity Review*, Vol. 4, Autumn 1985, pp. 327–344.

Under these conditions, it is probably the case that many nonproductive activities consume employees' time. Such messes are a gold mine of opportunity for improvement. Work sampling can be used to help a manager understand the nature of activities being performed and opportunities for improvement.

EXAMPLE 2 Using Work Sampling to Identify Improvement Opportunities.   One example involved about 30 clerical and professional people in a Hewlett-Packard office taking telephone orders.[9] Management felt that a large amount of the work being performed was related to resolving problems caused by mistakes in processing and shipping the orders. A work sampling study was performed to classify these activities and understand the nature of the problems better. The study was performed over three days and resulted in 130 observations of the activities of 10 people. The activities were grouped by major category and counted. The supervisor asked the following question about each activity: "If there were no errors in the process and everything were running perfectly, would you be working on this activity?" The results of the seven most frequently observed activities were:

Activity	Type	Frequency
Processing customer returns	Nonproductive	20
Entering orders into computer	Productive	14
Converting orders to fix a problem	Nonproductive	8
Making changes to orders	Productive	8
Expediting shipments	Nonproductive	7
Answering questions about order status	Nonproductive	6
Taking orders over the telephone	Productive	4

Sixty-one percent of these activities were classified as nonproductive work. The most frequent activity, processing customer returns, was a result of shipping the wrong product, duplicate shipment, or wrong quantity being delivered to customers. The amount of time spent on this activity was the equivalent of six people. The supervisor immediately made changes in the work procedures to improve the processing of returns. At the same time, a task force was formed to reduce the number of products returned.

In service organizations, customer complaints may provide a starting point for identifying quality-related problems.[10] Focus groups can be used effectively to learn about customer's experiences with a particular service. Another technique often used is called the *critical incident technique*. This involves an in-depth interview to generate a complete story about a service interaction. This method often reveals numerous issues relating to quality.

---

[9]Ibid.

[10]D. Randall Brandt and Kevin L. Reffett, "Focusing on Customer Problems to Improve Service Quality," *The Journal of Services Marketing*, Vol. 3, No. 4, Fall 1989, pp. 5–14.

Fact Finding

Understanding the true state of quality—that is, fact finding—depends on data collection, observation, and careful listening. Past and current data must be collected and analyzed to establish a base of information for problem identification and idea generation. As we saw in Chapter 3, a good quality cost reporting system can provide important information for identifying quality problems. Many aspects of the quality information system, including control charts, process capability studies, analyses of customer complaints, and warranty claims, all contribute to understanding the state of quality within an organization. As we observed in the Hewlett-Packard example earlier in this chapter, inspection of current production processes and practices will often provide important information. The opinions of supervisors and workers are also a good source of information, as is feedback from customers and field service employees. Such opinions, however, must be based on fact and not on emotion. Proper design of the quality information system and the organizational structure is a prerequisite for effective problem solving for quality improvement.

The first step in data collection, which aids fact finding, is to develop operational definitions for all quality measures that will be collected. For example, what does it mean to have "on-time delivery"? Does this mean within one day of the promised time? One week? One hour? What is an error? Is it wrong information on an invoice, a typographical mistake, or either? Clearly, any data are meaningless unless they are well defined and understood without ambiguity.

The Juran Institute suggests 10 important considerations for data collection:[11]

1. Formulate good questions that relate to the specific information needs of the project.

2. Use appropriate data analysis tools and be certain the necessary data are being collected.

3. Define comprehensive data collection points so that job flows suffer minimum interruption.

4. Select an unbiased collector who has the easiest and most immediate access to the relevant facts.

5. Understand the environment and make sure that data collectors have the proper experience.

6. Design simple data collection forms.

7. Prepare instructions for collecting the data.

8. Test the data collection forms and the instructions and make sure they are filled out properly.

9. Train the data collectors as to the purpose of the study, what the data will be used for, how to fill out the forms, and the importance of remaining unbiased.

10. Audit the data collection process and validate the results.

These guidelines can greatly improve the process of fact finding.

---

[11]"The Tools of Quality Part V: Check Sheets," *Quality Progress,* October 1990, p. 53.

Problem Finding

An old proverb says that a problem clearly stated is half solved. The purpose of problem finding is to understand what the true problem is, that is, to identify the problem from the "mess." A major flaw in traditional problem-solving approaches is a lack of emphasis on problem finding. Too often, we action-oriented Americans want to jump to the solution phase of a problem without fully understanding the nature of the problem. It is not uncommon to solve the wrong problem if this step of the process is ignored.

The creative thinking literature places heavy emphasis on the redefinition of the problem. This can be done by first asking "In what ways might I . . . ?" followed by "Why?" and to redefine the problem. For example, consider the following simplified scenario for: "In what ways might I reduce the cost of final inspection?":

Ask why: Why do I want to reduce the cost of final inspection?
Answer: To reduce total quality costs.
Redefine: In what ways might I reduce total quality costs?
Ask why: Why do I want to reduce total quality costs?
Answer: To improve profitability.
Redefine: In what ways might I improve profitability? etc.

As problems are restated in this fashion, new perspectives emerge. One must then converge to select the problem definition that best captures the real problem.

In services, a technique called *problem detection methodology* is often used to isolate critical problems.[12] Consumers assess each problem along several key dimensions such as frequency and bothersomeness. Consumers are asked to provide an estimate of how frequently they encounter a particular problem and also how bothersome the problem is to them. An example for food service problems is shown

FIGURE 9.1 Importance × Effectiveness for Food Service Problems

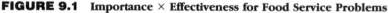

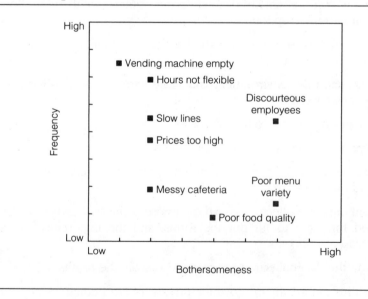

[12]Brandt and Reffett, "Focusing on Customer Problems."

in Figure 9.1. In this example, poor food quality and discourteous employees are particularly bothersome, but occur only infrequently. Slow lines occur frequently, but are not perceived as bothersome. On the other hand, inflexible hours and empty vending machines were relatively frequent and bothersome. Management must focus attention on these problems.

While this methodology is useful, it has two significant limitations. First, customer ratings are difficult to use to establish the relative impact on customer satisfaction and perceived quality. The problems customers find bothersome may not always be the ones that create the most dissatisfaction. Second, the ratings are subjective and not anchored to an absolute measurement system. More precise measures of customer satisfaction can be used.

Idea Finding

The purpose of the idea-finding step is to generate ideas for removing the problem. One of the difficulties in doing this is the natural instinct to prejudge ideas before thoroughly evaluating them. There is a natural fear of proposing a "silly" idea or looking foolish. However, it is not uncommon for such ideas to form the basis for a creative and useful solution. Effective problem solvers must learn to *defer judgment* and *develop the ability to generate a large number of ideas* at this stage of the process. A number of processes and tools to facilitate idea generation can be used. One of the most popular is brainstorming.

Brainstorming is a very useful group problem-solving procedure for generating ideas. It was proposed by Alex Osborn[13] "for the sole purpose of producing checklists of ideas" that can be used in developing a solution to a problem. With brainstorming, no criticism is permitted, and people are encouraged to generate a large number of ideas through combination and enhancement of existing ideas. Wild ideas are encouraged and often trigger other good ideas from someone else.

The process often works in the following manner. Each individual in the group suggests an idea relating to the problem at hand, working in a round-robin fashion. If a person cannot think of anything, he or she passes. A facilitator writes down all ideas on a blackboard or easel so that everyone can see them. Only one idea is presented at a time by each individual. The process is repeated until no further ideas can be generated. By writing down the ideas in plain view of the group, new ideas are usually built from old ones by combining or extending previous suggestions.

For example, suppose that a group is examining the problem of the reasons for damage due to parts handling. The first individual might suggest "lack of storage"; the second, "poor placement of machines"; the third, "poor design of racks." The next individual might combine the previous two ideas and suggest "poor placement of parts on racks." In this fashion, one individual's idea might spawn a new idea from someone else.

Checklists are often used as a guide for generating ideas. Osborn proposed about 75 fundamental questions based on the following principles:

1. Put to other uses?

2. Adapt?

---

[13]A. F. Osborn, *Applied Imagination* (New York: Scribner's, 1963).

3. Modify?

4. Magnify?

5. Minify?

6. Substitute?

7. Rearrange?

8. Reverse?

9. Combine?

By consciously seeking ideas based on this list, one can generate many unusual, and often very useful, ideas.

Several other methods for generating ideas have been suggested. One is to change the wording of a problem statement. Simple modification of a single word can dramatically change the meaning. For example, consider this statement: "In what ways might this company reduce quality costs by 30%?" Dropping the qualifier "by 30%" broadens the problem and potential solutions. Relaxing the "by 30%" by 5% produces a similar effect. Changing the action verb or goal can also change the problem perspective. Turning a negative statement into a positive one leads to different ideas, such as "reducing quality costs" to "increasing quality value." Reversing the focus of the problem is another technique. For instance, "how to reduce costs due to excessive scrap" can be reversed to "how to use excessive scrap to reduce costs." Does this give you any ideas?

Solution Finding

The purpose of solution finding is to evaluate ideas that have been proposed and select a method to remove the problem. Questions that must be addressed include what facilities or equipment are needed, what are the costs, how much time is required for implementation, what is the effect on supervisors and workers, what results are expected, and what are the barriers to implementation.

Implementation

To implement a solution, one must determine who will be responsible, what must be done, where it will be done, when it will be done, and how it will be done. The potential consequences of each action should also be evaluated. The implementation phase of problem solving must consider personnel planning, budget issues, facilities, scheduling, and methods. Goals and milestones for evaluating improvement should be established, plans for training personnel in new methods are often needed, and a control mechanism must be set up for monitoring the process.

To implement a solution, changes must be made in how things are done. A new procedure must be used, a new piece of equipment must be installed and debugged, or people must start paying attention to some aspect of quality that had been previously ignored. This step will not be too painful if problem-solving teams have been properly organized.

PROGRAMS FOR QUALITY IMPROVEMENT

Leaders in the quality revolution—Deming, Juran, and Crosby—have proposed specific methodologies for quality improvement. While the generic problem-solving process described in the last section is applicable to any situation, it is instructive to study and compare the different approaches to quality improvement that are advocated by these individuals and others.

The Deming Cycle

In Chapter 4 we discussed W. Edwards Deming's 14 Points for Management and his emphasis on the reduction of variation for quality improvement. The *Deming cycle* is a methodology for improvement. It was originally called the Shewhart cycle after its founder, Walter Shewhart, but was renamed the Deming cycle by the Japanese in 1950. The Deming cycle is composed of four stages: *Plan, Do, Study,* and *Act* (see Figure 9.2). (The third stage—Study—was formerly called Check, and the Deming cycle was known as the PDCA cycle. Deming made the change in 1990. Study is more appropriate; with only a "check," one might miss something.) This characterization of problem solving is considerably different from the process that we discussed in the last section in that much of the focus is on implementation. The Plan stage consists of studying the current situation, gathering data, and planning for improvement. Thus, it actually consists of the "understanding the mess" through "developing solutions" steps in the previous process. In the Do stage, the plan is implemented on a trial basis, for example, in a laboratory, pilot production process, or with a small group of customers. The Study stage is designed to determine if the trial plan is working correctly and if any further problems or opportunities are found. The last stage, Act, is the implementation of the final plan to ensure that the improvements will be standardized and practiced continuously. This leads back to the Plan stage for further diagnosis and improvement.

FIGURE 9.2 **The Deming Cycle**

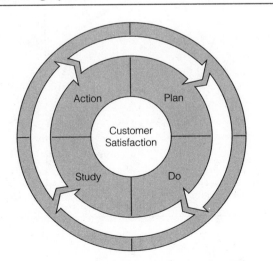

As Figure 9.2 illustrates, this cycle is never ending; that is, it is focused on *continuous improvement*. The improved standards are only a springboard for further improvements. This is what distinguishes it from more traditional problem-solving approaches and is one of the essential elements of the Deming philosophy.

Juran's Improvement Program

Joseph Juran emphasizes the importance of developing a habit of making annual improvements in quality and annual reductions in quality-related costs. Juran defines *breakthrough* as the accomplishment of any improvement that takes an organization to unprecedented levels of performance. Breakthrough is focused on attacking chronic losses or, in Deming's terminology, common causes of variation.

EXAMPLE 3 **Breakthrough at INCO, Ltd.** An example of break-through was reported by the Manitoba Division of INCO Limited.[14] The data entry department employed a staff of six operators and a full-time working supervisor,

FIGURE 9.3 Data Entry Overtime Hours

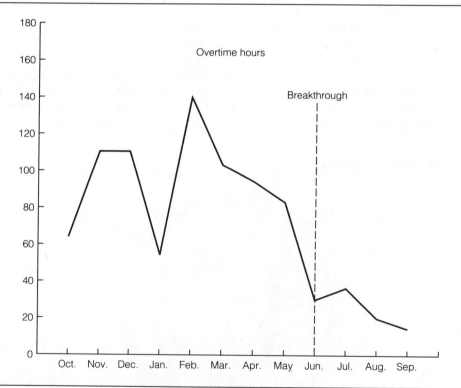

---

[14]L. M. Ames and W. D. Harwood, "People, Quality, and Process Improvement," Manitoba Division, INCO Limited (undated).

yet still required an average of 100 hours of overtime to handle the workload. After studying the processes and reviewing the needs with customers, data entry procedures were simplified, employees cross-trained themselves in different skills, and work loads were smoothed. As a result, overtime was virtually eliminated (see Figure 9.3) and the supervisor, who was an integral part of the improvement, was transferred to a more challenging and rewarding position in another department.

All breakthroughs follow a common sequence of discovery, organization, diagnosis, corrective action, and control. This "breakthrough sequence" is described and formalized in a 16-session videotape/workbook series entitled *Juran on Quality Improvement,* which is summarized below.

1. *Proof of the need:* Managers, especially top managers, need to be convinced that quality improvements are simply good economics. Through data collection efforts, information on poor quality, low productivity, or poor service can be translated into the language of money—the universal language of top management—to justify a request for resources to implement a quality improvement program. Improvements in quality lead to increased market share and higher profits; these are important objectives of top management.

2. *Project identification:* All breakthroughs are achieved project by project, and in no other way. By taking a project approach, management provides a forum for converting an atmosphere of defensiveness or blame into one of constructive action. Participation in a project increases the likelihood that the participant will act on the results. The Pareto principle provides the means of identifying the vital few problems from the trivial many and determining priorities.

3. *Organization for breakthrough:* Organization for improvement requires a clear responsibility for guiding the project. The responsibility for the project may be as broad as an entire division with formal committee structures or as narrow as a small group of workers at one production operation. These groups must provide the definition and agreement as to the specific aims of the project, the authority to conduct experiments, and implementation strategies.

   The path from problem to solution consists of two journeys: one from symptom to cause (the diagnostic journey) and the other from cause to remedy (the remedial journey). These must be performed by different individuals with the appropriate skills.

4. *The diagnostic journey:* Diagnosticians skilled in data collection, statistics, and other problem-solving tools are needed at this stage. Some projects will require full-time, specialized experts while others can be performed by the work force.

   Quality problems can be either management-controllable or operator-controllable. Like Deming, Juran believes that most problems are attributable to management. It is important to distinguish between the two types of problems because they require different methods of diagnosis and remedy. The attack on management-controllable problems begins with a description of the symptoms. Theories are proposed and tested for validity, often with controlled experimentation and statistical methods. We will discuss the basic tools used for diagnosis later in this chapter.

Operator-controllable errors often are caused by inattention, lack of skill, or willful behavior. Foolproofing the process can eliminate inadvertent errors, while comparing the work methods of good and poor workers often leads to a discovery of the differences in performance. Willful errors may be a result of the management system or lack of communication. Improved understanding and communication are necessary.

5. *The remedial journey:* The remedial journey consists of several phases: choosing an alternative that optimizes total cost (this is similar to one of Deming's points), implementing remedial action, and dealing with resistance to change. Motivation of both managers and workers is critical for success. Many techniques, especially participative programs, can improve motivation. As Juran states, "No one is against quality."

6. *Holding the gains:* This final step involves establishing the new standards and procedures, training the work force, and instituting controls to make sure that the breakthrough does not die over time.

Many companies have followed Juran's program religiously. A Xerox plant in Mitcheldean, England, for example, cut quality losses by 30% to 40% and won a national prize in Britain in 1984 for quality improvement using the Juran system.[15]

The Crosby Program

Philip Crosby proposes a 14-step program for quality improvement:

1. *Management commitment:* The program begins with obtaining commitment from management for quality improvement with an emphasis on the need for defect prevention. The personal commitment of management raises the visibility of a quality improvement program and ensures everyone's cooperation.

2. *Quality improvement team:* A quality improvement team is formed with representatives from each department. The team is oriented to the content and purpose of the program. This enhances the communication and ensures that everyone understands the scope and objectives of the program.

3. *Quality measurement:* Quality measurement for each activity must either be reviewed or established to show where improvement is possible, where corrective action is necessary, and to document actual improvement later. Formalizing the measurement system strengthens the inspection and test functions and allows for visibility of results.

---

[15]Jeremy Main, "Under the Spell of the Quality Gurus," *Fortune,* August 18, 1986, p. 31.

4. *Cost of quality evaluation:* Accurate figures should be obtained on the cost of quality as an indication of where corrective action will be profitable. This provides a company-wide measurement of quality management performance.

5. *Quality awareness:* Share with employees the measurements of what a lack of quality is costing. Provide visible evidence of concern for quality improvement through communications material such as booklets, films, and posters. This step gets supervisors and employees in the habit of talking positively about quality and changing existing attitudes.

6. *Corrective action:* As people are encouraged to talk about their problems, opportunities for correction come to light, particularly from the workers themselves. These problems must be brought to the attention of managers and resolved. As employees see that their problems are being corrected, they will learn to get in the habit of identifying further problems.

7. *Establish an ad hoc committee for the zero defects program:* Three or four members of the team are selected to investigate the "zero defects" concept and ways to implement the program. It is not a motivation program, but a program to communicate the meaning of "zero defects" and the concept of doing it right the first time.

8. *Supervisor training:* All managers must understand each step well enough to explain it to their people. This helps supervisors to understand the program and realize its value for themselves.

9. *Zero defects day:* The establishment of zero defects as the performance standard of the company should be done in one day so that everyone understands it the same way. It provides an emphasis and a long-lasting memory.

10. *Goal setting:* Each supervisor should establish goals to achieve. All should be specific and capable of being measured.

11. *Error cause removal:* Individuals are asked to describe any problem that keeps them from performing error-free work on a simple, one-page form. The appropriate functional group will develop the answer. Problems should be acknowledged quickly. People need to know that problems will be heard and develop trust in management.

12. *Recognition:* Establish award programs to recognize those who meet their goals or perform outstanding acts. The prizes or awards should not be financial; recognition is what is important. People appreciate recognition of performance and will support the program.

13. *Quality councils:* The quality professionals and team chairpersons meet regularly to discuss and determine actions necessary to upgrade and improve the quality program. These councils are the best source of information on the status of programs and ideas for action.

14. *Do it over again:* The typical program takes one year to 18 months. Changes in the organization require new organization efforts. Quality must be ingrained in the organization.

Harrington's Approach

Although more than 50% of the work force in the United States is engaged in information handling, processing, and/or dissemination, we frequently ignore the impacts that information-related processes can have on quality. H. James Harrington, formerly with IBM and now a partner in a major consulting firm, focuses on business process improvement.[16] He defines a *business process* as any service process that supports production, for example, order processing, engineering change processing, payroll processing, and manufacturing process design.

Harrington's unique contribution is that he strongly believes that the most urgent need for quality improvement is not in production processes, but in business processes. For example, he pointed out that Intel Corporation previously used a 91-step process costing thousands of dollars to purchase ballpoint pens—the same process that was used to purchase forklift trucks! The improved process was reduced to 8 steps. A similar philosophy was used by Motorola (see Chapter 5) to reduce cycle times for service quality improvement in all areas of the firm.

Harrington suggests a five-step process for improvement that is similar to, but simpler than Juran's and Crosby's approaches. The steps include:

- organizing for improvement
- understanding the process
- streamlining
- measurement and control
- continuous improvement.

Harrington advocates a hierarchy of employee involvement teams to improve business processes, including "executive improvement teams," "process improvement teams," "department improvement teams," and "task teams." (You might recall the discussion of the "three levels of quality" in Chapter 7.) These teams must include adequate representation of those individuals who own the process, not staff analysts. The teams need to be trained in:

- business process concepts
- flowcharts (discussed later in this chapter)
- measurement
- defining customer needs
- eliminating bureaucracy
- quality cost principles
- process simplification.

The teams are encouraged to identify projects, document current business processes, determine where steps should be added, deleted, or changed to simplify the process,

---

[16]H. James Harrington, *Business Process Improvement* (New York: McGraw Hill, 1991), p. 9.

establish and test the proposed process, and implement the new process with the approval and support of higher level improvement managers.

While Harrington may not be as well known as Deming, Juran, or Crosby, he presents many useful ideas for quality improvement that can be easily adopted by any organization. In the last several years as the quality revolution has continued to grow, numerous other authors have advocated similar approaches. For students, our message is that you must understand the various philosophies and stay abreast of current developments as you pursue your future business activities.

The quality improvement philosophies of Deming, Juran, Crosby, and Harrington differ considerably. The Deming cycle is a simple variation of the generic problem-solving process that can be understood and performed by individuals or groups at all levels of an organization. Juran's program is cast in traditional organizational structures and is replete with specific techniques and methods for problem identification, diagnosis, and remedy. Crosby's quality improvement program is a formal, company-wide program with a heavy emphasis on motivation. Harrington's approach builds on aspects of all the others. To reiterate our comment in Chapter 4, not every program is appropriate for all organizations. Managers must understand the differences and choose an approach that best fits their organization.

THE "SEVEN QC TOOLS" FOR QUALITY IMPROVEMENT

Seven simple quality control (QC) tools are used extensively to improve quality. These tools—flowcharts, check sheets, histograms, Pareto diagrams, cause-and-effect diagrams, scatter diagrams, and control charts—are fundamental to kaizen and Juran's approach to quality improvement. While Deming is an advocate of statistical thinking, his focus is primarily on variation and its analysis with control charts.

These tools also fit quite well within the creative problem-solving process that we presented in the last section. Figure 9.4 shows the seven tools in the context of this problem-solving process. These tools are deceptively simple, and designed this way so that workers at all levels can use them easily.

FIGURE 9.4 **Creative Problem Solving and the Seven Quality Improvement Tools**

Problem-Solving Step	Useful Tools
Understanding the mess	Flowcharts
Finding facts	Check sheets
Identifying problems	Pareto diagrams
	Histograms
Generating ideas	Cause-and-effect diagrams
Developing solutions	Scatter diagrams
Implementation	Control charts

Flowcharts

Understanding a "mess" often can be aided significantly through the development of flowcharts. A flowchart is simply a picture of a process that shows the sequence of steps for a process.

Flowcharts are best developed by having the people involved in the process—employees, supervisors, managers, and customers—construct the flowchart. A facilitator often is used to provide objectivity, to ask the right questions, and to resolve conflicts. The facilitator can guide the discussion through questions such as "What happens next?", "Who makes the decision at this point?", and "What operation is performed at this point?" Quite often, the group does not universally agree on the answers to these questions, due to misconceptions about the process itself or a lack of awareness of the "big picture."

Flowcharts help the people who are involved in the process understand it much better and more objectively. Employees realize how they fit into the process, and who is their supplier and customer. This leads to improved communication among all parties. By participating in the development of a flowchart, workers begin to feel a sense of ownership in the process, and hence become more willing to work on improving it. If flowcharts are used in training employees, then more consistency will be achieved.

Once a flowchart is constructed, it can be used to identify quality problems as well as areas for productivity improvement. Questions such as "How does this operation affect the customer?", "Can we improve or even eliminate this operation?" or "Should we control a critical quality characteristic at this point?" help to identify opportunities.

EXAMPLE 4   Parking Garage Operation Flowchart.   Figure 9.5 shows a simple flowchart of a parking garage operation. For example, we see that customers can become dissatisfied if the ticket machine does not work properly, if they must wait a long time at the cashier, or if the cashier is not friendly or does not make the correct change. Once such aspects of the process become apparent, managers might make decisions regarding preventive maintenance for the ticket machine such as a daily check for an adequate supply of tickets, a full ink well, accuracy of the time clock, and proper functioning of all mechanical parts. New procedures for customer interaction might be designed into the process. The cashier might be required to say hello, state the fee, and state the change returned.

Check Sheets

The fact-finding phase of problem solving for quality improvement typically involves some type of data collection. Data collection should not be performed blindly. One must first ask some basic questions, such as:

- What question are we trying to answer?

- What type of data will we need to answer the question?

FIGURE 9.5 Flowchart for Parking Garage Operation

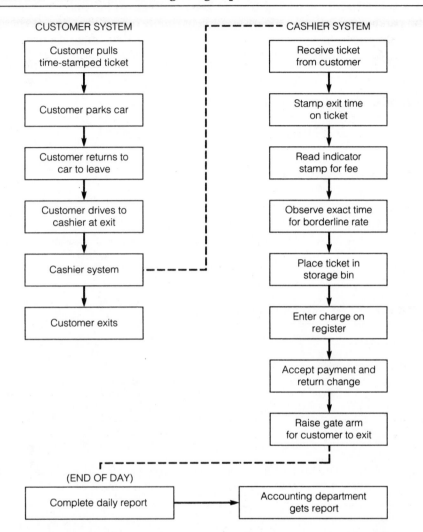

- Where can we find the data?

- Who can provide the data?

- How can we collect the data with minimum effort and with minimum chance of error?

Nearly any kind of form may be used to collect data. *Data sheets* are simple columnar or tabular forms used to record data. To generate useful information from raw data, further processing generally is necessary. *Check sheets* are special types of data collection forms in which the results may be interpreted on the form directly without additional processing.

EXAMPLE 5 **Parking Garage Data Collection Forms.** To collect data on parking garage rates, the cashier might simply record the amount charged to each customer on a data sheet shown in Figure 9.6. If the rates are fixed at $0.50, $1.00, $1.30, $1.60, $1.90, to a maximum of $2.00, a more useful form for

FIGURE 9.6 Data Collection Sheet for Parking Charges

Customer	Amount
1	1.00
2	0.50
3	1.30
4	1.30
5	2.00
6	1.60
.	.
.	.
.	.

FIGURE 9.7 Check Sheet for Garage Parking Rates

Amount	Tally
0.50	卌
1.00	卌 卌 ///
1.30	卌 卌 卌 卌 卌 //
1.60	卌 卌 卌 卌 //
2.00	卌 卌 ///

collecting this data might be the one shown in Figure 9.7. If the data are tallied in this fashion, it is easy to see which rates occur the most often.

In manufacturing, check sheets similar to Figure 9.7 are simple to use and easy to interpret by shop personnel. Another example is given in Figure 9.8. By including information such as specification limits, it is easy to see how many items are nonconforming. This provides immediate information about the quality of the process. For example, in Figure 9.8 we clearly see that a significant proportion of dimensions is out of specification, with a larger number on the high side than the low side.

A second type of check sheet for defective items is illustrated in Figure 9.9. This check sheet gives the type of defect and a tally in a resin production plant. Such a check sheet can be extended to include a time dimension so that data can be monitored and analyzed over time and trends and patterns, if any, can be detected.

Figure 9.10 shows an example of a defect location check sheet. Ishikawa relates how this check sheet was used to eliminate bubbles in laminated automobile

FIGURE 9.8 Check Sheet for Data Collection

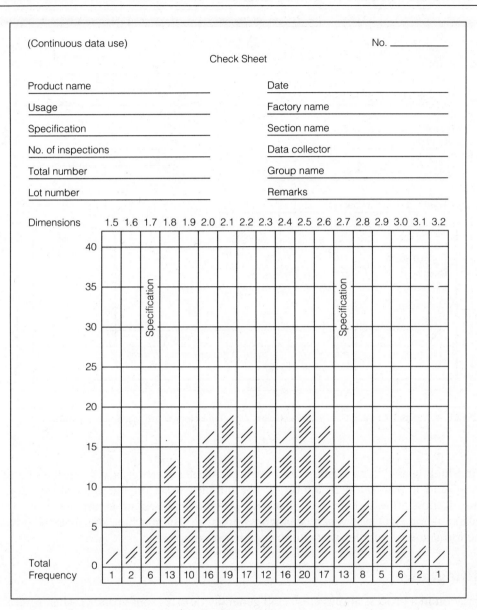

SOURCE: K. Ishikawa, *Guide to Quality Control* (Tokyo: Asian Productivity Organization, 1982), p. 31.

FIGURE 9.9 Defective Item Check Sheet

Check Sheet

Product:	Date:
	Factory:
Manufacturing stage: final insp.	Section:
Type of defect: scar, incomplete, misshapen	Inspector's name:
	Lot no.
	Order no.
Total no. inspected: 2530	
Remarks: all items inspected	

Type	Check	Subtotal
Surface scars	𝍸 𝍸 𝍸 𝍸 𝍸 𝍸 //	32
Cracks	𝍸 𝍸 𝍸 𝍸 ///	23
Incomplete	𝍸 𝍸 𝍸 𝍸 𝍸 𝍸 𝍸 𝍸 𝍸 ///	48
Misshapen	////	4
Others	𝍸 ///	8
	Grand total	115
Total rejects	𝍸 𝍸 𝍸 𝍸 𝍸 𝍸 𝍸 𝍸 𝍸 𝍸 𝍸 𝍸 𝍸 𝍸 𝍸 𝍸 𝍸 /	86

SOURCE: K. Ishikawa, *Guide to Quality Control* (Tokyo: Asian Productivity Organization, 1982), p. 33.

windshield glass.[17] The location and form of bubbles were indicated on the check sheet, and it was found that most of the bubbles were on the right side. Upon investigation, it was discovered that the pressure applied in laminating was off balance—the right side was receiving less pressure. The machine was adjusted, and the formation of bubbles was eliminated almost completely.

Histograms

Variation in a process always exists and generally displays some pattern. This pattern can be captured visually in a histogram. A histogram is a graphical representation of the variation in a set of data. It shows the frequency or number of observations of a particular value or within a specified group. Histograms provide clues about the characteristics of the parent population from which a sample is taken. Using a histogram, the shape of the distribution can be seen clearly and inferences can be made about the population. Patterns can be seen that would be difficult to see in an ordinary table of numbers.

[17]Ishikawa, Kaoru, *Guide to Quality Control,* 2nd revised ed., edited for clarity. (Tokyo: Asian Productivity Organization, 1986). Available from UNIPUB/Quality Resources, One Water Street, White Plains, NY 10601.

FIGURE 9.10 Defect Location Check Sheet

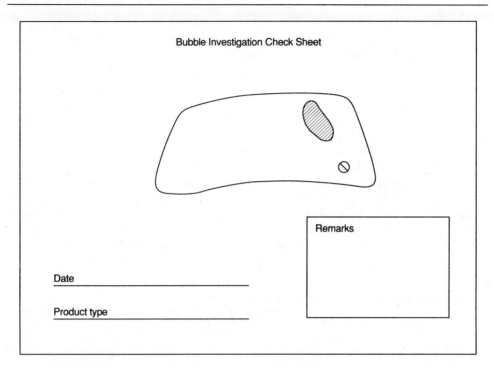

Bubble Investigation Check Sheet

Remarks

Date

Product type

SOURCE: K. Ishikawa, *Guide to Quality Control* (Tokyo: Asian Productivity Organization, 1982), p. 34.

EXAMPLE 6 **Histogram of Parking Garage Charges.** A histogram of the parking garage charge data in Figure 9.7 is shown in Figure 9.11. The histogram shows that $1.30 is the most frequent parking charge, and that more than half the charges are either $1.30 or $1.60. How might this information lead

FIGURE 9.11 Histogram of Parking Garage Charges

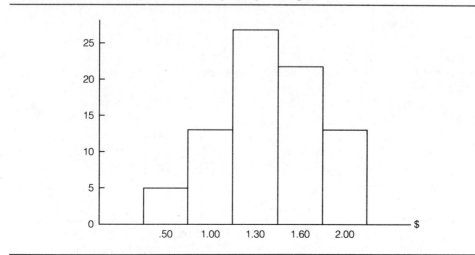

to improvements in the process? The cashier probably spends a considerable amount of time making change for these amounts. If the rate structure were simplified, the waiting times of customers might be reduced and the accuracy of the change-making process might be improved. Since the rates are closely related to parking times, the histogram provides information that can be used to study the revenue implications of such changes.

The check sheet in Figure 9.7 was designed to provide the visual appeal of a histogram as the data are tallied. For this data, it is easy to determine the proportion of observations that fell outside of the specification limits. Histograms are extremely useful in process capability analysis as we shall see in Chapter 13.

Figure 9.12 shows some typical patterns of histograms that are usually found in quality control applications. The bell-shaped pattern in (a) is symmetrical in shape and is the most common form of variation in process output. The process is centered around some value and observations are less frequent the further away one moves from this central value. Any deviation from this pattern is usually the result of some

FIGURE 9.12 Typical Histogram Patterns in Quality Control

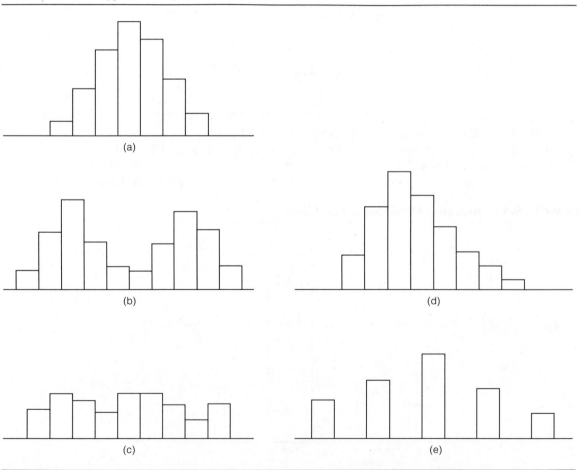

external influence, which should be investigated. A bimodal pattern in (b) suggests that two groups of bell-shaped measurements were combined. We would usually want to isolate the individual processes or conditions that cause this pattern. A uniform pattern in (c) shows much wider variability than (a) with no central tendency. Often, this is the result of combining the data of many different bell-shaped processes with different centers throughout the range of the data. A skewed pattern in (d) is like the bell-shaped pattern, but not symmetric; the distribution tails off in one direction. Skewed patterns arise when there is a natural limit on the data values. For instance, time measurements of a manual task have a lower limit governed by the physical characteristics of the task and most will be close to this value. Infrequently, however, observations will be large due to disturbing influences on the process. If the task is related to customer service, then a long tail should be examined to determine causes that result in long service times. Finally, a pattern such as that of (e) with alternating high and low values often results from systematic measurement error, the way in which data are grouped, or bias due to rounding data values.

Some cautions should be stated when interpreting histograms. First, the data should be representative of typical process conditions. If a new employee is now operating the equipment, or the equipment, material, method, etc., have changed, then it is best to collect new data. Second, the sample size should be large enough to provide good conclusions; the larger, the better. Various guidelines exist, but it is suggested that at least 50 observations be drawn. Finally, any conclusions drawn should be confirmed through further study and analysis.

Pareto Diagrams

Pareto analysis was introduced in Chapter 3 as a method for analyzing quality costs. The Pareto principle was observed by Joseph Juran in 1950. Juran found that most effects resulted from only a few causes. For instance, in analyzing costs in a paper mill, he found that 61% of total quality costs were attributable to one category—"broke," which is paper mill terminology for paper so defective that it is returned for reprocessing. In an analysis of 200 types of field failures of automotive engines, only 5 accounted for one-third of all failures; the top 25 accounted for two-thirds of the failures. In a textile mill, 3 of 15 weavers were found to account for 74% of the defective cloth produced. Pareto analysis clearly separates the vital few from the trivial many and provides direction for selecting projects for improvement.

Pareto analysis is often used to analyze the data collected in check sheets. A Pareto distribution is one in which the characteristics observed are ordered from largest frequency to smallest.

EXAMPLE 7 **Pareto Analysis of Defective Items.** In Figure 9.9, if the types of defects are ordered by their relative percentage, we have the following

	Number	Percent of Total
Incomplete	48	42%
Surface scars	32	28%
Cracks	23	20%
Others	8	7%
Misshapen	4	3%

The highest category of defects is "incomplete," accounting for 42% of the total. The top three categories account for 80% of all defects.

A Pareto diagram is a histogram of the data from the largest frequency to the smallest. Often one also draws a cumulative frequency curve on the histogram as shown in Figure 9.13. Such a visual aid clearly shows the relative magnitude of defects and can be used to identify opportunities for improvement. The problems that are the most costly or significant stand out. Pareto diagrams can also show the results of improvement programs over time. They are less intimidating to employees who are fearful of statistics.

Cause-and-Effect Diagrams

Variation in process output and other quality problems can occur for a variety of reasons, such as materials, machines, methods, and measurement. The goal of problem solving is to identify the *causes* of problems in order to correct them. An important tool for assisting in the generation of ideas for problem causes and hence for serving as a basis for solution finding is the cause-and-effect diagram.

FIGURE 9.13 **Pareto Diagram**

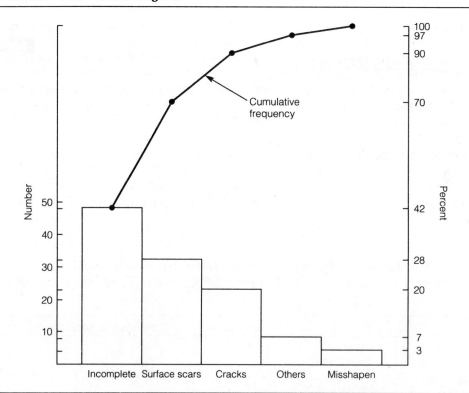

FIGURE 9.14 **General Structure of Cause-and-Effect Diagram**

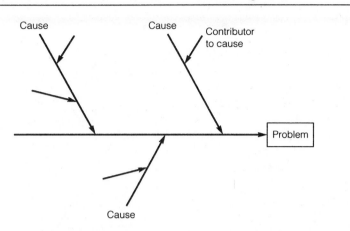

The cause-and-effect diagram was introduced in Japan by Kaoru Ishikawa. It is a simple, graphical method for presenting a chain of causes and effects and for sorting out causes and organizing relationships between variables. Because of its structure, it is often called a fishbone diagram.

The general structure of a cause-and-effect diagram is shown in Figure 9.14. At the end of the horizontal line, a problem is listed. Each branch pointing into the main stem represents a possible cause. Branches pointing to the causes are contributors to these causes. The diagram is used to identify the most likely causes of a problem so that further data collection and analysis can be carried out.

Two basic types of cause-and-effect diagrams are *dispersion analysis* and *process classification*. Dispersion analysis involves identifying and classifying possible causes for a specific quality problem. The fishbones in the diagram provide a chain of logical relationships among potential causes.

EXAMPLE 8 **Dispersion Analysis of Hospital Emergency Department Admissions.** A major hospital was concerned about the length of time required to get a patient from the emergency department to an in-patient bed. Significant delays appeared to be caused by beds not being available. A quality improvement team tackled this problem by developing a cause-and-effect diagram. Four major causes were identified: environmental services, emergency department, medical/surgery unit, and admitting. Figure 9.15 shows a cause-and-effect diagram with several potential causes in each category. This provided a basis for further investigations of contributing factors and data analysis to find the root cause of the problem.

A process classification cause-and-effect diagram is based on a flowchart of the process. The key factors that influence quality at each step are drawn on the flowchart.

FIGURE 9.15 Cause-and-Effect Diagram for Hospital Emergency Admission

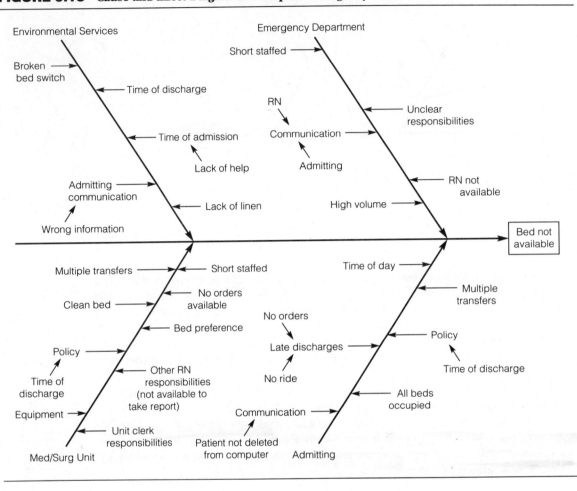

EXAMPLE 9 Process Classification Diagram for Parking Garage Operation. Figure 9.16 shows the customer system portion of the flowchart for the parking garage operation discussed earlier. Potential contributors to poor quality are listed on the chart in a manner similar to the dispersion cause-and-effect diagram.

Cause-and-effect diagrams are constructed in a brainstorming type of atmosphere. Everyone can get involved and feel they are an important part of the problem-solving process. Usually small groups drawn from manufacturing or management work with a trained and experienced facilitator. The facilitator must guide the discussion to focus attention on the problem and its causes, not opinions. As a group technique, the cause-and-effect method requires significant interaction

FIGURE 9.16 Process Classification Diagram

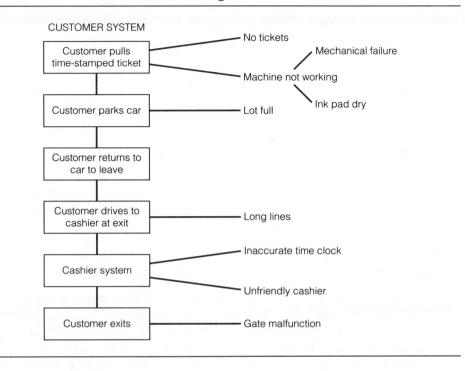

between group members. The facilitator must listen carefully to the participants and capture the important ideas. It is helpful to think of the problem broadly and to consider environmental factors, political factors, employee issues, and even government policies if appropriate.

Scatter Diagrams

Scatter diagrams are the graphical component of regression analysis. While they do not provide rigorous statistical analysis, they often point to important relationships between variables, such as the percent of an ingredient in an alloy and the hardness of the alloy. Typically, the variables in question represent possible causes and effects obtained from Ishikawa diagrams. For example, if it is suspected that the percent of an ingredient in an alloy is causing quality problems in meeting hardness specifications, one might collect data from samples on the amount of ingredient and hardness and plot the data on a scatter diagram as shown in Figure 9.17. This shows that there is very little effect on the hardness, and one would have to investigate other possible causes.

Statistical correlation analysis is used to interpret scatter diagrams. Figure 9.18 shows three types of correlation. If the correlation is positive, an increase in variable x is related to an increase in variable y; if the correlation is negative, an increase in x is related to a decrease in y; and if the correlation is close to zero, there is no linear relationship between the variables.

FIGURE 9.17 Scatter Diagram

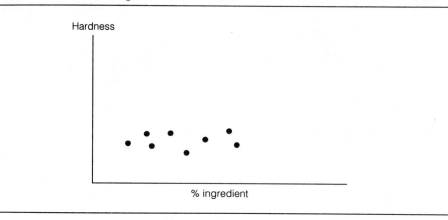

Control Charts

The concept of control was discussed in the previous chapter. Control charts are one of the most important tools for ensuring that a process is kept in control and will be studied extensively in Chapters 16 and 17. We provide only a brief introduction to control charts here and discuss their use as a problem-solving tool.

Control charts were first proposed by Walter Shewhart at Bell Laboratories in the 1920s. Shewhart was the first to make a distinction between common causes and special causes in process variation and developed the concept of a control chart to separate them. More recently, the control chart has been a principal tool in assisting the Japanese in their quality and productivity efforts. As a result of their success, interest in the use of control charts has been renewed throughout the world.

A control chart is a graphic tool for describing the state of control of a process. Figure 9.19 illustrates the general structure of a control chart. Time is measured on the horizontal axis, which usually corresponds to the average value of the quality

FIGURE 9.18 Three Types of Correlation

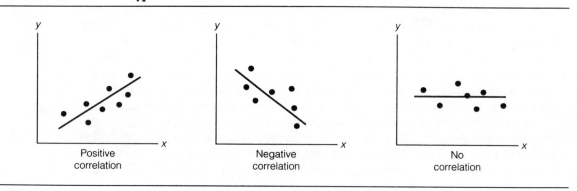

FIGURE 9.19 The Structure of a Control Chart

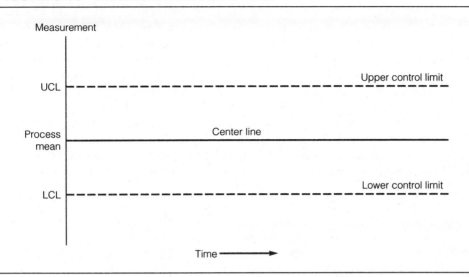

characteristic being measured on the vertical axis. Two other horizontal lines (usually dashed) represent the **upper control limit** (UCL) and **lower control limit** (LCL). These are chosen so that there is a high probability (generally greater than 0.99) that sample values will fall between these limits *if the process is in control.* Samples are chosen over time, plotted on the appropriate chart, and analyzed.

If sample values fall outside the control limits or if nonrandom patterns occur in the chart, then special causes may be affecting the process; the process is not stable. The process should be examined and corrective action should be taken as appropriate. If this is done in real time, then the chance of producing nonconforming product is minimized. Thus, as a problem-solving tool, control charts allow operators to identify quality problems as they occur. Of course, control charts alone cannot determine the source of the problem. Operators, supervisors, and engineers may have to resort to other problem-solving tools to seek the root cause.

There are many advantages to using control charts. A process that is in a state of statistical control will have improved quality of conformance, since there will be less product variation (more consistency) and a higher percentage of parts within specification. Scrap or rework will be reduced. More good parts will be produced, thus reducing cost and increasing productivity. The effect of productivity improvements in the design of a production system can be quantified and analyzed through control chart data. Control charts are easy to use and can be maintained by the operators themselves. The charts provide immediate feedback on when to take action and when to leave the process alone. This helps to eliminate confusion and frustration of misdirected problem-solving efforts. Also, control charts establish a common framework for communications between operators and supervisors, production and design personnel, and suppliers and consumers. They allow people to deal in facts, not emotions.

EXAMPLE 10 **Monitoring Surgery Infections.** The Joint Commission on Accreditation of Healthcare Organizations (JCAHO) monitors and evaluates health care providers with strict standards and guidelines. Improvement in the quality of care is a principal concern. Hospitals are required to identify and monitor important quality indicators that affect patient care and establish "thresholds for evaluation" (TFE), which are levels at which special investigations of problems should occur. TFEs provide a means of focusing attention on nonrandom errors (that is, special causes of variation). A logical way to set TFEs is through control charts.

For instance, a hospital collects monthly data on the number of infections arising from surgeries. These data are shown in Table 9.1. Hospital administrators

TABLE 9.1 **Montly Data on Infections Arising from Surgery**

Month	Surgeries	Infections	Percent
1	208	1	0.48
2	225	3	1.33
3	201	3	1.49
4	236	1	0.42
5	220	3	1.36
6	244	1	0.41
7	247	1	0.40
8	245	1	0.41
9	250	1	0.40
10	227	0	0.00
11	234	2	0.85
12	227	4	1.76
13	213	2	0.94
14	212	1	0.47
15	193	2	1.04
16	182	0	0.00
17	140	1	0.71
18	230	1	0.43
19	187	1	0.53
20	252	2	0.79
21	201	1	0.50
22	226	0	0.00
23	222	2	0.90
24	212	2	0.94
25	219	1	0.46
26	223	2	0.90
27	191	1	0.52
28	222	0	0.00
29	231	3	1.30
30	239	1	0.42
31	217	2	0.92
32	241	1	0.41
33	220	3	1.36
34	278	1	0.36
35	255	3	1.18
36	225	1	0.44
	7995	55	

FIGURE 9.20 **Control Chart for Surgery Infections**

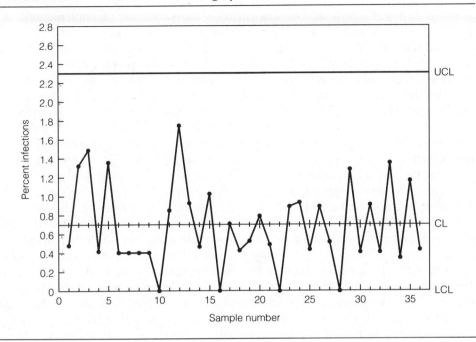

are concerned about whether the high percentages of infections (such as 1.76% in month 12) are caused by factors other than randomness. A control chart constructed from these data is shown in Figure 9.20. The average percent infections is 55/7995 = 0.688%. Using formulas that we describe in Chapter 16, the upper control limit is computed to be 2.35%. We see that none of the data points falls above the upper control limit. Thus we can conclude that the variation each month is due purely to chance and that the process is stable. To reduce the infection rate, management would have to attack the common causes in the process. The upper control limit would be a logical TFE to use, since any value beyond this limit is unlikely to occur by chance. Management can continue to use this chart to monitor future data.

The seven basic quality improvement tools that we have presented in this section have useful applications in the creative problem-solving process we discussed earlier. For example, identifying a mess can be aided by drawing a flowchart of a process. Check sheets, histograms, and control charts provide data for the fact-finding phase. Pareto analysis helps to identify the most important quality problems. Cause-and-effect diagrams help to facilitate idea finding. Scatter diagrams can be used to validate theories and find a solution. Finally, control charts help to maintain the improvements and gain acceptance from workers.

Seven "new" tools for quality improvement and problem solving have become popular in recent years. These are discussed in the next section.

THE "NEW SEVEN" QUALITY IMPROVEMENT TOOLS

James L. Brossert[18] pointed out that many of the problems of implementing the Deming cycle and quality function deployment (discussed in Chapter 6) are due to the way that American managers have become accustomed to planning and organizing businesses based on Frederick W. Taylor's philosophy. Process improvements often are not implemented because they are too complex to work in practice, or are not accepted by those who have the responsibility to carry them out. The barriers to effective planning and quality improvement efforts have been strict departmentalization that has separated the planners (staff specialists, such as QA and industrial engineers) from the doers; relegating planning to a seat-of-the-pants approach, due to the perception that it is either too theoretical to be of practical use or too detailed to be interesting or action oriented; and the lack of good tools for planning.

The "new seven" quality improvement tools provide simple means of assisting managers in implementing improvements through active involvement. They had their roots in post–World War II operations research developments in the United States, but were combined and refined by several Japanese companies over the past several decades as part of their CWQC planning processes. They were popularized in America by GOAL/QPC, a U.S. consulting firm, and have been used since 1984 by a number of U.S. firms to improve their TQM planning and quality improvement efforts. Thus, they are only "new" to managers who have neither been exposed to them nor seen what powerful aids they may be in improvement processes. Although they are more complex and sophisticated than the seven basic QC tools, they can be used to address problems typically faced by managers who are called on to structure unstructured ideas, make strategic plans, and organize and control large, complex projects. They have helped to overcome the barriers listed above, and have provided managers better tools for planning and implementing quality improvement efforts.

The seven "new" quality planning tools are briefly introduced below. The interested reader is referred to the books by Brossert, Brassard, and Mizuno that are listed in the bibliography at the end of this chapter for further details and examples.

Affinity Diagram/KJ Method

The affinity diagram/KJ method, developed in the 1960s by Kawakita Jiro, a Japanese anthropologist, is a technique for gathering and organizing a large number of ideas, opinions, and facts relating to a broad problem or subject area. ("KJ" is a trademark registered by the Kawayoshida Research Center.) Its purpose is to allow problem solvers to sift through large volumes of information efficiently and identify natural patterns or groupings in the information, allowing managers to focus on the key issues and their elements rather than an unorganized collection of information.

Interrelationship Diagraphs

The purpose of an interrelationship diagraph is to take a central idea and map out logical or sequential links among related categories. It shows that every idea can be

---

[18]James L. Brossert, *Quality Function Deployment: A Practitioner's Approach* (Milwaukee, WI: ASQC Quality Press/Marcel Dekker, 1991), Part 2.

logically linked with more than one idea at a time, and allows for "lateral thinking" rather than "linear thinking." This technique often is used after the affinity diagram has brought issues, problems, and opinions into clearer focus.

Tree Diagram

A tree diagram maps out the paths and tasks that need to be accomplished to complete a specific project or reach a specified goal. Thus, the planner seeks to answer the following questions by using this technique: "What is the sequence of tasks that need to be completed in order to best address the issue?" or "What are all of the factors that contribute to the existence of the key problem?"

Matrix Diagrams

Matrix diagrams are "spreadsheets" that show relationships in a graphical display between characteristics, functions, and tasks in such a way as to provide logical connecting points between each item. The "House of Quality" developed in Chapter 6 is an example of one of the many varieties of matrix diagrams now being used for planning and quality improvement.

Matrix Data Analysis

Matrix data analysis takes data from matrix diagrams and seeks to arrange them quantitatively to display the relationships and strengths of those relationships between variables. Basically, it is a rigorous, statistically based "factor analysis" technique. GOAL/QPC feels that this method, while worthwhile for many applications, is too quantitative to be used on a daily basis and has developed an alternative tool called a *prioritization matrix,* which is easier to understand and implement. The interested reader should consult Brassard's book for further details.

Process Decision Program Chart (PDPC)

This is a method for mapping out every conceivable event and contingency that can occur when moving from a problem statement to possible solutions. Its purpose is to anticipate possible problems and provide countermeasures that will (a) prevent the deviation from occurring, or (b) be in place if the deviation *does* occur.

Arrow Diagrams

These have been used by construction planners for years in the form of CPM and PERT project planning techniques. Arrow diagramming has also been taught extensively in quantitative methods, operations management, and other business and engineering courses in the United States for a number of years. Unfortunately, its use has been confined to the technical expert, rather than the general manager.

Quality Improvement for the Jacksonville Naval Aviation Depot[19]

The Navy's six aviation depots are large industrial plants that overhaul, repair, and modify aircraft, air-launched missiles, and related engines and components. Their customers include the Navy, other military services, foreign governments, and civilian agencies such as NASA. The Jacksonville and Alameda depots won a major $50 million bid to modify 89 Navy antisubmarine aircraft by offering the highest level of service at the lowest price. Jacksonville was assigned 39 of the aircraft, but found that the first few aircraft needed several hundred more man-hours than originally planned in the bid. Unable to sustain such losses, a meeting of managers, supervisors, and employees devised changes in sequencing the work that resulted in significant productivity improvements. However, in such labor-intensive jobs, further gains could only come from continuous improvement.

Depot managers developed a continuous improvement strategy designed to maximize worker improvement ideas and to implement them quickly. This strategy involved new information technology and management practices.

Information technology included:

- Linking performance data to subprocesses and swiftly sending this information to the shop floor.

- Using computer graphics to enhance the ease, accuracy, and speed of making, analyzing, and introducing improvement ideas.

Management practices involved:

- Freeing foremen and supervisors to concentrate on improvement.

- Eliminating barriers between shop personnel and customers and eliminating the transition problems between shifts.

- Allowing foremen to make some customer-authorized changes without higher approval.

[19]Adapted from Frederick G. Schobert, Jr., and Charles L. Brown, "A Strategy for Continuous Improvement," *Quality Progress,* October 1990, pp. 69–71.

- Organizing workers into teams to promote ownership and the fun of competition.

- Acting quickly on workers' improvement ideas.

The first task was to ensure that the project stayed in control. The depot started comprehensive monitoring of quality, schedule, and cost by means of an information system. As a result, data vital for controlling day-to-day operations went swiftly to the shop floor. This allowed shop personnel to spot and solve problems early. Computer graphics traced the project plans in flowchart form, which let people immediately link performance reports with subprocesses. This connection was significant in diagnosing problems. Computer graphics also made it easy to revise and distribute new procedures to workers. With printouts in hand, they could accurately follow new operating procedures just hours after they were established. Equally important, they could determine where further improvements were possible in a specific subprocess.

Many foremen complained that they did not have time to plan beyond the immediate demands of the day. Jacksonville assigned many tasks previously done by supervisors and foremen to work leaders in charge of small teams of employees. As the chief foreman stated: "This is the first time in my 24 years of work that I've actually been able to manage instead of just doing paperwork and putting out fires." When the foremen started to concentrate on improving processes, so did other employees.

Customers were included in the improvement process because Jacksonville knew that any problems that customers found were opportunities for improvement. Depot managers invited customer representatives to spot-check quality at any time, not just in mandatory inspections. Managers and foremen discussed performance reports not normally shown to outsiders with the representatives and asked for their suggestions. These practices saved time, money, and misunderstandings.

Keeping improvement a top priority among workers was not a matter of slogans and banners. Instead, it was a combination of instilling pride of ownership, making improvement fun, removing barriers to communication, and constant manage-

(continued)

ment attention to worker suggestions. Jacksonville managers actively encouraged workers to think of new ideas by assigning a work leader and team to each aircraft. This inspired a sense of ownership. Two teams were usually doing the same thing on different planes. If one team was faster or better, it won an informal contest for baseball caps or jackets, but mostly for the pride of teaching the other teams how it was accomplished. The transition problem between shifts was eliminated by overlapping shifts for 30 minutes to let one shift brief the other on the progress of the job and to compare notes and ideas.

This improvement strategy paid off handsomely. By the ninth aircraft, they had exceeded their best-case projection for man-hours, with record-breaking quality check results. By the thirtieth aircraft, the required man-hours was 40% less than the original bid amount, and continued to decrease. This meant savings of millions of dollars over the life of the contract.

Key Issues for Discussion

1. Discuss the elements of improvement at the Jacksonville depot. How do these relate to the Japanese concept of kaizen? What specific impacts on quality do you think these improvements made?

2. Were the improvements primarily a result of technology or management? List the important key themes that can be extracted from this experience and applied to other organizations.

QUALITY IN PRACTICE

Applications of Quality Improvement Tools at Rotor Clip[20]

Rotor Clip Company, Inc., of Somerset, New Jersey, is a major manufacturer of retaining rings and self-tightening hose clamps and is a believer in the use of simple quality improvement tools. Several years ago, one of its clamps was failing stress testing during final inspections. No reason was evident, so managers and supervisors decided to develop a cause-and-effect diagram to search for a solution. Every employee involved with the part was called to a meeting to discuss the problem. The group was encouraged to brainstorm reasons for the problem, resulting in the fishbone diagram shown in Figure 9.21.

After reviewing all the probable causes, they concluded that the salt temperature of the quenching tank (a heat-treating step) was too close to the martensite line. This was selected for further study, but raising the salt temperature did not alleviate the problem. The group met again and agreed to pursue the second possibility, seams in one wire, as a possible cause. Wire samples that failed inspection were examined metallographically and seams were confirmed as the major cause of the defective parts.

The material was returned to the supplier and new material yielded parts that passed the final inspection.

A second application involved the use of a Pareto diagram to study rising premium freight charges for shipping retaining rings. The study covered three months in order to collect enough data to draw conclusions. The Pareto diagram is shown in Figure 9.22. The results were startling. The most frequent cause of higher freight charges was customer requests. The decision was made to continue the study to identify which customers consistently expedite their shipments and to work closely with them to find ways of reducing costs. The second largest contributor was the lack of available machine time. Once a die was installed in a stamping press, it ran until it produced the maximum number of parts (usually a million) before it was removed for routine maintenance. While this policy resulted in efficient utilization of tooling, it tied up the press and ultimately accounted for rush shipments. The policy was revised to limit die runs to fill orders more efficiently.

A third application was the use of a scatter diagram by the advertising department. Traditionally, it had been difficult to prove the effect of advertising expenditures on the bottom line. Man-

[20]Adapted from Bruce Rudin, "Simple Tools Solve Complex Problems," Reprinted with permission from *Quality*, April 1990, pp. 50–51, a publication of Hitchcock Publishing, a Capital Cities/ABC, Inc. company.

(continued)

FIGURE 9.21 The Fishbone Diagram for the Rotor Clip Clamp Problem

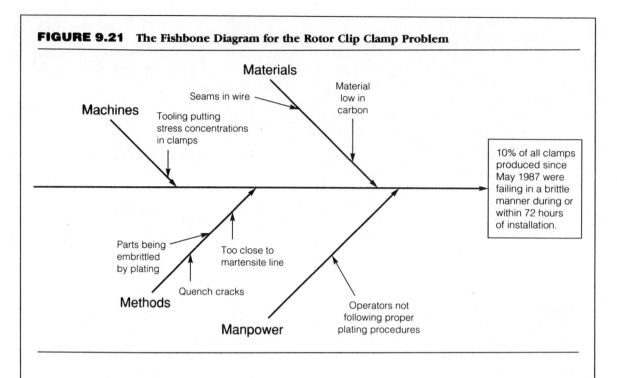

FIGURE 9.22 Pareto Diagram of Customer Calls

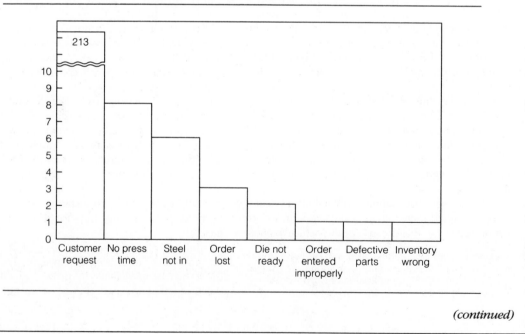

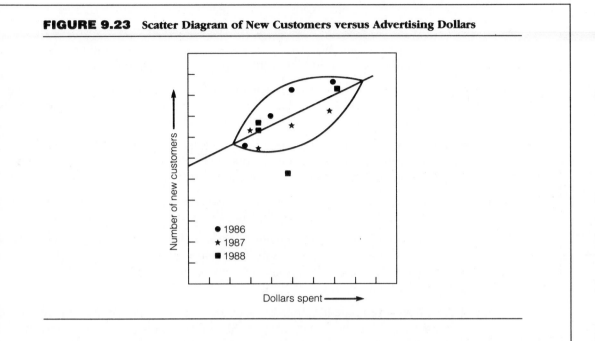

FIGURE 9.23 Scatter Diagram of New Customers versus Advertising Dollars

agement wanted to learn if the amount of advertising dollars spent correlated with the number of new customers gained in a given year. Advertising dollars spent by quarter were plotted against the number of new customers added for the same period for three consecutive years (see Figure 9.23). The positive correlation showed that heavy advertising was related to new customers. The results were fairly consistent from year to year except for the second quarter of 1988, an outlier that clearly stood out from the rest. Advertising checked the media schedule and discovered that experimental image ads dominated that particular period. This prompted the advertising department to eliminate image ads from its schedule.

Key Issues for Discussion

1. Once the seam problem in the clamps was understood, what controls should have been instituted to prevent the problem from occurring again?

2. In the freight charge example, what steps do you think the company should take with customers who consistently expedite shipments?

3. How might the advertising department continue to use scatter diagrams in the future? How might top management use the results in setting budget priorities?

Summary of Key Points

- *Kaizen,* the Japanese term for improvement, is a philosophy focused on improving quality in all areas of business using small, frequent, and gradual improvements over a long term.

- A problem is a deviation between what *is* actually happening and what *should be* happening. Problem solving is at the heart of quality improvement and is a highly creative effort, encompassing problem redefinition and analysis, idea generation, evaluation and selection of ideas, and implementation.

■ The creative problem-solving process consists of mess finding, fact finding, problem finding, idea finding, solution finding, and implementation.

■ The Deming cycle is a problem-solving methodology that consists of four stages: plan, do, study, and act. It is based on continuous improvement and has been the foundation of most Japanese problem-solving efforts.

■ Juran's quality improvement approach is based on *breakthrough*—improvement that takes an organization to unprecedented levels of performance. Breakthrough is focused on attacking common causes of variation.

■ Crosby proposes a 14-step program for quality improvement that is based more on a managerial/behavioral approach than on the use of analytical tools.

■ The "seven QC tools" for quality improvement are flowcharts, check sheets, histograms, Pareto diagrams, cause-and-effect diagrams, scatter diagrams, and control charts. These tools are used for problem diagnosis and idea generation in quality problem solving.

■ The "new seven" quality improvement tools are focused on the implementation process. They are the affinity diagram/KJ method, interrelationship diagraphs, tree diagrams, matrix diagrams, matrix data analyses, process decision program charts, and arrow diagrams.

Questions for Review and Discussion

1. Explain the Japanese concept of *kaizen*. How does it differ from traditional Western approaches to improvement?

2. What is the Kepner and Tregoe definition of a problem? How does this definition apply to quality assurance? Give some examples.

3. Explain the difference between structured, semistructured, and ill-structured problems. What implications do these classifications have for solving problems?

4. What are the four major components of any problem-solving process?

5. List and explain the six steps of the Osborn/Parnes problem-solving process.

6. Discuss some of the common sources of "messes."

7. Explain how work sampling can be used to identify quality improvement opportunities.

8. What techniques are useful to identify quality-related problems in service organizations?

9. Discuss the important considerations that must be taken into account when collecting data.

10. State five different problems that you face as "In what ways might I . . . ?" Use the Why technique to redefine the problems. Have your initial problem definitions changed?

11. Explain the technique of *problem detection methodology*. Develop an example at your school by interviewing your fellow students, such as registering for classes. Based on the data collected, what are the critical problems? Can you suggest some solutions?

12. Describe various methods used for idea finding.

13. What is the Deming cycle? How does it relate to the creative problem-solving process?

14. What is breakthrough? Describe Juran's breakthrough sequence for quality improvement.

15. Explain Crosby's program for quality improvement. How does it differ from the Deming cycle and Juran's breakthrough sequence?

16. What contributions has H. James Harrington made to quality improvement?

17. Explain the use of the seven QC tools for problem solving. Provide two examples of each that are different from those in the chapter based on your own experiences or research.

18. How are the "new seven" quality improvement tools used? Briefly explain the purpose of each.

Problems

1. A flowchart for a fast food drive-through window is shown in Figure 9.24. Discuss the important quality characteristics inherent in this process and suggest possible improvements.

2. A catalog order-filling process for personalized printed products can be described as follows[21]: Telephone orders are taken over a 12-hour period each day. Orders are collected from each person at the end of the day and checked for errors by the supervisor of the phone department, usually the following morning. Depending on how busy she was on the phone, this one-day batch of orders would not get to the data processing department until after 1:00 P.M. The next step is data processing. Orders are invoiced in the one-day batches. Then they are printed and matched back to the original orders. At this point, if the order was for a new customer, it was sent to the person who did the customer verification and setup of new customer accounts. This had to be done before the order could be invoiced. The next step involved order verification and proofreading. Once invoicing was completed, the orders with invoices attached were given to a person who verified that all required information was present and correct to permit typesetting. If there was a question, it was checked by computer or by calling the customer. Finally, the completed orders were sent to the typesetting department of the printshop.

   a. Develop a flowchart for this process.
   b. Discuss opportunities for improving the quality of service in this situation.

---

[21]Adapted from Ronald G. Conant, "JIT in a Mail Order Operation Reduces Processing Time from Four Days to Four Hours," *Industrial Engineering,* Vol. 20, No. 9, September 1988, pp. 34–37.

FIGURE 9.24 Flowchart for Problem 1

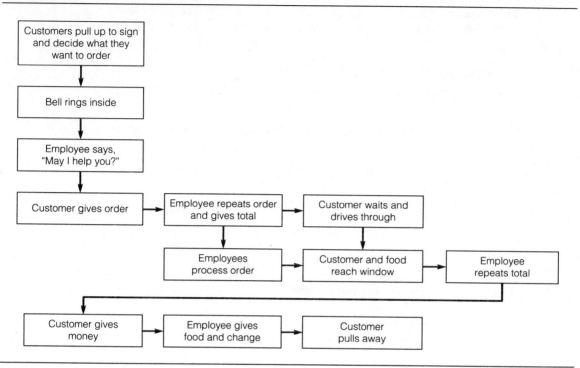

---

3. Develop a flowchart of your daily routine from getting up to going to school or work.

4. Design a check sheet to help a high school student who is getting poor grades on a math quiz determine the source of his or her difficulty.

5. The number of seconds waiting for a customer service representative on a telephone are listed below. Construct a histogram. What do the data tell you?

5	7	7	15	21	15	22	10	10	6
8	18	14	5	7	8	3	8	4	10

6. The number of hours that a machine ran until failure is given below. Construct a histogram and discuss any conclusions that you might reach.

10.5	5.0	15.3	16.8	9.2	20.2	27.5	8.9	12.2	18.2
4.2	12.6	7.8	11.5	12.6	14.5	14.0	5.5	15.5	8.9

7. Analysis of customer complaints for a large mail-order house revealed the following:

billing errors: 867
shipping errors: 1960
unclear charges: 9650
long delay: 6672
delivery error: 452.

Construct a Pareto diagram for these data. What conclusions would you reach?

8. Develop cause-and-effect diagrams for the following problems:

   a. poor exam grade
   b. no job offers
   c. too many speeding tickets
   d. late for work or school.

9. In a manufacturing process, the production rate (parts/hour) was thought to affect the number of defectives found during a subsequent inspection. To test this theory, the production rate was varied and the number of defects were collected for the same batch sizes. The results were:

Production Rate	Number of Defectives
20	21
20	19
40	15
30	16
60	14
40	17

Construct a scatter diagram for these data. What conclusions can you reach?

10. The number of defects found in 30 samples of 100 electronic assemblies taken on a daily basis over one month is given below. Plot these data on a control chart, computing the average value (center line), but ignoring the control limits. Do you suspect that any special causes were present? Why?

1	6	5	5	4	3	2	2	4	6	2	1	3	1	4
5	4	1	6	15	12	6	3	4	3	3	2	5	7	4

Case Problem A

Federal Express describes the process of sending a package from the United States to Amsterdam as follows:[22] Your call for a pick-up is answered at a Federal Express Customer Service Call Center. A trained customer service agent enters all the information about your shipment into the COSMOS information and tracking system. They make sure you have properly completed and included all applicable documentation. Your pick-up request is relayed to a courier near your address via the Federal Express on-board computer (DADS—Digitally Assisted Dispatch System) in every van. The courier plots your location on a pick-up schedule.

When the courier arrives to pick up your shipment, he or she verifies all the information on the international air waybill and determines that the required documentation is attached. A barcode scanner (SuperTracker) scans the barcode on the waybill and the information is relayed to the COSMOS system.

By evening, the courier transfers your shipment at the airport and, prior to loading, its status is again entered into the COSMOS system. Later, the shipment departs on a direct flight to the SuperHub sorting facility in Memphis and arrives around midnight. The moment one of the sorters comes in contact with it, the waybill is scanned again and the COSMOS system updates the shipment status. It proceeds to a computerized sort system. Location and sorting informa-

[22]Federal Express Worldwide Delivery System, International Priority Service, 1990. Due to changes in international operations, there are slight variations in this process.

tion is entered at this stage into computers. International shipment specialists recheck the shipment's documentation and prepare the required customs manifests. The COSMOS system is again updated by scanners.

To speed customs clearance time at the destination, the manifests and accompanying documentation are electronically transmitted to the freight sorting facility at the destination airport. Moments later your shipment arrives at the routing code and destination sort station. Here it is scanned again and the correct loading zone and departure gate are scheduled. The shipment is loaded onto the appropriate international flight. A specialist gives it one final check and the aircraft departs.

The direct Federal Express European flight arrives at Stansted Airport near London to unload shipments designated for Great Britain. The flight proceeds to Frankfurt where all shipments are sorted and scanned again to update the COSMOS system. They are placed on the appropriate vehicles to their final destinations.

Your shipment arrives at the final customs clearing facility. Customs officials have reviewed the facsimile of the documentation the night before when it was transmitted from Memphis. After clearance, the shipment is scanned and the COSMOS system is updated. A Federal Express van carries the package to its final destination. The courier scans the documentation for the last time and provides the COSMOS system with proof of performance information.

Questions

1. Construct a flowchart for this process. Discuss activities in the process where quality may break down. Are these within or beyond the control of Federal Express?
2. Highlight all steps of the process that are focused on improving quality. Do these activities completely eliminate quality problems?
3. What is the function of the COSMOS system? How can it achieve and maintain quality?

Case Problem B

Welz Business Machines sells and services a variety of copiers, computers, and other office equipment.[23] The company receives many calls daily for service, sales, accounting, and other departments. All calls are handled centrally through customer service representatives and routed to other individuals as appropriate. A number of customers had complained about long waits when calling for service. A market research study found that customers became irritated if the call was not answered within five rings. Scott Welz, the company president, authorized the customer service department manager, Tim, to study this problem and find a method to shorten the call-waiting time for its customers.

Tim met with the service representatives who answered the calls to attempt to determine the reasons for long waiting times. The following conversation ensued:

[23]This problem was developed from a classic example published in "The Quest for Higher Quality: The Deming Prize and Quality Control," by RICOH of America, Inc.

Tim: "This is a serious problem; how a customer phone inquiry is answered is the first impression the customer receives from us. As you know, this company was founded on efficient and friendly service to all our customers. It's obvious why customers have to wait: You're on the phone with another customer. Can you think of any reasons that might keep you on the phone for an unnecessarily long time?"

Robin: "I've noticed quite often that the party to whom I need to route the call is not present. It takes time to transfer the call and wait to see if it is answered. If the party is not there, I end up apologizing and transfer the call to another extension."

Tim: "You're right, Robin. Sales personnel often are out of the office for sales calls, absent on trips to preview new products, or not at their desks for a variety of reasons. What else might cause this problem?"

Ravi: "I get irritated at some customers who spend a great deal of time complaining about a problem that I cannot do anything about except to refer to someone else. Of course, I listen and sympathize with them, but this eats up a lot of time."

LaMarr: "Some customers call so often, they think we're long lost friends and strike up a personal conversation."

Tim: "That's not always a bad thing, you realize."

LaMarr: "Sure, but it delays my answering other calls."

Nancy: "It's not always the customer's fault. During lunch times, we're not all available to answer the phone."

Ravi: "Right after we open at 9:00 A.M., we get a rush of calls. I think that many of the delays are caused by these peak periods."

Robin: "I've noticed the same thing between 4 and 5 P.M."

Tim: "I've had a few comments from department managers that they were routed calls that didn't fall in their areas of responsibility and had to be transferred again."

Mark: "But that doesn't cause delays at our end."

Nancy: "That's right, Mark, but I just realized that sometimes I simply don't understand what the customer's problem really is. I spend a lot of time trying to get him or her to explain it better. Often, I have to route it to *someone* because other calls are waiting."

Ravi: "Perhaps we need to have more knowledge of our products."

Tim: "Well, I think we've covered most of the major reasons as to why many customers have to wait. It seems to me that we have four major reasons: the phones are short-staffed, the receiving party is not present, the customer dominates the conversation, and you may not understand the customer's problem. We need to collect some information next about these possible causes. I will set up a data collection sheet that you can use to track some of these things. Mark, would you help me on this?"

Over the next two weeks, the staff collected data on the frequency of reasons why some callers had to wait. This is summarized below.

Reason	Total number
A Operators short-staffed	172
B Receiving party not present	73
C Customer dominates conversation	19
D Lack of operator understanding	61
E Other reasons	10

Questions

1. From the conversation between Tim and his staff, draw a cause-and-effect diagram.
2. Perform a Pareto analysis of the data collected.
3. What actions might the company take to improve the situation?

Bibliography

Ackoff, R. L., and Vergara, E. "Creativity in Problem Solving and Planning: A Review," *European Journal of Operations Research,* Vol. 7 (1981), pp. 1–13.

Box, G. E. P., and Bisgaard, S. "The Scientific Context of Quality Improvement," *Quality Progress,* Vol. 20, No. 6, June 1987, pp. 54–61.

Brassard, Michael. *The Memory Jogger Plus+.* Methuen, MA: GOAL/QPC, 1989.

Brossert, James L. *Quality Function Deployment: A Practitioner's Approach.* Milwaukee, WI: ASQC Quality Press/Marcel Dekker, 1991, Part 2.

Burr, John T. "The Tools of Quality Part I: Going With the Flow (chart)," *Quality Progress,* June 1990, pp. 64–67.

Burr, John T. "The Tools of Quality Part VI: Pareto Charts," *Quality Progress,* November 1990, pp. 59–61.

Burr, John T. "The Tools of Quality Part VII: Scatter Diagrams," *Quality Progress,* December 1990, pp. 87–89.

Freeman, N. B. "Quality on the Mend," *American Machinist and Automated Manufacturing,* April 1986, pp. 102–112.

Gitlow, H., Gitlow, S., Oppenheim, A., and Oppenheim. R. *Tools and Methods for the Improvement of Quality.* Homewood, IL: Irwin, 1989.

Hradesky, John L. *Productivity and Quality Improvement.* New York: McGraw-Hill, 1988.

Juran Institute, Inc. "The Tools of Quality Part IV: Histograms," *Quality Progress,* September 1990, pp. 75–78.

Juran Institute, Inc. "The Tools of Quality Part V: Check Sheets," *Quality Progress,* October 1990, pp. 51–56.

Melan, E. H. "Process Management in Service and Administrative Operations," *Quality Progress,* June 1985, pp. 52–59.

Mizuno, Shigeru. *Management for Quality Improvement: The 7 New QC Tools,* Cambridge, MA: Productivity Press, 1988.

Ott, Ellis R. *Process Quality Control.* New York: McGraw-Hill, 1975.

Sarazen, J. Stephen. "The Tools of Quality Part II: Cause-and-Effect Diagrams," *Quality Progress,* July 1990, pp. 59–62.

Shainin, Peter D. "The Tools of Quality Part III: Control Charts," *Quality Progress,* August 1990, pp. 79–82.

Skrabec, Q. R. "Process Diagnostics," *Quality Progress,* Vol. 19, No. 11, November 1986, pp. 40–44.

Stratton, A. D. "Solving Problems with CEFA, *Quality Progress,* Vol. 19, No. 4, April 1986, pp. 65–70.

Human Resource Management for Quality

All businesses have three principal resources: capital, physical, and human. Many global competitors—both old and new—such as Japan, Taiwan, Singapore, and Switzerland, have few natural resources, but they use the same basic technologies as the United States. So they have been forced to develop their competitive edge primarily through the human resource. The human resource is the only one that competitors cannot copy, and is the only one that can synergize, that is, produce output whose value is greater than the sum of its parts.

Deming emphasizes that no organization can survive without good people, people who are improving. The essence of Deming's Point 1 is that profit is not the ultimate objective of the firm. In Japan and in Europe, corporations are social entities, not simply money-making machines. The objective of these corporations is to serve customers and their own employees. Businesses are beginning to learn that to provide satisfied customers, they must first provide satisfied employees.

The role of human beings in work has changed over the centuries and in recent decades. Skilled craftspeople in the village days had a major stake in the quality of their products because their families' livelihoods depended on the sale of those products. They were motivated by pride in their work as well as the need for survival. The departure from the craftsmanship concept was promulgated by Frederick W. Taylor. Taylor concluded that a factory should be managed on a scientific basis. He focused on work methods design, the establishment of standards for daily work, selection and training of workers, and piecework incentives. Taylor separated planning from execution, concluding that foremen and workers of those days lacked the education necessary to plan their work. The foreman's role was to assure that the work force met productivity standards. Other pioneers of scientific management, such as Frank and Lilian Gilbreth and Henry Gantt, further refined the system through motion study, methods improvement, ergonomics, scheduling, and wage incentive systems.

The Taylor system dramatically improved productivity. However, as the pressures to achieve better productivity increased, quality eroded. The Taylor philosophy also contributed to the development of labor unions and led to the establishment of an adversarial relationship between labor and management that has yet to be completely overcome. Most significantly, the Taylor system failed to make use of an organization's most important asset—the knowledge and creativity of the work force. Japan, in particular, has marshaled this asset and clearly demonstrated that attention to the human resource can improve quality and productivity far more than robots and automation. Konosuke Matsushita told[1] a group of U.S. executives in 1988:

> We will win, and you will lose. You cannot do anything about it because your failure is an internal disease. Your companies are based on Taylor's principles. Worse, your heads are Taylorized too. You firmly believe that good management means executives on one side, and workers on the other; on one side, men who think, and on the other side, men who can only work. For you, management is the art of smoothly transferring the executive's ideas to the workers' hands.
>
> We have passed the Taylor stage . . . . For us, management is the entire work force's intellectual commitment at the service of the company . . . without self-imposed functional or class barriers. . . . Only the intellects of all employees can permit a company to live with the ups and downs and requirements of its new environment. Yes, we will win and you will lose. For you are not able to rid your minds of the obsolete Taylorisms that we never had.

Clearly, we face a critical challenge in human resource management. The revolution in industrial psychology and human relations was begun at the Hawthorne Works of Western Electric Company in the late 1920s by a Harvard team that included Elton Mayo, Fritz Roethlisberger, and William Dickson. Both Deming and Juran were working for Western Electric at the time, which may have influenced their views on quality and the work force. A few years later, the work of Abraham Maslow, Douglas McGregor, and Frederick Herzberg helped to develop the concepts of motivation, leadership, employee development, and individual and group approaches to job design with an emphasis on human relations. New theories are continually proposed. The challenge is how to use these theories properly for quality improvement.

In this chapter, we focus on human resource management. We will consider the strategic and operational impact of values, business strategy, motivation, leadership, performance, and rewards on the implementation of human resource management processes within the context of total quality management.

THE SCOPE OF HUMAN RESOURCE MANAGEMENT

Human resource management (HRM) consists of those activities designed to provide for and coordinate the human resource of an organization.[2] Human resource management is a modern term for what has been traditionally referred to as personnel administration or personnel management. The traditional role of "personnel managers" in a business organization was to interview job applicants, negotiate contracts with the union, keep time cards on hourly workers, and occasionally teach a training course. Today, their role has changed dramatically. Human resource functions are the tasks and duties that human resource managers perform. They include determining the organization's human resource needs; recruiting, selecting, developing, counseling, and rewarding employees; acting as a liaison with unions and government organizations; and handling other matters of employee well-being.

---

[1]Cited in A. Richard Shores, *A TQM Approach to Achieving Manufacturing Excellence* (Milwaukee, WI: ASQC Quality Press, 1990), p. 270.

[2]Lloyd L. Byars and Leslie W. Rue, *Human Resource Management,* 3rd ed. (Homewood, IL: Richard D. Irwin, 1991), p. 6.

Human resource managers may still perform the traditional tasks of personnel managers, but the scope and importance of their area of responsibility have changed significantly. Human resource managers now are taking on a strategic role in their organizations. They are also being required to consider and plan for the development of the organization's corporate culture, as well as day-to-day operations involved with maintenance of HRM systems. If the organization has committed itself to a total quality management philosophy, both the process and content of the human resource department—the way that it carries out its mission and responsibilities—will be drastically changed.

An example of the strategic use of HRM can be seen at the Prudential Insurance company.[3] The Prudential has identified five critical success factors that must be consistently implemented well in order to widen its lead over competitors. One of these is superior service to its customers and field force. The ability to consistently deliver value-added service requires superior performance in eight areas, which have been determined as key to becoming customer- and market-driven. These areas are:

- people recruitment and retention

- training

- continuing education

- creative use of information technologies

- accessibility to customers

- performance measuring and monitoring

- recognition for superior performance

- customer satisfaction monitoring.

Five of these eight areas for superior performance involve HRM issues. All eight areas are also related to quality issues of excellence in selection and retention, internal performance, customer service, and continuous improvement.

A Framework for HRM

The complexity of human resource management has been noted by Skinner, who observed that HRM is based on no fewer than six theoretical perspectives, many of which are in conflict and work at cross purposes with each other.[4] These perspectives can be grouped into two basic areas: *human relations* and *systems*. Human relations includes individual, group behavior, and organization development approaches. Motivation is a key notion in understanding individual behavior. Group behavior approaches include social interaction, interpersonal relations, and authority theories. Organization development often centers around leadership.

Systems include industrial engineering, which involves designing jobs to fit technology and human capabilities and controlling performance based on industrial

---

[3]Ethan Davis, "Quality Service at the Prudential," in Spechler, Jay W. (ed.), *When America Does It Right* (Norcross, GA: Industrial Engineering and Management Press, 1988), pp. 225–226.

[4]Wickham Skinner, "Big Hat—No Cattle: Managing Human Resources," *Harvard Business Review*, September–October 1981, p. 109.

engineering studies; labor relations, which relies on labor laws, public policies, the economics of wages and costs, demographics and manpower management, collective administration and grievances to explain management-worker interactions; and personnel management, which includes activities involved in managing large numbers of people in the aggregate, including recruiting, selecting, training, compensating, and development.

Figure 10.1 summarizes this structure. In this chapter we focus on these themes, with the exception of group approaches. Because of the special role that groups play in quality, we shall devote the next chapter entirely to employee involvement and teamwork.

Despite the fact that the field is at least 100 years old, few companies have successfully resolved the conflicts between the human relations and systems perspectives. Many HRM departments tend to overemphasize one aspect in pursuit of the other. A classic case in which an individual human relations philosophy was permitted to overwhelm the need for systems was at a high-tech company called Non Linear Systems.[5]

Non Linear Systems (NLS) was founded as a manufacturer and marketer of digital electrical measuring instruments in the early 1950s. Initially, its stock was wholly owned by the president, Andrew F. Kay, and his family. In 1960–61 Kay decided to institute a series of radical changes in the structure and day-to-day processes of the company in the belief that he was implementing a field experiment in participative management based on some of the most current organizational behavior theories of the day. Some of the theorists referenced included Maslow, McGregor, and Drucker. Some of the corporate policies and participative procedures that were introduced included: (1) a flat three-level organization structure, consisting of an executive council of the president and seven vice presidents, a manager level consisting of 30 line and staff managers, and the worker level that also included a few assistant

---

[5]Edmund R. Gray, "The Non Linear Systems Experience: A Requiem," *Business Horizons,* February 1978, pp. 31–36.

FIGURE 10.1 TQM Model of Human Resource Management

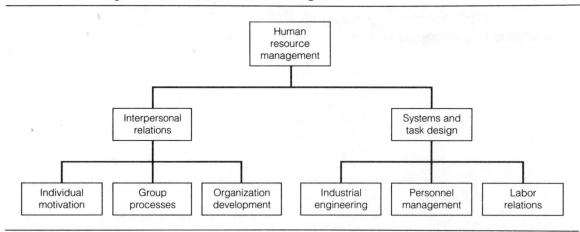

managers; (2) elimination of assembly lines and replacement by assembly teams; (3) establishment of a salary system for all employees, with accompanying elimination of time clocks, absence control, and layoffs; and (4) elimination of the accounting function, with the requirement for a minimum level of record-keeping (for governmental reporting purposes) placed on the departments. The new system seemed to work quite well for a period of three or four years, but the experiment was abandoned in 1965 when falling sales and increased competition forced the company back to a more conventional structure and process. What had been widely praised by a number of management scholars as a bold experiment in participative management was quickly denounced by conservative scholars as showing that participative management could only work in extremely favorable, but very limited, environmental conditions. The failure of NLS was not in the human relations theory, but in its misapplication in practice. The lesson learned was that change must be implemented slowly, evaluated carefully, and that participation must be applied to the problem of developing adequate control and coordination systems throughout the organization in order for business quality and quality of worklife to be simultaneously improved.

HUMAN RESOURCE MANAGEMENT IN A TQM ENVIRONMENT

The total quality management focus is changing the role of human resource management by changing the perspectives of employees, HRM professionals, and line-and-staff managers from an adversarial, control-oriented relationship to a cooperative position based on mutual organizational and individual goals, trust, and respect. Human resource managers tend to reflect the culture within which they are working, as well as influence it. Thus, values can and do play a key role in determining how the HRM function is carried out. Two typical philosophical positions[6] that seem to capture the managerial and HRM assumptions that affect the development of TQM within organizations can be seen in Table 10.1. We call these the "TQM/HRM" and the "traditional HRM" approaches.

The traditional norm in many industries over the years has been the formal, contractual approach to human resources management. It is identified with labor relations (with or without union involvement) and industrial engineering perspectives, within the framework of traditional personnel management systems. It has frequently led to rigid work rules, labor unrest, and "us-versus-them" thinking as management and labor attempted to get or keep the upper hand.

Specifically, the traditional HRM philosophy of "a fair day's work for a fair day's pay" was the driving force in many industries, such as in automobile manufacturing. At GM and Ford in the 1970s, for example, the business objectives were productivity and profits, while the quality objective was to meet minimum required standards or federal regulations. Information was only shared as needed. Constituencies consisted first of managers and stockholders; customers and employees were last in priority. Employee involvement programs were primarily of the suggestion plan approach

---

[6]Carla O'Dell, "Sharing the Productivity Payoff," reprinted from *Productivity Brief 24* with permission of the American Productivity and Quality Center (Houston, TX) in William B. Werther et al., *Productivity Through People* (St. Paul, MN: West Publishing Company 1986), p. 336.

TABLE 10.1 Characteristics of Philosophical Positions

	TQM/HRM Approach	Traditional HRM
Philosophy	Shared responsibility, commitment, rewards	Fair day's work for a fair day's pay
Business objectives	Increased quality, productivity, customer satisfaction, employee satisfaction, and loyalty	Increased productivity, profitability; quality is secondary; focus on labor
Quality objectives	Total quality management and continuous improvement at and across every level	Adequate quality to remain in business; staff-driven approaches to quality improvement
Business information sharing	Open books—share broad information on profits, productivity, quality, costs, capital spending plans	Limited to information on an as-needed basis for job performance
Major constituencies	Customers, all employees, stockholders	Managers, stockholders, customers, employees
Employee involvement	Extensive, within and between levels and functions; "way of life"	Programs—suggestion plans, individual employee awards; usually no formal system
Education and training	Quality and economic education; multiple skill training; problem solving and group process	On-the-job training; feedback on job performance
Reward structure	Designed and adjusted by management-employee committee; formal, early union involvement	Management designed and administered
Job security	Formal commitment; a key consideration in all decisions	Labor as a variable cost; layoffs common during business downturns

SOURCE: Adapted from Carla O'Dell, "Sharing the Productivity Payoff."

(although GM was experimenting with "Quality of Worklife" approaches in selected locations in the early 1970s). Education and training was strictly job-related, rather than broad in scope. Rewards were management-designed and driven by productivity requirements. Finally, layoffs and plant shutdowns without retraining undermined job security.

In contrast, the TQM/HRM approach has been used successfully in recent years by a number of small, medium, and a few large firms to develop a more cooperative, productive, flexible, and innovative work environment. This approach is based on recognizing the value of the human resource in meeting customer needs, with a focus on sharing information, responsibility, and rewards. The automotive industry in general and Ford in particular have made great strides in the last 10 years toward adopting a TQM/HRM approach. This is evident in the following discussion of the turnaround at Ford's Louisville plant, which produces Ranger and Bronco utility vehicles.[7]

When Tom Ryan came to the plant in 1976 as industrial relations manager, the plant had everything wrong with it that had ever been written about the U.S. auto industry: a history of bitter labor relations, autocratic managers who naturally confronted labor leaders, broken and discarded parts littered about, shouting matches between workers and supervisors, and forklift operators who dropped or smashed into their loads.

---

[7]Adapted from Jeremy Main, "Ford's Drive for Quality," *Fortune,* April 18, 1983.

In 1979, the night shift was laid off because of dwindling demand. Word spread that the plant was a prime candidate for closure when the LTD and light truck models it built were phased out. The first message from the new plant manager, Don Baker, was straight to the point: "Saying to hell with the company is just like saying to hell with yourself. What do you want? Do you want to make a good product or do you want to shut down? We've got about six months left."

Changes began with small things. The workers complained that they had nowhere to sit during breaks or meals (except on cases or parts, which as a result were sometimes damaged or stained with coffee or mayonnaise). Picnic tables quickly appeared all over the plant. The plant became, and remains, spotless. These and other improvements were developed by workers and managers talking to each other to solve problems. Without any change in the basic production facilities, these small steps—backed by the threat of a permanent shutdown—turned the plant around. By early 1980, the vehicles from Louisville were getting a high quality rating from corporate auditors. By the early 1980s, surveys had shown that the Ranger had narrowed, if not closed, the gap with the top-rated Toyota pickup truck.

The message from Ford's experience is clear. Unless labor and management can agree to work to solve problems cooperatively, organizations can find themselves in an increasingly dangerous competitive position. The TQM/HRM route offers a way for everyone to search for a "win-win" solution, in contrast to the traditional "win-lose" mentality that was previously held by managers and workers.

Although arguments are still being made for the traditional approach, we will focus on the TQM/HRM approach as the model toward which most enlightened companies with a TQM philosophy are moving. It is important to recognize that changes in corporate culture come slowly, and even managers who have adopted the TQM philosophy do not necessarily have the power to move their organization and its systems overnight.

Business Strategy and HRM

Until recently, most organizations neglected the strategic aspects of human resource management, relegating HRM to a support function. Today, most progressive firms are recognizing that HRM plays the key role in developing a viable competitive strategy. Schuler and Jackson explored the linkage between strategy and HRM structure.[8] In general, managers must make choices in five areas that affect the design and operation of the HRM system: planning, staffing, appraising, compensating, and training and development. Each of these five areas has dimensions that can be viewed on a continuum from very structured and rigid to very unstructured and flexible. These areas and their dimensions are shown in Table 10.2.

Schuler and Jackson outlined three typical competitive strategies that are used by companies: (1) cost reduction, (2) quality enhancement, or (3) innovation. Some companies, such as Honda of America, have pursued multiple strategies such as quality enhancement and innovation, although it appears that one of the three strategies tends to dominate in most organizations. Schuler and Jackson outlined

---

[8]Randall S. Schuler and Susan E. Jackson, "Linking Competitive Strategies With Human Resource Management Practice," *Academy of Management EXECUTIVE,* Vol. 1, No. 3, 1987, pp. 207–219.

TABLE 10.2 Human Resource Management Practice Continuae

Planning Choices

Informal	....	Formal
Short Term	....	Long Term
Explicit Job Analysis	....	Implicit Job Analysis
Job Simplification	....	Job Enrichment
Low Employee Involvement	....	High Employee Involvement

Staffing Choices

Internal Sources	....	External Sources
Narrow Paths	....	Broad Paths
Single Ladder	....	Multiple Ladders
Explicit Criteria	....	Implicit Criteria
Limited Socialization	....	Extensive Socialization
Closed Procedures	....	Open Procedures

Appraising Choices

Behavioral Criteria	....	Results Criteria
Purposes: Development, Remedial, Maintenance		
Low Employee Participation	....	High Employee Participation
Short-Term Criteria	....	Long-Term Criteria
Individual Criteria	....	Group Criteria

Compensating Choices

Low Base Salaries	....	High Base Salaries
Internal Equity	....	External Equity
Few Perks	....	Many Perks
Standard, Fixed Package	....	Flexible Package
Low Participation	....	High Participation
No Incentives	....	Many Incentives
Short-Term Incentives	....	Long-Term Incentives
No Employment Security	....	High Employment Security
Hierarchical	....	High Participation

Training and Development

Short Term	....	Long Term
Narrow Application	....	Broad Application
Productivity Emphasis	....	Quality of Work Life Emphasis
Spontaneous, Unplanned	....	Planned, Systematic
Individual Orientation	....	Group Orientation
Low Participation	....	High Participation

SOURCE: Adapted from R. S. Schuler, "Human Resource Management Practice Choices," in R. S. Schuler, S. A. Youngblood, and V. L. Huber (eds.), *Readings in Personnel and Human Resource Management,* 3rd ed. (St. Paul, MN: West Publishing Company, 1988).

specific employee role behaviors and human resource management practices that are required to ensure that each of the strategies fits within its competitive environment.

It is obvious that the cost reduction strategy fits a highly stable competitive environment, most often in a mature industry. The time frame, or strategic focus, is short term with routine, repetitive, predictable operations being the predominant work mode. Employees must "fit the mold," tolerate narrow skill use, be more concerned about quantity than quality, be comfortable with stability, avoid risks, and have a tendency to resist change. They do, however, have to interact with other employees on the line in order to perform their jobs successfully, although this interaction is primarily reactive, rather than proactive. HRM practices generally fall on the left side of each continuum shown in Table 10.2.

On the opposite side of the coin, an innovation strategy fits an unstable, unpredictable, turbulent environment where the emphasis is on creativity and flexibility. Employees must be comfortable with ambiguity and uncertainty, expect to use a variety of skills, seek risks, and embrace change. They tend to have a balanced concern for quality and quantity of output, high involvement with the job, and a very high concern for results. They also tend to be highly independent in their work, prefer the maximum possible level of autonomy, and prefer not to have to work closely with large groups of people on projects. HRM choices that tend to fit this strategy are on the right-hand side of each continuum in Table 10.2.

The majority of organizations do not find themselves in highly unstable or very stable environments, but tend to fall somewhere in between. Even the high-tech firms that typically find themselves in unstable environments, such as Motorola, Apple Computer, and 3M, have many processes that require more emphasis on systematic planning, control, and productivity enhancement than on continuous innovation. This is the environment in which a quality enhancement strategy is most appropriate. According to Schuler and Jackson[9]:

> The profile of employee behaviors necessary for firms pursuing a strategy of quality enhancement is (1) relatively modest and predictable behaviors, (2) a more long-term or intermediate focus, (3) a modest amount of cooperative, interdependent behavior, (4) a high concern for quality, (5) a modest concern for quantity of output, (6) high concern for process (how the goods or services are made or delivered), (7) low risk-taking activity, and (8) commitment to the goals of the organization. . . .
>
> In an attempt to gain competitive advantage through a quality-enhancement strategy, the key HRM practices include (1) relatively fixed and explicit job descriptions, (2) high levels of employee participation in decisions relevant to immediate work conditions and the job itself, (3) a mix of individual and group criteria for performance appraisal that is mostly short-term and results-oriented, (4) relatively egalitarian treatment of employees and some guarantees of employment security, (5) extensive and continuous training and development of employees.

While one may quarrel with the emphasis on one or more of the above factors, as a whole they provide a generally accurate composite of individual and organizational requirements associated with an overall corporate strategy of quality enhancement. An organization wishing to implement this strategy would have to align its planning, staffing, appraising, compensating, and training and development systems and processes to support these HRM requirements. The theory linking process to implementation is developed in the next section.

MOTIVATION

A general understanding of the concept of motivation and the context in which motivation takes place is necessary to see how motivation applies to quality. Human motivation may be defined simply as a response to a felt need by an individual. Thus,

---

[9]Ibid.

there must be some stimulus, or activating event, the felt need to respond to that stimulus, and the response itself. For example, an individual worker may be given the goal or quality task of achieving zero defects on the parts that he or she produces. The worker may feel a *need* to keep his or her job, be motivated by the *stimulus* of fear, and *respond* by carefully producing parts *to achieve* the goal. Another, less insecure, worker may feel the *need* for approval of his or her work by peers or superiors, be motivated by the *stimulus* of pride, and *respond* to that need and that stimulus by producing high-quality parts.

Thousands of studies have been performed over the years on human and animal subjects in attempts to define and refine the concept of motivation. It is an extremely complex phenomenon that still is not fully understood. The entire field of psychology is based on the study of individual behavior in living organisms, particularly humans. Sociology is a related discipline that is concerned with the study of group behavior. Both are important in the study of motivation.

One of the biggest motivators for quality today is the need to stay in business. The intense competition from both domestic and foreign firms provides the simple message quoted from *Business Week* in the introduction to Part 1: Get better or get beat.

An Overview of Motivation Theories

Two basic classes of motivation theories proposed by various researchers are **content models** and **process models.** While these theories typically are studied in traditional management courses, they are worth reviewing because of their important implications for quality.

Content Models of Motivation. Many of the theories of motivation that have been developed by behavioral scientists over the past 75 years have been simple content models that describe how and why people are motivated to work. Three of the best-known content models are those developed by Abraham Maslow, Frederick Herzberg, and Douglas McGregor,[10] each of which will be reviewed briefly.

Quality depends on employee commitment at every level of the organization. If employees are not provided with the proper motivating climate to align their efforts to meet organizational goals, the result can be conflict, poor performance, and low quality levels. Managers must understand that *there is no such thing as an unmotivated employee.* The key question is: What are employees being motivated to do? The models developed by Maslow, Herzberg, and McGregor help to explain motivation.

Maslow and Herzberg developed models describing various factors that motivate individuals to work. Maslow proposed a priority of human needs from basic physiological needs through the highest order needs of self-realization and fulfillment. Each level would have to be satisfied before an individual would be concerned about the next higher level. Herzberg postulated that two sets of factors affect motivation. Motivating factors, such as the work itself, responsibility, and recognition tend to cause individuals to work harder. Maintenance factors, such as

---

[10]See, for example, Abraham Maslow, "A Theory of Human Motivation," *Psychological Review,* Vol. 50, No. 4, July 1943, pp. 370–396; Abraham Maslow, *Motivation and Personality* (New York: Harper and Row, 1954); F. Herzberg, B. Mausner, and B. Snyderman, *The Motivation to Work,* 2nd. ed. (New York: John Wiley and Sons, 1959); and Douglas McGregor, *The Human Side of Enterprise* (New York: McGraw-Hill, 1960).

status, job security, working conditions, and salary are not positive motivators, but can be demotivators if not present. Figure 10.2 describes and compares Maslow's Hierarchy of Needs model with Herzberg's Motivation-Maintenance model. The five levels in Maslow's hierarchy correspond quite closely with Herzberg's categories. One major difference between Herzberg's and Maslow's models was that Herzberg worked to make his model operational so that it could be applied to actual organizations.

From Herzberg's model arose the concept of **job enrichment,** which is defined as increasing the areas of responsibility of workers so as to provide greater opportunities to use a range of skills, see the "big picture," and gain a sense of fulfillment from completion of every cycle of a task. For example, instead of a worker simply welding a few wires on a headlight for an automobile, the job might be enriched to include the tasks of ordering materials, complete assembly of the headlight, testing, and packing the finished item for shipment. This concept is used to tap the motivational needs of his model, specifically, advancement, responsibility,

FIGURE 10.2 **A Comparison of Maslow's Hierarchy of Needs Model with Herzberg's Motivation-Maintenance Model**

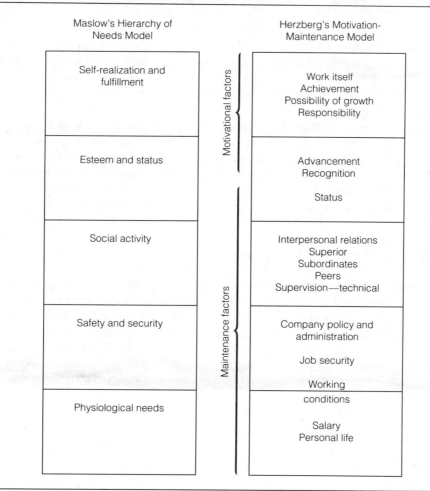

SOURCE: Adapted from Leslie W. Rue and Lloyd C. Byars, *Management: Theory and Application,* 4th ed. (Homewood, IL: Irwin, 1986), p. 363.

growth, a feeling of achievement, and identification with the job itself. These, of course, parallel Maslow's highest order need level for self-realization and fulfillment. Job enrichment is also an important component of employee involvement programs and self-managed work teams, which will be explored in the next chapter.

An interesting example of how Japanese managers in the air conditioning industry view job enrichment as important to quality is discussed by Garvin.[11] In Japan, newly hired workers are trained so that they can do *every* job on the line, before eventually being assigned to only one job. Training frequently requires 6 to 12 months, in contrast to the standard training time of one to two days for newly hired production workers in American air conditioning companies. The advantage to this "enriched" training is that workers are better able to track defects to their source and can frequently suggest remedies to problems since they understand the entire process from start to finish.

Herzberg's model has been criticized for having been developed on accountants and engineers. Some later studies of lower level workers have cast doubt on the ability to generalize Herzberg's original findings.[12] However, the model has been widely used and has stood the test of time.

Douglas McGregor's model, well known as Theory X–Theory Y, is shown in Figure 10.3. This model describes the role of managerial assumptions in motivating employees. While related to motivation, the model is actually a description of leadership styles, and has direct application to the TQM/HRM approach discussed earlier. Under Theory X, workers are assumed to have no interest in quality. Management must therefore provide incentives and penalties, as well as close supervision and control. Quality is achieved through inspectors and engineers. If Theory X assumptions guide managerial practice, then it is likely that adversarial conditions will exist. Theory Y, on the other hand, places trust in people, and establishes this trust through delegation of responsibility and reliance on employee self-control. Theory Y leads to participative approaches and continuous improvement.

Anecdotal cases exist to support both theories. However, most believe that organizations operating under Theory Y have improved levels of quality. Deming's philosophy is clearly Theory Y-oriented. However, it must be noted that Theory Y, by itself, cannot ensure quality improvements unless management takes the responsibility for improving the system and providing workers with the appropriate tools to perform their jobs.

Process Models of Motivation. The second major thrust in motivation theories was the development of process models. Process models tend to focus on the dynamic process of how people make choices in an effort to obtain desired rewards. Pioneering work in this area was performed by B. F. Skinner, who developed reinforcement theory (sometimes called *operant conditioning*) in 1953.[13]

Skinner's theory suggests that organisms (animals and humans) will respond positively to positive stimuli presented in their environment and will avoid negative

---

[11]David A. Garvin, *Managing Quality* (New York: The Free Press, 1988), pp. 202–203.

[12]J. Schneider and E. A. Locke, "A Critique of Herzberg's Incident Classification System and a Suggested Revision," *Organizational Behavior and Human Performance,* 1971, pp. 441–457.

[13]B. F. Skinner. *Science and Human Behavior,* New York: Free Press, 1953. See also, *Beyond Freedom and Dignity,* New York: Bantam Books, 1971.

FIGURE 10.3 McGregor's Theory X–Theory Y Model

Theory X	Theory Y
1. The average person has an inherent dislike of work and will avoid it if possible. 2. Because of the human characteristic of dislike for work, most people must be coerced, controlled, directed, or threatened with punishment to get them to put forth adequate effort toward achievement of objectives. 3. The average person prefers to be directed and avoid responsibility. He or she has relatively little ambition and seeks security above all.	1. The average person does not inherently dislike work. The expenditure of physical and mental effort is as natural as work or play. Depending on controllable conditions, work may be a source of satisfaction or a source of punishment. 2. External control and the threat of punishment are not the only means for bringing about effort toward organizational objectives. People will exercise self-direction and control in the service of objectives to which they are committed. 3. The average person can learn not only to accept but also to seek responsibility. Avoidance of responsibility, lack of ambition, and emphasis on security are generally consequences of experience, not inherent human characteristics. 4. The capacity to exercise a relatively high degree of imagination, ingenuity, and creativity in the solution of organizational problems is *widely,* not narrowly, distributed in the population. 5. Under conditions of modern industrial life, the intellectual potential of the average person is only partly used.

SOURCE: Adapted from Douglas McGregor, *The Human Side of Enterprise* (New York: McGraw-Hill, 1960), pp. 33, 34, 47, 48.

stimuli. Thus, positive reinforcement will lead to improved performance. Skinner's work was put to practical use in the early 1970s.[14] One of the most far-reaching and dramatic examples of the use of positive reinforcement in a work environment took place at Emery Air Freight. Emery applied behavior modification techniques to areas in which a low performance level was found, such as sales, customer service, and containerized shipping. The company used detailed measurement of performance factors coupled with daily feedback to their workers on their progress to increase performance and quality levels. Supervisors were taught to give positive reinforcement through praise and recognition of their employees' progress. They began applying this concept at least twice a week in the early stages of the program. Later, this was put on a variable interval schedule as workers became more consistent in meeting high performance targets. Over a three-year period, Emery estimated savings of three million dollars from a very minimal cost.

Victor H. Vroom, another innovator in the process approach to motivation, proposed his preference–expectancy theory in 1964.[15] Vroom's work forms the basis for one of the better known process theories, the Porter and Lawler model. This is one

---

[14]Edward J. Feeney, "At Emery Air Freight: Positive Reinforcement Boosts Performance," *Organizational Dynamics,* Winter, 1973, pp. 41–50.

[15]Victor H. Vroom, *Work and Motivation* (New York: John Wiley and Sons, 1964).

of the most widely accepted process models available today that also has applications to leadership theories.

The Porter and Lawler model is a *contingency model* that explains the conditions and processes by which motivation to work takes place.[16] A contingency model is one that defines variables, interactions between those variables, and dynamic conditions under which those variables work. The Porter and Lawler model was influenced heavily by the work of Vroom, but Porter and Lawler examined more closely the traits and perceptions of the individual and the nature and impact of rewards on motivation.

The Porter and Lawler model is shown in Figure 10.4. Tracing through this model, we see that effort (3) is dependent on value of reward (1) and perceived effort–reward probability (2). Effort leads to performance (6), which is affected by the abilities and traits (4) and the role perceptions (5) of the individual. Performance (6), in turn, has an influence on *actual* rewards—intrinsic (7A) or extrinsic (7B)—perceived equitable rewards (8), and a long-term influence (feedback) on perceived effort–reward probability. The rewards (7A and 7B) and their perceived equity (8) then influence satisfaction (9), which has a long-term influence (feedback) on the value of reward (1).

Components of the model are expectancy (which includes performance–outcome expectancy and effort–performance expectancy), instrumentality (the combination of abilities, traits, and role perceptions) and valence (preference for

---

[16]Lyman W. Porter and Edward E. Lawler, *Managerial Attitudes and Performance* (Homewood. IL: Irwin, 1968).

FIGURE 10.4   **Porter and Lawler Expectancy Model**

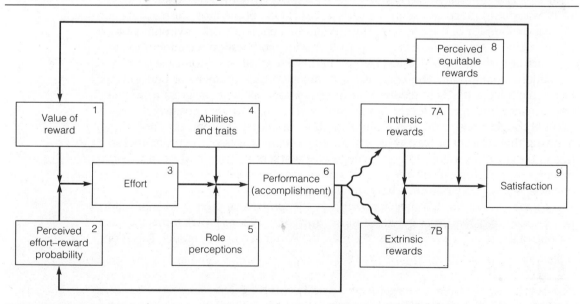

SOURCE: L. W. Porter and Edward E. Lawler, *Managerial Attitudes and Performance,* Homewood, IL: Irwin, 1968; used with permission.

anticipated outcomes). Valence is represented by the value of reward. Expectancy is included in the perceived effort–reward probability and is also related to perceived equitable rewards. Instrumentality is the linking of effort to performance (accomplishment) while moderated by abilities and traits and role perceptions. Successful performance then results in intrinsic rewards, such as a feeling of accomplishment, and extrinsic rewards, such as raises or bonuses. Given that rewards are equitable, satisfaction is the result, which in turn contributes to renewal of the motivation cycle. The model states that, depending on the actions of management, the expectations of employees, and the actual outcomes, a certain quantity and quality of employee motivation in an organization will result.

Porter and Lawler's model does not necessarily refute the Herzberg model; it merely brings in another dimension of motivation—the dynamic process—that is lacking in the Herzberg model. An example will tend to explain the various components of the model and how it works.

Suppose that a bank decides to install a statistical process control system in its check-clearing department. It performs the activities of planning the new system, organizing the work force, and training employees to use the new system. The bank even trains clerical workers in the details of recording information clearly and accurately. However, the bank emphasizes the detection of errors, the penalties for being caught making an error, and the advantages to the bank in reducing the costs brought on by the need to correct errors. No positive reinforcement is built into the system for making improvements in the process, reducing errors, or recording and using information. A few weeks after the system is installed, turnover and absentee rates have increased, new types of errors are being made, old error rates are increasing, and morale in the department is generally low.

For this situation, the Herzberg model would indicate that the motivating factors of status and the work (content) itself are missing. The Porter and Lawler model could be used to trace out the flaws in the motivating process. The model shows that the bank's system has a deficiency in perceived effort–reward probability and, perhaps, value of reward as well. Thus, if employees do not perceive a high effort–reward probability or do not see a high value in the rewards that are provided, they will not apply their best efforts to the task. Their abilities and traits will not be exercised to the fullest, and their perceptions of their role in the firm will be either negative or confused. These factors combine to result in low performance. This will have a negative impact on extrinsic (tangible) rewards and intrinsic (intangible) rewards and on the perception of equitable (fair) rewards and overall satisfaction with accomplishment of the task. The negative cycle and consequences are renewed each time the task is performed. To turn the situation around, an upward rather than a downward spiral of motivation would have to be introduced by providing a positive combination of expectancy, effort, and accomplishment.

From this discussion we can deduce that the value of the reward [(1) in the Porter and Lawler model in Figure 10.4], and the perceived effort–reward probability (2) were working in conjunction with intrinsic rewards, extrinsic rewards, and perceived equitable rewards (7A, 7B, and 8) to produce motivated effort (3), performance (6), and satisfaction (9). Thus, it can be seen that attention to the details of job design can have a significant impact on the quality level in a work setting.

The Porter and Lawler model is much more complex than the earlier, more popular theories of Maslow and Herzberg. As in any complex model, the purpose of added complexity is to permit a more accurate representation of the real process.

Although it is important to understand the content of human motivation theories that were presented by pioneers such as Maslow and Herzberg, Sink points out the dangers of using outdated theories:[17]

> It would appear that one of the biggest problems facing managers today with respect to motivating employees is that of outdated and overly simplistic concepts and models of motivation. In an audience of over 300 managers recently addressed on the topic of motivation, nearly all were familiar with Maslow's hierarchy of needs and Herzberg's two-factor theory. We would hope that this would be the case, for Maslow's theory is 30 years old and Herzberg's theory is at least 25. Yet less than 10 had heard of expectancy theory, or VIE (valence, instrumentality, expectancy) theory, although this theory is almost 20 years old. Managers today can ill afford to have overly simplistic and often quite outdated thinking on the art of motivation. Motivating employees for improved performance is simply too important a management skill to let atrophy.

The application of any behavioral approach to improve quality and productivity in any organization is never guaranteed to succeed. Despite a number of success stories reported in the literature, there are also reports of partial successes and even failures. For example, a Midwestern die-casting plant attempted to use behavior modification to improve quality and productivity of several dozen production workers. A target group and a control group were designated. Foremen were instructed on how to give proper feedback at a weekly meeting of production workers. The feedback consisted of information on individual and group performance on quality and quantity of output over the previous week. The foremen were also required to encourage good performers to maintain their performance and to suggest ways in which the average and poor performers could improve. The control group was given no information on quality and quantity of output.

At the end of 45 weeks when the project was stopped, the results were somewhat surprising. Attitudes of workers in both groups were the same, quality levels had remained the same, and output had increased significantly. However, management was somewhat disappointed that quality had not increased, although they were pleased that it had not *decreased* at the higher level of output.[18]

The debate between process and content theories of motivation centers on which theory is a more accurate representation of human motivation. Obviously, they represent two different views of the same reality. The content approach provides for a simple, static representation of components of motivation. The process approach focuses on the dynamic interaction between the components of effort, ability, rewards, and performance as perceived by individuals in the work environment. Understanding both content and process views can aid managers as they attempt to design work to enhance motivation for quality.

However, one must be cautious when applying motivation theories to quality. As Deming and Juran emphasize, workers *are* intrinsically motivated; management stands in the way. Management can motivate employees through good employee relations policies and practices. These include empowering employees to control

---

[17]D. Scott Sink, *Productivity Management: Planning, Measurement and Evaluation, Control and Improvement* (New York: John Wiley, 1985), p. 309.

[18]Everett Adam, Jr., "Behavior Modification in Quality Control," *Academy of Management Journal,* Vol. 18, 1975, pp. 662–679.

their own work and make important decisions that affect quality, eliminating fear and blame for uncontrollable variation, recruiting employees who demonstrate the ability and willingness to meet quality standards, providing adequate training and education that explains the why as well as the how of doing quality work, changing the role of supervisors to coaches and teachers, and keeping workers informed of management decisions and actions that affect quality, as well as opportunities for participation in solving quality problems.

Task Design for Motivation[19]

Task (or job) design is the key to understanding HRM systems. It is an integrating concept that ties together many different perspectives. Chapter 7 discussed task design from an organizational perspective; we now examine some motivational aspects of task design. Tasks must be designed to fit the technical needs of the organization and the human needs of the employees who must perform the task. When approached in a careful, systematic fashion, job design can result in improved quality and productivity as well as higher levels of employee motivation and morale.

The Hackman and Oldham model, shown in Figure 10.5, has been proposed to help explain the motivational properties of task design by tying together technical and

[19]Adapted from Chapter 4, "Motivation Through the Design of Work," in J. R. Hackman and G. R. Oldham. *Work Redesign* (Reading, MA: Addison-Wesley, 1980).

FIGURE 10.5   **The Complete Job Characteristics Model of Hackman and Oldham**

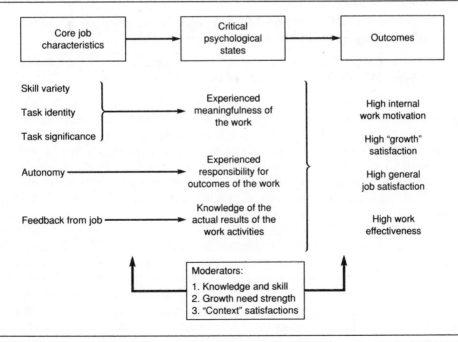

SOURCE: J. Richard Hackman and Greg R. Oldham, *Work Redesign.*© 1980, by Addison-Wesley Publishing Co., Inc., Reading, Massachusetts. Reprinted with permission of the publisher.

human components of a job. This model is an extremely effective operationalization of earlier motivation theories and research studies. It draws heavily on the work of Herzberg and others and has been validated in numerous organizational settings.

The Hackman and Oldham model contains four major segments:

1. critical psychological states

2. core job characteristics

3. moderating variables

4. outcomes.

Three **critical psychological states** drive the model: *Experienced meaningfulness* is the psychological need of workers to have the feeling that their work is a significant contribution to the organization and society. *Experienced responsibility* indicates the need of workers to be accountable for the quality and quantity of work produced. *Knowledge of results* implies that there is a need felt by all workers to know how their work is evaluated and what the results of the evaluation are.

Five **core job characteristics** have been identified as having an impact on the critical psychological states:

1. *Task significance*—the degree to which the job gives the participant the feeling that it has a substantial impact on the organization or the world.

2. *Task identity*—the degree to which the worker can perceive the task as a whole, identifiable piece of work from start to finish.

3. *Skill variety*—the degree to which the job requires the worker to have to use a variety of skills and talents.

4. *Autonomy*—the degree to which the task permits freedom, independence, and personal control to be exercised over the work.

5. *Feedback from the job*—the degree to which clear, timely information about the effectiveness of performance of the individual is available.

Quality is related in a primary or secondary sense to all five of the core job characteristics in the Hackman and Oldham model. Quality of a product or service undoubtedly is benefited by a worker's dedicated application of skills, enhanced by *task identity* and a feeling of *task significance*. More directly, quality of work is enhanced by a task design that incorporates *autonomy* and *feedback* relating to quality characteristics. The key outcomes of high general job satisfaction and high work effectiveness can then be seen as results that define and reinforce excellent quality.

An example illustrating characteristics of the Hackman and Oldham model is the case of workers in a small Delaware firm that produces space suits for astronauts. The work requires a great deal of hand crafting, using conventional sewing machinery as well as high technology in testing the suits for proper functioning. Task significance and task identity are evident in the workers' ability to see the job as being of extreme importance and as fitting into a complete unit (a space suit for an individual astronaut). Skill variety and autonomy are somewhat limited, since conventional sewing techniques must be used and rigid specifications must be precisely followed. However, other motivating aspects of the job may compensate for the lack of these characteristics. Feedback on results is timely and individualized. Comprehensive testing and inspection of the space suits is performed to assure that no defective units are produced.

LEADERSHIP

Leadership is frequently confused with motivation. Motivation is the internal desire to act in order to meet felt needs. Leadership, while often dependent on a focal person who is motivated to lead, is centered on the leader providing a motivating climate for a group or groups within an organization through task design and attention to desired outcomes. Thus if motivation can be said to be internally directed, leadership can be seen as externally focused.

Leadership can be defined as the right to exercise authority and the ability to achieve results from subordinates under one's authority. Current leadership theory is focusing on *contingency approaches,* which state that effective leadership depends on three variables: the leader, the led, and the situation. While it may be argued that the concept of leadership is properly treated under the category of human resource management, leadership is also an indispensable component of organizing human and capital resources in order to produce a quality product or service.

Intuition often fails us in describing the process of leadership. For example, one of the appealing approaches to the subject is the belief by many people that leaders must have certain traits to be effective. After many studies involving hundreds of leaders, academicians have had to give up on the trait theory.

Although the trait approach to discovering how to be a leader has been discredited in an academic context, it is still fascinating to study successful leaders to observe what they do and how they do it. Bennis and Nanus[20] interviewed 90 successful manager/leaders and determined that the leaders were an extremely diverse group, as indicated by the fact that:

> They were right-brained and left-brained, tall and short, fat and thin, articulate and inarticulate, assertive and retiring, dressed for success and dressed for failure, participative and autocratic.

Bennis and Nanus also talked about the need to lead others and manage yourself, thus separating the concept of management from leadership. The comparison of quality leadership versus management practices in Figure 10.6 shows that management too often relies on the practice of mechanistic planning and organizing, reaction to events, pushing products, and controlling people. Leadership involves envisioning the future, overseeing the development of products having exemplary quality and features, and providing a motivating climate for people while controlling things. The key need that drives the requirement for leadership in the organizational context is the situation. Many organizations today find themselves in a leadership vacuum because the environment has changed more rapidly than they ever dreamed was imaginable. Their leadership styles have not been able to keep pace and they find themselves falling back on the approaches that were good enough for their predecessors, but frequently inadequate today.

---

[20]Warren Bennis and Burt Nanus, *Leaders: The Strategies for Taking Charge* (New York: Harper & Row, 1985), pp. 25–26.

Organization Design Approach to Leadership

Henry Mintzberg did an extensive research project in which he studied managers who had formal authority and defined 10 managerial roles that leaders must play:[21] (1) figurehead, (2) leader, (3) liaison, (4) monitor, (5) disseminator, (6) spokesperson, (7) entrepreneur, (8) disturbance handler, (9) resource allocator, and (10) negotiator. Mintzberg highlighted the leader role, saying:

> The influence of the manager is most clearly seen in the leader role. Formal authority vests the manager with great potential power; leadership determines in large part how much of it he or she will in fact use.

He also pointed out that the importance of each role is contingent on the environmental and organizational factors that face managers who must lead. These include the industry or environmental surroundings of the organization, its age and size, the organizational level at which the leader operates, and the part of the organization where the leader resides. For example, in a pharmaceutical firm, where government regulation and the need for constant protection of the "ethical" quality image abounds, the top-management leader must spend a tremendous amount of time as figurehead, liaison, and spokesperson. In contrast, in a small, family-owned foundry with a history of labor unrest, the CEO would tend to spend much more time as entrepreneur, disturbance handler, and negotiator in order to develop a quality product and image. A middle-line manager in an automobile assembly plant would have duties that would require taking on the roles of disseminator, liaison, and spokesperson as he or she interprets and passes information from and to upper level managers, works with suppliers, and acts as a spokesperson inside and outside the plant on quality and other issues.

---

[21]Henry Mintzberg, *Mintzberg on Management* (New York: The Free Press, 1989), pp. 15–21.

FIGURE 10.6 TQM Leadership Contrasts

Managers	Leaders
Plan Projects	Practice
■ Make plans for the future (on paper)	■ Envision the future
■ Organize materials & methods	■ Optimize materials and methods
■ Preach MBO	■ Use participative management
Push Products	Produce
■ Give "lip-service" to quality	■ Exemplary quality
■ Sell to customers	■ Service to their customers
■ Cut costs	■ Less waste through better processes
■ Perform R&D	■ Innovative products and services
Control People	Motivate People
■ Control people and things through systems	■ Develop people's talents, control things with systems
■ Reward conformance, punish deviation	■ Reward effort, skill development, and innovation; use simultaneous loose-tight controls
■ Maintain status quo	■ Look to the future through continuous improvement

Tying the leadership concept more directly to quality, Peter R. Scholtes proposed the following principles of quality leadership:[22]

- customer focus
- obsession with quality
- recognizing the structure in work
- freedom through control
- unity of purpose
- looking for faults in the system
- teamwork
- continued education and training.

Customer focus starts with an emphasis by the quality leader on customers, rather than on internal goals of return on investment or cost minimization, as necessary as these objectives are for corporate survival. Obsession with quality means that quality is the force that drives organizational decisions by managers and other employees. For example, at corporations such as Motorola and the Budd Company, quality is the first item reported on and discussed at board meetings and monthly operations meetings. Recognizing the structure in the work requires that leaders support and empower employees to investigate, analyze, and improve methods for doing work in a systematic fashion. Freedom through control requires that leaders support the requirement to reduce variability in the product or service, while still encouraging all employees to look for better methods and practices. Unity of purpose is similar to Deming's Point 1 and implies that everyone in the organization is striving for the same goals and suggests that they work for more than a paycheck when they do their jobs. Looking for faults in the system is also based on Deming's observation that at least 85% of the quality problems in an organization are the fault of the system. However, it goes beyond this to require that leaders encourage correction of the system and not attempt to affix blame on individuals for its faults. Teamwork, of course, implies that leadership must delegate authority and responsibility for teams to make decisions and suggestions for improvement that will result in higher quality. Finally, leadership is needed to provide the continued education and training that is required to make the best use of the human resource available in the organization.

Leadership Models

The characteristics of a leader have been classified according to two typical managerial approaches: consideration and task maintenance. Consideration refers to empathy and concern for employee needs while employees are on the job. Task maintenance refers to the leader's focus on meeting deadlines and goals in completing work assignments. As we shall see, a proper blend of these approaches is necessary for effective leadership. Characteristics of the led include skills, motivation, and effort. Characteristics of the situation include the amount of power accorded to anyone holding the managerial responsibility in that part of the organization.

---

[22]Peter R. Scholtes, *The Team Handbook* (Madison, WI: Joiner Associates, 1988), pp. 1-11–1-13.

Quality depends on the correct mix of the leader's style of management, characteristics of the led, and the situation. Emery Air Freight[23] found that emphasis by the leader (supervisor) on daily performance measures, together with positive reinforcement, resulted in quality benefits within that organization. However, there is no guarantee that such an approach would work, for instance, for a leader in an R&D laboratory. In fact, current leadership research would suggest that the same outcome is unlikely.

One of the best known theories of leadership was developed by Fiedler.[24] While a number of criticisms have been aimed at his theory from researchers who have questioned the measures used in assessing the dimensions involved in his model, his conceptual development of the factors affecting leadership is straightforward and intuitively sound.

Fiedler's model (Figure 10.7) shows the effect of leadership styles on leader performance according to situational conditions. The vertical axis on the model shows the range of organizational performance achieved by the leader. The dotted V and

---

[23]Edward J. Feeney, "At Emery Air Freight."

[24]Frederick E. Fiedler. *A Theory of Leadership Effectiveness* (New York: McGraw-Hill, 1967).

FIGURE 10.7 **Model of the Effect of Leadership Styles on Leader Performance According to Situational Conditions**

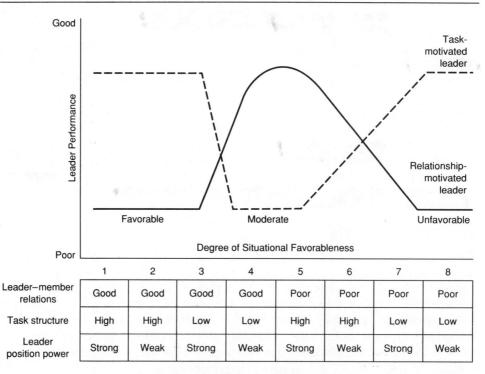

	1	2	3	4	5	6	7	8
Leader–member relations	Good	Good	Good	Good	Poor	Poor	Poor	Poor
Task structure	High	High	Low	Low	High	High	Low	Low
Leader position power	Strong	Weak	Strong	Weak	Strong	Weak	Strong	Weak

inverted V trace the effect of the task-motivated leader and the relationship-motivated leader on the performance level, depending on the degree of situational favorableness (high to low). Situational favorableness is directly related to leader–member relations, task structure, and leader position power, which can be clarified by answering the following questions:

- *Leader-member relations:* How well does the leader get along with his or her subordinates?

- *Task structure:* How well defined are the steps to perform the task?

- *Leader position power:* How much power does the organization give to the leader in this position (for example, the ability to reward or punish)?

Thus, the model predicts that the best leadership style to obtain good performance within an environment having high situational favorableness is the task-motivated leadership style (good leader–member relations, high task structure, and strong leadership position power). As the degree of situational favorableness falls to the moderate level, the relationship-oriented leader is most likely to obtain good performance from subordinates. Note that either the task-motivated or relationship-motivated leader may get along well (or poorly) with subordinates. The former type of leader focuses on getting the job done, while the latter type of leader focuses on getting people or groups motivated.

Fiedler's basic contention is that given technical qualifications, most people will be able to be successful leaders in at least some situations. He summarizes his position by saying ". . . the secret of improving leadership effectiveness lies in matching the leader and the situation or changing the leadership situation so that it fits the leader's personality."[25]

Some simple examples will serve to show the "prescriptions" of the model for appropriate leadership styles. The applicability of this model to quality management situations can be seen to vary over a range of possible situations that might occur in various organizational settings. For example, in a manufacturing area of a pharmaceutical company, where high quality is essential to the safety of the product, a highly task-oriented approach to leadership might be required. Managers at every level would be strongly oriented to the task of consistently meeting stringent quality standards. The three major variables from the model that apply to this situation would be good leader–member relations, a high task structure, and strong position power (position 1 on the model).

A contrasting situation might be seen in an R&D laboratory in the same firm, where experimental work is being performed on new drug products. Here, a highly task-oriented leader would be ineffective. Because the leader has moderate control over the work being done in the lab, certain standards of quality for routine work can be enforced. However, the leader is responsible for providing a motivating climate within which creative professional scientists and technicians can work. Supportive relations between the leader and professional subordinates are essential. It would be useless for the organization's leader to concentrate strongly on the task and control aspects while neglecting the motivational aspects of the work environment. Variables

---

[25]Frederick E. Fiedler, "Job Engineering for Effective Leadership: A New Approach," *Management Review,* Vol. 66, September 1977, pp. 29–31.

from the model that apply to this situation would be good leader–member relations, low task structure, and weak position power (position 4 on the model). The appropriate leadership style would be a permissive, passive, considerate leadership mode.

Vroom and Yetton's supervisory contingency model[26] is based in part on leadership propositions that follow from Vroom's VIE motivation theory. The model prescribes an appropriate leadership style based on various contingencies in a decision-making situation. The major focus of the model is on the problem-solving function of leadership. Vroom and Yetton theorize that the three major concerns of a leader in solving problems are (1) the quality of the decision, (2) the degree of acceptance of the decision by the subordinate(s), and (3) the time frame within which the decision must be made. Four principal assumptions are made:

1. Autocratic decisions are faster.

2. Subordinate participation creates acceptance.

3. Group decisions are most effective when applied to unstructured, shared issues.

4. Involvement develops subordinates' abilities.

Based on these assumptions, Vroom and Yetton developed a set of decision rules and a decision tree model to provide guidelines for managers who wish to use an appropriate form of decision making to maximize the effectiveness of their decisions. The application of these leadership assumptions will be clearly seen in the next chapter as we discuss employee involvement and team approaches to problem solving.

In summary, it is evident that numerous leadership theories have been developed to help explain differences in leadership styles and contexts. The well-informed manager, engineer, or technician should be aware of such approaches and use them to broaden his or her understanding of how leadership can affect behavior in the workplace. Good leadership can contribute substantially to high quality, while poor leadership is often a major cause of many quality problems in organizations.

SYSTEMS APPROACHES TO HUMAN RESOURCE MANAGEMENT

Systems approaches in HRM include **industrial engineering, labor relations,** and **personnel management.** Starting with Frederick W. Taylor's concept of "the one best way" of performing a task, these approaches have often been the basis for labor/management conflicts. In switching from an adversarial to a TQM/HRM approach, it is obvious that conflict will arise around philosophies, roles, and methods that have long been held by advocates of these approaches.

---

[26]Victor H. Vroom and Phillip W. Yetton, *Leadership and Decision Making* (Pittsburgh, PA: University of Pittsburgh Press), 1973.

Industrial Engineering

Industrial engineers (IEs) have been taught to perform detailed methods analysis, develop an improved method, determine the standard amount of time required to perform each repetition of a task via time study or other related techniques, and monitor the results by using some type of performance or productivity index. They have typically been required to support management as they bargain and battle with unions over wages, incentives, work methods, job specialization, and performance measurement review systems.

The traditional areas for which industrial engineers have been responsible are:

- productivity
- job design
- methods improvement
- quality control.

Classical industrial engineering practice is undergoing a transformation from a control orientation to a sociotechnical systems orientation. Instead of seeing first-line workers as extensions of machines, IEs must recognize them as capable assistants in the process of developing integrated systems. This means that they must become partners with line employees in problem solving and decision making. This also means that they must better understand human motivation and leadership principles.

In productivity measurement, IEs can now obtain assistance in defining output measures that are relevant to organizational objectives. For example, in service firms such as banks, employees from several different levels within a department have been asked to participate in a team project to define quality and productivity measures for their own department. By doing so, they have felt that they had valuable input into determining what was important and how they were to be rewarded for their efforts.

In job design and methods improvement, teams use some of the classical industrial engineering techniques, such as flowcharting, to analyze and improve their own work. Often IEs are called on to teach these techniques or consult on more complicated aspects of a team project.

In quality control, IEs have often played a technical role in developing the systems for measuring and improving quality. Now they are being called on to disseminate information about the techniques and the management and worker implications of quality systems.

Labor Relations

In the rapidly changing environment of HRM, it is very difficult for both managers and union leaders to come to grips with the need to share power with workers at every level. However, the TQM/HRM approach requires that unions and management cooperate in new and innovative ways if they are to survive.

Union leaders and their counterpart labor relations managers have their own culture. In the past, they have emphasized:

1. collective bargaining
2. work rules

3. grievance procedures

4. management and worker domains.

Many of these procedures and work rules are legally binding on the company and have arisen through years of negotiation and policy-making. To simplify and/or eliminate them, labor and management must first agree that a new paradigm is desirable.

Leventhal suggests that a joint problem-solving approach be substituted for the traditional adversarial approach between labor and management in the new total quality-oriented work systems that are being put into place by many firms.[27] The following labor-management issues have become at least as important, if not more so, than the traditional issues:

- work operations and design

- pay systems (beyond rates and scales)

- training

- system governance.

Work operations and design affect the day-to-day tasks of union members. With a team approach to problem solving, many of the problems and frustrations of job design by third parties, such as industrial engineers with a limited understanding of the requirements of a specific job, can be reduced.

Pay system design also requires input from the people who are going to be affected by the system. This can often prevent future headaches and grievances.

Participation in training program development can help union members meet personal goals as well as corporate goals and objectives. For example, Lawrence Cable Company has a trainer as a member of every team in the company.[28] The company has adopted a "pay for skills" approach, so the trainer is paid more once he or she has mastered certain training and analysis skills. Then the team trainer monitors the skills of the team members and helps design, refine, and deliver training courses in the needed skill areas.

System governance refers to the fact that many organizations have developed sufficient trust in their employees to turn over to them some of the traditional management functions. For example, Nucor Corporation, an innovative $1 billion steel-maker, allows teams to select their own members and allows workers to evaluate peers for bonuses and promotion opportunities. Other companies have peer review processes or committees that perform some of the disciplinary functions previously reserved for management.

To deal with the issues discussed above, both labor and management must become more flexible in their stance toward each other. This will require union members and leaders to: (1) take new approaches toward dispute resolution; (2) develop flexible work rules and means for accommodation to such rules by union stewards; (3) initiate peer performance feedback methods designed to improve work

---

[27]Robert B. Leventhal, "Union Involvement in New Work Systems," *The Journal for Quality and Participation,* June 1991, pp. 36–39.

[28]Jack D. Orsburn, Linda Moran, Ed Musselwhite, and John H. Zenger, *Self-Directed Work Teams* (Homewood, IL: Business One–Irwin, 1990), pp. 145–146.

operations; and (4) establish new contract language and ongoing labor-management negotiation. Management will also be required to adjust by doing the following:

- Work with union representatives on how—or whether—new work systems will be adopted.

- Examine values within a joint framework and adopt new ones to guide the transformed organization.

- Include labor representation at every level where process and job transformations are taking place.

- Fill key training and employee involvement (EI) facilitator positions with both union and management representatives (Ford Motor Company has a parallel EI structure of union-management facilitators from the plant level up to corporate headquarters).

- Recognize union strengths, such as the ability to take the pulse of its membership on various issues.

An example of the new level of cooperation between unions and management is the historic agreement reached between LTV and the United Steelworkers (USW) union in 1985.[29] The terms of the contract at that time provided for:

- Workers paid on salaries, with built-in wage increases, but no provision for "cost of living allowance" (COLA) wage increases. Wage increases were provided for learning new skills.

- Twice-yearly performance bonuses of up to 25% of salary, starting in 1987.

- Work divided into four skill levels, instead of rigid job classes; workers assigned to rotating teams of 10 to 12 workers on each shift.

- Overtime paid after 40 hours per week, instead of after 8 hours per day, thus improving flexibility in scheduling.

- Workers to have a voice in hiring, firing, grievance handling, work and vacation scheduling, and promotion.

- Layoff pay plus unemployment compensation amounts to 100% of regular income. When unemployment compensation ceases, the company pays 60% of salary for a limited time.

- Other benefits include nine holidays (versus ten previously), no vacations during first year of employment, pension program after two years, insurance "package" consisting of low-cost life insurance, medical and dental care.

This LTV-USW pact shows that change, when brought on by a competitive crisis, is possible, even in union-management systems that were once considered hopelessly adversarial.

In summary, changes in union-management relations are critical where new work structures are considered vital to corporate survival or competitiveness. Good

---

[29]John Hoerr, "LTV Steel Knocks the Rust Off Its Labor Relations," *Business Week,* December 23, 1985, pp. 57–58.

relations can aid in improving quality and productivity at every level. Poor relations can ensure that any changes will be cosmetic and that quality efforts will suffer.

Personnel Management

Job and position descriptions and task designs set the boundaries for the individual and system characteristics for any job and for the person selected to fill it. However, the way in which an individual performs his or her task within the boundaries of a particular position, the joint effects of team efforts and their interaction with technology on the job, and the appraisal of performance can and does have a profound effect on quality of output of goods or services. In this section we will consider these issues of the traditional personnel management function.

Recruitment. Lawler pointed out that strategic factors must drive the processes of recruitment, selection, performance appraisal, and especially pay.[30] Limited availability of people with the skills to perform complex, rapidly changing jobs is forcing HRM managers to rethink their selection strategies. In the past, the major criterion for selection for most jobs was a specific skill in the necessary area. Today, the criterion is shifting to the need for general skills and the flexibility to learn new skills rapidly. An example of how a firm integrates recruitment, performance of HRM activities, and quality is shown by the following example.

Motorola is tying recruitment and selection activities to results in order to gage the quality of their recruiting effort as they strive for TQM at every level.[31] Their recruiting department is now being measured by a new quality-oriented criterion— success of recruits on the job. Instead of using the old measure of how much it costs to hire each recruit, recruiters now measure whether new hires were well trained coming into the company, brought in at the right salary level, or left the company after the first six months for a better job. Based on these and other measures, the department decided that it had to increase, rather than decrease, the amount spent on each recruit. Thus, in recruiting activities, Motorola is planning and setting objectives for recruiting, charting progress over time in order to reduce "defects" in the hiring process, and ensuring that the "output" of the process (excellent employees) is under control, rather than just measuring inputs (dollar per recruit).

Performance Appraisal. Performance appraisal is an exceedingly difficult HRM activity to perform. The typical uses for performance appraisal include:[32]

- compensation
- counseling
- training and development
- promotion
- staff planning

---

[30]E. E. Lawler, Jr. *Strategic Pay* (San Francisco: Jossey-Bass Publishers, 1990), pp. 3–12.

[31]Ronald Henkoff, "Make Your Office More Productive," *Fortune,* February 25, 1991, p. 76.

[32]Adapted from a 1984 American Management Association survey, reported in Ronald D. Moen, "The Performance Appraisal System: Deming's Deadly Disease," *Quality Progress,* November 1989, p. 62.

- retention/discharge

- validation of the selection technique.

Conventional appraisal processes typically involve a manager or supervisor evaluating the work of a subordinate for a given time period. Steps and characteristics of the process may include some or all of the following:

- Objectives for a certain period of time (typically for the year ahead) are set unilaterally or jointly by the manager with his or her subordinate.

- At the end of the review period, the manager sits down with the subordinate and reviews accomplishments, strengths and weaknesses, and/or personal characteristics of the subordinate relating to the job.

- Frequently, the form used for performance rating has 10 to 15 tangible and intangible categories such as: quantity of work, quality of work, works well with others, takes initiative, etc., to be rated on a five- or seven-point scale from "excellent" to "unsatisfactory" or "poor."

- Usually, the manager is required to force a distribution on the ratings, based on company policies, such as "no more than 10% of any department's employees may be rated as excellent" or "merit raises or bonuses will only be paid to employees who are rated as excellent or very good."

- The standard form generally asks the rater to evaluate the ratee's capacity to handle greater responsibility and/or readiness for promotion.

- Often, the performance appraisal interview is accompanied by announcements of raises, bonuses, and/or promotions.

Dissatisfaction with conventional performance appraisal systems is common among both managers, who are the appraisers, and workers, who are the appraisees. Numerous research studies over the past several decades have pointed out the problems and pitfalls of performance appraisals.[33] Performance appraisals encourage the status quo and discourage autonomy, innovation, and creativity. They can create fear and anxiety for both the employee and supervisor.

W. Edwards Deming has condemned the performance appraisal process as one of the "seven deadly diseases" of management.[34] Deming suggests that management eliminate the use of performance appraisal because it is statistically unsound. For example, many salespersons' compensation is based on a sales quota. However, sales depends on more than the individual's contribution. Factors such as the economy, competition, customer interaction with other aspects of the company, and prior relationships all affect sales. These are *system* factors outside the control of the individual salesperson. Thus, Deming would point out that since sales *(Y)* is a function of both system *(S)* and individual *(I)* performance factors, or

---

[33]Douglas McGregor, "An Uneasy Look at Performance Appraisal," *Harvard Business Review,* September–October 1972; Herbert H. Meyer, Emanuel Kay, and John R. P. French, Jr., "Split Roles in Performance Appraisal, *Harvard Business Review,* January–February, 1965; Harry Levinson, "Appraisal of *What* Performance?," *Harvard Business Review,* January–February, 1965; A. M. Mohrman, *Deming Versus Performance Appraisal: Is There a Resolution?* (Los Angeles: Center for Effective Organizations, University of Southern California, 1989).

[34]W. Edwards Deming, *Out of the Crisis* (Cambridge, MA: MIT Center for Advanced Engineering Study, 1986).

$$Y = f(S, I)$$

it is impossible to solve for two unknowns with one equation. Yet this is precisely what traditional performance appraisal systems attempt to do.

Scholtes provides a summary of the objections against the use of performance appraisal, pointing out that some systems of appraisal may avoid *some,* but not all of these objections:[35]

1. Any employee's work, including the work of managers, is tied to many systems and processes. *But* performance evaluations focus on individuals, as if those individuals could be appraised apart from the systems in which they work.

2. Most work is the product of a group of people. *But* a process of evaluating an individual requires the pretense that the individual is working alone. As a result, performance evaluation encourages "lone rangers" and is a divisive influence.

3. Performance evaluation presumes consistent, predictable systems. *But* systems and processes are subject to constant changes, often beyond anyone's awareness or ability to predict.

4. Performance evaluation requires a process of appraisal that is objective, consistent, dependable, and fair. Otherwise, the evaluations will be seen as capricious and based on favoritism. *But* such objectivity and consistency simply do not exist.

TQM is based on the assumption that people want to do better and will, if given the opportunity to participate, are properly motivated, and are given adequate training and tools. With a shared vision of quality that goes beyond one's own workplace, a team concept emerges, where trust, effective communication, and cooperation are necessary to achieve success. Performance appraisals are most effective when they focus on the objectives of the work team that support the organization.[36] In this respect, they act as a diagnostic tool and review process for individual, team, and organizational development and achievement. The performance appraisal can also be a motivator when it is developed and used by the work team itself. Team efforts are harnessed when team members are empowered to monitor their own workplace activities.

It is also important to separate individual compensation from the performance appraisal. One method often used is **gainsharing,** an approach in which all employees share savings equally. Another way is to have pay tied closely to the acquisition of new skills. This can be done within the context of a continuous improvement program in which all employees are given opportunities to broaden their work-related competencies. In a TQM organization it is extremely important that the performance appraisal process be closely monitored and oriented toward "best practices" and continuous improvement of quality.

Training and Development. Training and development have become an essential responsibility for HRM departments in TQM organizations. A number of

---

[35]Peter R. Scholtes, *An Elaboration on Deming's Teachings on Performance Appraisal* (Madison, WI: Joiner Associates, 1987).

[36]Stanley M. Moss, "Appraise Your Performance Appraisal Process," *Quality Progress,* November 1989, p. 60.

recent studies have shown that businesses in the United States do not spend enough time and effort on training compared to similar organizations in other countries, such as Japan.

The stark realization that the United States has fallen behind Japan and other nations in quality has led to a significant interest in training and education, at both the managerial and operating levels. The leaders in quality—Deming, Juran, and Crosby—as well as many other consultants are actively engaged in quality training and education. Their approaches are not based on sophisticated statistics or new technologies. Rather, they are focused on the philosophical importance of quality and simple tools and techniques that are easy to apply and to understand. Once the basics are in place, more advanced statistical methods can be taught and applied.

For example, the Juran Institute in Wilton, Connecticut, provides a variety of educational services and products devoted to quality improvement, including courses and seminars, public and on-site training, and consulting. The institute offers a video-based training program—called Juran on Quality Improvement—which is a structured, project-by-project process designed to produce annual improvement in quality and annual reduction in quality-related costs. The program features 16 video cassettes and supporting materials. More than 100,000 managers at 1,000 locations have used the program; clients have included General Motors, Eastman Kodak, and General Dynamics.

Philip Crosby has engaged in similar ventures. Philip Crosby Associates (PCA) is widely regarded as the largest consulting and teaching firm in the quality area. Crosby opened Quality College in Winter Park, Florida, to teach his quality improvement philosophy to top management. Deming also conducts extensive programs for quality training.

Despite such programs, many workers still lack appropriate training in statistical quality control (SQC). A study conducted by Control Data Corporation revealed that three out of every four U.S. production workers lack formal training in SQC, even though there is a high awareness (83%) of SQC methods. One reason might be the inability of workers to learn the simple statistical tools because of very poor basic skills in mathematics. Even among engineers, there is a lack of statistical training that prevents the application of advanced methods such as experimental design and the Taguchi method. In contrast, both line workers and engineers in Japan are highly trained in statistical methods. Nevertheless, many companies in the United States are successfully developing SQC training programs, and the training gap is growing smaller each day.

Companies committed to TQM invest heavily in training. Motorola provides at least 40 hours of training to *every* employee. The Cincinnati Service Center of the Internal Revenue Service (see the Quality in Practice case in Chapter 7) devoted more than 420,000 hours (more than 70 hours and $500 per employee) in 1988 to classroom and on-the-job training as part of its quality improvement initiative. Specific approaches vary by company. For example, AT&T has presented a three-day training course to every manager.[37] The first day was aimed at creating an awareness of quality and productivity programs and progress throughout the world. Outside speakers were invited to review the challenges to American industry and the reasons for the Japanese success. Company vice presidents were asked to discuss the challenges facing their lines of business. The methods used by other companies to manage

---

[37]A. Blanton Godfrey, "Training and Education in Quality and Reliability—A Modern Approach," *Communications in Statistics—Theory and Methods,* Vol. 14, 1985, pp. 2621–2638.

quality and productivity were also reviewed. The second day focuses on Juran's approach to quality and productivity improvement and how to organize and manage an annual improvement program. The final day focuses on tools, such as statistical methods, software, and project management. In addition, AT&T has developed a number of courses specifically for product and process designers: a statistical reliability workshop, a reliability prediction workshop, an experimental design workshop, and a product and process design optimization workshop.

Rewards. The topic of rewards has already been introduced in the context of performance appraisal. Motivation, leadership, performance review, and training and development all ultimately lead to the question of "What's in it for me?" for each individual in every organization. Without willing, sustained individual effort, coordinated team efforts, and the sum total of the individual efforts that meet organizational goals, TQM is an impossible dream. Extrinsic and intrinsic rewards are the key to sustained individual efforts. A well-designed pay and benefit system can provide excellent extrinsic motivation. The design of the job itself is the key to intrinsic rewards. For example, at the IRS, employee recognition takes place in a number of ways. Team and individual recognition is publicized in a newsletter; certificates and pins are awarded for cooperative effort; and the Processing Division conducts an awards breakfast and end-of-year picnic at which contributors and teams are recognized. Financial awards for suggestions and innovative ideas for simplifying work are also given.

In the absence of performance appraisal, compensation must be based on new criteria. Many TQM-focused companies now base compensation on the market rate for an individual with proven capabilities, with adjustments as capabilities are increased; enhanced responsibilities; seniority; and business results. Walton describes how an organization can move from a traditional control approach to a TQM/HRM approach.[38] This is summarized in Table 10.3. Walton's model suggests that managers who are seriously concerned about moving from a traditional approach to a TQM/HRM approach must modify the assumptions and structure of compensation systems. Pay policies must move from an individual focus to a group focus using gainsharing and profit-sharing systems. Such programs reinforce the importance of group contributions instead of focusing only on individual contributions. Since it is unlikely that individual pay can or should be eliminated, it should be focused on development and mastery of skills, as opposed to traditional job evaluation. Finally in the new HRM/TQM approach, when the economy turns down, the pain of layoffs and pay cuts will be borne by managers and staff, not just by hourly employees.

It is not easy to make the transition to a TQM/HRM approach to compensation in a hostile environment in which organizations may be trying to react to competitors who already have demonstrated outstanding quality, high productivity, and lower wage rates. However, because of the aging work force, the need for general skills in broadly defined jobs, the trends toward group problem solving and team efforts, and continual economic pressures from foreign and domestic sources, managers may have no choice but to move to the TQM/HRM model.

A case study of one company that seems to have succeeded in attacking quality, productivity, participation, and compensation issues is that of Nucor Corporation,

---

[38]Richard E. Walton, "Toward a Strategy of Eliciting Employee Commitment Based on Policies of Mutuality," in Richard E. Walton and Paul R. Lawrence (eds.), *HRM Trends and Challenges* (Boston, MA: Harvard Business School Press, 1985), pp. 35–65.

TABLE 10.3 Characteristics of Compensation Management

	Traditional Control Approach	Transitional Approach	TQM/HRM Approach
Pay policies	Variable pay where possible to provide individual incentive	Typically no basic changes in compensation concepts	Variable rewards to create equity and to reinforce group achievements; gain-sharing, profit sharing
Individual pay	Geared to job evaluation		Linked to skills, mastery
Effects of economic downturns	Cuts concentrated on hourly payroll, not staff	Equality of sacrifice among employee groups	Equality of sacrifice among employee groups

SOURCE: Adapted from Richard E. Walton, "Toward a Strategy," Table 3–1, p. 38.

mentioned earlier.[39] Workers at Nucor's five nonunion steel mills earned base hourly rates in 1988 of $5.80 to $9.02 per hour, less than half of the going rate for unionized steelworkers. However, because of productivity/quality bonuses based on the number of tons of steel of acceptable quality that production teams produced, the average worker at Nucor earned about $2,000 per year *more* than the average worker in the industry, while the company was able to sell its steel at competitive worldwide market prices. In fact in 1982, Ken Iverson, chairman of the board of Nucor, said that the company was producing a ton of steel for approximately $60 of employment costs (wages, bonuses, fringe benefits), while the average U.S. steel company had employment costs of approximately $130 per ton.[40] Nucor required less than four hours of labor per ton, Japanese companies required about five hours per ton, and U.S. mills averaged over six hours per ton. This illustrates the use and benefits of team-based pay policies (point 1 in Walton's model).

While information on individual pay rates, levels, and the basis on which higher rates were paid was not directly available, a quote from Ken Iverson,[41] chairman of the board, suggests that individual pay is probably linked to skills and mastery in some way (point 2 in Walton's model). Iverson stated:

To keep a cooperative and productive work force you need, number one, to be completely honest about everything; number two, to allow each employee as much as possible to make decisions about that employee's work, to find easier and more productive ways to perform duties; and number three, to be as fair as possible to all employees.

During downturns, managers at Nucor frequently find that their bonuses are cut, even while hourly workers continue to receive theirs, based on production rates (point number 3 in Walton's model). In 1982, Nucor cut salaries for its 12 top executives by 5% and froze wages for its 3,500 employees. However, despite the tough times, they maintained their policy of *never* having a layoff during the history of the current company. By March 1983, when the United Steelworkers Union signed a

[39]Nancy J. Perry, "Here Come Richer, Riskier Pay Plans," *Fortune,* December 19, 1988, pp. 50–58.
[40]Frank C. Barnes, "Nucor (A)," in Robert R. Bell and John M. Burnham, *Managing Productivity and Change* (Cincinnati, OH: South-Western Publishing Company, 1991), p. 507.
[41]Ibid., p. 507.

contract to reduce wages and benefits in order to improve the competitiveness of the basic steel industry, Iverson was announcing a 5% wage *increase* for his workers.

The Individual-System Interface

Bounds and Pace[42] developed a model to show how *individual* activities of selection, performance, appraisal, development, and reward can be tied to the identical *system*

---

[42]Gregory M. Bounds and Larry A. Pace, "Human Resource Management for Competitive Capability," Chap. 26 in Michael J. Stahl and Gregory M. Bounds (eds.), *Competing Globally Through Customer Value* (New York: Quorum Books, 1991), pp. 648–684.

FIGURE 10.8   **Critical Individual-System Linkages: HRM Implications**

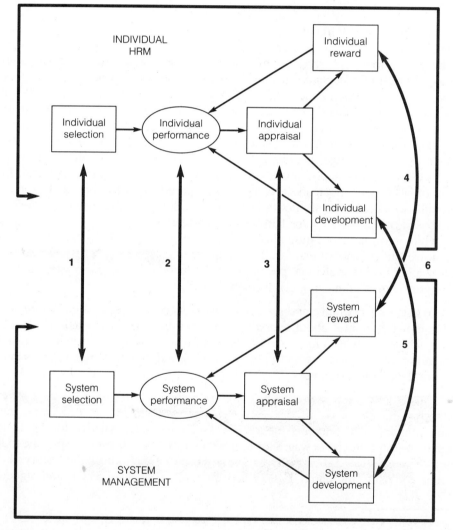

activities for a viable HRM process (see Figure 10.8). For example, a high-quality individual cannot be selected unless the HRM recruiter has determined what the relevant goals and objectives of the system or organization are, and how an individual's skills and characteristics will help to enhance the quality of that organization or department. This was shown in the case of Motorola when they defined the quality of their recruiting effort by how well selected individuals performed on the job in support of their system performance objectives.

The pitfalls of individual performance appraisal were discussed earlier. The HRM system in most organizations is geared primarily to individual, rather than group, appraisal and rewards, and must be modified to encourage and reward individuals to support team initiatives.

Finally, in system development and organizational improvement, HRM managers must ensure that individual development activities support and enhance the systems. The example of training in Japanese air conditioner manufacturing firms shows the incredible commitment of those firms to develop individuals to meet the corporate goal of quality improvement.

Human Resource Management at Disneyland[43]

Walt Disney's original vision of Disneyland was "a place where adults and children can experience together some of the wonders of life, of adventure, and feel better because of it." Achieving this vision has required a constant effort and near-fanatical attention to detail. Every foreman must have his maintenance report in every afternoon. Every defect—from ride problems to pigeon droppings—gets coded to different craft areas. Then every night after the park closes, everything gets fixed. Every morning the painters scrape the lead off the back of the shooting gallery and repaint it. Every morning every window in the park is washed. Every morning three groups of two women each will reapply makeup to every audio-animatronics figure in the park. The CEO has observed:

> It is interesting to note that our guests' comments have been consistent. . . . First, they comment about the cleanliness of our operation, second, they comment about the friendliness and courtesy of our employees, and third, they remark that we offer a good show. Cleanliness and friendliness are qualities of operation which can only be achieved by people. A strong employee program cannot be built on lip service. It takes time and money and effort to develop and maintain an understanding of our "Disney Ways." And then we work hard to protect our investment in human resources. On our Disney team, we stress pride and dignity in their job, in their company and its traditions . . . and in themselves.

> Let me assure you that this is not just a responsibility to be handed off to personnel administrators and forgotten by presidents. It must start at the top. It must permeate everyone throughout the organization. It must be practiced by everyone. Motivation—pride—dedication—responsibility—reward, these are the cornerstones of the organization Walt Disney built.

[43]Adapted from Lee Branst, "Disneyland—A Kingdom of Service Quality," Reprinted with permission from *Quality,* Vol. 23, February 1984, pp. 16–18; a publication of Hitchcock Publishing, a Capital Cities/ABC, Inc., company, and Brad Stratton, "How Disneyland Works," *Quality Progress,* July 1991, pp. 17–30.

Disney's Four C's for success are curiosity, confidence, courage, and constancy.

Disneyland interviews most prospective "cast members" (not "employees") in groups of three, a technique it adapted from the airline industry. For 45 to 60 minutes, the Disney interviewers ask the three a variety of questions. While their answers are important, so are their attitudes. The interviewer watches how the interviewees interact. Those who pay attention to what the others say, respect others' responses, engage in thoughtful conversation, and smile are the kind of people that Disneyland is looking for.

All new hires are given an eight-hour orientation describing the Disney experience. This includes a combination of presentations by highly trained in-costume cast members, slides and video presentations, and a tour of the park, both on stage and backstage. Disneyland wants their cast members to know that they are a business, what the product is, and how their role contributes to the product. Also included is training in safety, courtesy, show, and standards of what they are expected to exemplify as Disney employees. New on-stage cast members receive as many as 16 hours of classroom instruction, some of it after hours when the park is closed. Following this comes paired training, where experienced cast members work side by side with new ones for 16 to 48 hours.

At Disney, 85% of the managers have been promoted from within. A management training program combines on-the-job with classroom training in areas such as Disney management perspective, labor laws, and management skills. As part of the program, the class is divided into smaller groups to develop a Disneyland improvement proposal that must be presented in both verbal and written form to Disneyland executives.

To audit the effectiveness of training programs, focus groups meet regularly. Groups might be made up of cast members leaving Disney to work for different companies or those with 30 days of on-the-job experience. They are surveyed on issues such as training, wages, and their relationship with management. Action plans are developed from survey results.

(continued)

Current cast members are continually treated as special people. When a new orientation film was developed, it was shown to the cast first. When the introductory handbook was updated, it was mailed along with a personalized letter to their homes. When the Main Street electrical parade was refurbished, management felt it was important to preview the event before guests could see it, but there was no money budgeted for the preview. Instead, management decided to put on costumes and work the parade previews to pay for the cost.

The park sponsors the participation of hundreds of cast members in Disney-only sports leagues. Social events and after-hours treasure hunts based on Disney trivia build camaraderie and also raise money for charity.

Although the employees at the various Disney parks belong to almost 30 unions, there has been only one major strike in over 30 years. Many of the temporary Disney employees have been employed regularly at the parks during weekends, vacations, and holidays for periods of 20 years or longer.

Key Issues for Discussion

1. Discuss the approach taken by Disney to build quality through human resource management into their organization. What lessons can be applied to other organizations?

2. Since Disney is a service firm, what special challenges does it face as it attempts to emphasize quality to its employees?

Summary of Key Points

- HRM encompasses those activities designed to provide for and coordinate the human resources of an organization. Human resource management is a modern term for what has been traditionally referred to as personnel administration or personnel management.

- Human resource functions are tasks and duties that human resource managers perform, such as determining the organization's human resource needs; recruiting, selecting, developing, counseling, and rewarding employees; acting as a liaison with unions and government organizations; and handling other matters of employee well being.

- Approaches to HRM include human relations approaches, focusing on individual and group behavior, and organization development; systems approaches include industrial engineering, labor relations, and personnel management.

- The TQM/HRM approach is a progressive, often radical approach designed to focus the human resources of an organization on the philosophy, values, and techniques of total quality management. This can be done by adopting a *strategic* approach to HRM.

- Companies that adopt a quality improvement strategy as a major focus will align their quality philosophy and measurement with the following factors: objectives, motivation, leadership, employee selection and retention, training and development, appraisal systems, and compensation systems.

- Human relations factors of individual motivation, leadership, and organization design must be compatible with and support a quality focus in a TQM/HRM system.

- Industrial engineering and union/management relations must be adapted to the new philosophy of cooperation and shared goals and objectives if a TQM/HRM approach is to be successful.

- An effective and progressive compensation system depends on a policy of rewards to create equity and to reinforce group achievements, and a system of individual pay linked to skills and mastery.

Questions for Review and Discussion

1. Discuss the impact of the Taylor system on quality and productivity.

2. Define *human resource management*. Contrast it with the traditional role of personnel management.

3. Discuss Wickham Skinner's six different perspectives on HRM. Is it possible for someone to integrate these into a workable TQM approach to human resources management? Why or why not?

4. Contrast the traditional HRM approach with the TQM/HRM viewpoint.

5. How easy or difficult is it for a company to shift from the traditional HRM approach to the TQM/HRM approach? Which of the areas — philosophy, business objectives, quality objectives, business information sharing, inclusion of constituencies, or employee involvement — might be the most difficult for companies to change? Why?

6. Why must business strategy be considered when a quality approach is being developed? Isn't it obvious that companies must produce quality products or services if they are to remain in business?

7. Define the term *motivation*. What are the important components of this definition?

8. What is the difference between process and content theories of motivation? Which type is most essential to quality managers?

9. What relations do Maslow's and Herzberg's theories have to one another? What implications do they have for quality?

10. Of what significance to quality is McGregor's Theory X–Theory Y model? Point to specifics of the Deming philosophy that support either of these theories.

11. Explain the components of expectancy theory.

12. What insights on motivation that may be useful in quality management does the Porter and Lawler model give us?

13. What is the relevance of Hackman and Oldham's job characteristics model to quality?

14. Compare and contrast leadership with motivation. How do managers who are oriented to a TQM philosophy develop a motivating climate that enhances quality?

15. Compare the "traditional" manager with the quality-oriented *leader*. Discuss why people would prefer to be led rather than managed.

16. Discuss the traditional conflict between industrial engineers and union members. Can this rivalry be overcome in organizations that want to move to a TQM approach?

17. What is to be the new role of IEs and other technical experts in a TQM organization when information is open and shared and improvement techniques are taught to everyone?

18. Discuss the controversy over performance appraisal. Do you agree with Deming's approach, or take the more traditional viewpoint toward performance review? Why?

19. How do pay systems affect the likelihood of success or failure of a TQM/HRM system?

20. Discuss the conditions under which team incentives, gainsharing, and "pay for increased skills" reward systems may work. When may it *not* be a good idea to install such systems?

21. Briefly review the history of HRM. Conduct a thorough literature search of one of the "branches" of HRM and relate it to current quality management issues.

22. Survey several managers in one or two companies on the topic of motivation and/or leadership for quality. Try to find managers at each of the following levels to interview:

    a. quality control
    b. manufacturing or industrial engineering
    c. upper level management
    d. first-line supervision
    e. line employees (perhaps a union steward or officer).

Bibliography

Chung, Kae H., and Gray, Margaret Ann. "Can We Adopt Japanese Methods of Human Resources Management?" *Personnel Administrator,* Vol. 27, May 1982, p. 43.

Dowling, William F. "Job Redesign on the Assembly Line: Farewell to the Blue-Collar Blues?" *Organizational Dynamics,* Vol. 2, No. 2, 1973, p. 61.

Fiedler, Fred E., and Chemers, Martin M. *Leadership and Effective Management.* Glenview, IL: Scott-Foresman, 1975.

Herzberg, Frederick. *Work and the Nature of Man.* Cleveland, OH: World, 1966.

Herzberg, Frederick. "One More Time: How Do You Motivate Employees?" *Harvard Business Review,* Vol. 46, January–February 1968, pp. 53–62.

Kern, Jill P., Riley, John J., and Jones, Louis N. (eds.). *Human Resources Management, Quality and Reliability Series, Sponsored by the ASQC Human Resources Division,* New York: Marcel Dekker, Inc. and Milwaukee: ASQC Quality Press, 1987.

Lewin, Kurt. *A Dynamic Theory of Personality.* New York: McGraw-Hill, 1935.

Mayo, Elton. *The Human Problems of Industrial Civilization.* Cambridge, MA: Harvard Graduate School of Business, 1946.

Miner, John B. *Theories of Organizational Behavior.* Hinsdale, IL: Dryden Press, 1980.

Pierce, J. L., and Dunham, R. B. "The Measurement of Perceived Job Characteristics: The Job Diagnostic Survey Versus the Job Characteristics Inventory," *Academy of Management Journal,* Vol. 21, 1978, pp. 123–128.

Pierce, Jon L. "Job Design in Perspective," *Personnel Administrator,* Vol. 25, No. 12, 1980, p. 67.

Rubinstein, Sidney P. "Quality and Democracy in the Workplace," *Quality Progress,* April 1988, pp. 25–28.

Ryan, John. "Labor/Management Participation: The A. O. Smith Experience," *Quality Progress,* April 1988, pp. 36–40.

Taylor, Frederick W. *The Principles of Scientific Management.* New York: Harper & Row, 1911.

Teel, Kenneth S. "Performance Appraisal: Current Trends, Persistent Progress," *Personnel Journal,* Vol. 59, No. 4, April 1980, pp. 296–301.

Tolman, Edward C. *Purposive Behavior in Animals and Men.* New York: Appleton-Century-Crofts, 1932.

Turner, A. N., and Lawrence, P. R. *Industrial Jobs and the Worker.* Boston: Harvard Graduate School of Business Administration, 1965.

Wagel, William H. "Corning Zeros in on Total Quality," *Personnel,* July 1987.

Walton, Richard E. "From Control to Commitment in the Workplace," *Harvard Business Review,* Vol. 63, No. 2, March/April 1985, pp. 77–85.

Wexley, Kenneth N., and Latham, Gary P. *Developing and Training Human Resources in Organizations.* Glenview, IL: Scott Foresman, 1981.

Yukl, Gary A. *Leadership in Organizations.* Englewood Cliffs, NJ: Prentice-Hall, 1981.

CHAPTER 11

Employee Involvement and Participative Management

One of the most exciting and controversial trends in the total quality management movement during the 1980s has been the development of participative team approaches to problem solving and decision making for quality improvement. Participative team approaches involve transforming the culture of the entire organization to tap the creative energies of all employees.

Today, a number of labels are being applied to various participative team approaches used in organizations. Some of the broad behavioral management approaches have been labeled "quality of worklife (QWL)," "humanization of work," "work reform," "work restructuring," "work design," and "sociotechnical systems." Terms used for employee involvement teams within such behavioral management programs include QWL teams, productivity action teams (PATs), and quality circles. For the sake of consistency, we will generally use the terms participative problem solving for the broad concept and employee involvement (EI) for the team approach within which participative problem solving takes place.

EI is exciting because it offers unprecedented possibilities for tapping the knowledge, enthusiasm, and expertise of people. It promises workers autonomy over their jobs and gives managers a powerful approach to improve quality and productivity. The chief executive of Ford Motor Company has stated:[1]

> The magic of employee involvement [EI] is that it allows individuals to discover their own potential — and to put that potential to work in more creative ways. A survey last year of more than 750 EI participants at seven facilities found that a full 82 percent felt they had a chance to accomplish something worthwhile, compared with only 27 percent before EI was initiated. . . . People develop in themselves pride in workmanship, self-respect, self-reliance, and a heightened sense of responsibility.

However, EI also is controversial because it threatens old ways of working and could undermine managerial control. Many managers have difficulty understanding and accepting the notion of empowering employees. The president of a United Paperworkers Local has said:[2]

---

[1] Phillip Caldwell, "Cultivating Human Potential at Ford," *The Journal of Business Strategy,* Spring 1984, p. 75.

[2] "The Payoff From Teamwork," *Business Week,* July 10, 1989, p. 56.

What the company wants is for us to work like the Japanese. Everybody go out and do jumping jacks in the morning and kiss each other when they go home at night. You work as a team, rat on each other, and lose control of your destiny. That's not going to work in this country.

Despite the controversy, employee involvement and participative management are gaining increased acceptance as vital components of quality management and control. Many experts, however, believe that the movement is not spreading fast enough, especially considering the potential benefits. Many suggest that the federal government should reinforce employee involvement in public policy.

In this chapter we examine the history and development of employee involvement approaches for quality improvement and discuss ways of measuring and evaluating such programs.

THE IMPORTANCE OF EMPLOYEE PARTICIPATION

Effective quality assurance depends on good planning, organization, motivation, and control involving managers, supervisors, and workers. Since these three groups of employees must function together as a team, participative approaches to problem solving are important methods for improving quality and productivity. With some notable exceptions, the history of management-labor relations in U.S. firms has been largely adversarial. Lack of sensitivity to worker needs, exploitation of workers, and poor management practices and policies have frequently resulted in strained relations between managers and their subordinates. Labor leaders also must bear their share of the blame. They have had a tendency to resist any management effort to reduce rigid, rule-based tasks, preferring to adhere to the structured approaches that have their roots in Frederick W. Taylor's historical principles of scientific management.[3]

Participative problem-solving approaches continue to hold the promise of breaking down barriers between labor and management, designers and engineers, line and staff, and other groups that tend to relate to each other in an adversarial fashion.

EI offers many advantages over traditional management practices, including:[4]

- replacing the adversarial mentality with trust and cooperation

- developing the skills and leadership capability of individuals, creating a sense of mission and fostering trust

- increasing employee morale and commitment to the organization

- fostering creativity and innovation, the source of competitive advantage

- helping people understand quality principles and instilling these principles into the corporate culture

---

[3]"Detroit vs. the UAW: At Odds Over Teamwork," *Business Week,* August 24, 1987, pp. 54–55.

[4]Joseph J. Gufreda, Larry A. Maynard, and Lucy N. Lytle, "Employee Involvement in the Quality Process," in The Ernst & Young Quality Improvement Consulting Group, *Total Quality: An Executive's Guide for the 1990s* (Homewood, IL: Richard D. Irwin, 1990).

- allowing employees to solve problems at the source immediately

- improving quality and productivity.

An analysis of the findings of a large number of research studies on participation, job performance, and satisfaction showed that EI has many positive aspects, but that it is by no means a panacea for all of the problems of management.[5] Key studies of participation have concluded the following:

- Participation is consistently and significantly related to job satisfaction.

- People who have a high need for independence and low need for authoritarian control more strongly support and obtain satisfaction from the use of participative decision-making approaches.

- Participation is generally associated with group or unit effectiveness. Effectiveness criteria may include decision quality, likelihood of implementation, and decision time.

- Laboratory research on the quality of group versus individual decisions leaves uncertain the question of whether findings apply in the same manner within organizations.

- Participation is consistently and positively related to how well decisions are implemented.

- Participation takes time and money.

These findings generally support the advantages of EI listed earlier. They suggest that the satisfaction of subordinates with their jobs depends significantly on the extent to which they participate in and exert influence on decisions affecting them in their work situation. People who have different personality characteristics will respond differently to involvement opportunities. Those who want to be told what to do may be initially uncomfortable in group problem-solving situations. However, the benefits of participation tend to enhance group or unit effectiveness.

Laboratory findings show persistent differences in content between group and individual decisions, and the group decisions tend to be superior. Numerous studies also show that participative decisions tend to be more readily accepted and efficiently carried out than those that are imposed. Finally, participation requires time and effort. Only those directly associated with the problems at hand can decide whether these costs are outweighed by the improvement in quality, the additional commitment to implementation, the presumed reduction in needed surveillance, and (if satisfaction is allowed some weight in the equation) the increase in satisfaction of human needs.

Taken as a whole, the evidence seems strong that participative approaches are beneficial and frequently underused in organizational decision making today. This summary gives convincing reasons why quality managers must pursue a strategy of increasing participation in decisions in order to capture the benefits of improvements in quality. Most major corporations and thousands of small organizations in the United

---

[5]Robert L. Kahn, "In Search of the Hawthorne Effect," in Eugene Louis Cass and Frederick G. Zimmer (eds.), *Man and Work in Society* (New York: Van Nostrand Reinhold, 1975), pp. 56–58.

States and around the world have adopted these ideas and are making employee involvement an integral part of their efforts to improve quality and productivity.

HISTORICAL FOUNDATIONS OF EI PROGRAMS[6]

It is difficult to fit the philosophy of EI-teams into a specific category such as quality control, productivity improvement, or participative management. Quality control is designed to ensure that a product or service is fit for its intended use and conforms to specifications. Productivity improvement is an approach to increasing the output of conforming (high-quality) goods or services from some process while maintaining the same—or a lower—level of inputs of labor, materials, and other resources. Participative management provides opportunities for members of an organization to assist in making decisions concerning things that affect their area of work. EI programs have some of the elements of each of these labels and yet are unique in the way that the components are assembled.

Many of the early experiments in participative team problem solving focused on work improvement rather than quality improvement. Early work improvement activities took place at the Zeiss Company in Germany in the 1890s where workers were involved in work planning, design of precision machinery, and group problem solving.[7]

In 1913, the Lincoln Electric Company began to develop its unique mix of work improvement and employee incentive plans, including an employee advisory board, employee stock ownership, year-end bonuses, and a benefit package.[8] Lincoln Electric still boasts of outstanding productivity, quality, and employee loyalty, some 85 years after beginning its experiment. These examples show that early work innovations did recognize the value of employee inputs into improvement of productivity and quality.

Classical and Industrial Engineering Approaches

A number of productivity improvement programs were developed and successfully applied in the 1930s, 1940s, and 1950s that were based primarily on rational, often quantified, approaches to quality/productivity problem solving. Some of these approaches assumed that expert staff personnel would be used to implement changes, while others assumed that nonspecialist or operative-level employees could and should be involved in improvement projects. All of these approaches were based on a multifunctional process that cuts across boundaries of disciplines and organizational levels. The common theme in these approaches is a wholistic view of problem solving using systematic, rational analysis. The common label used for this approach is **productivity improvement.** Two productivity improvement approaches that we

---

[6]A more comprehensive review of history and the forerunners of quality circles from the early 1900s can be found in William M. Lindsay, "Quality Circles and Participative Work Improvement: A Cross-Disciplinary History," in Dennis F. Ray (ed.), *Southern Management Association Proceedings* (Mississippi State, MS: Mississippi State University, 1987), pp. 220–222.

[7]Sud Ingle, *Quality Circles Master Guide: Increasing Productivity with People Power* (Englewood Cliffs, NJ: Prentice-Hall, 1982), p. 7.

[8]Leslie W. Rue and Lloyd L. Byars, *Management Theory and Application,* 3rd ed. (Homewood, IL: Irwin, 1983), p. 45.

will review are **work simplification** and **planned methods change.** Work simplification is a concept developed by Allan H. Mogensen, an industrial engineer, writer, and consultant. It involves teaching basic analytic techniques, such as methods analysis, flowcharting, and diagramming, to every employee in a firm from the top down. Employees are then encouraged to use their newly acquired skills to analyze their own work procedures to improve quality and productivity and reduce costs. The Maytag Company's reputation for quality is said to have originated with a work simplification seminar that Mogensen gave to Maytag's corporate executives in 1947. Today, all employees in the firm are still being given work simplification training. Reported cost reduction in 1982 was $5.1 million.[9]

Planned methods change is a productivity improvement concept that is closely related to work simplification. It was developed at the Procter & Gamble Company in 1946 under the direction of Art Spinanger, then associate manager of the Management Systems Division. The program began with the concept of introducing deliberate methods change into manufacturing processes. This went beyond the idea of methods improvement, which asked the question "Can this operation be improved?", and instead asked the question "Can this operation be improved, replaced, or eliminated?" At the outset, all manufacturing managers were trained in work simplification techniques. They were then asked to set specific dollar goals as to how much of their cost they would try to eliminate through planned change. Gradually, the concept was broadened over several years' time to include nonmanufacturing areas of the firm and nonmanagement personnel. The approach includes the following three steps:

1. Form methods teams.

2. Establish dollar goals.

3. Provide positive recognition.

Spinanger reported that the company's noncumulative first-year profit increase from the program as a result of the savings stood at $1 billion.[10]

Statistical Quality Control

Statistical quality control (SQC), described more fully in Chapters 16 and 17, is often viewed merely as a productivity improvement tool. Actually, there is a long history of employee involvement in quality measurement and improvement activities. Many of the statistical quality control techniques that were developed at AT&T's Bell Labs in the 1930s by Drs. Shewhart, Dodge, and Romig as well as others were the result of group participation. The company's *Statistical Quality Control Handbook* was designed for operating-level people and was written in 1956 by a manufacturing engineering team. The book, which is still in print, has been and continues to be used in numerous companies for training in SQC basics.[11] The authors recommended continued use of

---

[9]"An Unsung Benefit from Work Simplification or Quality Circles," *National Productivity Report,* June 15, 1983. Wheaton, IL: The Improvement Institute.

[10]Arthur Spinanger, "Increasing Profits Through Deliberate Methods Change" (Lake Placid, NY: A. H. Mogensen Work Simplification Programs, undated).

[11]*Statistical Quality Control Handbook,* AT&T, 1956. Available from AT&T Technologies, Commercial Sales Clerk, Select Code 700-444, P.O. Box 19901, Indianapolis, IN 46219.

a quality team consisting of a manufacturing supervisor, a quality control manager, a manufacturing engineer, and a statistical clerk for coordination of quality improvement and control projects.

W. Edwards Deming's approach to quality has always been grounded in statistical quality control concepts but with a pioneering recognition that individuals and groups of managers and operating level employees had to be involved in making quality happen. During the 1940s, Deming gave the same series of courses on statistical quality control in the United States that he gave in Japan during the 1950s. The only difference was that top management *and* technicians attended the courses in Japan, while only quality control staff, engineers, and technicians attended the U.S. sessions.[12] The results of this difference in commitment are strikingly clear.

Behavioral Management Innovations

In the 1940s, 1950s, and 1960s, a number of work innovation experiments that focused on worker motivation and productivity took place. These behavioral experiments frequently, though not exclusively, relied on the use of group participation at the operating level to achieve organizational change. One of the most publicized cases of work innovation was the Weldon Company, a division of Harwood Manufacturing, a garment manufacturing firm. Weldon engaged in a multifaceted program to improve productivity and effectiveness by a combination of (1) improving personnel practices for hiring, training, and termination, (2) instituting group problem-solving sessions with first-line supervisors and employees, and (3) conducting attitude surveys and acting on results to make beneficial improvements.[13]

Texas Instruments (TI) instituted several work innovations in the 1960s. Most production employees in the firm participated in a work simplification training program. All the people from a given line were trained at the same time to encourage group interaction and problem solving. A performance review system that emphasized individual goal setting was established. An annual opinion survey was also implemented with 10% to 25% samples of TI employees. This survey provided a measure of employee attitudes for each of the factors identified in the Herzberg motivation/maintenance theory.

Walton lists large and small firms that have been leaders in work innovation experiments in the 1960s and 1970s.[14] He named General Motors, Procter & Gamble, Exxon, General Foods, TRW, Cummins Engine, Butler Manufacturing, Mars, Inc., Citibank, Prudential Insurance, Donnelly Mirrors, and Eaton Corporation. His basic conclusion from a review of work improvement experiments conducted over a 10-year period was that (1) most such experiments were neither extreme successes nor extreme failures, (2) such innovations must take into account the interrelation of techniques, outcomes, and corporate culture, and (3) work improvement efforts that have balanced goals of both productivity and quality of worklife improvement are the most likely to succeed. A recent text by Werther, Ruch, and McClure provides an

---

[12]"Dr. W. Edwards Deming: The Statistical Control of Quality," *Quality,* February 1980, pp. 13–15.

[13]Raymond A. Katzell and Daniel Yankelovich, *Work, Productivity, and Job Satisfaction* (New York: New York University, 1975), pp. 336–339.

[14]Richard E. Walton, "Work Innovations in the U.S.," *Harvard Business Review,* July/August 1979, pp. 88, 91. Copyright © 1979 by the President and Fellows of Harvard College; all rights reserved.

excellent set of readings and interpretation of productivity issues, organizational improvements, and recent innovations.[15]

Each of these approaches to participative team problem solving has influenced modern quality assurance efforts. The following section shows how the development of quality control circles in Japan affected the course of U.S. employee involvement programs.

Quality (Control) Circles in Japan and the United States

The term **quality control circles** (QCCs) was coined in Japan in the early 1960s and brought to the United States in the early 1970s. It took five years for the concept to begin to blossom in the United States. QCCs blend participative management approaches with classical problem solving, work simplification, and statistical quality control techniques to improve productivity as well as quality. The term *quality control circles* was shortened to *quality circles* (QCs), which is in common use in the United States.

A **quality circle** is a small group of employees from the same work area who meet regularly and voluntarily to identify, solve, and implement solutions to work-related problems. Quality circles have some unique characteristics:[16]

- Quality circles are small groups, ranging from 4 to 15 members. Eight members is considered the norm.

- All members come from the same shop or work area. This gives the circle its identity.

- The members work under the same supervisor, who is a member of the circle.

- The supervisor is usually, though not always, the leader of the circle. As leader, he or she moderates discussion and promotes consensus. The supervisor does not issue orders or make decisions. The circle members, as a group, make their own decisions.

- Voluntary participation means that everyone has an opportunity to join.

- Circles usually meet once every week on company time, with pay, and in special meeting rooms removed from their normal work area.

- Circle members receive training in the rules of quality circle participation, the mechanics of running a meeting and making management presentations, and techniques of group problem solving.

- Circle members, not management, choose the problems and projects that they will work on, collect all information, analyze the problems, and develop solutions.

- Technical specialists and management assist circles with information and expertise whenever asked to do so. Circles receive advice and guidance from an adviser who attends all meetings but is not a circle member.

---

[15]William B. Werther, William A. Ruch, and Lynne McClure, *Productivity Through People* (St. Paul, MN: West Publishing Company, 1986).

[16]Philip C. Thompson, *Quality Circles: How To Make Them Work In America* (New York: AMACOM, 1982).

■ Management presentations are given to those managers and technical specialists who would normally make the decision on a proposal.

As mentioned earlier, the quality circle concept as defined here evolved from the quality control circles developed in Japan in the 1960s.[17] Quality control circles were an outgrowth of the postwar education effort in Japan. Prior to the visits of Deming and Juran, U.S. engineers worked with the Japanese to improve production methods, particularly in the development of high-quality communications equipment. Initially, quality training was limited to engineers and middle-level supervisors. This resulted from the traditional American way of thinking regarding division of labor but was in direct contrast to the Japanese philosophy of relying on production workers for creative ideas. Japanese manufacturers considered quality control to be the responsibility of all employees, including management and line workers. In Japan, foremen are considered to be "working supervisors," who are much closer to the workers than in the United States. Not only were top and middle managers attending seminars, but foremen were being trained in basic quality concepts using nationwide radio broadcasts. Copies of the texts for quality control courses were sold on newsstands across the country. The push for quality was truly a national priority, and the results were dramatic.

This quality improvement effort and the cultural bias toward group activity resulted in the formation of the quality control circle concept, attributed to Dr. Kaoru Ishikawa, of the University of Tokyo. The initial growth of quality circles in Japan was phenomenal. The Japan Union of Scientists and Engineers (JUSE) estimated that registration in quality circles grew from 400 members in 1962 to 200,000 members in 1968 to more than 700,000 members in 1978. Today, millions of workers are involved.

Evidence exists that quality circle concepts were not only known but also used by some U.S. firms in the late 1960s.[18] The quality of worklife programs developed in the early 1960s were related to circle concepts but tended to emphasize behavioral interventions, reorganization of groups or tasks, or efforts to build or enhance morale. The quality circle movement became established and began to grow when a team of managers for Lockheed Missiles and Space Division in California made a trip to Japan in 1973 to view quality control circles in action. A manufacturing manager for Lockheed, Wayne S. Rieker, headed this team of six managers who visited eight Japanese firms and returned with an enthusiastic report about the use of quality circle programs there.

After the success of the Lockheed program became known, many other manufacturing firms established quality circle programs or began using similar team problem-solving approaches. They included Westinghouse, General Electric, Cincinnati Milacron, Ford Motor Company, Dover Corporation, and Coors Beer Company. Later, service organizations such as hospitals, school systems, and state and federal governmental units started their quality circle programs.

In 1977, the International Association of Quality Circles (IAQC), now the Association for Quality and Participation (AQP), was formed. Evidence of the increasing importance of QC teams in the United States can be measured partly by

---

[17]Much of the history in this section has been adapted from J. M. Juran, "The QC Circle Phenomenon," *Industrial Quality Control,* January 1967, pp. 329–336.

[18]Sidney P. Rubinstein, "QC Circles and U.S. Participative Movements," *1972 ASQC Technical Conference Transactions,* Washington, D.C., pp. 391–396.

attendance at the annual IAQC conference and in membership growth. According to a brochure produced by the association, conference attendance grew from 150 to 2,700 registrants in the six years from 1978 through 1983.[19] During this same period, membership grew from 200 to 6,000. It was during this time that the word "control" was dropped from "quality control circles" and the standard designation of "quality circles" was established in the United States.

Today, the term *quality circles* has become less popular as the notion of employee involvement has broadened in scope. In the early to middle 1980s, special-purpose teams emerged. Such teams might work on projects involving the design and introduction of work reforms and new technology, meeting with suppliers and customers, or linking separate functions. In union shops, labor and management collaborate on operational decisions at all levels, creating an improved atmosphere for quality and productivity improvements. The special-purpose team approach created a foundation for self-managed work teams, which are discussed in the next section.

Self-Managed Teams

Today, many companies are moving beyond the traditional team approaches to problem solving and decision making and adopting the self-managed team (SMT), or self-directed work team concept. In this participative management approach, employees are encouraged to take on many of the roles formerly held only by management. The focus on quality and improvement shifts from a passive, management-initiated one to a highly active, independent one.

A **self-managed team** is defined as "a highly trained group of employees, from 6 to 18, on average, fully responsible for turning out a well-defined segment of finished work. The segment could be a final product, like a refrigerator or ball bearing; or a service, like a fully processed insurance claim. It could also be a complete but intermediate product or service, like a finished refrigerator motor, an aircraft fuselage, or the circuit plans for a television set."[20]

The SMT concept was developed in Britain and Sweden in the 1950s. One of the early companies to adopt SMTs was Volvo, the Swedish auto manufacturer. Pioneering efforts in SMT development were made by Procter & Gamble in 1962 and by General Motors in 1975. These U.S. developments were concurrent with the Japanese quality team developments that, in many cases, cannot be classified as true SMTs because of their limited autonomy. SMTs began to gain popularity in the United States in the late 1980s.

A 1991 study of workgroups in 22 manufacturing facilities in the United States and Canada showed a widespread use of SMT-type work groups.[21] SMTs were used in many different industries, including food processing, auto-related businesses, petrochemicals, the glass industry, and other miscellaneous industries. The age of the workgroup programs ranged from 1 to 17 years. The average age was 6 years, and over half of the companies studied established workgroups only within the past 5 years. Of

---

[19]IAQC. Exhibitor Brochure for the 6th Annual IAQC Conference and Exhibition, 1984, at Cincinnati, Ohio.

[20]Jack D. Orsburn, Linda Moran, Ed Musselwhite, and John H. Zenger, *Self-Directed Work Teams* (Homewood, IL: Business One–Irwin, 1990), p. 8.

[21]Peter Lazes and Marty Falkenberg, "Workgroups in America Today," *The Journal for Quality and Participation,* Vol. 14, No. 3, June 1991, pp. 58–69.

the 22 cases studied, 15 (68%) established workgroups primarily for economic reasons (that is, to increase productivity, reduce costs, or improve product quality). Of these 15, 4 (all unionized) were established in response to threatened plant closures. Six of the cases (27%) established workgroups primarily to improve the work environment or to increase employee satisfaction. One company adopted a team system specifically to avoid a a union (ironically, that plant was organized a year after it opened and has remained union since).

IMPLEMENTING EMPLOYEE INVOLVEMENT TEAMS

Fairly standard procedures exist for establishing EI team programs and training participants. Because any employee involvement program requires a major commitment to organizational change by management and workers, it is likely to fail unless a systems viewpoint is taken. Figure 11.1 illustrates the process of planning and implementing EI programs.

FIGURE 11.1 **A Process Model for Establishing EI Programs**

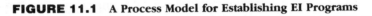

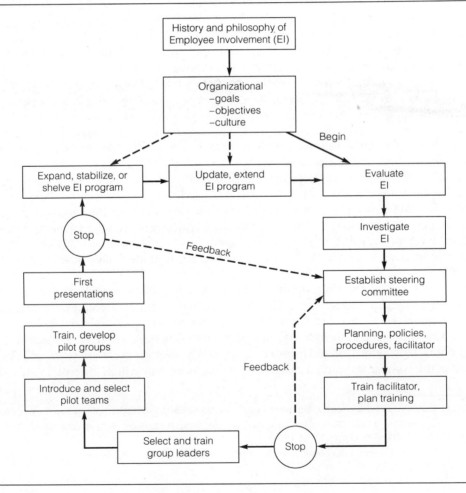

Initially, there should be a period of investigation, reflection, and soul searching before buying into the concept of EI. The process begins with understanding the history and philosophy of EI. By learning how Japanese and American firms have performed, an organization is in a better position to be its own expert rather than having to rely on the confusing, and sometimes contradictory, insights found in any single source written about the topic.

After gathering background information, managers must examine their organization's goals, objectives, and culture to evaluate readiness to install EI programs. This may be the most difficult step in the process, because it requires a hard self-appraisal of the organization as a whole. One enthusiastic manager can often get teams going, but it requires solid support of a number of managerial levels to *keep* them going.

Once it has been decided to move ahead, most organizations find it best to establish a steering committee made up of a group of interested, committed line and staff managers and, if a union exists, a union representative. The steering committee establishes initial policies and procedures for the EI program and chooses a person or persons to be the facilitator(s). Once first-line operative, clerical, or other candidate team members are given an introduction to team concepts, they are offered an opportunity to join a team. If employees choose to join the team, they are given 8 to 16 hours of initial or concurrent training before or during the first few group meetings. Usually, the facilitator or group leader will conduct the training.

Approaches to EI teams have become quite varied since the early 1980s as organizations have sought to fit the original quality circle idea to their specific needs. Many tried to structure teams according to a very rigid format. For example, *every* team had to be composed of *volunteers,* meet *regularly* for *one hour* per week, work to solve problems *chosen by them,* and limited to within their *own* work areas. Today, organizations exist with *mandatory* team membership, teams that meet irregularly for two or four (or more) hours every month, teams that work on problems chosen by management, teams that work across departments or the entire company, and teams that work on a problem in their own area and disband after the problem has been solved successfully.

The three main types of teams in use today can be classified as intraorganizational (the QC type), cross-functional (task type), and self-managed. The QC-type teams are the closest to the original quality circle concept in that they tend to work regularly on problems of limited scope in their own work areas. However, the importance of QC-type teams should not be downplayed. One Cincinnati-area company with about 500 workers reported that they had received over 10,000 suggestions from individuals and teams over an eight-year time span. This averaged 2.5 suggestions per worker per year, with more than 70% of the suggestions having been implemented.

Task-type teams may be either management-initiated or worker-initiated. They are made up of workers, staff, and others from various departments that may "own" part of a business or production process. They typically are asked by management to review a system problem that cuts across boundaries of several different departments or processes and to recommend improvements. Frequently, they will be given special training in advanced problem-solving techniques.

Problem solving drives the team concept. Figure 11.2 illustrates the typical process by which EI teams operate. The three basic functions are to identify, analyze, and solve quality and productivity problems. The methodology is essentially a process of creative problem solving. Problem-solving techniques are taught to members by team leaders with the assistance of a facilitator, who is a full-time or part-time resource person.

FIGURE 11.2 Functions of EI Teams RJP Tam - 6

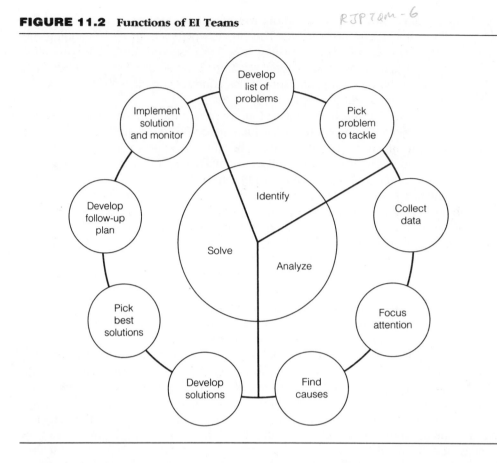

EI teams are taught to use brainstorming and the "Seven QC Tools" for problem solving, which were discussed at length in Chapter 9, as well as skills in presentation techniques and group leadership and motivation. Presentation skills are useful in presenting reports of solved problems to management; presentations are usually informal and serve to increase members' self-esteem. Leadership skills such as discussion leading, active listening, and role playing are taught as aids to enhancing the effectiveness of team meetings.

Examples of team problem solving can be illustrated with the Cincinnati Service Center (CSC) of the Internal Revenue Service, which was introduced in a Quality in Practice in Chapter 7. Some typical projects that have been undertaken by their quality improvement program teams included:

- Solve an entry related problem in one of the information systems that reduced the error rate to 1.6%.

- Recruit and retain seasonal employees.

- Reduce missing attachments from letters.

- Improve work flow in many areas.

- Computerize routing slips for internal use.

Criticism of Quality Circle Programs

Quality circles, as a formal concept, can rightfully be labeled a "fad" of the 1980s. A number of articles written in this decade criticized the quality circle movement, branding it as a limited success or an outright failure.[22] However, many failures of quality circle programs have been based on false hopes of management for finding a panacea for all of the ills that plagued U.S. businesses in the 1970s. In essence, management believed that quality circles represented a quick fix without providing their full support and commitment. As expounded in the Deming philosophy, inadequate funding of the program, lack of proper training, resistance of staff or middle managers, and lack of proposal implementation by management are all elements of the system of management beyond the control of the workers. Under such circumstances, workers quickly lose interest and initiative.

In a study of quality and productivity improvement in two plants of a U.S. manufacturer that was making sausage casings, researchers found that the use of quality circles to deal with a problem of the wire clips lost in the production process in one plant was superior to a "self-monitoring" approach applied to the same problem by workers in another plant.[23] Not only was there a significant improvement in performance at the plant using quality circles, but there were accompanying improvements in absenteeism and lost work time measures. The authors felt the need to defend the positive results found in their study in the face of much criticism of QC programs. They pointed out several factors that they believed have led to poorly designed QC programs in the United States including:

- Quality circles started out as a program designed to aid in improving quality and productivity in Japan and ended up being billed as a QWL program in the United States.

- The idea of Deming's approach was to make powerful statistical quality control techniques and ideas available to *every* employee at every level and to make quality part of everyone's job. The American approach has been to set up a separate program under the control of nonline personnel, such as staff people from the Human Resources Department.

- Under the direction of HRM-oriented staff, the dominant theoretical orientation is not Deming's, but a blend of Maslow, Herzberg, and McGregor, thus stressing self-actualization, communication, and employee development, rather than measurable improvements in quality and productivity.

- Sufficient reinforcement has not been built into the typical QC program for line management, middle management, facilitators, or participants to become strong supporters and believers in the process. Specifically, line management has frequently been asked to become involved without having adequate training as to how to shift responsibilities and redesign their own jobs. Middle managers have been asked for support, but have not been rewarded for or kept

[22]For a thorough discussion and additional sources, see Richard E. Kopelman, *Managing Productivity in Organizations* (New York: McGraw-Hill, 1986), pp. 133–135.

[23]Naomi Krigsman and Richard M. Obrien, "Quality Circles, Feedback and Reinforcement: An Experimental Comparison and Behavioral Analysis," *Journal of Organizational Behavior Management,* Vol. 9, No. 1, 1987, pp. 77–78.

informed about the results of their efforts. Quality circle facilitators have frequently found that they are in a dead-end job, with no path to move up in the organization. Participants have found that their ideas were listened to, but only implemented after a long delay, if at all.

The conclusion to be reached is that the success of quality circle and similar employee involvement programs is situational. If the organization is not ready to make changes and to struggle with the problems and opportunities of the philosophy, they will probably be dissatisfied with the results. If such an organization can develop patience, learn from its mistakes, and make evolutionary improvements, the EI approach will probably pay dividends in the long run.

In all fairness to management, failures can also be attributed to the teams. For example, members may not be able to learn adequately the necessary problem-solving or group process skills. They may fail to reach agreement on problems to address or may propose inadequate solutions. Ideas may be poorly presented. Group versus nongroup friction, running out of ideas, and pressure for financial rewards for improvements suggested by groups may arise. If the EI program begins to decline, it can be killed by cynicism about the program and a terminal case of burnout.[24] Thus, quality circle programs should be monitored and controlled to determine the benefits that are derived and to decide whether or not to modify them.

The Transition to Self-Managed Teams

Organizations that have SMTs have typically arrived at them through one of two routes —organizational start-up with SMTs in place or transformations from more limited participative management techniques to SMTs. The latter is often a next logical step after other types of employee involvement programs have reached maturity.

Donovan recommended seven steps in the design of SMTs during a transition from a quality circle type of program.[25] He recommends the establishment of a design team to analyze and change the work system of individual tasks, team tasks, and support functions. The steps involved include:

1. Create a work unit responsible for an entire task. This step requires defining a whole work unit based on identifying a customer, establishing a means of contact between the team and customer, and establishing the standard for the product or service.

2. Establish specific measures of the work unit's output. Establishing meaningful measures includes defining standards for outputs in terms of quality, quantity, cost, and timeliness, together with accountability and a feedback system.

3. Design multiskilled jobs. This requires systematic study of workflow functions and variances, followed by redesign of the jobs to enhance the development of multiple skills.

---

[24]Edward E. Lawler, and Susan A. Mohrman, "Quality Circles After the Fad," *Harvard Business Review*, January/February 1985, pp. 65–71. Copyright © 1985 by the President and Fellows of Harvard College; all rights reserved.

[25]J. Michael Donovan, "Self-Managing Work Teams: Extending the Quality Circle Concept,"*The Quality Circles Journal* (now *The Journal for Quality and Participation*), Vol. 9, No. 3, March 1986, pp. 15–20.

4. Create internal management and coordination tasks. These include coordination tasks of the work team, typically handled by managers in a conventional organization, such as scheduling, task assignments, hiring of new members, and cross-functional training, which must be addressed by designers and by the team itself.

5. Create boundary management tasks. These are processes and procedures for coordination outside of the group with managers, other departments, suppliers, and customers that must be established.

6. Establish access to information. This requires definition of the needed information and design of the processes, hardware, and software required to obtain direct, accurate, and timely performance-related feedback and information.

7. Establish support systems. This includes consideration of how the teams are to be supported and involves the "hows" of training, career progression (typically based on skills developed and used), team interfacing with management, and payments and rewards.

The design process used in transforming an existing organization to a team approach does not appear to be considerably different from that used for development of a start-up work team organizational structure with one exception. Lazes and Falkenberg found that 8 of 11 transformed plants had used shop floor-level workers on their design teams, while shop floor representatives were not generally included on the design team for start-up plants.[26] In summary, it appears that careful, systematic planning for both work design and coordination issues is required for successful introduction of self-managed teams.

There is no doubt that SMTs have attained many positive results. A *Business Week* article reported that when workers were organized into self-directed teams on a pilot production line for the Mercedes-Benz 400E at Stuttgart, Germany, defects were reduced by 50%.[27] Others have pointed out that companies routinely report that they have achieved as much as an 800% reduction in setup and teardown times for production machinery because self-directed teams have been able to find faster ways of doing the job with no adverse effects on quality or productivity.[28]

The study of 22 manufacturing plants using self-managed teams cited earlier in this chapter found, subject to a number of limitations, the following:[29]

■ Eleven of 22 cases reported quality improvements.

■ Twelve out of 22 cases reported productivity improvements.

■ Twelve facilities removed at least one layer of management and reduced or eliminated supervisors.

■ Of the 10 unionized plants, 6 reported a decrease in grievances, with one going from 130 per year to 10.

---

[26]Peter Lazes and Marty Falkenberg, "Workgroups in America Today," p. 59.

[27]David Woodruff and Jonathan B. Levine, "Miles Traveled, More to Go," *Business Week,* October 25, 1991, p. 71.

[28]Jack D. Orsburn et al., *Self-Directed Work Teams,* p. 15.

[29]Peter Lazes and Marty Falkenberg, "Workgroups in America Today," p. 66.

- Absenteeism and turnover decreased in most cases with rates dropping to around 1% per year.

An almost universal warning on the results of SMT studies, as well as other types of EI programs, is that too few objective studies have been performed. Also, those results that have been reported are frequently biased because of contamination with other improvement processes taking place in the same facility and/or the desire of those reporting the results to cast a favorable light on their efforts.

EVALUATING EMPLOYEE INVOLVEMENT PROGRAMS

A study of the literature on measurement of EI program effectiveness in the United States showed that of several thousand articles on productivity and quality written before 1983, very few dealt with EI program measurement issues.[30] Obviously, few managers have seen the need for measuring EI program activities despite the millions of dollars being poured into them by hundreds of U.S. firms.

Because many activities of EI team programs are intangible and difficult to measure, EI program coordinators and facilitators have generally avoided setting up an explicit measurement system. Despite the difficulties of measurement, there are many reasons that it should be performed, including the need to:

- Convince management to begin an EI program.
- Convince management to continue its support of the EI program.
- Convince workers that it's worthwhile to continue the EI program.
- Decide whether to implement a costly improvement project proposal from a team.
- Assess the need to modify an EI program to improve its effectiveness.
- Choose an EI program installation over some other competing program (based on cost/benefit results).
- Justify budgeting limited funds to the EI program.
- Choose a "winning" team to appear at a local, regional, or national EI convention from within an organization.
- Calculate financial rewards for team suggestions.
- Satisfy management expectations for measurement.[31]

Measurement Perspectives

There are at least three distinct perspectives from which the measurement process may be viewed: the human resources perspective, the quality perspective, and the cost improvement perspective.

[30]William M. Lindsay, *Measurement of Quality Circle Effectiveness: A Survey and Critique,* unpublished M.S. thesis, University of Cincinnati, College of Engineering, May 1986.

[31]Wayne S. Rieker and Shaun J. Sullivan, "Can the Effectiveness of QC Circles Be Measured?" *The Quality Circles Journal* (now *The Journal for Quality and Participation*), Vol. IV, May 1981, pp. 29–31.

Human Resources Perspective. The difficulties of measuring costs or benefits of personnel or human resources programs, a label under which EI programs are often placed, are well known. The difficulty arises, not from the fact that it is impossible to measure costs and benefits of personnel programs, but because the measurement process has not been made operational. EI programs are frequently labeled as programs that are "impossible" to measure.

Quantitative measures generally have not been applied in most human resources departments because of such reasons as the following:[32]

- Personnel people don't know *how* to measure their activity.

- Top management has bought the myth that personnel cannot be quantitatively evaluated.

- Some personnel managers do not *want* to be evaluated.

- A few brave souls would like to apply some measures to their function, but they haven't been able to do so.

A specific example of how quantified measures of effectiveness could be used is the measurement of training costs and benefits for EI programs. They could be measured by such data as pre-tests and post-tests of knowledge and skills, cost per person-hour of training for various courses, and cost reduction related to specific training. The objective would be to generate a meaningful set of measures that could be tracked over time. The result would be trend data that would tell objectively how well an organization is carrying out its responsibilities.

Quality Perspective. Adam, Hershauer, and Ruch developed a unique approach to the measurement of productivity and quality that involves calculation of a quality and productivity index.[33] The index is calculated in a regular, systematic fashion and is reported each period to managers and other employees in the organization in a timely fashion. The index uses multiple measures of outputs with specific, measurable definitions of acceptable units, scrap, and rework as well as system inputs of labor, materials, and capital cost per unit produced. This total quality/productivity system includes measurement of the following features:

- technology

- psychological or sociological dimensions of work

- economic performance variables.

Systematic use of the index allows managers to quantify and analyze the impact of simultaneous changes in quality and productivity. Managers can then assess both positive and negative results of changes in activity.

As noted in Chapter 3, productivity is usually defined as the ratio of units produced to units of input. Similarly, a quality ratio can be defined as the number of acceptable units produced divided by the total number of units produced, or the number of units scrapped or reworked divided by the total number of units produced.

---

[32]Jac Fitz-Enz, "Quantifying the Human Resources Function," *Personnel,* March/April 1983, pp. 41–52.

[33]Everett E. Adam, Jr., James E. Hershauer, and William A. Ruch, *Productivity and Quality: Measurement as a Basis of Improvement* 2nd. ed. (Columbia, MO: Research Center, College of Business and Public Administration, University of Missouri, 1986).

A new ratio, called the quality/productivity ratio (QPR), combines these separate quality and productivity measures into a single index as follows:

$$QPR = \frac{\text{number of acceptable units}}{\left(\begin{array}{c}\text{number}\\\text{processed}\end{array}\right)\left(\begin{array}{c}\text{cost to}\\\text{process}\end{array}\right) + \left(\begin{array}{c}\text{number}\\\text{rejected}\end{array}\right)\left(\begin{array}{c}\text{cost to}\\\text{correct rejects}\end{array}\right)}$$

This ratio differs from most productivity ratios because it measures the cost to correct rejected items instead of merely examining the ratio of units of output (some of which may have to be corrected—reworked) to units of output. An example of the effects of various changes in outputs are shown in Table 11.1.

If processing costs or quality costs decrease or if quality improves, the QPR increases. The example in Table 11.1 shows the following:

- Going from the base case to the higher volume case has no effect on the QPR, since processing costs and quality level remain constant.

- Going from the base case to the lower process cost case improves the QPR, since processing cost improved from $5/unit to $4/unit.

- Going from the base case to the lower correction cost case also improves the QPR, since quality cost for correction has improved from $10/unit to $7/unit.

- Going from the base case to the higher quality level case also improves the QPR, since the quality level has improved from three rejects to one reject for each 60 units produced.

This approach can be applied equally well to service operations. Consider the case of an airline baggage handling facility. Suppose it costs $2 to process a bag and $15 to trace a lost bag. The airline has recently experienced 10 losses per 1,000 bags. The QPR calculation is

$$QPR = \frac{990}{(1000 \times \$2) + (10 \times \$15)} = 990/2150$$
$$= 0.460$$

If new training is introduced and the baggage loss is cut in half, the impact would immediately show up, with a new QPR = 995/2075 = 0.48, a 4.3% increase. If a new method for processing bags was developed to reduce the cost of processing bags by

TABLE 11.1 Example of Quality–Productivity Index Calculation

Case	Number			No. Processed × $ Cost	No. Rejected × Correction $ Cost	Total Cost	QPR
	Good	Rejected	Total				
Base	19	1	20	20($5) = $100	1($10) = $10	$110	0.173
Higher volume	57	3	60	60($5) = $300	3($10) = $30	$330	0.173
Lower process cost	57	3	60	60($4) = $240	3($10) = $30	$270	0.211
Lower correction cost	57	3	60	60($5) = $300	3($7) = $21	$321	0.178
Higher quality level	59	1	60	60($5) = $300	1($10) = $10	$310	0.190

$0.0875/bag, the new ratio would also be a QPR = 990/2062.5 = 0.48. This shows the interdependence of quality level, productivity level, and cost. Thus, managers must be persuaded to strive to improve quality by simultaneously reducing reject rates, improve productivity by changing methods and procedures, and reduce processing and rework costs.

Quality and productivity must be understood as stemming from the same performance measure. Adam and the others stated, "There is no economic value in increased output levels if the increase is offset by lower quality. Any study of productivity should measure output as the number of usable, salable, acceptable goods or services produced."[34]

Quality Cost Perspective. Classical quality control theorists have consistently taken the approach that quality can be improved by detailed cost analysis and improvement efforts. We argued this viewpoint in Chapter 3. Quality cost data are useful for (1) measuring overall quality activities, (2) identifying high manufacturing loss areas, (3) programming available quality control personnel for corrective action, and (4) budgeting quality expenditures to balance prevention, appraisal, and failure costs.

If EI program costs are viewed as a major component of total quality costs, they fall into the category of prevention costs. The problem with the classical approach to quality control cost measurement is that it does not capture the full range of costs or benefits of EI programs, nor does it deal with the measurement issues that are inherent in the program. Some of these issues are as follows:

■ Classification of costs. Is EI activity considered to be a quality-productivity improvement program or a quality of worklife-human resources program?

■ To what extent can/should increases in productivity and/or quality indexes be attributed to EI program activities?

■ How should program variables, such as program growth and employees trained, be measured and reported?

■ How should nonfinancial results be measured and classified?

■ Should quality/productivity improvements be tied to the reward system for employees?

Clearly, measurement of EI program effectiveness must go beyond classical quality cost measurement approaches to meet the needs of managers involved in these programs.

An example of a measurement system that incorporates several of these principles is the one developed by the Michaud Division of Martin Marietta Aerospace in New Orleans.[35] The measurement process was divided into three parts, called program outcome, personal outcome, and organizational outcome measures. The program outcome measures were directed toward accounting for the growth and efficiency of the QC program. Some of the typical measures included the number of

[34]Ibid, p. 12.

[35]R. Tortorich et al., "Measuring Organizational Impact of Quality Circles," *The Quality Circles Journal* (now *The Journal for Quality and Participation*), Vol. IV, November 1981, pp. 24–33.

supervisors and circle members trained (totals and percentages of the work force), circles formed and average size, management presentations given, success rate for circles formed (active circles/total formed), direct cost savings, and percentages of problems falling into certain quality, cost, and safety categories. For personal outcomes, the firm measured attitudes of circle members and nonmembers toward such objects as the QC process, the job, individual self-esteem, coworkers, supervision, their own management and management in general, and the organization. Finally, for organizational outcomes, measures included production rates, defect rates, scrap rates, attrition rates, lost time, grievance rates, and accident rates. Three suggestions were offered by Martin-Marietta personnel for any measurement program:

1. Measure aggregated data, gathered by individuals. Report these data showing circle versus noncircle member results.

2. Measure trends over time periods.

3. Measure "before circle" versus "after circle" behavior for aggregates of individuals' results.

Measurement Practices in Japan and the United States

Two studies done at the end of the 1970s reported on some measurement practices and results of EI efforts in the Japanese automobile industry.[36] They should not be taken as typical of all measurement practices in Japanese industry, but they do show what is being done in one of the major industries. A number of the measures and measurement practices cited were drawn from the research that the authors had performed at Toyota.

One measure of the success of an EI program is the number of suggestions that employees make for productivity and quality improvements. Toyota, in particular, stressed the need to increase the number of suggestions per employee, with suggestion quotas being set for each work unit. The quota was usually based on the previous years' results, plus some small percentage increase. Fujita showed the following results from Japanese auto firms in 1980 and 1981:

Company	Suggestions	Suggestions per Employee
Toyota	1,412,500	31
Nissan	1,267,222	23
Toyo Kogyo	1,350,574	48
Honda	160,000	7

In contrast, General Motors was reported to have received 2.4 suggestions per employee in 1969 and 0.8 suggestion per employee in 1976. Both of these figures were reported before the installation of QWL teams, which several divisions of GM are now using.

---

[36]Robert E. Cole, *Work, Mobility and Participation* (Berkeley: University of California Press, 1979); Y. Fujita, "Participative Work Practices in the Japanese Auto Industry: Some Neglected Considerations," *The Quality Circles Journal* (now *The Journal for Quality and Participation*), Vol. VI, September 1983, pp. 15–19.

Cole describes other productivity/quality measures that were routinely gathered and reported to management at Toyota, including the following:

- value of suggestions per worker

- increasing productivity per employee

- decline in defects per car

- decline in man-hours per car

- decrease in accident rate per 1,000,000 man-hours

- decline in employee turnover.

In addition to the preceding tangible measures, a very important attitude survey was given nationally in Japan. The question was asked, "Do you believe that your job is worth doing?" Reported results for 1967 and 1973 included the following:

	1967			1973		
	Yes	Don't Know	No	Yes	Don't Know	No
National	32	20	46	N/A	N/A	N/A
Toyota	29	40	31	45	35	19

The dramatic improvement in the percentage of workers responding with "yes" was attributed to various team efforts, such as quality circle programs, which were introduced or changed during that six-year period at Toyota.

An extensive survey of 532 members of the IAQC (now AQP) provides insights into the nature of quality circle programs in the United States in the mid-1980s.[37] The survey responses covered a wide variety of manufacturing, service, government, and other organizations that had, or were planning to start, quality circle programs. The major purpose of the study was to analyze factors that contributed to effective versus less effective quality circle programs. Effectiveness factors were narrowed to three, including (1) size relationships, (2) savings-to-cost ratios, and (3) program factors. Effectiveness was defined primarily in terms of benefit-to-cost ratios. It was found that large organizations with the most effective programs were in nonmanufacturing environments. Large organizations had a higher proportion of staff specialists who worked with quality circles and tended to have the oldest quality circle programs in years of operation.

Concerning savings/cost ratios, average annual savings per program was estimated to be $438,730, while average annual costs per program were estimated to be $132,300. This gives a benefit/cost ratio of about 3.3 to 1. Average savings per circle member were estimated at $1,788, and average costs were $614. The benefit/cost ratio is estimated here at about 2.9 to 1. The two sets of figures do not yield the same ratio, because not all survey respondents responded to all four questions on costs and savings.

---

[37]William M. Lindsay, "Quality Circle Effectiveness," pp. 72, 117–120.

Concerning program factors, it was found that the maturity of the program was directly related to the program's financial success—the older the program, the higher the per-member savings. Interestingly, 75% of the programs in the highest success category had per-circle-member costs of less than $400 and a 6:1 or higher benefit/cost ratio. Both the Japanese and American studies of quality circle programs have some interesting implications for management, as discussed in the following section.

Implications for Management

From this discussion of EI measurement research, management should consider three areas: (1) the measurement process, (2) analysis and reporting of results, and (3) use of results in determining rewards for performance.

Measurement Process. The studies described in the previous section indicate that measurement of EI results can be done without harming commitment to the program. The literature also seems to suggest that such measurement may be beneficial and, in some cases, vital to the continued support and success of such programs. Obviously, measurement is a topic that has been neglected but is likely to receive increasing attention, given the continuing pressures for quality and productivity improvement by management and the likelihood of increased pressures for tangible rewards for productivity improvement by workers.

Management should consider incorporating the following factors in development of its measurement process:

- Multiple measurements of EI team activities and results should be made.

- The system should measure consistently, but be lenient, not rigid.

- Measurement should be tied to objectives of the program.

- Trends and long-term results should be emphasized.

- Key results should be communicated to employees.

Analysis and Reporting of Results. Reporting of EI program results must be tied in to the needs of management for information. Current information systems, with modifications as necessary to tailor the results to EI needs, can frequently be used. Managers should avoid creating an entirely separate reporting system just for measuring EI team results. A sound reporting system should include the following:

- Results should be regularly reported, perhaps monthly or quarterly, with a summary year-end report.

- Graphical reporting techniques should be used where possible.

- Detailed reports should go to lower level managers, showing results at their level. Summary reports should go to higher management levels.

- Specific action should be taken, based on reported results. Such action might include retraining in basic techniques, training in advanced techniques, contests, consideration of different types of rewards, or financial recognition of excellent EI projects.

Relation of Measurement to Rewards. One of the most controversial aspects of the employee involvement/participative management movement is the issue of rewards. Currently, most EI programs in the United States have operated on the assumption that EI activities and results provide sufficient intrinsic rewards to team members and that financial incentives are either unnecessary or actually a detriment to program success. Some writers have been very vocal in their disagreement with this conventional wisdom.[38] They have stated that the long-term success of EI programs depends on giving the circle members a share in the savings that they have generated.

One broad-based work improvement approach that has successfully tied together group problem solving, productivity improvement, and rewards has been a form of gainsharing known as the Scanlon plan. It has been adopted by a number of firms since it was developed in 1938 by Joseph Scanlon. It features (1) joint labor/management committees to discuss labor-saving improvements, (2) group rewards for adopted suggestions, and (3) employees sharing in reduced costs, not in increased profits.[39] One major disadvantage of the gainsharing formula used to calculate Scanlon payments is that it uses an economic definition for productivity (outputs divided by inputs). This means that workers will be rewarded or penalized in their profit-sharing earnings based partially on factors in the environment, such as the upward and downward movement of product prices, material costs, and product mix. There is evidence, however, that 80% of the installations of the Scanlon plan have been effective in improving labor efficiency.[40]

Another group incentive plan that appears to hold some promise of being successfully used in conjunction with EI programs is the Improshare® ("improved productivity through sharing") system developed and marketed since 1974 by Mitchell Fein, an industrial engineering consultant in New Jersey. Unlike the Scanlon plan, this plan is based on gains from physical process productivity improvement (ratio of actual to standard labor hours used to produce products), not on an economic definition of productivity. Thus, Improshare's calculation of gains to be shared between workers and the company is unaffected by factors in the business environment that are beyond the workers' control. A review of some 100 installations of Improshare indicated a median productivity improvement of about 20% and a success rate of 90% of all installations.[41]

Although a clear, unequivocable policy recommendation cannot be made on the applicability of incentive systems to EI programs, the following three points should be considered:

1. Historical precedence exists for giving workers a share in increased productivity and cost reduction that goes all the way back to Henry Gantt's (a contemporary of Frederick W. Taylor's in the early 1900s) "task and bonus" incentive plan.

---

[38]Robert E. Cole, "Rationale for Financial Incentives for Quality Circle Members," *The Quality Circles Journal,* Vol. IV, February 1981, p. 8; Robert I. Patchen, "Circles and Suggestion Plans" *The Quality Circles Journal* (now *The Journal for Quality and Participation*), Vol. IV, February 1981, pp. 9–10.

[39]Leslie W. Rue and Lloyd L. Byars, *Management Theory,* p. 46.

[40]Edward E. Lawler and Gerald E. Ledford, "Productivity and the Quality of Worklife," *National Productivity Review,* Vol. 1, Winter 1981–82, p. 30.

[41]Office of Economic Research, New York Stock Exchange, *People and Productivity: A Challenge to Corporate America,* (New York: New York Stock Exchange, 1982), p. 33.

2. Some research evidence suggests that financial rewards that are tied to and result from meeting clear objectives are effective in motivating workers to increase output.

3. Many of the developers and early supporters of EI programs insisted that such programs be seen as representing a change in management style rather than "merely" as a program. However, the fact remains that from a budgetary perspective, they must and will be seen as programs that can be cut out or supported, depending on results.

The conclusion that can be reached is that management must face the issue of appropriate rewards as a motivating factor in its EI program efforts. Measurement can and will play a significant part in reaching an appropriate conclusion in each organization.

Employee Involvement at Ford Motor Company[42]

One organization that was an early user of the term employee involvement (EI) for its participative team approach to problem solving was Ford Motor Company. In 1980, the auto and truck transmission plant at Sharonville, Ohio, had about 2,500 hourly workers and 435 salaried employees. With a backlog of 500 labor grievances and the worst quality index of any of Ford's plants, Sharonville was a prime candidate for a permanent plant shutdown. Late in the previous year during collective bargaining negotiations, the United Auto Workers (UAW) and Ford's management had signed a letter of agreement to cooperate in a sustained effort to increase the involvement of workers in making decisions on matters affecting their work. With the establishment of a National Joint Committee on Employee Involvement, cochaired by the UAW vice president and the vice president of labor relations at Ford, the stage was set for some dramatic changes to take place in such locations as the Sharonville plant.

Although no formal EI activities were launched at Sharonville until the fall of 1980, a number of informal communication and orientation activities were started. Supervisors began to extend weekly safety meetings to include problem-solving items. In addition, training in problem solving and team management was begun for first-line supervisors, and sessions were conducted by top management and union leaders on the competitive challenges brought on by the Japanese in the auto industry.

At the same time that these orientation activities were being started, two significant organizational changes were taking place that would impact the development of EI at Sharonville. They were the arrival of a new plant manager and the decentralization of staff activities into production areas. The new

[42]Adapted from Robert H. Guest, "The Sharonville Story: Worker Involvement at a Ford Motor Company Plant," in Robert Zarger and Michael P. Rosow, eds., *The Innovative Organization: Productivity Programs in Action* (Elmsford, NY: Permagon Press, 1982), and Michael J. Weiss, "Making Quality Work," *American Way,* November 12, 1985, p. 122. Reprinted by permission of *American Way,* inflight magazine of American Airlines. Copyright © 1985 by American Airlines.

plant manager had worked at Sharonville before and was known to be a skilled, tough, fair, and effective administrator. The decentralization of staff activities such as quality control, engineering, and other technical areas brought experts down to the shop floor and made their expertise more accessible to EI groups.

In September 1980, the division approved the selection of management consultants who were to guide the start-up of the EI program. After initial meetings with the top management team and union representatives, steps were taken to identify two departments in which pilot EI teams could be formed. Following the pattern set at headquarters, the plant decided to appoint two full-time facilitators, one from management and one from the union. In October, a plant EI coordinating committee consisting of the chairman of the union bargaining committee, three other union representatives, the manager of quality control, the manager of engineering and facilities, a supervisor in labor relations, and the night-shift manufacturing manager was formed. The last manager and the chairman of the union bargaining committee agreed to serve as cochairmen of the coordinating committee.

Despite these organizing efforts and attempts by both labor and management to set up a workable plan, a number of problems had to be overcome. The initial orientation had affected only a few first-line supervisors, the union had a skeptical wait-and-see attitude, and the plant was under enormous pressure to reduce costs and implement programs for quality improvement before the end of the year. The plant was still trying to adjust to massive layoffs that had occurred over the past year. The management facilitator responsibility was only a temporary appointment for the night-shift manufacturing manager, who was also the cochairman of the coordinating committee, as mentioned above. To add to his burden, he had no secretary who could assist him in coping with the added paperwork necessitated by the EI start-up.

Meanwhile, two problem-solving groups were formed. Each of the two groups had seven hourly members, an inspector, a supervisor, and a process

(continued)

engineer. Union representatives from the coordinating committee also sat in at each group meeting. After initial presentations on EI by the consultant and the coordinator, the group set its ground rules, elected a leader, brainstormed problems, and began to meet regularly for an hour each week on company time to search for solutions. There were some early successes: One of the groups solved more than 10 problems that resulted in substantial savings in scrap and downtime. Plant quality performance, measured by dealer warranty claims, was also improving. But difficulties in implementing recommendations developed as the groups found that several of the problems were related to maintenance hangups, and the Maintenance Department was short-handed, due to the recent layoffs.

One other significant event at the end of 1980 was the establishment of a committee to sponsor involvement activities for salaried workers. These workers chose to call their problem-solving groups "quality circles." Within a year, there were eight groups working on problems in nearly every administrative department.

With heavy support from the plant manager, visits from headquarters labor and management representatives, and encouragement from the consultants, the program gained momentum. In February 1981, a young, enthusiastic cost manager was chosen as the permanent management co-coordinator. In March, development of a master plan for expansion of the program throughout the plant was begun. In May, union elections were held with overwhelming support for the existing leaders. The chairman of the bargaining committee, who was also the coordinating committee cochairman, ran and was elected with no opposition. In the same month, he stated in an open meeting of top union and management representatives from headquarters that attitudes on the shop floor "had improved 90 percent." In July, an hourly co-coordinator was selected to fill the permanent facilitator position from the union side of the organization. By the end of the year, an additional 450 workers had to be laid off due to sluggish demand, but enthusiasm for the EI program continued to be strong. By May 1982, the program had grown to 43 groups covering two-thirds of the production departments. A new organization, decentralized to the level of area "minicoordinators," and self-directing coordinating committees had to be established to provide for orientation, training, and guidance of new groups.

By spring of 1982, overall plant quality was at its highest level in several years. There was a noticeable improvement in supervisor-to-worker communications. One group proved to engineers' satisfaction that two small hydraulic cylinders could be replaced by a larger worn-out cylinder on a machine, which resulted in a savings of more than $700 per week. A group of salaried nonmanagement personnel contacted computer vendors and did an extensive analysis of word-processing hardware before making their recommendation, which was adopted by management. In the zone where all six manufacturing departments had problem-solving groups in operation, there was a 22% increase in direct labor efficiency. The cost in lost time for EI team meetings was only 2.5%. By 1985, management reported that product quality had improved by 60%, grievances were down 90%, and the plant would almost certainly remain open for many years.

At the corporate level, Ford now has more than 86 EI programs in 15 states. Company officials estimate that between 1980 and 1983, the quality of Ford cars improved by 59% and the quality of Ford trucks increased by 47%. In 1987, the company's operating profits exceeded those of General Motors for the first time since the 1920s.

Key Issues for Discussion

1. What factors spurred the development of EI at the Ford Sharonville plant?

2. What factors do you believe were most responsible for the success of the EI program at Ford?

Total Employee Involvement at Burroughs Wellcome Co.[43]

One of the keystones of success in TQM is ongoing employee involvement and genuine commitment to participative problem solving and decision making at every level. Burroughs Wellcome Co., a pharmaceutical firm, has achieved a high level of employee involvement over an extended period of time.

Burroughs Wellcome Co. (B. W. Co.) is a research-oriented U.S. pharmaceutical firm that is owned by the British firm, Wellcome, plc, whose stock, in turn, is 75% owned by The Wellcome Trust, a charitable organization in Britain that funds medical libraries and research. The company's administrative and research headquarters are in Research Triangle Park, North Carolina (abbreviated as RTP). Their major manufacturing facility is at Greenville, North Carolina.

Among hundreds of prescription and over-the-counter products that it produces, two of its best-known products are the over-the-counter antihistamine/decongestants, Actifed and Sudafed. A well-known, but highly controversial product, for which the company obtained generally positive reviews in a recent *Fortune* magazine article is AZT, the first drug approved for use on AIDS victims.[44]

B. W. Co. began their development of quality circles as an initial step in involving their employees in problem solving by starting six pilot circles at their manufacturing site in Greenville in 1981.

After going through the typical start-up process similar to that shown in Figure 11.2, the six pilot teams were put to work identifying, analyzing, and solving problems in their own work areas. Initial projects were slow in completion; the first team presentation was made to management approximately seven months after volunteers were recruited. However, management persevered in their efforts to establish the program. Within a year or so, the program was showing projected savings-to-expenditure ratios of between 1.28 and 2.27 to 1. By the end of the fifth year of the program, projected project savings were exceeding $1 million annually.

By late 1986, the program had grown to 63 circles, with 17 of those at the headquarters in RTP. In recent years, the process has evolved and fully matured to the point where most of the teams are self-managed and many are cross-functional (working across organizational boundaries with team membership including people from several different departments, such as accounting, purchasing, and production). Most projects focus on "strategic areas of interest" to the firm.

The evolution of the process did not take place easily. Manning and Johnson[45] identified four stages that characterized the development of EI at B. W. Co. These were:

- resolving critical issues
- employee buy-in
- employee ownership
- employee self-direction.

Critical issues began to develop by the end of the first year of quality circle existence. These included leader and facilitator appointments and length of service, the question of management support, and documentation of circle activities.

Leader and facilitator length of service became an issue when circle leaders, who were first-line supervisors nominated by their superiors for the pilot circles, began to joke and later complain about being "volunteered for life" for their EI jobs. This issue was overcome by providing for an assistant leader who was a line employee. After the group had made three project presentations to management, the assistant leader was eligible to be nominated as a group leader, if confirmed by the steering committee that oversees all aspects of the EI program. Facilitators were nominated by the EI coordinator or area managers, usually from the ranks of successful group leaders.

[43]Appreciation is expressed to Mitch Manning, Section Head of EI Administration at Burroughs Wellcome Co. for providing numerous papers, materials, and editorial suggestions on the EI program at B.W. Co.

[44]Brian O'Reilly, "The Inside Story of the AIDS Drug," *Fortune,* November 5, 1990, pp. G112–129.

[45]Mitchell W. Manning and G. Wesley Johnson, Jr. "Evolution in Involvement," undated working paper.

(continued)

Management support became an issue during the second year. Managers in various areas of the plant reportedly were not supporting the groups in their areas. After investigation, it was found that the reason for nonsupport was a lack of training, since they had been appointed or transferred to their jobs after the EI process was under way. The solution to the problem involved regular training of new managers and a procedures manual to explain how the process worked and what their responsibilities were during various stages of group progress.

The third issue was documentation and administration of the progress of EI as more groups were added and projects mushroomed. Although many report forms were tried during the first couple of years, five reports are still consistently being used: (1) activity reports (meeting minutes), (2) attendance reports, (3) monthly reports, (4) annual reports, and (5) project summary reports (completed projects). Amazingly detailed, accurate records of every project under way and aggregate reports of all corporate EI activity are compiled on personal computers and stored within the coordinator's office by the coordinator and his one assistant, with some clerical assistance.

After the pilot groups had completed their initial projects, they were surveyed and asked about their feelings toward circles. They said that they had enjoyed the projects, felt good about their results and the opportunities for growth and development, and that they wanted to disband! However, by this time, many critical issues had been worked through, more circles were being formed, and management kept searching for solutions to make participation a permanent part of the way that the company does business. Soon, because of continued success, first-line supervisors began to ask to have awareness sessions presented in their areas, key staff people asked to become facilitators, and employees requested permission to develop the agenda for the annual Quality Circles Conference, a one-day company-wide meeting. The "buy-in" stage was under way.

From here it was only a short step to the employee ownership stage. Three employee advisory committees that reported to the steering committee were formed: publicity, training, and policies and procedures. The committees took over EI publicity inside and outside the company, development and implementation of training on a wide variety of topics, and keeping handbooks and procedures up to date.

The EI process continues to evolve as employees come up with ways to improve the work environment, quality, productivity, and the EI process itself. They are essentially in control of the process, with management providing resources, guidance, and rewards for accomplishments.

The process of continuous improvement of employee involvement requires that the coordinator and responsible managers address the need to *communicate, motivate, educate,* and *administrate.* At B. W. Co., this is accomplished by:

- administrative efficiency
- extensive, effective communications
- support of managers/employees
- integration with corporate values, goals, and objectives
- establishing involvement as the highest priority management function.

The directive that has come from top management, with support at every level, is:[46]

> Involvement will be made a part of the way that [this] company does business. Involvement must be approached the same way as any other business plan. It requires vision, a mission, goals and objectives, and strategies.

It seems apparent that a major change in the corporate culture has taken place at B. W. Co. Thus, it is not a process that is likely to be reversed in the future.

Key Issues for Discussion

1. Trace the development of EI at B. W. Co. from the program establishment to the current cross-functional EI teams working on "strategic areas of interest." Comment on how those steps conform to the "process model" for establishing EI programs that is shown in Figure 11.2.

2. What can you surmise about why the program at B. W. Co. has managed to stay in existence over a 10-year time frame when many other "quality circle" programs were abandoned after a year or two of operation? Do these results seem to be consistent with the findings on participation at the beginning of the chapter? Why or why not?

[46]Mitch Manning, "Map Your Processes," *Journal for Quality and Participation,* June 1989, pp. 46–53.

Summary of Key Points

■ Participative problem-solving approaches help to break barriers between labor and management; foster trust and cooperation; develop individual skills, creativity, and morale; and improve quality and productivity.

■ The historical roots of employee involvement (EI) grew out of classical management and industrial engineering, statistical quality control, and behavioral management concepts, all developed in the United States.

■ Japanese management and scientists made a major contribution by developing the Quality Control Circle concept to allow employees to participate in the process of systematically analyzing and solving problems in their own workplaces.

■ In the early 1980s many companies tried to import quality circles to the United States in the hope of getting the same positive benefits that the Japanese had obtained, but a number of unanticipated problems were often encountered, limiting the effectiveness of the movement.

■ Self-managed teams that take on many of the roles formerly reserved for management are having a positive impact on quality, continuous improvement, and effectiveness in more advanced organizations.

■ Effective organizations have frequently found ways to resolve the earlier problems and have gone on to use a variety of EI team approaches to spread the concept of participation in problem solving to every area.

■ Evaluation of EI programs and processes varies widely. To be effective, it should include attention to (1) the measurement process itself, (2) analysis and reporting of results (both quantitative and qualitative), and (3) use of the results for determining rewards for performance.

Questions for Review and Discussion

1. Define employee involvement (EI) teams. Explain how such teams, often made up of people with limited technical expertise, can have any noticeable impact on product quality.

2. Discuss some of the advantages of EI over traditional management practices.

3. Explain the key results and significance of the many research studies on participation, job performance, and satisfaction.

4. Briefly summarize the "roots" of EI from its U.S. and Japanese origins.

5. Define a quality circle. List the principal characteristics that differentiate quality circles from other group processes.

6. Summarize the history of quality control circles in Japan and quality circles in the United States.

7. What types of employee involvement and participative programs have evolved from the quality circle movement?

8. What is a self-managed team? How does it differ from a quality circle?

9. How should an EI program be started in an organization? Are there certain characteristics that might increase the likelihood of success in some organizations and other characteristics that would weigh against success? Discuss.

10. Discuss the criticisms of quality circle programs. Could many failures of quality circles have been prevented had organizations fully adopted the Deming philosophy? Why or why not?

11. Explain how self-managed teams can be developed. Does it matter whether or not an organization has had previous EI programs such as quality circles?

12. Find a company or plant in which self-managed teams are used. Interview a manager or worker to determine how the team's program was started and grew.

13. Why should measurement of EI effectiveness be important?

14. What are the difficulties in measuring effectiveness of EI programs?

15. Manufacturing and service firms measure work content and labor effectiveness using work standards derived from time and motion studies. Why can't similar concepts be used in the measurement of outputs of EI teams?

16. Discuss the three perspectives on EI measurement: (1) the human resources perspective, (2) the quality perspective, and (3) the cost improvement perspective.

17. Discuss Adam et al.'s approach to quality/productivity measurement. Explain what the QPR ratio tells managers and how it can be used.

18. Japanese managers are reputed to be more people oriented toward their workers than are American managers, yet Cole pointed out that suggestion quotas and other "hard" measures of success are regularly set and measured for quality control circles in Japan. Speculate on why such measurement approaches are successfully used in Japan but are frequently avoided as demotivating in EI programs in the United States.

19. Are intrinsic rewards (satisfaction with a job well done) likely to be sufficient to keep employees interested in EI teamwork, or will there be a need to move toward extrinsic (cash or other tangible rewards) as the EI team movement matures? Why or why not?

20. Do an in-depth analysis of incentive plans such as the Scanlon and Improshare plans. What are their strengths and weaknesses? Which one or ones seem to be best suited to aiding in the improvement of quality, not just productivity?

Case Problem

Conduct a telephone or personal interview of an EI coordinator at an organization that has had teams successfully in operation for three or more years. To what do they attribute their success? Compare their experiences to those at B. W. Co. in the Quality in Practice case to determine how they are similar or different. Report your findings to your class in the form of a case presentation or written report.

Bibliography

Garvin, David A. "Quality Problems, Policies, and Attitudes in the United States and Japan: An Exploratory Study," *Academy of Management Journal,* Vol. 29, 1986, pp. 653–673.

Griffin, Ricky W. "Consequences of Quality Circles in an Industrial Setting: A Longitudinal Assessment," *Academy of Management Journal,* Vol. 31, 1988, pp. 338–358.

Gryna, Frank M., Jr. *Quality Circles: A Team Approach to Problem Solving.* New York: AMACOM, 1981.

Lawler, E. E., and S. A. Mohrman. "Quality Circles: After the Honeymoon," *Organizational Dynamics,* Vol. 15, 1987, pp. 42–54.

Mohr, William L. and Harriet Mohr. *Quality Circles: Changing Images of People at Work.* Reading, MA: Addison-Wesley, 1983.

Munchus, G. III. "Employer-Employee Based Quality Circles in Japan: Human Resources Policy Implications for American Firms," *Academy of Management Review,* Vol. 8, 1983, pp. 255–261.

Ouchi, William G. *Theory Z.* New York: Avon Books, 1981.

Pascale, Richard Tanney, and Anthony G. Athos. *The Art of Japanese Management.* New York: Warner Books Inc., 1981.

QC Sources: Selected Writings on Quality Circles. Cincinnati, OH: Association for Quality and Participation (formerly IAQC), 1983.

PART THREE

The Technical System
Quality Measurement

MEASUREMENT IS ONE of the most critical functions in quality assurance. Without a means of measuring quality, it is impossible to control or improve it. Deming taught the Japanese to measure variation using basic statistical principles. Indeed, understanding and using elementary statistical tools is the foundation of his philosophy. The application of statistics to quality has become an area of much interest and activity within the statistical community. While the principal focus of this book is not on statistics, a basic knowledge of statistics is necessary to understand other important issues in the technical system such as product and process design and reliability. Chapter 12 provides a concise review of basic statistical concepts necessary to follow subsequent discussions. We emphasize that this is a *review;* it is not meant to substitute for a solid course in statistical methods. Most readers should be familiar with most of the material in this chapter. However, we do introduce a number of useful topics that perhaps are not normally covered in elementary statistics courses. The reader is encouraged to review these and think about their use in quality. Chapter 13 focuses on inspection and measurement, and discusses the role of inspection, methods of inspection, and statistical issues in measurement. We also introduce the important concept of *process capability,* which provides a measure of how well a process can conform to design requirements.

CHAPTER 12

Statistical Methods in Quality Assurance

The term *statistics* is used frequently in everyday conversation, yet many people would find it difficult to provide a working definition. Statistics is a science concerned with "the collection, organization, analysis, interpretation, and presentation of data."[1] Data usually come from some type of measurement process. The data may be dimensions of bolts being produced on a production line, order entry errors per day in an order entry department, or numbers of flight delays per week at an airport. Raw data such as the individual lengths of bolts does not provide information necessary for quality control or problem solving. Data must be organized, analyzed, and interpreted in a meaningful fashion. Statistics provides an efficient and effective way of obtaining meaningful information from data.

The importance of statistical concepts in quality assurance cannot be over-emphasized. Indeed, statistics is basic to the understanding and implementation of quality assurance. Frank H. Squires, himself a well-known expert in quality, has credited W. Edwards Deming with keeping statistics in the forefront on the worldwide quality improvement movement. Squires states:[2]

> The triumph of statistics is the triumph of Dr. Deming. When others have wavered or been lukewarm in their support for statistics, Dr. Deming has stood firm in his conviction that statistics is the heart of quality control. Indeed, he goes further and makes statistical principles central to the whole production process.

All managers, supervisors, and production and clerical workers must have some knowledge of the technical aspects of statistical quality control. Successful companies around the world have shown that if a total quality control philosophy is to be implemented, it is essential that employees at every level be trained in basic statistical problem-solving techniques.

This and later chapters provide some detailed examples of the many uses of statistics in controlling and improving quality. For example, data on the number of customer complaints and returns in a department store may be gathered and described using statistical methods as a basis for future decisions. Statistical methods

---

[1] J. M. Juran and Frank M. Gryna, Jr., *Quality Planning and Analysis,* 2d ed. (New York: McGraw-Hill, 1980), p. 35.

[2] Frank H. Squires, "The Triumph of Statistics," *Quality,* February 1982, p. 75.

may be used to determine the capability of machines to produce parts consistently so that a critical dimension will fall within a specified range, thus ensuring that the parts may be properly assembled with mating parts produced elsewhere. In food processing, statistical methods are used to ensure that filling machines do not put too much or too little product in the containers passing along the line.

The purpose of statistics in quality assurance is to assist managers, supervisors, and operators in controlling and improving the quality of manufacturing or service products. Readers of this text are assumed to have prior knowledge of elementary statistics. Thus, this chapter is designed as a review and refresher of the statistical concepts needed for the remainder of this text. In addition, we present a variety of examples that illustrate the application of statistics in quality assurance.

DESCRIPTIVE, INFERENTIAL, AND PREDICTIVE STATISTICS

The first major component of statistical methodology is the efficient collection, organization, and description of data, commonly referred to as **descriptive statistics.** Frequency distributions and histograms are used to organize and present data. Measures of central tendency (means, medians, proportions) and measures of dispersion (range, standard deviation, variance) provide important quantitative information about the nature of the data. For example, an airline might investigate the problem of lost baggage and determine that the major causes of the problem are lost or damaged identification tags, incorrect tags on the bags, and misrouting to baggage claim areas. An examination of frequencies for each of these categories might show that lost or damaged tags accounted for 50% of the problems, incorrect tags for 30%, and misrouting for only 20%. The airline might also compute the average number of baggage errors per 1,000 passengers each month. Such information is useful in identifying quality problems and as a means of measuring improvement.

The second component of statistical problem solving is **statistical inference.** Statistical inference is the process of drawing conclusions about unknown characteristics of a population from which data were taken. Techniques used in this phase include hypothesis testing and experimental design. For example, a chemical manufacturer might be interested in determining the effect of temperature on the yield of a new manufacturing process. In a controlled experiment, the manufacturer might test the hypothesis that the temperature has an effect on the yield against the alternative hypothesis that temperature has no effect. If the temperature is, in fact, a critical variable, steps will be required to maintain the temperature at the proper level and to draw inferences as to whether the process remains under control, based on samples taken from it. Statistical inference and hypothesis testing are also the basis for control charting (developed in Chapter 16).

The third component in statistical methodology is **predictive statistics,** the purpose of which is to develop predictions of future values based on historical data. Correlation and regression analysis are two useful techniques. Frequently, these techniques can also help to understand the characteristics of a process as well as predict future results. For example, in quality assurance, correlation is frequently used in test instrument calibration studies. In such studies, an instrument is used to measure a standard test sample that has known characteristics. The actual results are compared to standard results, and adjustments are made to compensate for errors.

Figure 12.1 summarizes statistical processes and methods commonly used in quality assurance. The remainder of the chapter discusses the details of the methods used to complete these processes.

DATA COLLECTION, ORGANIZATION, AND PRESENTATION

The application of statistical quality control invariably requires that data be collected from a manufacturing or service process. Collection of the correct data in the right amount at the right time is crucial to managers and workers who must make decisions every day.

Populations and Samples

The main objective of sampling is to choose a sample that is representative of the population in which we are interested. A **population** is a complete set or collection of objects of interest; a **sample** is a subset of objects taken from the population. As

FIGURE 12.1   **Statistical Methodology in Quality Assurance**

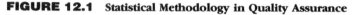

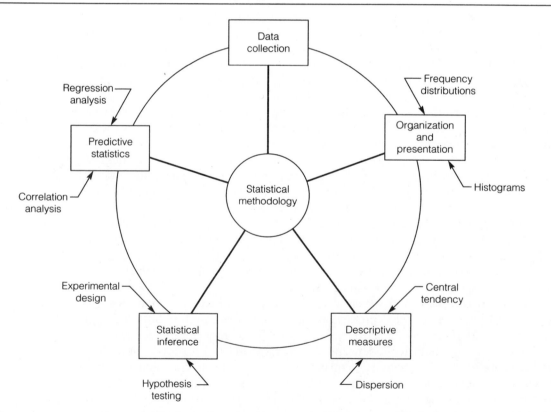

noted in Chapter 7, sampling is an important tool in quality assurance. It is used to obtain estimates of population parameters such as means, proportions, and standard deviations, which in turn are used to make decisions about the state of quality. Statistical process control (Chapters 16 and 17) is based on sampling during a production process. Other aspects of sampling will be discussed in Chapter 18.

Frequency Distributions and Histograms

Frequency distributions and histograms are simple methods for organizing and presenting data in a useful form and were briefly discussed in Chapter 9. A frequency distribution is a tabular summary of a set of data showing the frequency or number of observations of a particular value or within a specified group. It gives clues about the characteristics of the parent population from which the sample was taken. A histogram is a graphic representation of a frequency distribution. With a histogram, the shape of the distribution can be seen clearly and inferences can be made about the population. To illustrate the use of frequency distributions and histograms, consider the following example.

EXAMPLE 1 **A Drying Oven Temperature Study.** The data in Table 12.1 represent readings in degrees Celsius (C) taken from a drying oven in an enamel wire manufacturing process. The drying oven temperature is a critical variable that must be monitored to ensure that high-quality enamel coating is maintained.

A frequency distribution and histogram for these data are shown in Table 12.2 and Figure 12.2, respectively. The histogram shows that the temperature is centered around 45 to 50 degrees and that most of the observations lie between 37.5 and 57.5 degrees C. The largest frequency of values lies in class 5, ranging

TABLE 12.1 **Temperature of Drying Oven (Degrees C)**

56	46	48	50	42	43	49	48	56	50	52	47	48	56	41	37	47	47
45	44	52	55	52	44	50	45	44	65	48	48	32	40	52	52	51	59
63	59	47	38	50	49	40	54	46	51	48	54	49	50	50	56	50	52
37	61																

TABLE 12.2 **Frequency Distribution of Temperature Data**

Class	Boundaries	Mid-Point	Frequency Tally	Frequency
1	27.5–32.5	30	/	1
2	32.5–37.5	35	//	2
3	37.5–42.5	40	ЖНГ	5
4	42.5–47.5	45	ЖНГ ЖНГ //	12
5	47.5–52.5	50	ЖНГ ЖНГ ЖНГ ЖНГ ////	24
6	52.5–57.5	55	ЖНГ //	7
7	57.5–62.5	60	///	3
8	62.5–67.5	65	//	2
				N = 56

FIGURE 12.2 **Histogram of Temperature Data**

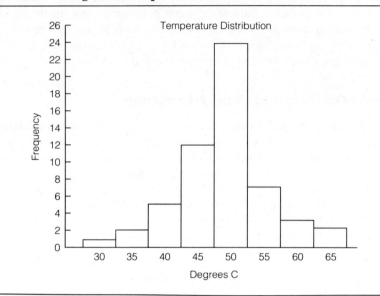

from 47.5 to 52.5 degrees. This information would aid a quality manager or technician in estimating the shape of the distribution of temperatures, where the distribution is centered, and how widely values are spread over the range of temperature readings. If there were specified limits within which the temperature had to be maintained for quality purposes, the plots could be used to estimate the ability of the process to operate within these limits. To obtain more accurate descriptions of the data, the analyst would have to compute specific numerical measures (discussed in the next section).

There are no hard-and-fast rules for the number of cells to use for a histogram. The number of cells should be large enough to display the general shape of the distribution, but not so large as to leave gaps in the histogram. Sturges's rule can be used to determine the approximate number of cells, k:

$$k = 1 + 3.322 \log_{10}n$$

Approximate guidelines are shown below.

Number of Observations, n	Number of Cells, k
0–9	4
10–24	5
25–49	6
50–89	7
90–189	8
>189	9 or 10

In Example 1, these guidelines suggest using seven cells. We used eight cells simply to allow midpoints to be whole numbers and increments of five.

DESCRIPTIVE STATISTICAL MEASURES

Although frequency distributions and histograms are effective tabular and visual aids for summarizing data, they do not give precise numerical information about the data that would be useful for further analysis. Many histograms that describe variation in production or service output in quality control applications have a rough bell-shaped pattern, as seen in Figure 12.2. The data typically are centered around some value and are spread out, or dispersed, over some range. **Measures of central tendency** describe the centering of the data. **Measures of dispersion** describe the spread of the data.

Measures of Central Tendency

The three most common measures of central tendency are the mean, the median, and the mode. The **mean** is the most commonly used measure of the center of a distribution and is simply the average value of the data. It is computed by adding the values of all the observations and dividing by the number of observations. The mean is usually denoted as $\bar{x}$ (x-bar). Mathematically, we write

$$\bar{x} = \frac{1}{n} \sum_{i=1}^{n} x_i$$

where x_i is the value of the ith observation and n is the number of observations. For the temperature data presented earlier, the sum of the observations is

$$\sum_{i=1}^{56} x_i = 2745$$

Therefore, the mean is

$$\bar{x} = \frac{2745}{56} = 49.02$$

The **median** is the value of the middle observation when the data are ordered from smallest to largest. This value is easily estimated from the frequency distribution. Since $n = 56$ (an even number of values), the middle two observations are the 28th and 29th. If we add the frequencies in Table 12.2, we find that these observations fall in class 5. We then use the midpoint of 50 as an estimate of the median. Although the mean is used as a measure of central tendency more often than the median, the median is not affected by very large or very small values in the data as much as the mean is. Hence, when data contain such outliers, the median usually provides a better measure of central tendency.

The final measure of central tendency often used is the mode. The **mode** is the value that occurs with the greatest frequency. For grouped data, we estimate the mode by using the midpoint of the class having the largest frequency. In Table 12.2, we can see that the class having the largest frequency is class 5, thus we estimate the mode as 50. In general, the mode is not as good a measure of central tendency as is the mean or the median. However, for large sets of data that are reasonably bell-shaped, the mode does provide a very quick estimate of the central value of the data.

By comparing the data from this sample with a standard of previous means, medians, or modes obtained from earlier samples, we can judge whether or not the dryer is operating in a normal fashion. If the usual operating temperature averages about 50, everything is fine. However, if the dryer should normally be expected to average 65 degrees C, there appears to be a problem.

Measures of Dispersion

Measures of dispersion describe the spread of the data. Three common measures of dispersion used in statistics are the range, the standard deviation, and the variance.

The **range,** commonly denoted as R, is simply the difference between the largest and smallest value in a set of data. In the example of the temperature data, we saw that the largest value was 65 and the smallest value was 32. Therefore, the range is

$$R = 65 - 32 = 33$$

The range is very simple to calculate and thus has found extensive use in quality control. However, since it uses only two pieces of data, it does not provide complete information about the set of data. The measure of dispersion that yields the most information about a distribution is the **standard deviation**—a measure of the distance of each observation from the mean. The formula for determining the sample standard deviation is

$$s = \sqrt{\frac{\sum_{i=1}^{n} (x_i - \bar{x})^2}{n - 1}}$$

Unlike the range, the sample standard deviation includes all observations in the sample, thus making it a more accurate measure of dispersion. In the preceding formula, the difference $(x_i - \bar{x})$ is called a **deviation about the mean.** The deviation about the mean is squared and averaged by dividing by $(n - 1)$, and the square root of the result is taken. Thus, the standard deviation provides a measure of the average deviation from the mean. If the data represented the entire population, we would divide by n instead of $(n - 1)$. The more the data are spread out, the larger the value of s will be.

Using a calculator, the standard deviation of the temperatures is computed as

$$s = \sqrt{\frac{\sum_{i=1}^{56} (x_i - \bar{x})^2}{56 - 1}} = \sqrt{\frac{2302.98}{55}} = 6.47$$

The standard deviation is a measure of the variability of the temperature of the oven. By itself, it is not a very useful number. It is only when it can be related to other values of the standard deviation that its use becomes apparent. For example, if a new drying oven with a temperature controller that could hold the variability to $s = 3.0$ could be purchased, its cost might be justified by avoiding production of scrap formerly caused by the amount of temperature variation in the present dryer. As shown in this and later chapters, the standard deviation is required for statistical inferences to be made about process conditions and capability in a wide variety of situations.

The **variance** is obtained by squaring the standard deviation and is denoted by s^2. Thus, the variance of the temperature data is $s^2 = (6.47)^2 = 41.86$. While the variance is an important statistical measure, the standard deviation is usually preferred in quality assurance applications.

Calculations Using Grouped Data

For a small number of values, it is easy to calculate the mean and standard deviation using a calculator. If there are several hundred values, a choice must be made whether to spend the time and effort to put the data into a computer or use a rough approximation method that is much easier to compute. The approximation method involves grouping the data prior to calculation of the mean and standard deviation. It is reasonably accurate when used with 50 or more observations.

We will illustrate this procedure with the temperature data grouped as shown in Table 12.2. The required calculations are shown in Table 12.3. We have added three additional columns: the "Scale x" column, the "fx" column, and the "fx^2" column. In the Scale x column, we chose an arbitrary origin from the data. This is usually selected as the class with the largest frequency (class 5). Each class with values below this zero class has a negative value and shows its relative distance in numbers of classes *below* the arbitrary origin. Similarly, classes 6, 7, and 8 are a distance of +1, +2, and +3 classes, respectively, *above* the mean. Values in the fx column are obtained by multiplying the frequency times the Scale x value for each class and summing the result. This yields $\Sigma fx = -13$. The fx^2 values are calculated by multiplying the Scale x value times its respective fx value for each class. The column total is obtained by summing the values in the column, yielding $\Sigma fx^2 = 103$.

The formulas we shall present for estimating the mean and standard deviation assume that the midpoint of each class is the representative value for that class and that the frequency specifies the number of observations having that representative value.

Definitions for the variables in the formulas for the mean and standard deviation are

m = midpoint of the class selected as arbitrary origin
i = class interval
Σfx = sum of frequencies in each class times Scale x
Σfx^2 = sum of frequencies in each class times Scale x^2
n = number of observations.

TABLE 12.3 Grouped Data Intermediate Values

Class	Midpoint	Frequency f	Scale x	fx	fx^2
1	30	1	−4	−4	16
2	35	2	−3	−6	18
3	40	5	−2	−10	20
4	45	12	−1	−12	12
5	50	24	0	0	0
6	55	7	1	7	7
7	60	3	2	6	12
8	65	2	3	6	18
		56		−13	103

The modified formulas are

$$\bar{x} = m + i\left(\frac{\Sigma fx}{n}\right)$$

and

$$s = i\sqrt{\frac{\Sigma fx^2}{n-1} - \left(\frac{\Sigma fx}{n-1}\right)^2}$$

For this problem, we find

$$\bar{x} = 50 + 5(-13/56) = 48.84$$

$$s = 5\sqrt{\frac{103}{55} - \left(\frac{-13}{55}\right)^2} = 6.74$$

Thus, it can be seen that these are reasonably accurate estimates of the values of these statistics that were calculated earlier using the complete set of data.

Interpreting Descriptive Statistics

Measures of central tendency, such as the mean, median, or mode, are easy to interpret but present an incomplete picture of a set of data. Thus, measures of dispersion such as the standard deviation, variance, or range are necessary. To illustrate how descriptive statistics can be used in quality assurance, let us consider an example comparing data from similar production processes.

EXAMPLE 2 Comparing Elevator Cable Breaking Strength. Suppose that two companies (Company A and Company B) manufacture elevator cable. An elevator contractor wishes to purchase cable from at least one of the firms and has specified that the breaking strength must average 30 thousand pounds per square inch (M psi). Company A has an estimated range of 30 M psi, while Company B has an estimated range of 10 M psi. One thousand cable samples of each company's product are tested for breaking strength. The results are shown in Table 12.4. We are interested in comparing these results to discover which manufacturer appears to be more reliable. First, we will compute the mean

TABLE 12.4 Breaking Strength of Cable Samples

Company A					Company B				
Strength		Scale			Strength		Scale		
M psi	Frequency	x	fx	fx^2	M psi	Frequency	x	fx	fx^2
15.0	50	−5	−250	1250	25.0	50	−2	−100	200
18.0	200	−4	−800	3200	27.5	200	−1	−200	200
30.0	500	0	0	0	30.0	500	0	0	0
42.0	200	4	800	3200	32.5	200	1	200	200
45.0	50	5	250	1250	35.0	50	2	100	200
	1000		0	8900		1000		0	800

and standard deviation for each product. Using the procedure for grouped data previously outlined, we have

$$\bar{x} = m + i\left(\frac{\Sigma fx}{n}\right)$$

and thus

$$\bar{x}_A = 30 + 3\left(\frac{0}{1000}\right) = 30$$

$$\bar{x}_B = 30 + 2.5\left(\frac{0}{1000}\right) = 30$$

Note that in the Company A data, the classes between the values of 18 and 30 and from 30 to 42 have been omitted. Since there are zero frequencies for each of these classes, they have no effect on the calculations. Note also that in both the Company A and Company B data, equal frequencies counterbalance each other at equal distances above and below the middle class, which contains the arbitrary origin. This explains why $\Sigma fx/n = 0$ for each set of data. Thus, the means have been shown to be equal. We next compute the standard deviations.

$$s = i\sqrt{\frac{\Sigma fx^2}{n-1} - \left(\frac{\Sigma fx}{n-1}\right)^2}$$

$$s_A = 3\sqrt{\frac{8900}{999} - \left(\frac{0}{999}\right)^2} = 8.95 \text{ M psi}$$

$$s_B = 2.5\sqrt{\frac{800}{999} - \left(\frac{0}{999}\right)^2} = 2.24 \text{ M psi}$$

We see that the dispersion of B is much less than that of A. We can sketch the distributions of both products as in Figure 12.3.

FIGURE 12.3 **Comparisons of Variation—Company A versus Company B**

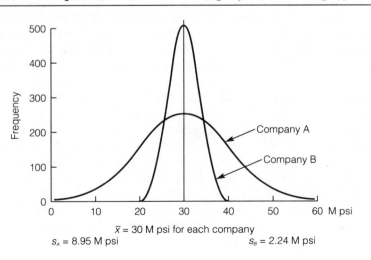

$\bar{x} = 30$ M psi for each company

$s_A = 8.95$ M psi $s_B = 2.24$ M psi

Obviously, Company B has tighter control over its manufacturing process than does Company A. Even though both companies average 30 M psi, the lower variability of the product produced by Company B means that its customers can expect to find a higher proportion of breaking strengths much closer to 30 M psi. If customers purchase cable from Company A, they can expect to find breaking strengths of less than 25 M psi as a fairly frequent occurrence. This decision can be both costly and dangerous if weak elevator cable from Company A is installed in a critical location.

PROBABILITY THEORY

Probability is important in quality control because it provides a mechanism for quantifying and analyzing uncertainties associated with future events. This section reviews a few basic concepts, including probability experiments, random variables, and probability distributions. These concepts are used in many applications in quality assurance.

A **probability experiment** is performed when a random process is observed and the results from the process are recorded. For example, we could perform an experiment of rolling a single die and recording the outcome (a value of 1, 2, 3, 4, 5, or 6) obtained from one roll. The values that represent all possible outcomes (one through six) are said to be mutually exclusive and collectively exhaustive. The term **mutually exclusive** means that only one value can be observed in any one roll. The term **collectively exhaustive** means that only this set of possible outcomes can occur. An event is a collection of sample outcomes. For example, we might roll a die 1,000 times to observe the number of times that each outcome occurs. One event might be: 161 ones, 172 twos, 153 threes, 149 fours, 167 fives, and 198 sixes.

Random Variables and Probability Distributions

The collectively exhaustive set of outcomes from an experiment makes up a **sample space.** A mathematical function that assigns numerical values to every possible outcome in a sample space is called a **random variable.** A random variable can be either **discrete** or **continuous,** depending on the specific numerical values it may assume. A discrete random variable can take on only finite values. An example would be the number of defects observed in a sample. A continuous random variable can take on any real value over a specified interval of real numbers. An example would be the diameters of bearings being manufactured in a factory. Of course, the actual observed values for the variable are limited by the precision of the measuring device. Hence, there would be only a finite number of actual observations. In theory, this would still be a continuous random variable. We next look at how random variables are used in the development of probability distributions.

A **probability distribution** represents a theoretical model of the relative frequency of a random variable. Relating probability distributions to the random variables that they represent allows us to classify the distributions as either discrete or continuous.

Discrete Probability Distributions. A **discrete probability distribution** is a table, graph, or equation that relates values of the discrete random variable to associated probabilities. Consider the roll of a single fair die. The values of possible outcomes, x, and the function describing the outcomes' probability of occurrence, $f(x)$, are uniformly distributed as follows:

x	f(x)
1	1/6
2	1/6
3	1/6
4	1/6
5	1/6
6	1/6

These data can also be represented as a graph, as shown in Figure 12.4. For a discrete probability distribution, two conditions must hold:

1. $f(x) \geq 0$ for all x

2. $\sum_{x} f(x) = 1$

This simply says that all probabilities must be greater than or equal to zero and that the sum of all values of the random variable x must equal one.

Continuous Probability Distributions. **Continuous probability distributions** are extremely important distributions in statistical quality control applications. A continuous random variable takes on all real values over some specified interval. Thus, we cannot calculate the probability of a specific value. Instead, we must talk about the probability that the random variable takes on some value within the interval. The function that describes the probability of ranges of values of a continuous

FIGURE 12.4 Probability Distribution for Rolls of One Die

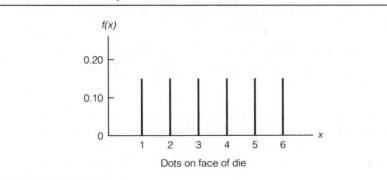

FIGURE 12.5 Probability Density Function for Applied Voltage

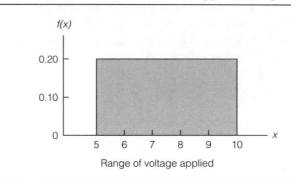

Range of voltage applied

random variable is called a **probability density function.** The probability that the random variable takes on a value within some interval between a and b corresponds to the area under the graph (or curve) of the probability density function between a and b. Applications of continuous probability distributions are discussed later in the chapter.

To illustrate the development of a continuous probability density function for use in estimating probabilities, let us assume that an electronics engineer is working on the quality specifications for a new microprocessor chip for which the incoming voltage is known to vary continuously over a range of between 5 and 10 volts. The engineer wishes to estimate the probabilities of various ranges of values of the incoming voltage to the chip. The probability distribution for this continuous random variable is a uniform distribution, as shown in Figure 12.5.

To find the area under a probability density function between two values of x, we must integrate the function over that interval. (If you have not studied calculus, you may skip any discussions of integrals relating to continuous probability distributions. They are not necessary to understand quality control applications in the following chapters.) For example, to find the probability of a value of the voltage falling between 5 and 7 volts, we would evaluate the following expression:

$$P(a \leq x \leq b) = \int_a^b f(x)dx = \int_5^7 0.20\,dx = 0.20x \Big|_5^7 = 0.20(7-5) = 0.40$$

Therefore, there is a 0.40 probability of the voltage falling between 5 and 7 volts. The probability density function can be plotted from values obtained from the previous function, as shown in Figure 12.6.

Expected Value. An extremely useful concept is that of the **expected value** of a random variable. Many statistical relationships and formulas depend on the use of this concept. The expected value of a random variable can be defined as its probability-weighted average value. Mathematically, this can be represented as follows:

FIGURE 12.6   **Cumulative Probability Distribution for Applied Voltage**

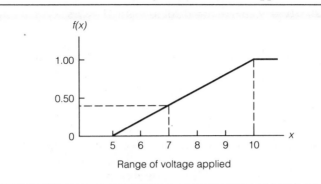

Range of voltage applied

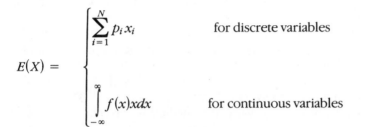

$$E(X) = \begin{cases} \sum_{i=1}^{N} p_i x_i & \text{for discrete variables} \\ \\ \int_{-\infty}^{\infty} f(x)x\,dx & \text{for continuous variables} \end{cases}$$

As an example of the expected value calculation for a discrete variable, let us extend the previous probability example using a single fair die. If a game of chance pays $0.50 for each dot that appears when the single die is rolled (i.e., $0.50 for a 1, $1.00 for a 2, $1.50 for a 3, $2.00 for a 4, $2.50 for a 5, and $3.00 for a 6), what will be the expected value of the amount the player will receive?

$$E(X) = 1/6 \ (\$0.50) + 1/6 \ (\$1.00) + 1/6 \ (\$1.50) + 1/6 \ (\$2.00)$$
$$+ 1/6 \ (\$2.50) + 1/6 \ (\$3.00) = \$1.75$$

The long-run average winnings per roll of the single die would be $1.75. For the game to be fair, each player should put in $1.75 each time the die is rolled, giving everyone an equal chance to break even. Note that for each round of play, it is not necessary that the expected value equal any of the possible outcomes. Thus, a player might win $1.50 or $2.00 but never $1.75 in any one round of play.

The expected value of a continuous variable can be found in a similar fashion. The major difference is the need to determine the appropriate probability function and integrate it to find the expected value over a relevant range. For example, the design engineer in the earlier example wishes to specify the expected value of the incoming voltage to the microprocessor chip. This will require the use of the expected value calculation

$$E(X) = \int_{-\infty}^{\infty} f(x)x\,dx \qquad \text{for continuous variables}$$

$$E(X) = \int_{5}^{10} 0.20 \, x dx = 0.20 \frac{x^2}{2} \Big|_{5}^{10} = 0.20(50 - 12.5) = 7.5$$

Thus, the expected value for this continuous variable is found to be 7.5 volts. As previously defined, the expected value is the probability-weighted average value of the voltage. Further applications of the expected value concept are developed in the discussion of the normal distribution later in the chapter.

Functions of Random Variables. It is sometimes desirable to be able to combine means and standard deviations of several random variables. The expected value of the sum of two random variables can be shown to be the sum of or difference between the individual expected values. For example, the probability that a machine will produce a defective part in a one-hour period was found to be 0.10. The probability of a second machine of the same type producing a defective part was found to be 0.07. If each machine produces 50 parts per hour, what is the expected total number of defective parts?

We simply take $[0.10 \times 50] + [0.07 \times 50] = 8.5$ defective parts. Of course, it is impossible to produce 0.5 defective part in any one-hour period, but the long-run average should be 8.5 if the process is stable.

As another example, if three parts having average lengths of 1″, 2″, and 3″ are to be assembled together, their overall average length is $x = 1'' + 2'' + 3'' = 6''$. As long as all items have the same units of measure, this method is correct.

To obtain a combined measure of variability requires a similar but slightly more complex process and is applicable only if the random variables are statistically independent. The variance of the sum of or difference between random variables can be shown to be the sum of the variances of the individual random variables. We may not add standard deviations but must first add the variances and then take the square root of the total variance if we wish to compute an overall measure of the standard deviation. Thus, if three independent random variables have standard deviations of $\sigma_1 = 0.283$, $\sigma_2 = 0.4$, $\sigma_3 = 0.5$, the total variance of the sum of the random variables is $\sigma_t^2 = \sigma_1^2 + \sigma_2^2 + \sigma_3^2$, and the standard deviation of the sum is

$$\sigma_t = \sqrt{(0.283)^2 + (0.4)^2 + (0.5)^2} = 0.7$$

Important Probability Distributions

Certain discrete distributions describe many natural phenomena and have broad applications in statistical process control. Two of them are the binomial distribution and the Poisson distribution, discussed next. Later, we will introduce some important continuous probability distributions.

Binomial Distribution. The **binomial distribution** describes the probability of obtaining exactly x successes in a sequence of n identical experiments, called trials. The probability of success in each trial is a constant value p. The binomial probability function is given by the following formula:

$$f(x) = \binom{n}{x} p^x (1 - p)^{n-x}$$

$$= \frac{n!}{x!(n - x)!} p^x (1 - p)^{n-x} \qquad x = 0, 1, 2, \ldots, n$$

where p is the probability of a success

$\quad n$ is the number of items in the sample

$\quad x$ is the number of items for which the probability is desired $(0, 1, 2, \ldots, n)$.

The expected value, variance, and standard deviation of the binomial distribution are

$$E(p) = \mu = np$$
$$\sigma^2 = np(1 - p)$$
$$\sigma = \sqrt{np(1 - p)}$$

Binomial probabilities for selected values of p and n have been tabulated in Appendix D. Naturally, computer programs are also available to make binomial computations easier.

EXAMPLE 3   Silicon Chip Defectives. To illustrate the use of the binomial distribution, suppose that a new process for producing silicon chips is averaging 40% defective items. If a quality supervisor takes a sample of five items to test for defectives, what is the probability of finding 0, 1, 2, 3, 4, or 5 defectives in the sample, and what is the expected number of defectives? For this problem, we have $n = 5$ and $p = 0.4$. Therefore, the binomial distribution for this experiment is

$$f(x) = \binom{5}{x}(0.4)^x (1 - 0.4)^{5-x}$$

$$= \frac{5!}{x!(5 - x)!} (0.4)^x (0.6)^{5-x}$$

Table 12.5 shows the detailed calculations required to compute individual probabilities. (You may wish to check the binomial probability table in Appendix D to verify these answers.)

TABLE 12.5   Binomial Probability Values

x	$\dfrac{5!}{x!(5-x)!}$	$(0.4)^x(0.6)^{5-x}$	f(x)
0	1	0.07776	0.0778
1	5	0.05184	0.2592
2	10	0.03456	0.3456
3	10	0.02304	0.2304
4	5	0.01536	0.0768
5	1	0.01024	0.0102
			1.0000

FIGURE 12.7   **Binomial Probability Distribution**

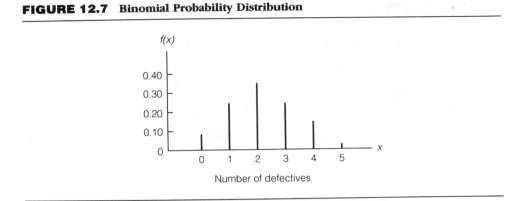

Thus, the probability of finding exactly zero defectives in the sample of five is 0.0778, the probability of finding one defective is 0.2592, and so on. The expected number of defectives and the variance are given by

$$\mu = np = 5(0.4) = 2.0$$
$$\sigma^2 = np(1 - p) = 2.0(0.6) = 1.2$$

Figure 12.7 shows a graph of this probability distribution.

Poisson Distribution.   The second discrete distribution often used in quality control is the **Poisson distribution.** The Poisson probability distribution is given by

$$f(x) = \frac{e^{-\mu}\mu^x}{x!}$$

where μ = expected value or average number of occurrences

   $x = 0, 1, 2, 3, \ldots$

   $e = 2.71828$, a constant.

The Poisson distribution is closely related to the binomial distribution. It is derived by allowing the sample size (n) to become very large (approaching infinity) and the probability of success or failure (p) to become very small (approaching zero) while the expected value (np) remains constant. Thus, when n is large relative to p, the Poisson distribution can be used as an approximation to the binomial. A common rule of thumb is if $p \leq 0.05$ and $n \geq 20$, the Poisson will be a good approximation with $\mu = np$. It is also used to calculate the number of occurrences of an event over a specified interval of time or space, such as the number of scratches per square inch on a polished surface.

Let us extend Example 3 to show how the Poisson distribution can be of use in quality control problems. Suppose that improvements are made in the production process that bring the average level of defects down to 5% from the previous level of 40%. The quality supervisor now decides to use a sample size of 30 parts to detect changes in the quality level of the process with a much longer time period between

TABLE 12.6 Poisson Probability Values

x	$e^{-1.5}$	$\dfrac{(1.5)^x}{x!}$	$f(x) = \dfrac{e^{-1.5}(1.5)^x}{x!}$
0	0.22313	1.00000	0.22313
1	0.22313	1.50000	0.33467
2	0.22313	1.12500	0.25102
3	0.22313	0.56250	0.12551
4	0.22313	0.21094	0.04707
5	0.22313	0.06328	0.01412
			0.99552

samples. What is the probability of finding five or fewer defective items in any randomly selected sample of 30 parts?

Since we must find discrete probabilities of 0, 1, 2, 3, 4, or 5 defectives, we must calculate each probability and add the results. This can be stated as

$$P(x \le 5) = P(x = 0) + P(x = 1) + P(x = 2)$$
$$+ P(x = 3) + P(x = 4) + P(x = 5)$$

As an approximation to the binomial, we can use the relationship to $\mu = np = 30(0.05) = 1.5$. This becomes the parameter μ for the Poisson distribution. The computations are given in Table 12.6.

Thus, it is highly likely that if the average value is 5% defectives, there will be five or fewer defectives in a sample of 30 parts. In fact, there is a 0.99552 probability that this will be the case. The probability of finding *more* than five defectives is very small. It would be only

$$1 - P(x \le 5) = 1 - 0.99552 = 0.00448$$

Note that our previously stated conditions under which the Poisson distribution is a good approximation of the binomial have been met; that is, $n \ge 20$ and $p \le 0.05$. Table 12.7 compares these probability values to the true values using the binomial distribution. We can see that the Poisson distribution does provide a good approximation to the binomial probabilities when the specified conditions are met. If the conditions for the Poisson approximation cannot be met, we may be able to use a normal approximation to the binomial, discussed in the next section.

TABLE 12.7 Binomial versus Poisson Probability Values

x	Binomial Probability	Poisson Probability
0	0.21464	0.22313
1	0.33890	0.33467
2	0.25864	0.25102
3	0.12705	0.12551
4	0.04514	0.04707
5	0.01235	0.01412
	0.99672	0.99552

Two of the most frequently used continuous probability distributions are the normal distribution and the exponential distribution. They form the basis for many of the statistical analyses performed in quality assurance today.

Normal Distribution. The probability density function of the **normal distribution** is represented graphically by the familiar bell-shaped curve. It should be recognized that not every symmetric, unimodal curve is a normal distribution, nor can all data from a sample or population be assumed to fit a normal distribution. However, it is often assumed that data are normally distributed to simplify certain calculations. In most cases, this assumption makes very little difference in the results but is important from a theoretical perspective.

The probability density function for the normal distribution is as follows:

$$f(x) = \frac{1}{\sqrt{2\pi\sigma^2}} e^{-(x-\mu)^2/2\sigma^2} \qquad -\infty < x < \infty$$

where μ = the mean of the random variable x

σ^2 = the variance of x

e = 2.71828 . . .

π = 3.14159 . . .

If a normal random variable has a mean $\mu = 0$ and a standard deviation $\sigma = 1$, it is called a **standard normal distribution.** The letter z is usually used to represent this particular random variable. Using the constants 0 and 1 for the mean and standard deviation, respectively, we are able to simplify the probability density function for the normal distribution to

$$f(z) = \frac{1}{\sqrt{2\pi}} e^{-z^2/2}$$

This standard normal distribution function is shown in Figure 12.8. Since $\sigma = 1$, the scale on the z axis is given in units of standard deviations. Special tables of areas under

FIGURE 12.8   **Standard Normal Distribution**

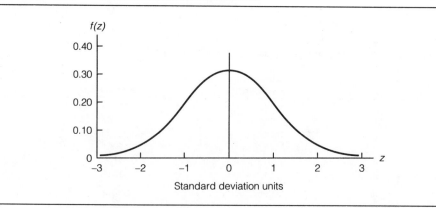

the normal curve have been developed as an aid in computing probabilities. Such a table is given in Appendix A.

Fortunately, it is easy to transform *any* normal distribution involving a random variable x with a known (or estimated) mean and standard deviation into a standard normal distribution. This is done using the formula

$$z = \frac{x - \mu}{\sigma}$$

This formula tells us that we must take the value of the variable in which we are interested (x), subtract the mean value (μ), and divide by the standard deviation (σ). This yields a random variable z, which has a standard normal distribution. Probabilities for this variable can then be found in the table in Appendix A.

Referring back to the problem of oven temperatures in Example 1, suppose that we had sufficient data to calculate the population mean and standard deviation of the oven temperatures. Let us assume that $\mu = 49$ and $\sigma = 7$ and that the population of values was normally distributed. Given this information, let us calculate three probabilities [shown in Figures 12.9 (a), (b), and (c), respectively]: (1) that a sample value x will fall between 42 and 49, (2) that it will be less than 42, and (3) that it will fall between 50 and 57.

Referring to Figure 12.9(a), to compute the probability that the random variable x will fall between 42 and 49, we must convert these values to standard normal deviates (z values):

$$z_1 = \frac{x - \mu}{\sigma} = \frac{42 - 49}{7} = -1.0 \quad \text{and} \quad z_2 = \frac{49 - 49}{7} = 0$$

Since this case is bounded on the right by the mean of the distribution, we can read the normal table for the z_1 value and obtain the probability without further calculations. From the table we find that the area under the curve between -1.0 and

FIGURE 12.9(a) Calculation of Probabilities from the Standard Normal Distribution

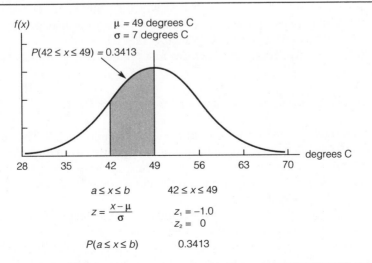

FIGURE 12.9(b)   **Calculation of Probabilities from the Standard Normal Distribution**

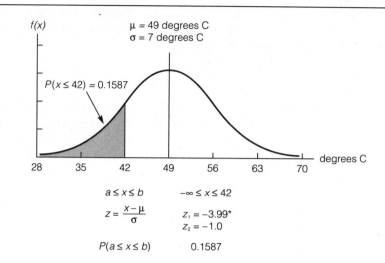

$$z = \frac{x - \mu}{\sigma}$$

$a \leq x \leq b$	$-\infty \leq x \leq 42$
$z = \dfrac{x - \mu}{\sigma}$	$z_1 = -3.99*$
	$z_2 = -1.0$
$P(a \leq x \leq b)$	0.1587

Note: The left (lower most) limit of the distribution using the standard normal table in Appendix A is a z value of -3.99. Actually, the lower limit of the distribution extends to $-\infty$.

0 is 0.3413. This means that we would expect 34.13% of the values taken from this population to fall in the specified interval and that we have a 34.13% probability of obtaining a value within that interval if we make a random observation of the oven temperature.

To compute the probability that x is less than 42 for the second case, we must find the area under the normal curve from minus infinity to:

$$z_2 = \frac{42 - 49}{7} = -1.0$$

This value is 0.5 minus the area from -1.0 to 0, which we find in Appendix A as 0.3413. Thus, the probability of obtaining a temperature reading of less than 42 degrees C is $0.5 - 0.3413 = 0.1587$. This is shown in Figure 12.9(b).

Finally, for the third case, we transform $x = 50$ and $x = 57$ to standard normal values and obtain:

$$z_1 = \frac{x - \mu}{\sigma} = \frac{50 - 49}{7} = 0.14 \quad \text{and} \quad z_2 = \frac{57 - 49}{7} = 1.14$$

The area from 0 to $z_2 = 1.14$ can be read from the table as 0.3729. The area from 0 to $z_1 = 0.14$ is 0.0557. We must then subtract the smaller area from the larger to obtain $0.3729 - 0.0557 = 0.3172$, the area of interest. Thus, we have a probability of 0.3172 of observing an oven temperature between 50 and 57 degrees C. These calculations are summarized in Figure 12.9(c).

The area under the curve that corresponds to one standard deviation from the mean is 0.3413; therefore, the probability that the value of a normal random variable falls within one standard deviation ($\pm 1\sigma$) of the mean is 0.6826. The corresponding x-values are often called **1-sigma limits** in statistical quality control terminology. Two

FIGURE 12.9(c) Calculation of Probabilities from the Standard Normal Distribution

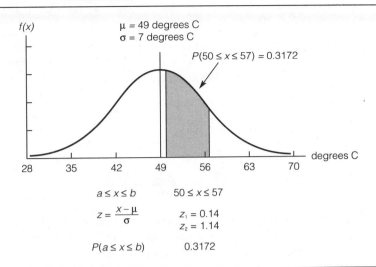

$$a \leq x \leq b \qquad 50 \leq x \leq 57$$

$$z = \frac{x - \mu}{\sigma} \qquad \begin{aligned} z_1 &= 0.14 \\ z_2 &= 1.14 \end{aligned}$$

$$P(a \leq x \leq b) \qquad 0.3172$$

standard deviations on one side of the mean corresponds to 0.4772 area under the curve, so the probability that a normal random variable falls within a **2-sigma limit** is twice that figure, or 0.9544. Three standard deviations encompasses 0.4986 area under the curve on either side of the mean, or a total area of 0.9972. Hence, the **3-sigma limit** encompasses nearly all of the normal distribution. These concepts form the basis for control charts discussed in Chapter 16.

Normal Approximation to the Binomial. Although the binomial distribution is extremely useful, it has a serious limitation when dealing with either small probabilities or large sample sizes—it is very tedious to calculate. In our discussion of the Poisson approximation to the binomial, we showed that when the probability of success or failure becomes very small, the Poisson distribution permits us to calculate similar probability values more easily than the binomial. It can also be shown that as the sample size gets very large (approaches infinity), the binomial distribution approaches the normal distribution as a limit. This means that for large sample sizes, we can obtain good approximations of probabilities that would have been calculated using the binomial distribution by using the normal distribution. The normal approximation holds well when $np \geq 5$ and $n(1 - p) \geq 5$. The following example illustrates this.

Let us use the silicon chip example with two changes in assumptions. Suppose, instead of using a small sample size, we chose a sample of 50. We still have a probability of 0.40 of finding a defective item. We wish to determine the probability of finding between 15 and 20 defective items in the sample. If we use the binomial distribution to calculate the probabilities, we would have

$$f(x) = \binom{50}{x}(0.4)^x (1 - 0.4)^{50-x}$$

$$= \frac{50!}{x!(50 - x)!} (0.4)^x (0.6)^{50-x}$$

This would have to be evaluated for $x = 15, 16, 17, 18, 19$, and 20, since

$$P(15 \leq x \leq 20) = P(x = 15) + P(x = 16) + P(x = 17) + P(x = 18)$$
$$+ P(x = 19) + P(x = 20)$$

This would be difficult and time-consuming, even with a good electronic calculator!

By using the normal approximation, we may obtain a reasonably accurate estimate of the probability. The calculations are as follows:

$$\mu = np = 50(0.40) = 20$$

$$\sigma_p^2 = np(1 - p) = 20(0.60) = 12$$

$$\sigma_p = \sqrt{12} = 3.46$$

$$z_1 = \frac{x - \mu}{\sigma_p} = \frac{15 - 20}{3.46} = -1.45 \qquad z_2 = \frac{20 - 20}{3.46} = 0$$

From the table for the standard normal distribution, we find that the value for $P(-1.45 \leq z \leq 0) = 0.4265$. Thus, we can say that the probability of obtaining between 15 and 20 defectives in a sample of 50 parts is 0.4265. This is shown in Figure 12.10.

Exponential Distribution. Another continuous distribution that is commonly used in quality assurance is the **exponential distribution.** The exponential distribution is used extensively in reliability estimation, discussed in Chapter 15. The probability density function for the exponential distribution is much simpler than the one for the normal distribution. Therefore, direct evaluation is easier, although tabulated values for the exponential distribution are also readily available (see Appendix F). The formula for the exponential probability density function is

$$f(x) = \frac{1}{\mu} e^{-x/\mu}, \; x \geq 0$$

FIGURE 12.10 Normal Approximation to the Binomial

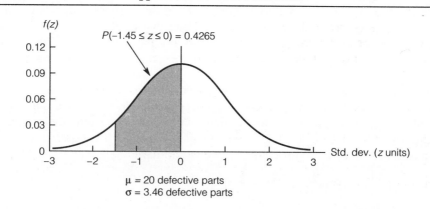

$\mu = 20$ defective parts
$\sigma = 3.46$ defective parts

where μ = mean value for the distribution

x = time or distance over which the variable extends

e = 2.71828 . . .

By integrating this function between 0 and x, we can obtain the cumulative distribution function

$$F(x) = 1 - e^{-x/\mu}$$

EXAMPLE 4   Distribution of Light Bulb Failure Times.   To illustrate an application of the exponential distribution, suppose that the maintenance manager of an office building is trying to schedule the maintenance crew that changes floodlights used to illuminate the exterior of the building. The manager is told by the light bulb supplier that the mean time between failure for the bulbs being used is 1,000 hours. What is the probability that the *actual* time between any two successive failures will be 750 hours or less? For this example, $\mu = 1000$ and $x = 750$. Thus,

$$F(x) = 1 - e^{-x/\mu} = 1 - e^{-0.75} = 1 - 0.4724 = 0.5276$$

Therefore, there is a 0.5276 probability that the time between two successive failures will be 750 hours or less. The problem is shown graphically in Figure 12.11.

Figure 12.12 summarizes the four important distributions reviewed in this section.

SAMPLING THEORY AND DISTRIBUTIONS

In statistical quality control, the purpose of sampling is to gain knowledge about the characteristics of the population from the information that is contained in a sample. Characteristics of a population, such as the mean μ, standard deviation σ, or

FIGURE 12.11   Exponential Distribution of Time between Failures

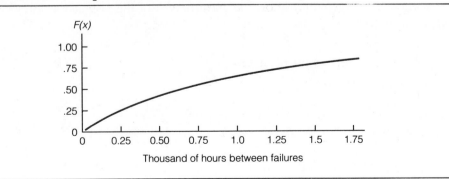

Thousand of hours between failures

FIGURE 12.12 Summary of Common Probability Distributions Used in Quality Assurance

Distribution	Form	Probability Function	Comments on Application
Normal	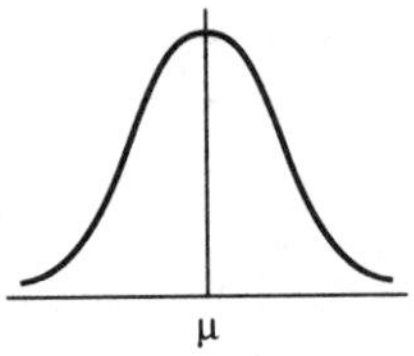	$y = \dfrac{1}{\sigma\sqrt{2\pi}}\, e^{-\frac{(x-\mu)}{2\sigma}}$ μ = Mean σ = Standard deviation	Applicable when there is a concentration of observations about the average and it is equally likely that observations will occur above and below the average. Variation in observations is usually the result of many small causes.
Exponential	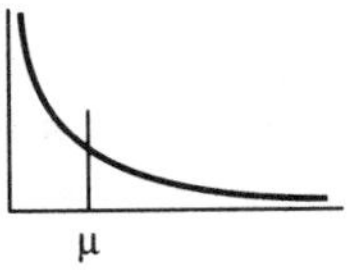	$y = \dfrac{1}{\mu}\, e^{-\frac{x}{\mu}}$	Applicable when it is likely that more observations will occur below the average than above.
Poisson	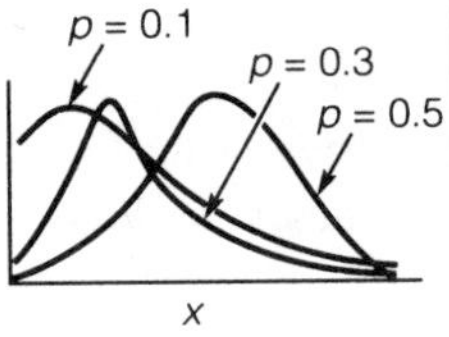	$y = \dfrac{e^{-\mu}\mu^{x}}{x!}$ n = Number of trials p = Probability of occurrence x = Number of occurrences $\mu = np$	Same as binomial but particularly applicable when there are many opportunities for occurrence of an event but a low probability (less than 0.10) on each trial.
Binomial	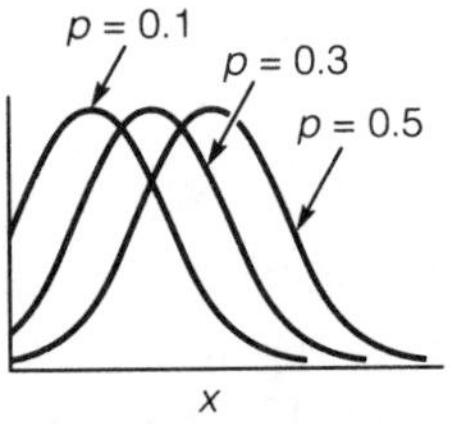	$y = \dfrac{n!}{x!(n-x)!}\, p^{x}q^{n-x}$ n = Number of trials x = Number of occurrences p = Probability of occurrence $q = 1 - p$	Applicable in defining the probability of x occurrences in n trials of an event that has a constant probability of occurrence on each independent trial.

SOURCE: Adapted from J. M. Juran and F. M. Gryna, Jr., instructor's manual to accompany *Quality Planning and Analysis* (New York: McGraw-Hill, 1980), p. 125. Copyright © 1980 by McGraw-Hill, Inc., used with permission.

proportion π, are generally known as **parameters** of the population. In statistical notation, we write

$$\text{population mean: } \mu = \frac{1}{N}\sum_{i=1}^{N} x_i$$

$$\text{population standard deviation: } \sigma = \sqrt{\frac{\sum_{i=1}^{N}(x_i - \bar{x})^2}{N}}$$

$$\text{population proportion: } \pi = \frac{Q}{N}$$

where N is the number of items in a population

Q is the number of items exhibiting a criterion of interest (e.g., defects, on-time departures of aircraft).

Earlier in the chapter we noted that the *sample* mean and standard deviation are computed as follows:

$$\bar{x} = \frac{1}{n}\sum_{i=1}^{n} x_i$$

$$s = \sqrt{\frac{\sum_{i=1}^{n}(x_i - \bar{x})^2}{n - 1}}$$

$$\text{sample proportion} = \frac{q}{n}$$

where n is the number of items in a sample

q is the number of items in the sample exhibiting a criterion of interest

Statistical theory is devoted to exploring the relationship between such **sample statistics** ($\bar{x}$, s, and p) and their corresponding **population parameters** (μ, σ, and π). For instance, we generally use the sample statistic $\bar{x}$ as a point estimator for the population parameter μ, and s as a point estimator for σ. The actual numerical values of $\bar{x}$ and s, which represent the single "best guess" for each unknown population parameter, are called **point estimates.**

Sampling Distributions

Different samples will produce different estimates of the population parameters. Therefore, sample statistics such as $\bar{x}$, s, and p are random variables that have their own probability distribution, mean, and variance. These probability distributions are called **sampling distributions.** Knowledge of these sampling distributions will help us make probability statements about the relationship between sample statistics and population parameters. In quality control, we are most often interested in the sampling distributions of $\bar{x}$ and p. Let us first consider the sampling distribution of $\bar{x}$.

It can be shown that when using simple random sampling, the expected value of $\bar{x}$ is the population mean μ, or

$$E(\bar{x}) = \mu$$

The standard deviation of $\bar{x}$ (often called the **standard error of the mean**) is given by the formula

$$\sigma_{\bar{x}} = \frac{\sigma}{\sqrt{n}} \qquad \text{(for infinite populations or sampling with replacement from an infinite population)}$$

$$\sigma_{\bar{x}} = \sqrt{\frac{N - n}{N - 1}}\frac{\sigma}{\sqrt{n}} \qquad \text{(for finite populations)}$$

When $n/N \leq 0.05$, $\sigma_{\bar{x}} = \sigma/\sqrt{n}$ provides a good approximation for finite populations.

The last step is to develop the form of the probability distribution of $\bar{x}$. If the true population distribution is unknown, we can rely on the **central limit theorem** to provide some useful insights. The central limit theorem (CLT) is stated as follows:

> If simple random samples of size n are taken from any population having a mean μ and a standard deviation σ, the probability distribution of the sample means approaches a normal distribution with mean μ and standard deviation (standard error) $\sigma_{\bar{x}} = \sigma/\sqrt{n}$ as n becomes very large. In more precise mathematical terms: As $n \rightarrow \infty$ the distribution of the random variable $z = (\bar{x} - \mu)/(\sigma/\sqrt{n})$ approaches that of a standard normal distribution.

The approximation to a normal distribution can be assumed for sample sizes of 30 or more. If the population is *known* to be normal, the sampling distribution of $\bar{x}$ is normal for any sample size.

Next, consider the sampling distribution of p. We can show that $E(p) = \pi$. Here π is used as the population parameter. This is not related to the *number π* $= 3.14159$ used in the calculation of the standard normal distribution.

The standard deviation of p is

$$s_p = \sqrt{\frac{\pi(1 - \pi)}{n}}$$

for infinite populations.

For finite populations or when $n/N \leq 0.05$, we modify s_p by

$$s_p = \sqrt{\frac{N - n}{N - 1}} \sqrt{\frac{\pi(1 - \pi)}{n}}$$

Applying the CLT to p, we may state that the sampling distribution of p can be approximated by a normal distribution for large sample sizes.

Chapters 13, 16, and 18 explore various applications of the CLT to statistical quality control in the areas of process capability determination, control charting, and the development of sampling plans. The following example illustrates an application of sampling distributions.

EXAMPLE 5 **Sampling Distribution of Shaft Lengths.** The mean length of shafts produced on a lathe has historically been 50 inches, with a standard deviation of 0.12 inch. If a sample of 36 shafts is taken, what is the probability that the sample mean would be greater than 50.04 inches?

The sampling distribution of the mean is approximately normal with mean 50 and standard deviation $0.12/\sqrt{36}$. Thus,

$$z = \frac{\bar{x} - \mu}{\sigma/\sqrt{n}} = \frac{50.04 - 50}{0.12/\sqrt{36}} = 2.0$$

When we look up this value in the standard normal table, we find the probability of 0.4772 between the mean and this value. The area for $z \geq 2.0$, in which we are interested, is found by

$$P(z \geq 2.0) = 0.5000 - 0.4772 = 0.0228$$

Thus, the probability of a value equal to or greater than 50.04 inches as the mean of a sample of 36 items is only 0.0228 if the population mean is 50 inches. The applicability of this to statistical quality control is that "shifts" in the population mean can quickly be detected using very small, representative samples to monitor the process. The procedure for finding the area under the curve is exactly the same as previously covered. However, the procedure for finding the z value differs in that the standard error term ($\sigma/\sqrt{n} = 0.12/\sqrt{36} = 0.02$) is substituted in the denominator of the equation for z.

Similarly, if a sample size of 64 is used, $\sigma/\sqrt{n} = 0.12/8 = 0.015$ and

$$z = \frac{\bar{x} - \mu}{\sigma/\sqrt{n}} = \frac{50.04 - 50}{0.015} = 2.67$$

and $P(z \geq 2.67) = 0.5000 - 0.4962 = 0.0038$. As the sample size increases, it is less likely that a mean value of at least 50.04 will be observed purely by chance. We probably would expect some special cause to be present.

HYPOTHESIS TESTING

Hypothesis testing is a method of statistical inference by which we can state an assumption about a population characteristic (usually a parameter). This assumption, called the **null hypothesis** (H_0), is taken to be true unless sufficient evidence can be found in a sample to reject it. Figure 12.13 summarizes the general procedure for hypothesis testing. From the sample data, we compute a point estimate and compare it with a critical value that is based on the sampling distribution. A decision is then made whether or not to reject the null hypothesis. If we reject the null hypothesis, we must conclude that the alternative hypothesis is true.

FIGURE 12.13 **Procedure for Hypothesis Testing**

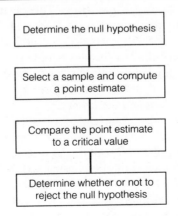

We may test several different types of hypotheses. If we are interested in the population mean μ, for example, we may wish to state our hypothesis in one of three ways:

1. $H_0 : \mu \geq \mu_0$ vs. $H_1 : \mu < \mu_0$

2. $H_0 : \mu \leq \mu_0$ vs. $H_1 : \mu > \mu_0$

3. $H_0 : \mu = \mu_0$ vs. $H_1 : \mu \neq \mu_0$

where μ_0 is a specific value for the true population mean. Forms 1 and 2 are called **one-sided tests of statistical significance,** while form 3 is called a **two-sided test of statistical significance.**

To illustrate, suppose that federal law requires that a container labeled as having 16 ounces must contain at least 15.9 ounces of a product. A quality control manager might test the hypothesis $H_0 : \mu \geq 15.9$ ounces against the alternative hypothesis $\mu < 15.9$ ounces to determine compliance. On the other hand, since constant overfilling contributes to unnecessary cost, the manager might wish to verify that no more than 16 ounces are packaged. In this case, the null hypothesis would be $H_0 : \mu \leq 16$ and $H_1 : \mu > 16$. These would be examples of *one-sided tests.*

As another example, it is frequently necessary to measure quality based on timely arrival of shipments of parts to an assembly plant. If trucks arrive behind schedule, the plant might have to shut down production because of lack of parts. If the trucks arrive ahead of schedule, unloading docks could become congested and accidents and mistakes would probably increase. A *two-sided test* would be used to determine whether the scheduled arrival times are within acceptable upper and lower limits.

There is an inherent risk of reaching an incorrect conclusion when testing hypotheses because of the nature of sampling. This risk can be classified in two ways:

1. Type I error—the risk of rejecting H_0 when, in fact, it is true.

2. Type II error—the risk of accepting H_0 when, in fact, it is false.

The probability of making a Type I error is referred to as α (alpha), while the probability of making a Type II error is called β (beta). Later chapters examine the relationship of these concepts to quality control.

Figure 12.14 gives an abbreviated summary of typical hypothesis tests that can be used in various quality assurance applications. This review of hypotheses does not include all the assumptions that must be considered for each hypothesis test. For example, when the random variable z is used, the underlying assumption is that the distribution is normally distributed or that the sample size $n > 30$. In performing tests where sigma is unknown and large sample sizes (where $n > 30$) are available, it is permissible to use the normal distribution as an approximation to the student's t distribution for cases where sigma is unknown.

Space does not permit consideration of all variations of two-sided and one-sided tests. For example, two-sided tests of a single population proportion, tests for differences between two population proportions, or tests for differences between two populations' standard deviations could be constructed. The cases involving one-sided lower-tailed and upper-tailed tests with sigma unknown have also been omitted from Figure 12.14. Readers who are interested in pursuing this topic may wish to consult standard statistics texts such as those referenced at the end of the chapter. Let us next illustrate these concepts with two examples of hypothesis tests in quality assurance.

FIGURE 12.14 **Summary of Typical Hypothesis Tests**

	Condition	Hypothesis	Test Statistic	Critical Values
Two-sided tests	Sigma known	$H_0: \mu = \mu_0$ $H_1: \mu \neq \mu_0$	$z = \dfrac{\bar{x} - \mu_0}{\sigma/\sqrt{n}}$	Reject if $z < z_{\alpha/2}$ or $z > z_{\alpha/2}$
		$H_0: \mu_1 = \mu_2$ $H_1: \mu_1 \neq \mu_2$	$z = \dfrac{\mu_1 - \mu_2}{\sqrt{\sigma_1^2/n_1 + \sigma_2^2/n_2}}$	Reject if $z < z_{\alpha/2}$ or $z > z_{\alpha/2}$
	Sigma unknown	$H_0: \mu = \mu_0$ $H_1: \mu \neq \mu_0$	$t = \dfrac{\bar{x} - \mu_0}{s/\sqrt{n}}$	Reject if $t < t_{\gamma,\alpha/2}$ or $t > t_{\gamma,\alpha/2}$
		$H_0: \mu_1 = \mu_2$ $H_1: \mu_1 \neq \mu_2$	$t = \dfrac{\bar{x}_1 - \bar{x}_2}{\sqrt{\left(\dfrac{(n_1-1)s_1^2 + (n_2-1)s_2^2}{n_1 + n_2 - 2}\right)\left(\dfrac{n_1 + n_2}{n_1 n_2}\right)}}$	Reject if $t < t_{\gamma,\alpha/2}$ or $t > t_{\gamma,\alpha/2}$ γ = degrees of freedom for t
One-sided tests	Lower-tailed test	$H_0: \mu \geq \mu_0$ $H_1: \mu < \mu_0$	$z = \dfrac{x - \mu_0}{\sigma/\sqrt{n}}$	Reject if $z < z_\alpha$
		$H_0: \pi_1 \geq \pi_0$ $H_1: \pi_1 < \pi_0$	$z = \dfrac{p - \pi_0}{\sqrt{p(1-p)/n}}$	Reject if $z < z_\alpha$
	Upper-tailed test	$H_0: \mu \leq \mu_0$ $H_1: \mu > \mu_0$	$z = \dfrac{x - \mu_0}{\sigma/\sqrt{n}}$	Reject if $z > z_\alpha$
		$H_0: \pi_1 \leq \pi_0$ $H_1: \pi_1 > \pi_0$	$z = \dfrac{p - \pi_0}{\sqrt{p(1-p)/n}}$	Reject if $z > z_\alpha$

NOTE: Not all possible conditions or assumptions are covered for each of the hypothesis tests in this table. There are also hypothesis tests involving standard deviations, variances, and "goodness of fit" of tests using other probability distributions besides the normal. See any basic statistics text.

EXAMPLE 6 **Testing Tire Durability.** Metro Transit Company is concerned about the quality of tires purchased for use on buses. The company wishes to be confident that the tires will last at least 20,000 miles. Therefore, it wishes to set the probability of a Type I error, α, at 0.05. The supplier tells the transit company that the standard deviation for all tires that it produces is 3,000 miles. A sample of 225 tires is taken, and the mean of the sample is found to be 19,700 miles. Can the company conclude that the tires will last 20,000 miles?

To find the solution, we must set up a one-sided hypothesis test of the form

$$H_0 : \mu \geq \mu_0 \text{ vs. } H_1 : \mu < \mu_0$$

or

$$H_0 : \mu \geq 20{,}000 \text{ mi. vs. } H_1 : \mu < 20{,}000 \text{ mi.}$$

$$z = \frac{x - \mu_0}{\sigma/\sqrt{n}} = \frac{19{,}700 - 20{,}000}{3{,}000/\sqrt{225}} = \frac{-300}{200} = -1.5$$

FIGURE 12.15   Hypothesis Test—Metro Transit Company

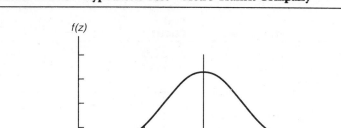

$\mu = 20,000$ miles (assumed)
$\sigma = 3,000$ miles

$\bar{x} = 19,700$
$\sigma_{\bar{x}} = 3,000/\sqrt{225} = 200$

From our standard normal table, we find that the critical value of $z_\alpha =$ -1.645 defines the boundary for a 0.05 probability (area under the curve). Since our calculated $z = -1.5$ is larger than the critical value (that is, to the right), we find that we cannot reject the hypothesis that the mean of the population is, in fact, greater than or equal to 20,000 miles. The graphic representation of the problem is shown on Figure 12.15.

Another example of hypothesis testing illustrates a test of equality of population means.

EXAMPLE 7 Testing Electrical Components. Suppose that two different suppliers make the same electrical part. Supplier 1 claims that his parts can withstand the same electrical load as Supplier 2's parts. A potential customer obtained 12 parts from Supplier 1 and 14 parts from Supplier 2. The parts were tested until they failed. Supplier 1's parts could handle an average of 21.85 amps of current with a standard deviation of 6.99, while Supplier 2's parts could handle an average of 20.0 amps with a standard deviation of 2.25. The customer wished to test the hypothesis that there is no significant difference in the average ability of the parts to handle the necessary electrical load, using a probability of Type I error of 0.05.

The hypothesis test, known as a test of the *difference between means,* is

$$H_0 : \mu_1 = \mu_2 \text{ vs. } H_1 : \mu_1 \neq \mu_2$$

or

$$H_0 : \mu_1 - \mu_2 = 0 \text{ vs. } H_1 : \mu_1 - \mu_2 \neq 0$$

We compute the test statistic as follows:

$$t = \frac{\bar{x}_1 - \bar{x}_2}{\sqrt{\left(\dfrac{(n_1 - 1)s_1^2 + (n_2 - 1)s_2^2}{n_1 + n_2 - 2}\right)\left(\dfrac{n_1 + n_2}{n_1 n_2}\right)}} = \frac{21.85 - 20.0}{\sqrt{\left(\dfrac{11(6.99) + 13(2.25)}{(12 + 14 - 2)}\right)\left(\dfrac{12 + 14}{(12)(14)}\right)}}$$

$$= \frac{1.85}{\sqrt{\left(\dfrac{106.14}{24}\right)\left(\dfrac{26}{168}\right)}} = \frac{1.85}{0.827} = 2.24$$

The null hypothesis must be rejected, since 2.24 is larger than the critical value of 2.064 (obtained from the student's t table in any statistics textbook) for $\gamma = n_1 + n_2 - 2 = 24$ degrees of freedom and a probability in each tail of the distribution of 0.025 (see Figure 12.16). It should be noted that the same formula may be used to calculate the z-value for large sample sizes by simply substituting z for t when $n \geq 30$.

These quality assurance examples used to illustrate hypothesis testing have been primarily limited to materials and suppliers coming into an organization. However, many other problems of control and improvement lend themselves to the use of hypothesis testing inside organizations. In fact, control charting, discussed in Chapter 16, is actually a graphical form of hypothesis testing.

TESTING DISTRIBUTIONAL ASSUMPTIONS

Most statistical procedures rely on certain distributional assumptions. For example, in analyzing the capability of a process to conform to specifications, we often assume that the data follow a normal distribution. In reliability computations, the exponential

FIGURE 12.16 Hypothesis Test—Electrical Parts Difference between Means

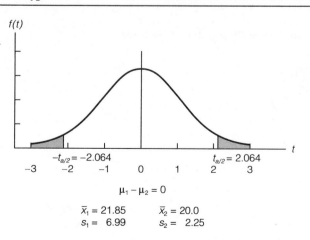

distribution often is assumed. One purpose of testing distributional assumptions is to decide whether it is meaningful to use a certain statistical procedure. If the distributional assumption is incorrect, then any conclusions drawn from the statistical procedure are likely to be wrong. A second purpose of distributional testing is to find a distribution that fits a given set of data. This is particularly important in reliability analysis where we need to determine the form of failure distributions.

To test a distributional assumption, we test the null hypothesis,

H_0 : the data follow the assumed distribution

against the alternate hypothesis,

H_1 : the data do not follow the assumed distribution

If we reject the null hypothesis, then we must either try a different distribution, transform the data, or use statistical procedures that do not rely on distributional assumptions, such as nonparametric tests. Two basic techniques are used to test distributional assumptions: probability plots and the chi-square test. We review these procedures in this section.

Probability Plots

Recall that the graph of a cumulative distribution function has a range from 0 to 1. The graphs of different cumulative distribution functions form many different patterns. Figure 12.17 shows the graphs of the cumulative distribution functions for a standard normal distribution and an exponential distribution. If one were to plot the cumulative distribution of some sample data, it would be difficult to determine solely by visual inspection whether or not the data "fit" one of these patterns. On the other hand, it is quite easy to assess the fit of data to a straight line. This is the basis for probability plotting.

The basic idea of a probability plot is to transform the cumulative probability scale (vertical axis) so that the graph of the cumulative distribution will be a straight line. This is illustrated in Figure 12.18 for a standard normal distribution. Probability paper with such transformed scales is available for many common distributions such

FIGURE 12.17 **Examples of Cumulative Distribution Functions**

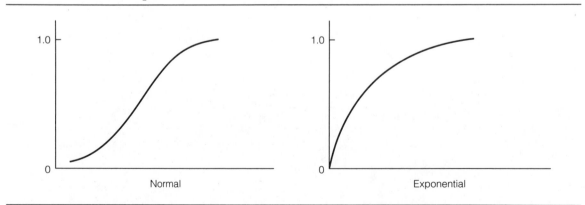

FIGURE 12.18   **Transformation of Cumulative Distribution Function**

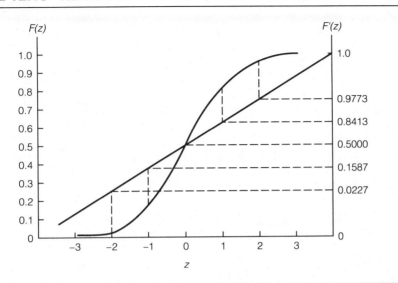

as the normal and exponential distribution. An example of normal probability paper is shown in Figure 12.19.

A probability plot provides a variety of information about a distribution, such as estimates of its parameters, percentiles, and cumulative probabilities. It also allows us to check on the validity of the data and the assumed distribution. To construct a probability plot, suppose we have n observations.

1. Order the data points from smallest to largest. Let $x(i)$ be the value in the ith position.

2. Let $F(i) = 100(i - 0.5)/n$ for $i = 1, 2, . . ., n$.

3. On probability paper for the assumed distribution, plot the value of the $x(i)$ against $F(i)$.

4. Draw a straight line through the plotted data. This line is an estimate of the cumulative distribution. The closer the points are to the straight line, the better the fit to the assumed distribution. If the distribution is appropriate, then the points will tend to fall on a straight line. If not, the points will deviate from a straight line, usually in some systematic manner.

If the distributional assumption is not rejected, then we can obtain estimates of percentiles, cumulative probabilities, and parameter estimates. To estimate a percentile, enter the probability scale at the desired percentage; move across to the fitted line, and down to the corresponding point on the data scale. For instance, to find the median, use the 50th percentile. To estimate a cumulative probability, enter the plot on the data scale at the given value, go to the fitted line, and then to the corresponding point on the probability scale.

Parameter estimates depend on the type of distribution. For a normal distribution, the mean is also the median (50th percentile), and the slope of the fitted

FIGURE 12.19 Normal Probability Paper

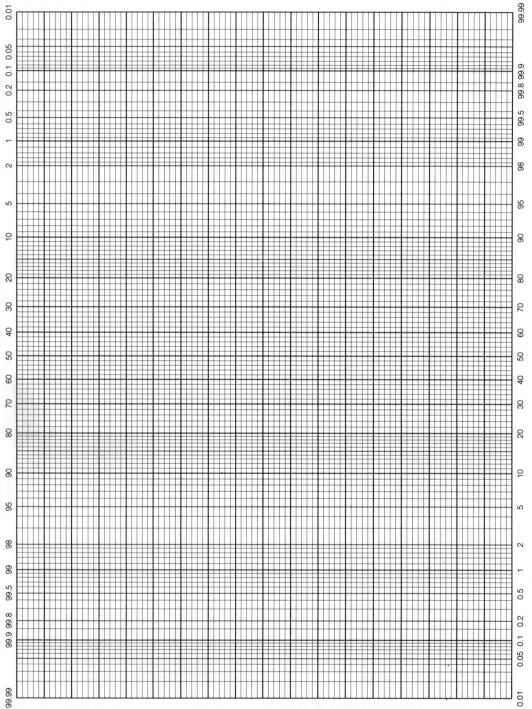

line corresponds to the standard deviation. An estimate of the standard deviation can be found by taking two-fifths of the difference between the 90th and 10th percentiles.

EXAMPLE 8   A Normal Probability Plot.   Fifteen samples of industrial wire are tested for breaking strength (in grams). After ordering the data from smallest to largest we have:

i	x(i)	F(i)
1	300	3.33
2	371	10.00
3	382	16.67
4	389	23.33
5	425	30.00
6	438	36.67
7	450	43.33
8	452	50.00
9	470	56.67
10	486	63.33
11	520	70.00
12	526	76.67
13	573	83.33
14	598	90.00
15	620	96.67

These data are plotted on normal probability paper in Figure 12.20. A straight line was visually estimated through the data. An estimate of the mean is the median, 452. The 90th percentile is approximately 580 and the 10th percentile is 355. Thus, an estimate of the standard deviation is $\frac{2}{5}(580 - 355) = 90$. The actual mean is 466.67 and the standard deviation is 89.44. The probability that the breaking strength is less than, say, 400 grams is found to be 0.22 (as shown in Figure 12.20).

Chi-Square Goodness-of-Fit Test

The chi-square goodness-of-fit test can be used to test a distributional assumption. The chi-square test is most useful for large samples; for small samples, other tests not described in this text are more appropriate.[3] Suppose the data are grouped into k cells. We may compute the number of observations that would be expected if the distributional assumption is valid. This is done by computing the probability associated with each cell and multiplying by the total number of observations. The chi-square test focuses on the difference between the observed and expected

---

[3]An excellent monograph on distributional testing is *How to Test Normality and Other Distributional Assumptions* by Samuel S. Shapiro, ASQC Basic References in Quality Control: Statistical Techniques (Milwaukee, WI: American Society for Quality Control, 1986).

FIGURE 12.20 Probability Plot of Company B Wire Break Strength

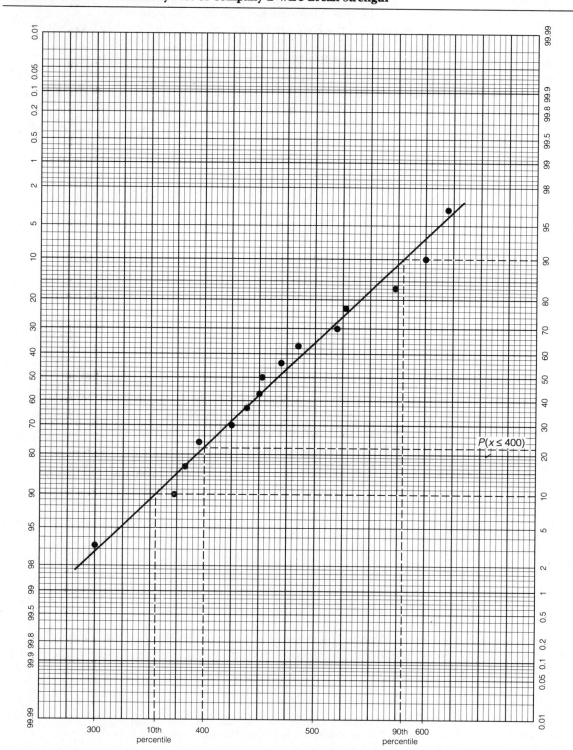

frequencies. Large differences suggest that the distributional assumption is invalid, whereas small differences will not provide sufficient evidence to reject the null hypothesis.

Let f_i be the observed frequency in cell i and e_i be the expected frequency. Let

$$\chi^2 = \Sigma (f_i - e_i)^2/e_i$$

This has a chi-square distribution with $k - 1 - t$ degrees of freedom, where k is the total number of cells and t is the number of parameters that are estimated from the data. We accept H_0 if $\chi^2 \leq \chi_\alpha^2$ and reject it if $\chi^2 > \chi_\alpha^2$, where α is the significance level of the test. Critical values of chi-square can be found in Appendix G.

In applying the chi-square test, the number of observations in each cell should be at least five. If any cell contains less than five data points, it should be combined with another cell.

EXAMPLE 9 **Applying the Chi-Square Goodness-of-Fit Test.** Let us reconsider the temperature data in Table 12.1. We will test the null hypothesis that the distribution is normal. Table 12.2 showed the frequency distribution. Since some cells contain less than five observations, we will combine the first three and the last two cells in the frequency distribution to satisfy this requirement.

Cell	Boundaries	Frequency
1	$-\infty - 42.5$	8
2	42.5–47.5	12
3	47.5–52.5	24
4	52.5–57.5	7
5	57.5–∞	5

Since we estimated the mean as 49.02 and the standard deviation as 6.47 from the data, we will have $5 - 1 - 2 = 2$ degrees of freedom. Let us choose a significance level of $\alpha = 0.05$.

To find the expected frequencies, we seek the areas under the normal density function defined by the cell boundaries as shown in Figure 12.21. These

FIGURE 12.21 **Areas under Normal Distribution for Chi-Square Test**

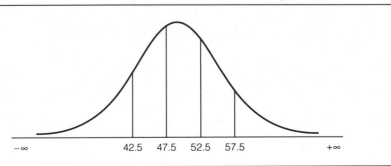

are found easily by converting the boundaries to standard normal values and using Appendix A. Multiplying these areas by the total number of observations (56), we find the expected frequencies and complete the calculations as shown below.

f_i	e_i	$(f_i - e_i)^2$	$(f_i - e_i)^2/e_i$
8	8.75	0.5625	0.0643
12	13.94	3.7636	0.2700
24	16.81	51.6961	3.0753
7	11.17	17.3889	1.5568
5	5.33	0.1089	0.0204
			4.9868

Since $\chi^2 = 4.9868 < \chi^2_{0.05} = 5.99$, we cannot reject the null hypothesis that the data are normally distributed.

CORRELATION AND REGRESSION

Linear regression and correlation are very closely related to one another. Regression tells *how* two or more variables are related to one another. In regression analysis, changes in one variable are assumed to be related to changes in the other variable(s). A mathematical function is derived to show the relationship between the designated *dependent* variable and the *independent* variable(s). Correlation measures *how strongly* variables are linearly related to one another. Correlation makes no assumption of a functional relationship but is merely used to show the degree of association between the variables. The degree of association is usually expressed as a

FIGURE 12.22 **Applying the Sign Test to a Scatter Diagram**

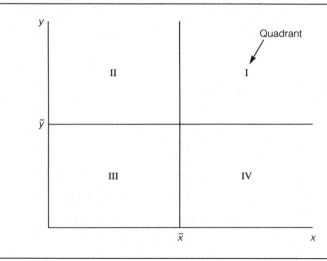

correlation coefficient, which is an abstract measure of the extent to which variables are linearly related. These two powerful statistical techniques—correlation and regression— are probably misused as frequently as they are correctly used. The temptation to misuse them stems from the fact that *any* two variables can be correlated with or regressed on each other. However, one may or may not *cause* a change in the other.

Many of the earlier statistical techniques reviewed here are descriptive in nature. Linear regression can also be used for prediction. Using historical data (for example, length of wire contained on a coil versus the weight of the coil), we may describe how closely the two variables are related at any point in time using correlation. By developing a regression equation, we may "predict" the length of wire on coils if we have information on the weight of the coils being processed.

TABLE 12.8 Sign Test Table

n	Lower limit 1%	Lower limit 5%	Upper limit 5%	Upper limit 1%	n	Lower limit 1%	Lower limit 5%	Upper limit 5%	Upper limit 1%	n	Lower limit 1%	Lower limit 5%	Upper limit 5%	Upper limit 1%
1					31	7	9	22	24	61	20	22	39	41
2					32	8	9	23	24	62	20	22	40	42
3				3	33	8	10	23	25	63	20	23	40	43
4				4	34	9	10	24	25	64	21	23	41	43
5			5	5	35	9	11	24	26	65	21	24	41	44
6		0	6	6	36	9	11	25	27	66	22	24	42	44
7		0	7	7	37	10	12	25	27	67	22	25	42	45
8	0	0	8	8	38	10	12	26	28	68	22	25	43	46
9	0	1	8	9	39	11	12	27	28	69	23	25	44	46
10	0	1	9	10	40	11	13	27	29	70	23	26	44	47
11	0	1	10	11	41	11	13	28	30	71	24	26	45	47
12	1	2	10	11	42	12	14	28	30	72	24	27	45	48
13	1	2	11	12	43	12	14	29	31	73	25	27	46	48
14	1	2	12	13	44	13	15	29	31	74	25	28	46	49
15	2	3	12	13	45	13	15	30	32	75	25	28	47	50
16	2	3	13	14	46	13	15	31	33	76	26	28	48	50
17	2	4	13	15	47	14	16	31	33	77	26	29	48	51
18	3	4	14	15	48	14	16	32	34	78	27	29	49	51
19	3	4	15	16	49	15	17	32	34	79	27	30	49	52
20	3	5	15	17	50	15	17	33	35	80	28	30	50	52
21	4	5	16	17	51	15	18	33	36	81	28	31	50	53
22	4	5	17	18	52	16	18	34	36	82	28	31	51	54
23	4	6	17	19	53	16	18	35	37	83	29	32	51	54
24	5	6	18	19	54	17	19	35	37	84	29	32	52	55
25	5	7	18	20	55	17	19	36	38	85	30	32	53	55
26	6	7	19	20	56	17	20	36	39	86	30	33	53	56
27	6	7	20	21	57	18	20	37	39	87	31	33	54	56
28	6	8	20	22	58	18	21	37	40	88	31	34	54	57
29	7	8	21	22	59	19	21	38	40	89	31	34	55	58
30	7	9	21	23	60	19	21	39	41	90	32	35	55	58

SOURCE: Reprinted from Kaoru Ishikawa, *Guide to Quality Control* (Tokyo: Asian Productivity Organization, 1982), p. 217. Reprinted by permission of the Asian Productivity Organization. Distributed in the U.S., Canada, and western Europe by Quality Resources, White Plains, NY.

Correlation Analysis

The starting point for correlation analysis is to obtain a set of pairs of data for two variables that are thought to be related. They are generally plotted on standard graph paper with the x axis used for one variable and the y axis used for the other variable. Designation of which variable will appear on each axis requires no judgment, since the variables are assumed to be two random variables. To obtain a measure of the degree of relationship between the variables, the correlation coefficient r is calculated. The value of r falls between -1 and 1. If two variables are perfectly linearly related and each increases proportionally to the other, they would have a correlation coefficient of 1. If they are perfectly linearly related so that as one increases, the other decreases proportionally, they would have a correlation coefficient of -1. If they are linearly unrelated to each other, they would have a correlation coefficient of 0. Since the correlation coefficient is a by-product of a regression analysis calculation, we will delay explanation of the calculation of the correlation coefficient until after we review regression analysis.

A simple test for correlation can be performed using a scatter diagram. This is called the **sign test.** On the scatter diagram, draw horizontal and vertical lines through the medians of the data and label the four quadrants I, II, III, and IV counterclockwise from the upper right as shown in Figure 12.22 (on page 392). Count the number of points in each quadrant and n, the total number of data points minus the number on one of the lines. Next, add the points in quadrants II and IV. Compare this value to critical values found in Table 12.8 (on page 393) corresponding to n. Table 12.8 provides critical values for both 1% and 5% levels of significance. For instance, if the total number of points (less those on a line) is 30 and the significance level is chosen to be 5%, then less than 9 or more than 21 points in quadrants II and IV would cause us to reject the hypothesis of no correlation and conclude that correlation exists.

EXAMPLE 10   Testing for Correlation in a Scatter Diagram.   Seventeen batches of a raw material were tested for the percentage of a certain chemical (x). It is believed that the amount of this chemical influences an important quality characteristic of the final product (y). The data are given below.

x	y	x	y
3.5	7.0	6.1	11.0
3.2	8.0	6.9	10.7
4.5	8.4	7.0	11.9
5.0	7.6	7.4	9.6
3.8	10.5	7.5	8.2
5.4	9.2	8.5	9.1
5.3	11.7	8.2	11.1
6.0	8.8	9.0	13.0
6.1	10.1		

Using a 5% level of significance, can we conclude that a correlation between these two variables exists?

The median value of x is 6.1; the median value of y is 9.6. Figure 12.23 shows the scatter diagram of this data and the median lines. In quadrants II and IV, we find four points. Since three points fall on the median lines, $n = 17 - 3 = 14$. The critical values at the 5% level for $n = 14$ are 2 and 12. Thus, we conclude that no correlation exists between these two variables.

Regression Analysis

Simple linear regression is used to examine the relationship between two variables that are thought to be related. A set of pairs of data are generally plotted on standard graph paper with the x axis used for the *independent* variable and the y axis used for the *dependent* variable. Designation of which variable is independent and which is dependent requires that judgment be exercised, since the independent variable is assumed to be a fixed, mathematical variable, while the dependent variable is assumed to be a random variable.

If the data follow a reasonably straight line, we can compute a linear regression equation $y = a_0 + a_1 x$ using the following formulas:

$$a_0 = \frac{\Sigma y \Sigma x^2 - \Sigma x \Sigma xy}{n \Sigma x^2 - (\Sigma x)^2}$$

$$a_1 = \frac{n \Sigma xy - \Sigma x \Sigma y}{n \Sigma x^2 - (\Sigma x)^2}$$

For any value of x, $a_0 + a_1 x$ represents the estimated or predicted value of y.

Another critical characteristic of regression analysis is how well the data fit the ideal, or theoretical, regression equation. If data points are scattered widely around

FIGURE 12.23 Scatter Diagram

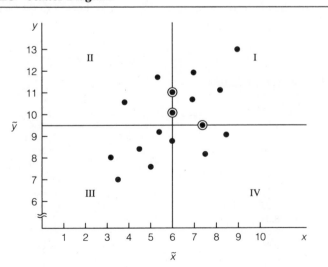

the regression equation, the degree of fit is low. However, if the points are rather tightly clustered near the regression line, the degree of fit will be high. The statistical measure used to estimate the degree of fit is called the **coefficient of determination.** The symbol r^2 is used to denote the measure. If the correlation coefficient r has already been calculated for the variables, the coefficient of determination can be easily obtained by squaring the correlation coefficient and vice versa if the coefficient of determination is calculated first.

We calculate r^2 and r using the formulas:

$$r^2 = \frac{a_0 \Sigma y + a_1 \Sigma xy - n(\bar{y})^2}{\Sigma y^2 - n(\bar{y})^2}$$

$$r = \sqrt{r^2}$$

Many computer programs are available that can easily calculate the regression and correlation coefficients.

EXAMPLE 11   **Calibrating a Voltmeter.**   A very common problem in the inspection departments of many quality assurance organizations is ensuring that instruments are properly calibrated. In principle, it is a simple matter to check this. One connects the instrument to a known source, such as an extremely accurate voltage generator to check a voltmeter or a precision gage block to check a micrometer. A reading is then obtained to determine if the instrument is capable of accurately measuring the known variable. In practice, there may be numerous sources of variation in the process that make this difficult (see Chapter 8).

The data in Table 12.9 represent the actual readings obtained from the calibration of a voltmeter versus the standard source readings from an accurate voltage generator. The source readings were purposely not set in even integer increments so as to minimize possible bias of the inspector taking the actual readings. The inspection supervisor wished to know if the instrument was

TABLE 12.9   **Voltmeter Readings**

Actual (y)	Source (x)	xy	y^2	x^2
1.09	1.05	1.1445	1.1881	1.1025
2.12	2.15	4.5580	4.4944	4.6225
3.08	3.12	9.6096	9.4864	9.7344
4.09	4.08	16.6872	16.7281	16.6464
5.11	5.11	26.1121	26.1121	26.1121
6.08	6.07	36.9056	36.9664	36.8449
7.20	7.23	52.0560	51.8400	52.2729
8.30	8.34	69.2220	68.8900	69.5556
9.59	9.66	92.6394	91.9681	93.3156
10.41	10.49	109.2009	108.3681	110.0401
57.07	57.30	418.1353	416.0417	420.2470

accurate. If it was not, what evidence was available and what "calibration function" could be applied to the voltmeter?

Figure 12.24 (on page 398) shows a plot of the actual reading y versus the source volts x. As can be seen, a straight line provides a very good fit for this data. The coefficients a_0 and a_1 are obtained by using the following calculations:

$$a_0 = \frac{\Sigma y \, \Sigma x^2 - \Sigma x \, \Sigma xy}{n\Sigma x^2 - (\Sigma x)^2}$$

$$= \frac{(57.07)(420.2470) - (57.30)(418.1353)}{10(420.2470) - (57.30)^2}$$

$$= \frac{24.3436}{919.1800} = 0.02648404$$

$$a_1 = \frac{n\Sigma xy - \Sigma x\Sigma y}{n\Sigma x^2 - (\Sigma x)^2} = \frac{10(418.1353) - (57.30)(57.07)}{10(420.2470) - (57.30)^2}$$

$$= \frac{911.242}{919.180} = 0.991364042$$

Thus, our estimated regression equation is

$$y = 0.0265 + 0.9914x$$

Using the data in Table 12.9 we can also calculate r and r^2, as follows:

$$r^2 = \frac{a_0\Sigma y + a_1\Sigma xy - n\bar{y}^2}{\Sigma y^2 - n\bar{y}^2}$$

$$= \frac{0.0265(57.07) + 0.9914(418.1353) - 10(5.707)^2}{416.0417 - 10(5.707)^2}$$

$$= \frac{90.33725527}{90.34321} = 0.999934198$$

and

$$r = \sqrt{0.9999} = 0.9999$$

With the value of $a_0 = 0.0265$, $a_1 = 0.9914$, and $r^2 = 0.9999$, the fit of the voltmeter with the calibration standard is excellent. The value of $a_0 = 0.0265$ indicates that the regression line has an intercept of very close to zero, which is where it should be. The value of $a_1 = 0.9914$ is very close to a perfect slope value of 1.0, and the $r^2 = 0.9999$ is also very close to a perfect coefficient of determination 1.0. Based on these data, the instrument appears to be in near-perfect calibration.

FIGURE 12.24 **Voltmeter Readings—Actual Versus Source**

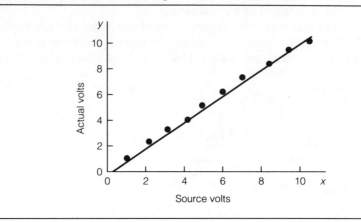

Statistical Applications for Quality at Colgate-Palmolive[4]

The Colgate-Palmolive Company dates back to 1806, or three years after the Louisiana Purchase. It started as a small shop in New York City that made and sold candles and soap. The business grew and prospered. Colgate and Company merged with the Palmolive Company in the late 1920s to form the present-day corporation, which now has annual sales in excess of $5 billion.

Most of Colgate's products are in the low-price, high-volume consumer market, which is known for its intense competition. Since the possibility of increasing a product's price is limited by the competition, Colgate's profitability is determined largely by the efficiency of its management techniques and production operations.

The slogan on Colgate's crest reads "Quality Products since 1806," and every department is touched by the demands of this central business principle. The Quality Assurance and Improvement Department within Colgate devotes full time toward achieving this goal and includes a wide variety of special services. At each manufacturing plant, a group of chemists, inspectors, engineers, and managers is involved with product quality levels. The data that are collected must be communicated to others throughout the organization. The format of the data summary is often vital to achieving the desired results.

A variety of statistical techniques is used. Relative frequency distributions and graphical techniques such as histograms are some of the most useful tools for communicating data and ideas. As an example of the use of these statistical techniques, consider the production of the familiar heavy-duty detergent used for home laundries. Television advertisements claiming the relative merits of the competing brands are widely seen throughout the country.

The regular size carton of the detergent has a stated weight of 20 ounces. In the manufacturing process great pains are taken to ensure that the label specifications of 20 ounces of detergent per carton

[4]Adapted from David R. Anderson, Dennis J. Sweeney, and Thomas A. Williams, *Statistics for Business and Economics,* 2nd ed. (St. Paul, MN: West Publishing Company, 1984), pp. 29–32.

are maintained. However, meeting the 20-ounce-per-carton weight is not the only aspect of quality assurance addressed in the manufacture of this product. Of particular concern, from the point of view of quality, is the density of the detergent powder that is placed in the carton. Even with rigid quality control standards in the powder production process, at times the powder varies in its weight per unit volume. For example, if the weight of the powder is on the heavy side (a high specific gravity), it will not take as much powder to reach the 20-ounce-per-carton weight limit, and the company can be faced with the problem of filling cartons with 20 ounces but having the carton appear slightly underfilled when it is opened by the user.

To reduce this problem and maintain the quality standards, the powder is sampled periodically prior to being placed in the cartons. When the powder reaches an unacceptably high density or specific gravity, corrective action is taken to reduce the specific gravity of the powder before the filling operation is permitted to resume.

Repeated samples provide more and more data about the specific gravity of powder. At some point, various parties in the company are interested in knowing how the powder production process is doing in terms of meeting density guidelines. Tabular and graphical summaries provide convenient ways to present the data to production, quality assurance and management personnel. Table 12.10

TABLE 12.10 Relative Frequency Distribution Showing the Specific Gravity of Heavy-Duty Detergent (Based on 150 Sample Results)

Specific Gravity	Relative Frequency
0.27 but less than 0.29	0.02
0.29 but less than 0.31	0.18
0.31 but less than 0.33	0.50
0.33 but less than 0.35	0.21
0.35 but less than 0.37	0.06
0.37 but less than 0.39	0.02
0.39 but less than 0.41	0.01

(continued)

FIGURE 12.25 Histogram Showing Relative Frequency of Specific Gravity of Heavy-Duty Detergent

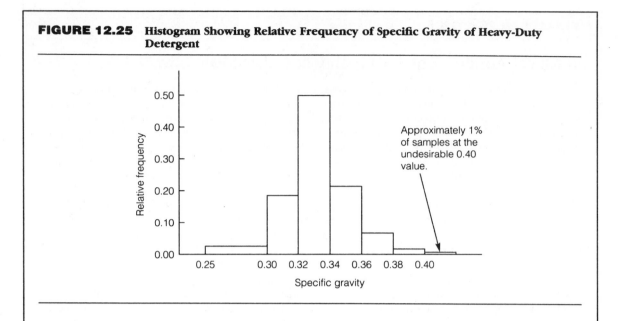

shows a relative frequency distribution for the specific gravity of 150 samples taken over a one-week period. Figure 12.25 shows a histogram of these sample data. Note that the specific gravity of the powder varies, with a specific gravity of 0.32 occurring most frequently. The undesirably high specific gravity occurs around 0.40. Thus the summaries show that the operation is meeting its quality guidelines, with practically all the data showing values less than 0.40. Production management personnel would be pleased with the quality aspect of the powder product as indicated by these statistical summaries.

In cases where the relative frequency distribution and/or histogram summaries do not support the above conclusion, managers and quality assurance personnel begin to monitor the powder production process closely. Engineers may be consulted on ways of reducing the specific gravity to a more satisfactory level. After making any change in the process, data are collected and summarized in similar tabular and graphical forms to determine how the modifications are affecting the quality of the product. The engineers' work continues until the statistical summaries show that the high quality level is once again obtained. The use of tabular and graphical methods of descriptive statistical summaries is essential in communicating data to the engineers, inspectors, and managers whose job it is to assure quality products at Colgate-Palmolive Company.

Key Issues for Discussion

1. Describe the important quality characteristics of laundry detergent that are monitored by Colgate-Palmolive.

2. Explain the use of frequency distributions and histograms in quality assurance at Colgate-Palmolive.

3. Compute the mean specific gravity from Table 12.10.

Applications of Statistical Analysis in Distribution Center Operations[5]

Quality control in distribution operations is important to assure that correct products, carton quantities, and pallet quantities are shipped to the customer. Statistical sampling can be applied to the daily order population as an auditing tool. Since many different types and sizes of orders are shipped from a warehouse, a good characteristic to monitor is the *line item*—a model number with an associated quantity. The statistic of interest is the number of line items in error divided by the number of line items checked. An inspection plan was developed to inspect 100% of the orders with 40 or fewer line items, and inspect only 40 line items in larger orders.

A flowchart of a typical distribution center operation is shown in Figure 12.26. The shift supervisor normally selects the orders to be checked. The key principle is to assure the random selection of orders from different order categories such as United Parcel and other small parcel orders, small orders containing less than 40 line items, and large orders having more than 40 line items. A few orders are selected from each category, with the exact number related to the number of line items that can reasonably be checked during the shift.

A photocopy of the picking list is used to perform the inspection. The line items to be checked are circled by the shift supervisor. After the order is complete, the checker is given the photocopied picking list and performs the inspection.

Each line item is checked for the following characteristics:

1. correct model number

2. correct carton count

3. correct address

4. general condition of the cartons

5. incidental characteristics of the entire order (such as pallet height, quantity, size, and correct staging).

[5]Adapted from J. W. Martin, "SQC at a Consumer Goods Distribution Center," *Quality Progress,* June 1985, pp. 36–39.

If an error is found, the individual responsible must correct the error. At the end of the shift the checker gives the photocopied picking list to the supervisor. This information is transferred to a data sheet kept for each individual on the shift.

The data are summarized for each individual by the week. A weekly shift summary is completed. At the end of the month, each shift reports a monthly quality rating to the distribution center manager, who summarizes all shift data into a center summary, which is sent to division at the end of the month.

The system allows direct comparison at any level (individual, shift, or center), which facilitates corrective action by management. Every week the distribution center manager reviews the shift quality level with the supervisor. Those supervisors whose groups are above the target quality goal can provide useful instruction for the entire group. Supervisors of groups below the goal should present corrective action on their shift.

More detailed statistical analyses can also be conducted. These include determinations of the randomness of the inspection (see discussion item 1) and significant differences in quality levels between individuals, shifts, or distribution centers (see discussion item 2). Other advanced techniques are used as necessary.

This statistical quality audit system forms the basis for improvements through corrective action. Normally, this involves worker training. By studying workers with exceptionally low error percentages, useful information can be obtained for the instruction of the entire group. Immediate corrective action is taken to improve the quality of the high error percentage group.

Key Issues for Discussion

1. In one shift, orders are checked for six individuals. Eight orders were checked for workers 1 and 2, and five orders were checked for the remaining four workers. Perform a chi-square test to determine if the audit performed was random; that is, if the distribution of the number of orders checked per worker is uniformly distributed.

(continued)

FIGURE 12.26   **Distribution Center Quality Plan Flowchart**

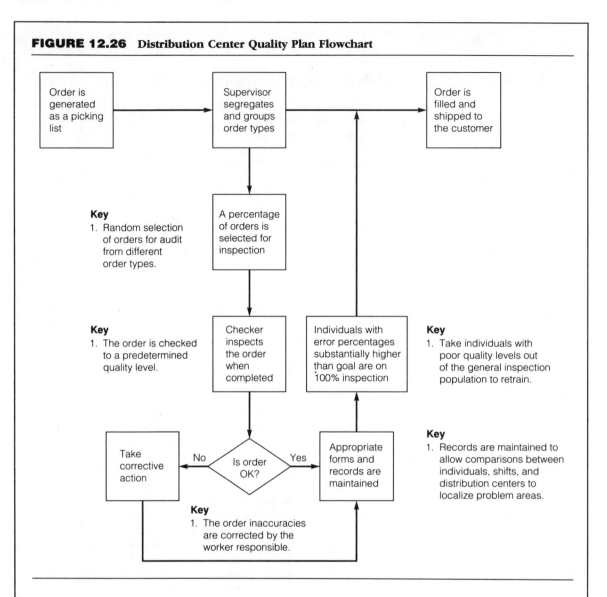

2. The following data were collected over time for two shifts:

Shift	Number of Line Items Audited	Number of Line Items Found to Be in Error
1	2848	18
2	1675	5

Test the hypothesis that the proportion of line items in error does not differ between shifts at a 5% significance level.

3. As improvements to the system lower the error percentage, what statistical implications arise with regard to the sample sizes that should be used?

4. Discuss how Pareto analysis might be used within this application.

Summary of Key Points

- Statistics is concerned with the collection, organization, analysis, interpretation, and presentation of data and has extensive applications in quality assurance.

- The three basic components of statistical methodology are descriptive statistics, statistical inference, and predictive statistics.

- Descriptive statistical tools include frequency distributions and histograms.

- Descriptive statistical measures include the mean, median, and mode for central tendency, and the range and standard deviation for dispersion.

- A variety of probability distributions is useful in quality assurance. They include the binomial, Poisson, normal, and exponential distributions.

- Sample statistics are used to obtain estimates of population parameters. To make probability statements about sample statistics, we need to know the sampling distribution and its standard deviation, called the standard error.

- Hypothesis testing is the basis of statistical inference. Many tools in quality control, such as control charts and acceptance sampling, are essentially tests of hypotheses.

- Since many statistical techniques depend on certain distributional assumptions, such as normality, it is convenient to be able to test for these assumptions. The use of probability paper and the chi-square test are simple means of doing this.

- Correlation and regression analysis are used to describe or predict the relationship between two variables. These techniques are important in relating causes and effects in quality problem solving.

Questions for Review and Discussion

1. Discuss the differences between the three major components of statistical methodology (descriptive statistics, statistical inference, and predictive statistics). Why might this distinction be important to a manager?

2. Define a population and a sample. What are their major characteristics?

3. What techniques can be used to present data in a systematic, understandable way?

4. Define the common measures of central tendency and dispersion used in statistical problem solving and discuss their uses.

5. Define the terms *random variable, mutually exclusive, collectively exhaustive,* and *outcome* in your own words.

6. What is a sample space? What is the difference between discrete and continuous random variables?

7. What is an expected value, and how is it used in statistical analysis?

8. How are the binomial and Poisson distributions related to one another? In what general category of probability distributions do they both fall?

9. How is the normal distribution used in statistical quality control applications? Why are assumptions of normality usually made?

10. How are normal and exponential distributions related? In what general category of probability distributions do they both fall?

11. For what applications is the binomial distribution typically used?

12. State the meaning of the central limit theorem in your own terms. How important is it to the development and use of statistical quality control techniques?

13. What is the standard error of the mean? How does it differ from the standard deviation?

14. How can hypothesis testing contribute to a manager's success in controlling quality in an organization?

15. What is the purpose of testing distributional assumptions? Of what value is it in quality-related studies?

16. Describe the construction and use of probability paper.

17. Explain the chi-square goodness-of-fit test.

18. How is correlation related to regression? Where can each be used?

19. Describe how the sign test is used in determining correlation in a scatter diagram.

Problems

1. Consider the following measurements taken when measuring the diameters of one-inch steel bar stock used to manufacture various machined parts in a plant.

Raw Data on Bar Stock Dimension ($n = 75$)

1.03	0.99	1.01	0.98	1.00	1.01	0.96	1.08	1.02	1.01
1.05	1.02	1.00	1.07	1.03	1.01	0.96	0.99	0.97	0.91
1.02	1.07	1.01	0.98	1.06	1.04	0.96	0.98	1.02	1.00
1.09	1.01	0.95	0.95	0.97	1.00	1.00	1.04	1.03	1.04
1.02	1.04	1.01	0.94	0.95	0.99	1.00	1.05	1.02	0.98
0.99	1.01	1.06	0.93	1.06	1.05	1.04	1.07	1.01	0.99
0.97	1.03	1.02	0.99	1.01	1.01	1.03	1.04	1.05	1.02
1.02	0.99	1.04	1.05	1.01					

a. Calculate the mean, median, mode, range, and standard deviation without grouping the data.
b. Group the data into 10 groups and construct a frequency histogram.
c. Using the groups developed in (b), recalculate the mean and standard deviation using the grouped data method. Compare the results with your calculations from (a). How similar are your answers?

2. The average time to failure for a machine in hours is recorded below:

20.0	22.5	15.0	26.1	31.4
23.0	25.9	16.2	17.6	20.7
34.0	23.6	24.1	21.1	25.6
22.0	16.1	18.4	24.9	28.3
26.0	21.3	25.9	17.3	21.7

  a. Develop a grouped frequency distribution and histogram.
  b. Estimate the mean, median, mode, and standard deviation using your answer to (a).
  c. Find the exact values of the mean and standard deviation. Compare these to your answer in (b).

3. Ten refrigerators are carefully examined for surface imperfections prior to shipment. The number of imperfections found is:

2 0 1 4 0 3 1 1 0 2

Compute the mean, median, and standard deviation.

4. Acme Corporation sells ice cream machines to fast-food chains in the South. The probability that a randomly chosen sales prospect will make a purchase is 0.2. If a salesperson calls on six prospects, what is the probability that exactly four sales will be made?

5. Auditing of outgoing invoices has revealed that on average, 2.5% of them contained errors.

  a. If a sample of 10 invoices is selected each week, what is the probability that none of them will contain any errors?
  b. What is the probability that more than three will contain errors?

6. A production process has an average level of 10% defective. If five parts are sampled, compute the probability of finding x defects, for $x = 1$ through 5.

7. The probability that an antimissile defense system will successfully destroy an approaching missile is 0.90.

  a. If 10 missiles are launched simultaneously, what is the probability that all 10 will be destroyed?
  b. What is the probability that at least 8 will be destroyed?

8. A delivery service for telephone books has a record of accurate delivery to 98% of the names in the telephone book. The telephone company randomly selects 100 callers to determine if they have received the book.

  a. What is the probability that all of them have received the book?
  b. What is the probability that exactly two have not received the book?
  c. What is the probability that at most five have not received it?

9. A supercomputer has an average of two system crashes per day.

  a. Assuming a Poisson distribution, what is the probability that the system will not crash in a given day?

b. What is the probability of exactly one crash in one day?

c. What is the probability of three or more crashes in one day?

10. A data entry process in an insurance firm has averaged a 2.5% error rate. A sample of 100 items was recently taken. What is the probability of finding between one and four defective items in the sample?

11. The useful life of a line of steel-belted radial tires has been found to be normally distributed with a mean of 38,000 miles and a standard deviation of 3,000 miles.

a. What is the probability that a randomly selected tire will have a value of at least 35,000 miles?

b. What is the probability that it will last between 35,000 and 45,000 miles?

c. What is the probability that it will last 45,000 miles or more?

12. The useful life of a printer in a university computer lab is 3.5 years with a standard deviation of 0.5 years.

a. What is the probability that the useful life will be at least 3 years?

b. What is the probability that the useful life will be between 2 and 3.25 years?

13. A hospital is trying to correct problems in its billing procedures, which have been averaging a 20% error rate. The comptroller requests that a 75-item sample be taken to determine if any progress is being made on improving the error rate. What is the probability of finding between 15 and 20 defectives in the sample if the error rate is still 20%? What is the probability if the error rate is now 10%? Use the normal approximation to the binomial to calculate your answers.

14. A sample of light bulbs manufactured by a bulb company yielded a mean time between failures of 1,400 hours. Use the exponential distribution to determine the probability that the time between any two bulb failures would be 700 hours or greater.

15. The time to failure of an airborne radar is exponentially distributed with a mean time of 8000 hours.

a. What is the probability of failure before 8000 hours?

b. What is the probability that it will last at least 10,000 hours without a failure?

16. The percentage defective output from a certain process varies, but is known to be normally distributed with a mean of 3% and a standard deviation of 0.4.

a. What is the distribution of the percent defective of samples of size 9? of size 25?

b. Find the probability that a sample of either size 9 or 25 will have a percentage defective of at least 3.2.

17. The mean of a sample of 64 measurements of a part's length was 4.03 inches. Historically, the population mean for this part has been 4.0 inches with a standard deviation of 0.16 inch. What is the probability of finding a sample mean of 4.03 or larger if the population mean is still the same?

18. The population mean for a critical dimension of a part has averaged 2.5 inches with a standard deviation of 0.6 inch. A sample of 36 parts was taken, and the

sample mean was found to be 2.75 inches. Test the hypothesis at the 5% significance level that the population mean is greater than 2.5 inches.

19. Construct your own probability plotting paper for an exponential distribution having a mean of 1,000. Illustrate its use for Example 4 in the text.

20. Determine if it can be concluded that the oven drying temperature data in Table 12.1 follows a normal distribution using a normal probability plot and the chi-square goodness-of-fit test. With the probability plot, estimate the mean and standard deviation and compare these estimates to the values computed in the text.

21. A hospital collected data on the number of medication errors per week versus the number of hours overtime worked by the nursing staff in a particular unit:

Hours Overtime	Number of Medication Errors
2	0
4	1
0	0.
0	1
5	5
1	0
6	1
0	1
2	0
3	2
4	3
0	2
6	6
5	2
5	2
3	1
1	0
2	1
4	1

  a. Plot the data on a scatter diagram and use the sign test to determine if a correlation exists at the 1% significance level.
  b. Calculate the regression equation and correlation coefficient.

22. The following data were obtained from tests of the relationship of mold temperature to breaking strength in a plastic injection molding process. The quality manager wanted to be able to estimate breaking strengths based on temperatures in order to determine if specifications for orders could be met. Calculate the regression equation and the coefficient of determination for this process. Comment on the degree of confidence that one could have in this analysis.

Breaking Strength	Temperature (Degrees C)
4.93	78
4.97	80
4.98	82
5.02	85
5.05	87
5.09	85
5.09	87
5.11	89
5.13	88
5.18	87
5.20	90
5.23	89

Case Problem[6]

The tragic loss of the space shuttle *Challenger* in January 1986 was attributed to failure in 0.280-inch-diameter O-rings in the booster rockets. The O-rings were designed to be forced into the small gap between two segments of the rocket assembly by the pressure of expanding gas immediately upon ignition of the rocket's fuel. A central question in discussions leading up to the decision to launch the *Challenger* was whether temperatures predicted for launch time would allow normal O-ring functioning. A year earlier O-rings of booster rockets of the shuttle (Flight 51-C) launched on January 24, 1985, had been found to be damaged. The only conclusion engineers could reach after examining the rocket's joints was that the unusually cold weather at the time of the launch had caused the O-rings to harden, allowing more gas to blow by and erode the rings. The temperature for that launch had been estimated at 53 degrees F, the lowest temperature of any launch up to that point. The predicted temperature for the *Challenger* launch (Flight 51-L) was 29 degrees F.

Table 12.11 provides some data regarding the temperature at time of launch and the actual depth of O-ring erosion that was found for each prior launch. What conclusions can you reach from these data? Use whatever statistical techniques you feel are appropriate.

[6]Adapted from Frederick F. Lighthall, "Launching the Space Shuttle Challenger: Disciplinary Deficiencies in the Analysis of Engineering Data," *IEEE Transactions on Engineering*

TABLE 12.11 Temperatures and Actual Depths (inches) of Field Joint Erosion for 22 Space Shuttle Flights

Flight Number	Temperature of O-rings	Actual Depth of Erosion (in thousandths)
1	66	0
2	70	53
3	69	0
4	80	–
5	68	0
6	67	0
7	72	0
8	73	0
9	70	0
10	57	40
11	63	0
12	70	28
13	78	0
14	67	0
15 51-C	53	48
16	67	0
17	75	0
18	70	0
19	81	0
20	76	0
21	79	0
22	75	0
23[a]	76	0
25 51-L	29	–

[a]Data from Flight 24 are omitted because they would not have been available for analysis by the eve of the Challenger launch.

Management, Vol. 38, No. 1, February 1991, pp. 63–74 © 1991 IEEE.

Bibliography

Chatfield, Christopher. *Statistics for Technology: A Course in Applied Statistics.* New York: Halstead Press, Div. of John Wiley & Sons, 1978.

Duncan, Acheson J. *Quality Control and Industrial Statistics,* 5th ed. Homewood, IL: Richard D. Irwin, 1986.

Ishikawa, Kaoru. *Guide to Quality Control.* Tokyo: Asian Productivity Organization, 1976.

Lapin, Lawrence L. *Statistics for Modern Business Decisions,* 4th ed. San Diego: Harcourt Brace Jovanovich, Inc., 1987.

Lipson, Charles, and Sheth, Narendra J. *Statistical Design and Analysis of Engineering Experiments.* New York: McGraw-Hill, 1973.

McGill, R., Tukey, J. W., and Larsen, W. A. "Variations of Box Plots," *The American Statistician,* Vol. 38, February 1978, pp. 12–16.

Nelson, Wayne. *How to Analyze Data With Simple Plots, ASQC Basic References in Quality Control: Statistical Techniques,* Vol. 1, Milwaukee, WI: American Society for Quality Control, 1986.

Statistical Quality Control Handbook. 2nd ed. Indianapolis, IN: AT&T Technologies, 1958.

Tukey, J. W. *Exploratory Data Analysis.* New York: Addison-Wesley, 1977.

Yamane, Taro. *Elementary Sampling Theory.* Englewood Cliffs, NJ: Prentice-Hall, 1967.

Zubairi, Mazhar M. "Statistical Process Control Management Issues," *1985 IIE Fall Conference Proceedings,* reprinted in Mehran Sepehri (ed.), *Quest for Quality: Managing the Total System.* Norcross, GA: Industrial Engineering & Management Press, 1987.

CHAPTER 13

Inspection and Measurement

Statistical thinking forms the basis for the reduction of variation and the improvement of quality. To collect data on which to assess the current state of quality and to make decisions, some form of inspection and measurement is necessary. In an often-repeated quote, Lord Kelvin stated "[If] you can measure what you are speaking about and can express it in numbers, you know something about it; but when you cannot measure it, when you cannot express it in numbers, your knowledge is of a meager and unsatisfactory kind." The principal reasons for inspection and measurement are to enable producers of goods and services to analyze and provide feedback on the quality of the product to permit short-term corrections or long-term improvements to be made. For example, we might inspect incoming raw materials and measure important quality characteristics to determine if they conform to purchasing specifications, inspect work in process to determine if any assignable causes of variation have crept into the production process, and inspect finished goods prior to shipment to avoid external failure costs.

Inspection serves as the control function that ties together quality of design with quality of conformance. The benefits of inspection are that it helps to evaluate the degree of conformance or nonconformance to specifications, provides for reporting of deficiencies early in the production process, and helps to assure that desired quality requirements have been met. Since quality decisions are based on inspection and measurement, undesirable consequences may result if these tasks are not performed properly.

In this chapter we will address the role of inspection in quality assurance, inspection planning activities, measurement technology and evaluation, and process capability—the application of inspection and measurement to evaluation of the ability of a process to meet specifications.

THE ROLE OF INSPECTION IN QUALITY ASSURANCE

Inspection is the judging of a product's conformance to specifications with feedback on the quality provided to the producer. Inspection has always been a vital part of manufacturing since the industrial revolution; however, the role of inspection has changed dramatically over the years. In this section we examine the traditional and modern roles of inspection.

Traditional Inspection Practices

Prior to the industrial revolution, inspection was not a separate function in production; craftspeople served as fabricators and inspectors and were entirely responsible for the quality of their products. Mass production and the interchangeability of parts made inspection a necessity. Separate job classifications for inspectors became common in industry. The task of the inspection department was to seek out defective items in production and remove them prior to shipment. Everyone knew that inspection was used simply to ensure that only good products would be shipped, because the pressure from management was for output, not quality. Inspectors became "policemen" who were to catch "lawbreakers"—the operators and others who contributed to poor quality products.

Traditional inspection practices typically involve heavy inspection of incoming materials and final product, with some off-line inspection of work in process. (Recall our discussion of acceptance inspection in Chapter 8.) As materials and components are received, they are routed to a staging area where each part of some sample is inspected for conformance to specifications. There is no trust in the supplier's ability to do what they are paid to do—supply conforming items. Rejected items or entire shipments are returned to the supplier. The labor cost and tied-up inventory add no value to the product, and delays incurred by inspection and returns make managing the production process more difficult. At final inspection, similar activities occur. The inspector's job is to separate good product from bad product. The bad product is either reworked or scrapped. In either case, unnecessary expense is incurred. In the case of rework, production flow must be disrupted. This adds unnecessary complexity to production control activities.

During the manufacturing process, inspectors typically make the rounds periodically, pick up some parts, bring them back to an inspection area, and check them. By the time the inspector determines that a problem exists, these parts have probably already made their way downstream in the production process or have been mixed with good parts waiting for transfer to the next operation. In the second case, a "hold for inspection" tag will be placed on the parts, and they will be moved to an inspection area for 100% inspection to separate the good parts from the bad. Note that this type of inspection does not directly involve the people who are actually making the parts.

Unfortunately, this scenario is all too common in many companies. Not only does it often result in poor quality, but it can also affect interpersonal relations. Inspectors are often promoted from the ranks of production workers and have close associations with shop personnel. When a part borders on being defective, an inspector may tend to err in favor of the operators to preserve their friendship and protect them from criticism or even loss of jobs because of consistently poor quality production. Conversely, the operators, believing that the inspection department will catch any nonconforming parts, may not take their own roles in producing quality products very seriously.

Modern Inspection Practices

Just as there are never enough officers to patrol every highway, there are never enough inspectors to inspect every part and catch every defect. Thus, the traditional practice of inspection is inefficient and ineffective. Deming clearly states that dependence on mass inspection as a means of quality control must cease. The Japanese have built their reputation around the phrase "Quality cannot be inspected into a product." We know today that companies that seek to *ship* only good product will not be competitive with those that seek to *produce* good product. Quality is everyone's responsibility. The new role of inspection is a means to an end, not the end in itself.

Figure 13.1 illustrates the role that inspection should play in quality assurance. Product specifications provide the basis for achieving quality in the production system. When materials and components are received, occasional inspection might be used to audit compliance. However, the suppliers themselves should be required to provide documentation and statistical evidence that they are meeting required specifications. If this is done properly, incoming inspection can be completely eliminated. Japan has been doing this for years, and many companies in the West now follow this practice.

Within manufacturing, inspection should be conducted in a statistical fashion and performed by the workers on the production line so that they have immediate feedback that can be used for process adjustment. The production operator and inspector become one again, similar to the way it was before the industrial revolution. If sufficient inspection and control are performed during the manufacturing process, then final inspection becomes unnecessary.

Inspection should be used as an auditing tool. The major role of inspection today should be for manufacturing process control. Unless inspection is performed as an integral part of the production process, time-based planning and organizing, as well as just-in-time material control, become impossible. Other reasons for inspection include generating documentation for customers on the factory's capability to produce consistent product that meets specifications and providing data for planning long-term improvements in both products and processes.

A number of radical reformers have argued that the total quality management concept eliminates the need for the inspection function and quality control departments at the operating level. However, this will probably never occur for a number of reasons. James A. Sears, manager of the Tire Division's quality assurance organization at The General Tire and Rubber Company, gave seven situations that

FIGURE 13.1 **The Inspection Process**

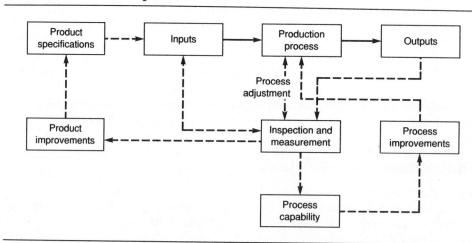

could cause an organization to maintain the traditional inspection function in operations areas despite the fact that a total quality concept had been adopted:[1]

1. Quality conformance may be required by government regulations.

2. Customer requirements specify an independent inspection activity.

3. Critical parts or materials require close scrutiny by an independent inspection function to prevent economic losses from defective items.

4. Centralized inspection is needed to accomplish testing using expensive inspection equipment in a timely and cost-effective fashion.

5. Inspection and testing activities require specialized skill or in-depth training for the person performing the work.

6. Strategically placed inspection personnel may be able to give early warnings of potentially catastrophic situations before they cause major damage.

7. Management audit and review requirements may necessitate an impartial inspection and quality assurance function.

Thus, although the nature of inspection has changed over time, inspection will always remain an important activity in quality assurance.

ISO 9000 Inspection Standards

Government contractors must adhere to rigid inspection system standards. Such standards have been in use for many years and provide a useful guideline for companies to implement formal inspection systems. Recently, the "Europe 1992" plan for free trade among 12 European nations, due to go into effect at the end of 1992, has had a major impact on standardization of quality systems, particularly those relating to inspection. The results have been felt not only in Europe, but in North America, Asia, and throughout the world.

The two major forces behind this worldwide impact are markets and common standards. The European market cannot be ignored by any firm seeking to do business outside of its own country. According to Boehling,[2]

> When . . . complete, the single integrated market will contain 320 million consumers, plus 30 million more from the six European Free Trade Association countries, which have bridging agreements. These 350 million citizens will represent the largest trade market in the free world. (The United States has 250 million and Japan has 120 million.)

To standardize requirements for European countries within the common market and those wishing to do business with those countries, a specialized agency for standardization, the International Organization for Standardization (ISO), adopted a series of written quality standards in 1987[3]. The ISO is a powerful body, comprised of

[1]James A. Sears, "Changing Role of the Quality Inspection Function," *Quality Progress,* July 14, 1983, pp. 12–17.

[2]Walter H. Boehling, "Europe 1992: Its Effect on International Standards," *Quality Progress,* June 1990, pp. 29–32.

[3]"World Quality: Making Connections Through Standards," *Quality Progress,* June 1990, pp. 16–17.

representatives from the national standards bodies of 91 nations. The written standards are called the ISO 9000 series. For instance, any telecommunications product that interfaces with the European telecommunications network must be purchased from manufacturers that have been certified to be in compliance with ISO 9000. The standards have been adopted in the United States by our national standards body, the American National Standards Institute (ANSI), with the endorsement and cooperation of the American Society for Quality Control. The American version of the ISO 9000 standards have been relabeled the ANSI/ASQC Q90-1987 series. They contain five sections on the topics shown in Table 13.1.[4]

The Q90 section of the ISO/ANSI standard provides an overview and description of the standards, and it suggests that suppliers and purchasers agree to choose either Q91, Q92, or Q93 as the quality standard model to be followed in their contracts with each other. The standard suggests that the choice of Q91, Q92, or Q93 should be

"based on the 'functional or organizational capability' required of a supplier for a product or service:

a) Q91 applies to companies that are involved in complete product development. This includes design, development, production, test, final inspection, installation, and service.

b) Q92 applies to companies that are involved only in manufacture, test, final inspection, and installation.

c) Q93 applies to companies that are involved only in the test and final inspection of a product.

The Q94 section of the ISO/ANSI standard provides general guidelines for internal use within supplier companies on how to design and develop an integrated total quality management system. It facilitates the specifications and requirements found in the Q91, Q92, and Q93 sections.

For example, in terms of product development, the standard requires a company to understand what customers want, verify and control the design to meet requirements, provide employees with the correct documentation, assume responsibility for vendor and internal quality, maintain material traceability throughout the

---

[4]Ibid, p. 17. Adapted from a table that originally appeared in the March 1990 issue of *Quality News,* which is published by the Institute of Quality Assurance, London, England.

TABLE 13.1 Quality Content of ISO 9000/Q90 Standards

Title by Section	ISO Number	ANSI/ASQC Number
Quality management and quality assurance standards: guidelines for selection and use	9000	Q90
Quality systems: model for quality assurance in design/development, production, installation, and servicing	9001	Q91
Quality systems: model for quality assurance in production and installation	9002	Q92
Quality systems: model for quality assurance in final inspection and test	9003	Q93
Quality management and quality system elements: guidelines	9004	Q94

assembly process, assure process stability and control, accomplish and document incoming, in-process, and final inspection, calibrate test equipment to ensure correct measurement, certify vendors, maintain an effective quality management system, and maintain appropriate product records and documentation.

Once the determination of the Q91–93 standard is agreed on, the supplier must prove that it is qualified to meet the standard requirements by demonstration and documentation of its capabilities. Demonstration of quality capability can be shown by reference to present and previous products and a track record in the marketplace. Documentation criteria are set by the purchaser and are subject to verification via examination of quality manuals, descriptions of quality-related procedures, and various other quality records. A provision in the standards allows the purchaser to use precontract assessment by an independent organization in lieu of individual purchaser certification of each supplier. In fact, an accreditation process has been developed by the British Standards Institute and has already been used by a large number of companies in Britain who are doing business in the 12 Common Market countries.[5] The British accreditation process may become the model for certification of quality assurance conformance to the ISO standards for future business in Europe. An equivalent certification process is under development in the United States under the auspices of the ASQC.

TECHNICAL SPECIFICATIONS

The basis for inspection lies in product specifications that are developed during product design. The description of product specifications is often aided by engineering drawings. Several types of engineering drawings are used. Two of the most important are the assembly drawing and detailed engineering drawing. Figure 13.2 is an example of an assembly drawing of a carburetor for a four-cycle lawnmower engine. An assembly drawing is an exploded view of the individual components of a product and their relationship to one another. Usually accompanying an assembly drawing is a parts list, such as the one shown in Figure 13.3. Parts lists include such items of information as part number, name, whether it is manufactured or purchased, and a detailed engineering drawing number. In addition, they may contain dimensional information, material specifications, and other manufacturing data.

Detailed engineering drawings, such as the one illustrated in Figure 13.4, provide the necessary technical specifications for manufacturing personnel to produce a part or for purchasing agents to procure an item from vendors. For purchased parts, engineering drawings provide a legal basis for the contract between the vendor and the company. Such drawings are also used to inspect finished parts and establish conformance to specifications. Assembly drawings and detailed drawings are important inputs to process design. They aid in determining what materials and machines are required, which establishes the feasibility of production with existing equipment or the need for new equipment.

Drawings represent the transition from a designer's concept to implementable manufacturing specifications. The key components are **nominal dimensions** and **tolerances.** These have a major influence on quality. Nominal refers to the ideal dimension, the target value in the context of the Taguchi loss function; tolerance

---

[5]John T. Burr, "The Future Necessity," *Quality Progress,* June 1990, pp. 19–23.

FIGURE 13.2   **Assembly Drawing of Lawnmower Carburetor**

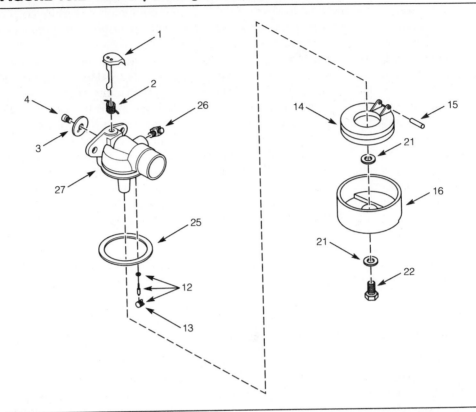

SOURCE: Courtesy of Sears, Roebuck and Co.

FIGURE 13.3   **Parts List for Lawnmower Carburetor**

Parts List for Carburetor 631928				
Ref. no.	Part no.	Name	Make or buy	Drawing file no.
1	631615	Throttle shaft and lever assy.	Make	26079
2	630731	Throttle return spring	Buy	26080
3	631616	Throttle shutter	Make	20091
4	650506	Screw slotted washer head	Buy	25030
12	631021	Inlet needle, seat & clip assy.	Make	26026
13	631022	Inlet needle clip	Make	26030
14	631023	Carburetor float	Make	26031
15	631024	Float shaft	Buy	26048
16	631700	Float bowl	Make	26032
21	631334	Bowl-to-body gasket	Buy	26049
22	631617	Float bowl bolt	Buy	26352
25	631028	Bowl-to-body gasket	Buy	26053
26	631775	Fuel inlet fitting	Make	26054
27	631927	Housing	Make	26058

FIGURE 13.4   Detailed Engineering Drawing

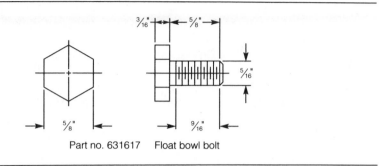

Part no. 631617   Float bowl bolt

refers to the permissible variation in a dimension or other quality characteristic. Figure 13.4 shows nominal dimensions for the bolt. The specification for the threaded diameter might be stated as 0.3125 ± 0.003. The nominal size is 0.3125 (5/16″); the tolerance of ±0.003 means that the dimension is permitted to vary between 0.3095 and 0.3155.

EXAMPLE 1   An Illustration of Tolerancing for a Microprocessor.
To further illustrate the notion of tolerance, consider a microprocessor. The drawing in Figure 13.5 shows some of the critical dimensions and tolerances for the microprocessor. A number of facts can be inferred about the design of the microprocessor based on an inspection of the tolerances.

Looking at the top view, it is obvious that the size of the base is not very critical, since the length is specified only as 2.100″ maximum and the width is permitted to vary by 0.074″ from a low of 0.514″ to a high of 0.588″. Looking at the side view, it can be seen that tighter tolerances are required on the dimensions of the pins (electrical leads) for the chip. The 0.230″ maximum from the top of

FIGURE 13.5   Microprocessor

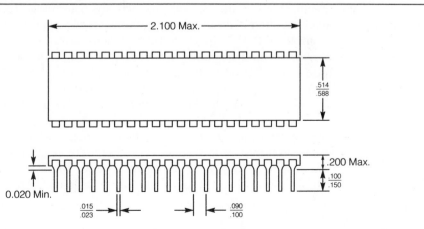

the chip to the neck of the pin is probably required to ensure that the pin is firmly attached to the base. On the opposite end, the 0.020″ minimum from the base to the neck of the pin is needed to provide clearance of the microprocessor above the socket into which the pins are to fit. Likewise, the length of the pin (0.100″ minimum to 0.150″ maximum) must be controlled so that a good fit is obtained. Spacing between the pins is very critical and is allowed to vary by only 0.01″ with the 0.090″ to 0.100″ tolerance. Finally, the most critical dimension is the width of each pin, which is permitted to have a precise 0.008″ tolerance, ranging from 0.015″ to 0.023″.

Tolerances are necessary because it is a fact of life that not all parts can be produced exactly to nominal specifications. This is a result of natural variations due to the "5 Ms": men and women, materials, machines, methods, and measurement. Design specifications must be made compatible with such inherent variation in the production process. Suppose, for example, that the natural variation of a machine is 0.3125 ± 0.004. Then the above specification cannot be achieved with 100% conformity. Some nonconforming parts will be made unless the production technology (at least one of the 5 Ms) is changed. The natural variation resulting from using a given combination of people, machinery, materials, methods, and measurements is known as **process capability.** If a process is incapable of producing within design specifications, management must weigh the cost of acquiring new technology against the consequences and related cost of allowing nonconformities to be produced. These costs may include, among others, requirements for 100% screening, allowing nonconforming parts further in the production process, and loss of present and future customers. Process capability is explored in more detail later in this chapter.

Both nominal specifications and tolerances relate design quality to quality of conformance. They are important concepts for managers and engineers because they provide a focal point for discussion of issues that relate design to manufacturing, manufacturing to plant engineering, plant operations to field service, and all of these back to redesign and product improvement. However, tolerances do not provide a license for simply meeting specifications. Efforts should be made to meet nominal values as closely as possible.

While the specifications of mechanical products are determined by designers, government regulations often determine specifications for food and pharmaceutical products. For example, the U.S. Food and Drug Administration sets standards regarding the number of unsavory items that find their way into food products.[6] Packaged mushrooms are allowed to contain up to 20 maggots of any size per 100 grams of drained mushrooms or 15 grams of dried mushrooms, while 100 grams of peanut butter may have an average of 30 insect fragments and one rodent hair. (Need we say more?)

In services, specifications are much more difficult to define and measure. They require extensive research into customer needs and attitudes regarding timeliness, consistency, accuracy, and other service attributes that we discussed in previous chapters. For example, Hertz advertises 54 quality standards including reservation

---

[6]Susan Dillingham, "A Little Gross Stuff in Food is OK by FDA," *Insight,* May 22, 1989, p. 25.

processing speed, courtesy shuttle, mechanical check of brake system and window washer operation, and an oil level check. Examples of service specifications by one of the airline industry leaders, Swissair, are:

- Ninety percent of calls are answered within 30 seconds.

- Ninety percent of passengers are checked in within 3 minutes of arrival.

- Eighty percent of flights are delayed no more than 15 minutes.

- Baggage claim time is only 10 minutes between the first and last customer.

- Complaints about meals are less than 3%.

- Complaints about staff are less than 1%.

While many product specifications developed for manufactured products are focused on meeting a target ("nominal is best" in the Taguchi philosophy), service targets typically are "smaller is better." Thus, the true service standard is zero defects, and any other standards (such as those of Swissair) should be construed as interim standards and targets only.

PLANNING INSPECTION ACTIVITIES

Inspection planning is the function of evaluating and determining inspection requirements, preparing for inspection, and defining methods and means for fulfilling those requirements. This includes the determination of facilities, equipment, personnel, procedures, and plans for inspection activities. The result of inspection planning is the **inspection plan,** a document that identifies what is to be inspected, how it is to be inspected, the location of inspection stations, frequency of inspection, and disposition of inspected items. Responsibility for inspection activities and coordination with other organizational groups, such as manufacturing, engineering, purchasing, and field service, must be determined.

What to Inspect

The purpose of inspection is to uncover nonconformities in products, that is, failures to meet specifications. Historically, the term *defect* was used instead of nonconformity. Because of the negative connotation of defect and its potential implications in liability suits, nonconformity has become widely accepted. However, we shall occasionally use these terms interchangeably to be consistent with current literature and practice.

Quality characteristics are those properties of a product that are to be evaluated against specifications. For example, if a specification states that the diameter, hardness, and weight of a ball bearing must lie within certain limits, then diameter, hardness, and weight are the quality characteristics that are inspected.

While specifications determine the quality characteristics that are designed into a product, inspection need not examine every possible quality characteristic. One way of determining what to inspect is to classify defects into three categories:[7]

---

[7]Glenn E. Hayes and Harry G. Romig, *Modern Quality Control* (Encino, CA: Benziger, Bruce & Glencoe, Inc., 1977).

1. *Critical defect:* A critical defect is one that judgment and experience indicate will surely result in hazardous or unsafe conditions for individuals using, maintaining, or depending on the product and will prevent performance of the function of the product.

2. *Major defect:* A major defect is one that is not critical but is likely to result in failure or to materially reduce the usability of the unit for its intended purpose.

3. *Minor defect:* A minor defect is one that is not likely to materially reduce the usability of the item for its intended purpose, nor will it have any bearing on the effective use or operation of the unit.

Critical defects should always be a basis for inspection at all costs, particularly since they may lead to serious consequences or product liability suits. Inspection of quality characteristics that may be classified as major defects depends on the strategic quality goals of the firm. One would expect that any company wishing to remain in business and achieve a competitive advantage in the marketplace would avoid major defects as much as possible. Minor defects, however, may escape inspection in many products, since they do not affect fitness for use. However, for many products, even minor defects may produce negative responses from customers. For example, a marred finish on a wrench would probably not cause much concern to a mechanic, while a similar defect on an automobile body would be unacceptable.

Type of Inspection

The type of quality characteristic to be inspected can be classified in one of two categories. An **attribute** is a characteristic of quality that is either present or absent in the unit or product under consideration. Attributes assume one of two values, for instance, conforming or not conforming, within tolerance or out of tolerance, complete or incomplete. An example of an attribute measurement would be the visual inspection of the color of an item from a printing process to determine whether or not it is acceptable. Another example is whether or not the correct ZIP code was used in shipping an order. A third example is whether or not the diameter of a shaft falls within specification limits of 1.60 ±0.01″.

The second type of quality characteristic is called a **variable.** Variables are appraised in terms of measurable values on a continuous scale, for instance, length or weight. With variables measurements, we are concerned with the *degree* of conformance to specifications. Thus, rather than determining whether or not the diameter of a shaft meets a specification of 1.60 ± 0.01″, we are concerned with the actual *value* of the diameter.

Inspection by attributes is usually simpler than inspection by variables for several reasons. The inspection itself can be done more quickly and easily, less information needs to be recorded, and administration of the inspection is easier. In a statistical sense, attributes inspection is less efficient than variables inspection. Thus, attributes inspection requires a larger sample than variables inspection to obtain the same amount of statistical information about the quality of the product. This difference can become significant when inspection is time-consuming or expensive. Most quality characteristics in services are attributes. This perhaps is one reason why service organizations have been slow to adopt quality control methods.

Locating Inspection Stations

In determining where to locate inspection stations, one must consider trade-offs between the explicit costs of detection, repair, or replacement and the implicit costs of unnecessary additional investment in a nonconforming item if inspection is not performed. While the location decision is fundamentally based on economics, it is a complex one, since it involves the trade-off between prevention and appraisal costs and failure costs as discussed in Chapter 3. It is not always easy or possible to quantify these costs.

Several rules of thumb have been proposed for the location decision. The more popular rules are:

- Locate before all processing operations, such as before every machine or assembly operation.

- Locate before relatively high cost operations or where significant value is added to the product.

- Locate before processing operations that may make detection of defectives difficult or costly, such as operations that may mask or obscure faulty attributes, for example, painting.

- Locate after operations likely to generate a high proportion of defectives.

- Locate after the finished product is completed.

No one rule is best in all situations. Simulation, economic analysis, and other quantitative tools often are used to evaluate a particular design for inspection activities.

Inspection Quantity

One important decision in inspection planning is the amount of inspection to be performed. Several factors should be considered: the type of product to be inspected, the quality characteristics to be examined for conformance, the quality history of the producer, the cost of inspection, and the effect of inspection on the product (for example, destructive testing). The decision is usually to use either 100% inspection or some form of sampling procedure.

One hundred percent inspection is the inspection of every unit that is produced. For critical quality characteristics, such inspection is usually required. While it provides the best assurance of conformance to specifications, it is not always perfect, because of such problems as human error, faulty measuring equipment, and use of incorrect standards. It is often not practical because of the time, effort, and costs involved. Clearly, it cannot be used when testing is destructive. With automated inspection techniques, 100% inspection is becoming more economical and feasible.

Sampling procedures involve inspecting only a portion of a production lot. They are useful in dealing with large quantities of noncritical quality characteristics. Sampling is more economical than 100% inspection but is subject to a higher degree of risk. The lower costs of sampling inspection must be weighed against the risk of greater cost incurred by permitting nonconforming products to be accepted. In practice, however, it has been shown that sampling inspection is generally superior to 100% inspection because of its ability to overcome systematic forms of human error.

Sampling procedures are based on concepts of probability and statistics and form the basis for most quality control procedures used in practice. Specific sampling methods for process control and inspection of incoming material or finished products are discussed in later chapters.

Inspection Methods

Traditional inspection activities include *acceptance inspection, classification inspection, control inspection,* and *audit inspection.* We shall illustrate each of these activities in the context of a policy preparation section of an insurance company.

As we discussed in Chapter 8, **acceptance inspection** is inspection of raw materials, parts, or components upon receipt from vendors, at any point in the production process, or after final production to decide whether or not to accept the items. The purpose of acceptance inspection is to ensure that products meet specified standards. The most common form of acceptance inspection is **receiving inspection,** in which materials or parts coming into an organization from an outside supplier are inspected for conformance to purchasing specifications. For example, the insurance company may purchase printed blank policy forms from an outside printer. When the blank forms arrive, they must be inspected to ensure that they are within the standards required in the purchase contract. If a certain number of forms are found to be defective during the sampling process, the entire shipment will be returned to the printer for rework.

Classification inspection is inspection required to separate parts into categories according to specifications. It is an in-process operation that may be located anywhere from the beginning to the end of a production process. Classification inspection is used in situations where a "grading" process is applicable. For example, policy applications coming in from field offices may have to be graded according to the information that they contain. Some forms may contain all information and be processed immediately. Other forms may have minor defects, such as missing information, for example, the name of the insurance agent who issued the policy. This piece of information could be obtained through a phone call to the field office. Vital information that is missing, such as the age of the customer or the customer's beneficiary, might require that the application be returned to the field office for reprocessing.

Control inspection is inspection of a periodic sample of work in process of an end product. Its purpose is to ensure that the process is operating within a state of statistical control and to provide timely feedback for correcting any deviations that indicate that the process is not producing to specifications. For example, a chart could be used to show the percentage of defective policies prepared within the department, and incentives could be provided for improvement. By tracking this statistic over time, managers can demonstrate the success of quality improvement initiatives.

Audit inspections are periodic, random inspections of plant or departmental quality processes and results. Audit inspections involve ensuring that procedures and processes are being followed so that the validity and reliability of the ongoing inspection operations of acceptance inspection, classification inspection, and control inspection may be maintained. In the insurance firm, this might include verification that sampling of incoming printed forms is being properly done, that insurance applications are being properly logged and classified, and that accurate data on error detection and correction is being gathered and used.

Human Factors Issues

Many inspection tasks are performed manually. Inspection is not always an easy task and is highly subject to error. Error rates of 10 to 50% are not uncommon. Ask three people to proofread a lengthy manuscript for typographical errors as an experiment. Rarely will everyone discover all errors, much less the same ones. The same is true of complicated industrial inspection tasks, especially those involving detailed microelectronics.

Inspection tasks are affected by several factors:

- *Complexity:* The number of defects caught by an inspector decreases with more parts and less orderly arrangement.

- *Defect rate:* When the product defect rate is low, inspectors tend to miss more defects than when the defect rate is higher. (This applies to the proofreading task.)

- *Repeated inspections:* Different inspectors do not miss the same defects. Therefore, if the same item is inspected by a number of different inspectors, a higher percentage of total defects will be caught.

- *Inspection rate:* The inspector's performance degrades rapidly as the inspection rate increases.[8]

As a result of understanding these factors, there are several ways to improve inspection:

- Minimize the number of quality characteristics considered in an inspection task. Five to six different types are approximately the maximum limit that the human mind can handle well at one time.

- Minimize disturbing influences and time pressures.

- Provide clear, detailed instructions for the inspection task.

- Design the workspace to facilitate the inspection task and provide good lighting.

MEASUREMENT

Measurement can be defined as the act of quantifying the amount of a characteristic that an item possesses. This term should be carefully distinguished from counting, which merely separates items into classes that exhibit or fail to exhibit the desired characteristic or characteristics. Measurement as well as counting provides important quantitative data on which to base decisions about quality. Before we can understand the measurement process, we must have a basic understanding of measurement systems.

Four levels, or scales, of measurement are commonly used in practice. They are the nominal, ordinal, interval, and ratio scales.

---

[8]Douglas H. Harris and Frederick B. Chaney, *Human Factors in Quality Assurance* (New York: John Wiley, 1969).

The **nominal scale** is used to name or identify objects and is not used in a dimensional sense. A common example is the use of numbers to identify players on a football team. Another example is the identification of part numbers in a product line.

The **ordinal scale** is used to rank objects on some characteristic or dimension. For example, a lumberyard may have bins where two-by-fours are ranked according to length. There may be bins for 12-, 10-, 8-, 6-, 3-, and 1-foot lengths. Notice that the rank ordering does not require that the dimension be equally spaced, or even accurately measured.

The **interval scale** requires equal intervals between adjacent units, although the scale has an arbitrary zero point. An example is the Fahrenheit or Celsius temperature scale. Each degree on each scale is the same size as on the other scale, although an arbitrary zero point has been established for each scale. On the Fahrenheit scale, zero is 32 degrees below the freezing point of water. On the Celsius scale, the freezing point of water has been arbitrarily established as the zero point.

The highest level of measurement is the **ratio scale.** On this scale, there must be an absolute, as opposed to an arbitrarily established, zero point. Examples of these scales are distance and weight. Figure 13.6 summarizes these four measurement scales and their differences.

Statistical quality control systems typically use a combination of measurement and counting to assess and improve the level of quality. For the purposes of this discussion, we will restrict ourselves to physical measurement systems, although many of these concepts and systems can be adapted to counting as well as to measurement. In measurement, the amount of a quality characteristic that an item possesses

FIGURE 13.6 **Four Classes of Measurement Scales**

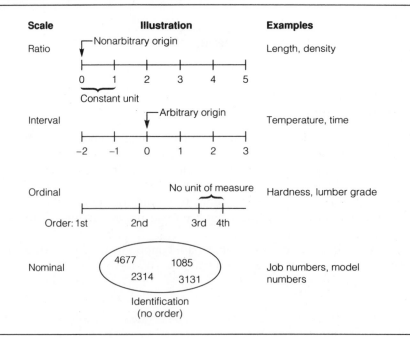

generally requires use of the human senses—seeing, hearing, feeling, tasting, and smelling—and the use of some type of instrument or gage to measure the magnitude of the quality characteristic in standard units.

The next section gives an overview of gages and measuring instruments and their applicability in manufacturing and service industries for quality monitoring and control.

Gages and Measuring Instruments

A number of "low-technology" and "high-technology" gages and measuring instruments are being used today in manufacturing and nonmanufacturing applications. By low-technology instruments we mean those devices that have been available for a number of years and that do not include recent high-technology advances such as microprocessors, lasers, or advanced optical devices. This section is confined to a discussion of such instruments. The impact of advanced technology on inspection is discussed later.

Gages can generally be divided into two basic categories: **variable gages** and **fixed gages.** Variable gages are adjusted to measure each individual part or dimension being inspected. Fixed gages are preset to a certain dimension, and parts being measured are classified according to whether or not they meet this dimension. The terms "go" and "no-go" are often used to signify this classification. We see that variable gages are used for variables inspection, and fixed gages are used for attributes inspection. The photographs in Figure 13.7 illustrate many of the types of gages discussed in this section.

There are several types of variable gages in use. **Line graduated gages** have graduated spacings representing known distances. They include rulers and tapes, various types of inside and outside calipers, and micrometers. Each instrument varies by function and precision of measurement. Rulers and tapes are used to measure length. They are generally accurate to within 1/64 inch. Vernier calipers are used to measure inside and outside diameters and are accurate to within 0.001 inch. Because of their construction, they require a considerable amount of skill to obtain accurate readings. Micrometers are also used to measure outside and inside diameters. Their usual accuracy is 0.001 inch, although some are made to measure in 0.0001-inch graduations. Micrometers have higher reliability in measuring than do vernier calipers.

Dial, digital, and **optical gages** show variations using a mechanical, electronic, or optical system to obtain dimensional readings. Dial gages use a mechanical system in which a movable contact touches the part to be measured and translates the dimensional characteristic through a gear train to the dial. The dimension is read from the face of the dial. Digital gages use electronic systems to translate the movement of the contact touching the part to be measured *directly* into a number or reading on a dial. This generally results in greater accuracy than a mechanical dial gage can provide. Optical gages use a lens system to magnify the profile of an object and to project it onto a screen so that it can be viewed and measured.

Fixed gages are much simpler than variable gages. Once they are set for a particular dimension, no adjustment is required as long as wear or deposits on the measuring surfaces are negligible. Types of fixed gages include plug gages, ring gages, snap gages, and gage blocks.

FIGURE 13.7 **Examples of Various Types of Gages**

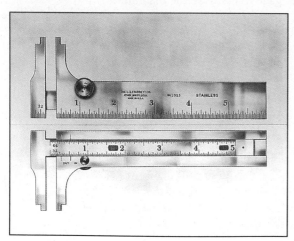

Line graduated gage

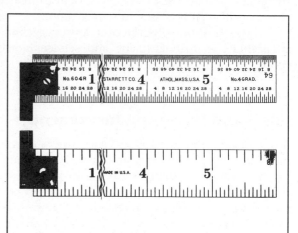

Steel hook rules

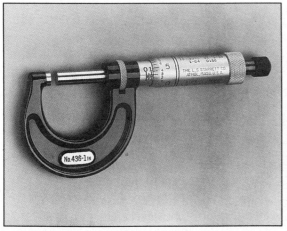

Micrometer

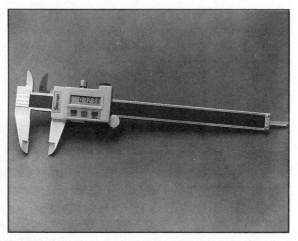

Digital caliper

Dial gage

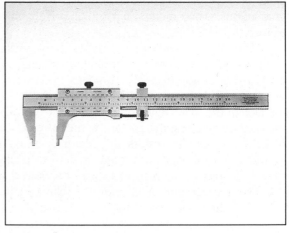

Vernier caliper

FIGURE 13.7 Continued

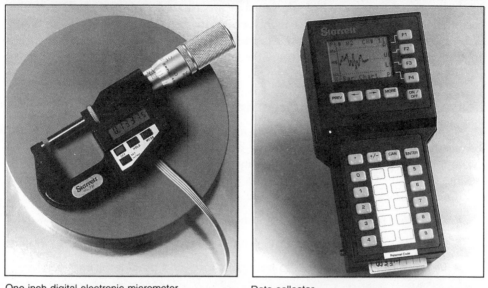

One-inch digital electronic micrometer   Data collector

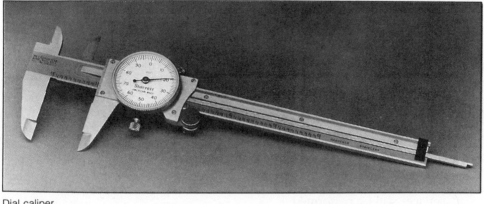

Dial caliper

SOURCE: Courtesy of the L. S. Starrett Company.

Plug gages are used to measure the inside diameters of bores. They have a machined diameter on one or both ends corresponding to go/no-go dimensions that have been specified for the bore being inspected. If the bore is larger than the no-go dimension of the plug gage, the part is rejected. If the bore is smaller than the go dimension, it must be rebored to meet the minimum size specification.

Ring gages are used to measure outside diameters of parts using a go/no-go principle. Typically, they are made in pairs, with a no-go ring being used for the minimum dimension and a go ring being used for the maximum size limit.

Snap gages are similar to ring gages in purpose but operate in a different fashion. They are used to measure outside diameters of parts but have an open-ended construction so that they can snap onto the diameter of the part.

Gage blocks are special types of fixed gages designed to be used as a precision measurement standard for calibration of other measuring and inspection instruments. Gage blocks are constructed of special steel in various lengths and have carefully machined, perfectly parallel, and highly polished measuring end surfaces. When stacked together, various combinations of lengths can be used to produce accurately any desired dimension to the nearest 0.0001 inch.

Measurement in Service Organizations

While the quality of goods can be measured objectively, service quality is more abstract and elusive. One approach for assessing service quality is to measure consumer's perceptions. Perceived quality is the consumer's judgment about a product's overall excellence. Research has shown that five key dimensions used by consumers in assessing service quality are

- *Tangibles:* physical facilities, equipment, and appearance of personnel
- *Reliability:* ability to perform the promised service dependably and accurately
- *Responsiveness:* willingness to help customers and provide prompt service
- *Assurance:* knowledge and courtesy of employees and their ability to inspire trust and confidence
- *Empathy:* caring, individualized attention the firm provides its customers.[9]

Measurement of service quality attributes typically is performed by using some type of survey questionnaire. Such an instrument would measure both consumer's expectations and perceptions about a service. For example, to measure expectations, one might solicit responses on a "strongly disagree" to "strongly agree" scale to statements such as the following:

- Equipment should be up-to-date.
- Physical facilities should be visually appealing.
- Firms in this industry should not be expected to tell customers exactly when services will be performed.

Measurement of perceptions about a particular firm would solicit responses to statements such as the following:

- This company has up-to-date equipment.
- This company's physical facilities are visually appealing.
- This company provides its services at the time it promises to do so.

By examining scores for items associated with particular quality dimensions, a service organization can determine gaps in their service levels and determine the relative importance of the various dimensions in influencing customers' quality perceptions.

---

[9]A. Parasuraman, V. A. Zeithaml, and L. L. Berry, "SERVQUAL: A Multiple-Item Scale for Measuring Consumer Perceptions of Service Quality," *Journal of Retailing,* Vol. 64, No. 1, Spring 1988, pp. 12–40.

In many service industries, very specific questions can be asked. For instance, a bank might ask how important each of the following service characteristics is on a "not important" to "extremely important" scale:

- Offers a variety of financial services.
- Does a good job of handling transactions by mail.
- Does a good job of handling transactions by phone.
- Does a good job of coordinating the different types of accounts a customer may have.

Internal measurement of service quality for purposes of control is commonly performed through some type of checklist. Most quality characteristics surveyed are attributes; thus, the observed data assume "yes" or "no" values. For example, a survey of pharmaceutical operations in a hospital might include the following questions:

- Are drug storage and preparation areas within the pharmacy under the supervision of a pharmacist?
- Are drugs requiring special conditions for storing properly stored?
- Are drug emergency boxes inspected on a monthly basis?
- Is the drug emergency box record book filled out completely?

Hotels, restaurants, and other service operations use similar survey information to measure and monitor quality. The form of the questionnaire or survey is not as important as collecting the right information. Thus, service organizations must understand what quality characteristics are important.

METROLOGY

Metrology is the science of measurement. Originally its use referred only to measurements of the physical attributes of an object. Today, metrology is defined broadly and is the collection of people, equipment, facilities, methods, and procedures used to assure correctness or adequacy of measurements. Metrology is vital to quality assurance because of the increasing emphasis on quality by government agencies, the implications of measurement error on safety and product liability, and the reliance on improved quality control methods such as statistical process control.

Every measurement is subject to error. Whenever variation is observed in measurements, some portion is due to measurement system error. Some errors are systematic (called *bias*); others are random. How large the errors are relative to the measurement value can significantly affect the quality of the data and resulting decisions. The evaluation of data obtained from inspection and measurement is not meaningful unless the measurement instruments are accurate, precise, and reproducible.

Accuracy is defined as the closeness of agreement between an observed value and an accepted reference value or standard. The lack of accuracy reflects a systematic bias in the measurement such as the gage being out of calibration, being worn, or being used improperly by the operator. Accuracy is measured as the amount of error in a measurement in proportion to the total size of the measurement. One measurement is more accurate than another if it has a smaller relative error. For example, suppose that two instruments measure a dimension whose true value is 0.250″. Instrument A may read 0.248″, while instrument B may read 0.259″. The relative error of instrument A is $(0.250 - 0.248)/0.250 = 0.8\%$, while that of instrument B is $(0.259 - 0.250)/0.250 = 3.6\%$. Thus, instrument A is said to be more accurate than instrument B.

Precision, or *repeatability,* is defined as the closeness of agreement between randomly selected individual measurements or results. Precision, therefore, relates to the variance of repeated measurements. A measuring instrument having a low variance is said to be more precise than another having a higher variance. Low precision is due to random variation that is built into the instrument, such as friction among its parts. This may be the result of a poor design or lack of maintenance.

A measurement system may be precise but not necessarily accurate at the same time. In the example above, suppose that each instrument is used to measure the dimension three times. Instrument A may record values of 0.248, 0.246, and 0.251, while instrument B may record values of 0.259, 0.258, and 0.259. Instrument B is therefore more precise than instrument A.

The relationships between accuracy and precision are summarized in Figure 13.8. The figure illustrates four possible frequency distributions of ten repeated measurements of some quality characteristic. In Figure 13.8(a), the average measure-

FIGURE 13.8 **Accuracy versus Precision**

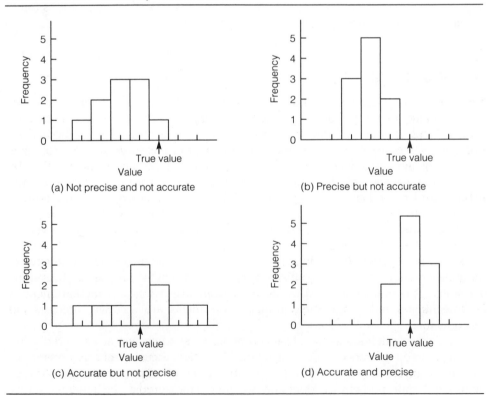

(a) Not precise and not accurate

(b) Precise but not accurate

(c) Accurate but not precise

(d) Accurate and precise

ment is not very close to the true value. Moreover, there is a wide range of values around the average. In this case, the measurement is neither accurate nor precise. In Figure 13.8(b), even though the average measurement is not close to the true value, there is a small range of variation. Thus, we say that the measurement is precise but not accurate. In Figures 13.8(c) and (d), the average value is close to the true value—that is, the measurement is accurate—but in 13.8(c) the distribution is widely dispersed and therefore not precise, while the measurement in 13.8(d) is both accurate *and* precise. Thus, it is vital that all instruments used for quality measurements be properly calibrated and maintained in good working order.

Reproducibility is the variation in the same measuring instrument when it is used by different individuals to measure the same parts. Causes of poor reproducibility include poor training of the operators in the use of the instrument or unclear calibrations on the gage dial.

The quality of a product depends on the use of accurate, precise, and reproducible measurement and test equipment for inspections. One of the most important functions of metrology is *calibration*. Calibration is the comparison of a measurement device or system having a known relationship to national standards to another device or system whose relationship to national standards is unknown. Calibration is necessary to ensure the accuracy of measurement and hence to have confidence in the ability to distinguish between conforming and nonconforming production. Measurements made with uncalibrated or inadequately calibrated equipment can lead to erroneous and costly decisions. For example, suppose that an inspector has a micrometer that is reading +0.002″ too low. When measurements are made close to the upper limit, parts that are as much as 0.002″ over the maximum tolerance limit will be accepted as good, while those at the lower tolerance limit or that are as much as 0.002″ above the limit will be rejected as nonconforming.

National standards are maintained and monitored by the National Bureau of Standards (NBS). The NBS works with various metrology laboratories in industry and government to assure that measurements made by different people in different places yield the same results. Thus, the measurement of "voltage" or "resistance" in an electrical component has a precise and universal meaning. This process is accomplished in a hierarchical fashion. The NBS calibrates the reference-level standards of those organizations requiring the highest level of accuracy. These organizations calibrate their own working-level standards and those of other metrology laboratories. These working-level standards are used to calibrate the measuring instruments used in the field. The usual recommendation is that equipment be calibrated against working-level standards that are 10 times as accurate as the equipment. When possible, there should be at least a four-to-one accuracy ratio between the reference- and working-level standards; that is, the reference standards should be at least four times as accurate as the working-level standards.

The ability to quantify a laboratory's measurement uncertainty in relationship to national standards is called *traceability*. Traceability is based on analyses of measurement error along each step of the calibration process, from the NBS standards, to the measurement laboratory, and finally to the measurement of the item itself. Such traceability is usually required in government contracts.

A typical calibration system involves the following activities:

■ evaluation of equipment to determine its capability

■ identification of calibration requirements

- selection of standards to perform calibration

- selection of methods and procedures to perform the calibration

- establishment of calibration frequency and rules for adjusting this frequency

- establishment of a system to ensure that instruments are calibrated according to schedule

- implementation of a documentation and reporting system

- establishment of an auditing process to evaluate the calibration system.

The accuracy, repeatability, and reproducibility of any measurement system must be quantified and evaluated. Accuracy can be measured by comparing the observed average of a set of measurements to the true value of a reference standard. Repeatability and reproducibility require a study of variation and can be addressed through statistical analysis. A repeatability and reproducibility study is conducted as follows:[10]

1. Select m operators and n parts. Typically at least two operators and 10 parts are chosen. Number the parts so that the numbers are not visible to the operators.

2. Calibrate the measuring instrument.

3. Let each operator measure each part in a random order and record the results. Repeat this for a total of r trials. At least two trials must be used. Let M_{ijk} represent the kth measurement of operator i on part j.

4. Compute the average measurement for each operator:

$$\bar{x}_i = \left(\sum_j \sum_k M_{ijk}\right)/nr$$

The difference between the largest and smallest average is

$$\bar{x}_D = \max_i\{\bar{x}_i\} - \min_i\{\bar{x}_i\}$$

5. Compute the range for each part and each operator:

$$R_{ij} = \max_k\{M_{ijk}\} - \min_k\{M_{ijk}\}$$

These values show the variability of repeated measurements of the same part by the same operator. Next, compute the average range for each operator:

$$\bar{R}_i = \left(\sum_j R_{ij}\right)/n$$

The overall average range is then computed as

$$\bar{\bar{R}} = \left(\sum_i R_i\right)/m$$

---

[10]ASQC *Automotive Division Statistical Process Control Manual* (Milwaukee, WI: American Society for Quality Control, 1986).

TABLE 13.2 Values of K_1 and K_2

Number of Trials	2	3	4	5
K_1	4.56	3.05	2.50	2.21
Number of Operators	2	3	4	5
K_2	3.65	2.70	2.30	2.08

6. Calculate a "control limit" on the individual ranges R_{ij}:

control limit $= D_4 \bar{\bar{R}}$

where D_4 is a constant that depends on the sample size (number of trials, r) and can be found in Appendix B at the end of this book. Any range value beyond this limit might result from some assignable cause, not random error. Possible causes should be investigated and, if found, corrected. The operator should repeat these measurements using the same part. If no assignable cause is found, these values should be discarded and all statistics in step 5 as well as the control limit should be recalculated.

Once these basic calculations are made, an analysis of repeatability and reproducibility can be performed. The repeatability, or equipment variation (EV) is computed as

$EV = K_1 \bar{\bar{R}}$

Reproducibility, or operator variation (OV) is computed as

$OV = \sqrt{(K_2 \bar{x}_D)^2 - (EV^2/nr)}$

The constants K_1 and K_2 depend on the number of trials and number of operators, respectively. Some values of these constants are given in Table 13.2. These constants provide a 99% confidence interval on these statistics.

An overall measure of repeatability and reproducibility is given by

$RR = \sqrt{(EV)^2 + (OV)^2}$

Repeatability and reproducibility are often expressed as a percent of the tolerance of the quality characteristic being measured. The American Society for Quality Control suggests the following guidelines for evaluating repeatability and reproducibility:

- *Under 10% error:* This is acceptable.

- *10 to 30% error:* This may be acceptable based on the importance of the application, cost of the instrument, cost of repair, and so on.

- *Over 30% error:* Generally, this is not acceptable. Every effort should be made to identify the problem and correct it.

EXAMPLE 2 A Gage Repeatability and Reproducibility Study.   The gage used to measure the thickness of a gasket having a specification of 0.50 to 1.0 mm is to be evaluated. Ten parts have been selected for measurement by three operators. Each part is measured twice with the following results:

Part Number\Trial	Operator 1		Operator 2		Operator 3	
	1	2	1	2	1	2
1	0.63	0.59	0.56	0.56	0.51	0.54
2	1.00	1.00	1.04	0.96	1.05	1.01
3	0.83	0.77	0.80	0.76	0.81	0.81
4	0.86	0.94	0.82	0.78	0.81	0.81
5	0.59	0.51	0.43	0.43	0.46	0.49
6	0.98	0.98	1.00	1.04	1.04	1.00
7	0.96	0.96	0.94	0.90	0.95	0.95
8	0.86	0.83	0.72	0.74	0.81	0.81
9	0.97	0.97	0.98	0.94	1.03	1.03
10	0.64	0.72	0.56	0.52	0.84	0.81

The average measurement for each operator, $\bar{x}_i$, is

$$\bar{x}_1 = 0.8295 \qquad \bar{x}_2 = 0.7740 \qquad \bar{x}_3 = 0.8285$$

Thus, $\bar{x}_D = 0.8295 - 0.7740 = 0.0555$. The range for each operator, R_{ij}, is shown below:

Part Number	Operator 1			Operator 2			Operator 3		
	1	2	Range	1	2	Range	1	2	Range
1	0.63	0.59	0.04	0.56	0.56	0.00	0.51	0.54	0.03
2	1.00	1.00	0.00	1.04	0.96	0.08	1.05	1.01	0.04
3	0.83	0.77	0.06	0.80	0.76	0.04	0.81	0.81	0.00
4	0.86	0.94	0.08	0.82	0.78	0.04	0.81	0.81	0.00
5	0.59	0.51	0.08	0.43	0.43	0.00	0.46	0.49	0.03
6	0.98	0.98	0.00	1.00	1.04	0.04	1.04	1.00	0.04
7	0.96	0.96	0.00	0.94	0.90	0.04	0.95	0.95	0.00
8	0.86	0.83	0.03	0.72	0.74	0.02	0.81	0.81	0.00
9	0.97	0.97	0.00	0.98	0.94	0.04	1.03	1.03	0.00
10	0.64	0.72	0.08	0.56	0.52	0.04	0.84	0.81	0.03

The average range for each operator is

$$\bar{R}_1 = 0.037 \qquad \bar{R}_2 = 0.034 \qquad \bar{R}_3 = 0.017$$

The overall average range is $\bar{\bar{R}} = (0.036 + 0.034 + 0.017)/3 = 0.029$. From Appendix B at the end of the book, $D_4 = 3.267$ since there are two trials. Hence the control limit is $(3.267)(0.029) = 0.095$. We see that all range values fall below this limit and, therefore, no assignable causes of variation are suspected. We compute the repeatability and reproducibility measures:

$$EV = (4.56)(0.029) = 0.132$$

$$OV = \sqrt{[(0.0555)(2.70)]^2 - (0.132)^2/(10)(2)} = 0.147$$

$$RR = \sqrt{(0.132)^2 + (0.147)^2} = 0.198$$

Since the tolerance of the gasket is $1.00 - 0.50 = 0.50$, these measures expressed as a percent of tolerance are:

equipment variation $= 100(0.132)/0.50 = 26.4\%$
operator variation $= 100(0.147)/0.50 = 29.4\%$
total R and R variation $= 100(0.198)/0.50 = 39.6\%$

While individually, the equipment and operator variation may be acceptable, their combined effect is not. Efforts should be made to reduce the variation to an acceptable level.

AUTOMATION AND INSPECTION TECHNOLOGY

Microprocessor technology has revolutionized the tasks of inspection and measurement. The potential uses of microprocessors in quality management and control are still being developed at an astonishing rate today. Processes as diverse as manufacturing and microwave cooking can be monitored for correct temperature and timing. Heart monitors and grocery checkout scanners automatically store data for later analysis. Handheld micrometers can run "instant" process capability studies from readings taken on the shop floor. If desired, the readings can be loaded into a desktop personal computer for more thorough analysis.

A variety of automated testing and measuring equipment has been introduced in recent years. One of the most highly accurate and sophisticated instruments with digital readouts is the *coordinate measuring machine*. This versatile machine, often costing $50,000 to $100,000 or more, combines optics and computer technology to measure dimensional characteristics that would be impossible to measure using conventional measuring instruments. *Photogrammetry* is an indirect, noncontact measurement process by which three-dimensional relationships in real space are determined through mathematical analysis of data extracted from photographic images. This process has applications in periodic inspection of assembly tools and real-time realignment of assembly tools.

Electro-optical measurements are based on *optical digitizing*. This is a technique for transforming the optical field of view into an n-dimensional matrix. The system requires an average of one second per measurement with an accuracy of $+0.001$ inch or less over a 24×24-inch measuring range. *Fluorescent penetrant inspection* consists of having parts treated with an electrostatic penetrant spray and inspected by blacklight.

Vision systems consist of a camera and video analyzer, a microcomputer, and a display screen. Computer vision systems can read symbols, identify objects, measure dimensions, and inspect parts for flaws. In quality control applications, vision systems are used to measure, verify, or inspect parts for dimensional tolerances, completeness of assembly, or mechanical defects.

In the automotive industry, vision systems are used in conjunction with robots to weld body seams of varying widths, tighten imprecisely located bolts, and mark indentification numbers on engines and transmissions using lasers. At a General Motors plant in Lansing, Michigan, a vision-equipped robot system finds the exact location of a dozen lower suspension-rail bolts, then uses a pneumatic nut-runner attachment to tighten the bolts to precise torque specifications. The system works by visually locating two gage holes on the underbody of the car. From these two points, the robot's control computer can calculate the exact locations of the 12 bolts and guide wrench sockets to the bolt heads. The system has resulted in more accurate bolt torquing and less manual rework downstream on the assembly line.[11]

PROCESS CAPABILITY

All quality leadership philosophies stress continuous improvement. Too many people believe that this concept refers only to products. Having the best designed product in the world cannot enable a business to succeed if the processes that produces that product are not capable of meeting product specifications. The philosophy of continuous improvement must be focused on *process* improvement. Process improvements reduce waste and thus reduce costs and improve productivity. Deming, Juran, and Taguchi all focus attention on reducing variation in process output. To do this, we must first be able to quantify that variation.

Process capability is the range over which the natural variation of a process occurs as determined by the system of common causes. It is the ability of the combination of people, machines, methods, materials, and measurements to produce a product or service that will consistently meet design specifications. Process capability is measured by the proportion of output that can be produced within design specifications; in other words, it is a measure of the uniformity of the process. Process capability can be measured only if all special causes have been eliminated and the process is in a state of statistical control. In subsequent discussions we shall generally assume that the process is in control.

Process capability is important to both product designers and manufacturing engineers. Process capability studies allow one to predict, quantitatively, how well a process will meet specifications and to specify equipment requirements. For example, if a design specification requires a length of metal tubing to be cut within one-tenth of an inch, a process consisting of a worker using a ruler and hacksaw will probably result in a large percentage of nonconforming product. In such a case, the process is not capable of meeting the design specifications. Management then has three possible decisions: (1) measure each piece and either recut or scrap nonconforming parts, (2) develop a better process by investing in new technology, or (3) change the design specifications.

Such decisions are usually based on economics. Scrap and rework are poor strategies, since labor and materials have already been invested in a bad product. Also, inspection errors will probably allow some nonconforming products to leave the production facility. New technology might require substantial investment that the firm cannot afford. Changes in design may sacrifice fitness-for-use requirements and result in a lower quality product. Thus, it is crucial that process capability be considered in product design and acceptance of new contracts. Many firms now require process capability data from their suppliers.

Product design often takes place in isolation, with inexperienced designers applying tolerances to parts or products while having little awareness of the capabilities of the production process to meet these design requirements. Even experienced designers may be hard pressed to remain up-to-date on the capabilities

---

[11]Stuart F. Brown, "Building Cars with Machines That See," *Popular Science,* October 1985.

of processes that involve constant equipment changes, shifting technology, and difficult-to-measure variations in methods at scores of plants located hundreds or thousands of miles away from a centralized product design department. Process capability should be carefully considered in determining design specifications.

Process capability information can also be used by production personnel to compare the natural variability to specifications and predict the amount of yield of conforming product in situations where it would not be practical to invest in new technology or to change the design specifications. Knowledge of existing process capability aids in planning production schedules and inspection strategies.

Process capability has three important components: (1) the design specifications, (2) the centering of the natural variation, and (3) the range, or spread, of variation. Figure 13.9 illustrates four possible outcomes that can arise when natural process variability is compared with design specifications. In Figure 13.9(a), the specifications are looser than the natural variation, and one would expect that the process will always produce conforming products as long as it remains in control. It may even be possible to reduce costs by investing in a cheaper technology that allows for a larger variation in the process output. In Figure 13.9(b), the natural variation and specifications are the same. A very small percentage of nonconforming products might be produced; thus, the process should be closely monitored.

In Figure 13.9(c), the range of natural variability is larger than the specification; thus, it will be impossible for the current process to meet specifications even when it is in control. This is often the result of a lack of adequate communication between the design department and manufacturing. If the process is in control but cannot produce according to the design specifications, the question should be raised whether the specifications have been correctly applied or if they may be relaxed without adversely affecting the assembly or use of the product. If the specifications are realistic, an effort must be made to improve the process to the point where it is capable of producing consistently within specifications.

FIGURE 13.9 Natural Variability versus Specifications for Process Capability

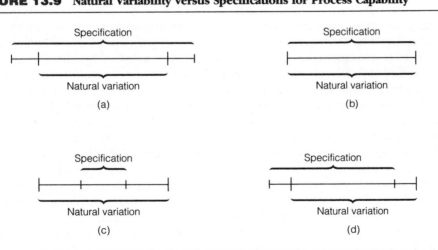

Finally, in Figure 13.9(d), the variability is the same, but the process average is off-center. This might result from a faulty machine setting or poorly calibrated inspection equipment. In such cases, adjustment is required to move the process back within specification. If no action is taken, a substantial portion of output will fall outside the specification limit even though the process may appear to be in control.

One might think that having the natural tolerance equal to design tolerance would be good quality. After all, if the distribution is normal, only 0.27% of the output would be expected to fall outside the design tolerance range. Consider what such a level of quality really means:

- at least 20,000 wrong drug prescriptions each year
- more than 15,000 babies accidently dropped each year by nurses and obstetricians
- no electricity, water, or heat for about nine hours each year
- 500 incorrect surgical operations each week
- 2,000 lost pieces of mail each hour.

Are you satisfied with such quality? Neither was Motorola, one of the first winners of the Malcolm Baldrige National Quality Award, which set the following goal in 1987:

> Improve product and services quality ten times by 1989, and at least one hundred fold by 1991. Achieve six sigma capability by 1992. With a deep sense of urgency, spread dedication to quality to every facet of the corporation, and achieve a culture of continual improvement to assure total customer satisfaction. There is only one ultimate goal: zero defects—in everything we do.

The concept of "six sigma" quality means that while the natural variation of a process is defined by $\pm 3\sigma$, the design tolerance should be $\pm 6\sigma$; that is, the design tolerance should be twice as large as the natural tolerance. Instead of 2.7 defects per thousand (2,700 defects per million) as represented by "three sigma" quality, six sigma quality translates to 3.4 defects per million. Defects per million is now the global standard for quality measurement.

Product specifications and process capability form an unbreakable link between design, manufacturing, and quality. If product specifications of parts and components are good (that is, not too tight and not too loose), manufacturing units will use the capability of their processes and equipment to produce good, standard high-quality parts and assemblies, although a small percentage may be nonconforming. However, if product specifications are too tight, the product will be seen as very difficult to make by manufacturing units, and a large proportion of nonconforming products may result. Close tolerances often are hard to achieve, hard to hold, and hard to measure and, of course, can be very costly. Although customers using such products often appreciate the apparent high quality, the products are often difficult to maintain.

On the other hand, one must be cautious about product specifications that are too loose. In this case, process capability and assembly of the product will be easy to achieve, but fitness for use may be negatively affected, resulting in frequent breakdowns and repairs. Designers and manufacturing engineers both must consider these issues very carefully in determining product specifications and processes to achieve the quality objectives of the firm.

Statistical Analysis of Process Variation

A *process capability study* is a carefully planned study designed to yield specific information about the performance of a process under specified operating conditions. Typical questions that are asked from a process capability study are

- Where is the process centered?
- How much variability exists in the process?
- Is the performance acceptable?
- Is the process stable?
- What factors contribute to variability?

Many reasons exist for conducting a capability study. Manufacturing may wish to determine a performance baseline for a process, to prioritize projects for quality improvement, or to provide statistical evidence of quality for customers. Purchasing might conduct a study at a supplier plant to evaluate a new piece of equipment or to compare different suppliers. Engineering might conduct a study to determine the adequacy of R&D pilot facilities or to evaluate new processes.

Three types of studies are often conducted. A *peak performance study* is focused on determining how a process performs under ideal conditions. A *process characterization study* is designed to determine how a process performs under actual operating conditions. A *component variability study* has the goal of determining the relative contribution of different sources of total variation. The methods by which each study is conducted vary. A peak performance study is conducted under very carefully controlled conditions over a short time interval to ensure that no special causes can affect variation. A process characterization study is performed over a longer time interval under actual operating conditions to capture the variations in materials, operators, etc. A component variability study is based on a designed experiment to control the sources of variability. We will consider a process characterization study in this section, although the general approach applies to a peak performance study with appropriate modifications.

The six steps involved in making a process capability study are similar to any systematic study and include the following:

1. Choose a representative machine or segment of the process.
2. Define the process conditions.
3. Select a representative operator.
4. Provide materials that are of standard grade, with sufficient materials for uninterrupted study.
5. Specify the gaging or measurement method to be used.
6. Provide for a method of recording measurements and conditions, in order, on the units produced.

Two statistical techniques are commonly used to establish process capability. One is the frequency distribution histogram, the other is the control chart. We will discuss

TABLE 13.3 Measurements of U-Bolts

Sample	Observations				
1	10.65	10.70	10.65	10.65	10.85
2	10.75	10.85	10.75	10.85	10.65
3	10.75	10.80	10.80	10.70	10.75
4	10.60	10.70	10.70	10.75	10.65
5	10.70	10.75	10.65	10.85	10.80
6	10.60	10.75	10.75	10.85	10.70
7	10.60	10.80	10.70	10.75	10.75
8	10.75	10.80	10.65	10.75	10.70
9	10.65	10.80	10.85	10.85	10.75
10	10.60	10.70	10.60	10.80	10.65
11	10.80	10.75	10.90	10.50	10.85
12	10.85	10.75	10.85	10.65	10.70
13	10.70	10.70	10.75	10.75	10.70
14	10.65	10.70	10.85	10.75	10.60
15	10.75	10.80	10.75	10.80	10.65
16	10.90	10.80	10.80	10.75	10.85
17	10.75	10.70	10.85	10.70	10.80
18	10.75	10.70	10.60	10.70	10.60
19	10.65	10.65	10.85	10.65	10.70
20	10.60	10.60	10.65	10.55	10.65
21	10.50	10.55	10.65	10.80	10.80
22	10.80	10.65	10.75	10.65	10.65
23	10.65	10.60	10.65	10.60	10.70
24	10.65	10.70	10.70	10.60	10.65

the use of histograms in this section and defer the discussion of control charts to a later chapter.

To illustrate the use of histograms for process capability, let us consider the data in Table 13.3 for Consolidated Auto Supply Company. The company is a primary supplier of U-bolts for one of the major auto manufacturers. Table 13.3 shows a large sample of 120 measurements of the inside distance (a critical dimension in auto assembly) between ends of a U-bolt (illustrated in Figure 13.10) and are accurate to 0.05 centimeter. For the purpose of process capability estimates, we will assume that

FIGURE 13.10 U-Bolt Produced by Consolidated Auto Supply Company

Dimension measured in Table 13.3

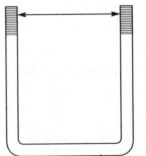

FIGURE 13.11 **Histogram of U-Bolt Dimensions**

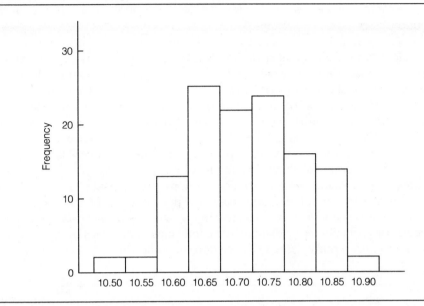

these 120 measurements are representative of the population from which they were drawn, that is, the process is in statistical control.

Figure 13.11 shows a histogram of the data presented in Table 13.3. We see that the dimensions are spread out between 10.50 and 10.90 centimeters, with a high proportion of values toward the center of the distribution. We can compute descriptive measures for this data using either Table 13.3 directly or the histogram in Figure 13.11. Calculations using grouped data from the histogram are as follows:

Midpoint	Frequency, f	Arbitrary Scale, x	fx	fx^2
10.50	2	−4	−8	32
10.55	2	−3	−6	18
10.60	13	−2	−26	52
10.65	25	−1	−25	25
10.70	22	0	0	0
10.75	24	+1	24	24
10.80	16	+2	32	64
10.85	14	+3	42	126
10.90	2	+4	8	32
	120		41	373

Using the formulas from Chapter 12, we find

$$\bar{x} = 10.70 + 0.05(41/120) = 10.7171$$

$$s = 0.05\sqrt{373/119 - (41/119)^2} = 0.0868$$

Hence, the mean is $\bar{x} = 10.7171$, and the sample standard deviation is $s = 0.0868$. Oftentimes, frequency distributions of the output from a production process follow some common probability distribution. The most common distribution that models many production processes or is assumed in many applications is the normal distribution.

The histogram in Figure 13.11 appears to be close to a normal distribution. If this is true, calculations using the normal distribution can be used to predict the yield of conforming product for various manufacturing specifications. As discussed in Chapter 12, testing for normality can be done in several ways. The simplest and most practical method is to use normal probability paper. Normal probability paper is a special type of graph paper scaled so that the plot of a cumulative normal distribution will be a straight line. Usually the "straightness" of the line can be determined by visual inspection, and one can reach valid conclusions most of the time. Many computer packages have the ability to draw normal probability plots.

To test whether a frequency distribution is normal, we must first convert the data to a cumulative frequency distribution, that is, the number of observations less than or equal to a specified value. These cumulative frequencies are next converted to relative frequencies or probabilities by dividing the cumulative frequencies by the number of observations (120). From Figure 13.11 we have the following.

Dimensional Value	Frequency	Cumulative Frequency	Cumulative Relative Frequency
10.50	2	2	0.017
10.55	2	4	0.033
10.60	13	17	0.142
10.65	25	42	0.350
10.70	22	64	0.533
10.75	24	88	0.733
10.80	16	104	0.867
10.85	14	118	0.983
10.90	2	120	1.000

A plot of the cumulative relative frequencies on normal probability paper is shown in Figure 13.12. Since this results in approximately a straight line, we can reasonably conclude that the process output follows a normal distribution.[12]

One of the properties of a normal distribution is that 99.73% of the observations will fall within three standard deviations from the mean. Thus, we expect a process that is in control to produce a large percentage of output between $\mu - 3\sigma$ and $\mu + 3\sigma$, where μ is the process average. Therefore, we say that the *natural tolerance limits* of the process are $\mu \pm 3\sigma$. We use 6σ as a measure of process capability.

For the Consolidated example we use the sample statistics $\bar{x} = 10.7171$ and $s = 0.0868$ as estimates of the population parameters μ and σ. We therefore expect nearly all of the U-bolt dimensions to fall between $10.7171 - 3(0.0868) = 10.4566$ and $10.7171 + 3(0.0868) = 10.9766$. This tells the production manager that if the design specifications are between 10.45 and 11.00, for instance, the process will be capable of producing nearly 100% conforming product. Suppose, however, that design

---

[12]The point (10.90,1.000) is not plotted, since the normal curve extends to infinity and there is no finite value that has a cumulative probability of 1.0.

FIGURE 13.12 Normal Probability Plot

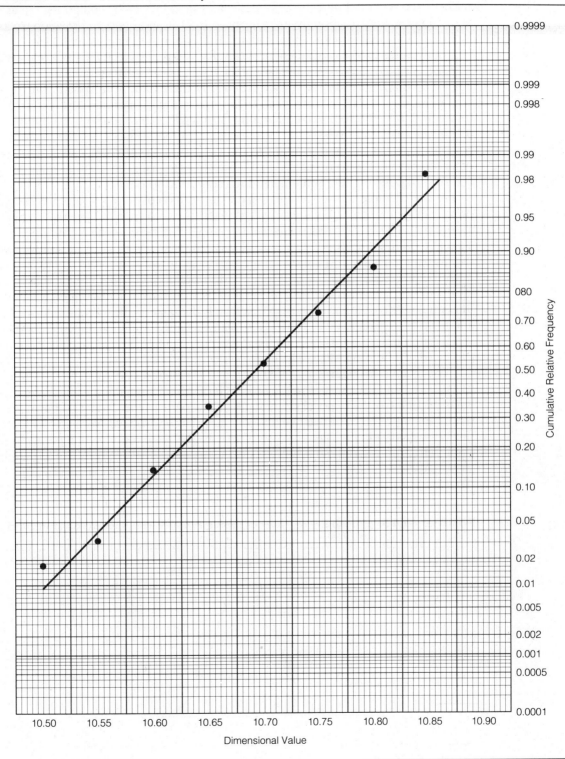

specifications are such that the dimension must lie between 10.55 and 10.90. We may calculate the expected percentage of nonconforming U-bolts by computing the area under a normal distribution having a mean of 10.7171 and standard deviation 0.0865 to the left and right of these specifications. This is illustrated in Figure 13.13.

Converting 10.55 to a standard normal value yields $z = (10.55 - 10.7171)/0.0868 = -1.93$. Using Appendix A at the end of the book, we find that the area to the *left* of $z = -1.93$ is $0.5000 - 0.4732 = 0.0268$. Similarly, the z value corresponding to 10.90 is $z = (10.90 - 10.7171)/0.0868 = 2.11$. The area to the *right* of $z = 2.11$ is $0.5000 - 0.4826 = 0.0174$. Therefore, the probability that a part will not meet specifications is $0.0268 + 0.0174 = 0.0442$ or, expressed as a percentage, is 4.42%. Similar computations can be used to estimate the percentage of nonconforming parts for other tolerances. This information can be used to help management determine scrap and rework policies, new equipment justification, and so on.

As this example showed, examining the distribution of output from a process can provide evidence of whether the actual characteristics of the products being produced are within, outside, or overlapping the tolerances that must be met. One need not attempt to fit the distribution to a normal curve, however, but can work directly with the histogram. Figure 13.14 shows some typical examples of process variations that might be detected by the use of frequency distribution plots. In 13.14(a), we see an ideal situation in which the natural variation is well within the specified tolerance limits. In 13.14(b), the variation is approximately the same as the tolerance limits. The graph in 13.14(c) shows a distribution with a natural variation greater than the specification limits; in this case, the process is not capable of meeting specifications and there will be some nonconforming output.

The graphs in Figures 13.14(d), (e), and (f) correspond to those in Figures 13.14(a), (b), and (c), except that the process is off-center from the specified tolerance limits. In 13.14(g), the bimodal shape suggests that perhaps the data were drawn from two different machines or that two different materials or products were involved. The small distribution to the right in 13.14(h) may be the result of including pieces from a trial setup run while the machine was being adjusted. The graph in 13.14(i) might

FIGURE 13.13 **Probability of Nonconforming Product with Specifications of 10.55 to 10.90**

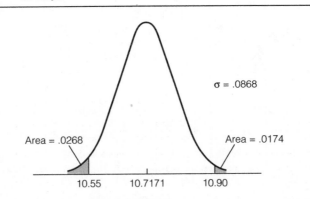

FIGURE 13.14 Examples of Process Variation Histograms and Specifications

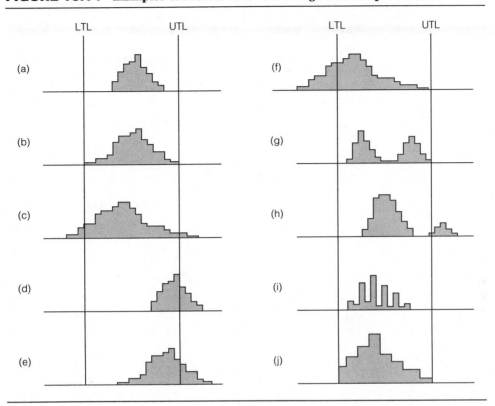

be the result of inadequate gaging or rounding values during inspection. Finally, the truncated distribution in 13.14(j) is often the result of sorting nonconforming parts.

It should be recognized that not all of the conditions shown in Figure 13.14 are due to a lack of process capability. Some may simply occur because a process that is in control drifts out. Others may be indicators of various types of process capability problems, technical mistakes, or system problems that should be corrected to improve long-term quality of the products. Thus, a good control system is a necessity, since a histogram alone will not provide complete information.

An important issue that is often ignored in process capability studies is the error resulting from using the sample standard deviation, s, rather than the true standard deviation, σ. A simple table can be constructed to find confidence intervals on the true value of σ for a given sample size. Such a table is shown in Table 13.4. and is easily explained by an example. For a given sample size, σ will be less than or equal to s times the factor in that row with probability p, where p is the column heading. Thus, for a sample of size 30, $\sigma \leq 0.744s$ with probability 0.005; $\sigma \leq 1.280s$ occurs 95% of the time; and so on. A 90% confidence interval for σ can be found by using the factors in the columns corresponding to $p = 0.050$ and $p = 0.950$. Thus, for a sample size of 30, a 95% confidence interval would be $(0.825s, 1.280s)$. The interpretation of process capability information should be tempered by such an analysis.

TABLE 13.4 Ratio of Population to Sample Standard Deviation

Number of Samples	Fraction of Population Less than or Equal to Value in Table							
	0.005	0.010	0.025	0.050	0.100	0.950	0.975	0.995
2	0.356	0.388	0.446	0.510	0.608	15.952	31.911	159.516
3	0.434	0.466	0.521	0.578	0.659	4.407	6.287	14.142
4	0.483	0.514	0.567	0.620	0.693	2.919	3.727	6.468
5	0.519	0.549	0.599	0.649	0.717	2.372	2.875	4.396
6	0.546	0.576	0.624	0.672	0.736	2.090	2.453	3.484
7	0.569	0.597	0.644	0.690	0.751	1.918	2.202	2.979
8	0.588	0.616	0.661	0.705	0.763	1.797	2.035	2.660
9	0.604	0.631	0.675	0.718	0.774	1.711	1.916	2.440
10	0.618	0.645	0.688	0.729	0.783	1.645	1.826	2.278
11	0.630	0.656	0.699	0.739	0.791	1.593	1.755	2.154
12	0.641	0.667	0.708	0.748	0.798	1.551	1.698	2.056
13	0.651	0.677	0.717	0.755	0.804	1.515	1.651	1.976
14	0.660	0.685	0.725	0.762	0.810	1.485	1.611	1.910
15	0.669	0.693	0.732	0.769	0.815	1.460	1.577	1.854
16	0.676	0.700	0.739	0.775	0.820	1.437	1.548	1.806
17	0.683	0.707	0.745	0.780	0.824	1.418	1.522	1.764
18	0.690	0.713	0.750	0.785	0.828	1.400	1.499	1.727
19	0.696	0.719	0.756	0.790	0.832	1.385	1.479	1.695
20	0.702	0.725	0.760	0.794	0.836	1.370	1.461	1.666
21	0.707	0.730	0.765	0.798	0.839	1.358	1.444	1.640
22	0.712	0.734	0.769	0.802	0.842	1.346	1.429	1.617
23	0.717	0.739	0.773	0.805	0.845	1.335	1.415	1.595
24	0.722	0.743	0.777	0.809	0.848	1.325	1.403	1.576
25	0.726	0.747	0.781	0.812	0.850	1.316	1.391	1.558
26	0.730	0.751	0.784	0.815	0.853	1.308	1.380	1.542
27	0.734	0.755	0.788	0.818	0.855	1.300	1.370	1.526
28	0.737	0.758	0.791	0.820	0.857	1.293	1.361	1.512
29	0.741	0.762	0.794	0.823	0.859	1.286	1.352	1.499
30	0.744	0.765	0.796	0.825	0.861	1.280	1.344	1.487
31	0.748	0.768	0.799	0.828	0.863	1.274	1.337	1.475
36	0.762	0.781	0.811	0.838	0.872	1.248	1.304	1.427
41	0.774	0.792	0.821	0.847	0.879	1.228	1.280	1.390
46	0.784	0.802	0.829	0.854	0.885	1.212	1.260	1.361
51	0.793	0.810	0.837	0.861	0.090	1.199	1.243	1.337
61	0.808	0.824	0.849	0.871	0.898	1.179	1.217	1.299
71	0.820	0.835	0.858	0.879	0.905	1.163	1.198	1.272
81	0.829	0.844	0.866	0.886	0.910	1.151	1.183	1.250
91	0.838	0.852	0.873	0.892	0.915	1.141	1.171	1.233
101	0.845	0.858	0.879	0.897	0.919	1.133	1.161	1.219

SOURCE: Thomas D. Hall, "How Close Is s to σ?" *Quality*, December 1991, p. 45. Note: The table published in this article was incorrect. An error notice was published in a subsequent issue and the correct table was made available by *Quality* magazine.

Process Capability Index

The importance of process capability is in assessing the relationship between the natural variation of a process and the design specifications. This is often quantified by a measure known as the **process capability index.** The process capability index,

C_p, is defined as the ratio of the specification width to the natural tolerance of the process. C_p relates the natural variation of the process with the design specifications in a single, quantitative measure.

In numerical terms, the formula is

$$C_p = \frac{\text{UTL} - \text{LTL}}{6\sigma}$$

where

UTL = upper tolerance limit
LTL = lower tolerance limit
 σ = standard deviation of the process

C_p is often used in objective setting by managers and in discussions of contracts with suppliers.

To illustrate the computation and interpretation of C_p, suppose that the design specifications of a dimension have a tolerance spread (UTL − LTL) of 6 units and that the standard deviation of the process is 1.00. The process capability is therefore 6σ = 6(1.00) = 6.00. Therefore

C_p = (UTL − LTL)/6σ = 6/6(1) = 1.00

If σ = 2, then

C_p = 6/6(2) = 0.50

Finally, if σ = 0.50, then

C_p = 6/6(.5) = 2.00.

Figure 13.15 illustrates these three cases. Note that a C_p value of 1.0 occurs when the natural variation equals the design tolerance spread. A value less than one indicates that the process is not capable of meeting specifications; a value greater than one corresponds to a process that is highly capable of meeting specifications.

Let us show how the process capability index can be used for setting objectives and improving processes. Suppose that a quality manager in a firm has a process with a standard deviation of one and a tolerance spread of 8. The value of C_p for this situation is 1.33. The manager realizes that the natural spread is within specifications at this time, but new contracts call for increasing the value of the capability index. Targets are set for increasing the index to 1.66 within three months, to 2.00 within six months, and to 3.00 within a year. Given that the tolerance spread (UTL − LTL) is held at the previous level of 8, the following table shows the required process standard deviation for each phase of the project.

C_p	UTL − LTL	6σ	σ
1.33	8	6	1
1.66	8	4.8	0.8
2.00	8	4	0.67
3.00	8	2.67	0.44

Operationally, this involves reducing the variability in the process from a standard deviation of 1.000 to 0.444, which results in the desired increase of C_p from the current

FIGURE 13.15   Illustrations of Process Capability Indexes

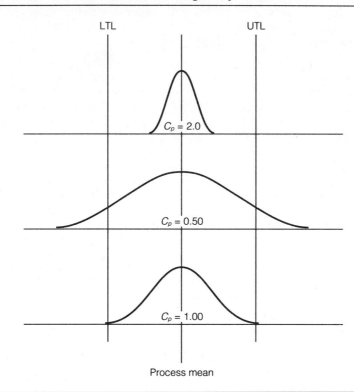

level of 1.33 to the final level of 3.00. This will be done using process improvement and minor equipment upgrades.

Two important facts about the C_p index should be pointed out. One relates to process conditions and the other relates to interpretation of the values that have been calculated. First, the calculation of the C_p has no meaning if the process is not under statistical control. The natural spread (6σ) should be calculated using a sufficiently large sample to get a meaningful estimate of the population standard deviation (σ). Second, a C_p of 1.00 would require that the process be perfectly centered on the mean of the tolerance spread to prevent some units from being produced outside the limits. It is much easier to achieve the goal of all units being produced within specifications with a C_p of 1.33, and still easier with a C_p of 2.00. Based on the experience of a number of practitioners, it has been suggested that a "safe" lower limit of C_p is 1.5. A value above this level will practically guarantee that all units produced by a controlled process will be within specifications. It is not uncommon for firms to require C_p values of 2 or greater from their suppliers.

The previous discussion assumed that the process was centered; clearly the value of C_p does not depend on the mean of the process. To include information on process centering, one-sided indexes are often used. One-sided process capability indexes are as follows:

$$C_{pu} = \frac{\text{UTL} - \mu}{3\sigma} \quad \text{(upper one-sided index)}$$

$$C_{pl} = \frac{\mu - \text{LTL}}{3\sigma} \quad \text{(lower one-sided index)}$$

$$C_{pk} = \min(C_{pl}, C_{pu})$$

For example, consider a process having a lower tolerance limit of 5.0, an upper tolerance limit of 9.0, and a standard deviation of 0.33. The process capability index, $C_p = (9.0 - 5.0)/6(0.33) = 2.0$. If the process mean is 7.0, both the lower and upper one-sided capability indexes (and also C_{pk}) are also 2.0, indicating that the process is centered with respect to the specifications. If, however, the process mean shifts up to 8.0, then

$$C_{pu} = (9-8)/3(0.33) = 1.0$$

$$C_{pl} = (8-5)/3(0.33) = 3.0$$

$$C_{pk} = \min(3.0, 1.0) = 1.0$$

These indexes indicate that the process would have difficulty meeting its upper tolerance limit but that it would easily meet the lower tolerance limit. C_{pk} summarizes the upper and lower capability indexes into a single number reflecting the worst case; it is often used in specifying quality requirements in purchasing contracts.

Some controversy exists over C_p and C_{pk} as measures of process capability, particularly with respect to the economic loss function philosophy of Taguchi.[13] These measures do not adequately account for how well the process can achieve the target value. Several alternative measures have been proposed. One is to adjust C_p by a factor $(1 - k)$ as follows:

$$C_{pk} = C_p(1 - k)$$

where $k = 2|\text{mean} - \text{target}|/\text{tolerance}$. When the sample mean is equal to the target, $k = 0$ and $C_{pk} = C_p$. As the sample mean deviates from the target, the absolute difference between them increases and k increases. Specification limits are used only to determine the tolerance; thus the focus of this measure is on the target value rather than on acceptable specification limits. Another index that has been proposed is

$$C_{pm} = C_p/\sqrt{1 + (\text{mean} - \text{target})^2/\sigma^2}$$

This measure also accounts for deviations from the target value.

Finally, we wish to point out that Motorola's "six sigma" concept implies a C_p of 2.0, with a minimum acceptable C_{pk} of 1.5. That is, the process mean is allowed to shift by as much as $\pm 1.5\sigma$.

---

[13]Paul F. McCoy, "Using Performance Indexes to Monitor Production Processes," *Quality Progress,* February 1991, pp. 49–55; see also Fred A. Spiring, "The Cpm Index," *Quality Progress,* February 1991, pp. 57–61.

A Process Capability Study[14]

The Hydraulic Lift Company (HLC) manufactures freight elevators and automotive lifts used in garages and service stations. Figure 13.16 shows a simplified diagram of a hydraulic lift. The check valve is an important component in the system. Its purpose is to control the flow of hydraulic oil from the oil reservoir to the cylinder when the elevator is rising. As the elevator descends, the rate at which oil flows from the cylinder back to the reservoir is also controlled by the check valve.

One of the most important parts of the check valve is the piston, which moves within the valve body as the valve is opened or closed. The quality manager at HLC noticed that scrap rates on the piston had been very high over the past three years. Two models (part numbers 117227 and 117228) of check valve pistons are being manufactured. Because of extremely critical tolerances, these parts are among the most difficult ones produced in the machine shop.

[14] This example has been adapted from an actual study in an organization within which one of the authors worked.

A study to determine the magnitude of the problem revealed that approximately $2,200 per month worth of parts had been scrapped over the past three years (Figure 13.17). This translates to about 14% of total production of the parts, a scrap rate that is considered unacceptable. About half of the defective items were scrapped due to inability of the process to hold a 0.4990/0.4985 inch tolerance on the valve stem (see Figure 13.18). The machining operation used to shape the valve stem is performed on a grinding machine, which should have the capability of holding a tolerance within 0.0001–0.0002 inch under standard operating conditions. Manufacturing engineers and the quality manager decided to do a process capability study on one part (no. 117227) to gather statistical data on the stem problem and make a recommendation for improvements.

The first step was to have an operator run 100 parts using the standard production methods. Results of the study [see the histogram in Figure 13.19(a)] revealed that a machine problem existed. The data showed that there were a few parts being produced outside the specifications. In addition, the strange shape of the histogram for dimensions

FIGURE 13.16 **Simplified Diagram of a Hydraulic Lift**

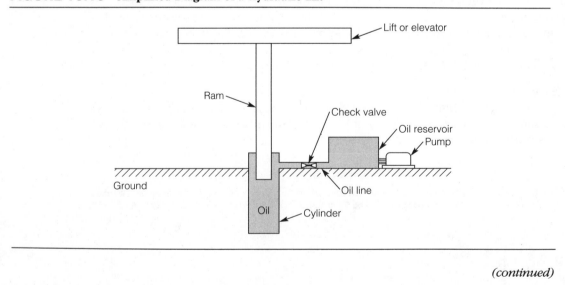

(continued)

FIGURE 13.17   Average Scrap Cost per Month

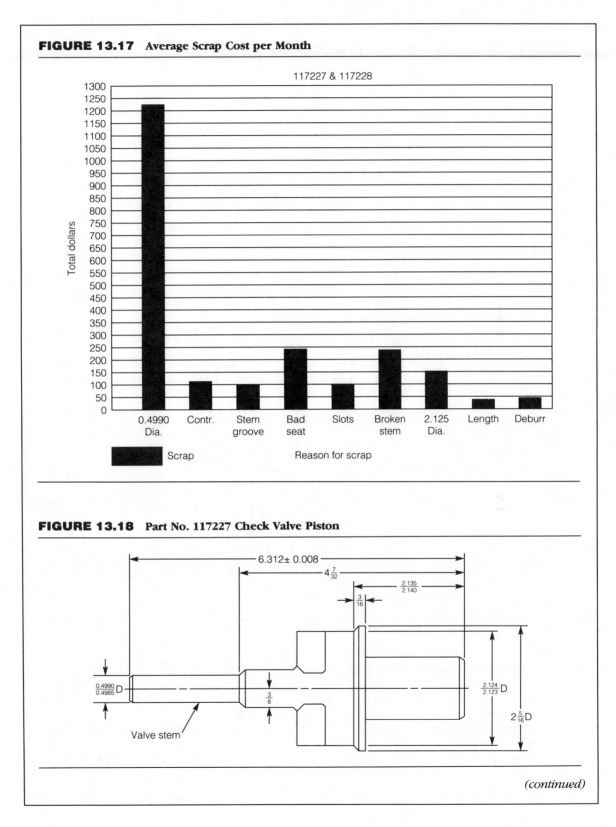

FIGURE 13.18   Part No. 117227 Check Valve Piston

(continued)

FIGURE 13.19 Process Capability Data for the Hydraulic Lift Company

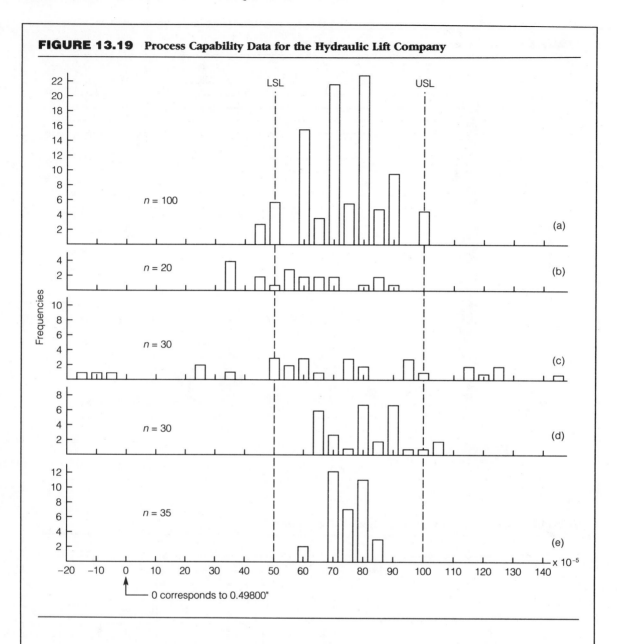

within the specification limits prompted an investigation into the possibility of instability of the process. It was observed that the operator was constantly adjusting the machine setting to try to hold to the specified tolerance.

As a check on machine capability, the operator was asked to run 20 parts without adjusting the machine. This resulted in scrapping 6 of 20 parts, a 30% scrap rate [see Figure 13.19(b)]. This test verified that the machine needed some major adjustments.

The machine manufacturer was contacted and a technician was dispatched to the plant. A run of 30 parts was made to show how the machine operated.

(continued)

Twelve of the thirty pieces were defective, with the stem dimension out of tolerance [see Figure 13.19(c)]. The technician made the following adjustments:

- Installed new gaskets.

- Cleaned machine, adding oil and coolant.

- Loaded hand wheel bearing for more positive control.

- Reset retard pressure on grind wheel.

- Adjusted stone dresser mechanism.

- Reset dwell time (time the grindstone stays on the work piece after reaching final diameter).

The results of these adjustments were significant. Another 30 parts were run, with only two falling outside the tolerance limits [Figure 13.19(d)]. The process was still not considered to be fully satisfactory. The manufacturer's technician said that the grinder "ways" (channels on which the machine head travels) would have to be reground and that some parts in the machine would have to be replaced. This recommendation was made to management, who agreed to have the machine overhauled as required.

After the work was completed, a run of 35 parts was made with results shown in Figure 13.19(e). These showed that all parts were well within tolerance limits. As a final step, operators and maintenance personnel were instructed on the proper use and care of the machine.

Key Issues for Discussion

1. Using the histograms in Figure 13.19, estimate the process capability indexes for each situation.

2. Discuss the approach used in this case in terms of the general problem-solving process presented in Chapter 9.

Summary of Key Points

- Inspection is a key control function that ties together quality of design with quality of conformance. Inspection helps to evaluate the degree of conformance or nonconformance to specifications, provides for reporting of deficiencies early in the production process, and helps to ensure that desired quality requirements are met.

- Traditional inspection practices involve heavy inspection of incoming materials and final product, with a focus on separating the good from the bad. These practices are inefficient and ineffective. Inspection should be used as an auditing tool to control processes and identify opportunities for improvement.

- The ISO 9000 series of standards has been adopted worldwide as a guide for quality practice, particularly in the areas of inspection. They provide important guidelines as the global economy continues to expand.

- Technical specifications provide the basis for inspection. The key components are nominal dimensions and tolerances.

- Planning inspection activities include determining what to inspect, the type of inspection (attribute or variable), location of inspection stations, inspection quantity, and human factors issues.

- Measurement is the act of quantifying the amount of a characteristic that an item possesses. Various types of gages, measuring instruments, and automated technology are used in manufacturing to measure quality characteristics. In services, measurement typically is conducted by surveys and other forms of observation.

■ Metrology is the science of measurement, and includes determining the accuracy, precision, and reproducibility of measurement instruments, as well as calibration relative to known standards. Statistical methods can be used to assess instrument precision and reproducibility.

■ Process capability is the range over which the natural variation of a process occurs as determined by the system of common causes. It is determined through statistical analysis of variation in a production process and measured relative to specifications by process capability indexes.

Questions for Review and Discussion

1. What is the purpose of inspection and measurement?

2. Contrast traditional and modern inspection practices. How do modern practices support the quality philosophies of Deming and others?

3. For what reasons will inspection always be around to some extent, despite the total quality management philosophy?

4. Of what use are global and national standards such as ISO 9000 and Q90-1987?

5. Explain the concepts of nominal dimensions and tolerances. Of what use are tolerances?

6. Why are specifications more difficult to define in services than in manufacturing?

7. Describe the common classification system for defects.

8. Explain the difference between attributes inspection and variables inspection. What relative advantages does each method have?

9. Discuss the problem of locating inspection stations. What guidelines should be used?

10. What are the advantages and disadvantages of 100% inspection and sampling inspection?

11. Explain the terms *acceptance inspection, classification inspection, control inspection,* and *audit inspection.*

12. Define and give examples of the four scales of measurement commonly used.

13. What is the difference between accuracy, precision, and reproducibility?

14. Briefly describe the different types and applications of variable and fixed gages.

15. What is metrology? Describe the activities associated with this science.

16. What is calibration and why is it important to quality assurance?

17. What are the important human factors issues that affect inspection?

18. Describe some of the uses of automated technology in inspection and measurement.

19. What types of inspection are used in airline operations? Hospitals? Police departments? Universities? Talk to a manager or administrator to check your assumptions.

20. Should an inspection department have to cost-justify an expensive piece of inspection equipment based on estimated savings, or should the inspection department manager simply point to "increased competition" as his justification? To support your conclusion, try to find an actual case in which each method was used.

21. Explain the term *process capability*.

22. Explain how a process can be in control but simultaneously outside design specifications. Relate this to process capability and to product design specifications.

23. Discuss the methodology of conducting a process capability study.

24. Define the process capability index C_p and explain how it may be used to establish or improve quality policies in operating areas or with vendors.

25. Discuss service quality standards that would be applicable to the following:

    a. local and intercity buses
    b. sightseeing tours
    c. department stores
    d. electric power company
    e. hotel and motels.

26. The use of Universal Product Code (UPC) scanners in supermarkets has become common in recent years. The scanners read the UPC code, and the item description and price are read from a central computer. Discuss the advantages and the disadvantages of these systems to both the stores and the customers, focusing on quality.

Problems

1. Consider the following measurements for an airline. Would they be attributes or variables measurements? Explain your answers.

    a. passengers bumped per flight
    b. delay times of departures
    c. time spent at check-in counter
    d. customers with lost baggage
    e. delivery time for baggage.

2. In a bank, the following measures are taken. Are these attributes or variables? Explain your answers.

    a. time spent waiting for teller
    b. errors made in check handling

    c. customer inquiries

    d. turnaround time for mail transactions

    e. computer breakdowns.

3. Ten parts are measured using two different instruments. The nominal specification for the part is 0.05. Which instrument is more accurate? More precise? Which one is the better instrument?

Instrument A					Instrument B				
0.06	0.07	0.06	0.05	0.06	0.05	0.07	0.07	0.06	0.04
0.05	0.06	0.06	0.07	0.06	0.05	0.04	0.07	0.04	0.05

4. A gage repeatability and reproducibility study collected the following data. Analyze these data. The part specification is 1.0 ± 0.06.

	Operator 1			Operator 2		
Part/Trial	1	2	3	1	2	3
1	0.97	0.99	0.99	0.96	0.99	1.00
2	0.94	0.96	0.97	0.95	1.00	1.00
3	1.00	1.00	0.99	1.02	1.03	1.00
4	0.97	1.00	0.99	0.96	0.98	0.98
5	0.99	1.00	1.00	1.01	1.01	1.03
6	1.02	1.04	1.03	0.99	1.02	1.02
7	0.96	1.01	0.98	0.97	0.97	0.99
8	1.00	1.02	0.97	1.07	1.02	1.00
9	1.03	1.01	1.00	1.04	1.02	0.98
10	0.96	0.98	0.95	0.99	0.95	0.95

(Except as indicated, all of the following problems assume that the quality characteristics are normally distributed.)

5. Jamaican Punch is sold in 11-ounce cans. The mean number of ounces placed in a can is 10.75 with a standard deviation of 0.1 ounce. Assuming a normal distribution, what is the probability that the filling machine will cause an overflow in a can, that is, the probability that more than 11 ounces will be placed in the can?

6. The standard deviation of the weight of filled containers is 0.7 ounce. If 3% of the containers contain less than 20 ounces, what is the mean filling weight of the containers?

7. In filling bottles of cola, the average amount of overfilling should be kept as low as possible. If the mean fill volume is 16.05 ounces and the standard deviation is 0.03 ounce, what percentage of bottles will have less than 16 ounces? More than 16.10 ounces (assuming that this does not overflow)?

8. The data and histogram on page 457 show the weight of castings (in kilograms) being made in a foundry. Based on this sample of 100 castings, find the mean and standard deviation of the sample.

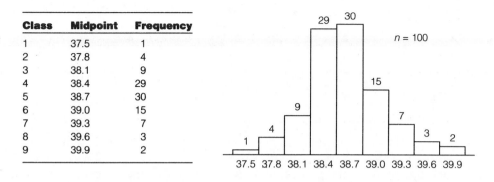

Class	Midpoint	Frequency
1	37.5	1
2	37.8	4
3	38.1	9
4	38.4	29
5	38.7	30
6	39.0	15
7	39.3	7
8	39.6	3
9	39.9	2

9. Plot the data from Problem 8 on normal probability paper to determine if the distribution of the data is approximately normal.

10. Referring again to Problem 8, if the upper tolerance limit (UTL) of the process is 40.5 and the lower tolerance limit (LTL) is 36.9, calculate the process capability index. Is it within satisfactory limits? How much reduction in the *sample* standard deviation would be required to bring the process capability index up to 2.00?

11. Sets of precision weights are being manufactured for use with pharmaceutical scales. One of the set is a 100-gram weight with a tolerance of ± 0.05 gram. Two production lines manufacture the weights. The following values (obtained by subtracting 100 from the measured values and then multiplying by 100) were observed when a sample of 60 weights was taken from each line.

Line 1						Line 2					
4	5	3	2	1	3	−4	−1	−1	−4	−3	1
4	−1	4	3	1	3	3	−1	−1	1	−2	−2
−1	2	1	0	1	2	2	−5	0	0	−6	3
2	2	3	3	2	3	−3	1	2	−1	2	−1
2	3	5	0	0	1	0	0	−4	−2	0	−1
5	0	2	3	0	3	−1	1	0	−3	−1	−2
0	−1	4	2	−1	4	1	0	−3	0	−6	1
7	1	4	1	2	1	−2	0	0	−3	−2	−2
4	1	3	5	4	5	−4	2	−5	0	2	0
6	3	2	−2	4	3	−3	1	−1	−1	−2	1

a. Construct histograms for each line and for the two lines combined.
b. Check the relationships of the distributions to the tolerance limits using the histograms and calculated means and standard deviations.
c. Interpret your results.

12. A machining process has a required dimension on a part of 0.575 ± 0.007″. Five samples of five parts each were measured as given below. What is its capability for producing within acceptable limits?

		Sample		
1	**2**	**3**	**4**	**5**
0.557	0.574	0.573	0.575	0.576
0.566	0.587	0.578	0.565	0.577
0.576	0.578	0.577	0.582	0.576
0.564	0.573	0.579	0.573	0.572
0.580	0.584	0.580	0.578	0.574

13. Adjustments were made in the process discussed in Problem 12 and five more samples of five parts each were measured. The results are given below. What can you observe about the process now? What is its capability for producing within acceptable limits now?

		Sample		
1	**2**	**3**	**4**	**5**
0.571	0.575	0.573	0.576	0.576
0.578	0.575	0.574	0.571	0.574
0.576	0.573	0.571	0.577	0.575
0.579	0.577	0.575	0.570	0.575
0.574	0.576	0.579	0.575	0.576

14. Samples for three parts were taken as shown below. Data set 1 is for part 1, data set 2 is for part 2, and data set 3 is for part 3.

Data set 1				
1.74831	1.7574	1.75134	1.73316	1.75134
1.71498	1.75437	1.73619	1.73922	1.73619
1.74528	1.74831	1.76346	1.74528	1.76952
1.70892	1.75134	1.71195	1.74831	1.77861
1.7574	1.73619	1.74225	1.74528	1.73922
Data set 2				
2.01144	2.00448	2.01492	2.00448	2.00448
2.001	2.00796	2.001	1.98708	1.99752
1.99752	2.001	1.99404	2.00796	2.00448
2.00448	2.001	1.99752	2.001	2.001
1.98708	1.99404	1.98708	1.9836	2.001
Data set 3				
1.25426	1.24775	1.24558	1.24992	1.23907
1.2586	1.25643	1.25209	1.25426	1.24341
1.25643	1.24775	1.24341	1.24558	1.23907
1.24124	1.24558	1.24992	1.25209	1.24992
1.24992	1.24558	1.24992	1.24775	1.24775

a. Calculate the mean and standard deviations for each part and compare them to the specification limits given below:

Part	Nominal	Tolerance
1	1.750	±0.045
2	2.000	±0.060
3	1.250	±0.030

b. Will the production process permit an acceptable fit of all parts into the slot at least 99.73% of the time?

15. A utility requires service operators to answer telephone calls from customers in an average time of 0.1 minute, with a tolerance of +0.04 and − 0.06 minute. A sample of 50 actual operator times was drawn, and the results are given in the following table. In addition, operators are expected to ascertain customer needs and either respond to them or refer the customer to the proper department within 0.5 minute with a tolerance of +0.20 and −0.30 minute. Another sample of 50 times was taken for this activity and is also given in the table. If these variables can be considered to be independent, how often can the total time be expected to vary from 0.6 minute, with a tolerance of +0.24 and −0.36 minute?

Component	Mean Time	Standard Deviation
Answer	0.1023	0.0183
Service	0.5044	0.0902

16. For the following data, construct a histogram and estimate the process capability. If the specifications are 24 ± 0.03, estimate the percentage of parts that will be nonconforming. Finally, compute C_p, C_{pu}, and C_{pl}.

24.029	24.003	24.020	23.991	24.008
23.996	23.991	24.000	24.005	24.011
23.989	24.023	24.020	24.004	24.004
24.002	23.998	23.993	24.016	24.010
23.991	24.008	24.015	23.990	24.013
24.010	23.995	23.997	23.988	23.996
23.995	24.004	23.994	24.001	24.006
23.986	24.001	23.995	24.013	23.990
24.008	23.996	24.010	24.002	24.005
23.999	24.000	23.991	24.007	23.992
23.994	23.997	23.995	23.994	24.001
24.000	24.001	24.007	23.995	24.000
23.984	24.001	23.996	24.013	23.999
23.984	24.000	23.994	23.971	24.008
24.011	24.015	23.998	23.997	24.009
23.995	23.999	24.005	23.985	24.002
23.994	24.010	23.988	24.003	24.009
24.005	24.009	24.018	24.003	23.998
23.983	24.001	24.003	24.006	23.996
24.000	24.013	24.009	24.019	24.007

17. An agricultural fertilizer is packed in 100-pound bags. The weights of 15 randomly selected bags are given below. Using normal probability paper, determine whether or not the data are normal and estimate the process capability.

94.75	97.05	97.70	97.75	98.60
99.60	99.65	99.75	100.50	100.75
101.00	101.75	101.80	102.00	102.50

18. Suppose that a process with a normally distributed output has a mean of 50.25 and a variance of 2.25.

a. If the specifications are 50.25 ± 4.00, compute C_p and the one-sided process capability indexes and interpret their meaning.

b. Suppose the mean shifts to 50.00. Recompute and interpret the process capability indexes.

c. If the variance can be reduced to 81% of its original value, how do the process capability indexes change (using the original mean of 50.25)?

19. A process has upper and lower tolerance limits of 5.60 and 5.20, respectively. If the customer requires a demonstrated C_p of 2.0, what must the process capability be? If both C_{pu} and C_{pl} must also be 2.0, determine the mean and standard deviation of the process, assuming a normal distribution of output.

20. Ten samples of five items each were taken on a drilled hole dimension in an engine block, as given below. What is the estimated population process capability (6-sigma spread) based on these samples?

1	2	3	4	5	6	7	8	9	10
0.207	0.211	0.206	0.207	0.210	0.205	0.206	0.210	0.206	0.208
0.209	0.207	0.208	0.209	0.210	0.207	0.210	0.208	0.208	0.209
0.207	0.208	0.210	0.208	0.205	0.211	0.211	0.206	0.206	0.209
0.206	0.207	0.203	0.209	0.207	0.208	0.212	0.207	0.208	0.207
0.211	0.207	0.231	0.209	0.213	0.211	0.204	0.206	0.210	0.209

21. Prepare a frequency distribution histogram for the data in Problem 20. Show the mean and standard deviation and the estimated 6-sigma spread for the process.

22. If the required tolerance in Problem 20 is 0.210 ± 0.005, calculate and interpret the process capability indexes C_p and C_{pk}.

Bibliography

American National Standard: Guide to Inspection Planning. ANSI/ASQC E-2-1984. American Society for Quality Control, 310 W. Wisconsin Ave., Milwaukee, WI 53203.

Boser, Robert B., and Christ, Cheryl L. "Whys, Whens and Hows of Conducting a Process Capability Study," presented at the ASQC/ASA 35th Annual Fall Technical Conference, Lexington, Kentucky, 1991.

Boznak, Rudolph G., "Manufacturers Must Prepare for International Quality Initiative," *Industrial Engineering,* October 1991, pp. 13-14.

Case, Kenneth E., and Jones, Lynn L. *Profit Through Quality: Quality Assurance Programs for Manufacturers.* Norcross, GA: American Institute of Industrial Engineers, 1978.

Ferdeber, Charles J. "Measuring Quality and Productivity in a Service Environment," *Industrial Engineering,* July 1981, pp. 193-201.

Griffith, Gary. *Quality Technician's Handbook.* New York: John Wiley, 1986.

Gunter, Bert. "Process Capability Studies Part 1: What Is a Process Capability Study?" *Quality Progress,* February 1991, pp. 97-99.

Holm, Richard A. "Fulfilling the New Role of Inspection," *Manufacturing Engineering,* May 1988, pp. 43-46.

MIL-HDBK-53-1A, *Military Handbook, Guide for Attribute Lot Sampling Inspection and MIL-STD-105.* Washington, D.C.: Department of Defense, June 30, 1965.

Puma, Maurice. "Quality Technology in Manufacturing," *Quality Progress,* August 1980, pp. 16-19.

Rice, George O. "Metrology," in *Quality Management Handbook,* Loren Walsh, Ralph Wurster, and Raymond J. Kimber (eds.), New York: Marcel Dekker, 1986, pp. 517–530.

Sherman, William H. "Inspection: Do We Need It?" *Manufacturing Engineering,* May 1988, pp. 39–42.

Tomas, Sam. "Six Sigma: Motorola's Quest for Zero Defects," *APICS, The Performance Advantage,* July 1991, pp. 36–41.

Tomas, Sam. "What Is Motorola's Six Sigma Product Quality?" *American Production and Inventory Control Society 1990 Conference Proceedings,* Falls Church, VA: APICS, pp. 27–31.

Troxell, Joseph R. "Service Time Quality Standards," *Quality Progress,* Vol. 14, No. 9, September 1981, pp. 35–37.

Troxell, Joseph R. "Standards for Quality Control in Service Industries," *Quality Progress,* Vol. 12, No. 1, January 1979, pp. 32–34.

PART FOUR

The Technical System
Quality of Design and Performance

IN CHAPTER 1 we noted that one important area of quality is *quality of design and performance*. Quality of design establishes a product's fitness for use and performance characteristics. This is a critical issue for customer satisfaction. How products are designed affects how they can be produced. Thus, attention to quality in the design of production processes is an important parallel activity. In Chapter 14 we focus on product and process design issues, especially the role that product design plays in manufacturability. In Chapter 15, our emphasis is on reliability, from a managerial, as well as from a technical, viewpoint.

Quality in Product and Process Design

The design of a manufactured product or service begins with an idea and continues through a variety of development and testing phases until production begins and the product is made available to the customer. Product design involves all activities performed to determine the functional specifications for a product and its fitness for use. Besides having the features expressed in the "voice of the customer" (see Chapter 6), products should

- be affordable,

- be easy to install and operate,

- perform to customer expectations,

- be reliable and durable,

- have well-documented instructions, and

- be easy to fix and maintain.

These attributes require that serious attention be paid to the technical aspects of engineering design.

Process planning is similar in nature to product design. Process planning involves the planning and design of both the physical facilities and the information and control systems required to manufacture a good or deliver a service. The goal of process planning is to ensure that the product conforms to design specifications and is produced in an economical and productive fashion.

Quality of design, coupled with quality of conformance in production, determines the ultimate performance, reliability, and value of the product. These attributes determine the overall quality as perceived by the user. The design influences the efficiency of manufacture, speed of repair and service, and flexibility of sales strategies. Thus, product design and process planning must be coordinated and concurrent activities. The methodology of quality function deployment discussed in Chapter 6 provides a structured approach to coordinating product and process planning activities. In this chapter we focus on other aspects of product design and process planning, particularly issues of quality engineering.

THE PRODUCT DEVELOPMENT PROCESS

Figure 14.1 shows the typical product development process. This process consists of idea generation, initial screening and economic analysis, preliminary product design and development, prototype testing, final product design, pilot runs, and, finally, release to production. Clearly, the first step in product design is to come up with new ideas. As we discussed in Chapter 6, new or redesigned product ideas should focus on customer needs and expectations. Initial screenings and economic analyses are performed to determine the feasibility of new ideas and eliminate those that do not appear to have a high potential for success and thus avoid expensive development costs.

The actual design process consists of determining engineering specifications for all materials, components, and parts. Engineering specifications consist of the nominal, or target, values as well as tolerances. The nominal specifications, sometimes called *product parameters,* determine the functional ability and performance characteristics of the product. Tolerances specify the precision required to achieve the desired performance. The preliminary design is often followed by prototype testing. A prototype model is constructed to test the product's physical properties or use under actual operating conditions. These tests might include performance tests, stress tests, environmental tests, wearout tests, and other reliability tests. Road testing an

FIGURE 14.1 **Product Design and Development Process**

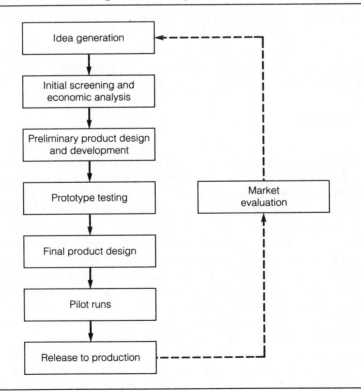

automobile or using a consumer panel to test a new food product are some examples. Such testing is important in uncovering any problems and correcting them prior to full-scale production.

The construction of physical prototypes has been reduced as a result of new technologies such as computer-aided design (CAD) in which computer simulations can predict the actual performance of a product to a high degree of accuracy without physical testing. Often 40 to 50% of design time can be saved through CAD, and potential quality problems can be found sooner in the design process than when using physical prototypes.

After any changes resulting from prototype testing are made, detailed drawings are developed for production, pilot runs are performed, and—provided no serious problems are found—the product is released to full-scale production. As Deming and Juran both advocate, this process should never end and it should rely on market evaluation and customer feedback to initiate continuous improvements.

Despite such structured attention to product development, companies invariably make numerous engineering changes after full-scale production begins. Design changes are costly in both time and money. Time has become perhaps the most important competitive strategy in the 1990s. As new and improved products are continually developed, and as foreign competitors shorten product life cycles, the pressure to reduce the time to market becomes greater each day. Design changes greatly increase the time until the product can be released to the market; this can result in a significant competitive disadvantage. Furthermore, design changes are costly, and these costs increase as the product moves through the product development cycle.

Engineering changes often are the result of poor planning in the development process. The use of quality function deployment, as we discussed in Chapter 6, can reduce the lead time of the product development process significantly. The time spent on designing, testing, and redesigning can be improved through techniques of quality engineering that we shall discuss in this chapter.

Process Planning

Process planning should be conducted concurrently with product development. Designing the physical facilities for manufacturing encompasses at least five different activities—product analysis, selection of appropriate technology, selection of specific production processes, selection of equipment, and layout of facilities. In addition, information and control systems must be designed to provide feedback on productivity and quality.

To design a production process for manufacturing a product, manufacturing engineers must first conduct a thorough analysis of the product. Engineers use assembly drawings and parts lists (discussed in Chapter 13) as aids in planning and designing a process. An assembly chart that defines the sequence in which components must be assembled and where inspections must take place is usually constructed. These drawings and charts are useful in selecting technology and equipment as well as for defining manufacturing operations.

The type of technology used in production, whether *manual, mechanized,* or *automated* technology, greatly influences the quality of the product and the productivity of the process. The relative roles that humans and machines have played in production have changed during the course of history. Recent advances in automated technology have removed the human element from many manufacturing processes and have significantly increased the quality of products. Technology is rapidly changing, and manufacturers must keep pace to provide quality products at a low cost. Unfortunately, technology is a long-term strategic decision that is not easily changed and is an issue for research and development. At the plant level, process and equipment selection are the principal decisions.

To select the appropriate production process to manufacture a product, manufacturing engineers must have the technical knowledge of materials and their properties, existing technology, and the desired properties of the final product as specified in the design. For example, one of the growing areas of current research in manufacturing is high-speed machining (HSM). Cutting speeds depend on the type of material being cut and the cutting tool itself. Typical cutting speeds might be 600 meters per minute for aluminum and 50 meters per minute for titanium alloys used in aircraft production. HSM speeds can reach as high as 9,000 meters per minute. The engineer needs to know the effects of such speeds on the structural properties of the materials being cut, such as in the construction of an airplane wing that incurs high stresses. Obviously, quality can be adversely affected if the wrong process is selected.

The goal of selecting a specific piece of equipment is to assure that the production process can produce the required quantity of output with the appropriate quality at the most economical cost. Often, similar equipment is available from several different vendors. Manufacturing engineers must take into account the equipment's performance, reliability, and cost in making selection decisions.

The layout of facilities is usually viewed as a productivity issue. However, quality may be affected if products undergo unnecessary handling that could result in damage. Hence, quality considerations should also be taken into account during facility layout studies.

Information and control systems are important components of process planning but are sometimes viewed as secondary in importance to machines and hardware. This is unfortunate, since like the design of physical facilities, the design of information and control systems revolves around productivity and quality issues. Routine documents such as operation sheets and route sheets are used to communicate the details of a manufacturing process to shop floor personnel. Methods and procedures for production scheduling are also required to control the flow of materials in production.

One of the most important control systems in production is the quality control system, the design of which must answer the following questions:

- Where should inspection take place?

- How should testing be performed?

- What instruments should be used for testing?

- How often should inspections and tests be performed?

- How is inspection/test data evaluated?

- What corrective action should be taken based on unfavorable test results?

In the discussion of organization in Chapter 7, we stated that in a well-structured organization, information and advice on technical matters must flow up the organizational ladder, just as orders and directives flow down the organizational chart.

Thus, efficient and effective reporting systems that provide feedback on production activities must also be designed. Written records—consisting of regular reports on critical variables relating to quality, scrap, and rework totals, process capability findings and recommendations, and employee involvement team presentations and reports—can all contribute to the internal intelligence system on how a process is running and where corrective actions need to take place.

QUALITY ISSUES IN PRODUCT DESIGN

To understand the importance of quality in product design, one must examine the history of quality assurance. Quality control in manufacturing originated primarily as an inspection activity that became necessary because of nonconformities in production output. Quality control departments consisted chiefly of inspectors who monitored production after the fact in an effort to reach acceptable quality levels—allowable percentages of defects. Only later was it realized that quality cannot be assured by inspection alone, and techniques of statistical process control (Chapters 16 and 17) found widespread use. The burden of quality assurance thus was placed where it truly belongs: on the production personnel themselves. However, while inspection and control can virtually eliminate defects in a capable manufacturing process, these activities alone cannot make a product fit for use. Intense global competition now demands continuous improvement in design quality.

The complexity of today's products make design a difficult activity. "Traditional" products such as bicycles, hand tools, and hydraulic pumps require less complex design aids and manufacturing procedures than do "modern" products, which frequently involve the use of sophisticated electronics. For example, a single state-of-the-art integrated circuit may involve more than 200 manufacturing steps.

Some of the major differences between traditional and modern products are listed in Table 14.1. As a result of these differences, new approaches to quality assurance are required that complement traditional inspection and process control methods. High quality can be achieved in complex products only by starting at the source of the production cycle—the design of the product and manufacturing process.

In addition, there are other reasons why quality of design cannot be neglected. These include the relationship of design to cost and manufacturability, and product liability.

Cost and Manufacturability

Product design affects the costs of manufacturing (direct and indirect labor, materials, and overhead), the costs of warranty and field repair, and the amount of redesign activities. General Electric, for example, found that 75% of its manufacturing costs are determined by design. With products in which parts alone are 65 to 80% of the manufacturing cost, design may account for 90% or more of the total manufacturing cost. Other companies exhibit similar figures. For Rolls Royce, design determines 80% of the final production costs; at General Motors, 70% of the cost of truck transmissions is design related. These statistics imply that significant reductions in manufacturing cost are possible through careful attention to design.

TABLE 14.1 Aspects of Traditional versus Modern Products

Aspects of Products	Traditional	Modern
Simplicity	Simple, static	Complex, dynamic
Precision	Low	High
Need for interchangeability	Limited	Extensive
Consumables or durables	Mainly consumables	Mainly durables
Environment in which used	Natural	Unnatural
User understanding of product	High	Low
Importance to human health, safety, and continuity of life	Seldom important	Often important
Life-cycle cost to user	Similar to purchase price	Much greater than purchase price
Life of a new design	Long; decades, even centuries	Short; less than a decade
Scientific basis of design	Largely empirical	Largely scientific
Basis of reliability, maintainability, etc.	Vague: "best effort"	Quantified
Volume of production	Usually low	Often high
Usual cause of field failures	Manufacturing errors	Design weaknesses

SOURCE: J. M. Juran and Frank M. Gryna, Jr., *Quality Planning and Analysis*, 2d ed. (New York: McGraw-Hill, 1980), p. 190; used with permission.

Improvements in cost and quality often are the result of simplifying the design. Simplicity of design leads to simplicity in manufacturing and assembly. By cutting the number of parts, material costs are reduced, inventories are lowered, the number of suppliers can be reduced, and production time can be shortened. For instance, General Electric found that assembly time and cost are roughly proportional to the number of parts assembled. The cost of carrying a part number in inventory might range from $500 to $2,500 annually. Costs of establishing and qualifying a new vendor for a new part might be as much as $5,000. Making design changes after release to manufacturing may cost $5,000 to $10,000 per design change. Clearly, the effect on total cost can be significant. IBM, for example, realized many benefits by designing a new dot matrix printer, the Proprinter. IBM had been buying its dot matrix printers from Seiko Epson Corporation, then the world's low-cost producer. IBM developed a printer with 65% fewer parts. All parts and subassemblies were designed to snap together during final assembly without the use of fasteners. This resulted in a 90% reduction in assembly time and major cost reductions.

Quality problems often arise when product design engineers are held to rigid schedules and cost goals for direct material and labor and do not work together with manufacturing personnel. The pressure to meet deadlines can often result in an inferior design that, while meeting functional requirements, may cause quality problems during or after manufacture. Product designers are chiefly concerned with performance and cost. Their responsibility is to create a design that meets performance criteria at the lowest possible cost. Traditionally, the only costs that concerned product designers were direct material and labor costs. Such costs were minimized, often at the expense of incurring higher quality costs. Designers must be aware that total cost is the important issue, not simply cost of direct labor and material. Quality costs are highly dependent on the design of the product and process. Poor design can lead to significant internal and external failure costs. The role of the quality engineer is to provide the link between design and manufacture so that total costs can be minimized.

Design must be coordinated with manufacturing to produce products of consistent quality with minimum waste. For example, it is typical for a company to replace failing parts during product testing by more expensive counterparts. This action only increases manufacturing costs. The alternative is to *redesign* the product around the less expensive parts. A Japanese watchmaker, for example, found that using expensive quartz crystals was not necessary to achieve high accuracy. The use of an inexpensive capacitor was found to compensate for variations in cheaper crystals and still achieve high accuracy.

Many aspects of product design can adversely affect manufacturability and, hence, quality.[1] Some parts may be designed with features that are difficult to fabricate repeatedly or with tolerances that are unnecessarily tight. Some parts may lack details for self-alignment or features that prevent insertion in the wrong orientation. In other cases, parts may be so fragile or so susceptible to corrosion or contamination that a fraction of the parts may be damaged in shipping or by internal handling. Sometimes a design, due to lack of refinement, simply has more parts than are really needed to perform the desired functions, so there is a greater chance of assembly error. Thus, problems of poor design may show up as errors, poor yield, damage, or functional failure in fabrication, assembly, test, transport, and end use.

A product's design affects quality in two major areas: at the supplier's plant and in the manufacturer's own plant. A frequent cause of supplier quality problems is incomplete or inaccurate specification of the item to be provided by the supplier. This often occurs with custom parts due to either weakness in the design process, engineers who do not follow set procedures, or sloppiness in the procurement and purchasing process. The greater the number of different parts and the more suppliers involved, the more likely it is that a supplier will receive an inaccurate or incomplete parts specification. Such problems can be reduced by designing a product around preferred parts (those already approved based on their reliability and qualified source of supply), minimizing the number of parts in the design, and procuring parts from a minimum number of vendors.

In manufacturing and assembly, many of the same problems described above for a supplier can occur. In addition, there will be problems in the area of assembly and test. For instance, designs with numerous parts may cause part mixups, missing parts, and more test failures. If some parts are similar but not identical, the chances of an assembler's using the wrong part are increased. Parts without details to prevent insertion in the wrong orientation may be assembled improperly. Complicated assembly steps or tricky joining processes may lead to incorrect, incomplete, unreliable, or otherwise faulty assemblies. Finally, the designer's failure to consider conditions to which parts will be exposed during assembly such as temperature, humidity, vibration, static electricity, and dust may lead to failures during testing or use.

---

[1]Adapted from Douglas Daetz, "The Effect of Product Design on Product Quality and Product Cost," *Quality Progress,* June 1987, pp. 63–67. Copyright © 1987, Hewlett-Packard Co. All rights reserved. Reprinted with permission.

Design for manufacturability (DFM) is the process of designing a product so that it can be produced efficiently at the highest level of quality. The main goals of DFM are to improve product quality, increase productivity, reduce lead time (the time to bring the product to market as well as manufacturing lead time), and maintain flexibility to adapt to future market conditions. DFM is intended to prevent product designs that may simplify assembly operations but require more complex and expensive components, designs that may simplify component manufacture while complicating the assembly process, and simple and inexpensive product designs that are difficult or expensive to service or support.

Some key design practices include the following[2]

- *Analyze All Design Requirements.* Since different manufacturing methods differ greatly in their ability to hold tolerances, it is important to review design specifications critically. Specifications should be as loose and flexible as realistically possible. Statistical analysis of the tolerances of multiple-part assemblies can assist in this effort.

- *Determine Process Capability.* Process capability was introduced in the previous chapter. If the process is capable of meeting all design and quality requirements, then little is left to do. If not, the engineer must make difficult decisions about changing design requirements, identifying different manufacturing processes, or reducing the variability in the existing processes.

- *Identify and Evaluate Potential Manufacturing Quality Problems.* This can include problems caused by equipment, procedures, the work force, and materials. Special emphasis should be placed on those problems that can result in serious or catastrophic failure in the product during use.

- *Select Manufacturing Processes that Minimize Technical Risks.* For example, in electronic assembly, automated component insertion generally is preferred to manual methods, regardless of production volume because of its low cost and high quality. For other types of products, the decision might not be so easy. In mechanical manufacturing, one has the choice of using metal or plastic components. Metal castings can produce very complex designs and hold relatively tight tolerances. Casting is much less expensive than machining. Another alternative is plastics. Plastics are less expensive, but have wider dimensional tolerances, are affected by thermal expansion, and have lower strength than comparable metal parts.

- *Evaluate Selected Processes under Actual Manufacturing Conditions.* Actual "pilot runs" may expose conditions that are not apparent during design or in simulated testing. Manufacturing research laboratories are sometimes used to perform this testing. In addition to identifying potential problems, such laboratories can perform research on improving manufacturing methods through experimentation.

Table 14.2 summarizes many important design guidelines for improving manufacturability and thus improving quality and reducing costs. Many industries

---

[2]John W. Priest, *Engineering Design for Producibility and Reliability* (New York: Marcel Dekker, 1988).

TABLE 14.2 Design Guidelines for Quality Improvement

Minimize Number of Parts	
▪ Fewer part & assembly drawings	→ Less volume of drawings & instructions to control
▪ Less complicated assemblies	→ Lower assembly error rate
▪ Fewer parts to hold to required quality characteristics	→ Higher consistency of part quality
▪ Fewer parts to fail	→ Higher reliability
Minimize Number of Part Numbers	
▪ Fewer variations of like parts	→ Lower assembly error rate
Design for Robustness (Taguchi method)	
▪ Low sensitivity to component variability	→ Higher first-pass yield
	→ Less degradation of performance with time
Eliminate Adjustments	
▪ No assembly adjustment errors	→ Higher first-pass yield
▪ Eliminates adjustable components with high failure rates	→ Lower failure rate
Make Assembly Easy and Foolproof	
▪ Parts cannot be assembled wrong	→ Lower assembly error rate
▪ Obvious when parts are missing	→ Lower assembly error rate
▪ Assy. tooling designed into part	→ Lower assembly error rate
▪ Parts are self-securing	→ Lower assembly error rate
▪ No "force fitting" of parts	→ Less damage to parts, better serviceability
Use Repeatable, Well-Understood Processes	
▪ Part quality easy to control	→ Higher part yield
▪ Assembly quality easy to control	→ Higher assembly yield
Choose Parts that Can Survive Process Operations	
▪ Less damage to parts	→ Higher yield
▪ Less degradation of parts	→ Higher reliability
Design for Efficient and Adequate Testing	
▪ Less mistaking "good" for "bad" product and vice versa	→ Truer assessment of quality, less unnecessary rework
Lay Out Parts for Reliable Process Completion	
▪ Less damage to parts during handling and assembly	→ Higher yield, higher reliability
Eliminate Engineering Changes on Released Products	
▪ Fewer errors due to changeovers & multiple revisions/versions	→ Lower assembly error rate

SOURCE: Daetz, op. cit.

have developed specific guidelines. For example, in designing printed circuit boards, some guidelines are:

- All components should be on the top side of the board.

- Similar components should be grouped together whenever possible.

- Clearance for insertable components must be 0.60 inch.

Design for Disassembly

Today's environmental concerns are having an unprecedented impact on product and process designs. The requirements brought on by pressures from environmental groups who are clamoring for "socially responsive" designs, states and municipalities that are running out of space for landfills, and consumers who want to get the most for their money are causing designers and managers to look carefully at the concept of "design for disassembly."[3] Design for disassembly consists of two components—recyclability and repairability.

Recyclable products must be designed to be taken apart in order for their components to be repaired, refurbished, melted down, or otherwise salvaged for reuse. *Business Week* cites several U.S. firms that are already working on, or have marketed such products, including Whirlpool, Digital Equipment, 3M, and General Electric.[4] The latter's plastics division, which serves the durable goods market, uses only thermoplastics in its products. Unlike many other varieties of plastics, thermoplastics can be melted down and recast into other shapes and products, thus making them recyclable.

The recyclability feature appeals to environmentalists as well as city and state officials, both of whom are fighting the effects of waste disposal. At the same time, however, it creates new issues for designers and consumers. For example, designers must strive to use fewer types of materials, such as plastics, and the materials must have certain characteristics, such as thermal properties, that allow them to be reused. They must also refrain from using certain methods of fastening, such as glues and screws, in favor of quick connect-disconnect bolts or other such fasteners. These changes in design will have an impact on tolerances, durability, and quality of products. Consumers will be affected by such design changes because they will be asked to recycle products, even though it may be an inconvenience for them to transport them to a recycling center. To provide further incentives for recycling, there have been discussions of requiring a deposit to be paid when a durable product is purchased, which would be returned when the product is recycled.

Repairable products are not a new idea, but the concept went out of fashion in the 1960s and 1970s in the United States, when we became known as the "throwaway society." Now design for disassembly promises to bring back easy, affordable product repair. For example, Whirlpool Corporation is developing a new appliance that will be designed for repairability, with its parts sorted for easy coding. Thus, repairability has the potential of pleasing customers, who will frequently find it easier and less costly to repair a product, rather than discard it. At the same time, companies will be challenged to consider new approaches to design in order to build both cost-effectiveness and quality into the product.

Product Liability

Safety in consumer products is a major issue in design, and quality assurance is an important defensive mechanism against liability claims. Industry has become increasingly concerned about product liability for a number of reasons. First, manufactured products are more complex and in widespread use today than ever before. Second, consumerism has become popular; there has been a shift from the traditional "let the buyer beware" to "let the supplier beware" philosophy. Third, the publicity around major liability suits and million-dollar judgments has increased

---

[3]Bruce Nussbaum and John Templeton, "Built to Last—Until It's Time to Take It Apart," *Business Week,* September 17, 1990, pp. 102–106.

[4]Ibid.

consumer awareness and generated more lawsuits. All parties responsible for design, manufacture, sales, and service of a defective product are now being held liable for damages.

It is useful to trace some of the history and background of product liability issues.[5] In 1916, the courts decided that a manufacturer should be liable for an injury to a product's user if the injury resulted from the manufacturer's negligence. This ruling was followed by the *theory of implied warranty,* which has two variations:

1. Fitness for a particular use, wherein the seller knows the use to which the buyer will put the product and the buyer relies on the seller's expertise and advice in the purchase.

2. Merchantability, wherein a product offered for sale will be suitable for the normal use of such product.

In this ruling, it was decided that losses should be borne by those in a position to control the danger.

In 1963, the theory of strict liability was established. According to this law, anyone who sells a product that is defective or unreasonably dangerous is subject to liability for any physical harm caused to the user, the consumer, or the property of either. This law applies when the seller is in the business of selling the product, and the product reaches the consumer without a substantial change in the condition in which it was sold even if the seller has exercised all possible care in the preparation and sale of his or her product. The principal issue is whether or not a defect, direct or indirect, exists. If it can be established that a defect does exist, the manufacturer usually will be held liable. A plaintiff need prove only that (1) the product was defective, (2) the defect was present when the product changed ownership, and (3) the defect resulted in injury.

Strict liability was used as a basis for the 1978 ruling against Ford in the Pinto automobile case. In the initial product liability case, the plaintiff was awarded $125 million. The damages awarded were punitive in nature. Evidence was established from Ford's own engineering documents that the company had determined that it was less expensive to pay a few product liability claims than to change the fuel tank design.

With the doctrine of strict liability, it is up to the manufacturer to prove innocence. That is, the manufacturer must prove that it would be highly unlikely for a product to be shipped in defective condition. *Defective condition* could refer to a design defect, poor design implementation, inadequate warnings, improper instructions, failure to anticipate misuse, improper materials, assembly errors, inadequate testing, or failure to take corrective action. Thus, we see that liability extends throughout the production organization.

Records and good documentation are the best evidence in product liability claims. The manufacturer must be prepared to present evidence of safety precautions and quality action steps. Design records should include reference to various standards, including company standards, used as guides in formulating a design. A record of rejected design approaches and the reason for rejection can be of great value when questions arise as to why a particular design path was chosen instead of other options. Documentation of design reviews, failure mode and effects analysis,

---

[5]John H. Farrow, "Product Liability Requirements," *Quality Progress,* May 1980, pp. 34–36; Mick Birmingham, "Product Liability: An Issue for Quality," *Quality,* February 1983, pp. 41–42.

and fault tree analysis (see Chapter 15) are extremely valuable in defending the product.

There is much that quality assurance can do to reduce the possibility of product liability claims and provide supporting evidence in defense arguments. Documentation of quality control procedures is a necessity. Evidence should exist that shows the designer has established test procedures to ensure that critical product characteristics are monitored. Feedback on test and inspection results along with corrective actions taken must be documented. Even adequate packaging and handling procedures are not immune to examination in liability suits, since packaging is still within the manufacturer's span of control.

Exorbitant liability judgments are one of Deming's Seven Deadly Diseases. Liability is causing many companies to forego product development activities. For example, Monsanto developed a phosphate fiber it says is safer than asbestos and more effective. They decided not to develop it further because they were not prepared to accept the potential liability risks despite the fact that research had shown it was safe. Unison Industries, Inc., of Rockford, Illinois, developed a new solid-state electronic ignition system for piston-engine aircraft. The company dropped the product after prototype testing. Unison says it was sued over crashes involving aircraft on which its products were not even installed. Getting removed from the lawsuits proved costly in itself.[6] In a survey of more than 500 chief executives, more than one-third of all firms surveyed have canceled introduction of new products because of liability concerns. Many have closed plants and laid off workers, and more than 20% believe they have lost market share to foreign competitors because of product liability costs.

QUALITY ENGINEERING

Quality engineering is concerned with the plans, procedures, and methods for the design and evaluation of quality in goods and services. Quality engineering consists of two principal methods: *on-line quality methods,* which focus on control in the manufacturing process, and *off-line quality methods,* which are technical aids for improving quality in product and process design. On-line quality control methods will be studied in Chapters 16 and 17. The objectives of off-line quality methods are to improve product manufacturability and reliability and to reduce product development and lifetime costs. Off-line quality methods include prototype tests, reliability tests, and various other techniques described later in this chapter.

Many modern approaches to quality engineering stem from the work of Genichi Taguchi. Taguchi proposes three principal tools for quality engineering: system design, parameter design, and tolerance design.

System Design

System design is the process of applying scientific and engineering knowledge to produce a basic functional design. It is the search for the best available technology. This consists of initial settings of product or process parameters and requires an

[6]Carolyn Lochhead, "Liability's Creative Clamp Holds Firms to the Status Quo," *Insight,* August 29, 1988, pp. 38–40.

understanding of both customer needs and the manufacturing environment. Three major factors must be taken into account in designing a product: (1) the function of the product, (2) technical requirements and specifications, and (3) economics of production.

Functional Influences. Important design considerations that relate to a product's function are the product's size, weight, appearance, safety, life, serviceability, and maintainability. Not all products are designed with the same level of features and characteristics. This is easily seen by contrasting a luxury car with a no-frills production model; each is designed to satisfy the needs of different groups of consumers and thus has different standards. In each case, it is the responsibility of quality engineering to assure that quality is achieved.

Technological Influences. The materials used in a manufactured product and the method of production affect the quality of a product and must be selected by the designer to meet specific quality objectives. For example, certain materials can be milled or bored to much closer tolerances than can others. Thus, parts that require close tolerances must be made from the appropriate materials, or serious quality problems will result. Different materials may require different manufacturing methods. In aircraft production, for instance, many parts are made from aluminum or titanium because of the requirement for strong, lightweight structures. However, titanium cannot be processed on many conventional machines, has different performance characteristics than aluminum, and includes potential fire hazards during processing. Thus, it is important to consider production processes in the design of a product.

Economic Influences. Products are targeted to specific consumer markets; hence, cost is an important factor in design. It would make little sense for a company to produce a product for mass consumer appeal if the costs of manufacturing were very high. The selection of materials and design alternatives should be made with the idea of avoiding any unnecessary cost that does not contribute to the performance of the product.

Parameter Design

A product's performance is affected by manufacturing imperfections, environmental factors, and human variations in operating the product. For example, military helicopters were found to be very sensitive to sand during the Iranian hostage rescue attempt. They simply were not designed for such environments. A high-quality product performs near its performance target consistently throughout the product's life span and under all different operating conditions. Parameter design is the process of identifying the settings of product or process parameters that reduce the sensitivity of designs to sources of variation in the factory and in use. Products that are insensitive to sources of variation are called *robust*. For example, a television whose picture sharpness varies with environmental conditions such as the room temperature would not be regarded as robust. An example of a robust design is the "gear effect" designed into modern golf clubs. This has the effect of bringing the ball back on line, even if it is hit off the "sweet spot" of the club. As another example, AT&T developed an integrated circuit that could be used in many products to amplify voice signals. As originally designed, the circuit had to be manufactured very precisely to avoid variations in the strength of the signal. Such a circuit would have been costly to make because of stringent quality controls needed during the manufacturing process. But AT&T's engineers, after testing and analyzing the design, realized that if the resistance of the circuit were reduced—a minor change with no associated costs—the circuit would be far less sensitive to manufacturing variations. The result was a 40% improvement in quality.[7]

Taguchi proposes the use of statistically planned experiments for parameter design. Experimental design techniques, developed by R. A. Fisher in England, date back to the 1920s. Historically, experimental design has not been widely used in industrial quality improvement studies. A major reason for this is that engineers found that it was difficult to work with the large number of variables, their interactions, and many different levels present in industrial problems. In such situations, the number of experiments that had to be conducted was very large. Taguchi was involved in improving the quality of the Japanese telephone system after World War II and recognized these limitations. He developed a new approach to designing experiments that focuses on the critical factors while deemphasizing their interactions, an approach that reduces greatly the number of required experiments. Another important difference in the Taguchi versus traditional methods is that, in most applications of experimental design, the objective is to optimize the mean value of an important response variable, such as yield in a chemical process. Parameter design experiments are aimed at reducing the variability caused by manufacturing variations. In industrial processes, controlling variability is much harder than controlling the average value.

Taguchi classifies variables that affect the performance characteristics into two categories: design parameters and sources of noise. Design parameters are those whose nominal settings can be chosen by the design engineer. The sources of noise are all those variables that cause the performance characteristics to deviate from their target values. The noise factors are those sources of noise that can be systematically varied in a designed experiment. The key factors that affect the product's performance in the field and process performance in manufacturing should be identified and included in the experiment.

One objective of the experiment is to identify settings of design parameters at which the effect of noise factors on the performance characteristic is minimum. These settings are determined by systematically varying the settings of the design parameters in the experiment and comparing the effect of the noise factors. The experiments can be done either through physical experiments or by computer simulation if a function that relates performance characteristics to design parameters and noise factors can be constructed and evaluated.

A celebrated case involves the Ina Tile Company, a Japanese ceramic tile manufacturer.[8] The company had purchased a new $2 million kiln from West Germany in 1953. Tiles were stacked inside the kiln and baked. Tiles toward the outside of the stack tended to have a different average and more variation in dimensions than those inside the stack. The cause was obvious: uneven temperature inside the kiln. Temperature is an uncontrollable factor, a noise factor. To try to

---

[7]John Mayo, "Process Design as Important as Product Design," reprinted with permission from *The Wall Street Journal,* © October 29, 1984, p. 29, Dow Jones & Co., Inc. All rights reserved.

[8]N. Raghu Kackar, "Off-Line Quality Control, Parameter Design, and the Taguchi Method," *Journal of Quality Technology,* Vol. 17, No. 4, October 1985, pp. 176–188.

eliminate the effects of temperature would require redesign of the kiln itself, a very costly alternative.

A group of engineers, chemists, and others who knew this manufacturing process brainstormed and identified seven major controllable variables that could affect the tile dimensions:

1. limestone content

2. fineness of additive

3. content of agalmatolite

4. type of agalmatolite

5. raw material quantity

6. content of waste return

7. content of feldspar.

A designed experiment was conducted using these factors. The experiment showed that the first factor, the content of limestone was the most significant factor and that other factors had smaller effects. By increasing the limestone content from 1 to 5% and by choosing better levels for other factors, the percentage of size defects was reduced from 30% to less than 1%. Limestone was the cheapest material in the tile. In addition, the experiment revealed that a smaller amount of agalmatolite, the most expensive material in the tile, could be used without adversely affecting the tile dimension. Both the effect of the noise factor and the cost of the product were reduced at the same time! This discovery was a breakthrough for the ceramic tile industry.

Other objectives of Taguchi experiments include identifying the settings of design parameters that reduce cost without sacrificing quality, identifying design parameters that have a large influence on the mean value of the performance characteristic but have no effect on its variation, and identifying those design parameters that have no detectable influence on the performance characteristics. The tolerances on such parameters can be relaxed.

Another concept that plays an important role in Taguchi methods is the signal-to-noise (S/N) ratio. This term stems from electrical engineering and measures the sensitivity of an effect (the signal) to the noise factors. The effect, or signal, is measured by its mean value, while the variability of the signal represents the effect of noise. This is measured by the standard deviation. Thus the S/N ratio essentially is the ratio of the mean to the standard deviation. Such a measure incorporates both the controllable and uncontrollable factors. High signal-to-noise ratios mean that the sensitivity to noise factors is low.

The signal and noise terminology can be extended to any type of product or service. The signal is what the product or component is intended to deliver. Noise is interference that is created by outside environmental factors, or even internal components in the system, that affect the quality of the signal. For example, the signal for a package delivery service is on-time delivery of an undamaged package to its destination. Noise that might cause variations in the expected delivery time or conditions would be such internal factors as misrouted, damaged, or incorrectly coded packages. External noise could be caused by incorrect or incomplete addresses furnished by the sender or weather-related delays of aircraft or delivery vehicles. If steps are taken to improve the systems within the company and to guard against external noise-producing factors, the signal will be stronger and clearer a higher percentage of the time, thus improving customer service and perceived quality.

As a practical tool for quality improvement the Taguchi methods have achieved considerable success in many different industries. For example, ITT Avionics Division, a leading producer of electronic warfare systems, has successfully used Taguchi methods.[9] ITT was experiencing a high defect rate using a wave solder machine to solder assemblies on printed circuit boards. The wave solder machine, developed to eliminate hand soldering, transports printed circuit boards through a wave of solder under computer control. Fourteen process variables were identified during a brainstorming session. Three sets of designed experiments were run. The data resulted in decisions that lowered the defect rate from 7 or 8 per board to 1.5 per board. With 2500 solder connections per board, the defect rate now translates to 600 defects per million connections and is being constantly improved. ITT conducted more than 2,000 Taguchi experiments between 1984 and 1986 to improve production processes. ITT's Suprenant Company, a supplier to Ford and an electrical wire and cable manufacturer, saved an estimated $100,000 per year in scrap, reduced product variability by a factor of 10, and improved the run rate of an extruding operation by 30% using Taguchi methods. Many other companies such as Xerox and Ford have been using Taguchi methods since the early 1980s.

We should point out that Taguchi's approach to experimental design violates some traditional statistical principles and has been criticized by the statistical community.[10] Among the shortcomings of his approach are the fact that Taguchi neglected to explain the assumptions underlying his methodology, introduced some statistically invalid and misleading analyses, ignored modern graphical approaches to data analysis, failed to advocate randomization in performing the experiments, and spawned a cult of extremists that accept only his teachings. While many of these issues are subject to debate, Taguchi must be recognized for having pioneered the simultaneous study of both the mean and variability, popularized the concept of robust product design, attracted a significant level of attention for education in quality engineering, demonstrated that experimentation produces results, focused attention on the cost associated with variability, and expanded the role of quality beyond that of control, thus winning the attention of a whole new audience.

Tolerance Design

Tolerance design is the process of determining tolerances around the nominal settings identified by parameter design.

Development of tolerances to specify how a part or product will be produced requires understanding of the trade-offs required. Narrow tolerances tend to increase manufacturing costs but perform the useful function of increasing interchangeability of parts, performance of the product, and product life. Factors operating to reduce tolerances include product function, durability, and appearance requirements; interchangeability requirements within the plant and in the field; and the need for a

---

[9]Bruce D. Nordwall, "ITT Uses Process Control Methods to Increase Plant Productivity," *Aviation Week & Space Technology,* May 11, 1987, pp. 69–74.

[10]Joseph J. Pignatiello, Jr., and John S. Ramberg, "The Top-10 Triumphs and Tragedies of Genichi Taguchi," presented at the 35th ASQC/ASA Fall Technical Conference, Lexington, Kentucky, 1991.

tolerance reserve or factor of safety to account for engineering uncertainty regarding maximum variation compatible with satisfactory product performance.

Wide tolerances, on the other hand, increase material utilization, machine throughput, and labor productivity while having the negative impact on product functioning characteristics previously mentioned. Thus, factors operating to enlarge tolerances include production planning requirements; tool design, fabrication, and setup; tool adjustment and replacement; process yield; inspection and gage control and maintenance; and labor and supervision requirements.

Setting inappropriate tolerances can also cause serious manufacturing problems and result in a high rate of defects. For instance, in one company, a bearing seat had to be machined on a large part costing over $1,000. Because of the precision tolerance specified by design engineers, one or two parts per month had to be scrapped when the tolerance was exceeded. A study undertaken by the quality manager revealed that the bearings being used did not require such precise tolerances. When the tolerance was relaxed, the problem disappeared. This one design change resulted in approximately $20,000 in savings per year.

Traditionally, tolerances are set by convention rather than scientifically. A designer might use the tolerances specified on previous designs or base the decision on judgment from past experience. All too often, tolerance settings do not account for the impact of variation on product functionality, manufacturability, or economic consequences. A more scientific approach to tolerance design can be performed using the Taguchi loss function introduced in Chapter 3.

EXAMPLE 1   Using the Taguchi Loss Function for Tolerance Design.   The speed of a cassette tape should be 1.875 inches per second. Any deviation from this value causes a change in pitch and tempo and thus poor sound quality. Suppose that it costs a manufacturer $20 to adjust the tape speed under warranty when a customer complains and returns a cassette player. (This does not include other costs due to customer dissatisfaction and therefore is at best a lower bound on the actual loss.) Based on past information, the average customer has returned a player if the tape speed is off the target by at least 0.15 inch per second. The loss function constant is computed as

$$20 = k(0.15)^2$$

$$k = 888.9$$

and thus the loss function is

$$L(x) = 888.9(x - 1.875)^2$$

At the factory, an adjustment can be made at a much lower cost, say $3, which consists of the labor to make the adjustment and additional testing. What should the tolerance be before an adjustment should be made at the factory?

We can use the loss function by setting $L(x) = \$3$ and solving for the tolerance:

$$3 = 888.9 \, (\text{tolerance})^2$$

$$\text{tolerance} = \sqrt{3/888.9} = 0.058$$

Therefore, if the tape speed is off by more than 0.058 inch per second, it is more economical to make the adjustment in the factory. Thus, the specifications should be 1.875 ± 0.058 or 1.817 to 1.933.

Applications in Process Design

The concepts of system, parameter, and tolerance design can be extended to the design of production processes. In system design, the manufacturing process is selected from knowledge of the relevant technology. In parameter design, the optimum working conditions for each of the component processes are decided. The purpose of this step is to improve process capability by reducing the influence of harmful factors. In tolerance design, the focus is on removing variation by removing the sources of variability from the process. All the methods and techniques of quality engineering apply. For example, many AT&T products contain hundreds or even thousands of circuit packs.[11] (A circuit pack is a collection of electronic components mounted on a printed circuit board.) A critical step in circuit-pack fabrication is the mass soldering of up to several hundred components to a printed circuit board. This mass soldering process can be cumbersome to control, since the optimum soldering machine settings depend on many factors, such as the physical layout of the printed circuit board, the type of components and their orientation, and the total number of components.

Rather than continually striving to control this process, AT&T designed a soldering technique that was much less sensitive to the variations in the manufacturing process. A new flux (a chemical that prepares the surface for soldering) was developed to increase the effectiveness of the mass soldering process without requiring a change in the soldering machine settings. The key idea is that it is cheaper to reduce the influence of manufacturing line variability than to try to control it. That is, the cause is allowed to go uncontrolled, but the resulting effect is controlled.

TECHNIQUES OF QUALITY ENGINEERING

Many useful methods can be considered tools of quality engineering. To conclude this chapter we will review three of them: value engineering and value analysis, design reviews, and experimental design.

Value Analysis

Value engineering and value analysis involve analyzing the function of every component of a product, system, or service to determine how that function can be accomplished most economically without degrading the quality of the product or service.

---

[11]John Mayo, "Process Design."

The term *value engineering* means cost avoidance or cost prevention before production. *Value analysis* is cost reduction during production. Typical questions that are asked during value engineering and value analysis studies include:

- What are the functions of a particular component? Are they necessary? Can they be accomplished in a different way?

- What materials are used? Can a less costly material be substituted? For example, can off-the-shelf items be used in place of custom-specified components?

- How much material is wasted during manufacturing? Can waste be reduced by changing the design?

Siver illustrates several examples of value analysis.[12] One of them involves the use of rope in explosion-proof seals in an electrical installation. The rope had always been sold on a weight basis. It was bought in ⅛-inch diameter, 50-pound spools, and cut to length and weighed for ¼-, ½-, and 1-pound packages. After studying the availability of standard products, it was found that if the customer would accept ¼ inch rope, the rope could be purchased in ¼-, ½-, or 1-pound balls for substantially less cost. In addition to the materials cost saving, the labor and cost of cutting, weighing, and packaging were eliminated.

Other examples are provided by Reuter.[13] An exhaust manifold in an air compressor was originally made from cast iron and required several machining steps. By switching to a powder metal process, four machine steps were reduced to one. The savings amounted to $50,000 per year. Bottles of shampoo for distributors were formerly packed in plain chipboard cartons. By changing to a six-pack holder similar to that used in the beverage industry, more than $100,000 was saved in the first year. Even simple ideas such as using packing material from incoming shipments to pack outgoing shipments resulted in over $600,000 in savings.

In addition to lower costs and higher profits, value engineering and value analysis result in better products, improved product performance and reliability, improved quality, improved delivery through reduced lead times, and increased standardization that leads to improved maintenance and lower repair costs.

Value analysis and value engineering are recognized corporate functions. Of the top 20 Japanese industrial firms in the mid-1980s, 17 had value analysis executives at the vice-presidential level. In 1983, Japan instituted the Miles Award, named after Larry B. Miles of General Electric, who originated the value analysis concept in the United States.

Value analysis programs are typically organized by project teams consisting of design engineers, manufacturing engineers, purchasing specialists, financial analysts, and others who possess relevant skills. The Pareto principle often is used to identify the products or components with cost or quality problems that deserve the most attention. The team familiarizes themselves with the item using engineering drawings, operation sheets, specifications, and sample items during the fact-finding phase. The evaluation phase consists of analyzing the function of the item and trying to find another item that could do the job better at a lower cost. This requires a tremendous amount of creativity, and creative thinking principles often are used to break habits

[12]D. L. Siver, "Standards in Value Engineering," Tech. Paper SP65-07, ASTME, 1964.
[13]Vincent G. Reuter, "What Good Are Value Analysis Programs?" *Business Horizons,* Vol. 29, March–April 1986, pp. 73–79.

and narrow mindsets. Once alternative ideas are generated, they are evaluated and submitted to decision makers for approval.

Successful value analysis programs require top management support; close coordination between engineering, production, purchasing, accounting, and quality control; availability of necessary data; and, finally, training.

Design Reviews

To ensure that all important design objectives are taken into account during the design process, many companies have instituted formal design reviews. The purpose of a design review is to stimulate discussion, raise questions, and generate new ideas and solutions to problems. The outcome of this process is a better product and lower costs. Design reviews help to facilitate standardization and reduce the costs associated with frequent design changes by assisting designers to anticipate problems before they occur. Hence, design reviews are nothing more than good planning.

Design reviews should be planned, scheduled, and documented and should involve all aspects of the production system. Generally, there are three major design reviews: preliminary, intermediate, and final. The preliminary design review establishes early communication between marketing, engineering, manufacturing, and purchasing personnel and provides better coordination of their activities. It usually involves higher levels of management and concentrates on strategic issues in design that relate to customer requirements and thus the ultimate quality of the product. Included in a preliminary design review are the following issues:

- function of the product

- conformance to customer needs

- completeness of specifications

- manufacturing costs

- process capability

- value and appearance

- marketing considerations

- make or buy decisions

- environmental conditions and product testing

- reliability requirements

- testing plans

- liability issues

- engineering documentation

- scheduling of the design and development process.

After the design is well established, an intermediate review takes place to study the design in more detail in order to identify potential problems and suggest corrective action. Personnel at lower levels of the organization are more heavily involved at this stage. Finally, just before release to production, a final review is held.

Materials lists, drawings, and other detailed design information are studied with the purpose of preventing costly changes after production startup.

Quality assurance personnel can play an important role in design reviews. Quality personnel have the expertise to classify quality characteristics and to determine quality levels and standards for verifying conformance to specifications. They can aid design engineers in the analysis of product function, life, interchangeability of components, and specifications. They can establish plans for inspection and testing and standardize criteria for product acceptance. Quality personnel can assist engineering and production personnel in understanding customer requirements and can help purchasing personnel to select materials and parts having the correct performance characteristics. Finally, they can also help to analyze serviceability in the field and to determine the need for inventories of replacement parts.

Experimental Design

A designed experiment is a test or series of tests that can enable the experimenter to draw conclusions about the situation under study. Designed experiments are fundamental to the Taguchi philosophy of product and process improvement. The objective is to determine the best settings for product or process parameters. For example, a paint company might be interested in determining if different additives have an effect on the drying time of paint and to select the additive that results in the smallest drying time. As another example, suppose that two different machines are used to produce the same part. The material used in processing can be loaded onto the machines either manually or using an automatic device. The experimenter might wish to determine whether or not the type of machine and the type of loading process affect the number of defectives and to select the machine type and loading process combination that minimizes the number of defectives.

A full discussion of experimental design is beyond the scope of this text. It is worthwhile to note that Taguchi has brought the attention of experimental design from the realm of statistics to a much broader segment of the engineering community. The importance of experimental design in product and process design and analysis has grown significantly in recent years and should continue to grow in the future.

MANAGING THE DESIGN PROCESS

All departments play a crucial role in the design process. The designer's objective is to design a product that achieves the desired functional requirements. The manufacturing engineer's objective is to produce it efficiently. The salesperson's goal is to sell the product, and that of the finance person is to make a profit. Purchasing must ensure that purchased parts meet quality requirements. Packaging and distribution are important to ensure that the product reaches the customer in good operating condition. Even the quality of user manuals and after-sales service is critical to a successful product. Such issues need to be considered during the design phase. Many personal computers, for example, were not successful when introduced simply because users, particularly those without technical background, could not understand the instruction manuals. Graphical user interfaces introduced on the MacIntosh and in Microsoft Windows are important design features for user-friendliness.

Clearly all business functions have a stake in the product; therefore, all should work together. Whitney relates the consequences of lack of understanding and cooperation in the design process.[14] A manufacturer of a household appliance depended on close tolerances for proper operation. The styling department demanded designs having a particular shape and appearance which prevented such tolerances and would not listen to manufacturing's concerns. The product was built from single parts on one long production line and could not be tested until complete. The finished product had to be adjusted to work, or taken apart to find out why it did not work. No one who understood the problem had enough authority to solve it, and no one with enough authority understood the problem. The company is no longer in business.

Involving manufacturing engineers from the beginning of a product development project has benefits for the product and the process. By asking the designer questions such as "Can you combine those two parts?" or "Can you use just one common screw type instead of three different types?" will help to improve the manufacturability of the product.

Whitney relates an example of a company that wanted to be able to respond in 24 hours to worldwide orders for its electronic products line.[15] Orders were small and required a large variety of different features. Engineers decided to redesign the products in modules, with different features in each module. All versions of each module were identical on the outside so that assembly machines could handle them. The company can now make up an order for any set of features by selecting the correct modules and assembling them, all without human intervention, from electronic order receipt to packaging. This is an example of successful cooperation between design and manufacturing.

Unfortunately, the product development process often is performed without such cooperation. In many large firms, product development is accomplished in a serial fashion. In the early stages of development, design engineers dominate the process. Later, the prototype is transferred to manufacturing for production. Finally, marketing and sales personnel are brought into the process. This approach has several disadvantages. First, product development time is long. Second, up to 90% of manufacturing costs may be committed before manufacturing engineers have any input to the design. Third, the final product may not be the best one for market conditions at the time of introduction.

An approach that alleviates these problems is called *concurrent engineering,* or *simultaneous engineering.* Basically, concurrent engineering is a process in which all major functions involved with getting a product to market are continuously involved with the product development from conception through sales.

Concurrent engineering involves multifunctional teams, usually consisting of 4 to 20 members and including every specialty in the company. The functions of such teams include the following:

1. Determine the character of the product to decide what design methods and production methods are appropriate. Ensure that the product can be repaired easily.

2. Analyze product functions so that all design decisions can be made with full knowledge of how the item is supposed to work and all team members understand it well enough to contribute. Understand product function in

---

[14]Daniel E. Whitney, "Manufacturing by Design," *Harvard Business Review,* July–August, 1988, pp. 83–91.
[15]Ibid.

relation to production methods. CAD tools allow a designer to simulate a product's performance by varying assumptions about materials, speeds, loads, and other operating conditions within a computer model.

3. Perform a design for manufacturability study to determine if the design can be improved without affecting performance. Manufacturing flexibility is an important characteristic of business strategy. Rapid changeover is important to meet changing demands and just-in-time environments. Flexibility can be improved through jigless production. Jigs and fixtures are usually designed to fit each part. If parts are designed with common jigging features or if products can be designed so that no jigs are needed, then manufacturing flexibility is improved.

4. Design an assembly sequence, identifying subassemblies, integrating quality control, and designing each part so that its quality is compatible with the assembly method. Questions such as the following need to be considered: What is the best combination of machines and people? How much can be saved if extra design effort eliminates the need for extensive appraisal and internal failure? Where should testing take place?

5. Design a factory system that fully involves workers in the production strategy, operates on minimal inventory, and is integrated with vendor's methods and capabilities. For instance, NUMMI, the joint GM-Toyota venture, attributes its success to careful analysis of failures of the previous GM operation: low-quality parts from suppliers, an attitude that repair and rework were expected, high absenteeism resulting in poor workmanship, damage to parts because of material handling, nonstandardized work methods, excessive inventory, and crowded work areas. Process changes in the new plant included permitting workers to stop the production line when problems were found and designing machines that could sense problems and automatically provide a signal or stop if necessary. Job classifications were simplified, displays showing how to do each job were developed, and extensive employee involvement programs were implemented.

Quality assurance personnel are in a unique position to perform such design coordination. Quality engineers can assist designers in developing products that can be consistently manufactured in conformance to specifications. They can better relate design standards to production, have access to vendor quality histories, and are aware of problem areas on the production floor. Quality personnel have knowledge of scrap, rework, and service records in the field. They also know the scope of various quality costs and can assist the designer in determining specifications that balance such costs against design costs. Process capability analysis, discussed in Chapter 13, provides valuable information about the ability of production equipment to meet design specifications.

A total approach to product development and process design involves the following activities:[16]

1. Constantly thinking in terms of how one can design or manufacture products better, not just solving or preventing problems.

---

[16]Don Clausing and Bruce H. Simpson, "Quality by Design," *Quality Progress,* January 1990, pp. 41–44.

2. Focusing on "things gone right" rather than "things gone wrong."

3. Defining customer expectations and going beyond them, not just barely meeting them or just matching competition.

4. Optimizing desirable features or results, not just incorporating them.

5. Minimizing the overall cost without compromising quality of function.

QUALITY AND PROCESS DESIGN FOR SERVICES

We have addressed the role of quality in service organizations throughout the preceding chapters. Because of the unique nature of services, the design of the "product"—that is, the service process itself—must be approached in a different fashion from manufactured goods.

In the design of a tangible product, technical specifications are defined precisely, and quality of conformance can be assessed through inspections and measurements. In many services, defining a quantitative standard may be difficult. For example, while it may be possible to set a standard for the maximum amount of waiting time in an emergency room, it is more difficult to assess the quality of the actual medical care. Usually surrogate (substitute) measures such as number of staff physicians, time to recovery, percentage of correct diagnoses, and appropriateness of medication are used to measure such quality. In hotel management, surrogate measures of quality might be the number of employees, size of rooms, or dollars spent in maintenance. Thus, much of the quality of service delivery is based on the customer's perception of the *process* used.

To design effective service quality control systems, service industries often use flowcharts and other methods similar to those used in manufacturing. For example, Figure 14.2 shows a typical insurance process. In this illustration, a quality check has been included at the end of the process. Such an analysis of a service process enables managers first to understand better the sequence of activities that make up the service,

FIGURE 14.2 **Typical Insurance Process**

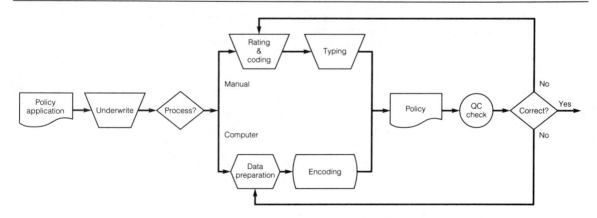

SOURCE: Adapted from A. C. Rosander, *Applications of Quality Control in the Service Industries* (New York: Marcel Dekker and ASQC Quality Press, 1985), p. 37.

and second to incorporate quality controls within the process. The use of flowcharts was discussed fully in Chapter 9.

Several researchers have suggested that services have three basic components: physical facilities, processes, and procedures; people's behavior; and professional judgment.[17] The design of a service process essentially involves choosing the relative balance among these components. The goal is to provide a service whose elements are internally consistent and focused to meet the needs of a specific target market segment. Too much or too little emphasis on one component may lead to problems. For example, too much emphasis on procedures might result in timely and efficient service, but might also suggest insensitivity and apathy with respect to the customer. Too much emphasis on behavior might provide a friendly and personable environment at the expense of slow, inconsistent, or chaotic service. Too much emphasis on professional judgment might lead to good solutions to problems, while resulting in slow, inconsistent, and insensitive service.

Service designers must ask some important questions: What is our service concept? What do customers expect? Are we aiming our service at the correct market segment? Are the components of the service compatible with customers' expectations? A useful approach to designing effective services is first to recognize that services can be viewed along a three-dimensional classification scheme as shown in Figure 14.3. Examples of services in each octant are

1. transportation

2. postal service

3. stockbrokers

4. retailing

5. public transit

---

[17]John Haywood-Farmer, "A Conceptual Model of Service Quality," *International Journal of Operations and Production Management,* Vol. 8, No. 6, 1988, pp. 19–29.

FIGURE 14.3 **Three-dimensional Classification of Service Organizations**

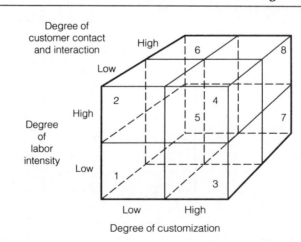

6. fast food

7. hospitals

8. design services.

Services low in all three dimensions of this classification are very similar to manufacturing organizations. The emphasis in quality control should be focused on the physical facilities and procedures; behavior and professional judgment are relatively unimportant. As contact and interaction between the customer and the service system increases, we must take two factors into account. In services low in labor intensity, the customer's impression of the physical facilities, processes, and procedures is important. Special care must be taken to make sure that equipment is reliable and easy to use. As high contact and interaction increase, more attention must be paid to making sure the staff behave appropriately.

As labor intensity increases, variations between individuals become more important; however, the elements of personal behavior and professional judgment will remain relatively unimportant as long as the degrees of customization and contact and interaction remain low. As customization increases, professional judgment will become more important in the customer's perception of service quality. In services high in all three dimensions, facilities, behavior, and professional judgment must all be equally balanced.

The Taurus-Sable Experience[18]

When Donald Petersen, Ford Motor Company's Chairman and CEO, became president in 1980, he inherited a company that could best be described as a "basket case." Overcapacity, uninspiring products, increasing competition from abroad, and poor quality all contributed to an incredible $1.54 billion loss. Petersen was quoted as saying: "Reestablishing our reputation was paramount. . . . We simply had to give quality an overriding priority." Wrenching decisions were made to close 15 North American plants, shrink the work force more than 25%, and introduce cost-cutting automation and technological change designed to shrink operating costs. According to the *Barron's* article, Ford had to rethink and revamp its way of doing things and make a bold gamble away from then mainline auto styling.

The Ford Taurus and Mercury Sable, introduced in 1986, became the hottest sellers since the Mustang in the mid-1960s. Ford took a lesson from the Japanese by studying customer wants and needs, making quality the top priority, and streamlining its operations and organization.

1980 was the year in which "Team Taurus" was born, under the direction of Lewis C. Veraldi, later vice-president of car programs management. Little did they realize that the products of their efforts, the Taurus and Sable, would be the #1 and #2 choices for *Motor Trend's* Car of the Year award in 1986, or that Taurus would be the second best-selling car in the United States (after Ford's Escort) in 1987.

Ford's Team Taurus approach was developed from the program management concept that had been used for many years in the aerospace industry. Program managers head product teams, which include representatives from design, engineering, purchasing, marketing, quality assurance, sales, and

service. It provides for concurrent, rather than sequential, input by all representatives. This, in itself, was a radical departure from previous Ford practice of independent responsibility for concept design, development of engineering specifications, and manufacturing process design.

The design process did not end with style and appearance. Ford went into painstaking detail to ensure that form followed function. Even before the Taurus-Sable line was introduced, Ford touted their unique design process:[19]

> In the early planning stages, a list of more than 800 significant improvements, from both customers and the people at Ford who actually build the cars, was drawn up to be incorporated into the cars' (Taurus-Sable) design and production. The result: vehicles that combine a dynamic shape with interior utility, fitting the car to the customer and his or her needs. Taurus and Sable also will bring to market a new powertrain, good fuel economy, advanced safety features and excellent "ergonomics"—the adaptation of such things as seats, controls and instruments to the driver.

Business Week reported:[20]

> The company bought a Honda Accord and a Toyota Corolla and "tore them down layer by layer, looking for things they could copy or make better," Veraldi says. All told, engineers combed over 50 comparable midsize cars. They found that the Audi 5000 had the best accelerator-pedal feel. The Toyota Supra grabbed top honors for fuel-gauge accuracy. The award for best tire and jack storage went to the BMW 528e. Of the 400 "best in class" features, Ford claims that 80% are met or exceeded in Taurus-Sable.

In 1984, the company implemented an innovation in manufacturing technology called "modular assembly" and began using it in the Atlanta and Chicago plants to produce the Taurus and Sable:[21]

[18]The factual data in this discussion are taken from: Richard Rescigno, "Spectacular Drive: What's Fueling Ford's Powerful Surge to the Top," *Barron's,* June 15, 1987, pp. 8–9; Ford Motor Company, *Annual Report,* 1986, p. 2, and *Annual Report,* 1987, p. 3; Richard Johnson, "Ford Moves to Speed Cars to Market," *Automotive News,* May 5, 1987, p. 57; Richard Rescigno, "Designing a Success: Of Bell Curves, Eagles and New Ideas," *Barron's,* June 15, 1987, pp. 8–9; Ford Motor Company, *Annual Report,* 1984, pp. 7, 11–12; Robert H. Waterman, Jr., *The Renewal Factor* (New York: Bantam Books, 1987), pp. 82–83.

[19]Ford Motor Company, *Annual Report,* 1984, p. 7.
[20]Russell Mitchell, "How Ford Hit the Bull's-Eye with Taurus," *Business Week,* June 30, 1986, pp. 69–70.
[21]Ford Motor Company, *Annual Report,* 1984, p. 7.

(continued)

. . . Modular assembly is the production of sub-assemblies or "modules" of the vehicle on automated ancillary lines feeding the main assembly line. This system reduces the chance of human or machine error, thus improving quality, because employees and robots can build modules without being paced by the moving assembly line. In addition, the system lessens the need for costly plant expansion by reducing the number of robots or machines that have to be incorporated into the main line, and also allows greater use of less expensive forms of automation on the ancillary lines.

An example of modular assembly is the "door-off-line" system. In this, the car's doors are removed after the body is painted. All door components, wiring and trim are applied in a separate system and the doors are reinstalled at the end of the final line. This process improves access to the vehicle interior and the doors for both employees and robots, saves time and reduces door scratching and other minor damage.

In his recent book, Waterman related how John Risk, who worked under Veraldi during the Taurus program, obtained worker input in the early days of Team Taurus. He would ride down the assembly line on a car body and ask workers for suggestions for improvement. Over an extended period, over 1,400 ideas were received. One idea was to attach a locator pin to the instrument panel so that it could be easily assembled. Previously, two people were needed to attach the panel. The new method required only one person to perform the job.

One operator suggested that a one-piece door and body module be developed, instead of the typical 12- to 15-piece design. Designers who worked on the project were unable to reduce the number of parts below two, but this still produced a substantial improvement in quality and productivity.

Suppliers were also consulted on design specifications. *Business Week* noted:[22]

Typically, an auto maker turns to its suppliers almost as an afterthought. Only when a car's design has been cast in concrete does the manufacturer send out specifications for parts and solicit bids in search of the lowest cost. The companies that are chosen keep the business only until a lower price comes along. Team Taurus, on the other hand, signed long-term contracts with contractors and invited them to participate in product planning. "We never had the supplier input we had on this car," says Veraldi. "Now we'll never do it any other way."

It is clear that integrating quality throughout the product design process as well as consideration of organizational issues was a major factor in Ford's success of the Taurus-Sable project.

Key Issues for Discussion

1. How did Ford change its approach toward product design with the Taurus/Sable?

2. What techniques were used to improve the quality of design of the automobiles?

---

[22]Russell Mitchell, *Business Week,* p. 70.

A Tale of Failure in Product Development[23]

In 1981, market share and profits in General Electric's appliance division were falling. The company's technology was antiquated compared to that

[23]Thomas F. O'Boyle, "GE Refrigerator Woes Illustrate the Hazards in Changing a Product." Reprinted by permission of *The Wall Street Journal,* © May 7, 1990, pp. A1, A6. Dow-Jones & Co., Inc. All rights reserved worldwide.

of foreign competitors. For example, making refrigerator compressors required 65 minutes of labor in comparison with just 25 minutes by competitors in Japan and Italy. Moreover, their labor costs were lower. The alternatives were obvious: Either purchase compressors from Japan or Italy or design and build a better model. By 1983, the decision to build a new rotary compressor in-house was made, along

(continued)

with a commitment for a new $120 million factory. GE was not a novice in rotary compressor technology; they had invented it and had been using it in air conditioners for many years. A rotary compressor weighed less, had one-third fewer parts, and was more energy-efficient than the current reciprocating compressors. Also, it took up less space, thus providing more room inside the refrigerators and therefore helped meet customer requirements better.

However, some engineers had argued to the contrary. Rotary compressors run hotter. In most air conditioners, this is not a problem since the coolant cools the compressor. In a refrigerator, the coolant flows only one-tenth as fast, and the unit runs about four times longer in one year than in an air conditioner. GE had problems with the early rotary compressors in air conditioners. Although the bugs had been eliminated in smaller units, GE quit using rotaries in larger units after frequent breakdowns in hot climates.

GE managers and design engineers were concerned about other issues. Rotary compressors make a high-pitched whine, and managers were afraid that this would adversely affect consumer acceptance. Many hours were spent by managers and consumer test panels on this issue. The new design also required key parts to work together with a tolerance of only 50 millionths of an inch. Nothing had been mass produced with such precision before, but manufacturing engineers felt sure they could do it.

The compressor they finally designed was nearly identical to that used in air conditioners, with one change. Two small parts inside the compressor were made out of powdered metal, rather than the hardened steel and cast iron used in air conditioners. This was chosen because it could be machined to much closer tolerances and reduced machining costs. This was tried a decade earlier on air conditioners and did not work. This fact was told to the design engineers who were new to designing compressors, and they did not pay attention.

A consultant suggested that GE consider a joint venture with a Japanese company who had a rotary refrigerator compressor already on the market. This idea was rejected by management. The original designer of the air conditioning rotary compressor, who had left GE, had offered his services as a consultant. GE declined this offer, writing to him that they had sufficient technical expertise.

About 600 compressors were tested in 1983 without a single failure. They were run continuously for two months under elevated temperatures and pressures that were supposed to simulate five years of operation. GE normally conducts extensive field testing of new products; their original plan to test models in the field for two years was reduced to nine months to meet time pressures to complete the project.

After testing, the technician who disassembled and inspected the parts thought they did not look right. Parts of the motor were discolored, a sign of excessive heat. Bearings were worn, and it appeared that high heat was breaking down the lubricating oil. The technician's supervisors discounted these findings and did not relay them to upper levels of management. Another consultant who evaluated the test results believed that something was wrong because only one failure was found in two years, and he recommended that test conditions be intensified. This too was rejected by management.

By 1986, only 2.5 years after board approval, the new factory was producing compressors at a rate of 10 per minute. By the end of the year, over 1 million had been produced. Market share rose and the new refrigerator appeared to be a success. In July 1987 the first compressor failed. Soon after, reports of other failures in Puerto Rico arrived. By September, the appliance division knew it had a major problem. By December, the plant stopped making the compressor. It was not until 1988 that the problem was diagnosed as excessive wear in the two powdered-metal parts that burned up the oil. The cost in 1989 alone was $450 million. By mid-1990, GE had voluntarily replaced nearly 1.1 million compressors with new ones purchased from six suppliers, five of them foreign.

Key Issues for Discussion

1. What factors in the product development process caused this disaster? What individuals were responsible?

2. Discuss how techniques of quality engineering might have improved the product development process for the compressor.

3. What lessons do you think GE learned for the future?

Summary of Key Points

- Quality of design, coupled with quality of conformance in production, determines the ultimate performance, reliability, and value of the product. Product design and process planning must be coordinated to ensure a quality product.

- The product development process consists of idea generation, initial screening and economic analysis, preliminary product design and development, prototype testing, final product design, pilot runs, and release to production. Competitive pressures are forcing companies to reduce the time to market. This can be reduced by eliminating design changes and improving the manufacturability of products.

- Quality assurance must be an inherent part of the design process, not simply an inspection activity. The complexity of today's products makes this a critical issue.

- Improvements in cost and quality often are the result of simplifying designs. Design for manufacturability is the process of designing a product so that it can be produced efficiently at the highest level of quality.

- Recently, environmental concerns have made "design for disassembly" an important feature of products, enabling components to be easily removed for recycling or repair.

- Product liability has forced manufacturers to pay increased attention to quality in design. As one of Deming's Seven Deadly Diseases, liability is a serious threat to competitiveness.

- Quality engineering consists of on-line methods focused on control in the manufacturing process and on off-line methods for improving quality in product and process design.

- Taguchi's three principal tools for quality engineering are system design, parameter design, and tolerance design. System design is focused on producing a basic functional design. Parameter design involves identifying the nominal settings of product or process parameters that reduce variation. Tolerance design is the process of determining tolerances around the nominal settings.

- Tolerance design is aided by the application of statistical methods as well as the Taguchi loss function.

- Tools of quality engineering include value analysis, design reviews, and experimental design.

- Concurrent engineering is a process involving all major functions of an organization working together to move a product from conception to market. Multifunctional teams help to remove organizational barriers between departments and therefore reduce the product development time.

- In designing services, one must consider physical facilities, processes, and procedures; behavior; and professional judgment. Classification of services along dimensions of customer contact and interaction, labor intensity, and degree of customization helps focus attention on the proper balance of these design elements.

Questions for Review and Discussion

1. Describe the product design and development process.

2. Discuss the importance of, and impediments to, reducing the time for the product development process.

3. How is process planning similar to product planning? What are the key elements that must be considered?

4. Discuss the major differences between "traditional" and "modern" products.

5. What are some of the factors that must be considered in the design of a product, both technically and managerially?

6. Explain the concept and importance of *design for manufacturability*.

7. What has been the traditional relationship between design engineers and manufacturing engineers during and after the design of a new product? How can quality assurance personnel assist in coordination of design improvements between these two groups of engineers?

8. Summarize the key design practices for high quality in manufacturing and assembly.

9. Why has design for disassembly become an important concept? Find some recent examples in the popular press.

10. Why should product liability be of concern to quality engineers in the design stage? What can be done to reduce the risk of product liability lawsuits?

11. Define the term *quality engineering*. What are its two principal methods?

12. Explain the role of system, parameter, and tolerance design in quality engineering.

13. What are "Taguchi methods" and how are they used in product design?

14. Explain the concept of the "signal-to-noise ratio."

15. What problems may be incurred in assembling mating parts if tolerances are not correctly and carefully specified?

16. Discuss value analysis and value engineering. Why are these activities important?

17. What is the purpose of a design review?

18. Discuss the principal tools used in design reviews.

19. Explain the role of experimental design in quality engineering.

20. What is concurrent engineering? What functions do concurrent engineering teams perform?

21. Explain the differences between designing manufactured products and services. How should the design of services be approached?

Problem

1. In the production of transformers, any output voltage that exceeds ±25 volts is unacceptable to the customer. Exceeding these limits results in an estimated loss of $400. However, the manufacturer can adjust the voltage in the plant by changing a resistor that costs $1.50.

   a. What is the Taguchi loss function?

   b. Suppose the nominal specification is 120 volts. At what tolerance should the transformer be manufactured?

Bibliography

Barker, Thomas B. "Quality Engineering by Design: Taguchi's Philosophy," *Quality Progress,* December 1986, pp. 32–42.

Byrne, Diane M., and Taguchi, Shin. "The Taguchi Approach to Parameter Design," *Quality Progress,* December 1987, pp. 19–26.

Case, Kenneth E., and Jones, Lynn L. *Profit Through Quality: Quality Assurance Programs for Manufacturers,* AIIE-QC & RE-78-2. Norcross, GA: Institute of Industrial Engineers, 1978.

Chaparian, Albert P. "Teammates: Design and Quality Engineers," *Quality Progress,* Vol. 10, No. 4, April 1977, pp. 16–17.

Clausing, Don, and Simpson, Bruce H. "Quality by Design," *Quality Progress,* January 1990, pp. 41–44.

Crow, Kenneth A. "The Role of Product Design in Competitive Manufacturing," in A. Richard Shores, *A TQM Approach To Achieving Manufacturing Excellence,* Milwaukee, WI: ASQC Quality Press, 1990, pp. 223–233.

Evans, James R. *Applied Production and Operations Management,* 4th ed., St. Paul: West Publishing Company, 1993.

Feigenbaum, A. V. *Total Quality Control,* 3rd ed. New York: McGraw-Hill, 1983.

Hopkins, David, "New Product Planning," *Quality Progress,* Vol. 13, No. 5, May 1980, pp. 24–25.

Ishikawa, Kaoru, "Quality and Standardization: Program for Economic Success," *Quality Progress,* Vol. 17, No. 1, January 1984, pp. 16–20.

Kackar, Raghu N. "Off-Line Quality Control, Parameter Design, and the Taguchi Method," *Journal of Quality Technology,* Vol. 17, No. 4, October 1985, pp. 176–188.

Kackar, Raghu N. "Taguchi's Quality Philosophy: Analysis and Commentary," *Quality Progress,* December 1986, pp. 21–29.

King, Carol A. "Service Quality Assurance Is Different," *Quality Progress,* Vol. 18, June 1985, pp. 14–18.

Michalek, Joseph M., and Holmes, Richard K. "Quality Engineering Techniques in Product Design/Process," *Quality Control in Manufacturing,* Society of Automotive Engineers, SP-483, pp. 17–22.

Montgomery, Douglas C. *Introduction to Statistical Quality Control.* New York: John Wiley, 1985.

Pettijohn, Caryl L. "Achieving Quality in the Development Process," *AT&T Technical Journal,* Vol. 65, No. 2, March/April 1986, pp. 85–93.

Ross, Philip J. *Taguchi Techniques for Quality Engineering,* New York: McGraw-Hill, 1988.

Ryan, Thomas P. "Taguchi's Approach to Experimental Design: Some Concerns," *Quality Progress,* May 1988, pp. 34–36.

van Gigch, John P. "Quality—Producer and Consumer Views," *Quality Progress,* Vol. 10, No. 4, April 1977, pp. 30–33.

Whitney, Daniel E. "Manufacturing by Design," *Harvard Business Review,* July–August 1988, pp. 83–91.

Ziemke, M. Carl, and Spann, Mary S. "Warning: Don't Be Half-Hearted in Your Efforts to Employ Concurrent Engineering," *Industrial Engineering,* February 1991, pp. 45–49.

Reliability

R*eliability* is one of Garvin's eight principal dimensions of quality that were discussed in Chapter 1. Reliability refers to the ability of a product to perform as expected over time. Reliability is one of the most important aspects of both product and process design. Sophisticated equipment used today in such areas as transportation, communications, and medicine require high reliability. For example, high reliability is absolutely necessary for safety in space and air travel and for medical products such as pacemakers and artificial organs. High reliability can provide a competitive advantage for many consumer goods. Japanese automobiles gained large market shares in the 1970s primarily due to high reliability. As the overall quality of products continues to improve, consumers expect higher reliability with each purchase; they simply are not satisfied with products that fail unexpectedly. However, the increased complexity of modern products makes high reliability more difficult to achieve. Likewise in manufacturing, the increased use of automation, complexity of machines, low profit margins, and time-based competitiveness make reliability in production processes a critical issue for survival of the business.

The subject of reliability became a critical issue during World War II. Sixty percent of the aircraft destined for the Far East proved unserviceable; 50% of electronic devices failed while still in storage; the service life of electronic devices used in bombers was only 20 hours; and 70% of naval electronics devices failed.[1] An *ad hoc* group was established by the Department of Defense in 1950 to study reliability of electronic equipment and components for the armed forces. The official report was released in 1952 and led to the development of the Advisory Group on Reliability of Electronic Equipment (AGREE) to further study issues involving reliability, testing, military contracts, packaging, and storage. Military specifications, coded MIL-R for military-reliability, were issued as requirements for military contracts, directed toward the procurement of equipment and components meeting reliability requirements. This military research spread rapidly throughout the industrial world and reliability engineering has become a distinct area of expertise.

The American Society for Quality Control provides a certification program for reliability engineering. The certified reliability engineer

---

[1] *Reliability Guidebook,* The Japanese Standards Association, Tokyo: Asian Productivity Organization, 1972, p. 4.

is a professional who can understand and apply the principles of performance evaluation and prediction to improve product/systems safety, reliability and maintainability. This body of knowledge and applied technologies include but are not limited to design review and control; prediction, estimation and apportionment methodology; failure mode; the planning operation and analysis of reliability testing and field failures, including mathematical modeling; understanding of human factors in reliability; the knowledge and ability to develop and administer reliability information systems for failure analysis, design and performance improvement, and reliability program management over the entire product life cycle.

In this chapter we shall formally define reliability, present various techniques for measuring and computing reliability, and discuss methods of reliability engineering.

BASIC CONCEPTS AND DEFINITIONS

Like quality, reliability is often defined in a similar, "transcendent" manner as a sense of trust in a product's ability to perform satisfactorily or resist failure. We need to deal with reliability in a more objective, quantitative fashion. Formally, reliability is defined as *the probability that a product, piece of equipment, or system performs its intended function for a stated period of time under specified operating conditions.* This definition has four important elements: probability, time, performance, and operating conditions.

First, reliability is defined as a *probability,* that is, a value between 0 and 1. Thus, it is a numerical measure that has a precise meaning. Expressing reliability in this way provides a valid basis for comparison of different designs for products and systems. For example, a reliability of 0.97 indicates that, on average, 97 of 100 items will perform their function for a given period of time and under certain operating conditions. Often we will express reliability as a percentage simply to be more descriptive.

The second element of the definition is *time.* Clearly a device having a reliability of 0.97 for 1,000 hours of operation is inferior to one having the same reliability for 5,000 hours of operation, assuming that the mission of the device is long life.

Performance is the third element. This refers to the objective for which the product or system was made. The term *failure* is used when performance of the intended function is not met. There are two types of failures: *functional failure* at the start of product life due to manufacturing or material defects such as a missing connection or a faulty component, and *reliability failure* after some period of use. Examples of reliability failures include the following: A device might not work at all (car will not start); the operation of a device might be unstable (car idles rough); or the performance of a device deteriorates (shifting becomes difficult). Since the nature of failure in each of these cases is different, the failure must be clearly defined.

The final component of the reliability definition is *operating conditions.* This involves the type and amount of usage and the environment in which the product is used. For example, Texas Instruments once manufactured electronic digital and analog watches (they have since eliminated these products as part of their strategic business plan). The typical operating conditions and environments for a watch are summarized in Table 15.1. Notice that reliability must include extreme environments and conditions as well as the typical on-the-arm use.

TABLE 15.1 Some Typical Watch Environments

Environment	Condition	Quantifiable Characteristics	Exposure Time
Typical use	On-the-arm	31°C (88°F)	16 hours/day
Transportation	In packing box	Vibration and shock (−20°C to +80°C)	Specifications for truck/rail/air shipping
Handling accident	Drop to hard floor	1200 g, 2 milliseconds	1 drop/year
Extreme temperature	Hot, closed automobile	85°C (185°F)	4−6 hours 5 times/year
Humidity and chemicals	Perspiration, salt, soaps	35°C (95°F) with 90% pH, rain	500 hours/year
Altitude	Pike's Peak	15,000 feet, −40°C	1 time

SOURCE: Adapted from William R. Taylor, "Quality Assured in New Products Via Comprehensive Systems Approach," *Industrial Engineering,* Vol. 13, No. 3, March 1981, pp. 28–32.

By defining a product's intended environment, performance characteristics, and lifetime, tests can be designed and conducted to measure the probability of survival (or failure). The analysis of such tests enable manufacturers to predict reliability better and improve product and process designs.

We often distinguish between *inherent reliability,* which is the predicted reliability determined by the design of the product or process, and the *achieved reliability,* which is the actual reliability observed during use. Actual reliability can be less than the inherent reliability due to the effects of the manufacturing process and the conditions of use.

The field of reliability has evolved through three distinct phases, much like the evolution of quality assurance. Initial efforts were directed at the measurement and prediction of reliability through statistical studies. The major focus was on the determination of failure rates of individual components such as transistors and resistors. Knowledge of component failure rates helps to predict the reliability of complex systems of these components. As knowledge about reliability grew, new methods of analysis were developed to help build reliability into products and processes. A new discipline called *reliability engineering* was established. Like total quality management, reliability must become an integrated part of all organizational functions: marketing, design, purchasing, manufacturing, and field service. We call the total process of establishing, achieving, and maintaining reliability objectives *reliability management.*

RELIABILITY MEASUREMENT

In practice, reliability is determined by the number of failures per unit time during the duration under consideration (called the *failure rate*). The reciprocal of the failure rate is used as an alternative measure. Some products must be scrapped and replaced upon failure; others can be repaired. For items that must be replaced when a failure occurs, the reciprocal of the failure rate (having dimensions of time units per failure) is called the *mean time to failure* (MTTF). For repairable items, the *mean time between failures* (MTBF) is used.

Failure Rate and Product Life Characteristics Curve

Let us first consider the failure rate. Suppose that a very large group of items is tested or used until all fail, and that the time of failure is recorded for each item. If we plot the cumulative percent of failures against time, we might get a curve as shown in Figure 15.1. The slope of the curve at any point (that is, the slope of the straight line tangent to the curve) gives the instantaneous failure rate (failures per unit time) at any point in time. Figure 15.2 shows the failure rate curve, generally called a *product life characteristics curve,* corresponding to the cumulative failure curve in Figure 15.1. This curve was obtained by plotting the slope of the curve at every point. Notice that the slope of the curve and thus the failure rate may change over time. Thus, in Figure 15.2, the failure rate at 500 hours is 0.2 failures per hour while the failure rate at 4,500 hours is 0.4 failures per hour. The *average failure rate* over any interval of time is the slope of the line between the two endpoints of the interval on the curve. As shown in Figure 15.3, the average failure rate over the entire 5,000 hour time period is .02 failures per hour. Many research institutes and large manufacturers conduct extensive statistical studies to identify distinct patterns of failure over time.

It is not always possible to gather enough data about failures to generate as smooth a curve as that shown in Figure 15.3. If limited data are available, the failure rate is computed using the following formula:

$$\text{failure rate} = \lambda = \frac{\text{number of failures}}{\text{total unit operating hours}}$$

or alternatively,

$$\lambda = \frac{\text{number of failures}}{(\text{units tested}) \times (\text{number of hours tested})}$$

There is a fundamental assumption in this definition that allows for different interpretations. Since the total unit operating hours equal the number of units tested

FIGURE 15.1 **Cumulative Failure Curve over Time**

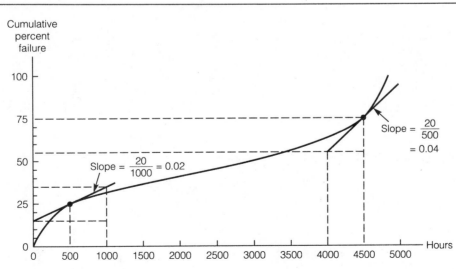

FIGURE 15.2 Failure Rate Curve

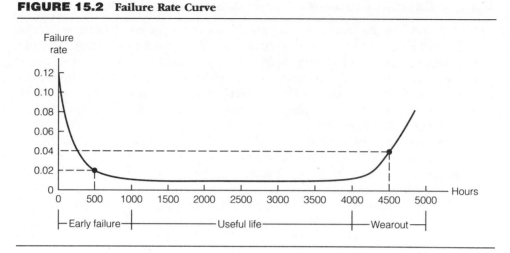

times the number of hours tested, there is no difference in total unit operating hours between testing 10 units for 100 hours or one unit for 1,000 hours. However, in view of Figure 15.2, clearly it would make a difference, since the failure rate varies over time. For example, if useful life began at 10 hours and the wearout period began at 200 hours, there would almost certainly be a failure before 1,000 hours, whereas this would not be the case for 100-hour tests. During a product's useful life, however, the failure rate is assumed to be constant, and different test lengths during this period of time should show little difference. This is why time is an important element of the definition of reliability.

To illustrate the computation of λ, suppose that 10 units are tested over a 100-hour period. Four units failed with one unit each failing after 6, 35, 65, and 70

FIGURE 15.3 Average Failure Rate over a Time Interval

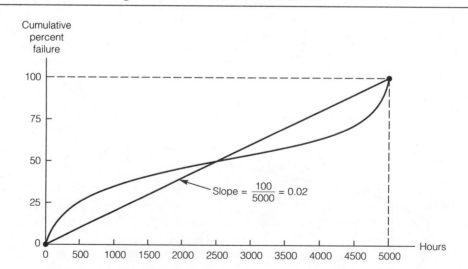

hours; the remaining six units performed satisfactorily until the end of the test. The total unit operating hours are

$$
\begin{array}{rcl}
1 \times 6 & = & 6 \\
1 \times 35 & = & 35 \\
1 \times 65 & = & 65 \\
1 \times 70 & = & 70 \\
6 \times 100 & = & \underline{600} \\
& & 776
\end{array}
$$

Therefore, λ = (4 failures)/(776 unit operating hours) = 0.00515 failure per hour. This means that in a one-hour period, about 0.5% of the units would be expected to fail. On the other hand, over a 100-hour period, we would expect about (0.00515)(100) = 0.515 or 51.5% of the units to fail. In this actual test, only 40% failed.

It is not uncommon for an electronic component such as a semiconductor to have a high, but decreasing, failure rate early in its life (as evidenced by the steep slope of the curve), followed by a period of a relatively constant failure rate, and ending with an increasing failure rate. The failure rate curve in Figure 15.2 is an example of a typical product life characteristics curve for such components.

In Figure 15.2, three distinct time periods are evident: early failure (from 0 to about 1,000 hours), useful life (from 1,000 to 4,000 hours), and wearout period (after 4,000 hours). The first is the early failure period, sometimes called the **infant mortality period.** Weak components resulting from poor manufacturing or quality control procedures will often lead to a high rate of failure early in a product's life. This usually cannot be detected through normal test procedures. This is particularly true for electronic semiconductors. Such components or products should not be permitted to enter the marketplace. The second phase of the life characteristics curve describes the normal pattern of random failures during a product's useful life. This period usually has a low, relatively constant failure rate that is determined by uncontrollable factors, such as sudden and unexpected stresses resulting from complex interactions in materials or the environment. These factors are usually impossible to predict on an individual basis. However, it is possible to model the collective behavior of such failures statistically, as we'll see later in the chapter. Finally, as age takes over, the wearout period begins, and the failure rate increases. You may have experienced such phenomena with automobile components or other consumer products.

Knowing the product life characteristics curve for a particular product helps engineers predict behavior and make decisions accordingly. For instance, if we know that the early failure period for a microprocessor is 600 hours, we can test the chip for 600 hours (or more) under actual or simulated operating conditions before releasing it to the market.

Knowledge of a product's reliability is also useful in developing warranties. To illustrate this, consider a tire manufacturer who must determine a mileage warranty policy for a new line of tires. From engineering test data, the reliability curve shown in Figure 15.4 was constructed. This graph shows the probability of tread separation within a certain number of miles. We see that half the tires will fail by 36,500 miles, 87% will wear out by 42,000 miles, and only 14% will wear out by 31,000 miles. Thus, if a 31,000-mile warranty is established, management can compute the expected cost of having to replace 14% of the tires. On the other hand, these data may indicate a

FIGURE 15.4 Cumulative Probability Distribution for Tire Mileage

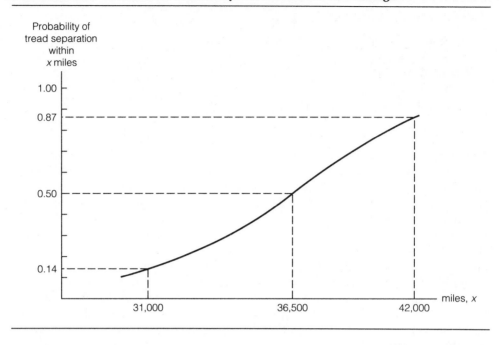

poor design in relation to similar products of competitors. Design changes might be necessary to improve reliability. Note that in this example time is not measured chronologically, but in terms of product usage.

Reliability Function

We defined reliability as the probability that an item will *not* fail over a given period of time. It is usually more convenient to use the probability distribution of failures in reliability computations. Recall that during the useful life of a product the failure rate is assumed to be constant. Thus, the fraction of good items that fails during any time period is constant. Under this assumption, it follows mathematically that the probability of failure over time can be modeled by an exponential probability distribution. Not only is this mathematically justified, but it has been empirically validated for many observable phenomena, such as failures of light bulbs, electronic components, and repairable systems such as automobiles, computers, and industrial machinery.

If λ is the failure rate, the probability density function representing failures is given by the exponential density

$$f(t) = \lambda \, e^{-\lambda t} \qquad t \geq 0$$

The probability of failing during a time interval (t_1, t_2) can be shown to be

$$e^{-\lambda(t_2 - t_1)}$$

Specifically, the probability of failure in the interval $(0, T)$ is given by the cumulative distribution function

$$F(T) = 1 - e^{-\lambda T}$$

Since reliability is the probability of *survival,* we have the *reliability function*

$$R(T) = 1 - F(T) = e^{-\lambda T}$$

This represents the probability that the item will not fail within T units of time.

Consider, for example, an item having a reliability of 0.97 for 100 hours of normal use. We may determine the failure rate λ by solving the equation $R = e^{-\lambda T}$ for λ. Substituting $R = 0.97$ and $T = 100$ into this equation, we have

$$0.97 = e^{-\lambda(100)}$$
$$\ln 0.97 = -100\lambda$$
$$\lambda = -(\ln 0.97)/100$$
$$= 0.0304/100$$
$$\approx 0.0003 \text{ failure per hour}$$

Thus, the reliability function is $R(T) = e^{-.0003T}$. We may tabulate the cumulative fraction of items that are expected to fail and survive after each 10-hour period. This is given in Table 15.2. Note that the fraction failing in any 10-hour period is constant.

The reciprocal of the failure rate is often used in reliability computations. For nonrepairable items, we define $\theta = 1/\lambda$ as the mean time to failure (MTTF). Thus, in the preceding example for $\lambda = 0.0003$ failure per hour, $\theta = 1/.0003 = 3,333$ hours. That is, one failure can be expected every 3,333 hours on the average. The probability distribution function of failures and the reliability function can be equivalently expressed using the MTTF as

$$F(T) = 1 - e^{-T/\theta}$$

and

$$R(T) = e^{-T/\theta}$$

Suppose, for example, that an electronic component has a failure rate of $\lambda = 0.0001$ failure per hour. The MTTF is $\theta = 1/0.0001 = 10,000$ hours. The probability that the component will not fail in 15,000 hours is

$$R(15,000) = e^{-15000/10000}$$
$$= e^{-1.5}$$
$$= 0.223$$

TABLE 15.2 Cumulative Fraction Failing and Surviving

Time, T	Failures, F(T)	Survivors, R(T)
10	0.003	0.997
20	0.006	0.994
30	0.009	0.991
40	0.012	0.988
50	0.015	0.985
60	0.018	0.982
70	0.021	0.979
80	0.024	0.976
90	0.027	0.973
100	0.030	0.970

For repairable items, θ is usually called the mean time between failures (MTBF). For example, suppose that a machine is operated for 10,000 hours and experiences four failures that are immediately repaired. The mean time between failures is

MTBF = 10,000/4 = 2500 hours

and the failure rate is

λ = 1/2500 = 0.0004 failure per hour

MTBF is a very useful statistic in many management decisions. Consider a company like Xerox, which leases copying equipment and maintains a service staff throughout the United States. The MTBF can be used to predict the volume of service calls expected, determine labor requirements for service and geographical assignments, and plan the purchase or manufacture of spare parts. In fact, Xerox actually has used an analytical model to determine service staff size. One of the parameters in the model is the average rate at which machines need service.[2]

The failure distribution can also be used to establish preventive maintenance policies for repairable systems.

EXAMPLE 1 Determining a Preventive Maintenance Policy. A part of a bathroom tissue production system is a saw/wrapper machine, which cuts long rolls into smaller pieces and wraps them into packages before they are placed into cartons. Historical data on the time between failures are presented in Table 15.3. From this information we calculate MTBF by taking an expected value, that is, we multiply the midpoint of each time interval by its associated probability and sum:

MTBF = 27.5(0.2) + 32.5(0.4) + 37.5(0.3) + 42.5(0.1)

= 34 hours

At present, the machine is repaired only when it fails, at an average cost of $50. The company is considering a preventive maintenance program that will cost $30 for each inspection and adjustment.

To determine whether this is economically justified, we compute and compare average annual costs. Consider, for instance, the current policy. Assuming 260 working days per year and one shift per day, there are 2,080 hours of available time. If the mean time between failures is 34 hours, we expect 2080/34 = 61.2 breakdowns per year. Hence, the annual cost will be 61.2 × $50 = $3,060. Now suppose that the machine is inspected every 25 hours and adjusted. If we assume that the time until the next failure after adjustment follows the distribution in Table 15.3, the probability of a failure under this policy is zero. However, inspection every 25 hours will occur 2080/25 = 83.2 times per year, resulting in a cost of 83.2 × $30 = $2,496. Next suppose we inspect every 30 hours. From Table 15.3, the probability of a failure occurring before the next inspection is 0.20. Thus, the total expected annual cost will be the cost of

---

[2]W. H. Blevel, "Management Science's Impact on Service Strategy," *Interfaces,* Vol. 6, No. 1, Pt. 2, November 1975, pp. 4–12.

TABLE 15.3 Historical Data on Time between Failures

Hours between Failures	Probability
25–30	0.2
30–35	0.4
35–40	0.3
40–45	0.1
Total	1.0

TABLE 15.4 Cost Computation for Preventive Maintenance

Time between Inspection	Number of Inspections Per Year	Probability of Failure before Next Inspection	Inspection Cost	Failure Cost	Total Cost
25	83.2	0.0	$2,496	$ 0	$2,496
30	69.3	0.2	$2,080	$ 693	$2,773
35	59.4	0.6	$1,782	$1,782	$3,564
40	52	0.9	$1,560	$2,340	$3,900

inspection, $30 \times 2080/30 = \$2,080$, plus the expected cost of emergency repair, $50 \times 2080/30 \times 0.20 = \$693$. The total cost is therefore $2,773. Table 15.4 summarizes similar calculations for other maintenance intervals. We see that a maintenance interval of 25 hours results in a minimal cost policy.

Other probability distributions are often used for modeling reliability. One of the most common is the Weibull distribution, whose probability density function is

$$f(t) = \alpha\beta t^{\beta-1}e^{-\alpha t^{\beta}} \qquad t > 0$$

The constants α and β are called the **scale** and **shape** parameters, respectively. By varying these constants, the Weibull distribution assumes a variety of shapes as illustrated in Figure 15.5. Thus, it is a very flexible modeling tool for fitting empirical failure data to a theoretical distribution. The Weibull distribution is often used in modeling failure data for memory components and structural elements in automobiles and airplanes. The reliability function based on the Weibull distribution is

$$R(T) = e^{-\alpha T^{\beta}}$$

To illustrate the use of the Weibull distribution, suppose that a particular electric component has a Weibull failure distribution with $\alpha = 0.02$ and $\beta = 0.5$. (Determining α and β is an exercise in curve fitting.) Then

$$R(T) = e^{-0.02\sqrt{T}}$$

The fraction of components expected to survive 400 hours is thus

$$R(400) = e^{-0.02\sqrt{400}} = e^{-0.4} = 0.67$$

FIGURE 15.5   **Weibull Distribution for $\alpha = 1$ and $\beta = 0.5, 1, 2,$ and 4**

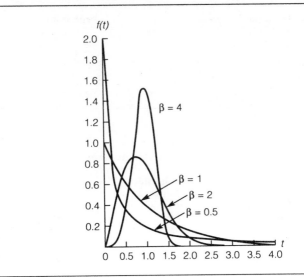

The following table presents some values of $R(T)$ for selected values of T:

T	R(T)
100	0.82
200	0.75
300	0.71
400	0.67
500	0.64
1000	0.53
5000	0.24
10000	0.14

For example, only 24% of the components will be expected to survive 5,000 hours or more.

RELIABILITY PREDICTION

Random failures during useful life are uncontrollable, but, as we have seen, they can be described by probability distributions. Many systems are composed of individual components with known reliabilities. We can use the reliability data of individual components to predict the reliability of the system. Systems of components may be configured in *series,* in *parallel,* or in some mixed combination. This section presents formulas and techniques for determining system reliability for each of these situations.

FIGURE 15.6 Series System

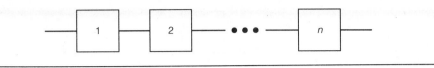

Series Systems

A **series system** is illustrated in Figure 15.6. In such a system, all components must function or the system will fail. If the reliability of component i is R_i, the reliability of the system is the product of the individual reliabilities, that is

$$R_s = R_1 R_2 \ldots R_n$$

This follows from the multiplicative law of probability. For example, suppose that a personal computer system is composed of the processing unit, modem, and printer with reliabilities of 0.997, 0.980, and 0.975, respectively. The reliability of the system is therefore given by

$$R_s = (0.997)(0.980)(0.975) = 0.953$$

Note that since reliabilities are less than one, system reliability decreases as additional components are added in series. Thus, the more complex a series system is, the greater the chance of failure.

If the reliability function is exponential, i.e., $R_i = e^{-\lambda_i T}$, then

$$R_s = e^{-\lambda_1 T} e^{-\lambda_2 T} \cdots e^{-\lambda_n T}$$
$$= e^{-\lambda_1 T - \lambda_2 T \cdots -\lambda_n T}$$
$$= e^{-\left(\sum_{i=1}^{n} \lambda_i\right) T}$$

Suppose that a two-component series system has failure rates of 0.004 and 0.001 per hour. Then

$$R_s(T) = e^{-(0.004 + 0.001)T}$$
$$= e^{-0.005T}$$

The probability of survival for 100 hours would be

$$R_s(100) = e^{-0.005(100)}$$
$$= e^{-0.5}$$
$$= 0.6065$$

Parallel Systems

A **parallel system** is illustrated in Figure 15.7. In such a system, failure of an individual component is less critical than in series systems; the system will successfully operate as long as one component functions. Hence, the additional components are **redundant.** Redundancy is often built into systems to improve their reliability. However, as mentioned earlier, trade-offs in cost, size, weight, and so on must be taken into account.

FIGURE 15.7   Parallel System

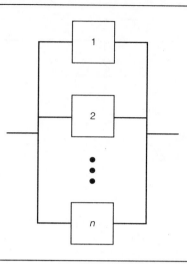

The reliability of the parallel system in Figure 15.7 is derived as follows. If $R_1, R_2, \ldots, R_n$ are the reliabilities of the individual components, the probabilities of failure are $1 - R_1, 1 - R_2, \ldots, 1 - R_n$, respectively. Since the system fails only if each component fails, the probability of system failure is

$$(1 - R_1)(1 - R_2) \ldots (1 - R_n)$$

Hence, the system reliability is computed as

$$R_s = 1 - (1 - R_1)(1 - R_2) \ldots (1 - R_n)$$

If all components have identical reliabilities R, then

$$R_s = 1 - (1 - R)^n$$

The computers on the space shuttle were designed to provide for redundancy in case of failure. Five computers were designed in parallel. Thus, for example, if the reliability of each were 0.99, the system reliability is

$$R_s = 1 - (1 - 0.99)^5 = 0.9999999999$$

Series-Parallel Systems

Most systems are composed of combinations of series and parallel systems. Consider the system shown in Figure 15.8(a). To determine the reliability of such a system, first compute the reliability of the parallel subsystem B:

$$R_B = 1 - (1 - 0.9)^3 = 0.999$$

This is equivalent to replacing the three parallel components B with a single component B having a reliability of 0.999 in series with A, C, and D [Figure 15.8(b)]. Next, compute the reliability of the equivalent series system:

$$R_s = (0.99)(0.999)(0.96)(0.98) = 0.93$$

FIGURE 15.8   Series-Parallel System and Equivalent Series System

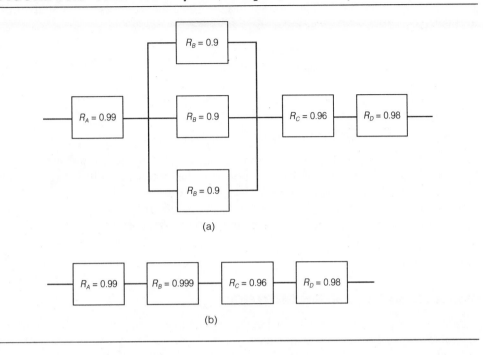

(a)

(b)

FIGURE 15.9   Series-Parallel System and Equivalent Series System

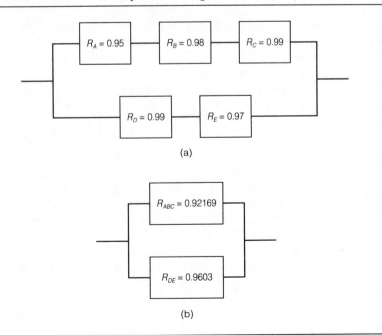

(a)

(b)

A second type of series-parallel arrangement is shown in Figure 15.9(a). System reliability is determined by first computing the reliability of the series systems ABC and DE:

$$R_{ABC} = (0.95)(0.98)(0.99) = 0.92169$$
$$R_{DE} = (0.99)(0.97) = 0.9603$$

The result is an equivalent parallel system shown in Figure 15.9(b). The system reliability is then computed as

$$R_s = 1 - (1 - 0.92169)(1 - 0.9603) = 0.9969$$

From these examples, we see that by appropriately decomposing complex systems into series and/or parallel components, the system reliability can be easily computed. Reliability requirements are determined during the product design phase. The designer may use techniques such as these to determine the effects of adding redundancy, substituting different components, or reconfiguring the design.

RELIABILITY ENGINEERING

Reliability engineering is a relatively new discipline that is concerned with the design, manufacture, and assurance of products having high reliability. Many techniques of reliability engineering have been developed. We will review some of the common methods of reliability engineering in this section.

Standardization

One method of ensuring high reliability is to use components with proven track records of reliability for years of actual use. If failure rates of components can be established, then standard components can be selected and used in the design process. The use of standardized components not only helps to achieve high reliability, but also reduces costs since standardized components are used in many different products.

Redundancy

Redundancy is providing backup components that can be used when the failure of any one component in a system can cause a failure of the system. In the previous section we saw how redundant components can increase reliability dramatically. Redundant components are designed either in a standby configuration or a parallel configuration. In a standby system, the standby unit is switched in when the operating unit fails; in the parallel configuration, both units operate normally but only one is required for proper functioning. Redundancy is crucial to systems in which failures can be extremely costly, such as aircraft or satellite communications systems. Redundancy, however, increases the cost, size, and weight of the system. Therefore, designers must trade off these attributes against increased reliability.

Physics of Failure

Many failures are due to deterioration because of chemical reactions over time, which may be aggravated by temperature or humidity effects. Understanding the physical properties of materials and their response to environmental effects helps to eliminate potential failures or to make the product robust with respect to environmental conditions that affect reliability. Reliability engineers must work closely with chemists, materials science engineers, and others who can contribute to a better understanding of failure mechanisms.

Reliability Testing

The reliability of a product is principally determined by the design and the reliability of the components of the product. However, reliability is such a complex issue that it cannot always be determined from theoretical analysis of the design alone. Hence, formal testing is necessary, which involves simulating environmental conditions to determine a product's performance, operating time, and mode of failure.

Testing is useful for a variety of other reasons. Test data are often necessary for liability protection, as means for evaluating designs or vendor reliability, and in process planning and selection. Often, reliability test data are required in military contracts. Testing is necessary to evaluate warranties and to avoid high costs related to early field failure. Good testing leads to good reliability and hence good quality.

Product testing is performed in various ways. The purpose of *life testing,* that is, running devices until they fail, is to measure the distribution of failures to better understand and eliminate their causes. However, such testing can be expensive and time-consuming. For devices that have long natural lives, life testing is not practical. *Accelerated life testing* involves overstressing components to reduce the time to failure and find weaknesses. This might involve running a motor faster than would be found in normal operating conditions. However, failure rates must correlate well to actual operating conditions if accelerated life testing is to be useful.

Other testing is designed to study the robustness of products. For example, Tandy Corporation performs a variety of tests on its computers.[3] Products are disassembled and destructive testing is performed on the electromechanical, mechanical, and physical properties of components. *Environmental testing* consists of varying the temperature from −40 degrees (the temperature inside trucks in the northern United States and Canada) to 165 degrees (the temperature inside trucks in the southwest United States) to shock the product to see if it can withstand extremes. Since old wiring exhibits a wide range of variation, ac power is varied from 105 to 135 volts. *Vibration and shock testing* are used to simulate trucks driving from the East to the West Coast to determine the product's ability to withstand rough handling and accidents.

Burn-in

Semiconductors are the basic building blocks of numerous modern products such as videocassette recorders, automotive ignition systems, computers, and military weapons systems. Semiconductors have a small proportion of defects, called *latent defects,* that

---

[3]Keith Denton, "Reducing DOAs (and other Q.C. Problems)," *P&IM Review with APICS News,* December 1989, pp. 35–36.

can cause them to fail during the first 1,000 hours of normal operation. After that, the failure rate stabilizes, perhaps for as long as 25 years, before beginning to rise again as components begin to wear out. These infant mortalities can be as high as 10% in a new technology or as low as 0.01% in proven technologies. The sooner a faulty component is detected, the cheaper it is to replace or repair it. A correction on a integrated circuit fabrication line costs about 50 cents; at the board level it might cost $5; at the system level about $50; and in the field, $500. If a printed circuit board contains 100 semiconductors, a failure rate of 0.01% would cause a board failure rate of 1%.

Burn-in, or component stress testing, involves exposing integrated circuits to elevated temperatures in order to force latent defects to occur. For example, a device that might normally fail after 300 hours at 25°C might fail in less than 20 hours at 150°C. Survivors are likely to have long, trouble-free operating lives.

Studies and experience have proven the economic advantages of burn-in. For example, a recent large-scale study of the effect of burn-in on enhancing reliability of dynamic MOS memories was conducted in Europe. The failure rate without burn-in conditioning and testing to eliminate infant mortality was 0.24% per thousand hours, while burn-in and testing reduced the rate to 0.02% per thousand hours. This improvement translates into a significant profit enhancement for users. When considering the cost of field service and warranty work, for instance, reduction of semiconductor failure rates in a large system by an order of magnitude translates roughly into an average of one repair call per year versus one repair call per month.

Since burn-in requires considerable time—48 to 96 hours is common— designers attempt to produce equipment that can perform some functional tests during the burn-in cycle rather than after. Modern systems exist to test and burn-in integrated circuits. One system has the capacity of 18,000 64K DRAMs (dynamic random access memory) per load and is flexible in its burn-in and test procedures to accommodate future types without modification of the hardware. The system can accumulate and display information on the devices under test, both for real-time evaluation and for lot documentation.

Failure Mode and Effects Analysis

The purpose of failure mode and effects analysis (FMEA), is to identify all the ways in which a failure can occur, to estimate the effect and seriousness of the failure, and to recommend corrective design actions. An FMEA usually consists of specifying the following information for each critical component:

- failure mode (i.e., how the component can fail)

- cause of failure

- effect on the product or system within which it operates (safety, downtime, repair requirements, tools required)

- corrective action (design changes, better user instructions)

- comments.

Figure 15.10 gives an (incomplete) example of a typical FMEA for an ordinary household light socket.

FIGURE 15.10   FMEA on Common Household Lamp

Failure Mode and Effects Analysis
Analyst *J.A. White*

Product *2C Lamp*   Date *10 Jan. 1992*

Component Name	Failure Mode	Cause of Failure	Effect of Failure on System	Correction of Problem	Comments
Plug part no. P-3	Loose wiring	Use vibration, handling	Will not conduct current. May generate heat.	Molded plug and wire	Uncorrected, could cause fire
	Not a failure of plug per se	User contacts prongs when plugging or unplugging	May cause severe shock or death.	Enlarged safety tip on molded plug	Children
Metal base and stem	Bent or nicked	Dropping, bumping, shipping	Degrades looks	Distress finish, improve packaging.	Cosmetic
Lamp socket	Cracked	Excessive heat, bumping, forcing	May cause shock if contacts metal base and stem. May cause shock upon bulb replcmt.	Improve material used for socket.	Dangerous
Wiring	Broken, frayed, from lamp to plug	Fatigue, heat, carelessness, childbite	Will not conduct current. May generate heat, blow breakers, or cause shock.	Use wire suitable for long life in extreme environment anticipated.	Dangerous Warning on instructions
	Internal short circuit	Heat, brittle insulation	May cause electrical shock or render lamp useless.	Use wire suitable for long life in extreme environment anticipated.	
	Internal wire broken	Socket slipping and twisting wires	May cause electrical shock or render lamp useless.	Use indent or notch to prevent socket from turning.	

SOURCE: K. E. Case and L. L. Jones, *Profit Through Quality: Quality Assurance Programs for Manufacturers,* QC & RE Monograph Series No. 2 (New York: Institute of Industrial Engineers, 1978).

Fault Tree Analysis

Fault tree analysis (FTA), is a logical procedure that begins with a list of potential hazards or undesired states and works backward to develop a list of causes and origins of failure. Its purpose is to show logical relationships between failures and causes. In this fashion, ways to avoid potential dangers can be uncovered.

An example of an FTA is given in Figure 15.11 for an industrial brake that is assumed to operate as a regular drum type of automobile brake. The fault tree is composed of branches connected to two different types of nodes: AND nodes, denoted by the symbol

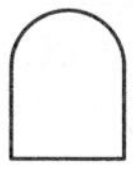

and OR nodes, depicted by

FIGURE 15.11 Fault Tree Analysis

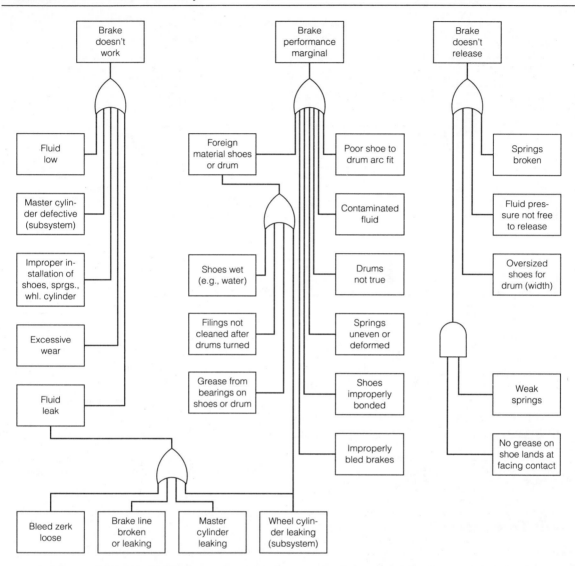

SOURCE: K. E. Case and L. L. Jones, *Profit Through Quality: Quality Assurance Programs for Manufacturers,* QC & RE Monograph Series No. 2 (New York: Institute of Industrial Engineers, 1978).

If a set of events are connected below an AND node, then *all* events must occur for the event above the node to occur. Below an OR node, *at least one* of the events must occur. Thus, in Figure 15.11 the event "brake doesn't release" can occur if any of the following conditions hold:

> broken springs
> OR fluid pressure not free to release
> OR oversize shoe for drum (width)

OR   weak springs

AND

no grease on shoe lands at facing contact.

RELIABILITY MANAGEMENT

Effective reliability management should include the following steps:

- Define customer performance requirements.

- Determine important economic factors and assess their relationship with reliability requirements.

- Define the environment and conditions in which the product will be used.

- Select components, designs, and vendors that meet reliability as well as cost criteria.

- Determine reliability requirements for machines and equipment as well as their impacts on product reliability during manufacturing.

- Analyze field reliability data as a method for quality improvement.

High reliability results in lower costs to society in the context of Taguchi's loss function. Consumers would like products to be 100% reliable and, indeed, this is a worthy goal for manufacturers. However, it is impractical to produce a product having perfect reliability under all conditions. To achieve high reliability, better materials and more precise manufacturing processes must be used. This will increase manufacturing costs to the point that consumers are unwilling to pay the price. Thus, management must balance these economic factors and seek to minimize total cost, keeping in mind that too low a reliability may damage the firm's reputation and result in lost sales or product liability suits. Such decisions must be addressed strategically by upper management.

Reliability is of concern in many areas of the production system and should be an important consideration in design, manufacturing, storage, and transportation, as well as supporting functions such as purchasing, field service, and maintenance.

As a fundamental dimension of quality, reliability must be *designed* into a product. The performance characteristics, operating conditions, and performance duration specified for the product or system drive the technical design. Variations in product performance arise because of the way it is used or because of environmental conditions. Changes take place over time because of chemical changes in components, vibration and stress, or expansion and contraction of materials due to fluctuations in temperature or humidity, for example. Sooner or later, products fail. To attempt to create products that will not fail is nearly impossible. The problem is not whether a product will fail, but when. Designers must decide to what extent failure is acceptable and establish specifications for reliability.

Many consumers will not always use a product correctly or follow suggested maintenance procedures. Designers must account for operating errors that will not result in failure, or they must maintain safety when failure does occur. Fail-safe designs provide safety in the event of failure. An example is a railway signal that turns red when a failure occurs. Foolproof designs prevent operation in the event of an operating error, thus avoiding failure. An example is a temperature control that prevents overheating by not allowing the heating switch to be closed without prior closure of the fan switch.

Whatever is done in the manufacturing process can and does have an effect on the reliability of the final product sold to customers. To manufacture reliable products from good designs, companies must use good materials, well-maintained machines, and trained workers. The greater the capability of a process to conform to design specifications and targets, the more likely it is that the product will have high reliability. Preventive maintenance in manufacturing is crucial to equipment reliability. Manufacturing, marketing, and financial managers must work together to ensure adequate time, schedules, and budgets for preventive maintenance activities. Operations control strategies such as just-in-time, the use of inspection, and statistical process control all contribute to the achievement of reliability objectives.

Packaging and transportation cannot be neglected. Poor protection and handling can adversely affect the reliability of the product when it reaches the customer. Denton relates a situation in which Tandy Corporation accidently packed a half-full load of computers in a 40-foot truck.[4] The boxes dropped from 12 feet high and tumbled around inside the truck from South Carolina to Boston. The cartons were demolished and it was thought that all the computers were destroyed. However, not one computer was damaged because of the careful attention to and testing of packaging.

As we have noted elsewhere in this book, purchasing plays an active role in the final quality of a product. Purchasing must understand the reliability requirements of purchased parts and components and clearly communicate these to suppliers.

Field service personnel must understand the nature of failures for preventive maintenance and maintain an adequate supply of spare and replacement parts. Feedback on failures completes the never-ending cycle of product improvement, leading to improved market knowledge and better designs.

RELIABILITY IN COMPUTER SOFTWARE

Many consumer goods are becoming more and more dependent on computers (strictly speaking, microprocessors), which in turn depend on the accompanying software. Reliability failures in computer software are unacceptable departures from requirements. Estimates have been made that the average software product in the United States contains between 8 and 10 errors per thousand lines of code.

Software reliability problems can cause considerable inconvenience or harm. On January 15, 1990, a software flaw in one programming statement controlling some AT&T switching systems caused a nine-hour nationwide saturation in their telephone network because the switches abnormally shut down.[5]

A more serious problem involved a radiation therapy machine problem that resulted in the deaths of several patients.[6] The accidents were caused by software

---

[4]Keith Denton, "Reducing DOAs."

[5]Peter G. Neumann, "Some Reflections on a Telephone Switching Problem," *Communications of the ACM,* Vol. 33, No. 7, 1990, p. 154.

[6]Jonathan Jacky, "Risks in Medical Electronics," *Communications of the ACM,* 33, No. 12, 1990, p. 138.

controlling the machine. If the operator entered an unusual but nonetheless possible sequence of commands, the computer control would place the machine into an erroneous and very hazardous state, subjecting the patient to a massive overdose. It was learned that the Food and Drug Administration had no requirements and performed no reviews regarding software development practices or software quality in medical devices. Only after these incidents occurred did the FDA announce that it would begin reviewing software in medical devices.

Software with high quality and reliability is becoming increasingly important for global competitiveness. While the United States has been the leader in the software and related services market, worldwide competition is growing. According to *Business Week*:[7]

> Quality could be the Achilles' heel of the U.S. software industry—and industry executives know it. "In the U.S., we have a history of shipping the product and getting the details right later," concedes David Reed, chief scientist at Lotus. "The Japanese seem to focus on getting every detail right."

Techniques used in quality control of manufacturing can be applied to software as well. Countries from Japan to India to a $400 million European consortium called the Eureka Software Factory are racing to try to find ways to design software quickly, while improving quality and reducing costs. Most of these approaches revolve around ways to use pretested blocks of code as building blocks for the final software product.

Estimating and predicting software reliability is not easy. Software failures result from inherent design flaws that only reveal themselves under appropriate operational circumstances. Software "bugs" arise from flaws in design specifications, routine coding errors, testing errors, or a variety of incompatibilities with hardware or other support software.

Computer software bears more similarity to services than to manufactured goods. With software, it is impractical to simply inspect the end product. Once the program is completed and stored on magnetic media, any bugs have already been included in the product. Hence, particular care must be taken in the design phase. Unfortunately, many software producers are under great pressure to ship products before they are fully tested. This results in expensive after-market support, not to mention damage to the company's reputation.

The environment in which software is produced has certain characteristics that negatively affect software quality:[8]

- Programmers of widely varying levels of skill.

- Small project staffs (often one person).

- Software-naive customers who are usually interested only in software output.

- Poorly defined but often highly complex customer objectives.

- A high turnover rate for programmers.

---

[7]Richard Brandt, with Evan I. Schwartz and Neil Gross, "Can the U.S. Stay Ahead in Software?," *Business Week,* March 11, 1991, pp. 98–105.

[8]G. G. Gustafson and R. J. Kerr, "Some Practical Experience with a Software Quality Assurance Program," *Communications of the ACM,* Vol. 25, No. 1, January 1982, pp. 4–12. Copyright 1982, Association for Computing Machinery, Inc.

- Externally or internally generated constraints such as cost and time.

- Hardware complexities that occasionally force the applications programmer to operate as a systems programmer, not directly working toward the actual goals outlined by the customer.

- Poor quality of existing programs that were produced without the benefit of modern support tools.

Building quality and reliability into software begins with good planning. A software quality assurance system must be integrated into existing practices and procedures. When software quality assurance is isolated from the software design system, such procedures can be easily ignored or forgotten. All functional groups involved must participate under the guidance of quality assurance personnel. Since quality assurance programs are usually new to software design groups, behavioral and motivational techniques for gaining acceptance are often necessary.

Several techniques have been developed to guide the software development process and help to ensure quality and reliability. These techniques include configuration management, reviews and audits, and a variety of testing methods. Each of these activities is based on objective measurement and feedback to the project manager or development team members.

Configuration management has been used extensively for hardware projects in the aerospace and defense industries and has been adapted to software projects. It is an essential requirement in government contracts. Configuration management is a process for designing and maintaining software by keeping tight controls of the set of software components, which make up a complex system. It provides an effective means of incorporating changes during development and use. The process consists of three activities:

1. Establishing approved baseline configurations (i.e., designs) for computer programs (configuration definition). These baselines support systematic evaluation, coordination, and disposition of all proposed changes.

2. Maintaining control over all changes in the baseline programs (change control). Many software problems arise during frequent changes. A rigorous system for monitoring changes is an important quality control function.

3. Providing traceability of baselines and changes (configuration accounting). Maintaining a paper trail of configurations and modifications is essential for ensuring that specifications are being met and for determining sources of errors and means of correction.

Independent reviews are used to discover and report problems or potential problems. Software quality assurance groups are responsible for maintaining control over specifications, documentation, and code to assure that performance and design requirements are being met. They also review software designs prior to coding, audit development activities, review and approve testing plans, and monitor tests to ensure that all requirements are tested.

A variety of methods for software verification are used. These include inspection for requirements that cannot be verified through operational testing such as examination of flow diagrams and program listings; comparing the execution of a program with a standard program with known results; analysis of program outputs to validate complex equations whose results are not directly related to inputs; and conducting tests with known inputs that should generate known outputs.

Achieving reliable software is expensive. One of the most ambitious projects was the software for the space shuttle. NASA paid $1,000 for each line of code; a total of $500 million. However, the space shuttle software has been found to contain only 0.1 errors per thousand lines.[9] Correcting software defects is often so expensive that it is usually cheaper to rewrite the code than to attempt to modify it. Errors not removed until the maintenance phase of a product's life cycle can cost up to 10 times more to correct than if discovered earlier. Today, more than 50% of a data processing department's budget goes to maintenance of software.

In some cases, it is believed that reliable software is not even possible. The Strategic Defense Initiative had been criticized by many computer scientists because the software required for space-based weapons is supposedly too complex to be developed reliably using current technology. Clearly, further research is necessary into better methods for achieving quality and reliability in software as we progress toward the twenty-first century.

MAINTAINABILITY AND AVAILABILITY

Failures will eventually occur, resulting in equipment shutdown and downtime. The amount of downtime is affected by the diagnosis effort required to determine the cause of failure, the ease of access to components, repair procedures, and the availability of spare parts. **Maintainability** is the totality of design factors that will enable maintenance to be accomplished easily. Maintenance is usually of two types: preventive or corrective. Preventive maintenance such as oiling equipment can reduce the risks of failure even though it results in downtime and is usually economically justified. Corrective maintenance is the response to failures and is a function of the reliability. Good maintenance adds to reliability, since it will increase the probability that the equipment will operate satisfactorily over a period of time. However, there is a trade-off between reliability and maintainability. Higher reliability will usually result in less frequent maintenance but higher design and production costs. It may be more economical to design for frequent repair or replacement.

Several design issues are related to maintainability.

- *Access of parts for repair:* One of the biggest consumer complaints about today's automobiles over those before the early 1970s is the difficulty of accessing many parts without special tools. While automotive reliability has increased, the complexity of today's engines makes maintenance difficult for a nonprofessional. For good maintainability, components must be easily accessible to maintenance personnel.

- *Modular construction and standardization:* Electronic equipment, such as televisions, is now designed with easily replaceable modular components. This makes diagnosis much easier, since problems can be isolated at the board level rather than for individual components. Of course, this increases the cost of replacement parts. Design effort also increases. Hence, these trade-offs must be

---

[9]Edward J. Joyce, "Is Error Free Software Achievable?" *Datamation,* February 15, 1989, pp. 53, 56.

considered on an economic basis. Standardization results in interchangeability of components between products, reducing inventory requirements for spare parts and the chances that they may not be available when needed.

■ *Diagnostic repair procedures:* During the design process, provisions must be made for diagnosis and repair. Clear instructions need to be written. For complex equipment, diagnosis can be very time-consuming. Modern information technology and artificial intelligence techniques, known as *expert systems,* are being developed to assist personnel in diagnosis of equipment.

Availability is the probability that equipment is not down due to failure. There are two principal definitions of availability: **Operational availability** is defined as

$$A_O = \frac{\text{MTBM}}{\text{MTBM} + \text{MDT}}$$

where MTBM = mean time between maintenance, including both corrective and preventive maintenance, and MDT = mean downtime. MDT includes such time as that needed for corrective and preventive maintenance and waiting time. This definition of availability is useful to operations managers in planning equipment utilization but is difficult to employ in design. Instead, we define **inherent availability** as

$$A_I = \frac{\text{MTBF}}{\text{MTBF} + \text{MTTR}}$$

where MTBF and MTTR represent mean time between failures and mean time to repair, respectively, as previously defined. This assumes no preventive maintenance downtime, waiting time, etc., since these variables cannot be determined in a design environment. Inherent availability assumes ideal conditions and can be used to establish trade-offs between reliability (as measured by MTBF) and maintainability (as measured by MTTR). To illustrate, suppose that availability is specified as 0.99. We then have

$$0.99 = \frac{\text{MTBF}}{\text{MTBF} + \text{MTTR}}$$

or

$$\text{MTBF} = 99 \text{ MTTR}$$

Thus, if MTTR = 2 hours, MTBF must equal to 198 hours. The designer can use such information to evaluate a proposed design and make appropriate modifications. On the other hand, this information can also be used to reduce MTTR through maintainability improvements given a specified reliability.

Testing Audio Components at Shure Bros., Inc.[10]

The philosophy at Shure Bros., Inc., is reliability oriented. Microphones and phonograph cartridges are tested for reliability well beyond the warranty period, with the goal of providing the customer long-term service and satisfaction. Audio transducers, for example, are sensitive and rather fragile devices. Stylus shanks for some cartridges are formed from 0.0005-inch beryllium foil. A precisely cut and polished diamond weighing only 20 micrograms is attached to the shank. Dynamic microphone coils are wound with fine wire only one-fifth the diameter of a human hair. Although their sensitivity ranks them along with the finest of laboratory instruments, they must be able to perform under conditions much less than ideal in locations all over the world.

These types of audio components have four major classes of end-use environments:

1. *The home:* There is much potential for damage ranging from accidental dropping of the cartridge onto the turntable or scraping the stylus across the record to cleaning the cartridge with various agents. There are also extremes of temperature and humidity.

2. *Public address systems:* Microphones are found in environments as diverse as churches, schools, bars, stores, and the outdoors. All these places represent potential challenges to the integrity of the microphone, which can be damaged by handling, mishandling, or long-term abuse. Random drops from a height of several feet are not uncommon.

3. *Mobile applications:* In vehicles, extremes of heat and cold, vibration, shock, and repeated switch actuation and cable flexing must be considered. Sand and dust are likely to be present. Reliability is critical, since backup is not usually available in an emergency on the road.

4. *Professional recording and sound reinforcement:* Sound professionals require reliability and cannot tolerate a dead or noisy microphone in the middle of a live performance or recording session. Yet repeated setups and teardowns during concert tours pose many problems.

Many standardized destructive tests developed by the military, the Electronic Industry Association, and the American Society for Testing and Materials are employed to gain knowledge of product failure. In addition, the following specialized environmental tests are conducted:

- *Cartridge drop test:* This test simulates the accidental dropping of the tone arm and cartridge onto a moving record. The vertical tracking force is set to the maximum recommended for the unit under test, and the minimum required number of drops is 100. This test simulates and exceeds the normal type of abuse accidentally given to a stylus.

- *Cartridge scrape test:* This test consists of moving the cartridge mounted in a tone arm across a moving record 100 times. The tone arm is pushed down hard enough to bottom out the cartridge.

- *Microphone drop test:* This is an unpackaged test consisting of a random free fall onto the floor. The test height is six feet, designed to simulate a fall from a tall shelf or an accidental drop by a very tall person at shoulder height. Ten drops must be sustained without significant loss of performance.

- *Barrel tumble:* A specially constructed barrel is used to tumble small microphones without packaging. This test is designed to simulate and exceed the roughest treatment expected in handling or transporting microphones loose in a case.

- *Stair tumble test:* A shipping carton is packed with a dozen units, sealed with tape, and tumbled down 17 steel stairs onto a concrete

[10]Adapted from Roger Franz, "Audio Component Reliability." Reprinted with permission from *Quality,* June 1983, pp. 50–51, a publication of Hitchcock Publishing, a Capital Cities/ABC Inc., Company.

(continued)

floor. Ten tumbles must be sustained without loss of function or severe loss of appearance of the packaging. This test allows for evaluation of possible damage during shipping.

■ *Outside weathering test:* This test actually exposes test units to outside weather. It aids in evaluating finishes and the performance of products that might actually be used outside such as microphones and sound reinforcement equipment.

The preceding are some examples of in-house reliability testing designed to simulate actual operating conditions. They help to assure the company's goal of marketing products with a long life of useful service.

Key Issues for Discussion

1. Which tests are used to study the reliability of the product in each of the four end-use environments?

QUALITY IN PRACTICE

Software Quality Assurance at Los Alamos National Laboratory[11]

A quality assurance program was created at Los Alamos National Laboratory to develop software that contained fewer defects and was more maintainable and flexible while also speeding program development. During management planning sessions, objectives were defined that would help produce a quality product, including developing methods for optimizing software maintainability, flexibility, and reliability; facilitating the creation of an environment whereby these goals can be accomplished; and monitoring improvement over time. The software features selected for optimization were the ones causing the most problems and therefore representing the greatest opportunity for payoff.

To assure true quality, the quality assurance program was fully integrated into the development process. The program included a structure for project planning, peer reviews of software products, availability of current sets of standards and guidelines, cost-effective testing procedures, accurate measurements of actual effort, and reliable project estimating tools.

Effective product reviews were the most significant element of the quality assurance process. Peer reviews, commonly called walkthroughs, consisted

of the developer's presenting the product to a small group of peers to discover errors or potential defects. The results and actions taken during a walkthrough were formally recorded and sent to the developers after the review. Further walkthroughs were scheduled until no defects could be found.

It was decided that the standards to be used had to be current and easily accessible. Before development of the quality assurance program, standards manuals sat unopened and gathering dust. The reason was that the methods in the manuals rarely conformed with the way business was normally conducted. The effort involved in writing, editing, and printing such a manual almost guaranteed that a significant portion of the contents would be obsolete before publication. The solution was to enter and update all guidelines and standards using computerized word processing equipment, with read-only access to all software development personnel.

Traditional software quality assurance programs typically place a great deal of emphasis on testing the operation of software in an actual computing environment; this is commonly called machine testing. Machine testing uncovers symptoms of problems, not the causes. Unlike the walkthrough process, no amount of machine testing can provide a cure for poorly designed and written computer programs. Dynamic testing is not 100% effective for uncovering all possible symptoms of problems, since all possi-

[11]Adapted from John Connell and Linda Brice, "Practical Quality Assurance," *Datamation,* March 1, 1985, pp. 106–114. Copyright © 1985 by Cahners Publ. Co.

(continued)

ble paths through a program are never exercised in testing. Thus, many problems occur when the program is actually used.

The plan developed at Los Alamos called for taking machine testing out of the hands of developers by creating a separate testing group and rewarding the members on the basis of the number of programs they could break. Testing teams were made responsible for creating test beds as well as for testing programs using live data. Performance evaluations were geared to finding the best new methodologies for testing.

During preliminary management discussions of the plan, management recognized that when projects are estimated accurately from the beginning, quality assurance can be built into the development schedule, allowing a more maintainable, flexible, and reliable product to be delivered. This addressed the problem of budget and schedule slips causing quality assurance deterioration. An auto-

mated estimating system was desired that would generate accurate estimates from historical data.

True quality assurance at Los Alamos is achieved by developing reliable methods to detect and remove defects early in the development process and by measuring the actual quality of finished products. By integrating the program into the development process, the entire staff is responsible for producing a quality product, and the program can be accepted by the software organization as a whole.

Key Issues for Discussion

1. Describe the approach used by Los Alamos National Laboratory to assure the quality and reliability of their software.

2. Does the use of the separate testing group conflict with TQM principles? Why or why not?

Summary of Key Points

- Reliability is the probability that a product, piece of equipment, or system performs its intended function for a stated period of time under specified operating conditions.

- Failures in products include functional failure at the start of product life and reliability failure after some period of use.

- Inherent reliability is the predicted reliability determined by the design of the product or process, and achieved reliability is the actual reliability observed during use.

- Reliability is measured by the number of failures per unit time, called the failure rate. The reciprocal of the failure rate is the mean time to failure, or for repairable items, the mean time between failures.

- The product life characteristics curve shows the instantaneous failure rate at any point in time. These curves are used to determine design and testing policies as well as for developing warranties.

- The probability of survival as a function of time is called the reliability function, and typically is modeled using an exponential distribution. Reliability functions of individual components can be used to predict reliability for complex systems of series, parallel, or series-parallel configurations.

- Reliability engineering involves techniques such as standardization, redundancy, failure physics, various testing methods, failure mode and effects analysis, and fault tree analysis.

- Reliability management should include the consideration of customer performance requirements, economic factors, environmental conditions, cost, and analysis of field data.

- Reliability in computer software is a difficult, but important issue. Many techniques have been developed to help ensure reliability in software.

Questions for Review and Discussion

1. What is the importance of reliability and why has it become such a prominent area within the quality disciplines?

2. Define reliability. Explain the definition thoroughly.

3. What is the difference between a functional failure and a reliability failure?

4. What is the definition of failure rate? How is it measured?

5. Explain the differences and relationships between the cumulative failure rate curve and the failure rate curve. How is the average failure rate over a time interval computed?

6. Explain the product life characteristics curve and how it can be used.

7. What is a reliability function? Discuss different ways of expressing this function.

8. Explain how to compute the reliability of series, parallel, and series-parallel systems.

9. What is reliability engineering? Briefly discuss some of the major techniques of reliability engineering.

10. Describe different forms of product testing.

11. What does the term "latent defect" mean?

12. Explain the purpose of failure mode and effects analysis and fault tree analysis.

13. What should be included in an effective reliability management program?

14. Discuss the importance of reliability in computer software. Why is it difficult to achieve?

15. What is configuration management? How is it used in quality assurance for software?

16. What is maintainability? Discuss the principal design issues related to it.

17. Discuss the two definitions of availability. What are the differences between them?

Problems

1. Given the following cumulative failure curve, sketch the failure rate curve:

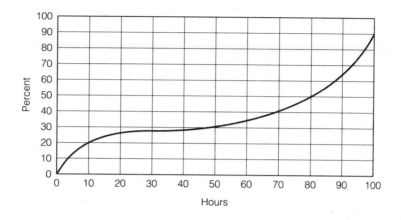

2. For the figure in Problem 1, compute the average failure rate during the intervals 0 to 50, 50 to 100, and 0 to 100.

3. The life of a battery is normally distributed with a mean of 1,200 days and standard deviation of 60 days.

    a. What fraction of batteries is expected to survive beyond 1,300 days?
    b. What fraction will survive less than 900 days?
    c. Sketch the reliability function.
    d. If a warranty is to be developed so that no more than 10% of the batteries will be expected to fail during the warranty period, how long should the warranty period be?

4. Five transformers were tested for 500 hours each, and two failed after 40 and 220 hours. Compute the failure rate.

5. A test of 10 items is conducted for 200 hours. Three items fail at 8, 54, and 162 hours. What is the failure rate?

6. Assuming an exponential distribution, a particular light bulb has a failure rate of 0.001 unit per hour. What is the probability of failing within 800 hours? What is the reliability function?

7. An electrical component has a reliability of 0.90 over 500 hours of normal use. What is the failure rate? What fraction will survive after 100, 200, and 500 hours?

8. Find the mean time to failure for the data in Problems 4 and 5.

9. A piece of equipment operated for 4,500 hours and experienced two failures. What is the MTTF?

10. The MTBF of a circuit is 1,000 hours. What is the failure rate?

11. The MTBF for a computer's central processing unit is normally distributed with a mean of 14 days and a standard deviation of 3 days. Each failure costs the company $500 in lost computing time and repair costs. A shutdown for preventive maintenance can be scheduled during nonpeak times and will cost only $100. As the manager in charge of computer operations, you are to determine if a preventive maintenance program is worthwhile. What is your recommendation? Assume 260 operating days per year.

12. Refer to the failure data for the equipment maintenance example in Table 15.3. What preventive maintenance period would you recommend if the preventive maintenance cost were $50 and the average cost for an equipment failure were $30? How many breakdowns a year should you expect under your preventive maintenance program?

13. For a particular piece of equipment, the probability of failure during a given week is as follows:

Week of Operation	Probability of Failure
1	0.20
2	0.10
3	0.10
4	0.15
5	0.20
6	0.25

Management is considering a preventive maintenance program that would be implemented at the end of a given week of production. The production loss and downtime costs associated with an equipment failure are estimated to be $1,500 per failure. If it costs $100 to perform the preventive maintenance, when should the firm implement the preventive maintenance program? What is the total maintenance and failure cost associated with your recommendation, and how many failures can be expected each year? Assume 52 weeks of operation per year.

14. An electronic missile guidance system consists of the following components:

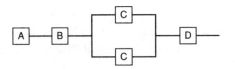

Components A, B, C, and D have reliabilities of 0.95, 0.98, 0.90, and 0.99, respectively. What is the reliability of the entire system?

15. A manufacturer of portable radios purchases major electronic components as modules. The reliabilities of components differ by supplier. Suppose that the configuration of the major components is given by

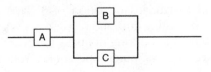

The components can be purchased from three different suppliers. The reliabilities of the components are as follows:

	Supplier		
Component	1	2	3
A	.95	.92	.94
B	.80	.86	.90
C	.90	.93	.85

Transportation and purchasing considerations require that only one supplier be chosen. Which one should be selected if the radio is to have the highest possible reliability?

16. In a complex manufacturing process, three operations are performed in series. Because of the nature of the process, machines frequently fall out of adjustment and must be repaired. To keep the system going, two identical machines are used at each stage; thus, if one fails, the other can be used while the first is repaired (see accompanying figure). The reliabilities of the machines are as follows:

Machine	**Reliability**
A	.60
B	.75
C	.70

a. Analyze the system reliability, assuming only *one* machine at each stage.
b. How much is the reliability improved by having two machines at each stage?

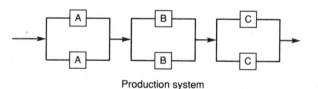

Production system

17. An automated production system consists of three operations: turning, milling, and grinding. Individual parts are transferred from one operation to the next by a robot. Hence, if one machine or the robot fails, the process stops.

a. If the reliabilities of the robot, turning center, milling machine, and grinder are 0.99, 0.98, 0.99, and 0.96, respectively, what is the reliability of the system?
b. Suppose that two grinders are available and the system does not stop if one fails. What is the reliability of the system?

18. Military radar and missile detection systems are designed to warn a country of enemy attacks. A system reliability question deals with the ability of the detection system to identify the attack and perform the warning correctly. Assume that a particular detection system has a 0.90 probability of detecting a missile attack.

a. What is the reliability of the system?

b. Assume that two detection systems are installed in the same area and that the system operates satisfactorily if at least one of the two detection systems performs correctly. Assume that the probability of detecting an attack is 0.90 for each system. What is the reliability of the two systems?

Bibliography

Bernstein, Amy, "Putting Software to the Test," *Business Computer Systems,* December 1984, pp. 48–51.

Buck, Carl N. "Improving Reliability," *Quality,* February 1990, pp. 58–60.

Chowdhury, A. R. "Reliability As It Relates to QA/QC," *Quality Progress,* Vol. 18, No. 12, December 1985, pp. 27–30.

Halpern, S. *The Assurance Sciences, An Introduction to Quality Control and Reliability.* Englewood Cliffs, NJ: Prentice-Hall, 1978.

Juran, J. M., and Gryna F. M. *Quality Planning and Analysis,* 2nd ed. New York: McGraw-Hill, 1980.

Lawrence, Jr., Joseph D. "Semiconductor Quality Considerations," *Quality,* December 1983, pp. 39–41.

Posedel, Rhea J. "Burn-in: The Way to Reliability," *Quality,* August 1982, pp. 22–23.

Singh, B. P. "Reliability, Availability, and Maintainability Program in a Metal Processing Facility," *Proceedings, AIIE 1978 Spring Annual Conference.* Norcross, GA: American Institute of Industrial Engineers, 1978.

Smith, Charles O. *Introduction to Reliability in Design.* New York: McGraw-Hill, 1976.

PART FIVE

The Technical System
Quality of Conformance

IN THIS LAST section of the book we concentrate on statistical methods for quality control. Statistical Process Control, or SPC, has been the foundation of Japanese quality control since Deming introduced it to Japan in 1950. Control charts were briefly discussed in Chapter 9. In Chapter 16 we present a thorough treatment of SPC at an elementary level. These concepts are expanded upon from a more theoretical perspective in Chapter 17. We also introduce some advanced concepts of SPC. Chapter 18 concludes with a treatment of sampling techniques in quality control. These have many useful applications, particularly in service organizations.

CHAPTER 16

Fundamentals of Statistical Process Control

In Chapter 8 we introduced the concepts of common causes and special causes of variation as well as the idea of statistical control. To recall, a process is in statistical control if the variation in the process is due to common causes alone. When special causes are present, the process is deemed to be out of control. Process improvement is based on reducing common cause variation; process control is the process of identifying and eliminating special causes of variation. Process capability cannot be determined unless the process is in statistical control.

Control charts were introduced in Chapter 9 as one of the seven fundamental tools of quality. *Statistical process control,* or *SPC,* is a methodology using control charts for assisting operators, supervisors, and managers to monitor the output from a process to identify and to eliminate special causes of variation. SPC is a proven technique for reducing scrap and rework, thus, increasing productivity. It also provides the basis for determining process capability and predicting the yield from a process. In many industries, suppliers are *required* to provide evidence of statistical process control to their customers. Survivors in highly competitive markets will be those firms that can demonstrate their quality capability. SPC provides the means to do this. In this chapter we provide the details of how control charts are developed and used.

THE NEED FOR SPC

There are two basic reasons for using SPC: First SPC allows us to determine *when to take action* to adjust a process that has fallen out of control. Second, SPC tells us when to *leave a process alone.* Knowing when to take action on a process is an important step in defect prevention and eliminates inspection and sorting of product after a large batch has been made. Knowing when to leave a process alone is equally important in keeping variation at a minimum. Many production workers have difficulty with this concept because they do not understand the nature of variation and the difference between common and special causes of variation. Often, they believe that whenever process output is off-target, some adjustment must be made. Such overadjustment will actually *increase* the variation in the process output. This can be seen through the following simulation.

530

Suppose that we have a process in which 60% of the output will fall exactly on the process mean; the remaining 40% of the time; however, it is off in either direction by 0.1. If the process mean is 5.0, for example, then out of ten parts, on the average, six will have a value of 5.0, two will have a value of 4.9, and two will have a value of 5.1. Under these assumptions, all of the output will fall between 4.9 and 5.1 if the process is left alone.

We will assume that the operator can make adjustments in the process mean, but cannot determine its true value; he or she can only measure the output, which may differ from the mean because of the natural variation of the process. Suppose that the operator inspects and measures each part and decides to make an adjustment to the process mean if the measurement is off-target. If the value is above the target, the operator will adjust the process setting downward by the difference; if the value is below the target, an adjustment upward will be made.

Assume the process mean is equal to a target value of 5.0. Let us see what would happen if the process variation would result in the following sequence of deviations away from the process mean:

Mean	5.0	5.0	5.0	5.0	5.0	5.0	5.0	5.0	5.0	5.0
Deviation	−0.1	+0.1	0	0	−0.1	0	0	0	+0.1	0
Output	4.9	5.1	5.0	5.0	4.9	5.0	5.0	5.0	5.1	5.0

Notice that the distribution of process output follows our assumptions if we leave the process mean alone.

Now let us use the same sequence of deviations, but adjust the process up or down after each part is produced according to the rule stated earlier. Assume that the initial mean is 5.0. Since the first measurement is 4.9, the operator would adjust the process setting up by 0.1. This actually changes the process mean to 5.1, but the operator really thinks that he or she is adjusting it "back" to 5.0. Applying this rule for all ten parts, we would have:

Mean	5.0	5.1	4.9	5.0	5.0	5.1	5.0	5.0	5.0	4.9
Deviation	−0.1	+0.1	0	0	−0.1	0	0	0	+0.1	0
Output	4.9	5.2	4.9	5.0	4.9	5.1	5.0	5.0	5.1	4.9

We see that only three of the ten parts now meet the target; four have a value of 4.9; two have a value of 5.1; and one has a value of 5.2. Clearly, the variation in the process output actually has increased.

The second use of SPC is that of knowing when it is necessary to adjust a process. Table 16.1 shows 150 measurements of a quality characteristic from a manufacturing process. Each row corresponds to a sample of size 5 taken every 15 minutes. The mean of each sample is also given in Table 16.1. A histogram of these data is shown in Figure 16.1. We see that the data form a relatively symmetric distribution around the overall mean of 10.7616. From the histogram alone, what can you conclude about the state of control for this process? Very little, because histograms do not allow you to distinguish between common and special causes of variation. In a histogram, the dimension of *time* is not considered. This is an important factor, since special causes

TABLE 16.1 Sample Observations

Sample	Observations					Mean
1	10.682	10.689	10.776	10.798	10.714	10.7318
2	10.787	10.860	10.601	10.746	10.779	10.7546
3	10.780	10.667	10.838	10.785	10.723	10.7586
4	10.591	10.727	10.812	10.775	10.730	10.7270
5	10.693	10.708	10.790	10.758	10.671	10.7240
6	10.749	10.714	10.738	10.719	10.606	10.7052
7	10.791	10.713	10.689	10.877	10.603	10.7346
8	10.744	10.779	10.660	10.737	10.822	10.7484
9	10.769	10.773	10.641	10.644	10.725	10.7104
10	10.718	10.671	10.708	10.850	10.712	10.7318
11	10.787	10.821	10.764	10.658	10.708	10.7476
12	10.622	10.802	10.818	10.872	10.727	10.7682
13	10.657	10.822	10.893	10.544	10.750	10.7332
14	10.806	10.749	10.859	10.801	10.701	10.7832
15	10.660	10.681	10.644	10.747	10.728	10.6920
16	10.816	10.817	10.768	10.716	10.649	10.7532
17	10.826	10.777	10.721	10.770	10.809	10.7806
18	10.828	10.829	10.865	10.778	10.872	10.8344
19	10.805	10.719	10.612	10.938	10.807	10.7762
20	10.802	10.756	10.786	10.815	10.801	10.7920
21	10.876	10.803	10.701	10.789	10.672	10.7682
22	10.855	10.783	10.722	10.856	10.751	10.7934
23	10.762	10.705	10.804	10.805	10.809	10.7770
24	10.703	10.837	10.759	10.975	10.732	10.8012
25	10.737	10.723	10.776	10.748	10.732	10.7432
26	10.748	10.686	10.856	10.811	10.838	10.7878
27	10.826	10.803	10.764	10.823	10.886	10.8204
28	10.728	10.721	10.820	10.772	10.639	10.7360
29	10.803	10.892	10.741	10.816	10.770	10.8044
30	10.774	10.837	10.872	10.849	10.818	10.8300

occur sporadically over time. For example, tools wear out after a period of use, materials from different shipments may vary, or a substitute operator may run a process when the regular operator is absent.

Let us plot the mean of each sample against the time at which the sample was taken. Since the time increments between samples are equal, the sample number is an appropriate surrogate for time. This is shown in Figure 16.2. We clearly see that the mean has shifted up at about sample 17. Some special cause has probably caused this shift and some adjustment is necessary to bring the process back on target. The histogram does not indicate this.

We may summarize this discussion in Table 16.2. SPC can be viewed as making a test of a hypothesis:

H_0: the process is in control

versus

H_1: the process is out of control.

FIGURE 16.1   **Histogram of Quality Measurements**

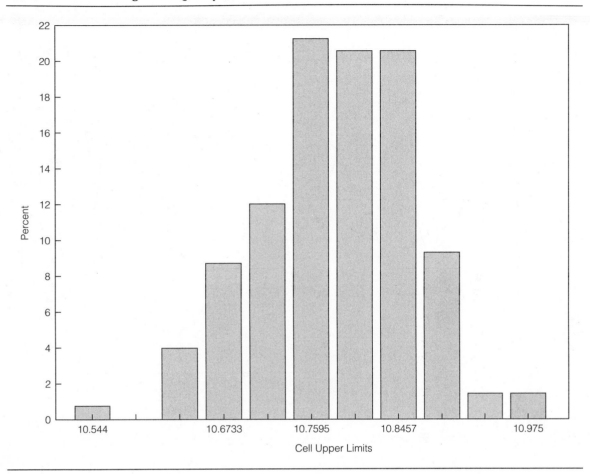

The correct decisions are to adjust the process when it is out of control and to leave the process alone when it is in control. Of course, incorrect decisions may be made due to sampling error or errors in interpreting the data. The risk of unnecessarily adjusting a process in control is equivalent to a Type I error; not correcting a process that is out of control is a Type II error. The correct use of SPC minimizes these risks.

CONTROL CHARTS FOR VARIABLES DATA

Variables data are those that are measured along a continuous scale. Examples of variables data are length, weight, and distance. The charts most commonly used for variables data are the $\bar{x}$-chart ("x-bar" chart), and the R-chart (range chart). The $\bar{x}$-chart is used to monitor the centering of the process, and the R-chart is used to monitor the

FIGURE 16.2   **Graph of Sample Means Versus Time**

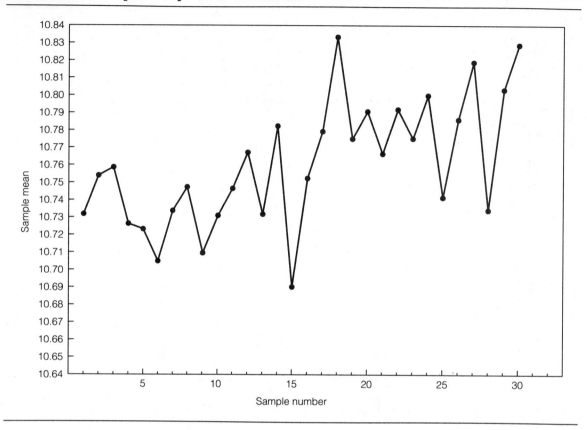

variation in the process. These charts are used together for the analysis of variables data. The range is used as a measure of variation simply for convenience, particularly when workers on the factory floor perform control chart calculations by hand. For large samples and when data are analyzed by computer programs, it is better to use the standard deviation as a measure of variability. We discuss this in the next chapter. In this section we discuss the construction, interpretation, and use of variables control charts. Control charts have three basic applications: (1) to establish a state of statistical control, (2) to monitor a process and signal when the process goes out of control, and (3) to determine process capability.

TABLE 16.2   **Decisions and Risks in Process Control**

Decision	Process State	
	In Control	Out of Control
Adjust process	Type I error	Correct decision
Leave alone	Correct decision	Type II error

Constructing Variables Control Charts and Establishing Statistical Control

The first step in developing $\bar{x}$- and R-charts is to gather data. Usually, about 25 to 30 samples are collected. Samples between size 3 and 10 are generally used, with 5 being the most common. We let k denote the number of samples and n denote the sample size. For each sample i, we compute the mean (denoted $\bar{x}_i$) and the range (R_i). These values are then plotted on their respective control charts. Next, we compute the *overall mean* and *average range*. These values specify the center lines for the $\bar{x}$- and R-charts, respectively. The overall mean is the average of the sample means $\bar{x}_i$:

$$\bar{\bar{x}} = \frac{\sum_{i=1}^{k} \bar{x}_i}{k}$$

The average range is similarly computed, using the formula

$$\bar{R} = \frac{\sum_{i=1}^{k} R_i}{k}$$

The average range and average mean are used to compute control limits for the R- and $\bar{x}$-charts. Control limits are easily calculated using the following formulas:

$$\text{UCL}_R = D_4 \bar{R} \qquad \text{UCL}_{\bar{x}} = \bar{\bar{x}} + A_2 \bar{R}$$
$$\text{LCL}_R = D_3 \bar{R} \qquad \text{LCL}_{\bar{x}} = \bar{\bar{x}} - A_2 \bar{R}$$

where the constants D_3, D_4, and A_2 depend on the sample size and can be found in Appendix B at the end of the book.

The control limits represent the range between which all points are expected to fall if the process is in statistical control. If any points fall outside of the control limits or if any unusual patterns are observed, then we would suspect that some assignable cause has affected the process. The process should be studied to determine the cause. If special causes are present, then they are *not* representative of the true state of statistical control, and the calculations of the center line and control limits will be biased. The corresponding data points should be eliminated, and new values for $\bar{\bar{x}}$, $\bar{R}$, and the control limits should be computed.

In determining whether a process is in statistical control, the R-chart should always be analyzed first. Since the control limits in the $\bar{x}$-chart depend on the average range, special causes in the R-chart may produce unusual patterns in the $\bar{x}$-chart, even when the centering of the process is in control. (An example of this is given later in this chapter.) Once statistical control is established for the R-chart, we may turn our attention to the $\bar{x}$-chart.

Figure 16.3 shows a typical data sheet used for recording data and drawing control charts, which is available from the American Society for Quality Control. This form provides space for descriptive information about the process, recording of sample observations and computed statistics, and drawing the control charts. On the back of this form (Figure 16.4), is a work sheet for computing control limits and process capability information. The construction and analysis of control charts is best seen by example. We will use this chart in the following example.

FIGURE 16.3 ASQC Control Chart Data Sheet

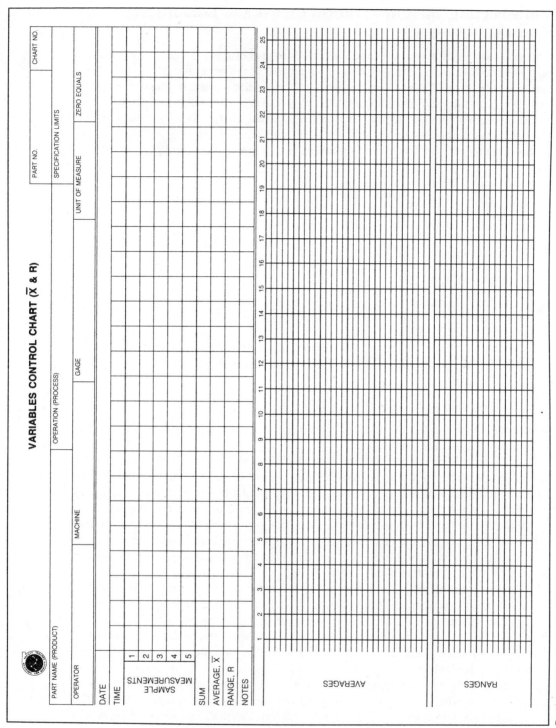

FIGURE 16.4 ASQC Control Chart Calculation Work Sheet

CALCULATION WORK SHEET

CONTROL LIMITS						LIMITS FOR INDIVIDUALS
SUBGROUPS INCLUDED						COMPARE WITH SPECIFICATION OR TOLERANCE LIMITS

$\bar{R} = \dfrac{\Sigma R}{k} = \underline{\hspace{2cm}} \quad = \quad \underline{\hspace{2cm}} \quad =$

$\bar{\bar{X}} = \dfrac{\Sigma \bar{X}}{k} = \underline{\hspace{2cm}} \quad = \quad \underline{\hspace{2cm}} \quad =$

OR

$\bar{X}'$ (MIDSPEC. OR STD.) $= \hspace{3cm} =$

$A_2\bar{R} = \hspace{1cm} x \hspace{2cm} = \underline{\hspace{1.5cm}} \hspace{1cm} x \hspace{1cm} = \underline{\hspace{1.5cm}}$

$UCL_{\bar{x}} = \bar{\bar{X}} + A_2\bar{R} \hspace{1cm} = \hspace{2cm} =$

$LCL_{\bar{x}} = \bar{\bar{X}} - A_2\bar{R} \hspace{1cm} = \hspace{2cm} =$

$UCL_R = D_4\bar{R} = \hspace{1cm} x \hspace{1cm} = \hspace{1cm} x \hspace{1cm} =$

LIMITS FOR INDIVIDUALS — COMPARE WITH SPECIFICATION OR TOLERANCE LIMITS:

$\bar{\bar{X}} \hspace{4cm} =$

$\dfrac{3}{d_2}\bar{R} = \hspace{1cm} x \hspace{1cm} = \underline{\hspace{2cm}}$

$UL_x = \bar{\bar{X}} + \dfrac{3}{d_2}\bar{R} \hspace{1cm} =$

$LL_x = \bar{\bar{X}} - \dfrac{3}{d_2}\bar{R} \hspace{1cm} =$

$US \hspace{4cm} =$

$LS \hspace{4cm} = \underline{\hspace{2cm}}$

$US - LS \hspace{2cm} =$

$6\sigma = \dfrac{6}{d_2}\bar{R} \hspace{1.5cm} =$

MODIFIED CONTROL LIMITS FOR AVERAGES

BASED ON SPECIFICATION LIMITS AND PROCESS CAPABILITY. APPLICABLE ONLY IF: $US - LS > 6\sigma$.

$US \hspace{2cm} = \hspace{2cm} LS \hspace{2cm} =$

$A_M\bar{R} = \hspace{1cm} x \hspace{1cm} = \underline{\hspace{1.5cm}} \hspace{1cm} A_M\bar{R} \hspace{1cm} = \underline{\hspace{1.5cm}}$

$URL_{\bar{x}} = US - A_M\bar{R} \hspace{1cm} = \hspace{2cm} LRL_{\bar{x}} = LS + A_M\bar{R} \hspace{1cm} =$

FACTORS FOR CONTROL LIMITS

n	A_2	D_4	d_2	$\dfrac{3}{d_2}$	A_M
2	1.880	3.268	1.128	2.659	0.779
3	1.023	2.574	1.693	1.772	0.749
4	0.729	2.282	2.059	1.457	0.728
5	0.577	2.114	2.326	1.290	0.713
6	0.483	2.004	2.534	1.184	0.701

Reprinted with permission of ASQC.

EXAMPLE 1 **Control Charts for Silicon Wafer Production.** The thickness of silicon wafers used in the production of semiconductors must be controlled very carefully. The tolerance of one such product is specified as ±0.0050 inches. In one production facility, three wafers were selected each hour and the thickness measured carefully to within one ten-thousandth of an inch. Figure 16.5 shows the results obtained for 25 samples. For example, the mean of the first sample is

$$\bar{x}_1 = \frac{41 + 70 + 22}{3} = \frac{133}{3} = 44$$

The range of sample 1 is $70 - 22 = 48$. (Note: we have rounded the calculations to the nearest integer.)

The calculations of the average range, overall mean, and control limits are shown in Figure 16.6. The average range is the sum of the sample ranges (676) divided by the number of samples (25); the overall mean is the sum of the sample averages (1221) divided by the number of samples (25). Since the sample size is 3, the factors used in computing the control limits are $A_2 = 1.023$ and $D_4 = 2.574$. (For sample sizes of 6 or less, factor $D_3 = 0$; therefore, the lower control limit on the range chart is zero.) The center lines and control limits are drawn on the chart in Figure 16.7.

FIGURE 16.5   Silicon Wafer Thickness Data

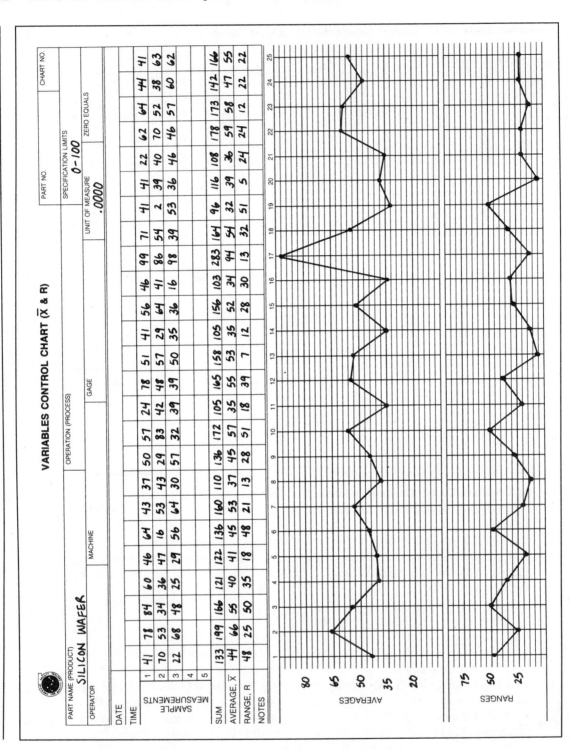

FIGURE 16.6 Control Limit Calculations

CALCULATION WORK SHEET

CONTROL LIMITS	LIMITS FOR INDIVIDUALS

SUBGROUPS INCLUDED __ALL__

COMPARE WITH SPECIFICATION OR TOLERANCE LIMITS

$\bar{R} = \dfrac{\Sigma R}{k} = \dfrac{676}{25}$ = **27** _____ =

$\bar{\bar{X}} = \dfrac{\Sigma \bar{X}}{k} = \dfrac{1221}{25}$ = **48.8** _____ =

OR

$\bar{X}'$ (MIDSPEC. OR STD.) = **50** _____ =

$A_2\bar{R}$ = **1.023** $\times$ **27** = **27.6** $\times$ = _____

$UCL_{\bar{X}} = \bar{\bar{X}} + A_2\bar{R}$ = **76.4** =

$LCL_{\bar{X}} = \bar{\bar{X}} - A_2\bar{R}$ = **21.2** =

$UCL_R = D_4\bar{R} = $ **2.574** $\times$ **27** = **69.5** $\times$ =

$\bar{X}$ =

$\dfrac{3}{d_2}\bar{R} =$ x = _____

$UL_x = \bar{\bar{X}} + \dfrac{3}{d_2}\bar{R}$ =

$LL_x = \bar{\bar{X}} - \dfrac{3}{d_2}\bar{R}$ =

US =

LS = _____

US − LS =

$6\sigma = \dfrac{6}{d_2}\bar{R}$ =

MODIFIED CONTROL LIMITS FOR AVERAGES

BASED ON SPECIFICATION LIMITS AND PROCESS CAPABILITY.
APPLICABLE ONLY IF: US − LS > 6σ.

US = LS =

$A_M\bar{R}$ = x = _____ $A_M\bar{R}$ = = _____

$URL_{\bar{X}} = US - A_M\bar{R}$ = $LRL_{\bar{X}} = LS + A_M\bar{R}$ =

FACTORS FOR CONTROL LIMITS

n	A_2	D_4	d_2	$\dfrac{3}{d_2}$	A_M
2	1.880	3.268	1.128	2.659	0.779
3	1.023	2.574	1.693	1.772	0.749
4	0.729	2.282	2.059	1.457	0.728
5	0.577	2.114	2.326	1.290	0.713
6	0.483	2.004	2.534	1.184	0.701

Examining the range chart first, it appears that the process is in control. All points lie within the control limits and no unusual patterns exist. In the $\bar{x}$-chart, however, we see that sample 17 lies above the upper control limit. On investigation, we found that some defective material was used. These data should be eliminated from the control chart calculations. Figure 16.8 shows the calculations after sample 17 was removed. The revised center lines and control limits are shown in Figure 16.9. It is customary to note the out-of-control points on the chart. The resulting chart appears to be in control.

Interpreting Patterns in Control Charts

When a process is in statistical control, the points on a control chart should fluctuate randomly between the control limits with no recognizable pattern. The following checklist provides a set of general rules for examining a process to determine if it is in control:

1. No points are outside control limits.

2. The number of points above and below the center line is about the same.

3. The points seem to fall randomly above and below the center line.

4. Most points, but not all, are near the center line, and only a few are close to the control limits.

FIGURE 16.7   Initial Control Chart

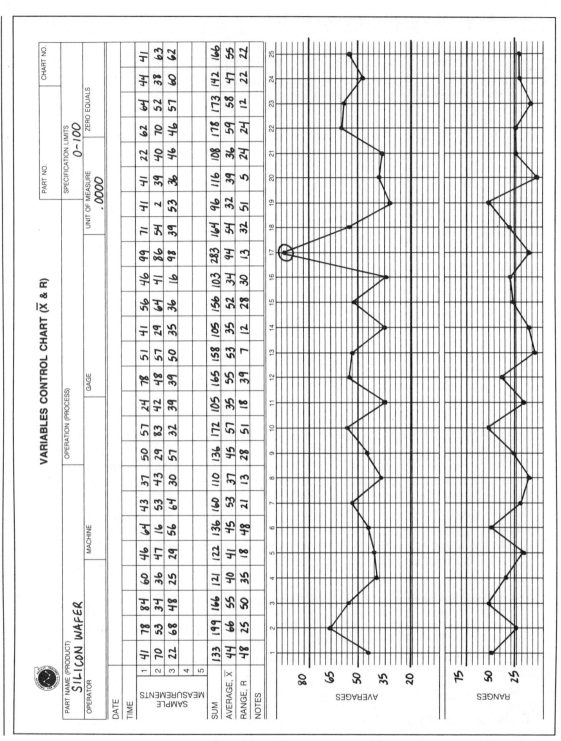

FIGURE 16.8   **Revised Control Chart Calculations**

CALCULATION WORK SHEET

CONTROL LIMITS

SUBGROUPS INCLUDED __ALL__   #17 REMOVED

$\bar{R} = \dfrac{\Sigma R}{k} = \dfrac{676}{25}$ = 27 $\dfrac{663}{24}$ = 27.6

$\bar{\bar{X}} = \dfrac{\Sigma \bar{X}}{k} = \dfrac{1221}{25}$ = 48.8 $\dfrac{1127}{24}$ = 47.0

OR

$\bar{X}'$ (MIDSPEC. OR STD.) = 50   = 50

$A_2\bar{R} = 1.023 \times 27$ = 27.6 1.023×27.6 = 28.2

$UCL_{\bar{X}} = \bar{\bar{X}} + A_2\bar{R}$ = 76.4   = 75.2

$LCL_{\bar{X}} = \bar{\bar{X}} - A_2\bar{R}$ = 21.2   = 18.8

$UCL_R = D_4\bar{R} = 2.574 \times 27$ = 69.5 2.574×27.6 = 71.0

LIMITS FOR INDIVIDUALS

COMPARE WITH SPECIFICATION OR TOLERANCE LIMITS

$\bar{\bar{X}}$ =

$\dfrac{3}{d_2}\bar{R} =$ $\times$ =

$UL_x = \bar{\bar{X}} + \dfrac{3}{d_2}\bar{R}$ =

$LL_x = \bar{\bar{X}} - \dfrac{3}{d_2}\bar{R}$ =

US =

LS =

US − LS =

$6\sigma = \dfrac{6}{d_2}\bar{R}$ =

MODIFIED CONTROL LIMITS FOR AVERAGES

BASED ON SPECIFICATION LIMITS AND PROCESS CAPABILITY. APPLICABLE ONLY IF: US − LS > 6σ.

US   =   LS   =

$A_M\bar{R} =$ $\times$ = $A_M\bar{R}$ =

$URL_{\bar{X}} = US - A_M\bar{R}$ = $LRL_{\bar{X}} = LS + A_M\bar{R}$ =

FACTORS FOR CONTROL LIMITS

n	A_2	D_4	d_2	$\dfrac{3}{d_2}$	A_M
2	1.880	3.268	1.128	2.659	0.779
3	1.023	2.574	1.693	1.772	0.749
4	0.729	2.282	2.059	1.457	0.728
5	0.577	2.114	2.326	1.290	0.713
6	0.483	2.004	2.534	1.184	0.701

The underlying assumption behind these rules is that the distribution of sample means is normal. This follows from the central limit theorem of statistics, which states that the distribution of sample means approaches a normal distribution as the sample size increases regardless of the original distribution. Of course, for small sample sizes, the distribution of the original data must be reasonably normal for this assumption to hold. The upper and lower control limits are computed to be three standard deviations from the overall mean. Thus, the probability that any sample mean falls outside of the control limits is very small. This is the origin of rule 1.

Since the normal distribution is symmetric, we should find about the same number of points above and below the center line. Also, since the mean of the normal distribution is the median, we should find about half the points on either side of the center line. Finally, we know that about 68% of a normal distribution falls within one standard deviation of the mean; thus, most points should be close to the center line. These characteristics will hold provided that the mean and variance of the original data have not changed during the time the data were collected; that is, the process is *stable*.

Several types of unusual patterns often arise in control charts. We will review these and indicate the typical causes of such patterns.[1]

---

[1]This discussion is adapted from James R. Evans, *Statistical Process Control for Quality Improvement: A Training Guide to Learning SPC* (Englewood Cliffs, NJ: Prentice-Hall, © 1991). Reprinted with permission of Prentice-Hall, Englewood Cliffs, NJ.

FIGURE 16.9 Revised Control Chart

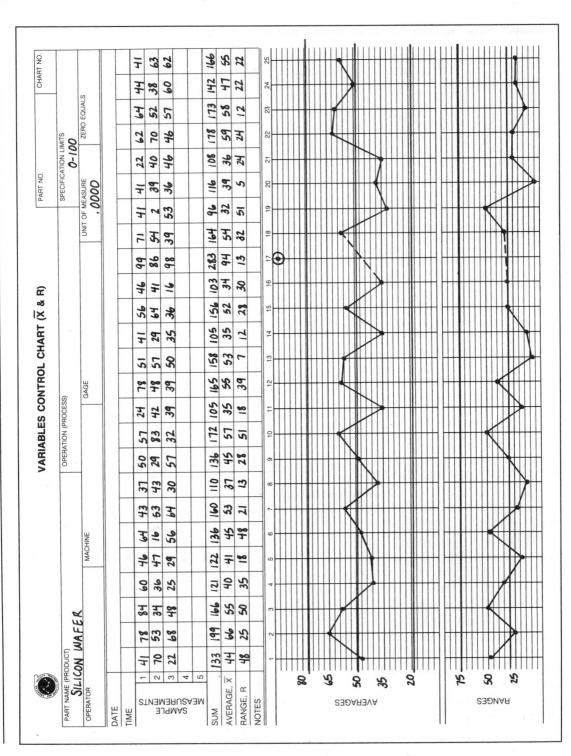

One Point Outside Control Limits

A single point outside the control limits (see Figure 16.10) is usually produced by a special cause. Often, there is a similar indication in the R-chart. Once in a while, however, they are a normal part of the process and occur simply by chance.

A common reason for a point falling outside a control limit is an error in the calculation of $\bar{x}$ or R for the sample. You should always check your calculations whenever this occurs. Other possible causes are a sudden power surge, a broken tool, measurement error, or an incomplete or omitted operation in the process.

Sudden Shift in the Process Average

An unusual number of consecutive points falling on one side of the center line (see Figure 16.11) is usually an indication that the process average has suddenly shifted. Typically, this is the result of an external influence that has affected the process; this would be a special cause. In both the $\bar{x}$- and R-charts, possible causes might be a new operator, a new inspector, a new machine setting, or a change in the setup or method.

If the shift is up in the R-chart, the process has become less uniform. Typical causes are carelessness of operators, poor or inadequate maintenance, or possibly a fixture in need of repair. If the shift is down in the R-chart, the uniformity of the process has improved. This might be the result of improved workmanship or better machines or materials. As we have said, every effort should be made to determine the reason for the improvement and to maintain it.

Three rules of thumb are used for early detection of process shifts. A simple rule is that if eight consecutive points fall on one side of the center line, one could

FIGURE 16.10   **Single Point Outside Control Limits**

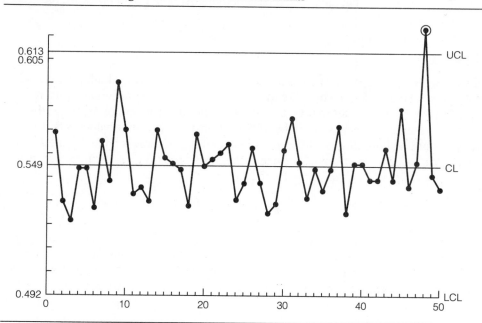

FIGURE 16.11 Shift in Process Average

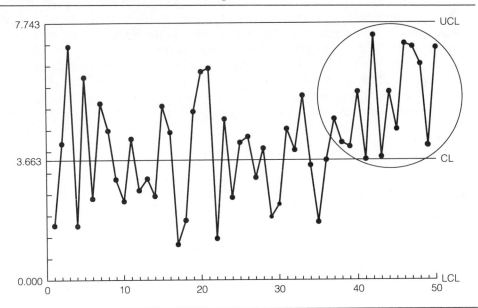

conclude that the mean has shifted. Second, divide the region between the center line and each control limit into three equal parts. Then if (1) two of three consecutive points fall in the outer one-third region between the center line and one of the control limits or (2) four of five consecutive points fall within the outer two-thirds region, one would also conclude that the process has gone out of control. Examples are illustrated in Figure 16.12.

Cycles

Cycles are short, repeated patterns in the chart, having alternative high peaks and low valleys (see Figure 16.13). These are the result of causes that come and go on a regular basis. In the $\bar{x}$-chart, cycles may be the result of operator rotation or fatigue at the end of a shift, different gages used by different inspectors, seasonal effects such as temperature or humidity, or differences between day and night shifts. In the R-chart, cycles can occur from maintenance schedules, rotation of fixtures or gages, differences between shifts, or operator fatigue.

Trends

A trend is the result of some cause that gradually affects the quality characteristics of the product and causes the points on a control chart to gradually move up or down from the center line (see Figure 16.14). As a new group of operators gains experience on the job, for example, or as maintenance of equipment improves over time, a trend may occur. In the $\bar{x}$-chart, trends may be the result of improving operator skills, dirt or chip buildup in fixtures, tool wear, changes in temperature or humidity, or aging

FIGURE 16.12   **Examples of Out-of-Control Processes**

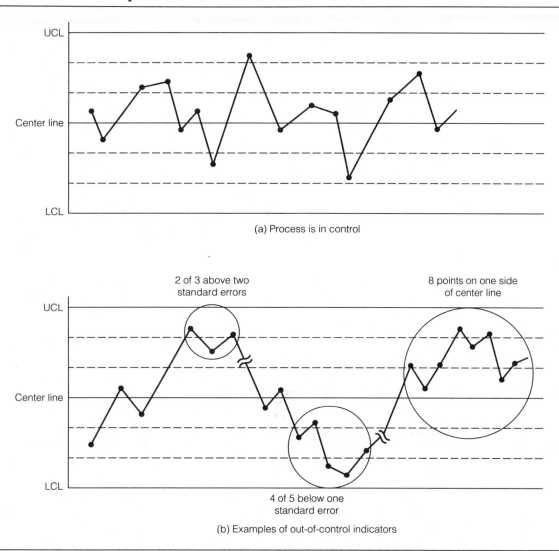

(a) Process is in control

2 of 3 above two
standard errors

8 points on one side
of center line

4 of 5 below one
standard error

(b) Examples of out-of-control indicators

of equipment. In the *R*-chart, an increasing trend may be due to a gradual decline in material quality, operator fatigue, gradual loosening of a fixture or a tool, or dulling of a tool. A decreasing trend often is the result of improved operator skill, improved work methods, better purchased materials, or improved or more frequent maintenance.

Hugging the Center Line

Hugging the center line occurs when nearly all the points fall close to the center line (see Figure 16.15). In the control chart, it appears that the control limits are too wide. A common cause of this occurrence is when the sample is taken by selecting one

FIGURE 16.13 Cycles

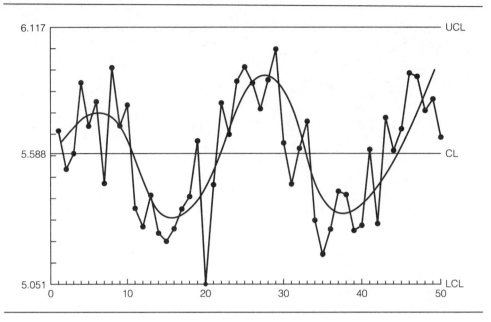

FIGURE 16.14 Gradual Trend

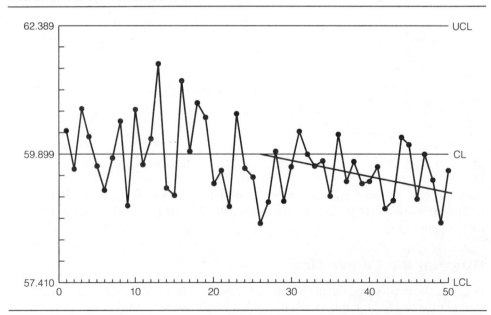

FIGURE 16.15   Hugging the Center Line

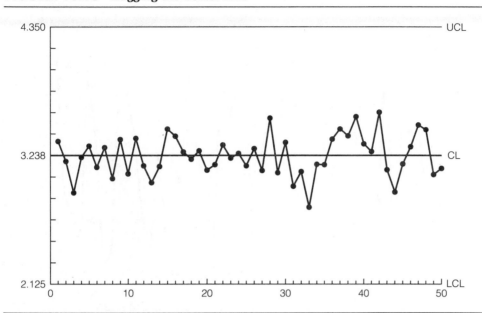

item systematically from each of several machines, spindles, operators, and so on. A simple example will serve to illustrate this. Suppose that one machine produces parts whose diameters average 7.508 with variation of only a few thousandths; a second machine produces parts whose diameters average 7.502, again with only a small variation. Taken together, you can see that the range of variation would probably be between 7.500 and 7.510, and average about 7.505. Now suppose that we sample one part from *each* machine and compute a sample average to plot on an $\bar{x}$-chart. The sample averages will consistently be around 7.505, since one will always be high and the second will always be low. Even though there is a large variation in the parts taken as a whole, the sample averages will not reflect this. In such a case, it would be more appropriate to construct a control chart for *each* machine, spindle, operator, and so on.

An often overlooked cause for this pattern is miscalculation of the control limits, perhaps by using the wrong factor from the table, or misplacing the decimal point in the computations.

Hugging the Control Limits

This pattern shows up when many points are near the control limits with very few in between (see Figure 16.16). It is often called a mixture, and is actually a combination of two different patterns on the same chart. A mixture can be split into two separate patterns, as Figure 16.17 illustrates.

A mixture pattern can result when different lots of material are used in one process, or when parts are produced by different machines but fed into a common inspection group.

FIGURE 16.16 Hugging Control Limits

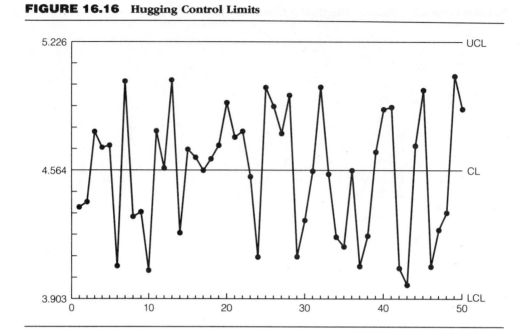

FIGURE 16.17 Illustration of Mixture

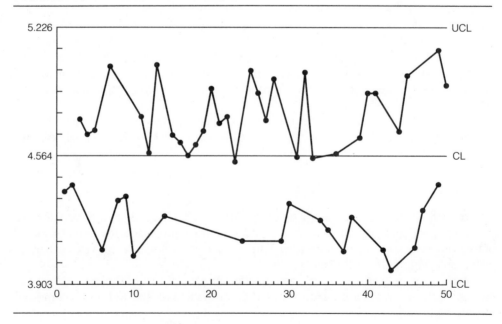

Instability

Instability is characterized by unnatural and erratic fluctuations on both sides of the chart over a period of time (see Figure 16.18). Points will often lie outside of both the upper and lower control limits without a consistent pattern. Assignable causes may be more difficult to identify in this case than when specific patterns are present. A frequent cause of instability is overadjustment of a machine, or the same reasons that cause hugging the control limits.

Recall that we had stated that the R-chart should be analyzed before the $\bar{x}$-chart. This is because some out-of-control conditions in the R-chart may *cause* out-of-control conditions in the $\bar{x}$-chart. Figure 16.19 gives an example of this. You can see a rather drastic trend down in the range. If you examine the $\bar{x}$-chart, you will notice that the last several points seem to be hugging the center line. As the variability in the process decreases, all the sample observations will be closer to the true population mean, and therefore their average, $\bar{x}$, will not vary much from sample to sample. If this reduction in the variation can be identified and controlled, then new control limits should be computed for both charts.

Process Monitoring and Control

After a process is determined to be in control, the charts should be used on a daily basis to monitor production, identify any special causes that might arise, and make corrections as necessary. More importantly, the chart tells when to leave the process alone. Unnecessary adjustments to a process result in nonproductive labor, reduced production, and increased variability of output.

FIGURE 16.18   Instability

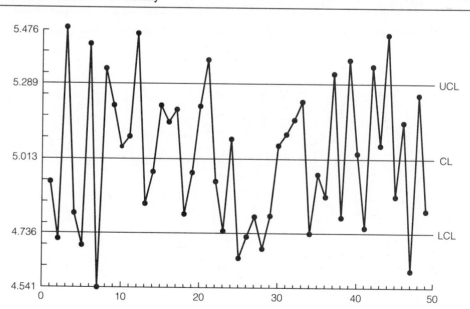

FIGURE 16.19(a) Trend Down in Range . . .

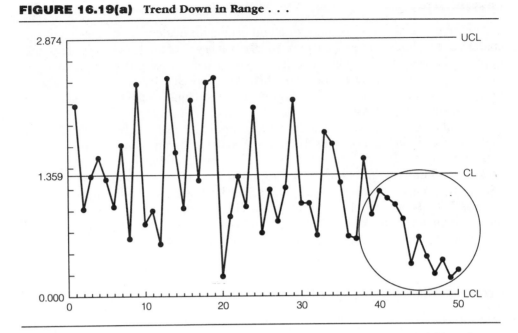

FIGURE 16.19(b) . . . Causes Smaller Variation in $\bar{x}$

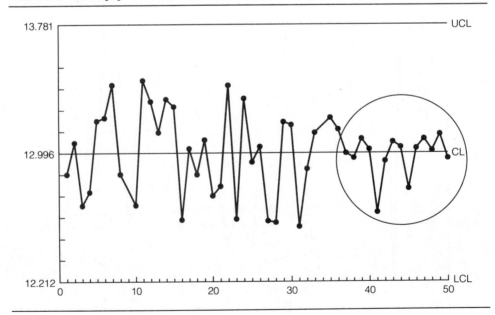

It is more productive if the operators themselves take the samples and chart the data. In this way, they can react quickly to changes in the process and immediately make adjustments. To do this effectively, training of the operators is essential. Many companies conduct in-house training programs to teach operators and supervisors the elementary methods of statistical quality control. Not only does this provide the mathematical and technical skills that are required, but it also gives the shop-floor personnel increased quality-consciousness.

It is not uncommon for improvements in conformance to follow the introduction of control charts on the shop floor, particularly when the process is labor intensive. Apparently, the involvement of management in operators' work often produces positive behavioral modifications (as first demonstrated in the famous Hawthorne studies). Under such circumstances, and as good practice, it is advisable to revise the control limits periodically and determine a new process capability as improvements take place.

Control charts are designed to be used by production operators rather than by inspectors or quality control personnel. Under the philosophy of statistical process control, the burden of quality rests with the operators themselves. The use of control charts allows opreators to react quickly to special causes of variation. This is why the range is used in place of the standard deviation: shop-floor personnel can easily make the necessary computations to plot points on a control chart. Only simple calculations are required.

Estimating Process Capability

After a process has been brought to a state of statistical control by eliminating special causes of variation, we can use the data to estimate process capability. This approach is not as accurate as that described in Chapter 13 since it uses the average range rather that the estimated standard deviation of the original data. Nevertheless, it is a quick and useful method, provided that the distribution of the original data is reasonably normal.

Under the normality assumption, the standard deviation of the original data can be estimated as follows:

$$\sigma = \bar{R}/d_2$$

where d_2 is a constant that depends on the sample size and is also given in Appendix B. Process capability is therefore given by 6σ. The natural variation of individual measurements is given by $\bar{\bar{x}} \pm 3\sigma$. The back of the ASQC control chart form provides a work sheet for determining this. We illustrate these calculations in the following example.

EXAMPLE 2   Estimating Process Capability for the Silicon Wafer Thickness.   Figure 16.20 shows the calculations for the silicon wafer example discussed earlier in the "Limits for Individuals" section of the form. For a sample of size 3, $d_2 = 1.693$. In Figure 16.20, UL_x and LL_x represent the upper and lower limit on individual observations, based on 3σ limits. Thus, the scaled thickness is expected to vary between -1.9 and 95.9. Since the zero point of the data is the lower specification, this means that the thickness is expected to vary from 0.0019

FIGURE 16.20 Process Capability Calculations

CALCULATION WORK SHEET

CONTROL LIMITS				LIMITS FOR INDIVIDUALS

SUBGROUPS INCLUDED __ALL__   **# 17 REMOVED**

COMPARE WITH SPECIFICATION OR TOLERANCE LIMITS

$\bar{R} = \dfrac{\Sigma R}{k} = \dfrac{676}{25}$ = 27 $\dfrac{663}{24}$ = 27.6 $\bar{\bar{X}}$ = 47.0

$\bar{\bar{X}} = \dfrac{\Sigma \bar{X}}{k} = \dfrac{1221}{25}$ = 48.8 $\dfrac{1127}{24}$ = 47.0 $\dfrac{3}{d_2}\bar{R} = 1.772 \times 27.6 = $ __48.9__

OR

$\bar{X}'$ (MIDSPEC. OR STD.) = 50   = 50 $UL_x = \bar{\bar{X}} + \dfrac{3}{d_2}\bar{R}$ = 95.9

$A_2\bar{R} = 1.023 \times 27$ = __27.6__ $1.023 \times 27.6 = $ __28.2__ $LL_x = \bar{\bar{X}} - \dfrac{3}{d_2}\bar{R}$ = -1.9

$UCL_{\bar{x}} = \bar{\bar{X}} + A_2\bar{R}$ = 76.4   = 75.2   US = 100

$LCL_{\bar{x}} = \bar{\bar{X}} - A_2\bar{R}$ = 21.2   = 18.8   LS = __0__

$UCL_R = D_4\bar{R} = 2.574 \times 27$ = 69.5 $2.574 \times 27.6 = 71.0$ US − LS = 100

     $6\sigma = \dfrac{6}{d_2}\bar{R}$ = 97.8

| MODIFIED CONTROL LIMITS FOR AVERAGES | | FACTORS FOR CONTROL LIMITS | | | | |

BASED ON SPECIFICATION LIMITS AND PROCESS CAPABILITY. APPLICABLE ONLY IF: US − LS > 6σ.

US =   LS =

$A_M\bar{R}$ =   x   = _____ $A_M\bar{R}$ =

$URL_{\bar{x}} = US - A_M\bar{R}$ = $LRL_{\bar{x}} = LS + A_M\bar{R}$ =

n	A_2	D_4	d_2	$\dfrac{3}{d_2}$	A_M
2	1.880	3.268	1.128	2.659	0.779
3	1.023	2.574	1.693	1.772	0.749
4	0.729	2.282	2.059	1.457	0.728
5	0.577	2.114	2.326	1.290	0.713
6	0.483	2.004	2.534	1.184	0.701

below the lower specification to 0.0959 above the lower specification. The process capability index (see Chapter 13) is

$$C_p = 100/97.8 = 1.02$$

However, the lower and upper capability indexes are

$$C_{pl} = (47 - 0)/48.9 = 0.96$$
$$C_{pu} = (100 - 47)/48.9 = 1.08$$

This analysis suggests that both the centering and the variation must be improved.

If the individual observations are normally distributed, then we may compute the probability of being out of specification. In the example above, let us assume that the data are normal. The mean is 47 and the standard deviation is 97.8/6 = 16.3. Figure 16.21 shows the calculations for specification limits of 0 and 100. From Appendix A, we see that the area between 0 and the mean (47) is 0.4980. Thus 0.2% of the output would be expected to fall below the lower specification. The area to the right of 100 is approximately zero. We would therefore expect all of the output to meet the upper specification.

There is one word of caution we wish to emphasize. Control limits are often confused with specification limits. Specification dimensions are usually stated in relation to individual parts for "hard" goods, such as automotive hardware. However, in other applications, such as in chemical processes, specifications are stated in terms

FIGURE 16.21   **Process Capability Probability Computations**

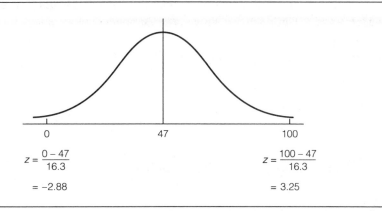

$$z = \frac{0 - 47}{16.3}$$

$$z = \frac{100 - 47}{16.3}$$

$$= -2.88$$

$$= 3.25$$

of average characteristics. Thus, control charts might mislead one into thinking that if all sample averages fall within the control limits, all output will be conforming. This is not true. Control limits relate to *averages,* while specification limits relate to individual measurements. It is possible that a sample average falls within the upper and lower control limits and yet some of the individual observations are out of specification. Since $\sigma_{\bar{x}} = \sigma/\sqrt{n}$, control limits are narrower than the natural variation in the process and do not represent process capability.

Modified Control Limits

The calculation work sheet on the back of the ASQC control chart form has one additional section entitled "Modified Control Limits for Averages." Modified control limits often are used when process capability is good. For example, suppose that the process capability is 60% of tolerance ($Cp = 1.67$) and that the mean can be controlled by a simple adjustment. It may not be practical to investigate every isolated point that falls outside of the usual control limits because the output is probably well within specifications. In such cases, the usual control limits may be replaced with the following:

$$\text{URL}_x = \text{US} - A_m \bar{R}$$

$$\text{LRL}_x = \text{LS} + A_m \bar{R}$$

where URL_x is the upper reject level, LRL_x is the lower reject level, and US and LS are the upper and lower specifications, respectively. Factors for A_m are found on the work sheet. These modified control limits allow for more variation than the ordinary control limits and still provide high confidence that the product produced is within specifications. While the ASQC chart states that these modified limits apply only if the tolerance is greater than 6σ, many suggest that process capability should be at least 60 to 75% of tolerance. If the mean must be controlled closely, a conventional $\bar{x}$-chart should be used even if the process capability is good. Also, if the standard deviation of the process is likely to shift, then modified control limits are not appropriate.

EXAMPLE 3 **Computing Modified Control Limits for the Silicon Wafer Case.** Figure 16.22 shows the completed work sheet for the silicon wafer thickness example we have studied in this chapter. Since the sample size is 3, $A_m = 0.749$. Therefore, the modified limits are

$$URL_x = US - A_m\bar{R} = 100 - 0.749(27.6) = 79.3$$

$$LRL_x = LS + A_m\bar{R} = 0 + 0.749(27.6) = 20.7$$

FIGURE 16.22 Modified Control Limit Calculations

CALCULATION WORK SHEET

CONTROL LIMITS

SUBGROUPS INCLUDED	ALL		#17 REMOVED	
$\bar{R} = \dfrac{\Sigma R}{k}$	$\dfrac{676}{25}$	= 27	$\dfrac{663}{24}$	= 27.6
$\bar{\bar{X}} = \dfrac{\Sigma \bar{X}}{k}$	$\dfrac{1221}{25}$	= 48.8	$\dfrac{1127}{24}$	= 47.0
OR				
$\bar{X}'$ (MIDSPEC. OR STD.)		= 50		= 50
$A_2\bar{R} = 1.023 \times 27$		= 27.6	$1.023 \times 27.6 =$	28.2
$UCL_{\bar{x}} = \bar{\bar{X}} + A_2\bar{R}$		= 76.4		= 75.2
$LCL_{\bar{x}} = \bar{\bar{X}} - A_2\bar{R}$		= 21.2		= 18.8
$UCL_R = D_4\bar{R} = 2.574 \times 27$		= 69.5	$2.574 \times 27.6 =$	71.0

LIMITS FOR INDIVIDUALS

COMPARE WITH SPECIFICATION OR TOLERANCE LIMITS

$\bar{\bar{X}}$		= 47.0
$\dfrac{3}{d_2}\bar{R} = 1.772 \times 27.6 =$		48.9
$UL_x = \bar{\bar{X}} + \dfrac{3}{d_2}\bar{R}$		= 95.9
$LL_x = \bar{\bar{X}} - \dfrac{3}{d_2}\bar{R}$		= -1.9
US		= 100
LS		= 0
US − LS		= 100
$6\sigma = \dfrac{6}{d_2}\bar{R}$		= 97.8

MODIFIED CONTROL LIMITS FOR AVERAGES

BASED ON SPECIFICATION LIMITS AND PROCESS CAPABILITY.
APPLICABLE ONLY IF: US − LS > 6σ.

US	= 100	LS	= 0
$A_M\bar{R} = .749 \times 27.6 =$ 20.7		$A_M\bar{R} =$	20.7
$URL_{\bar{x}} = US - A_M\bar{R}$	= 79.3	$LRL_{\bar{x}} = LS + A_M\bar{R} =$	20.7

FACTORS FOR CONTROL LIMITS

n	A_2	D_4	d_2	$\dfrac{3}{d_2}$	A_M
2	1.880	3.268	1.128	2.659	0.779
3	1.023	2.574	1.693	1.772	0.749
4	0.729	2.282	2.059	1.457	0.728
5	0.577	2.114	2.326	1.290	0.713
6	0.483	2.004	2.534	1.184	0.701

Observe that if the process is centered on the nominal, these control limits are looser than the ordinary control limits. In this example, the centering would first have to be corrected from its current estimated value of 47.0.

CONTROL CHARTS FOR ATTRIBUTES

Attributes data assume only two values—good or bad, pass or fail, and so on. Attributes usually cannot be measured, but they can be counted and are useful in many practical situations. For instance, in printing packages for consumer products, color quality can be rated as acceptable or not acceptable, or a sheet of cardboard either is damaged or is not. Usually, attributes data are easy to collect, often by visual inspection. Many accounting records, such as percent scrapped, are readily available. However, one drawback in using attributes data is that large samples are necessary to obtain valid statistical results.

Several different types of control charts are used for attributes data. One of the most common is the *p-chart* (introduced in this section). Other types of attributes charts are presented in the next chapter. One distinction that we must make is between the terms **defects** and **defectives**. A *defect* is a single nonconforming quality characteristic of an item. An item may have several defects. The term *defective* refers to items having one or more defects. Since certain attributes charts are used for defectives while others are used for defects, it is important to understand the difference. As pointed out in Chapter 13, the term *nonconforming* is often used instead of defective.

A **p-chart** monitors the proportion of nonconforming items produced in a lot. Often it is also called a **fraction nonconforming** or **fraction defective** chart. As with variables data, a *p*-chart is constructed by first gathering 25 to 30 samples of the attribute being measured. The size of each sample should be large enough to have several nonconforming items. If the probability of finding a nonconforming item is small, a large sample size is usually necessary. Samples are chosen over time periods so that any special causes that are identified can be investigated.

Let us suppose that k samples, each of size n, are selected. If y represents the number nonconforming in a particular sample, the proportion nonconforming is y/n. Let p_i be the fraction nonconforming in the ith sample; the average fraction nonconforming for the group of k samples then is

$$\bar{p} = \frac{p_1 + p_2 + \ldots + p_k}{k}$$

This statistic reflects the capability of the process. We would expect a high percentage of samples to have a fraction nonconforming within three standard deviations of $\bar{p}$. An estimate of the standard deviation is given by

$$s_{\bar{p}} = \sqrt{\frac{\bar{p}(1 - \bar{p})}{n}}$$

Therefore, upper and lower control limits are given by

$$\text{UCL}_p = \bar{p} + 3s_{\bar{p}}$$

$$\text{LCL}_p = \bar{p} - 3s_{\bar{p}}$$

IF LCL_p is less than zero, a value of zero is used.

Analysis of a *p*-chart is similar to that of an $\bar{x}$- or R-chart. Points outside the control limits signify an out-of-control situation. Patterns and trends should also be sought to identify special causes. There are two important differences, however. If a point on a *p*-chart is below the lower control limit or if a trend below the center line develops, this indicates that the process might have improved, since ideally we seek zero defectives. However, caution is advised before such conclusions are drawn, because errors may have been made in computation. An example of a *p*-chart is presented next.

EXAMPLE 4 **Constructing an Attribute Chart.** The operators of automated sorting machines in a post office must read the ZIP code on a letter and divert the letter to the proper carrier route. Over one month's time, 25 samples of 100 letters were chosen, and the number of errors was recorded. This information is summarized in Table 16.3. The fraction nonconforming is found

TABLE 16.3   **Sorting Errors at a Post Office**

Sample	1	2	3	4	5	6	7	8	9	10	11	12	13	14	15
Errors	3	1	0	0	2	5	3	6	1	4	0	2	1	3	4

Sample	16	17	18	19	20	21	22	23	24	25
Errors	1	1	2	5	2	3	4	1	0	1

by dividing the number of errors by 100. The average fraction nonconforming, $\bar{p}$, is determined to be

$$\bar{p} = \frac{0.03 + 0.01 + \ldots + 0.01}{25} = 0.022$$

The standard deviation is computed as

$$s_{\bar{p}} = \sqrt{\frac{0.022(1 - 0.022)}{100}} = 0.01467$$

FIGURE 16.23   **p-Chart for Post Office**

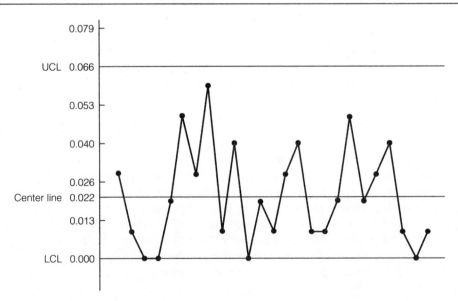

Thus, the upper control limit, UCL_p, is $0.022 + 3(0.01467) = 0.066$, and the lower control limit, LCL_p, is $0.022 - 3(0.01467) = -0.022$. Since this latter figure is negative, zero is used. The control chart for this example is shown in Figure 16.23. The sorting process appears to be in control. If any values are found above the upper control limit or if an upward trend is evident, this might indicate the need for more experience or training of the operators.

Variable Sample Size

Often 100% inspection is performed on process output during fixed sampling periods; however, the number of units produced in each sampling period may vary. In this case, the p-chart would have a variable sample size. One way of handling this is to compute a standard deviation for each individual sample. Thus, if the number of observations in the ith sample is n_i, control limits are given by

$$\bar{p} \pm 3 \sqrt{\frac{\bar{p}(1 - \bar{p})}{n_i}} \quad \text{where } \bar{p} = \frac{\sum \text{number nonconforming}}{\sum n_i}$$

To illustrate this, suppose that data were recorded over 10 shifts as given in Table 16.4. Upper and lower control limits are also shown in the table. Figure 16.24 illustrates the resulting control chart.

Another approach is to use the average sample size, $\bar{n}$, to compute approximate control limits. Using the average sample size, the control limits are computed as

$$UCL_p = \bar{p} + 3 \sqrt{\frac{\bar{p}(1 - \bar{p})}{\bar{n}}}$$

and

$$LCL_p = \bar{p} - 3 \sqrt{\frac{\bar{p}(1 - \bar{p})}{\bar{n}}}$$

TABLE 16.4 Data for Variable Sample Sizes

Shift	n_i	Number Nonconforming	Fraction Nonconforming	3-sigma	UCL	LCL
1	40	2	0.050	0.114	0.175	0
2	55	3	0.055	0.097	0.158	0
3	45	3	0.067	0.107	0.168	0
4	40	4	0.100	0.114	0.175	0
5	65	3	0.046	0.089	0.150	0
6	60	3	0.050	0.093	0.154	0
7	35	2	0.057	0.122	0.183	0
8	70	3	0.043	0.086	0.147	0
9	50	4	0.080	0.102	0.163	0
10	45	4	0.089	0.107	0.168	0
	505	31				

$$\bar{p} = 31/505 = 0.0614$$

FIGURE 16.24 Control Chart for Variable Sample Size

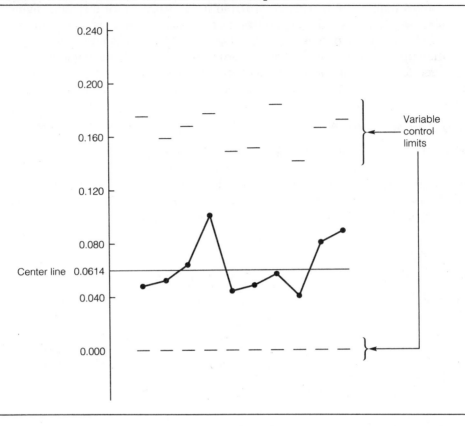

These result in an approximation to the true control limits. For the data in Table 16.4, the average sample size is $\bar{n} = 50.5$. Using this value, the upper control limit is calculated to be 0.1627, and the lower control limit is zero. However, this approach has several disadvantages. Since the control limits are only approximate, points that are actually out of control may not appear to be so on this chart. Second, runs or nonrandom patterns are difficult to interpret because the standard deviation differs between samples as a result of the variable sample sizes. Hence, this approach should be used with caution. We recommend a constant sample size whenever possible.

DESIGNING CONTROL CHARTS

In designing control chart procedures, there are four things to consider: (1) the basis for sampling, (2) the sample size, (3) the frequency of sampling, and (4) the location of the control limits.

Basis for Sampling

Samples should be chosen to be as homogeneous as possible so that each sample reflects the system of common causes or assignable causes that may be present at that point in time. That is, if assignable causes are present, the chance of observing differences between samples should be high, while the chance of observing differences within a sample should be low. Samples that satisfy these criteria are called **rational subgroups.**

One approach to constructing rational subgroups is to use consecutive measurements from a machine over a short period of time. This minimizes the chance of variability within the sample while allowing variation between samples to be detected. This approach is useful when control charts are used to detect shifts in process level. A second approach is to take a random sample of all units produced since the last sample was taken. This would allow one to make a decision on the acceptance of all units produced since the last sample was taken. However, care must be taken when interpreting the R-chart using this method, since a shift in the process level would cause points on the R-chart to be out of control, even if there was no change in the actual variability of the process. One must also be careful not to overlap production shifts, different batches of material, and so on, when selecting the basis for sampling. Thus, the method of selecting samples should be carefully chosen so as not to bias the results.

Sample Size

Sample size is a second critical design issue. A small sample size is desirable so that there is not much opportunity for within-sample variation due to special causes. This is important, since each sample should be representative of the state of control at one point in time. In addition, the cost of sampling should be kept low. When an operator is taking the sample measurements and plotting a control chart, it represents nonproductive time (in a strict accounting sense only!). On the other hand, control limits are based on the assumption of a normal distribution of the sample means. If the process is not normal, this assumption is valid only for large samples. Large samples also allow smaller changes in process characteristics to be detected with higher probability. In practice, samples of about five have been found to work well in detecting process shifts of two standard deviations or larger. To detect smaller shifts in the process mean, larger sample sizes of 15 to 25 must be used.

For attributes data, too small a sample size can make a p-chart meaningless. While many guidelines such as "use at least 100 observations" have been suggested, the proper sample size should be determined statistically. This is particularly true when the true portion of nonconformances is small. If p is small, n should be large enough to have a high probability of detecting at least one nonconformance. For example, if $p = .01$, then to have at least a 95% chance of finding at least one nonconformance, the sample size must be at least 300. Other approaches for determining attribute data sample sizes include choosing n large enough so that there is a 50% chance of detecting a process shift of some specified amount, or choosing n so that the control chart will have a positive lower control limit. The reader is referred to the book by Montgomery in the bibliography for details on these calculations.

Sampling Frequency

The third design issue is the sampling frequency. We would like to take large samples on a frequent basis, but clearly this is not economical. No hard and fast rules exist for the frequency of sampling. Samples should be close enough so that there is an opportunity to detect changes in process characteristics as soon as possible and reduce the chances of producing a large amount of nonconforming output. However, they should not be so close that the cost of sampling outweighs the benefits that can be realized. This decision depends on the individual application and production volume.

Location of Control Limits

The location of control limits is closely related to the risk involved in making an incorrect assessment about the state of control. A Type I error occurs when an incorrect conclusion is reached that a special cause is present when in fact one does not exist. This results in the cost of trying to find a nonexistent problem. A Type II error occurs when special causes are present but are not signaled in the control chart because points fall within the control limits by chance. Since nonconforming products have a greater chance to be produced, a cost will eventually be incurred as a result. The size of a Type I error depends only on the control limits that are used; the wider the limits, the less chance of a point falling outside the limits, and consequently there will be a smaller chance of making a Type I error. A Type II error, however, depends on the width of the control limits, the degree to which the process is out of control, and the sample size. For a fixed sample size, wider control limits increase the risk of making a Type II error.

The traditional approach of using three-sigma limits implicitly assumes that the cost of a Type I error is large relative to that of a Type II error; that is, a Type I error is essentially minimized. This will not always be the case. Much research has been performed on economic design of control charts.[2] Cost models attempt to find the best combination of design parameters (center line, control limits, sample size, and sampling interval) that minimize expected cost or maximize expected profit.

There are costs associated with making both Type I and Type II errors. A Type I error results in unnecessary investigation for an assignable cause. This may include costs of lost production time and special testing. A Type II error can be more significant. If an out-of-control process is not recognized, defectives that are produced may result in higher costs of scrap and rework in later stages of production or after the finished good reaches the customer. Unfortunately, the cost of a Type II error is nearly impossible to estimate, since it depends on the amount of nonconforming products—a quantity that is unknown.

The costs associated with Type I and Type II errors conflict as the size of the control limits are changed. The tighter the control limits, the greater the probability that a sample will indicate that the process is out of control. Hence, the cost of a Type I error increases as control limits are reduced. On the other hand, tighter control limits will reduce the cost of a Type II error, since out-of-control states will be more easily identified and the amount of defective output will be reduced.

The costs associated with sampling and testing may include lost productive time when the operator takes sample measurements, performs calculations, and plots the points on the control chart. If testing is destructive, the value of lost products would also be included. Thus, larger sample sizes and more frequent sampling result in higher costs.

---

[2]D. C. Montgomery, "The Economic Design of Control Charts: A Review and Literature Survey," *Journal of Quality Technology,* Vol. 12, No. 2 (1980), pp. 75–87.

TABLE 16.5 **Economic Decisions for Control Chart Construction**

Source of Cost	Sample Size	Sampling Frequency	Control Limits
Type I error	large	high	wide
Type II error	large	high	narrow
Sampling and testing	small	low	———

The sample size and frequency also affect the costs of Type I and Type II errors. As the sample size or frequency is increased, both Type I and Type II errors are reduced, since better information is provided for decision making. Table 16.5 summarizes this discussion of the three-way interaction of costs. In the economic design of control charts, we must consider these simultaneously. Most models for such decisions can become quite complex and are beyond the scope of this text.

As a practical matter, one often uses judgment about the nature of operations and the costs involved in making these decisions. Mayer suggests the following guidelines:[3]

1. If the cost of investigating an operation to identify the cause of an apparent out-of-control condition is high, a Type I error becomes important, and wider control limits should be adopted. Conversely, if that cost is low, narrower limits should be selected.

2. If the cost of the defective output generated by an operation is substantial, a Type II error is serious, and narrower control limits should be used. Otherwise, wider limits should be selected.

3. If the cost of a Type I error and the cost of a Type II error for a given activity are both significant, wide control limits should be chosen, and consideration should be given to reducing the risk of a Type II error by increasing the sample size. Also, more frequent samples should be taken to reduce the duration of any out-of-control condition that might occur.

4. If past experience with an operation indicates that an out-of-control condition arises quite frequently, narrower control limits should be favored because of the large number of opportunities for making a Type II error. In the event that the probability of an out-of-control condition is very small, wider limits will be preferred.

Length of Production Run

Control charts are most applicable to high-volume manufacturing situations. In some industries, particularly as the pressures for increased manufacturing flexibility increase, short production runs are common. In such situations, it may not even be possible to collect enough initial data to compute control limits. By the time the data are collected, the production run might be over, thus defeating the purpose of the chart.

---

[3]Raymond R. Mayer, "Selecting Control Limits," *Quality Progress,* Vol. 16, No. 9, pp. 24–26.

One method of overcoming this problem is to change the definition of the measurements. For example, consider a drill press in which each run requires varying depths of cut. Instead of measuring values of the actual depth for a particular part, one can measure the deviation of depth from the target. In this way, differences between products and production runs are removed. In effect, this approach monitors *process* characteristics rather than *product* characteristics.

IMPLEMENTING STATISTICAL PROCESS CONTROL

Control charts, like the other basic tools for quality improvement, are relatively simple to use. The following is a summary of the methodology for developing and using control charts:

1. Preparation

    a. Choose the variable or attribute to be measured.
    b. Determine the basis, size, and frequency of sampling.
    c. Set up the control chart.

2. Data collection

    a. Record the data.
    b. Calculate relevant statistics: averages, ranges, proportions, and so on.
    c. Plot the statistics on the chart.

3. Determination of trial control limits

    a. Calculate average mean and range for $\bar{x}$- and R-charts or the average proportion for p-charts.
    b. Draw the center line on the chart.
    c. Compute the upper and lower control limits.

4. Analysis and interpretation

    a. Investigate the chart for lack of control.
    b. Eliminate out-of-control points.
    c. Recompute control limits if necessary.
    d. Determine process capability.

5. Use as a problem-solving tool

    a. Continue data collection and plotting.
    b. Identify out-of-control situations and take corrective action.

Control charts can provide significant benefits to a company. For example, Edgewood Tool and Manufacturing Company in Taylor, Michigan, had a problem with misformed parts on hood hinges for Ford trucks.[4] One critical dimension, the distance from the edge of a pierced hole to the edge of the part, was monitored with a control chart. They found that the variation increased whenever the operator loaded a new coil onto the machine. The solution was an inexpensive gaging block, which made loading and positioning the coil a more precise operation.

---

[4]Jerry Houston, "Start Small for Successful SPC," *Quality* (August 1985), p. Q12.

A number of reasons exist explaining why control charts sometimes fail in organizations. Operators might not trust a new tool. Old methods, such as correcting a process only if production is out of specification or adjusting the machine after every batch, are difficult habits to break. Perhaps operators did not receive enough training or practice or do not fully understand the benefits. Another reason is the lack of a corrective action plan. The concept of control requires that assignable causes be identified and corrected. Failure to act on control chart signals increases variability, reduces the importance of the chart, and undermines the entire quality program.

One must also be careful to use the appropriate chart. Attributes charts are easier to use. However, using an attributes chart when a variables chart is more appropriate leads to loss of sensitivity, loss of information for corrective action, and quality being interpreted in terms of defects, rather than uniformity to a target.

Management has the responsibility to show commitment, not simply give lip service. Their commitment will become evident in cases where the use of control charts means that corrective action will delay a shipment. If not supported by management, operators will quickly see that they are wasting their time and stop using SPC. In addition, management must accept the fact that control charts require maintenance. Control limits must be periodically updated as elements of the process change and as assignable causes are eliminated—an outdated chart is useless. Upper management must commit financial resources for measurement instruments, calculators, or computers and software, as well as training for workers to learn the mechanics of SPC. Management must demonstrate that SPC is not a fad that will disappear in a few months, but an ongoing commitment to improve quality. Integrating SPC into daily work will disrupt production to some extent, and managers must recognize and prepare for this.

Second, successful SPC projects need a champion, that is, some individual in the company who has both the responsibility and the authority to make it work. Any kind of new business venture invariably fails if there is no champion to promote it and ensure its success.

Third, only one problem should be addressed at a time. If a company has never used SPC before, it makes little sense to try to introduce it throughout an entire plant or even an entire department at once. Mistakes will be made at the beginning from which the company will learn. In choosing an initial project, managers should select one that stands to benefit the most from SPC and that will have high visibility both to top management and other workers. One good success story will lead others to try SPC; therefore, they need to be well publicized within the company. Pareto diagrams and cause-and-effect diagrams are useful tools for choosing projects to tackle.

Fourth, education and training of all employees is absolutely necessary. Everyone needs to understand why SPC is being used and what it can do to improve quality and help the worker do a better job. Workers must understand that SPC will benefit them and is not a scheme set up by management to place blame on them.

Finally, the gaging and measurement system must first be evaluated for accuracy, repeatability, and reproducibility before implementing SPC. These features must be evaluated statistically, not on the basis of intuition or "experience."

Numerous implementation problems can arise because of poor planning. A case in point is the Uniroyal Goodrich Tire Plant in Fort Wayne, Indiana.[5] The plant began

---

[5]Frank X. Cantello, John E. Chalmers, and James E. Evans, "Evolution to an Effective and Enduring SPC System," *Quality Progress* (February 1990), pp. 60–64.

its process of implementing SPC by sending managers to an SPC seminar sponsored by an automobile manufacturer. In-house training began in 1982 and several tracking charts (not true control charts) had been established by 1983 to monitor various quality characteristics. With some positive results, it appeared that SPC was working and that the initial success would multiply. In 1984, a full-time coordinator was assigned to implement SPC. A basic course was developed for first-line supervisors. Next, one or two hours of training in basic control charting were given to small groups of hourly employees. By 1985, the number of charts used in production increased. Soon afterward however, management realized that insufficient resources existed to follow up on the information being collected. Some employees began to question the value of keeping the charts. It became obvious that something had gone wrong.

In 1985, the plant manager took a different direction. He established a seven-member steering committee consisting of two production managers, the SPC coordinator, an SPC instructor, the QA manager, and two department facilitators. In reviewing the history to that point, the committee reached several conclusions:

1. The charts being developed were tracking documents, not control charts, and had limited value.

2. The SPC process was primarily an educational exercise. Much of the training had not been put to practical use.

3. SPC was not made a part of daily business.

4. They did not understand the factors that led to successful implementation of SPC.

One of their first tasks was to visit a local company that had an established SPC program and an excellent reputation for quality. As a result they developed a six-step implementation process that involved a project group approach instead of traditional classroom training, with heavy emphasis on employee participation. This process is outlined in the following:

1. *Define the process:* What are the important parts of an operation? We have seen that flowcharts provide a useful visual means of characterizing a process. This is not a trivial exercise. Conflicting opinions often abound, and these must be resolved. Bringing people together in this task produces a sharing of perceptions and insights and can be an enlightening experience for all participants. A focus on customer satisfaction—and identification of the customer—helps to clarify the process and break down barriers to communication.

2. *Identify characteristics to study:* What are the important quality parameters? Most processes have many characteristics; all of them cannot be monitored. Pareto analysis is one method for prioritizing these characteristics. Are they machine-controllable or operator-controllable? For operator-controllable parameters, the operators must monitor themselves. A good management-employee relationship is necessary.

3. *Determine the ability to measure the characteristic:* A shortcoming of many SPC programs is the failure to assess the measurement tools. If the measurement system is unsatisfactory, all subsequent SPC activities may be

useless. Many employees often resist the idea of performing such studies. SPC groups should be trained in the methods and importance of gage studies (see Chapter 13).

4. *Perform capability studies:* We discussed this topic in Chapter 13 and in this chapter. One of the fundamental purposes of SPC is to establish a state of statistical control so that process capability can be determined. Knowing process capability is the first step toward resolving chronic problems and reducing common causes of variation. Workers must be taught the concept of variation, the use of control charts, and their role in capability studies. Process capability studies can become quite popular with employees since they show the variation that is management-controllable and for which the workers cannot be blamed.

5. *Study process performance:* This is an extension of capability studies to determine what actual variation is present. Using control charts to monitor performance and identify special causes leads to identification of various sources of variation and, eventually, to their elimination.

6. *Implement process control:* This is where most companies start their SPC programs after formal training is provided, and why many programs are not successful. Starting with steps 1 through 5 provides a foundation of training, employee involvement, and problem solving. By the time an SPC group reaches this step, they are thoroughly familiar with using control charts, and little training, if any, is needed to make the transition to real-time control using SPC. Because of the extensive employee participation in the previous steps, implementation is usually quite easy.

SPC IN SERVICE ORGANIZATIONS

In earlier chapters, we observed that service organizations all share common features that differ from manufacturing. These features include direct contact with the customer, large volumes of transactions and processing, and often large amounts of paperwork. It is easy to see that the sources of error are considerable in recording transactions and in processing. It is not unusual to see a newspaper report of a large error in billing that amounts to thousands or hundreds of thousands of dollars.

Although control charts were first developed and used in a manufacturing context, they are easily applied to service organizations. The major difference is the quality characteristic that is controlled. Many of the standards used in service industries form the basis for quality control charts. Table 16.6 lists just a few of the many potential applications of control charts for services.

To illustrate the application of SPC in service organizations, we discuss how it was applied at IBM's Kingston, New York, facility.[6] IBM Kingston tests and ships mainframe computers in addition to developing hardware and software products. Meeting customer requirements and reducing costs are principal goals that extend to the

---

[6]Adapted from W. J. McCabe, Manager of Quality Programs, IBM Corp., "Improving Quality and Cutting Costs in a Service Organization," *Quality Progress* (June 1985), pp. 85–89.

TABLE 16.6 Control Chart Applications in Service Organizations

Organization	Quality Measure
Hospital	lab test accuracy
	insurance claim accuracy
	on-time delivery of meals and medication
Bank	check-processing accuracy
Insurance company	claims-processing response time
	billing accuracy
Post office	sorting accuracy
	time of delivery
	percent express mail delivered on time
Ambulance	response time
Police department	incidence of crime in a precinct
	number of traffic citations
Hotel	proportion of rooms satisfactorily cleaned
	checkout time
	number of complaints received
Transportation	proportion of freight cars correctly routed
	dollar amount of damage per claim
Auto service	percent of time work completed as promised
	number of parts out of stock

purchasing, security, administration, maintenance, and personnel departments. Each department was asked to identify objectives for its business and user customers, and then to develop a set of measurements to provide senior management with a quarterly indication of progress toward the objectives. Almost 200 key service processes were identified. For example, in personnel safety, the objectives were to develop and administer the Kingston site's personnel safety and health programs, to assist management in complying with government requirements and good safety and health practices, and to make and keep IBM a safe and healthy place to work without interfering with employee's jobs. Measurements included days lost, workman's compensation cases, OSHA recordable accidents, and first-aid cases.

The IBM site services management decided to try control charts as an aid toward improvement. Managers needed to be educated, but most texts treated the subject in manufacturing terms. Examples of how control charts could be used in a site services environment had to be developed. Concepts had to be taken out of the statistical realm and put in practical terms. Examples of the areas in which control charts were used follow.

Speak-Up! The Speak-Up! program is an employee communications channel. It provides a way for employees to pass along a grievance, an idea, a comment, or a thank you to management. An employee forwards an informal letter to the Speak-Up! administrator. The administrator has the letter typed, deleting the employee's name to ensure confidentiality. The letter is routed to the appropriate functional manager who investigates and drafts a reply for the signature of a senior manager. The administrator mails the signed response to the employee.

Response time is very critical to the program. Those assigned to answer the letters must meet a number of requirements. Responses must admit when mistakes have occurred, describe any change that will be implemented, not be defensive, answer all questions raised, be short, and be written in a style used by the senior manager. A deficiency in any of these areas can cause a delay because the response will have to be revised. In looking at historical data, management noticed that certain functional areas appeared to take longer to reply than others. Control charts were used to track response time by functional area. A workshop was also set up to assure that people writing answers knew how to do so.

Control charts were set up using samples of five letters per week for 20 weeks. The average was found to be below the previous average, showing the impact of the tracking and the workshop. As the chart continued to be used, two consecutive weeks with sample averages beyond two standard errors were noted. The cause was found to be vacation coverage—the answers were being written by people who had not attended the workshop.

Preemployment Medical Exams.   Preemployment medical exams took too long and taxed the medical staff assigned to conduct them. Examinations were vital to assure that employees could do the job without excess stress and pose no clinical threat to other employees. The challenge IBM faced was to maintain the quality of the exam while reducing the time required for it. They did so by identifying and eliminating waiting periods between various parts of the exam.

Preliminary control charts revealed that the average time required for the physical was 74 minutes; the range, however, varied greatly. New equipment and additional training of the medical staff were suggested as a means of shortening the time. Initial charts were out of control, but continued monitoring and process improvements lowered the average time to 40 minutes, and both the average and range charts were brought into statistical control.

Purchase Orders.   The steps involved in processing purchase orders were fairly routine. The person requesting an item or service filled out a requisition and forwarded it to a buyer who translated it into an order. The buyer selected a vendor, usually after a number of bids.

Time and money were being lost by human error. Both requesters and buyers were contributing to the situation. Of great concern to the purchasing organization were nonconforming documents originating from the purchasing department itself. The department started to count them. Data on weekly purchase orders and orders in error were monitored, and a p-chart was constructed that showed an average error rate of 5.9%. After the buyers reviewed the data, they found that the process had actually changed during the data collection period, resulting in a shift in the mean to 3.7%. The use of the chart also showed out-of-control conditions resulting from vacations. Substitute buyers created a high percentage of rework because of the workload and their unfamiliarity with particular aspects of the process. Preventive measures were created for peak vacation periods to provide sufficient coverage and to ensure that temporary replacements understood the process better.

These examples show how control charts can be used to improve both quality and productivity. The key is in defining the appropriate quality measures to monitor. Once this is done and agreed on by management, the use of control charts becomes routine. You can undoubtedly think of many other applications in service processes with which you are familiar.

Using SQC for Process Improvement at Dow Chemical Company[7]

The magnesium department of the Dow Chemical Company in Freeport, Texas, has produced magnesium, a silvery light metal, for the past 70 years. This was the first major group in Texas Operations to train all its technical people and managers in the use of statistical quality control (SQC) techniques, following the example set by the automobile industry.

Some of the earliest successful applications of SQC were in chemical process areas. Figures 16.25 and 16.26 show the improvement in the drier analysis after SQC and retraining were implemented. In addition to the fact that the process control required significant improvement, it was found that differences between operators existed. The blackened circles in Figure 16.25 represent one operator in question; the open circles represent the other operators. On examination, it was found that the operator had not been properly trained in the use of SQC even though he had been performing this analysis for two years. There was an immediate improvement in the consistency of the analysis between the operators after retraining.

The use of control charts in the control room made the operators realize that their attempts to fine tune the process introduced a great deal of unwanted variation. A comparison of the before and

[7]Adapted from Clifford B. Wilson, "SQC + Mg: A Positive Reaction," *Quality Progress* (April 1988), pp. 47–49.

after range charts shows the improvement (see Figure 16.26).

As with many chemical and manufacturing operations, when the variability of the feedstock to one operation is reduced, it is possible to reduce the variability of the basic operation. With tighter control over the concentration of magnesium hydroxide from the filter plant, Dow was able to exert much tighter control of the subsequent neutralization operation. As seen in Figure 16.27, the differences are substantial. The upper control limit on the second range chart is about where the center line is on the first range chart. A similar situation exists on the $\bar{x}$ charts. These improvements resulted without any additional instrumentation or operators.

Another application involved the casting operation. On primary magnesium, for example, Dow calculated a process capability index C_{pk} of meeting a minimum magnesium content of 99.8% purity and found it to be over 10, based on over 10,000 samples. Thus, there has been little incentive to use control charts in this operation because of the comfortable level of compliance. However, ingots are also graded according to their surface quality. Using control charts, Dow found that the process was in control but that the number of rejects was much higher than desired. After several months of

FIGURE 16.25   **Before and After *x*-Bar Charts on Drier Analysis**

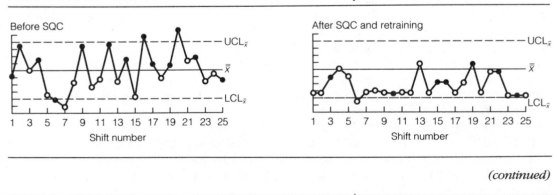

(continued)

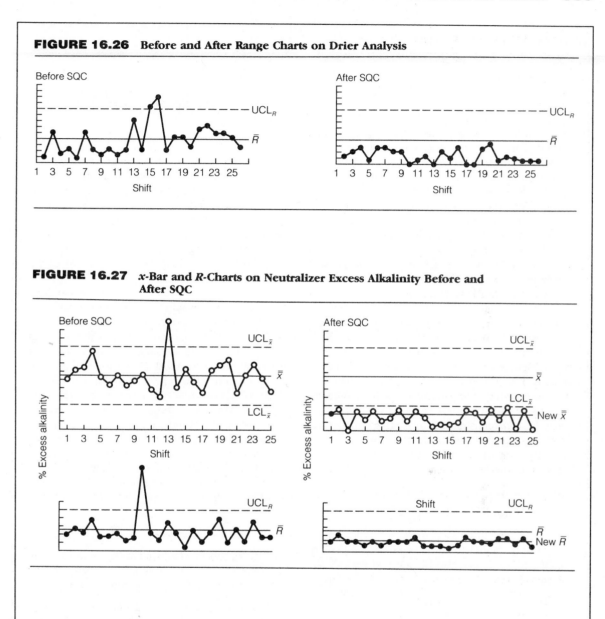

FIGURE 16.26 Before and After Range Charts on Drier Analysis

FIGURE 16.27 *x*-Bar and *R*-Charts on Neutralizer Excess Alkalinity Before and After SQC

analysis and modifications, this process was improved.

Dow Chemical Company has experienced success everywhere that SQC has been used in the magnesium process. Documented savings of several hundred thousand dollars per year have been realized, and new applications are continually being discovered.

Key Issues for Discussion

1. What conclusions do you reach upon interpreting the control charts in Figures 16.25, 16.26, and 16.27?

2. For primary magnesium, the high C_{pk} value suggested that control charts were not needed. How might the company maintain control of the process at this level without them?

Process Capability Analysis at John Deere[8]

John Deere, a major manufacturer of farm equipment, uses SPC to assess the capability of machine tools that it purchases. At Deere Harvester Works, almost all machine tool purchases have been subjected to SPC analysis since the late 1970s. Deere had decided to acquire a vertical column bandsaw that could make angle as well as straight cuts. A Marvel 81A PC bandsaw produced by Armstrong-Blum Manufacturing Company was selected. Before it was shipped, however, Deere studied its ability to meet performance criteria.

Figure 16.28 shows the basic analysis. Process capability is measured by testing the machine with the materials and tooling that will be used in its intended application. The natural variation must be less than two-thirds of the tolerance to be acceptable. Deere engineers begin testing at the supplier's plant if possible. The Deere quality or engineering staff observes the test and records the data for analysis. They prefer to send the operator who will use the machine at the supplier's plant to perform the tests. In addition to testing for process capability, reliability is demonstrated by operating the machine for 8 hours continuously without a failure.

Deere's capability study sets up very specific guidelines. The key elements are:

- No change in operators during the test.

- No change in raw material batches.

- No change in measuring devices. The devices must be calibrated at the beginning and end of the test and may also be checked periodically during the test. Repeatability is also verified.

- No change in inspectors.

[8]Adapted from Jean V. Owen, "Picking a Marvel at Deere," Society of Manufacturing Engineers, *Manufacturing Engineering Magazine* (January 1989), pp. 74–77.

- No change in temperature of equipment, material, or coolant.

- No change in coolant level.

Deere has developed a patented software package for collecting, storing, and analyzing the data collected. This system, called CAIR (Computer-aided Inspection and Reporting System), generates reports to analyze variability and control. Control charts from tests on the Marvel saw to check cut length on an 875-mm rectangular steel tube are shown in Figure 16.29. Figure 16.30 shows the results of the process capability analysis.

One of Deere's managers noticed that suppliers often learn more about their machine's capabilities during the testing. In one case, a CNC punch press supplier's chief engineer discovered that the machine's capability deteriorated as steel shafts of heavier weight were used. By reprogramming the machine control, the vendor was able to improve the machine's capability on heavy sheets. The tests also showed that the flatness of the sheet was crucial and could be correlated with process capability.

While this process consumes time, Deere believes that the long-term benefits far outweigh the costs. As one manager stated, "Usually we end up with a better supplier and a better machine than we would have gotten otherwise."

Key Issues for Discussion

1. From the control chart data in Figure 16.29, verify the control limits and estimate of the standard deviation using the formulas in this chapter.

2. Discuss the data found in Figure 16.30. What is the process capability index? What conclusions do you reach about the machine tool?

3. Discuss the guidelines set for Deere's capability test. Why are such guidelines strictly adhered to?

(continued)

FIGURE 16.28   **Quality Control at John Deere**

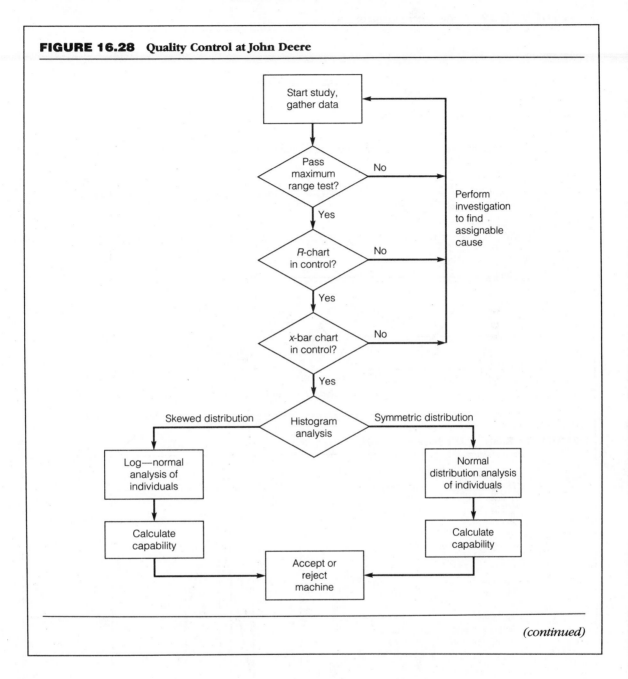

(continued)

FIGURE 16.29 CAIR System Control Analysis

Default select range used: 1 to 15

Number of pieces per sample: 3

Upper limit on x-bar: 875.400208
Average of x-bars: 875.275800
Lower limit on x-bar: 875.151917
R-bar/D2 estimate: 0.071666

Upper limit on R: 0.312424
Average of R's: 0.121330
Lower limit on R: 0.000000

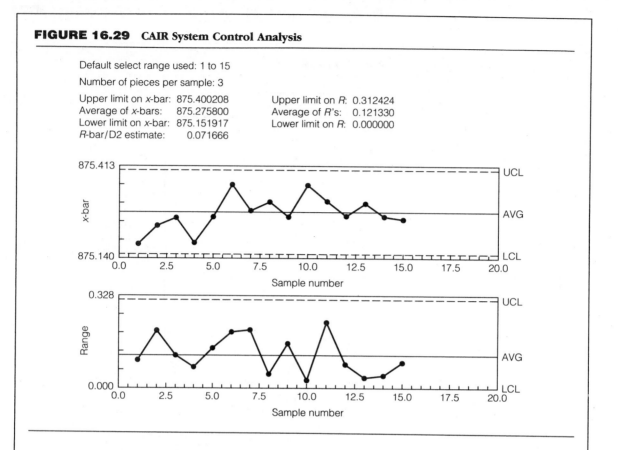

FIGURE 16.30 CAIR System Capability Analysis

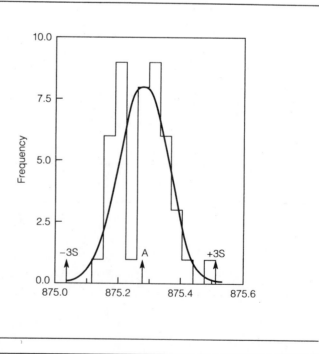

Normal probabilities
Nominal: 875.0000
+ TOL: 1.0000
– TOL: 1.0000
Sample size: 45

Probability predictions:
Process as is
% in spec: 100.00
% under: 0.00
% over: 0.00

Six sigma: 0.4758
Total tolerance: 2.0000
Capability ratio: 23.7900
Avg + 3S: 875.5138
Avg – 3S: 875.0379

Target: 875.0000
Average: 875.2758
Adjustment needed: –0.2758

Process after adjustment
% in spec: 100.00
% under: 0.00
% over: 0.00

Summary of Key Points

- Statistical process control (SPC) helps workers determine when to adjust a process and when to leave it alone. This reduces the incidence of Type I and Type II errors resulting from incorrect decisions.

- Overadjustment of a process actually increases the variation. This is an important fact that production workers must understand.

- Control charts have three basic applications: (1) establishing a state of statistical control, (2) monitoring a process to identify special causes, and (3) determining process capability.

- For variables data, $\bar{x}$- and R-charts are commonly used. For attributes data, the p-chart is used.

- A process is in control if no points are outside control limits; the number of points above and below the center line is about the same; the points seem to fall randomly above and below the center line; and most points (but not all) are near the center line, with only a few close to the control limits.

- Typical out-of-control conditions are represented as sudden shifts in the mean value, cycles, trends, hugging of the center line, hugging of the control limits, and instability.

- Modified control limits can be used when the process capability is known to be good. These wider limits reduce the amount of investigation of isolated points that would fall outside the usual control limits.

- In designing control charts, one must be concerned with how the sample data are taken, the sample size, the sampling frequency, and the location of the control limits.

- Successful implementation of SPC requires top management commitment; a project champion; an initial, workable project; employee education and training; and an accurate measurement system.

- Service organizations can benefit from the use of control charts. The difficult steps are identifying the appropriate variables or attributes measurements to track and helping users understand the nature of control charts outside of a manufacturing context.

Questions for Review and Discussion

1. What is statistical process control? What are the advantages of using it?

2. Discuss the two basic reasons for using SPC.

3. Why is it important for quality to be consistent in a production process?

4. What do we mean by the term *in statistical control?*

5. Explain the decisions and risks facing managers in process control decisions.

6. What are the disadvantages of simply using histograms to study process capability?

7. Discuss the three primary applications of control charts.

8. What is the difference between variables and attributes data? What types of control charts are used for each?

9. Briefly describe the methodology of constructing $\bar{x}$- and R-charts and establishing statistical control.

10. What does one look for in interpreting control charts? Explain the possible causes of different out-of-control indicators.

11. How should control charts be used by shopfloor personnel?

12. What are modified control limits? Under what conditions should they be used?

13. How are control charts used to determine process capability?

14. What is the difference between control limits and specification limits?

15. What risks and costs are involved in using control charts? Discuss guidelines for setting control limits that consider such risks and costs.

16. Explain the difference between defects and defectives.

17. Briefly describe the process of constructing a p-chart.

18. Discuss the concept of *rational subgroups*.

19. What trade-offs exist when selecting the sample size for a control chart?

20. Discuss the implications of control limit location in terms of Type I and Type II errors.

21. Explain the economic trade-offs that must be considered when designing a control chart.

22. What factors are necessary for successful implementation of SPC? Why?

23. Discuss applications of control charts to service organizations.

24. Discuss the lessons learned by Uniroyal in implementing SPC.

25. List 10 applications of control charts in service organizations that are not discussed in this chapter.

Problems

1. Thirty samples of size 3 listed in the following table were taken from a machining process over a 15-hour period.

Sample	Observations		
1	3.55	3.64	4.37
2	3.61	3.42	4.07
3	3.61	3.36	4.34
4	4.13	3.50	3.61
5	4.06	3.28	3.07
6	4.48	4.32	3.71
7	3.25	3.58	3.51
8	4.25	3.38	3.00
9	4.35	3.64	3.20
10	3.62	3.61	3.43
11	3.09	3.28	3.12
12	3.38	3.15	3.09
13	2.85	3.44	4.06
14	3.59	3.61	3.34
15	3.60	2.83	2.84
16	2.69	3.57	3.28
17	3.07	3.18	3.11
18	2.86	3.69	3.05
19	3.68	3.59	3.93
20	2.90	3.41	3.37
21	3.57	3.63	2.72
22	2.82	3.55	3.56
23	3.82	2.91	3.80
24	3.14	3.83	3.80
25	3.97	3.34	3.65
26	3.77	3.60	3.81
27	4.12	3.38	3.37
28	3.92	3.60	3.54
29	3.50	4.08	4.09
30	4.23	3.62	3.00

  a. Compute the mean and standard deviation of the data and plot a histogram.
  b. Compute the mean and range of each sample and plot them on control charts. Does the process appear to be in statistical control? Why or why not?

2. Thirty samples of size 6 yielded $\bar{\bar{x}} = 480$ and $\bar{R} = 34$. Compute control limits for $\bar{x}$- and R-charts and estimate the standard deviation of the process.

3. Twenty-five samples of size 5 resulted in $\bar{\bar{x}} = 5.42$ and $\bar{R} = 2.0$. Compute control limits for $\bar{x}$- and R-charts and estimate the standard deviation of the process.

4. Use the following sample data and construct $\bar{x}$- and R-charts. The sample size used is $n = 4$.

Sample	$\bar{x}$	R	Sample	$\bar{x}$	R
1	95.72	1.0	11	95.80	0.6
2	95.24	0.9	12	95.22	0.2
3	95.18	0.8	13	95.56	1.3
4	95.44	0.4	14	95.22	0.5
5	95.46	0.5	15	95.04	0.8
6	95.32	1.1	16	95.72	1.1
7	95.40	0.9	17	94.82	0.6
8	95.44	0.3	18	95.46	0.5
9	95.08	0.2	19	95.60	0.4
10	95.50	0.6	20	95.74	0.6

5. In testing the resistance of a component used in a microcomputer, the following data were obtained:

Sample	Observations		
1	414	388	402
2	408	382	406
3	396	402	392
4	390	398	362
5	398	442	436
6	400	400	414
7	444	390	410
8	430	372	362
9	376	398	382
10	342	400	402
11	400	402	384
12	408	414	388
13	382	430	400
14	402	409	400
15	399	424	413
16	460	375	445
17	404	420	437
18	375	380	410
19	391	392	414
20	394	399	380
21	396	416	400
22	370	411	403
23	418	450	451
24	398	398	415
25	428	406	390

Construct $\bar{x}$- and R-charts for these data. Determine if the process is in control. If not, eliminate any assignable causes and compute revised limits.

6. Construct $\bar{x}$- and R-charts for the following data. What conclusions do you reach?

Sample	Observations				
1	1.45	−0.15	−0.93	−1.55	−2.96
2	0.79	−1.02	−2.61	−0.85	−1.89
3	1.08	−0.54	−1.34	−2.03	−1.48
4	0.32	−0.41	−0.52	−1.87	−1.70
5	0.21	0.41	−1.09	−1.44	−2.34
6	−0.12	0.00	−1.56	−2.40	−1.19
7	1.66	−0.50	−1.62	−2.25	−2.87
8	−1.28	0.44	−2.29	−1.20	−1.75
9	−0.23	−1.41	−0.15	0.33	−2.61
10	0.65	−1.21	−0.54	−1.74	−1.59
11	0.55	−0.77	−2.08	−1.99	−1.72
12	−0.61	−0.40	−0.81	−2.07	−0.99
13	0.01	−0.50	−1.10	−0.71	−3.24
14	−0.46	−0.82	−1.28	−1.37	−2.05
15	0.80	−0.52	−1.77	−1.16	−2.09
16	0.84	−0.39	−0.16	−1.50	−2.47
17	0.41	−0.91	−2.04	−2.60	−1.26
18	−0.30	0.01	0.09	−1.12	−2.54

(continued)

Sample	Observations				
19	−0.16	0.44	−0.64	−1.94	−3.81
20	−0.83	0.59	−1.68	−2.73	−1.19
21	−0.02	−0.83	−0.68	−1.52	−1.58
22	−0.02	0.81	−1.42	−1.62	−2.97
23	1.26	−0.64	−0.44	−0.73	−1.80
24	0.00	1.13	−1.09	−2.04	−1.89
25	−0.13	−0.27	−1.41	−1.40	−3.55
26	−0.66	−0.97	−0.75	−2.13	−1.73
27	1.21	−0.28	0.33	−2.38	−1.61
28	−0.98	0.40	−1.85	−2.40	−2.89
29	0.39	−0.12	−1.55	−3.99	−2.49
30	−0.45	0.63	−1.57	−2.36	−3.26

7. General Hydraulics, Inc., is a manufacturer of hydraulic machine tools. It has had a history of leakage trouble resulting from a certain critical fitting. Twenty-five samples of machined parts were selected, one per shift, and the diameter of the fitting was measured. The results are given in the following table:

Sample	Diameter Measurement (cm) Observations			
	1	2	3	4
1	10.94	10.64	10.88	10.70
2	10.66	10.66	10.68	10.68
3	10.68	10.68	10.62	10.68
4	10.03	10.42	10.48	11.06
5	10.70	10.46	10.76	10.80
6	10.38	10.74	10.62	10.54
7	10.46	10.90	10.52	10.74
8	10.66	10.04	10.58	11.04
9	10.50	10.44	10.74	10.66
10	10.58	10.64	10.60	10.26
11	10.80	10.36	10.60	10.22
12	10.42	10.36	10.72	10.68
13	10.52	10.70	10.62	10.58
14	11.04	10.58	10.42	10.36
15	10.52	10.40	10.60	10.40
16	10.38	10.02	10.60	10.60
17	10.56	10.68	10.78	10.34
18	10.58	10.50	10.48	10.60
19	10.42	10.74	10.64	10.50
20	10.48	10.44	10.32	10.70
21	10.56	10.78	10.46	10.42
22	10.82	10.64	11.00	10.01
23	10.28	10.46	10.82	10.84
24	10.64	10.56	10.92	10.54
25	10.84	10.68	10.44	10.68

a. Construct control charts for these data.

b. It was discovered that the regular machine operator was absent when samples 4, 8, 14, and 22 were taken. How will this affect the results in part (a)?

c. The following table represents measurements taken during the next 10 shifts. What information does this provide to the quality-control manager?

Additional Sample	Observations			
	1	2	3	4
1	10.40	10.76	10.54	10.64
2	10.60	10.28	10.74	10.86
3	10.56	10.58	10.64	10.70
4	10.70	10.60	10.74	10.52
5	11.02	10.36	10.90	11.02
6	10.68	10.38	10.22	10.32
7	10.64	10.56	10.82	10.80
8	10.28	10.62	10.40	10.70
9	10.50	10.88	10.58	10.54
10	10.36	10.44	10.40	10.66

8. Discuss the interpretation of each of the following control charts:

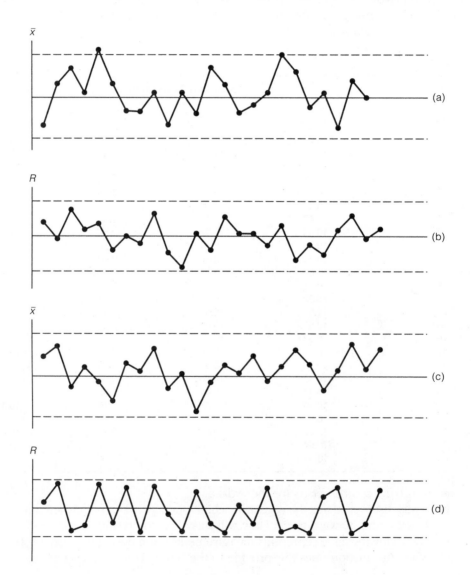

9. For each of the following control charts, assume that the process has been operating in statistical control for some time. What conclusions should the operators reach at this point?

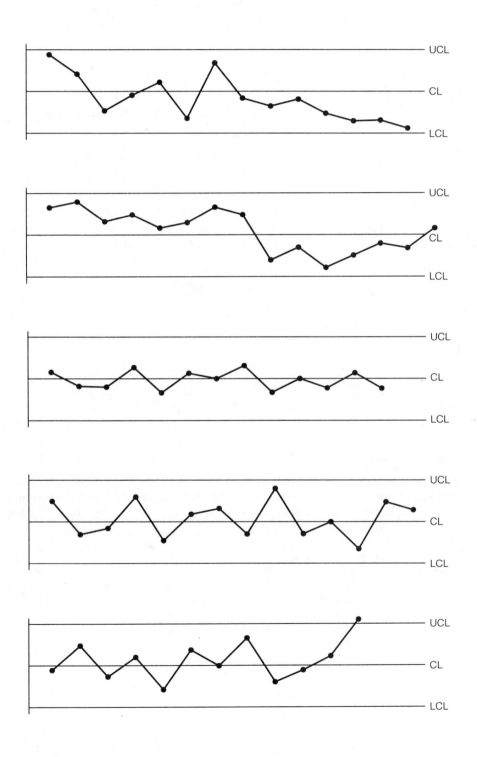

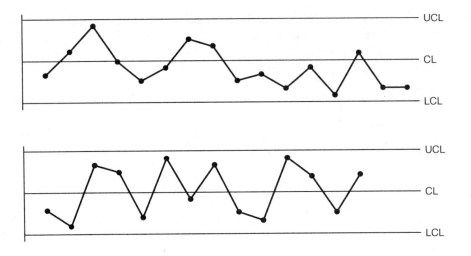

10. Consider the following 10 samples of size 5. Compute control limits for $\bar{x}$- and R-charts using the statistic $\bar{R}/d_2$ as an estimate of the standard deviation. Then construct the chart and plot the data, interpreting the results.

Sample	Observations				
1	0.077	0.080	0.078	0.072	0.078
2	0.076	0.079	0.073	0.074	0.073
3	0.076	0.077	0.072	0.076	0.074
4	0.074	0.078	0.075	0.077	0.077
5	0.080	0.073	0.075	0.076	0.074
6	0.078	0.081	0.079	0.076	0.076
7	0.075	0.077	0.075	0.076	0.077
8	0.079	0.075	0.078	0.077	0.076
9	0.076	0.075	0.074	0.075	0.075
10	0.071	0.073	0.071	0.070	0.073

11. For problem 10, estimate the process capability by using both the sample standard deviation and $\bar{R}/d_2$. Why is there a difference?

12. Suppose that a process is normally distributed and that the following sample means and ranges have been computed for eight samples of size 5. Determine process capability limits. If specifications are determined to be 46 ± 5, what percentage will be out of specification?

Sample	$\bar{x}$	R
1	51.6	5.2
2	40.1	7.1
3	42.3	5.4
4	48.9	5.0
5	36.5	6.3
6	53.1	3.9
7	47.3	4.8
8	49.6	5.9

13. Estimate the standard deviation of the individuals from the control chart constructed in Problem 5.

14. Suppose that in Problem 5, USL = 500 and LSL = 300. Compute the process capability and the modified control limits.

15. Twenty-five samples of 100 items each were inspected, and 68 were found to be defective. Compute control limits for a p-chart.

16. The fraction defective for an automotive piston is given here for 20 samples. Two hundred units are inspected each day. Construct a p-chart and interpret the results.

Sample	Fraction Defective	Sample	Fraction Defective
1	0.11	11	0.16
2	0.16	12	0.23
3	0.12	13	0.15
4	0.10	14	0.12
5	0.09	15	0.11
6	0.12	16	0.11
7	0.12	17	0.14
8	0.15	18	0.16
9	0.09	19	0.10
10	0.13	20	0.13

17. One hundred insurance claim forms are inspected daily over 25 working days, and the number of forms with errors have been recorded in the following table. Construct a p-chart. If any points occur outside the control limits, assume that assignable causes have been determined. Then construct a revised chart.

Day	Number Defective	Day	Number Defective
1	3	14	4
2	3	15	1
3	3	16	2
4	2	17	4
5	0	18	0
6	3	19	1
7	0	20	1
8	1	21	0
9	7	22	2
10	3	23	8
11	2	24	2
12	0	25	1
13	0		

18. Samples of size 100 have been randomly selected during each shift of 25 shifts in a production process. The data are given in the following table. Construct a p-chart and determine if the process is in control. If not, eliminate any data points that appear to be due to assignable causes and construct a new chart.

Sample	Number of Defectives	Sample	Number of Defectives
1	10	14	16
2	14	15	13
3	22	16	18
4	17	17	20
5	27	18	23
6	42	19	27
7	49	20	59
8	36	21	52
9	17	22	25
10	20	23	16
11	35	24	45
12	39	25	68
13	12		

19. A hospital surveys all outgoing patients by means of a patient satisfaction questionnaire. The number of patients surveyed each month varies. Control charts that monitor the proportion of unsatisfied patients for key questions are constructed and studied. Construct a p-chart for the following data, which represent responses to a question on satisfaction with hospital meals.

Month	Number of Patients	Number Unsatisfied
1	256	10
2	202	11
3	234	8
4	307	10
5	280	7
6	298	15
7	231	22
8	201	9
9	314	12
10	223	6
11	300	13
12	245	14
13	224	9
14	278	16
15	215	10
16	287	16
17	234	11
18	310	17
19	285	26
20	251	8

Case Problem

The Bell Vader Company, which produces heavy-duty electrical motors, machines a part called an end cap. To meet competitive pressures, the company began to apply statistical quality control to its processes. Because each motor produced by the company uses two end caps that could cost as much as $200 each, it is important that the process be brought under control. Figure 16.31 shows data collected to construct a control chart.

FIGURE 16.31 End Cap Control Chart

VARIABLES CONTROL CHART ($\overline{X}$ & R)

PART NO.	CHART NO.
21819	

PART NAME (PRODUCT)	OPERATION (PROCESS)	SPECIFICATION LIMITS
END CAP	BORE	3.9375 - 3.9380

OPERATOR	MACHINE	GAGE	UNIT OF MEASURE	ZERO EQUALS
		BORE GAUGE	.0000	

		1	2	3	4	5	6	7	8	9	10	11	12	13	14	15	16	17	18	19	20	21	22	23	24	25
DATE																										
TIME				12	19						12	20					12	15								
SAMPLE MEASUREMENTS	1	75	77	76	76	70	73	77	75	78	76	70	81	79	74	76	80	75	80							
	2	76	80	76	78	76	72	78	76	79	77	78	77	76	84	82	81	84	75							
	3	77	79	82	70	77	82	79	79	80	81	75	78	78	79	74	75	78	75							
	4	79	83	74	73	78	75	77	70	76	81	76	76	70	84	81	78	80	76							
	5	75	80	75	76	74	74	75	75	71	75	80	80	70	75	75	76	74	70							
SUM																										
AVERAGE, $\overline{X}$																										
RANGE, R																										
NOTES																										

AVERAGES

RANGES

Questions

1. Compute control limits and construct and analyze the $\bar{x}$- and R-charts for this process. What conclusions can you reach about the state of statistical control?

2. Using the control chart, estimate the process capability. Determine what percentage of end caps would be expected to fall outside specifications. What conclusions and recommendations can you make?

Bibliography

American National Standard, Definitions, Symbols, Formulas, and Tables for Control Charts, ANSI/ASQC A1–1987, American Society for Quality Control, 310 W. Wisconsin Ave., Milwaukee, WI 53203.

Brown, Bradford S. "Control Charts—The Promise and the Performance." Presented at the ASQC/ASA 35th Annual Fall Technical Conference, Lexington, Kentucky, 1991.

Mayer, Raymond R. "Selecting Control Chart Limits," *Quality Progress,* Vol. 16, No. 9, September 1983, pp. 24–26.

Montgomery, D. C. *Introduction to Statistical Quality Control,* 2nd Edition, New York: John Wiley & Sons, 1991.

Rosander, A. C. *Applications of Quality Control in the Service Industries.* New York: Marcel Dekker and ASQC Quality Press, 1985.

Squires, Frank H. "What Do Quality Control Charts Control?" *Quality,* November 1982, p. 63.

Vance, Lonnie C. "A Bibliography of Statistical Quality Control Chart Techniques, 1970–1980," *Journal of Quality Technology,* Vol. 15, No. 12, April 1983.

CHAPTER 17

Additional Topics in Statistical Process Control

The previous chapter introduced the fundamental concepts of statistical process control. It showed how control charts can be used to track process variation over time and signal the need for corrective action by identifying special causes. For variables data, $\bar{x}$- and R-charts were introduced; for attributes data, the p-chart was discussed. This chapter presents several other types of control charts for both variables and attributes data, as well as alternatives to the traditional $\bar{x}$- and R-charts. For readers interested in the theory behind control charts, we also discuss the statistical foundations for many of the charts and the rules used to interpret the charts. Since this material depends extensively on statistics, the reader is advised to refer to Chapter 12 when necessary.

SPECIAL CONTROL CHARTS FOR VARIABLES DATA

There are several alternatives to the popular $\bar{x}$- and R-charts for process control of variables measurements. This section discusses some of these alternatives.

$\bar{x}$ and s-Charts

An alternative to using the R-chart along with the $\bar{x}$-chart is to compute and plot the standard deviation s of each sample. Although the range has traditionally been used, since it involves less computational effort and is easier to understand by shopfloor personnel, there are advantages to using s instead of R. The sample standard deviation is a more sensitive and better indicator of process variability, especially for larger sample sizes. Thus, when tight control of variability is required, s should be used. With the use of modern calculators and microcomputers, the computational burden of computing s is reduced or eliminated and has thus become a viable alternative to R.

The sample standard deviation is computed as

$$s = \sqrt{\frac{\sum_{i=1}^{n}(x_i - \bar{x})^2}{n - 1}}$$

To construct an s-chart, we compute the standard deviation for each sample. Next, we compute the average standard deviation $\bar{s}$ by averaging the sample standard deviations over all samples. (Notice that this computation is analogous to computing $\bar{R}$.) Control limits for the s-chart are given by

$$\text{UCL}_s = B_4 \bar{s}$$

$$\text{LCL}_s = B_3 \bar{s}$$

where B_3 and B_4 are constants found in Appendix B.

For the associated $\bar{x}$-chart, the control limits derived from the overall standard deviation are

$$\text{UCL}_{\bar{x}} = \bar{\bar{x}} + A_3 \bar{s}$$

$$\text{LCL}_{\bar{x}} = \bar{\bar{x}} - A_3 \bar{s}$$

where A_3 is a constant found in Appendix B.

Observe that the formulas for the control limits are equivalent to those for $\bar{x}$- and R-charts except that the constants differ.

EXAMPLE 1   **Constructing $\bar{x}$- and s-Charts.**   To illustrate the use of the $\bar{x}$- and s-charts, consider the data given in Table 17.1. These data represent measurements of deviations from a nominal specification for some machined part. Samples of size 10 are used; for each sample, the mean and standard deviation have been computed.

FIGURE 17.1 $\bar{x}$-Chart

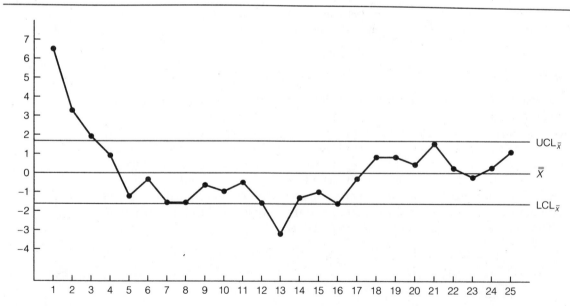

TABLE 17·1 Data for $\bar{x}$- and s-Chart Example

Data Row	1	2	3	4	5	6	7	8	9	10	11	12	13	14
1	1	9	0	1	-3	-6	-3	0	2	0	-3	-12	-6	-3
2	8	4	8	1	-1	2	-1	-2	0	0	-2	2	-3	-5
3	6	0	0	0	0	0	0	-3	-1	-2	2	0	0	5
4	9	3	0	2	-4	0	-2	-1	-1	-1	-1	-4	0	0
5	7	0	3	1	0	2	-1	-2	-3	-1	1	-1	-8	-5
6	9	0	-1	1	1	-1	-1	1	0	0	-2	4	-4	1
7	2	3	2	2	0	2	-3	-3	1	-1	-2	2	-6	5
8	7	4	0	0	-2	0	0	0	-3	-2	-1	-3	-1	-4
9	9	8	2	0	0	-3	-2	-3	-1	-2	1	-4	-1	-1
10	7	3	3	1	-2	0	-2	-2	0	0	1	0	-2	-5
Mean	6.5	3.4	1.9	0.9	-1.1	-0.4	-1.5	-1.5	-0.6	-0.9	-0.6	-1.6	-3.1	-1.2
Standard deviation	2.83823	3.13404	2.46981	0.73786	1.59513	2.50333	1.08012	1.43372	1.57762	0.87559	1.71269	4.52646	2.80673	3.91010

	15	16	17	18	19	20	21	22	23	24	25
	-1	-1	-2	0	0	1	1	-1	0	1	2
	-1	-2	2	4	3	2	2	0	0	0	2
	-1	-2	-1	0	-3	1	2	2	-1	1	1
	-2	0	0	0	3	1	-1	-1	0	-1	2
	-1	-4	-1	0	3	-3	2	2	1	1	-1
	0	0	-1	3	1	2	2	2	0	2	2
	-2	-2	2	0	0	-1	-1	-1	0	0	2
	-1	-4	-1	0	1	-2	-1	0	0	0	1
	0	-1	1	1	2	3	-1	0	-1	-1	-1
	-1	0	-2	0	-2	0	2	-1	0	0	2
Mean	-1	-1.6	-0.3	0.8	0.8	0.6	1.5	0.2	-0.1	0.4	1.2
Standard Deviation	0.66666	1.50554	1.49443	1.47572	2.09761	1.83787	0.52704	1.31656	0.56764	0.84327	1.22927

FIGURE 17.2 *s*-Chart

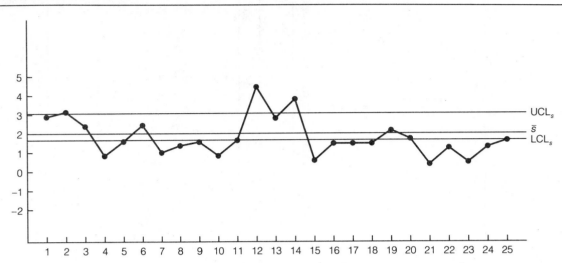

The average (overall) mean is computed to be $\bar{\bar{x}} = 0.108$, and the average standard deviation is $\bar{s} = 1.791$. Since the sample size is 10, we have $B_3 = 0.284$, $B_4 = 1.716$, and $A_3 = 0.975$. Control limits for the *s*-chart are

$$\text{LCL}_s = 0.284(1.791) = 0.509$$

$$\text{UCL}_s = 1.716(1.791) = 3.063$$

For the $\bar{x}$-chart, the control limits are

$$\text{LCL}_{\bar{x}} = 0.108 - 0.975(1.791) = -1.638$$

$$\text{UCL}_{\bar{x}} = 0.108 + 0.975(1.791) = 1.854$$

The $\bar{x}$- and *s*-charts are shown in Figures 17.1 and 17.2, respectively. It is evident that this process is not in control, and an investigation as to the reasons for the variation, particularly in the $\bar{x}$-chart, is warranted.

Charts for Individuals

With the development of automated inspection for many processes, manufacturers can now easily inspect and measure quality characteristics on every item produced. Hence, the sample size for process control is $n = 1$, and a control chart for *individual measurements* can be used. This is also called an *x-chart*. Other examples in which *x*-charts are useful include accounting data such as shipments, orders, absences, and accidents; production records of temperature, humidity, voltage, or pressure; and the results of physical or chemical analyses.

With individual measurements, we can estimate the process standard deviation and use three-sigma control limits. As we saw in Chapter 16, we use $\bar{R}/d_2$ as an estimate of the process standard deviation. Thus, an x-chart for individual measurements would have three-sigma control limits defined by

$$\text{UCL}_x = \bar{x} + 3\bar{R}/d_2$$

$$\text{LCL}_x = \bar{x} - 3\bar{R}/d_2$$

With samples of size 1, however, we do not have enough information to measure process variability. This can be determined by using a *moving average* of ranges, or a **moving range,** of n successive observations. For example, a moving range for $n = 2$ is computed by finding the absolute difference between two successive observations. The number of observations used in the moving range determines the constant d_2; hence, for $n = 2$, from Appendix B, $d_2 = 1.128$. In a similar fashion, larger values of n can be used to compute moving ranges. The moving range chart has control limits defined by

$$\text{UCL}_R = D_4\bar{R}$$

$$\text{LCL}_R = D_3\bar{R}$$

which is comparable to the ordinary range chart.

EXAMPLE 2   Constructing an x-Chart with Moving Ranges.   To illustrate; consider a set of observations measuring the percent cobalt in a chemical process as given in Table 17.2. The moving range is computed as shown by taking absolute values of successive ranges. Using the constants in Appendix B, we find

$$\text{LCL}_R = 0$$

$$\text{UCL}_R = (3.267)(0.377) = 1.232$$

TABLE 17.2   Individual Observations and Moving Ranges

Sample	Percent Cobalt	Moving Range	
1	3.75		
2	3.80	$0.05 = \lvert 3.80 - 3.75 \rvert$	
3	3.70	$0.10 = \lvert 3.70 - 3.80 \rvert$	
4	3.20	0.50	
5	3.50	0.30	
6	3.05	0.45	
7	3.50	0.45	etc.
8	3.25	0.25	
9	3.60	0.35	
10	3.10	0.50	
11	4.00	0.90	
12	4.00	0.00	
13	3.50	0.50	
14	3.00	0.50	
15	3.80	0.80	
	$\bar{x} = 3.517$	$\bar{R} = 0.377$	

FIGURE 17.3 Moving Range Chart

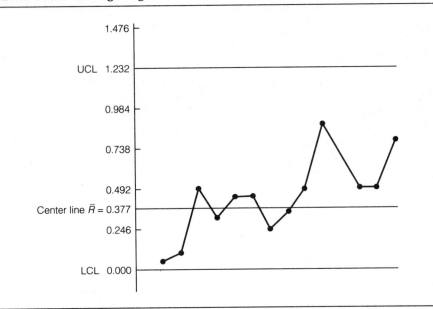

FIGURE 17.4 x-Chart for Individuals

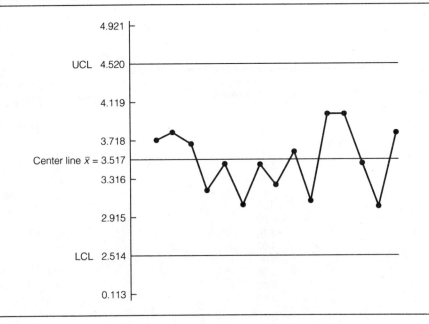

The moving range chart, shown in Figure 17.3 appears to be in control. We next construct the x-chart for the individual measurements:

$$LCL_x = 3.517 - 3(0.377)/1.128 = 2.514$$

$$UCL_x = 3.517 + 3(0.377)/1.128 = 4.520$$

This is shown in Figure 17.4 and also appears to be in control.

Some caution is necessary when interpreting patterns on the moving range chart. Points beyond control limits are signs of assignable causes. Successive ranges, however, are correlated, and they may cause patterns or trends in the chart that are not indicative of out-of-control situations. On the x-chart, individual observations are assumed to be uncorrelated; hence, patterns and trends should be investigated.

Moving averages of individual observations can also be computed and plotted like moving ranges. This is common in the chemical industry when batches of chemical are produced. Control limits are computed as for $\bar{x}$-charts. For example, using $n = 2$ in Table 17.2, we compute the moving average as shown in Table 17.3. For $n = 2$, we find in Appendix B that $A_2 = 1.880$. Therefore, the control limits for the moving average chart are

$$UCL_{\bar{x}} = 3.498 + 1.880(0.377) = 4.207$$

$$LCL_{\bar{x}} = 3.498 - 1.880(0.377) = 2.789$$

Note that these limits are tighter than those computed for individual measurements, since we are considering samples of size 2, whose sampling distribution has a smaller variance.

Control charts for individuals have the advantage that specifications can be drawn on the chart and compared directly with the control limits. Some disadvantages also

TABLE 17.3 Two-Sample Moving Average

Sample	Percent Cobalt	Moving Average
1	3.75	
2	3.80	3.775
3	3.70	3.75
4	3.20	3.45
5	3.50	3.35
6	3.05	3.275
7	3.50	3.275
8	3.25	3.375
9	3.60	3.425
10	3.10	3.35
11	4.00	3.55
12	4.00	4.00
13	3.50	3.75
14	3.00	3.25
15	3.80	3.40
		$\bar{\bar{x}} = 3.498$

exist. Individuals' charts are less sensitive to many of the conditions that can be detected by $\bar{x}$- and R-charts; for example, the process must vary a lot before a shift in the mean is detected. Also, short cycles and trends may appear on an individual's chart and not on an $\bar{x}$- or R-chart. Finally, the assumption of normality of observations is more critical than for $\bar{x}$- and R-charts; when this is not the case, there is greater chance for error.

Control Charts for Medians

Besides the mean, $\bar{x}$, the median, $\tilde{x}$, is another popular measure of central tendency and can be used as a statistic for controlling variables data. The median chart is often used for small sample sizes and is easier to use on the shop floor because it requires only a visual scan of the observations (for odd sample sizes). The formulas for control limits are as follows and use the factors given in Table 17.4:

$$UCL_{\tilde{x}} = \tilde{\tilde{x}} + A_5 \tilde{R}$$

$$LCL_{\tilde{x}} = \tilde{\tilde{x}} - A_5 \tilde{R}$$

where $\tilde{\tilde{x}}$ is the grand median (median of the medians) and $\tilde{R}$ is the median range. The mean of the medians, $\bar{\tilde{x}}$, can be substituted for $\tilde{\tilde{x}}$.

The range chart can be constructed using the median range $\tilde{R}$ instead of the average range $\bar{R}$. The control limits are

$$LCL_R = D_5 \tilde{R}$$

$$UCL_R = \tilde{\tilde{x}} - D_6 \tilde{R}$$

The range for each sample is plotted just as on the ordinary range chart.

The median chart is not as efficient from a statistical point of view as the $\bar{x}$-chart. Nelson notes that roughly the same amount of statistical information can be obtained from two-thirds as large a sample if the mean is used instead of the median.[1] He notes

TABLE 17.4 Factors for Computing 3σ Control Limits for Median and Range Charts from the Median Range

Subgroup Size	A_5	D_5	D_6	d_3
2	2.224	0	3.865	0.954
3	1.265	0	2.745	1.588
4	0.829	0	2.375	1.978
5	0.712	0	2.179	2.257
6	0.562	0	2.055	2.472
7	0.520	0.078	1.967	2.645
8	0.441	0.139	1.901	2.791
9	0.419	0.187	1.850	2.916
10	0.369	0.227	1.809	3.024

SOURCE: P. C. Clifford, "Control Charts Without Calculations," *Industrial Quality Control*, Vol. 15, No. 6, May 1959, p. 44.

---

[1]Lloyd S. Nelson, "Control Chart for Medians," *Journal of Quality Technology*, Vol. 14, No. 4, October 1982, pp. 226–227.

that the median is nevertheless better than no statistic at all. Thus, in some situations, the median chart can be a very useful tool.

EXAMPLE 3   Constructing a Median Chart.   Let us illustrate median charts using the silicon wafer data of Chapter 16 (Figure 16.5). The median for each sample is:

Sample	Median	Sample	Median
1	41	14	35
2	68	15	56
3	48	16	41
4	36	17	98
5	46	18	54
6	56	19	41
7	53	20	39
8	37	21	40
9	50	22	62
10	57	23	57
11	39	24	44
12	48	25	62
13	51		

The grand median is $\tilde{\tilde{x}} = 48$, and the median range is $\tilde{R} = 24$. For a sample size of three, $A_5 = 1.265$, $D_5 = 0$, and $D_6 = 2.745$. The control limits on the R-chart are

$$\text{LCL}_R = 0$$

$$\text{UCL}_R = 2.745(24) = 65.88$$

FIGURE 17.5 $\tilde{x}$-Chart

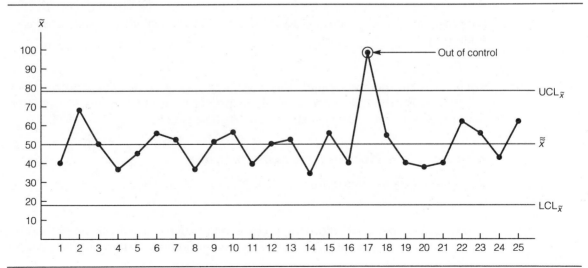

FIGURE 17.6 *R*-Chart

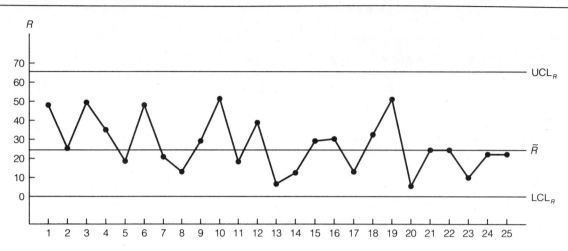

For the $\tilde{x}$-chart, we have

$$\text{LCL}_{\tilde{x}} = 48 - 1.265(24) = 17.64$$

$$\text{UCL}_{\tilde{x}} = 48 + 1.265(24) = 78.36$$

Figures 17.5 and 17.6 display the $\tilde{x}$- and *R*-charts for this example. The charts provide the same conclusions as the $\bar{x}$- and *R*-charts in Figure 16.7.

SPECIAL CONTROL CHARTS FOR ATTRIBUTES DATA

The *p*-chart, or fraction nonconforming chart, was discussed in Chapter 16 for process control of attributes measurements. Recall that the *p*-chart measures the proportion of nonconforming items produced in a lot. The fraction nonconforming of the ith sample is given by

$$p_i = y_i/n$$

where y_i is the number found nonconforming and n is the sample size. Many situations exist where it is not desirable or proper to use the *p*-chart. This section introduces variations of the *p*-chart used in such situations.

np-Charts for Number Nonconforming

If we multiply both sides of the equation $p_i = y_i/n$ by n, we get

$$y_i = np_i$$

That is, the number nonconforming is equal to the sample size times the proportion nonconforming. Instead of using a chart for the fraction nonconforming, we can use an equivalent alternative, a chart for the *number* of nonconforming items. Such a control chart is called a ***np*-chart.**

The *np*-chart is a control chart for the number of nonconforming items in a sample. To use the *np*-chart, the size of each sample must be constant. This is easy to see by considering the following situation. Suppose that two samples of sizes 10 and 15 each have four nonconforming items. Clearly, the fraction nonconforming in each sample is different, and this would be reflected in a *p*-chart. An *np*-chart, however, would indicate no difference between samples. Thus, equal sample sizes are necessary to have a common base for measurement. This need not hold for *p*-charts, since the fraction nonconforming is invariant to the sample size. Recall, though, that a *p*-chart with variable sample size will have variable control limits as explained in Chapter 16. Therefore, constant samples are much preferred.

The *np*-chart is a useful alternative to the *p*-chart because it is often easier to understand for production personnel—the number of nonconforming items is more meaningful than a fraction. Also, since it requires only a count, the computations are simpler.

The control limits for the *np*-chart, like the *p*-chart, are based on the binomial probability distribution. The center line is the average number of nonconforming items per sample. This is denoted by $n\bar{p}$, calculated by taking M samples of size n, summing the number of nonconforming items y_i in each sample, and dividing by M. That is,

$$n\bar{p} = \frac{y_1 + y_2 + \ldots + y_M}{M}$$

An estimate of the standard deviation is

$$s_{n\bar{p}} = \sqrt{n\bar{p}(1 - \bar{p})}$$

where $\bar{p} = (n\bar{p})/n$. Using three-sigma limits as before, the control limits are specified by

$$\text{UCL}_{n\bar{p}} = n\bar{p} + 3\sqrt{n\bar{p}(1 - \bar{p})}$$
$$\text{LCL}_{n\bar{p}} = n\bar{p} - 3\sqrt{n\bar{p}(1 - \bar{p})}$$

EXAMPLE 4   An *np*-Chart for a Post Office.   To illustrate the *np*-chart, we use the post office example discussed in Chapter 16. Table 16.3 showed the number of errors found in 25 samples of 100 letters over a month's period. We have

$$n\bar{p} = \frac{3 + 1 + \ldots + 0 + 1}{25} = 2.2$$

$$\bar{p} = \frac{2.2}{100} = 0.022$$

$$s_{n\bar{p}} = \sqrt{2.2(1 - .022)}$$
$$= \sqrt{2.2(0.978)}$$
$$= \sqrt{2.1516} = 1.4668$$

FIGURE 17.7 *np*-Chart for a Post Office

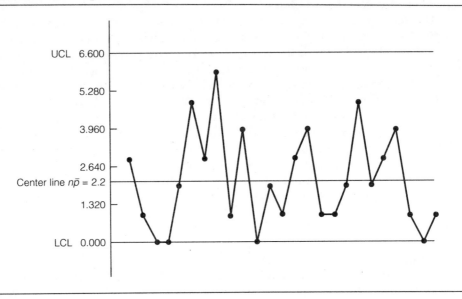

The control limits are then computed as

$$\text{UCL}_{n\bar{p}} = 2.2 + 3(1.4668) = 6.6$$

$$\text{LCL}_{n\bar{p}} = 2.2 - 3(1.4668) = -2.20$$

Since the lower control limit is less than zero, a value of 0 is used. The control chart for this example is given in Figure 17.7.

Charts for Defects

Chapter 16 made an important distinction between a *defect* and a *defective*. Recall that a defect is a single nonconforming characteristic of an item, while a defective refers to an item that has one or more defects. In some situations, quality assurance personnel may be interested not only in whether an item is defective but also in how many defects it has. For example, in complex assemblies such as electronics, the number of defects is just as important as whether or not the product is defective. Two charts can be applied in such situations. The **c-chart** is used to control the total number of defects per unit when subgroup size is constant. If subgroup sizes are variable, a **u-chart** is used to control the average number of defects per unit.

The c-chart is based on the Poisson probability distribution. To construct a c-chart, we must first estimate the average number of defects per unit, $\bar{c}$. This is done by taking at least 25 samples of equal size, counting the number of defects per sample, and finding the average. Since the standard deviation of the Poisson distribution is the square root of the mean, we have

$$s_c = \sqrt{\bar{c}}$$

Thus, three-sigma control limits are given by

$$UCL_c = \bar{c} + 3\sqrt{\bar{c}}$$
$$LCL_c = \bar{c} - 3\sqrt{\bar{c}}$$

To illustrate these computations, consider the inspection of the finish on a particular auto. Any surface imperfections, such as burrs in the body, scratches, and dents, are considered defects. A sample of 30 autos revealed a total of 81 defects. Thus,

$$\bar{c} = 81/30 = 2.7 \text{ defects/car}$$

Since $\sqrt{2.7} = 1.64$, the control limits would be

$$UCL_c = 2.7 + 3(1.64) = 7.62$$
$$LCL_c = 2.7 - 3(1.64) = -2.22 \text{ or } 0$$

Such a chart can be used for continued control or for monitoring the effectiveness of a quality improvement program.

As long as the subgroup size is constant, a c-chart is appropriate. In many cases, however, the subgroup size is not constant or the nature of the production process does not yield discrete, measurable units. For example, suppose that in an auto assembly plant, several different models are produced that vary in surface area. The number of defects will not then be a valid comparison among different models. In other applications, such as the production of textiles, photographic film, or paper, there is no convenient set of items to measure. In such cases, a standard unit of measurement is used, such as defects per square foot or defects per square inch. The control chart used in these situations is called a **u-chart.**

The variable u represents the average number of defects per unit of measurement, that is, $u = c/n$, where n is the size of the subgroup (such as square feet). We compute the center line $\bar{u}$ for M samples each of size n_i as follows:

$$\bar{u} = \frac{c_1 + c_2 + \ldots + c_M}{n_1 + n_2 + \ldots + n_M}$$

The standard deviation of the ith sample is estimated by

$$s_u = \sqrt{\bar{u}/n_i}$$

The control limits, based on three standard deviations for the ith sample, are then

$$UCL_u = \bar{u} + 3\sqrt{\bar{u}/n_i}$$
$$LCL_u = \bar{u} - 3\sqrt{\bar{u}/n_i}$$

Note that if the size of the subgroups varies, so will the control limits. This is similar to the p-chart with variable sample sizes. In general, whenever the sample size n varies, the control limits will also vary.

EXAMPLE 5 Constructing a *u*-Chart for Automotive Surface Defects. To illustrate, suppose that an automobile manufacturer produces two models in one of its assembly plants. The first is a compact that has a surface area of 11 square yards; the second is a mid-size model whose surface area is 15 square yards. Historical data have established that $\bar{u} = 0.25$ defect per square

TABLE 17.5 Number of Surface Defects in a Sample of Ten Autos

Sample	Size (n)	No. Defects, c	u = c/n	3-sigma	LCL	UCL
1	15	3	0.200	0.387	0.137	0.637
2	11	4	0.364	0.452	0.202	0.702
3	11	5	0.455	0.452	0.202	0.702
4	15	3	0.200	0.387	0.137	0.637
5	15	6	0.400	0.387	0.137	0.637
6	11	8	0.727	0.452	0.202	0.702
7	15	10	0.667	0.387	0.137	0.637
8	11	3	0.273	0.452	0.202	0.702
9	11	2	0.182	0.452	0.202	0.702
10	15	3	0.200	0.200	0.137	0.637

FIGURE 17.8 u-Chart for Surface Defects

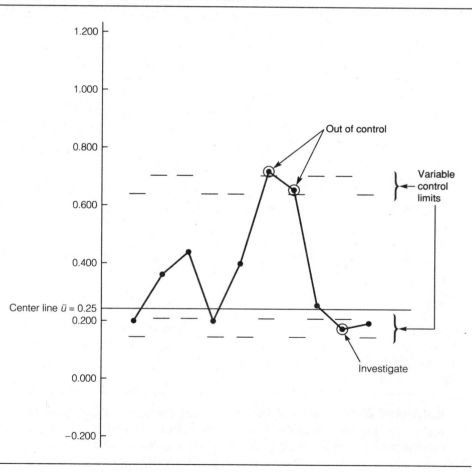

yard. Ten consecutive autos are inspected after painting. The number of defects found is recorded in Table 17.5. For each sample, the table also shows the upper and lower control limits. These limits and the sample value of the variable u are graphed in the control chart in Figure 17.8.

One application of c-charts and u-charts is in a quality rating system. When some defects are considered to be more serious than others, they can be rated, or categorized, into different classes. For instance,

A—very serious

B—serious

C—moderately serious

D—not serious

Each category can be weighted using a point scale, such as 100 for A, 50 for B, 10 for C, and 1 for D.[2] These points, or demerits, can be used as the basis for a c- or u-chart that would measure total demerits or demerits per unit, respectively. Such charts are often used for internal quality control and as a means of rating vendors and suppliers.

SUMMARY OF CONTROL CHART CONSTRUCTION

Table 17.6 summarizes the formulas used for constructing the different types of control charts we have discussed thus far.

TABLE 17.6 Summary of Control Chart Formulas

Type of Chart	LCL	CL	UCL
$\bar{x}$ (with R)	$\bar{\bar{x}} - A_2\bar{R}$	$\bar{\bar{x}}$	$\bar{\bar{x}} + A_2\bar{R}$
R	$D_3\bar{R}$	$\bar{R}$	$D_4\bar{R}$
p	$\bar{p} - 3\sqrt{\bar{p}(1-\bar{p})/n}$	$\bar{p}$	$\bar{p} + 3\sqrt{\bar{p}(1-\bar{p})/n}$
$\bar{x}$ (with s)	$\bar{\bar{x}} - A_3\bar{s}$	$\bar{\bar{x}}$	$\bar{\bar{x}} + A_3\bar{s}$
s	$B_3\bar{s}$	$\bar{s}$	$B_4\bar{s}$
x	$\bar{\bar{x}} - 3\bar{R}/d_2$	$\bar{\bar{x}}$	$\bar{\bar{x}} + 3\bar{R}/d_2$
np	$n\bar{p} - 3\sqrt{n\bar{p}(1-\bar{p})}$	$n\bar{p}$	$n\bar{p} + 3\sqrt{n\bar{p}(1-\bar{p})}$
c	$\bar{c} - 3\sqrt{\bar{c}}$	$\bar{c}$	$\bar{c} + 3\sqrt{\bar{c}}$
u	$\bar{u} - 3\sqrt{\bar{u}/n}$	$\bar{u}$	$\bar{u} + 3\sqrt{\bar{u}/n}$
$\tilde{x}$	$\tilde{\bar{x}} - A_5\tilde{R}$	$\tilde{\bar{x}}$	$\tilde{\bar{x}} + A_5\tilde{R}$
R (with $\tilde{x}$)	$D_5\tilde{R}$	$\tilde{R}$	$D_6\tilde{R}$

[2]H. F. Dodge and M. N. Torrey, "A Check Inspection and Demerit Weighting Plan," *Industrial Quality Control,* Vol. 13, No. 1, July 1956, pp. 5–12.

OTHER SPECIAL CONTROL CHARTS

Chapter 16 and this chapter have discussed a variety of control charts: $\bar{x}$ and $\bar{R}$, $\bar{x}$ and s, p, np, c, u, and charts for individuals and medians. Several other types of control charts are used in industry. This section briefly reviews three of them: exponentially weighted moving average charts, cumulative sum control charts, and zone control charts. The reader is encouraged to study more advanced books on statistical quality control for further details on these and other types of control charts.

EWMA Charts

The exponentially weighted moving average (EWMA) chart was introduced for applications in chemical and process industries in which only one observation per time period may be available. These are the same situations in which charts for individuals are used, except that the EWMA chart incorporates information on all the past data, not simply the last observation. The term *exponentially weighted* refers to the fact that the data are weighted, with more weight being given to the most recent data. (You may have studied exponential smoothing as a forecasting technique; the same principle applies.)

The statistic that is plotted on the chart is

$$z_t = \alpha \bar{x}_t + (1 - \alpha)z_{t-1}$$

Here, z_t is the exponentially weighted moving average after observation t is taken; $\bar{x}_t$ is the value of observation t; z_{t-1} is the previous exponentially weighted moving average; and α is a weighting factor between 0 and 1. This formula can be written in an alternative fashion:

$$z_t = z_{t-1} + \alpha(\bar{x}_t - z_{t-1})$$

which states that the current value of the statistic is equal to the previous value plus some fraction of the difference between the current observation and its last estimate. Note that when $\alpha = 1$, the formula reduces to the ordinary $\bar{x}$-chart.

The standard error of the exponentially weighted moving average is

$$\sigma_{zt} = \sigma_{\bar{x}} \sqrt{\frac{\alpha}{2 - \alpha}} = \frac{\sigma_x}{\sqrt{n}} \sqrt{\frac{\alpha}{2 - \alpha}}$$

Therefore the control limits are given by

$$\text{UCL}_z = \bar{\bar{x}} + 3\frac{\sigma_x}{\sqrt{n}} \sqrt{\frac{\alpha}{2 - \alpha}}$$

$$\text{LCL}_z = \bar{\bar{x}} - 3\frac{\sigma_x}{\sqrt{n}} \sqrt{\frac{\alpha}{2 - \alpha}}$$

The EWMA chart is more sensitive to small process level shifts than $\bar{x}$- or individual charts. The smaller the value of α, the easier it is to detect smaller shifts. This chart is useful when the acceptable process limits are very narrow. However, this sensitivity can lead to an excessive number of unnecessary adjustments to the process and, consequently, unnecessary costs.

Cumulative Sum Control Charts

The cumulative sum control chart (CuSum chart) was designed to identify small but sustained shifts in a process level much faster than ordinary $\bar{x}$-charts. Because it gives an early indication of process changes, it is consistent with the management philosophy of doing it right the first time and not allowing the production of nonconforming products.

The CuSum chart incorporates all past data by plotting cumulative sums of the deviations of sample values from a target value; that is,

$$S_t = \sum_{i=1}^{t} (\bar{x}_i - \bar{x}_0)$$

where $\bar{x}_i$ is the average of the ith subgroup, $\bar{x}_0$ is the standard or reference value, and S_t is the cumulative sum when the ith observation is taken. Note that when $n = 1$, $\bar{x}_i$ is the value of the ith observation.

The CuSum chart looks very different from ordinary $\bar{x}$ and R charts. In place of a center line and horizontal control limits, a "mask" is constructed that consists of a location pointer and two angled control limits as illustrated in Figure 17.9. The mask is located on the chart so that the point P lies on the last point plotted. The distance d and the angle θ are the design parameters of the mask. [We do not discuss how these are computed but refer the reader to Chapter 10 of Grant and Leavenworth or Chapter 7 of Montgomery (cited in the bibliography at the end of the chapter) for details.]

If no previous points lie outside the control limits, the process is assumed to be in control. If, for example, there is a shift in the process mean above the reference value, each new value that is added to the cumulative sum will cause S_t to increase and result in an upward trend in the chart. Eventually a point will fall outside the upper control limit, indicating that the process has fallen out of control (illustrated in Figure 17.10). The opposite will occur if the mean shifts downward.

FIGURE 17.9 CuSum Chart for Sample Averages

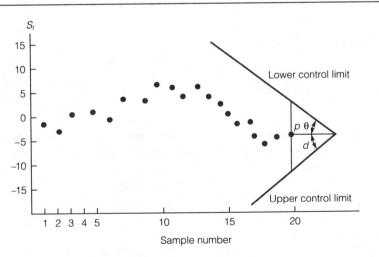

FIGURE 17.10 CuSum Chart Illustration of Lack of Control

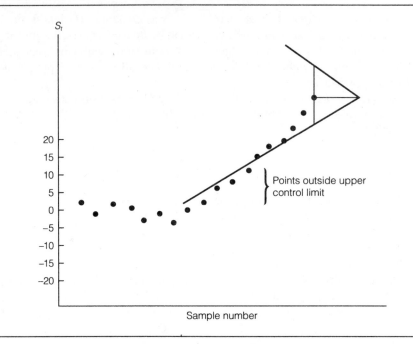

Zone Control Charts

A new type of control chart, called a *zone control chart,* has been proposed recently as a simpler alternative to the $\bar{x}$- and R-chart.[3] The $\bar{x}$- or R-chart is divided into eight zones as shown in Figure 17.11. As initially developed, scores are assigned to data points falling in each zone as follows:

Zone	Score
A	1
B	2
C	4
D	8

For the first data point, the score corresponding to the initial observed value is placed in a circle near the point. As new observations are plotted on the chart, the scores are added to the previous point *until* an observation falls on the other side of the center line. At this point, the score is reinitialized to that of the last observation. If the score for any point reaches or exceeds 8, then this is a signal that the process has gone out

[3]A. H. Jaehn, "Improving QC Efficiency With Zone Control Charts," *ASQC Chemical and Process Industries Division News,* Vol. 4, pp. 1–2; "Zone Control Charts—SPC Made Easy," *Quality,* October 1987, pp. 51–53; A. H. Jaehn, "The Zone Control Chart," *Quality Progress,* July 1991, pp. 65–68.

FIGURE 17.11   Zone Control Chart

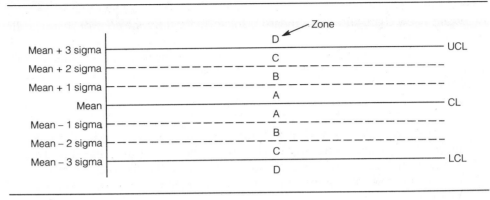

of control. Since the cumulative score determines when a signal is produced, no study of patterns or counts of points is necessary by personnel monitoring the chart. Thus, it is much simpler to analyze than traditional $\bar{x}$- and R-charts.

The concept behind the zone control chart is to allow for automatic signaling of the following out-of-control indicators in the Shewart chart:

1. a point falling outside the 3σ limits,

2. two of three successive points falling outside the 2σ limits on the same side of the center line,

3. four of five successive points falling outside the 1σ limits on one side of the center line, and

4. eight consecutive points falling on the same side of the center line.

A study of the performance of the chart has shown that it is only slightly better than using ordinary control chart interpretation rules.[4] In particular, the false alarm rate (Type I error) is very high, even though it detects shifts in the mean very quickly. However, a simple modification in which a score of 0 is assigned to points within one standard deviation of the center line greatly improves the performance of the chart, and actually outperforms charts analyzed using the standard interpretation rules. Thus, the following scoring system is recommended:

Zone	Score
A	0
B	2
C	4
D	8

Zone control charts provide several important benefits. They are easy to understand and use; the process of tediously seeking where to plot points is

[4]Robert B. Davis, Anthony Homer, and William H. Woodall, "Performance of the Zone Control Chart," *Communications in Statistics—Theory and Methods,* Vol. 19, No. 5, 1990, pp. 1581–1587.

eliminated; when to take action is automatically decided by the control charting procedure; changes in targets and control limits can be made easily without the need to rescale a new chart; and one standard blank form for the zone control chart usually meets all needs. Operators' acceptance of the zone control chart has been exceptional. The chart has been successfully used in production operations at Consolidated Papers, Inc. in Wisconsin, Lake Superior Paper Industries in Duluth, MN, and other companies.

EXAMPLE 6   Analyzing a Zone Control Chart.   We will illustrate the use of the modified zone control chart using the $\bar{x}$-chart from the silicon wafer example in Chapter 16. From Figure 15.6 we see that the range between the center line and the control limits is 27.6. Thus, the zones are partitioned as follows:

Zone	Range
D	>76.4
C	67.2–76.4
B	58–67.2
A	39.6–58 (center line = 48.8)
B	30.4–39.6
C	21.2–30.4
D	<21.2

The first point, 44, falls in zone A and therefore is assigned a score of 0. The second point, 66, falls in zone B. However, it is on the other side of the center line, so the process starts anew with its score of 2. The third point, 55, is in zone A; thus the cumulative score for this point is 2. Figure 17.12 shows the complete results. An out-of-control condition is signaled at point 17.

Pre-Control[5]

Pre-control is an alternative to $\bar{x}$- and R-charts that is useful for short manufacturing runs and in other applications in which operators do not have time to record, calculate, and plot data. A major advantage of pre-control is that it requires no recording, calculating, or plotting of data, and it relates directly to specifications.

The idea behind pre-control is to divide the tolerance range into zones by setting two *pre-control lines* halfway between the center of the specification and the tolerance limits (see Figure 17.13). The center zone, called the *green zone,* comprises one-half of the total tolerance. Between the pre-control lines and the tolerance limits are the *yellow zones.* Outside the tolerance limits are the *red zones.*

Pre-control is applied as follows. As a manufacturing run is initiated, five consecutive parts must fall within the green zone. If not, the production setup must be

[5]Robert W. Traver, "Pre-Control: A Good Alternative to $\bar{X}$-R Charts," *Quality Progress* (September 1985).

FIGURE 17.12 Zone Control Chart for Silicon Wafer Example

VARIABLES CONTROL CHART ($\bar{X}$ & R)

PART NO.				CHART NO.
PART NAME (PRODUCT) SILICON WAFER	OPERATION (PROCESS)		SPECIFICATION LIMITS 0-100	
OPERATOR	MACHINE	GAGE	UNIT OF MEASURE .0000	ZERO EQUALS

		1	2	3	4	5	6	7	8	9	10	11	12	13	14	15	16	17	18	19	20	21	22	23	24	25
DATE																										
TIME																										
SAMPLE MEASUREMENTS	1	41	78	84	60	46	64	43	37	50	57	24	78	51	41	56	46	99	71	41	41	22	62	64	44	41
	2	70	53	34	36	47	16	53	43	29	83	42	48	57	29	64	41	86	54	2	39	40	70	52	38	63
	3	22	68	48	25	29	56	64	30	57	32	39	39	50	35	36	16	98	39	53	36	46	46	57	60	62
	4																									
	5																									
SUM		133	199	166	121	122	136	160	110	136	172	105	165	158	105	156	103	283	164	96	116	108	178	173	142	166
AVERAGE, $\bar{X}$		44	66	55	40	41	45	53	37	45	57	35	55	53	35	52	34	94	54	32	39	36	59	58	47	55
RANGE, R		48	25	50	35	18	48	21	13	28	51	18	39	7	12	28	30	13	32	51	5	24	24	12	22	22
NOTES																										

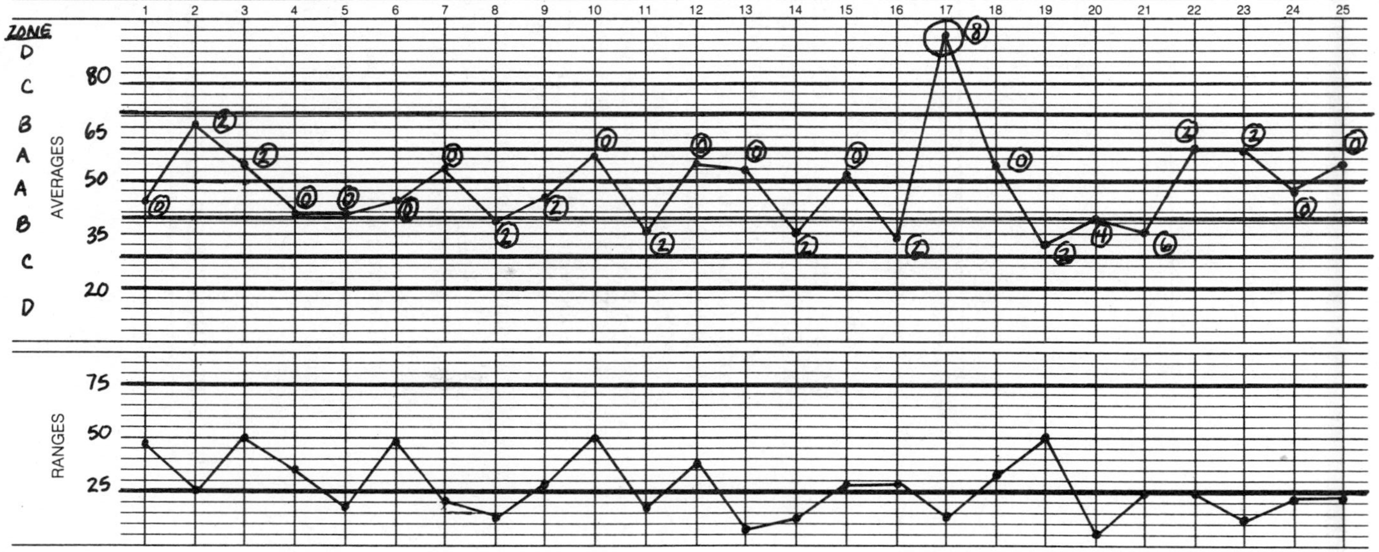

FIGURE 17.13 Pre-Control Ranges

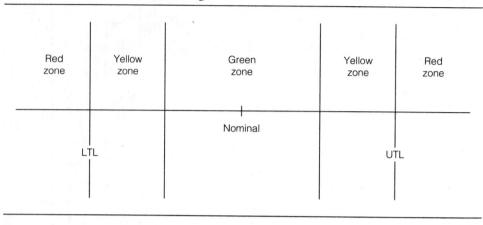

reevaluated before the full production run can be started. Once regular operations commence, two parts are sampled, and if the first falls within the green zone, production continues and there is no need to measure the second part. If the first part falls in a yellow zone, the second part is inspected. If the second part falls in the green zone, production can continue; if not, production should stop and a special cause should be investigated. If any part falls in a red zone, then action should be taken.

The rationale behind pre-control can be explained using basic statistical arguments. Suppose that the process capability is equal to the tolerance spread (see Figure 17.14). The area of each yellow zone is approximately 0.07, while that of the red zone is less than 0.01. The probability of two consecutive parts falling in a yellow zone is $(0.07)(0.07) = 0.0049$ if the process mean has not shifted. If $C_p > 1$, this probability is even less. Such an outcome would more than likely indicate a special cause. If both parts fall in the same yellow zone, you would conclude that the mean has shifted; if in different yellow zones, you would conclude that the variation has increased.

The frequency of sampling is often determined by dividing the time period between two successive out-of-control signals by six. Thus, if the process deteriorates, sampling frequency is increased; if it improves; the frequency is decreased.

FIGURE 17.14 Basis for Pre-Control Rules

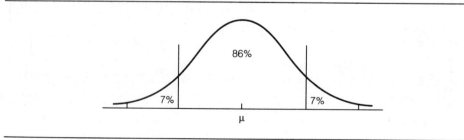

EXAMPLE 7 An Example of Pre-Control. The force necessary to break a wire used in electrical circuitry has a specification of 3 gm–7 gm. Thus, the pre-control zones are

Range	Zone
<3	Red
3–4	Yellow
4–6	Green
6–7	Yellow
>7	Red

The following samples were collected:

Sample	First Measurement	Second Measurement
1	4.7	
2	4.5	
3	4.4	
4	4.2	
5	4.2	
6	4.0	
7	4.0	
8	3.7	3.6
9	6.5	3.5

For samples 1 through 7, the first measurement falls in the green zone; thus no further action need be taken. For sample 8, however, the first measurement falls in a yellow zone. The second measurement also falls in a yellow zone. The process should be stopped for investigation of a shift in the mean. At the next time of inspection, both pieces also fall in a yellow zone. In this case, the probable cause is a shift in variation. Again, the process should be stopped for investigation.

Pre-control should only be used when process capability is no greater than 88% of the tolerance, or equivalently, when C_p is at least 1.14. If the process mean tends to drift, then C_p should be higher. Also, if managers or operators are interested in detecting process shifts even though the product output falls within specifications, pre-control should not be used because it will not detect such shifts.

STATISTICAL FOUNDATIONS OF CONTROL CHARTS

Control charts are defined by the center line, upper control limit, and lower control limit. These values are related to the expected value and variance of the statistics plotted on the charts. In Chapter 16 we saw that upper and lower control limits are specified through the use of certain constants given in Appendix B. This section shows how these factors are developed and discusses the statistical basis for the rules used to interpret control charts.

Variables Control Charts

When a process is in control, the distribution of *individual measurements* for variables data is assumed to have a mean μ and a variance σ_x^2. If a sample of size n is chosen, the sampling distribution of $\bar{x}$ will also have a mean μ but will have a variance $\sigma_{\bar{x}}^2 = \sigma_x^2/n$. If the original distribution of individuals is normal, the sampling distribution of averages will also be normal. If not, the central limit theorem states that the sampling distribution of averages will be approximately normal for large sample sizes. Since control chart samples are usually small ($n = 4$ or 5), we cannot always rely on the central limit theorem. However, normality is usually assumed in developing variables control charts.

Under this assumption, we expect $100(1 - \alpha)$ percent of the sample means to fall between $\mu - z_{\alpha/2}\sigma_{\bar{x}}$ and $\mu + z_{\alpha/2}\sigma_{\bar{x}}$; these values become the lower and upper control limits. We typically choose $z_{\alpha/2} = 3$. This gives a six-standard deviation range with $\alpha/2 \approx 0.0014$. Thus, only about 0.3% of the sample observations will be expected to fall outside these limits. If the process is in control, the likelihood that a sample will fall outside the control limits is extremely small. On the other hand, if the true mean has shifted, this probability will be much larger. This is the theoretical basis for assigning three-sigma control limits.

The value of $z_{\alpha/2}$ can, of course, be chosen arbitrarily. In the United States, the value of 3 is commonly accepted. In England, however, $z_{\alpha/2}$ is selected by first setting the probability of a Type I error; this is usually chosen as $\alpha/2 = 0.001$. Thus, $z_{0.001} = 3.09$ is commonly used to establish control limits. Such limits are called **probability limits.**

R-Chart. Let us first consider the *R*-chart. The range is used as a substitute for the standard deviation primarily because of its simplicity. As noted in Chapter 16, the factor d_2 in Appendix B is used to relate the range to the actual process standard deviation. The factor d_2 is determined as follows. Consider an experiment in which samples of size n are drawn from a normal distribution having a known standard deviation σ_x. If the range R of each sample is computed, the distribution of the statistic R/σ_x can be determined. The expected value of this statistic is the factor d_2, that is

$$E(R/\sigma_x) = d_2$$

or, since R is a random variable and σ_x is known,

$$E(R)/\sigma_x = d_2$$

This experiment can be performed for each n, and corresponding values of d_2 can be computed.

The hypothesis tested in the *R*-chart is $H_0: R = E(R)$. We estimate the expected value of R by the sample range $\bar{R}$. Thus $\bar{R}/d_2$ is an estimate of the process standard deviation σ_x. To establish control limits for an *R*-chart, we need to estimate the standard deviation of the random variable R, namely σ_R. From the distribution of the statistic R/σ_x, the ratio σ_R/σ_x can be computed for each n. This results in another constant d_3 that has been tabulated. We therefore have

$$\sigma_R = d_3 \sigma_x$$

If we now substitute the estimate for σ_x, $\bar{R}/d_2$, into this equation, we find that an estimate for σ_R is $d_3\bar{R}/d_2$. The control limits for the R-chart are based on three standard deviations about the estimate of the mean. Thus, we have

$$\text{UCL}_R = \bar{R} + 3d_3\bar{R}/d_2 = (1 + 3d_3/d_2)\bar{R} = D_4\bar{R}$$

$$\text{LCL}_R = \bar{R} - 3d_3\bar{R}/d_2 = (1 - 3d_3/d_2)\bar{R} = D_3\bar{R}$$

For convenience, the constants $1 + 3d_3/d_2$ and $1 - 3d_3/d_2$ are computed as D_4 and D_3, respectively. The control limits for the R-chart are therefore based on the distribution of the process standard deviation, adjusted to correspond to the range.

$\bar{x}$-Chart. Let us now turn our attention to the $\bar{x}$-chart. The statistic $\bar{\bar{x}}$ is an estimate of the population mean μ. Since $\bar{R}/d_2$ is an estimate of σ_x, an estimate of the sample standard deviation is

$$\sigma_{\bar{x}} = \frac{\bar{R}}{d_2\sqrt{n}}$$

Three-sigma limits on $\bar{x}$ are then given by

$$\bar{\bar{x}} \pm \frac{3\bar{R}}{d_2\sqrt{n}}$$

By letting $A_2 = 3/d_2\sqrt{n}$, we have the control limits presented in Chapter 16:

$$\text{UCL}_x = \bar{\bar{x}} + A_2\bar{R}$$

$$\text{LCL}_x = \bar{\bar{x}} - A_2\bar{R}$$

Fraction Nonconforming Control Charts

The theory underlying the p-chart is based on the binomial distribution, since attributes data assume only one of two values: conforming or nonconforming. If p represents the probability of producing a nonconforming item and a sample of n items is selected, the binomial distribution

$$f(x) = \binom{n}{x} p^x (1 - p)^{n-x} \qquad x = 0, 1, 2 \ldots, n$$

gives the probability of finding x nonconforming items in the sample.

The sample statistic $\bar{p}$ is an estimate of the population parameter p. An estimate of the standard deviation σ_p is given by

$$\sigma_p = \sqrt{\bar{p}(1 - \bar{p})/n}$$

Three-sigma limits on the parameter p are therefore given by

$$\text{UCL}_p = \bar{p} + 3\sqrt{\bar{p}(1 - \bar{p})/n}$$

$$\text{LCL}_p = \bar{p} - 3\sqrt{\bar{p}(1 - \bar{p})/n}$$

The critical assumptions in using a p-chart are the constant probability of a defective and independence of the trials. If these assumptions cannot be assured, the p-chart is not appropriate. (A previous section contained examples of other attributes charts that are based on different assumptions.) There is no substantive difference in these formulas when standards are given. One simply replaces the estimate $\bar{p}$ by the known fraction nonconforming p in the preceding formulas.

Basis for Control Chart Interpretation Rules

The use of a control chart represents a statistical test of hypothesis each time a sample is taken and plotted on the chart. In general, the null hypothesis, H_0, is that the process is in control, and the alternate hypothesis, H_1, is that the process is out of control. Specifically, we are testing the hypothesis that the sample statistic used in the chart— $\bar{x}$, R, or p—is drawn from a population having specified parameters. For example, in an $\bar{x}$-chart, to determine whether or not the process mean has shifted, we can test the hypothesis.

$$H_0: \mu = \mu_0$$

against the alternative hypothesis

$$H_1: \mu \neq \mu_0$$

where μ is the population mean and μ_0 is a specified value. Other hypotheses—for example, that the distribution is normal or the pattern above and below the center line is random—can also be tested.

Chapter 16 presented several rules based on such hypotheses for analyzing and interpreting control charts. For example, a point outside the control limits indicates the possibility that the process is out of control. Under the normality assumption, there is a 0.9973 probability that any sample value will fall within three-sigma limits. Thus, under H_0, there is only a $1 - 0.9973 = 0.0027$ probability of exceeding these limits. Unless the process mean, range, or fraction nonconforming has shifted, it will be highly unlikely that a point will fall outside the control limits. There is a chance, however remote, that the process is still under control even though a sample point falls outside the control limits. Since we would conclude that the process is out of control, this is the probability of a Type I error.

A second rule for interpreting control charts discussed in Chapter 16 was that about two-thirds of the points should fall within the middle one-third of the region between the control limits. This follows from the normality assumption. We know that about 68% of a normal distribution falls within one standard deviation on either side of the mean (see Figure 17.15). Therefore, if the process is in control and all samples

FIGURE 17.15   **Area under the Normal Curve within One Standard Deviation of the Mean**

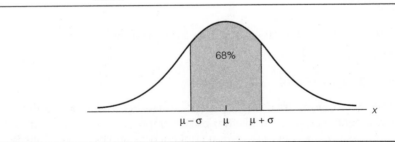

are chosen from a common population, this should be true. If, however, there has been a shift in the value of the population parameter, the distribution of sample statistics will also change. In such a case, we seek an assignable cause.

Another significant indication of an out-of-control situation is the presence of patterns in the control chart over time. If the process is in control, the distribution of sample values should be randomly distributed above and below the center line. A disproportionate number of points either above or below the center line should be suspect. For example, the probability that a point will fall either above or below the center line is 0.5. The probability of obtaining k successive points on one side of the center line is $(0.5)^k$. Thus, the probability that eight consecutive points will fall on one side of the center line is only $(0.5)^8 = 0.0039$. The probability that 10 of 11 consecutive points will fall on one side of the center line can be computed using the binomial formula:

$$f(10) = \binom{11}{10}(0.5)^{10}(0.5)^1 = 0.00537$$

If the process is in control, either of these events is highly unlikely.

The rules of thumb presented in Chapter 16 are based on statistical theories of randomness. Sample data collected over time are not random if there is a dependency between successive values. Statistical tests for randomness can be performed that verify if the observations obtained are similar to what might be expected from a truly random sequence. One such test is a nonparametric procedure called the **number-of-runs test.**

The number-of-runs test is used when sample data can be separated into two mutually exclusive categories. Let a denote the event that the sample belongs to the first category and b the event that it belongs to the second. A **run** is a string of consecutive a's or b's. Thus the sequence

aababbbaabbbbabaaabaabbb

consists of 12 runs, six runs of a's and six runs of b's.

The test for randomness is based on the number of runs. If there are n_a a's and n_b b's, one can show that if n_a and n_b are greater than or equal to 10, the sampling distribution of the random variable T, the total number of runs, is approximately normal with mean

$$\mu = E(T) = \frac{2n_a n_b}{n_a + n_b} + 1$$

and variance

$$\sigma^2 = \text{var}(T) = \frac{2n_a n_b(2n_a n_b - n_a - n_b)}{(n_a + n_b)^2(n_a + n_b - 1)}$$

The standardized variable $z = (T - \mu)/\sigma$ can be used in a two-tailed test of the hypothesis:

H_0: the sequence is random

H_1: the sequence is not random

where T is the observed number of runs. If z falls above or below the critical values of the normal distribution for a specified Type I error, the hypothesis is rejected.

FIGURE 17.16 A Run of Seven Consecutive Observations Up

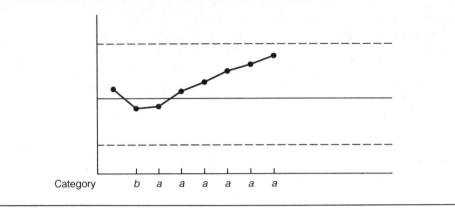

In a control chart, category a can represent sample points that fall *above* the previous point, and category b can represent sample points that fall *below* the previous point. The number-of-runs test can be applied directly to the number of runs up and down that are observed. To illustrate, let us use this test (as an approximate test of the hypothesis) to determine if the pattern in Figure 17.16 appears to be random. The figure shows a run of seven consecutive points up and, according to our heuristics, indicates a lack of control. The second point is below the first, so we assign it to category b; the remaining points are above the previous ones, so each is assigned to category a. We have $n_a = 6$ and $n_b = 1$. Using the formulas above, we have $E(T) = 2.714$ and $var(T) = 0.204$. Since there are two runs, $T = 2$ and $z = (2 - 2.714)/(0.204) = -3.5$. For a level of significance of 0.05, this value of z falls well beyond the critical value of $z_{0.025} = 1.96$; therefore, we reject the null hypothesis of randomness.

We have not examined every rule that was presented in Chapter 16, but these examples have shown how some of the interpretive rules of thumb in common practice are derived through fundamental principles of statistics.

Using a u-Chart in a Receiving Process[6]

Cincinnati Belting and Transmission is a distributor of electrical and power transmission products. The company began to implement a Total Quality Management process in early 1990. One manager was eager to collect data about the organization's receiving process because of a decrease in the organization's on-time delivery process. The manager suspected that the data entry person in the purchasing department was not entering data in the computer in a timely fashion; consequently, packages could not be properly processed for subsequent shipping to the customer. A preliminary analysis indicated that the manager's notion was inaccurate. In fact, the manager was able to see that the data entry person was doing an excellent job. The analysis showed that the handling of packages that were actually destined for a branch operation in the same fashion as other packages created significant delays. A simple process

TABLE 17.6 Packing Slip Error Counts

Date	Packing Slips	Errors	Date	Packing Slips	Errors
21 Jan	87	15	4 Mar	92	8
22 Jan	79	13	5 Mar	69	13
23 Jan	92	23	6 Mar	86	6
24 Jan	84	3	9 Mar	85	13
27 Jan	73	7	10 Nar	101	5
28 Jan	67	11	11 Mar	87	5
29 Jan	73	8	12 Mar	71	3
30 Jan	91	8	13 Mar	83	8
31 Jan	94	11	16 Mar	103	4
3 Feb	83	12	17 Mar	82	6
4 Feb	89	12	18 Mar	90	7
5 Feb	88	6	19 Mar	80	4
6 Feb	69	11	20 Mar	70	4
7 Feb	74	8	23 Mar	73	11
10 Feb	67	4	24 Mar	89	13
11 Feb	83	10	25 Mar	91	6
12 Feb	79	8	26 Mar	78	6
13 Feb	75	8	27 Mar	88	6
14 Feb	69	3	30 Mar	76	8
17 Feb	87	8	31 Mar	101	9
18 Feb	99	13	1 Apr	92	8
19 Feb	101	13	2 Apr	70	2
20 Feb	76	7	3 Apr	72	11
21 Feb	90	4	6 Apr	83	5
24 Feb	92	7	7 Apr	69	6
25 Feb	80	4	8 Apr	79	3
26 Feb	81	5	9 Apr	79	8
27 Feb	105	8	10 Apr	76	6
28 Feb	80	8	13 Apr	92	7
2 Mar	82	5	14 Apr	80	4
3 Mar	75	3	15 Apr	78	8

[6]We are grateful to Mr. Rick Casey for supplying this application.

(continued)

change of placing a branch designation letter in front of the purchase order number communicated to the receiving clerk to place those packages on a separate skid for delivery to where they should be received.

However, this analysis revealed a variety of other problems. Generally, anywhere from 65 to 110 packing slips are processed on a daily basis. These were found to contain many other errors in addition to the wrong destination designation that contributed to the delays. These included:

- wrong purchase order
- wrong quantity
- purchase order not on the system
- original order not on the system
- parts do not match
- purchase order was entered incorrectly

- double shipment
- wrong parts
- no purchase order

Many packing slips contained multiple errors. Table 17.6 shows the number of packing slips and total errors during early 1992. A u-chart was constructed for each day to track the number of packing slip errors—defects—found. A u-chart was used because the sample size varied each day. Thus, the statistic monitored was the number of errors per packing slip. Figure 17.17 shows the u-chart that was constructed for this period. (The change in the branch designation described above took place on January 24, resulting in significant improvement, as shown on the chart.)

Although the chart shows that the process is in control (since the branch designation change), the average error rate of over 9% still was not consid-

FIGURE 17.17 *u*-chart for Cincinnati Belting and Transmission Packing Slip Errors

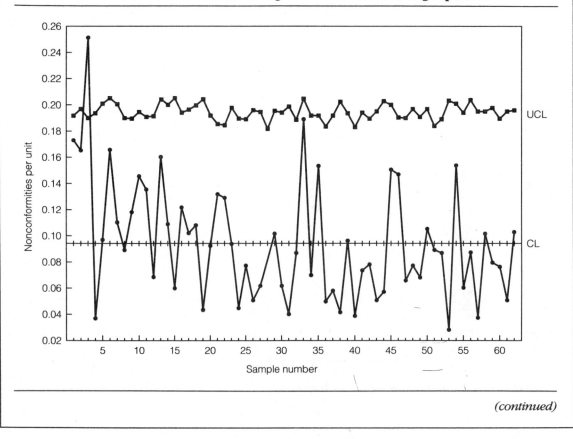

(continued)

FIGURE 17.18   **Pareto Analysis of Packing Slip Errors**

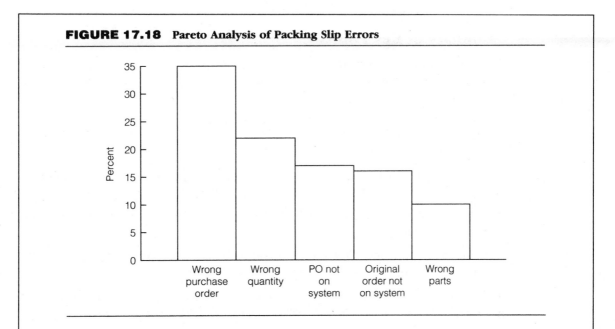

ered acceptable. After consolidating the types of errors into five categories, a Pareto analysis was performed. This analysis showed the following:

Category	Percentage
Purchase order error	35
Quantity error	22
No purchase order on system	17
Original order not on system	16
Parts error	10

This is illustrated in Figure 17.18.

The first two categories accounted for over half of the errors. The remedy for these problems was to develop a training module on proper purchasing methods to ensure that vendors knew the correct information needed on the purchase orders. The third category—no purchase order on the computer system—caused receiving personnel to stage the orders until an investigation could find the necessary information. This led the company to realize that the original order-writing process needed to be revamped. Specifically, the order-writing and purchase order activities needed to be improved.

An analysis of the control chart in Figure 17.17 shows that the average error rate has gradually improved. To a large extent, this was due to the recognition of the problems and improved communication among the constituents. While the full training program has not been implemented at the time this case was written, the company believes that a significant reduction in the error rate will result once the training is completed.

Key Issues for Discussion

1. Verify the computation of the center line and control limits in Figure 17.17.

2. What information might a separate chart for each error category provide? Would you recommend spending the time and effort to do this?

Summary of Key Points

- $\bar{x}$- and s-charts are alternatives to $\bar{x}$- and R-charts for larger sample sizes. The sample standard deviation provides a better indication of process variability than the range.

- Individuals charts are useful when every item can be inspected and when a long lead time exists for producing an item. Moving ranges are used to measure the variability in individuals charts.

- Charts for medians are often used for small sample sizes and are easier to implement on the factory floor.

- The np-chart is an alternative to the p-chart, and controls the number nonconforming for attributes data.

- Charts for defects include the c-chart and u-chart. The c-chart is used for constant sample size while the u-chart is used for variable sample size.

- Additional charts used in special situations include exponentially weighted moving average charts, cumulative sum control charts, and zone control charts.

- Pre-control is useful for short manufacturing runs and in applications in which operators do not have the time to construct conventional control charts.

- Rules for control chart interpretation that were presented in Chapter 16 are based on simple arguments from probability and statistics.

Questions for Review and Discussion

1. Why is the s-chart sometimes used in place of the R-chart?

2. Describe some situations in which a chart for individual measurements would be used.

3. Explain the concept of a moving range. Why is it difficult to interpret a moving range chart?

4. Why is a median chart easier to use on a factory floor than an $\bar{x}$-chart?

5. Does an np-chart provide any different information than a p-chart? Why would an np-chart be used?

6. Explain the difference between a c-chart and a u-chart.

7. Discuss how to use charts for defects in a quality rating system.

8. Explain the concept behind zone control charts. Why might it be preferred to the usual $\bar{x}$-chart?

9. Describe the use of pre-control. Why is pre-control not appropriate when process capability is poor?

10. Explain why three-sigma control limits are used in control charts.

11. What are probability limits and how are they used in control chart construction?

12. List the null and alternate hypotheses corresponding to the rules used in interpreting control charts.

13. Explain how the number-of-runs test is used in developing decision rules for determining out-of-control conditions in a control chart.

Problems

1. Suppose that the following sample means and standard deviations are observed for samples of size 5:

$\bar{x}$	s	$\bar{x}$	s
2.15	0.14	2.10	0.17
2.07	0.10	2.19	0.13
2.10	0.11	2.14	0.07
2.14	0.12	2.13	0.11
2.18	0.12	2.14	0.11
2.11	0.12	2.12	0.14
2.10	0.14	2.08	0.07
2.11	0.10	2.18	0.10
2.06	0.09	2.06	0.06
2.15	0.08	2.13	0.14

Construct $\bar{x}$- and s-charts for these data.

2. Construct an s-chart for the data given in Table 16.1.

3. Construct an $\bar{x}$- and s-chart for the data in Problem 1 of Chapter 16.

4. Construct an $\bar{x}$- and s-chart for the data in Problem 6 of Chapter 16.

5. Construct charts for individuals using both two-period and three-period moving ranges for the following observations:

   9.0, 9.5, 8.4, 11.5, 10.3, 12.1, 11.4, 11.4, 10.0, 11.0, 12.7, 11.3, 17.2, 12.6, 12.5, 13.0, 12.0, 11.2, 11.1, 11.5, 12.5, 12.1

6. Assume that the data in Problem 10 of Chapter 16 represent individual measurements instead of samples. Construct an x-chart and R-chart using a five-sample moving range.

7. Construct a median chart for the data in Problem 1 of Chapter 16.

8. Construct a median chart for the data in Problem 5 of Chapter 16.

9. Construct an np-chart for the data in Problem 17 of Chapter 16.

10. Construct an np-chart for the data in Problem 18 of Chapter 16.

11. Construct both a c-chart and a u-chart for a situation involving 25 samples of size 9 and having a total of 400 defects.

12. Consider the following data:

Sample	Number of Defects
1	4
2	15
3	13
4	20
5	17
6	22
7	26
8	17
9	20
10	22

Construct a c-chart for these data.

13. Find three-sigma control limits for a c-chart with an average number of defects equal to 9.

14. Find three-sigma control limits for a u-chart with $c = 9$ and $n = 4$.

15. Develop and analyze a zone control chart for Problem 1 of Chapter 16.

16. Develop and analyze a zone control chart for Problem 5 of Chapter 16.

17. Suppose that the specification limits for Problem 5 in this chapter are 9.0 to 12.0. Illustrate how pre-control would operate in this situation.

18. If control limits are based on 2.75 standard deviations, what percentage of observations will be expected to fall beyond the limits?

19. What are the probability limits corresponding to a Type I error of $\alpha = 0.04$?

20. Write a computer program to sample three observations from a normal distribution with mean 0 and variance 1. Use this simulation to estimate the value of d_2 in Appendix B and compare your result.

21. What is the probability of observing 11 consecutive points on one side of the center line if the process is in control? 10 of 11 points? 9 of 11 points? How many points out of 11 on one side of the center line would indicate lack of control?

Case Problem

Forty drivers deliver packages. A total of 240 mistakes were made in one year. The mistakes per driver varied from 0 to 24 as shown below:

Driver	1	2	3	4	5	6	7	8	9	10	11	12	13	14
Mistakes	6	1	0	14	0	2	18	2	5	13	1	4	6	5

Driver	15	16	17	18	19	20	21	22	23	24	25	26	27	28
Mistakes	0	0	1	3	15	24	3	4	1	2	3	22	4	8

Driver	29	30	31	32	33	34	35	36	37	38	39	40
Mistakes	2	6	8	0	9	20	9	0	3	14	1	1

The manager in charge of this operation has been issuing a "disciplinary citation" to drivers for each mistake.

(a) What do you think of this manager's approach? How does it compare with the Deming philosophy?

(b) Show how a control chart could be used to help this manager analyze the performance of this group of drivers. Explain how this can be used to reward good performance or provide a basis for improvement.

Bibliography

American National Standard, Definitions, Symbols, Formulas, and Tables for Control Charts, ANSI/ASQC A1-1987, American Society for Quality Control, 310 W. Wisconsin Ave., Milwaukee, WI 53203.

Grant, Eugene L., and Leavenworth, Richard S. *Statistical Quality Control,* 6th ed. New York: McGraw-Hill, 1988.

Montgomery, Douglas C. *Introduction to Statistical Quality Control.* New York: John Wiley, 1985.

Nelson, Lloyd S. "Control Charts for Individual Measurements," *Journal of Quality Technology,* Vol. 14, No. 3, July 1982, pp. 172–173.

Wadsworth, Harrison M., Stephens, Kenneth S., and Godfrey. A. Blanton. *Modern Methods for Quality Control and Improvement.* New York: John Wiley, 1986.

CHAPTER 18

Sampling Techniques for Quality Control

Inspection provides a means for controlling quality. We discussed the role of inspection in quality assurance in Chapters 8 and 13. Inspection is necessary to assess the quality of incoming materials, as a means of process control (as discussed in Chapters 16 and 17), and for verifying the quality of finished goods.

Since performing 100% inspection is generally not practical or economical, sampling is used. Sampling techniques in quality assurance form the subject of this chapter. We focus on the two principal uses of sampling: (1) estimating population parameters and (2) acceptance sampling. As we discussed in Chapter 8, many arguments exist against acceptance sampling; however, it is still used by many firms. Thus, it is useful to study the fundamentals.

SAMPLING PROCEDURES FOR STATISTICAL INFERENCE

The objective of statistics is to draw inferences about a population from information contained in a sample. Two factors affect the amount of information contained in a sample and, thus, the quality of the inferences drawn from the information. One factor is the method of selecting the sample. Various methods for sample selection exist. The most common method is simple random sampling. Other methods that we shall briefly discuss are stratified sampling, systematic sampling, and cluster sampling. The second factor is the sample size, which influences the precision of an estimate.

Practical Sampling Issues

Suppose that you worked in a 1,000-bed hospital and wanted to determine the attitude of a certain group of patients toward the quality of care they had received while in the hospital. Several factors should be considered before making this study:

1. What is the objective of the study?

2. What type of sample should be used?

3. What possible error might result from sampling?

4. What will the study cost?

One approach to tackling this problem would be to take a complete census—a survey of every person in the entire population. But it is important to first focus on the objective of the study to ensure that it is performed in an effective and efficient manner. This requires sensitivity to the needs of the user and an understanding of the strengths and weaknesses of the specific techniques being used. Would sampling work just as well? If the user needs the results next week to make a decision involving the expenditure of $1,000, the study will require a much different design from one where the expenditure is $1,000,000 and the decision will not be made for six months. Sampling provides a distinct advantage over a complete census in that much less time and cost are required to gather the data. In many cases, such as inspection, sampling may be more accurate than 100% inspection because of reduction of inspection errors. However, sampling is frequently subject to a *higher degree* of error.

The second issue relates to different methods of sampling. The following are some of the most common:

- *Simple random sampling:* Every item in the population has an equal probability of being selected.

- *Stratified sampling:* The population is partitioned into groups, or strata, and a sample is selected from each stratum.

- *Systematic sampling:* Every *n*th (4th, 5th, etc.) item is selected.

- *Cluster sampling:* A typical group (division of the company, for example) is selected, and a random sample is taken from within the group.

- *Judgment sampling:* Expert opinion is used to determine the location and characteristics of a definable sample group.

In choosing the appropriate type of sampling method, an analyst must consider what the sample is designed to do. A sampling study has a goal of selecting a sample at the lowest cost that will provide the best possible representation of the population, consistent with the objectives of precision and reliability that have been determined for the study.

Suppose that your objective is to provide a report to top management of the hospital to help them decide whether or not to expand the use of quality control measures within the hospital. Some issues that would have to be considered before choosing a sample would be the time frame for completing the study, the size and cost limitations of the sample, the accessibility of the population of patients, and the desired accuracy.

Assume that you have six weeks to complete the study, with a limited operating budget of $1,500, and that there are 800 maternity patients (the category in which you are interested) who could be involved in the quality study. Further assume that the accuracy of your study requires a sample of at least 400 patients and that the cost of each response would vary from $2 to $4, depending on how the survey is administered. Obviously, you would have to select a sample, since a complete census of all patients would not be feasible because of the budget limitation. Time limitations would make travel to conduct face-to-face interviews virtually impossible. Thus, the only feasible alternatives would be mailed questionnaires, telephone interviews, or a combination of the two.

Given this information, what type of sample should be chosen? Each type has advantages and disadvantages. A simple random sample would be easy to select but might not include sufficient representation by floor or ward. If a list of the patients, perhaps in alphabetical order, was available, a systematic sample of every fourth name could be easily selected. It would have the same disadvantages as the random sample, however. On the other hand, a cluster sample or judgment sample could be selected to include more representatives from floors or wards. However, cluster and judgment samples frequently take more time to identify and select appropriate sampling units. Also, because more subjective judgment is involved, it is more likely that a biased, nonrepresentative sampling plan would be developed.

The third issue in sampling relates to error. Errors in sampling generally stem from two causes: sampling error and systematic (often called nonsampling) error. Sampling error occurs naturally and results from the fact that a sample may not always be representative of the population, no matter how carefully it is selected. The only way to reduce sampling error is to take a *larger* sample from the population. Systematic errors, however, can be reduced or eliminated by design.

Sources of systematic error include the following:

- *Bias*—the tendency to see problems and solutions from one's own viewpoint.

- *Noncomparable data*—data that come from two populations but are erroneously considered to have come from one.

- *Uncritical projection of trends*—the assumption that what has happened in the past will continue into the future.

- *Causation*—the assumption that because two variables are related, one must be the cause of changes in the other.

- *Improper sampling*—the use of an erroneous method for gathering data, thus biasing results (for example, using telephone surveys to get opinions from a population having few phones).

Sources of error can be overcome through careful planning of the sampling study. **Bias** can be reduced by frequent interaction with end-users of the study as well as cross-checking of research designs with knowledgeable analysts. **Noncomparable data** can be avoided by a sensitivity to conditions that could contribute to development of dissimilar population segments. In the hospital example, data gathered from different floors, wards, or shifts could prove to be noncomparable. In production firms, different shifts, machines, or products may define different populations, even though the characteristics being measured are the same for each. **Uncritical projection of trends** can be avoided by analysis of the underlying causes of trends and a constant questioning of the assumption that tomorrow's population will be the same as yesterday's. **Reasons for causation** must be investigated. Relationships between variables alone is not sufficient to conclude that causality exists. Causation can often be tested by holding one variable constant while changing the other to determine effects of the change. Finally, **improper sampling** can be avoided by a thorough understanding of sampling techniques and determining whether the method being used is capable of reaching any unit in the population in an unbiased fashion.

Let us now turn to specific issues in sampling.

Simple Random Sampling

A *simple random sample* is a small sample of size n drawn from a large population of size N in such a way that every possible sample of size n has an equal chance of being selected. For example, if a box of 1,000 plastic components for electrical connectors is thoroughly mixed and 25 parts are selected randomly without replacement, we can see that we have satisfied this definition. Simple random sampling forms the basis for most scientific statistical surveys such as auditing and is a useful tool for quality assurance studies. Many statistical procedures depend on taking random samples. If random samples are not used, bias may be introduced. For instance, if the items are rolled in coils, sampling only from the beginning of the coil (a *convenience sample*) can easily result in bias if the production process that produced the coils varies over time.

Simple random samples can be selected by using a table of random numbers (see Appendix C). We assign a unique number to each element of the population. This might be accomplished by using serial numbers, by placing the items in racks or trays with unique row and column numbering, or by associating with each item a physical distance (such as depth in a card file). We then select numbers from the table in a systematic fashion, selecting as our sample the items that correspond to the chosen random numbers. We may begin at any point in the table and move in any direction, using any set of digits that serves our purpose. An illustration of the use of the random number table for simple random sampling follows.

EXAMPLE 1 Sampling Medical Patient Records. A particular nursing unit has 30 patients. Five patient records are to be sampled to verify the correctness of a medical procedure. To determine which patients to select, we assign numbers 1 through 30 to the 30 patients. Suppose we select the first row in Appendix C. We examine consecutive two-digit integers until five different numbers between 01 and 30 are found. (Any two-digit number greater than 30 is rejected since it does not correspond to an item in our population.) Thus, we have the following sequence of random numbers and decisions:

Number	Decision
63	reject
27	select
15	select
99	reject
86	reject
71	reject
74	reject
45	reject
11	select
02	select
15	duplicate
14	select

We therefore select patients 2, 11, 14, 15, and 27.

Simple random sampling is generally used to estimate population parameters such as means, proportions, and variances. Estimators for important population parameters for both variables and attributes data were reviewed in Chapter 12. The most common estimators uses in quality assurance are:

Sample mean: $\bar{x}$ (variables data)

Sample standard deviation: s (variables data)

Sample proportion: p (attributes data)

When we use $\bar{x}$ to estimate a population mean, for example, we also need to know how close the estimate is to the true population mean. The error due to sampling variability is given by the standard error of the mean. We use this to construct a confidence interval on the true population mean. The amount of error is determined by the sample size and is a critical issue in sampling.

Variables Data. Let us first consider the sample size when using $\bar{x}$ to provide a point estimate of the population mean. A $100(1 - \alpha)$ percent confidence interval on $\bar{x}$ is given by

$$\bar{x} \pm z_{\alpha/2}\sigma/\sqrt{n}$$

Thus, there is a $1 - \alpha$ probability that the value of the sample mean will provide a sampling error of $z_{\alpha/2}\sigma/\sqrt{n}$ or less. Let us denote this sampling error by E. Solving the equation

$$E = z_{\alpha/2}\sigma/\sqrt{n}$$

for n, we obtain

$$n = (z_{\alpha/2})^2\sigma^2/E^2$$

Thus, a sample size n will provide a point estimate having a sampling error of E or less at a confidence level of $100(1 - \alpha)$ percent.

To use this formula, we need to specify the confidence level (from which $z_{\alpha/2}$ is obtained); the maximum sampling error E; and the standard deviation σ. If σ is unknown, we need at least a preliminary value in order to compute n. We might either take a preliminary sample to estimate σ or use a good guess based on prior data or similar studies.

EXAMPLE 2 **Sample Size for a Process Capability Study.** A firm conducting a process capability study on a critical quality dimension wishes to determine the sample size required to estimate the process mean with a sampling error of at most 0.1 at a 95% confidence level. From control chart data, an estimate of the standard deviation of the process was found to be 0.47. To find the appropriate sample size, we have

$$n = (z_{\alpha/2})^2\sigma^2/E^2$$

$$= (1.96)^2(0.47)^2/(0.1)^2$$

$$= 84.86 \text{ or } 85 \text{ units}$$

Attributes Data. We next consider determining the sample size for estimating a population proportion for attributes data. A point estimate of the population proportion, p, is given by the sample proportion $\bar{p}$. The standard error of the proportion is

$$\sigma_{\bar{p}} = \sqrt{p(1-p)/n}$$

Thus, a $100(1-\alpha)$ percent confidence interval for the population proportion is

$$\bar{p} \pm z_{\alpha/2}\sqrt{p(1-p)/n}$$

The sampling error is given by $E = z_{\alpha/2}\sqrt{p(1-p)/n}$. Solving this equation for n provides the following formula for the sample size:

$$n = (z_{\alpha/2})^2 p(1-p)/E^2$$

To apply this formula, we need a prior estimate of p. If a good estimate is not known, we suggest using $p = 0.5$, since this value provides the largest sample size recommendation that guarantees the required level of precision.

EXAMPLE 3 Sample Size Determination for Attributes Data. Suppose that we wish to sample from a large finished goods inventory to determine the proportion of nonconforming product. Historically, we have found about 0.5% to be nonconforming. We wish to have a 90% confidence level with an allowable error of 0.25%. Thus, $E = 0.0025$, $p = 0.005$, $z_{0.05} = 1.645$.

$$n = (1.96)^2 0.005(1 - 0.005)/(0.0025)^2 = 3058$$

In some situations, certain activities are so critical that only a small number of nonconformances is tolerable. A typical example is in health care, where compliance with rigorous procedures must be adhered to 100% of the time. A nursing manager, for instance, will need to determine a sample size necessary to reveal at least one error in the sample if the population occurrence rate is equal to or greater than a specified critical rate of occurrence.

A technique used in such situations is called *discovery sampling*. Discovery sampling is a statistical sampling plan used for attributes where the expected rate of occurrence in most cases is zero, and the maximum tolerable rate of occurrence is critical and thus very small. Discovery sampling tables have been published for selecting the appropriate sample size.[1] An example is shown in Table 18.1. One must know the population size and critical rate of occurrence and must specify the desired confidence level. The table gives the probability of finding at least one occurrence in the sample.

---

[1] H. P. Hill, J. L. Roth, and H. Arkin, *Sampling in Auditing: A Simplified Guide and Statistical Tables* (New York: Copyright © Ronald Press 1962). Reprinted by permission of John Wiley & Sons, Inc.

TABLE 18.1 Discovery Sampling Table

	Critical Occurrence Rate						
	0.05%	0.1%	0.5%	1%	2%	5%	10%
Sample Size	Probability of Finding at Least One Occurrence						
		Population Size: 1,000					
10		1.0%	4.9%	9.6%	18.4%	40.3%	65.3%
25		2.5	11.9	22.5	40.0	72.7	93.1
50		5.0	22.7	40.3	64.5	92.8	99.6
100		10.0	41.0	65.3	88.1	99.6	100.0
200		20.0	67.3	89.4	98.9	100.0	100.0
400		40.0	92.3	99.4	100.0	100.0	100.0
		Population Size: 2,000					
10	0.5%	1.0%	4.9%	9.6%	18.3%	40.2%	65.2%
50	2.5	4.9	22.4	39.9	64.0	92.6	99.5
100	5.0	9.8	40.2	64.3	87.4	99.5	100.0
200	10.0	19.0	65.2	88.0	98.6	100.0	100.0
400	20.0	36.0	89.3	98.9	100.0	100.0	100.0
600	30.0	51.0	97.2	99.9	100.0	100.0	100.0

Adapted from: H. P. Hill, J. L. Roth and H. Arkin. *Sampling in Auditing: A Simplified Guide and Statistical Tables,* (New York: Ronald Press) 1962.

EXAMPLE 4 **An Application of Discovery Sampling.** Suppose that a nursing manager wants to be 95% confident of finding at least one incident where nursing personnel have failed to comply with a critical procedure. If 1,000 patient charts were prepared during the period under consideration and the critical rate of occurrence is 2%, Table 18.1 shows that 200 charts must be examined. If one occurrence is found in this random sample, the manager can conclude with 98.9% confidence that the quality of patient care in this area is unacceptable.

Other Types of Sampling Procedures

In this section we briefly discuss alternatives to simple random sampling. These methods have distinct advantages over simple random sampling in many situations.

Stratified Random Sampling. A *stratified random sample* is one obtained by separating the population into nonoverlapping groups, and then selecting a simple random sample from each group. The groups might be different machines, wards in a hospital, departments, and so on. For example, suppose that we have a population of 28,000 items produced on three different machines:

Machine	Group Size
1	20,000
2	5,000
3	3,000

Assume that we have determined that a sample of 525 units should be selected. We could draw these units randomly from the entire population. Under stratified random sampling, we might take a simple random sample of 250 units from machine 1, 150 units from machine 2, and 125 units from machine 3. Formulas are available for combining the results of individual samples into an overall estimate of the population parameter of interest. This will allow us to discover quality differences that may exist between machines.

Stratified random sampling will provide results similar to simple random sampling but with a smaller total sample size. It produces a smaller bound on the error of the estimation that would be produced by a simple random sample of the same size. These statements are particularly true if measurements within each group are homogeneous, that is, if the units within strata are alike.

Systematic Sampling. In some situations, particularly with large populations, it is impractical to select a simple random sample using random number tables and searching through the population for the corresponding element. With systematic sampling, we divide the population size by the sample size required, yielding a value for n. The first item is chosen at random from among the first n items. Thereafter, every nth item is selected. For example, suppose that a population has 4,000 units and a sample of size 50 is required. We select the first unit randomly from among the first 80 units. Every 80th (4000/50) item after that would be selected.

Systematic sampling is based on the assumption that since the first element is chosen at random, the entire sample will have the properties of a simple random sample. This method should be used with caution since quality characteristics may vary in some periodic fashion with the length of the sampling interval and thus bias the results.

Cluster Sampling. In cluster sampling, the population is first partitioned into groups of elements called clusters. A simple random sample of the clusters is selected. The elements within the clusters selected constitute the sample. For example, suppose that products are boxed in groups of 50. Each box can be regarded as a cluster. We would draw a sample of boxes and inspect all units in the boxes selected.

Cluster sampling tends to provide good results when the elements within the clusters are not alike (heterogeneous). In this case, each cluster would be representative of the entire population.

Judgment Sampling. With judgment sampling, an arbitrary sample of pertinent data is examined and the percentage of nonconformances is calculated. Since judgment sampling is not random, it is not possible to quantify the risks associated with making an incorrect conclusion. Thus, it is not a preferred method of sampling.

In the remainder of this chapter we discuss acceptance sampling.

ACCEPTANCE SAMPLING PLANS

Acceptance sampling, introduced in Chapter 8, may be performed for attributes or variables measurements. Recall that attributes measurements assume only two values (conforming or nonconforming) while variables are measured on a continuous numerical scale. We consider only acceptance sampling for attributes in this chapter.

A **sampling plan** for attributes is a description of the sample size or sizes used and an associated acceptance and/or rejection number. The acceptance number is the maximum number of nonconforming items in the sample that will permit acceptance of the lot; the rejection number is the minimum number of nonconforming items in the sample that will cause rejection of the lot. There are four basic types of attributes sampling plans: single, double, multiple, and sequential.

A **single sampling plan** is one in which the acceptability of a lot is determined from a single sample. A sampling plan for a lot of size N consists of a sample of size n and an acceptance number c. If the number of nonconforming items in the sample, x, is less than or equal to c, the lot is accepted; otherwise it is rejected. This logic is illustrated by the flowchart in Figure 18.1. An alternative is to specify a rejection number r, such that if x is greater than or equal to r, the lot is rejected. Note that the rejection number r is equal to $c + 1$. For example, a lot size of 700 units might have a sample size $n = 80$ and an acceptance number $c = 3$. The rejection number, if specified, would be $r = 4$.

A **double sampling plan** is illustrated by the flowchart in Figure 18.2. First, a sample of n_1 items is selected at random from the lot and inspected. If the number nonconforming is less than or equal to an acceptance number c_1, the lot is accepted. If the number nonconforming is greater than or equal to a rejection number r_1, the lot is rejected. However, if the number nonconforming is greater than c_1, but less than r_1, a second sample of n_2 items is taken. The number of nonconforming items in the second sample is added to that from the first sample. If this cumulative number is less than or equal to a second acceptance number c_2, the lot is accepted. If it is greater than c_2, the lot is rejected. Note that the second rejection number $r_2 = c_2 + 1$.

A **multiple sampling plan** is a generalization of double sampling plans; that is, three, four, five, or more samples may be taken. The sample sizes are smaller than for double sampling plans, but the procedures are similar to those just described. In the limiting case when items are inspected one at a time and a decision is made on whether to accept the lot, reject the lot, or continue sampling, we have an item-by-item

FIGURE 18.1 Single Sampling Plan Logic

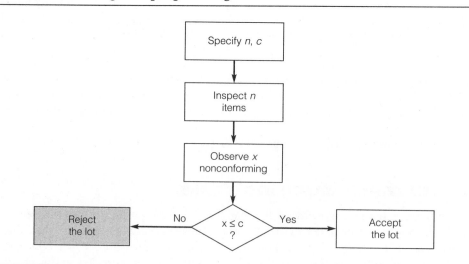

FIGURE 18.2 Double Sampling Plan Logic

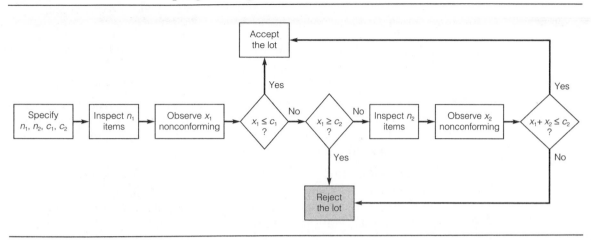

sequential sampling plan. The sampling procedure continues until the cumulative results of inspection determine that an acceptance or rejection decision should be made. Hence, the sample size is not specified in advance but depends on the actual results.

Equivalent single and multiple sampling plans can be constructed that give the same degree of protection. However, among these acceptance sampling procedures, double sampling is perhaps the most popular. Double sampling plans usually have smaller first-sample sizes than the corresponding single sampling plans. Lower sampling costs can result when the fraction nonconforming is either high or low and the decision is made on the basis of the first sample. Double sampling plans are also psychologically more appealing, since they are designed to provide more information in borderline cases. Finally, they are easier to implement and to understand than multiple or sequential plans, which require more training and record keeping.

FACTORS IN SELECTING A SAMPLING PLAN

The selection of a particular sampling plan depends on a variety of factors:

■ *The purpose of sampling:* Is the objective to guarantee specific levels of quality with prescribed levels of risk, maintain a certain quality level, ensure an average quality level, reduce inspection after good quality history, check inspection after an excellent quality history, or comply with contractual specifications? Different types of sampling plans are appropriate for different situations.

■ *The degree of risk and protection afforded by the plan:* In using sampling inspection, there is an inherent statistical, or sampling, risk that the sample will not reflect the quality of the population from which it is drawn. Hence, a chance exists that an incorrect decision is made, that is, accepting a lot of poor quality or rejecting a lot of good quality. We shall later see how we can quantify these risks.

- *The ease of administering the sampling plan:* As noted earlier, multiple and sequential sampling plans require more expertise and record keeping.

- *The amount of inspection required:* On the average, double sampling plans usually require less inspection than single sampling plans, and multiple sampling plans usually require less inspection than double sampling plans, particularly when the product is of very good or very poor quality.

- *The cost of inspection, manufacturing, and failure:* Plans involving a high degree of inspection can be costly; however, the costs must be weighed against the costs that result from allowing a nonconforming product to continue on in production or to reach the customer.

- *The size and number of lots inspected:* Are lots infrequently obtained from a variety of sources, or are they continually obtained from the same producer? As experience with the quality history from a particular producer is gained, the amount of inspection can often be reduced.

- *The cost of delayed shipments and availability of a product from other sources:* A firm might not be able to afford to reject entire lots and must then resort to in-house screening.

In general, it must be recognized that a plan selected for one product may not be right for another. This is especially true when inspection is dependent on the physical layout of the manufacturing facility or the production methods.

Risk in Acceptance Sampling

In any sampling procedure, one runs the risk of making an incorrect decision. Based only on sample observations, one might accept a poor quality lot or reject a good quality lot. We may view acceptance sampling as a statistical test of hypothesis: The null hypothesis is that the lot is of "good" quality, and the alternate hypothesis is that the lot is of "poor" quality. We will define the notions of "good" and "poor" quality more precisely later. A Type I error refers to rejecting the null hypothesis when it is true, while a Type II error refers to accepting the null hypothesis when it is false.

In quality control terminology, the probability of a Type I error—rejecting a lot of good quality—is commonly referred to as **producer's risk.** Type I errors create a risk for the producer, because a customer may erroneously reject a lot based on a small sample and return it to the producer. Upon performing a screening inspection, the producer will find that the lot is within permissible quality limits. The probability of a Type II error—accepting a lot of poor quality—is called **consumer's risk.** In a similar fashion, a consumer may test a lot and erroneously accept it as good. When the product is put into the production process, it is usually discovered that there is an unacceptable number of defectives. The analogy between these common statistical and quality control terminologies is summarized in Table 18.2.

The traditional value used for producer risk is 0.05. This means that there is a 5% chance that a good quality lot will be rejected by the acceptance sampling plan and returned to the vendor. At the same time, a 95% chance exists that the lot will be accepted. The consumer's risk is usually set at 0.1. This means that there is a 10% chance that a lot of poor quality will be accepted by the sampling plan and thus will find its way into production. Alternatively, there is a 90% chance that a poor quality lot will be rejected. Published acceptance sampling tables often use these values in

TABLE 18.2 Statistics and Quality Control

Statistical Concept	Notation	Quality-Control Concept
Null hypothesis	H_0	Lot is of good quality
Alternate hypothesis	H_1	Lot is of poor quality
Reject H_0 when H_0 is true	Type I error	Reject a good lot
Accept H_0 when H_0 is false	Type II error	Accept a bad lot
Probability of Type I error	α	Producer's risk
Probability of Type II error	β	Consumer's risk

defining sampling plans. However, with the current focus on quality, these levels are unacceptable in most plants today. Computer programs now allow the selection of any value.

Severity of Inspection

Severity of inspection refers to the total amount of inspection and the acceptance/rejection criteria specified by a sampling plan. Three levels of inspection are commonly used in practice:

1. **Normal inspection** is used when there is no evidence that the quality of a product under consideration is any better or worse than the specified quality level. Normal inspection is usually used at first and is continued as long as product quality is consistent with specified requirements.

2. **Tightened inspection** is more stringent than normal inspection and is used when there is evidence that quality is deteriorating. Usually it results in decreasing the acceptance number for the sampling plan. It also increases the producer's risk and reduces the consumer's risk.

3. **Reduced inspection** uses a smaller sample size than does normal inspection. It slightly reduces the producer's risk while greatly increasing the consumer's risk. Reduced inspection is often done when there is sufficient history to indicate good quality; however, if quality begins deteriorating, normal inspection is resumed.

The use of these three levels of inspection allows for switching from normal to tightened or reduced and back again as quality changes. The switching rules proposed in ANSI/ASQC Z1.9(1980) and ANSI/ASQC Z1.4(1981) are illustrated in Figure 18.3.[2]

OPERATING CHARACTERISTIC CURVES

In analyzing the risks involved in sampling, we need to answer the following question: Assuming that the lot has a given percentage of nonconforming items, what is the probability that it will be accepted or rejected by a particular sampling plan? Clearly,

---

[2]ANSI (American National Standards Institute)/ASQC (American Society for Quality Control) standards are published tables and procedures of industry standards for attributes and variables inspection, respectively.

FIGURE 18.3 Switching Rules for ANSI/ASQC Z1.9(1980) and ANSI/ASQC Z1.4(1981) (Z1.4 Limit Number Option Exercised)

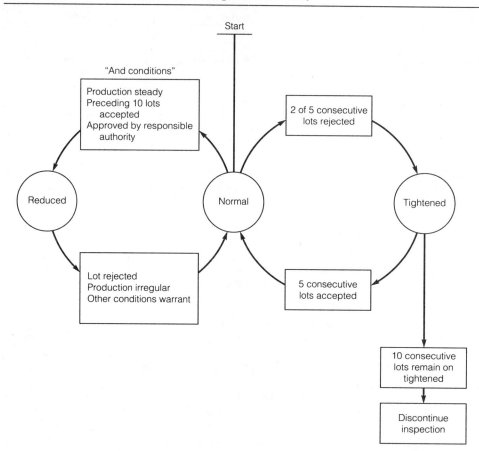

Reprinted with permission of ASQC.

this information is necessary in order to choose an appropriate plan. It is assumed that there are no inspection errors. When quality is good, both the consumer and the producer are interested in accepting the lot a high percentage of the time. When quality is poor, the consumer is particularly interested in rejecting the lot a high percentage of the time. These probabilities can be computed from the **operating characteristic (OC) curve** associated with the sampling plan.

A typical OC curve is shown in Figure 18.4. The x axis represents the actual percentage of nonconforming items in the lot (which is generally unknown); the y axis gives the probability of accepting a lot. The probability that a lot with 0% nonconformities will be accepted is 1; the probability that a lot with 100% nonconformities will be accepted is zero. Therefore, an OC curve always passes through the points (0, 1) and (100, 0).

As shown in Figure 18.4, if the percent nonconforming is 4%, we estimate the probability of acceptance to be about 0.70. If this is considered "good quality," the

FIGURE 18.4 **Illustration of an OC Curve**

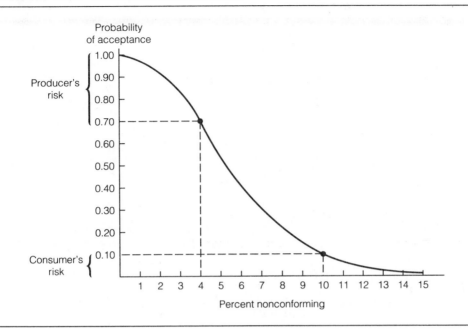

probability of rejecting the lot is $1 - 0.70 = 0.30$; this is the producer's risk. If the percent nonconforming is 10%, the probability of acceptance is only about 0.10. If this is considered "poor quality," this value represents the consumer's risk.

EXAMPLE 5 **Constructing an OC Curve.** OC curves are determined by fundamental probability calculations. To illustrate how an OC curve is constructed, let's consider a problem faced by Robertson Electronics, which purchases an important component for missile guidance systems that it manufactures for the Air Force. The components must withstand high temperatures and are tested by being subjected to temperatures much higher than those anticipated in normal service. Lots of 500,000 are purchased.

Suppose that 10 components are sampled ($n = 10$) from a large lot and that management decides to accept the lot using a single sampling plan only if no nonconforming items are found. Thus, the acceptance number is $c = 0$. We do not know the actual percentage of nonconforming items in the lot, but let us assume that this value is 5%. We can compute the probability that the lot will be accepted using the binomial formula[3]

$$f(x) = \binom{n}{x} p^x (1-p)^{n-x} = \frac{n!}{(n-x)!\,x!} p^x (1-p)^{n-x}$$

---

[3]The use of the binomial probability distribution assumes that the size of the lot is theoretically infinite; for large lot sizes, it is usually a good approximation.

TABLE 18.3 OC Curve Computations for
$n = 10, c = 0$

p	Probability of Acceptance, $f_{(0)}$
0.01	0.9044
0.02	0.8171
0.03	0.7374
0.04	0.6648
0.05	0.5987
0.10	0.3487
0.15	0.1969
0.20	0.1074
0.25	0.0563
0.30	0.0282

Since the probability of a nonconforming item is 0.05, we have $p = 0.05$. Thus, the probability of zero failures in the sample of 10 components is given by

$$f(0) = \binom{10}{0}(0.05)^0(0.95)^{10-0}$$

$$= \frac{10!}{(10-0)!\,0!}\,(1)(0.95)^{10}$$

$$= (1)(1)(0.95)^{10} = 0.5987$$

FIGURE 18.5 Operating Characteristic Curve for $n = 10, c = 0$

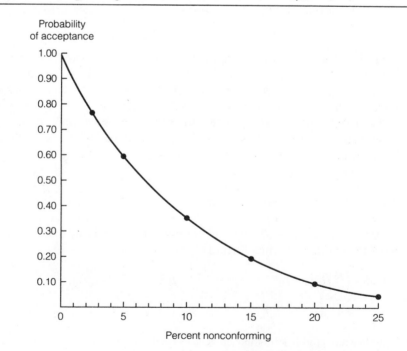

(Recall that 0! is defined to be 1.) If the actual percentage of nonconforming items is 10%, the probability of accepting the lot is

$$\binom{10}{0}(0.10)^0(0.90)^{10} = 0.3487$$

Table 18.3 gives the probability of acceptance for various values of p. If we plot these, we obtain the OC curve shown in Figure 18.5.

OC curves can be computed and plotted for other sampling plans (characterized by different sample sizes and acceptance numbers). In this fashion, we obtain a family of curves for different sampling plans. For example, when $n = 10$, $c = 1$, and $p = 0.05$, the probability of accepting the lot is $f(0) + f(1)$, since the lot is accepted if *at most* one defective item is found. Thus, we find:

$$f(0) + f(1) = 0.5987 + 0.3151 = 0.9138$$

This value is plotted on the OC curve in Figure 18.6 along with OC curves for other sampling plans.

In general, an increase in sample size results in a steepening of the OC curve, as shown in Figure 18.7. The steeper the curve, the greater the power of the sampling plan to discriminate between lots of good and poor quality. The general effect of increasing the acceptance number is to shift the curve to the right, as illustrated in Figure 18.8. This increases the probability of accepting a lot at a given quality level.

FIGURE 18.6 **Alternate Sampling Plans for Robertson Electronics**

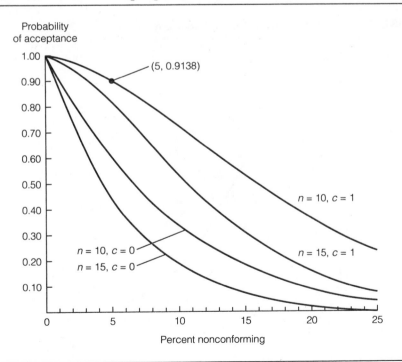

FIGURE 18.7 **Effect of Increasing Sample Size**

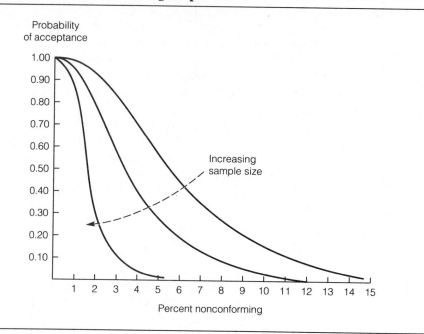

FIGURE 18.8 **Effect of Increasing Acceptance Number**

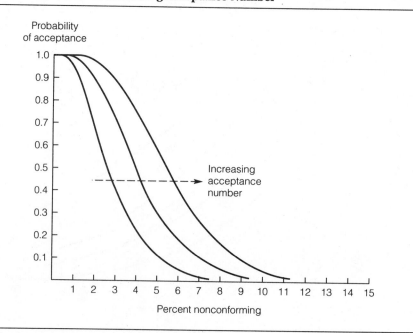

Appendix D at the end of the book gives values for the binomial distribution for use in constructing OC curves. However, for large values of n, binomial probability tables are usually not available and it is too cumbersome to compute them. When n is large and p is small, the Poisson distribution with $\mu = np$ provides an approximation to the binomial distribution. A good rule of thumb is that when $p \leq 0.05$ and $n \geq 20$, the approximation will be good. The Poisson distribution can be used to compute OC curves for sampling plans for which the computation of binomial probabilities is impractical.

OC curves are classified as two types: *type A* and *type B*. In the Robertson Electronics example, we assumed a very large lot size. When this is true, or when we are sampling from a stream of lots selected at random, we calculate the probability of lot acceptance using the binomial distribution. This gives a type B OC curve. If the lot size is finite (or not considered "large"), the exact probability of lot acceptance is calculated using the hypergeometric probability distribution. The resulting curve is called a type A OC curve. We often use type B curves as approximations to exact type A curves. When we do this, the probability of acceptance will always be larger than the true value. Unless the lot size is small relative to the sample size, the difference will be minor.

INDEXING SAMPLING PLANS

We have noted that sampling plans are uniquely defined by their operating characteristic curves. Suppose that we fix the probability of acceptance for a specific percent nonconforming. As illustrated in Figure 18.9, many different OC curves exist (and consequently many different sampling plans) that pass through this particular

FIGURE 18.9 A Collection of Sampling Plans

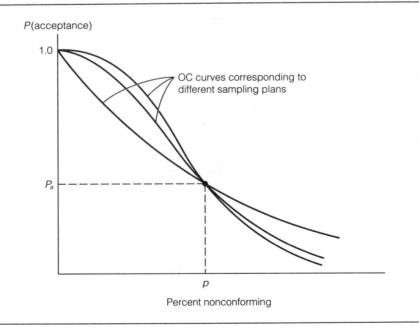

point. Usually this point is related to the producer or consumer risk desired. Such a collection of sampling plans is said to be *indexed* by the degree of consumer or producer protection that is afforded by the plans. Four common methods are used for indexing sampling plans: (1) indifference quality level, (2) limiting quality (lot tolerance percent defective), (3) acceptable quality level, and (4) average outgoing quality limit.

Indifference Quality Level

Sampling plans based on indifference quality are often called 50% plans. The indifference quality level (IQL) is that level of lot quality at which the probability of acceptance of the lot is 0.5 (see Figure 18.10). For example, one might determine that a lot having 2% nonconforming items be accepted with a probability of 0.5. Lots of better quality are accepted more often than they are rejected, while lots of poorer quality are rejected more often than they are accepted.

The following equation can be used to determine the approximate sample size n for a single sampling plan with a predetermined acceptance number c and indifference quality level p percent:

$$n = \frac{100c + 67}{p}$$

Thus, with $c = 4$ and $p = 2$ (percent), we have

$$n = \frac{100(4) + 67}{2}$$

$$= \frac{467}{2}$$

FIGURE 18.10   Indifference Quality Level Plans

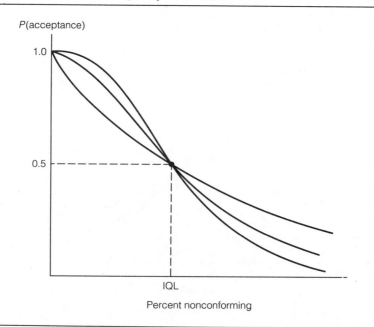

or about 234 units. Thus, from a sample of 234 units, the lot would be accepted if four or fewer nonconforming units are found.

Indifference quality is a very simple approach to sampling inspection but does not take into consideration producer or consumer risks.

Limiting Quality/Lot Tolerance Percent Defective

Limiting quality indexing is based on specifying a level of consumer's risk (see Figure 18.11). Recall that consumer's risk is the probability of accepting a lot of poor quality. "Poor quality" is some level of nonconformance that the consumer is willing to tolerate a small percentage of the time. This value is called the limiting quality (LQ), or alternatively, lot tolerance percent defective (LTPD). Thus, the consumer might state that he or she is willing to accept a maximum of 4% nonconforming items no more than 10% of the time. In this case, LQ = 4%, and the consumer's risk is 0.10. Thus, LQ sampling plans protect the consumer from accepting more lots of poor quality than he or she is willing to tolerate. Different plans, however, offer different degrees of producer risk. They are most commonly used for lots produced on an intermittent basis where there is little or no opportunity to tighten inspection if quality falls to an unacceptable level.

Acceptable Quality Level

Acceptable quality level (AQL) indexing is based on specifying a level of producer risk—the probability of rejecting a lot of good quality (see Figure 18.12). This "good quality" is called the acceptable quality level (AQL); that is, it is the maximum percent nonconforming considered satisfactory for sampling inspection. An example of an

FIGURE 18.11   **LQ/LTPD Plans**

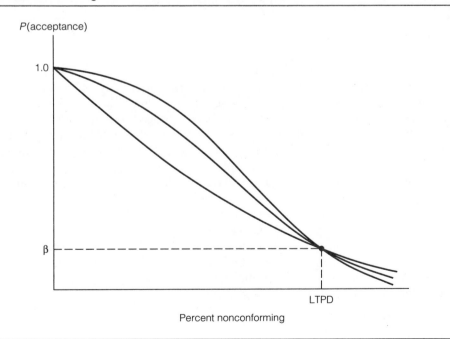

FIGURE 18.12 AQL Plans

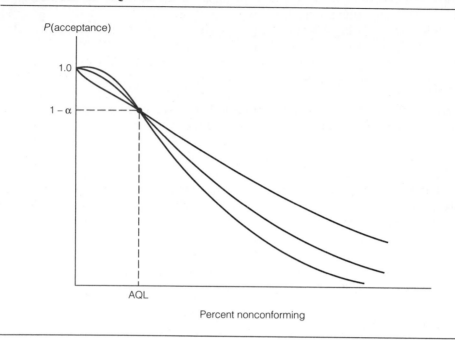

AQL plan might be based on the consumer's desire to accept lots 95% of the time when the percent nonconforming is no worse than 3%. In this case, AQL = 3%, and the producer's risk is $1 - 0.95 = 0.05$, or 5%. Different plans offer different degrees of consumer risk. AQL sampling plans are commonly used to inspect a continuous series of lots rather than infrequently produced lots.

Average Outgoing Quality Limit

The average outgoing quality (AOQ) is the average quality of outgoing product, including all accepted lots plus all rejected lots after they have been effectively screened and nonconforming items have been removed and replaced by conforming items. Thus, in AOQ plans, rejected lots must be 100% inspected and all nonconforming items replaced. The resulting lot will have zero nonconforming items. However, lots that are accepted will still have some percentage of nonconformities. The *average* quality of outgoing lots will nevertheless be better than the quality of the incoming lots.

To illustrate this, suppose that incoming lots have a 4% (fraction nonconforming) quality level and the sampling plan is designed so that there is a 90% chance of accepting the lot. Ninety percent of the lots will be accepted and have an average of 4% nonconforming items. The remaining 10% that are rejected will be screened and have 0% nonconformities upon removal of nonconforming items. This step is called **rectification.** The average outgoing quality is

$$(0.90)(0.04) + (0.10)(0) = 0.036, \text{ or } 3.6\%$$

If incoming lots have 12% nonconforming but are accepted only 5% of the time by the plan, the average outgoing quality is significantly improved:

$$(0.05)(0.12) + (0.95)(0) = 0.006, \text{ or } 0.6\%$$

The **average outgoing quality limit (AOQL)** is the maximum AOQ for all possible incoming qualities for a given sampling inspection plan. AOQ plans assure that the average outgoing quality will not exceed the AOQL on the average, but not for individual lots. Since sampling plans selected to assure a desired AOQL assume that rejected lots are screened, they cannot be used for destructive testing.

Comparison of Sampling Plans

Table 18.4 summarizes these methods of indexing. Sampling plans can be designed to combine two of the types of quality levels just described. For example, we might combine AQL/LQ protection or LQ/indifference quality protection. The most common combination is AQL/LQ, which provides a high probability (0.9 to 0.95) of accepting an AQL lot and a low probability (0.05 to 0.1) of accepting an LQ lot.

Under each category, a wide variety of specific plans can be chosen. For example, some AQL plans with an acceptable quality level of 0.012 and a producer risk of 0.05 are $n = 30$ and $c = 1$, $n = 68$ and $c = 2$, and $n = 274$ and $c = 6$. Each of these plans has different levels of consumer risk; the higher the sample size, the lower the risk. Hence, the user must trade off higher inspection costs against the lower risk of accepting poor quality lots. The basic issue in selecting a sampling plan is the determination of the level of protection to be offered and the quality level or levels. In selecting the quality level, design requirements, quality protection required, unit costs, cost of inspection, process capabilities, and available quality data must be considered. Selecting low quality levels might result in expensive inspection and final product costs or unnecessary frequent rejection of lots. High quality levels, on the other hand, might result in the delivery of many unsatisfactory lots to the customer.

The process capability may limit the selection of a quality level. One must determine the level of product quality that can be reasonably expected under existing production capabilities. Also, if the production or use of nonconforming items early in the production process will result in expensive rework or scrap later in the process, the quality level values should be tighter (smaller) than would normally be expected.

TABLE 18.4 Comparison of Sampling Plan Indexing Methods

Indexing Method	Purpose	User Specifications
Indifference quality	Ensure a high probability of accepting good and rejecting poor quality lots	Percentage nonconforming to be accepted 50% of the time
Limiting quality	Maintain level of consumer risk	Maximum percentage nonconforming willing to tolerate; consumer risk
Acceptable quality level	Maintain level of producer risk	Maximum satisfactory percentage nonconforming; producer risk
Average outgoing quality limit	Ensure average quality	Maximum acceptable level of output quality

Quality levels also affect the cost of inspection. A low quality level (for example, 15% nonconforming) may require a very small sample, while a high quality level (for instance, 0.02% nonconforming) would require a much larger sample size and thus increased costs.

APPLICATIONS OF OC CURVES

The OC curve allows the determination of producer and consumer risks for alternative sampling plans. Thus, considering the type of indexing method along with these risks, one can select a plan that meets specified criteria. For the Robertson Electronics problem, suppose that the quality assurance manager wants a plan with a specified producer and consumer risk, that is, an LQ/AQL plan. The manager specifies AQL = 0.03, LQ = 0.15, the producer's risk = 0.25, and the consumer's risk = 0.2. If we plot the points (0.03, 0.75) and (0.15, 0.2) in Figure 18.6, we see that these points lie on the OC curve corresponding to $n = 10$ and $c = 0$. Therefore, this is the appropriate plan to select.

Computing Average Outgoing Quality

We can use OC curves to compute the average outgoing quality (AOQ) and to determine the average outgoing quality limit (AOQL) for sampling plans in which rejected lots are rectified. The AOQ for incoming lots having a fraction nonconforming p is computed using the expected value formula

$$AOQ = P_a p + (1 - P_a)(0) = P_a p$$

where P_a is the probability of accepting a lot with quality level p. The first term corresponds to lots that are accepted. The second term corresponds to lots that are rejected; these lots will have zero nonconformities after screening and will be rejected with probability $1 - P_a$. The formula follows from the definition of expected value.

Let us compute the AOQ for Robertson Electronics using Table 18.3:

p	P_a	$P_a p$ = AOQ
0.01	0.9044	0.0090
0.02	0.8171	0.0163
0.03	0.7374	0.0221
0.04	0.6648	0.0266
0.05	0.5987	0.0299
0.10	0.3487	0.0349
0.15	0.1969	0.0295
0.20	0.1074	0.0215
0.25	0.0563	0.0141
0.30	0.0282	0.0085

Thus, for instance, if $p = 0.05$, the average outgoing quality after screening rejected lots will be 2.99%. If we plot AOQ versus p, we obtain the graph shown in Figure 18.13. Note that the curve achieves a maximum value around $p = 0.10$. If we refine our computations, we find that the maximum AOQ actually occurs for $p = 0.09$ and is

FIGURE 18.13 Average Outgoing Quality Curve for Robertson Electronics

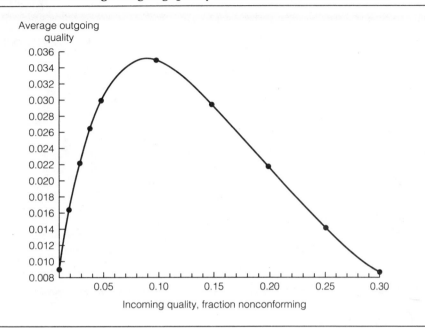

equal to 0.0350. This is the value of AOQL. Therefore, *in the long run* (and this is important to remember), the average outgoing quality of all lots will not exceed 0.0350.

The formula given above assumes that the lot size is very large relative to the sample size. To account for smaller lot sizes, the formula should be modified to be

$$AOQ = P_a p (1 - n/N)$$

For the Robertson example, since $n = 10$ and $N = 500,000$, the difference is unimportant.

Computing Average Total Inspection

OC curves are also useful in computing the total amount of inspection that will be expected by a sampling plan that includes rectifying rejected lots. If lots contain no nonconforming items, the amount of inspection will clearly be equal to n, the sample size. If all items are nonconforming, every lot will be 100% inspected, and the amount of inspection per lot will be N, the lot size. For quality levels between these two extremes, the average amount of inspection per lot will be between n and N.

The average total inspection (ATI) per lot is computed by the formula:

$$ATI = n + (1 - P_a)(N - n)$$

The first term represents the sample inspected. If the lot is rejected with probability $1 - P_a$, the remaining $N - n$ items must be inspected. Hence, the second term represents the expected amount of inspection beyond the initial sample.

The ATI for the Robertson Electronics example is computed as follows:

P	P_a	$10 + (1 - P_a)(499{,}990) = ATI$
0.01	0.9044	47,809
0.02	0.8171	91,458
0.03	0.7374	131,307
0.04	0.6648	167,607
0.05	0.5987	200,656
0.10	0.3487	325,653
0.15	0.1969	401,552
0.20	0.1074	446,301
0.25	0.0563	471,851
0.30	0.0282	485,900

A plot of ATI versus p is given in Figure 18.14.

FIGURE 18.14 Average Total Inspection Curve for Robertson Electronics

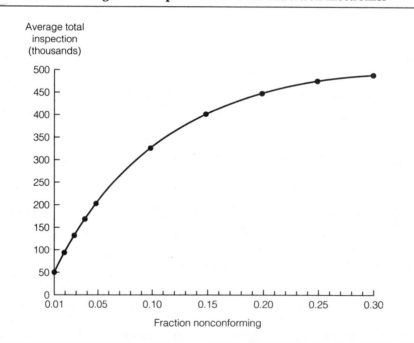

PUBLISHED SAMPLING PLANS

A variety of different acceptance sampling plans, indexed according to the methods described in the previous section, have been published and are widely used. In this section we briefly describe some of the most popular types of plans.

MIL-STD-105 Sampling Tables

Acceptance sampling plans developed with the concepts discussed thus far have been translated into standard charts and tables for easy use by industrial personnel. Different sets of tables have been indexed according to different criteria. MIL-STD-105E is a sampling scheme that was developed for government procurement as an outgrowth of efforts during World War II. It was revised five times (hence the label "E"), with the latest revision occurring in 1989. In 1973, it was adopted by the International Organization for Standardization and designated International Standard ISO/DIS-2859. An updated version was adopted in 1981 by the American National Standards Institute and the American Society for Quality Control, called ANSI/ASQC Z1.4.

MIL-STD-105E is designed for lot-by-lot attributes sampling. Its major purpose is to accept with a high probability lots whose quality level is greater than or equal to an AQL. AQLs ranging from 0.10% to 10% are used in the plans. AQL plans are most effective if (1) the plan rejects sufficient lots to make it worthwhile to improve product quality when the manufacturer is producing at a quality that is worse than the AQL and (2) the plan rejects very few lots when the manufacturer is producing at a quality level better than the AQL.

There are three types of sampling plans: single, double, and multiple, and three levels of inspection for each: normal, reduced, and tightened. Switching rules between each of these levels is also incorporated into the plan. In addition, there are four special inspection levels, designated as S-1, S-2, S-3, and S-4. These are used for small sample sizes and large levels of risk. The standard provides sampling plans for fraction defective inspection and defects per 100 units inspection.

The typical sequence of operations in using MIL-STE-105E can be stated as follows for a single sampling plan:

1. *Establish the value of AQL:* This is a management decision.

2. *Determine the lot size:* Usually this is established by agreement between the supplier and the customer.

3. *Determine the inspection level:* Initially, Level II (normal inspection) is chosen unless there is reason to use one of the other levels as previously discussed.

4. *Determine the sampling plan:* Single, double, or multiple samplings may be used.

5. *Determine the sample size code:* The sample sizes are coded by letter and are based on lot size and inspection level.

6. *Determine the sample size and acceptance number:* Assuming normal inspection and given the sample size code letter and the AQL value, the sample size and acceptance number are found in a table.

7. *Select the sample:* The sample should be selected at random from the lot.

8. *Inspect the sample:* The nonconforming items are counted. If the resulting number does not exceed the acceptance number found in the table, the lot is accepted; otherwise it is rejected.

9. *Record the results:* A record of accept and reject decisions should be maintained so that switching rules can be followed.

FIGURE 18.15 Using MIL-STD-105D Tables

TABLE I — Sample size code letters

(normal inspection)

Lot or batch size			Special inspection levels				General inspection levels		
			S-1	S-2	S-3	S-4	I	II	III
2	to	8	A	A	A	A	A	A	B
9	to	15	A	A	A	A	A	B	C
16	to	25	A	A	B	B	B	C	D
26	to	50	A	B	B	C	C	D	E
51	to	90	B	B	C	C	C	E	F
91	to	150	B	B	C	D	D	F	G
151	to	280	B	C	D	E	E	G	H
281	to	500	B	C	D	E	F	H	J
501	to	1200	C	C	E	F	G	J	K
1201	to	3200	C	D	E	G	H	(K)	L
3201	to	10000	C	D	F	G	J	L	M
10001	to	35000	C	D	F	H	K	M	N
35001	to	150000	D	E	G	J	L	N	P
150001	to	500000	D	E	G	J	M	P	Q
500001	and	over	D	E	H	K	N	Q	R

TABLE II-A — Single sampling plans for normal inspection (Master table)

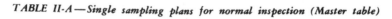

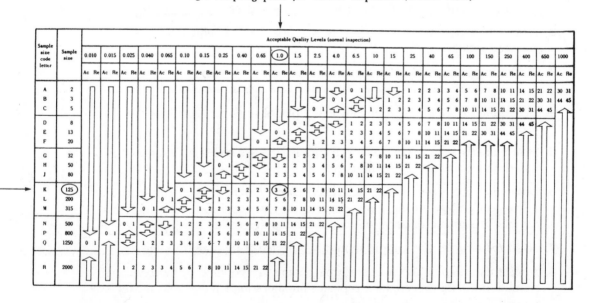

Acceptable Quality Levels (normal inspection): 0.010, 0.015, 0.025, 0.040, 0.065, 0.10, 0.15, 0.25, 0.40, 0.65, (1.0), 1.5, 2.5, 4.0, 6.5, 10, 15, 25, 40, 65, 100, 150, 250, 400, 650, 1000

Sample size code letter	Sample size
A	2
B	3
C	5
D	8
E	13
F	20
G	32
H	50
J	80
K	(125)
L	200
M	315
N	500
P	800
Q	1250
R	2000

⇩ = Use first sampling plan below arrow. If sample size equals, or exceeds, lot or batch size, do 100 percent inspection.
⇧ = Use first sampling plan above arrow.
Ac = Acceptance number.
Re = Rejection number.

To illustrate the use of MIL-STD-105D, suppose that a company receives an integrated circuit component in lots of 2,500 and that the AQL is determined to be 1.0. Using normal inspection, we find from Table I of Figure 18.15 that the sample size code letter is K. In Table II-A, we see that the corresponding sample size is 125. Under the AQL value of 1.0, we see that the acceptance number (Ac) is 3 and the rejection number (Re) is 4 (see Figure 18.15).

As a further illustration, suppose that the AQL is only 0.025. In Table II-A, the arrow directs us down to the plan corresponding to code letter N. In this case, we would choose a sample of size 500 and an acceptance number of zero.

The tables are also organized by code letter ("X" or eXtended tables). For example, Table X-K-2 gives sampling plans for code letter K. The plan for the first example we gave could have been found in this table as shown in Figure 18.16. In the second example, we are directed to use the next subsequent table for which the appropriate AQL appears; this leads us to Table X-N-2, and we find the same plan.

The extended tables also present information about OC curves. For example, in Table X-K, Chart K gives OC curves for plans corresponding to specified AQL values; Table X-K-1 gives tabulated values for these curves. Thus, for the first plan illustrated above (AQL = 1.0), we see from Table X-K-1 that if the incoming quality level is

FIGURE 18.16 Using Extended Tables in MIL-STD-105D

TABLE X-K-2 - SAMPLING PLANS FOR SAMPLE SIZE CODE LETTER: K

Type of sampling plan	Cumulative sample size	Acceptable Quality Levels (normal inspection): Less than 0.10	0.10	0.15	×	0.25	0.40	0.65	(1.0)	1.5	2.5	×	4.0	×	6.5	×	10	Higher than 10	Cumulative sample size
		Ac Re	Ac Re	Ac Re	Ac Re	Ac Re	Ac Re	Ac Re	Ac Re	Ac Re	Ac Re	Ac Re	Ac Re	Ac Re	Ac Re	Ac Re	Ac Re	Ac Re	
Single	(125)	▽	0 1	Use Letter J	Use Letter M	Use Letter L	1 2	2 3	(3 4)	5 6	7 8	8 9	10 11	12 13	14 15	18 19	21 22	△	125
Double	80	▽	•				0 2	0 3	1 4	2 5	3 7	3 7	5 9	6 10	7 11	9 14	11 16	△	80
	160						1 2	3 4	4 5	6 7	8 9	11 12	12 13	15 16	18 19	23 24	26 27		160
Multiple	32	▽	•				* 2	* 2	* 3	* 4	0 4	0 4	0 5	0 6	1 7	1 8	2 9	△	32
	64						* 2	0 3	0 3	1 5	1 6	2 7	3 8	3 9	4 10	6 12	7 14		64
	96						0 2	0 3	1 4	2 6	3 8	4 9	6 10	7 12	8 13	11 17	13 19		96
	128						0 3	1 4	2 5	3 7	5 10	6 11	8 13	10 15	12 17	16 22	19 25		128
	160						1 3	2 4	3 6	5 8	7 11	9 12	11 15	14 17	17 20	22 25	25 29		160
	192						1 3	3 5	4 6	7 9	10 12	12 14	14 17	18 20	21 23	27 29	31 33		192
	224						2 3	4 5	6 7	9 10	13 14	14 15	18 19	21 22	25 26	32 33	37 38		224
	Acceptable Quality Levels (tightened inspection)	Less than 0.15	0.15	×	0.25	0.40	0.65	1.0	1.5	2.5	×	4.0	×	6.5	×	10	×	Higher than 10	

△ = Use next preceding sample size code letter for which acceptance and rejection numbers are available.
▽ = Use next subsequent sample size code letter for which acceptance and rejection numbers are available.
Ac = Acceptance number
Re = Rejection number
• = Use single sampling plan above (or alternatively use letter N).
* = Acceptance not permitted at this sample size.

actually 2.03 (the fourth value in the column with heading 1.0), the probability of acceptance will be 0.75. Chart K can be used to estimate acceptance probabilities that are not tabulated in the table. For instance, if the incoming quality is actually 3.4, the probability of acceptance is about 38% (see Figure 18.17).

Dodge-Romig Sampling Plans

Dodge-Romig sampling plans were introduced in the 1920s for lot-by-lot inspection of attributes in the Bell Telephone system. As opposed to MIL-STD-105D plans, which are indexed by AQL, Dodge-Romig plans are indexed by either LQ (LTPD) or AOQL. AOQL should be chosen if interest centers on the general level of quality of product *after* inspection. AOQL plans are more useful than LTPD plans when a continuing supply of product is inspected. An LTPD plan is more pessimistic than AOQL. LTPD quality will be met by almost every lot, while AOQL quality will be met only on the average.

FIGURE 18.17 OC Curve Data in MIL-STD-105D

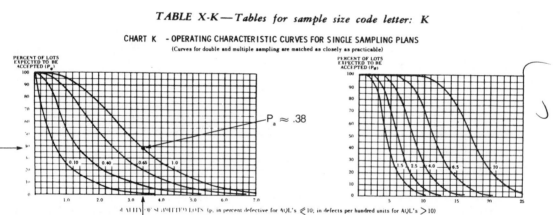

TABLE X-K—Tables for sample size code letter: K

CHART K - OPERATING CHARACTERISTIC CURVES FOR SINGLE SAMPLING PLANS
(Curves for double and multiple sampling are matched as closely as practicable)

TABLE X-K-1 - TABULATED VALUES FOR OPERATING CHARACTERISTIC CURVES FOR SINGLE SAMPLING PLANS

P_a	Acceptable Quality Levels (normal inspection)												
	0.10	0.40	0.65	1.0	1.5	2.5	✕	4.0	✕	6.5	✕	10
	p (in percent defective or defects per hundred units)												
99.0	0.0081	0.119	0.349	0.658	1.43	2.33	2.81	3.82	4.88	5.98	8.28	10.1
95.0	0.0410	0.284	0.654	1.09	2.09	3.19	3.76	4.94	6.15	7.40	9.95	11.9
90.0	0.0840	0.426	0.882	1.40	2.52	3.73	4.35	5.62	6.92	8.24	10.9	13.0
75.0	0.230	0.769	0.382	2.03	3.38	4.77	5.47	6.90	8.34	9.79	12.7	14.9
50.0	0.554	1.34	2.14	2.94	4.54	6.14	6.94	8.53	10.1	11.7	14.9	17.3
25.0	1.11	2.15	3.14	4.09	5.94	7.75	8.64	10.4	12.2	13.9	17.4	20.0
10.0	1.84	3.11	4.26	5.35	7.42	9.42	10.4	12.3	14.2	16.1	19.8	22.5
5.0	2.40	3.80	5.04	6.20	8.41	10.5	11.5	13.6	15.6	17.5	21.4	24.2
1.0	3.68	5.31	6.73	8.04	10.5	12.8	18.3	16.1	18.3	20.4	24.5	27.5
	0.15	0.65	1.0	1.5	2.5	✕	4.0	✕	6.5	✕	10	✕
	Acceptable Quality Levels (tightened inspection)												

Note: All values given in above table based on Poisson distribution as an approximation to the Binomial.

Dodge-Romig plans are often preferred over AQL plans, especially for critical components in assemblies. Plans for both single and double sampling are available. The plans are designed so that the average total inspection is minimized. As noted earlier, the AOQL concept is meaningless unless rejected lots are 100% inspected and nonconforming units are replaced; thus, these plans apply only to this situation.

A Dodge-Romig table is reproduced in Figure 18.18. Note that the relative sample sizes decrease as the lot sizes increase. Let us look at an example of an AOQL plan. Suppose that the lot size is $N = 2,500$, the process average is 0.75, and AOQL is specified to be 2.5% We find that a plan with $n = 55$ and $c = 2$ should be used. The corresponding LTPD is 9.4%. This is the point on the OC curve for which $P_a = 0.10$. Thus, the plan gives an average outgoing quality limit of 2.5% and assures that 90% of the lots with quality as bad as 9.4% nonconforming will be rejected.

LTPD plans are designed so that $P_a = 0.10$ at the value of LTPD. To illustrate such a plan, suppose that $N = 8,000$, the process average is 0.35, and LTPD = 1.0. From Figure 18.19, the plan $n = 1,150$ and $c = 7$ should be used. The corresponding AOQL is 0.34.

FIGURE 18.18 A Dodge-Romig AOQL Plan

Single Sampling Table for
Average Outgoing Quality Limit (AOQL) = 2.5%

2.5%

Lot Size	Process Average 0 to 0.05%			Process Average 0.06 to 0.50%			Process Average 0.51 to 1.00%			Process Average 1.01 to 1.50%			Process Average 1.51 to 2.00%			Process Average 2.01 to 2.50%		
	n	c	p_t %	n	c	p_t %	n	c	p_t %	n	c	p_t %	n	c	p_t %	n	c	p_t %
1–10	All	0	–	All	0	–	All	0	–	All	0	–	All	0	–	All	0	–
11–50	11	0	17.6	11	0	17.6	11	0	17.6	11	0	17.6	11	0	17.6	11	0	17.6
51–100	13	0	15.3	13	0	15.3	13	0	15.3	13	0	15.3	13	0	15.3	13	0	15.3
101–200	14	0	14.7	14	0	14.7	14	0	14.7	29	1	12.9	29	1	12.9	29	1	12.9
201–300	14	0	14.9	14	0	14.9	30	1	12.7	30	1	12.7	30	1	12.7	30	1	12.7
301–400	14	0	15.0	14	0	15.0	31	1	12.3	31	1	12.3	31	1	12.3	48	2	10.7
401–500	14	0	15.0	14	0	15.0	32	1	12.0	32	1	12.0	49	2	10.6	49	2	10.6
501–600	14	0	15.1	32	1	12.0	32	1	12.0	50	2	10.4	50	2	10.4	70	3	9.3
601–800	14	0	15.1	32	1	12.0	32	1	12.0	50	2	10.5	50	2	10.5	70	3	9.4
801–1000	15	0	14.2	33	1	11.7	33	1	11.7	50	2	10.6	70	3	9.4	90	4	8.5
1001–2000	15	0	14.2	33	1	11.7	55	2	9.3	75	3	8.8	95	4	8.0	120	5	7.6
2001–3000	15	0	14.2	33	1	11.8	55	2	9.4	75	3	8.8	120	5	7.6	145	6	7.2
3001–4000	15	0	14.3	33	1	11.8	55	2	9.5	100	4	7.9	125	5	7.4	195	8	6.6
4001–5000	15	0	14.3	33	1	11.8	75	3	8.9	100	4	7.9	150	6	7.0	225	9	6.3
5001–7000	33	1	11.8	55	2	9.7	75	3	8.9	125	5	7.4	175	7	6.7	250	10	6.1
7001–10,000	34	1	11.4	55	2	9.7	75	3	8.9	125	5	7.4	200	8	6.4	310	12	5.8
10,001–20,000	34	1	11.4	55	2	9.7	100	4	8.0	150	6	7.0	260	10	6.0	425	16	5.3
20,001–50,000	34	1	11.4	55	2	9.7	100	4	8.0	180	7	6.7	345	13	5.5	640	23	4.8
50,001–100,000	34	1	11.4	80	3	8.4	125	5	7.4	235	9	6.1	435	16	5.2	800	28	4.5

n = sample size; c = acceptance number
"All" indicates that each piece in the lot is to be inspected
p_t = lot tolerance percent defective with a Consumers Risk (P_c) of 0.10

SOURCE: *Sampling Inspection Tables, Single and Double Sampling*, 2d ed. (New York: John Wiley, 1959). Copyright © 1959, American Telephone and Telegraph Company. Reprinted by permission of John Wiley & Sons, Inc.

FIGURE 18.19   A Dodge-Romig LTPD Plan

1.0%   Single Sampling Table for
Lot Tolerance Per Cent Defective (LTPD) = 1.0%

Lot Size	Process Average 0 to 0.010%			Process Average 0.011 to 0.10%			Process Average 0.11 to 0.20%			Process Average 0.21 to 0.30%			Process Average 0.31 to 0.40%			Process Average 0.41 to 0.50%		
	n	c	AOQL %	n	c	AOQL %	n	c	AOQL %	n	c	AOQL %	n	c	AOQL %	n	c	AOQL %
1–120	All	0	0	All	0	0	All	0	0	All	0	0	All	0	0	All	0	0
121–150	120	0	0.06	120	0	0.06	120	0	0.06	120	0	0.06	120	0	0.06	120	0	0.06
151–200	140	0	0.08	140	0	0.08	140	0	0.08	140	0	0.08	140	0	0.08	140	0	0.08
201–300	165	0	0.10	165	0	0.10	165	0	0.10	165	0	0.10	165	0	0.10	165	0	0.10
301–400	175	0	0.12	175	0	0.12	175	0	0.12	175	0	0.12	175	0	0.12	175	0	0.12
401–500	180	0	0.13	180	0	0.13	180	0	0.13	180	0	0.13	180	0	0.13	180	0	0.13
501–600	190	0	0.13	190	0	0.13	190	0	0.13	190	0	0.13	190	0	0.13	305	1	0.14
601–800	200	0	0.14	200	0	0.14	200	0	0.14	330	1	0.15	330	1	0.15	330	1	0.15
801–1000	205	0	0.14	205	0	0.14	205	0	0.14	335	1	0.17	335	1	0.17	335	1	0.17
1001–2000	220	0	0.15	220	0	0.15	360	1	0.19	490	2	0.21	490	2	0.21	610	3	0.22
2001–3000	220	0	0.15	375	1	0.20	505	2	0.23	630	3	0.24	745	4	0.26	870	5	0.26
3001–4000	225	0	0.15	380	1	0.20	510	2	0.24	645	3	0.25	880	5	0.28	1000	6	0.29
4001–5000	225	0	0.16	380	1	0.20	520	2	0.24	770	4	0.28	895	5	0.29	1120	7	0.31
5001–7000	230	0	0.15	385	1	0.21	655	3	0.27	780	4	0.29	1020	6	0.32	1260	8	0.34
→ 7001–10,000	230	0	0.16	520	2	0.25	660	3	0.28	910	5	0.32	(1150	7	0.34)	1500	10	0.37
10,001–20,000	390	1	0.21	525	2	0.26	785	4	0.31	1040	6	0.35	1400	9	0.39	1980	14	0.43
20,001–50,000	390	1	0.21	530	2	0.26	920	5	0.34	1300	8	0.39	1890	13	0.44	2570	19	0.48
50,001–100,000	390	1	0.21	670	3	0.29	1040	6	0.36	1420	9	0.41	2120	15	0.47	3150	23	0.50

n = sample size; c = acceptance number
"All" indicates that each piece in the lot is to be inspected
AOQL = Average Outgoing Quality Limit

SOURCE: *Sampling Inspection Tables, Single and Double Sampling*, 2d ed. (New York: John Wiley, 1959). Copyright © 1959, American Telephone and Telegraph Company. Reprinted by permission of John Wiley & Sons, Inc.

The concept of indexing sampling plans was developed to provide practitioners with an easy means of selecting a plan. Since there are virtually an infinite number of sampling plans, tables could not be developed for all of them. Consequently, tables of plans were developed for fixed values of consumer risk or producer risk. Practitioners had no means of varying these parameters when using these plans. Today, however, because of the widespread availability of microcomputers and software, it is easy to generate plans having any desired characteristics. Hence the need for such tables of sampling plans is becoming obsolete. Nevertheless, the long-standing tradition of using indexed plans such as MIL-STD-105D is still ingrained in many companies.

The Proper Use of Acceptance Sampling

Note that acceptance sampling plans should only be used to pass sentence on lots, not to estimate the lot quality. Most acceptance sampling plans are not designed for estimation. Acceptance sampling does not provide any *control* of quality; it simply accepts and rejects lots. Even if all lots are of the same quality, sampling plans will reject some of them and accept others. This is quite different from concepts of SPC.

TABLE 18.5 Life Cycle of Acceptance Sampling Application

Stage	Step	Method
Preparation	Choose appropriate plan	Analysis of quality system to define exact need
	Determine producer capability	Performance evaluation using control charts
	Determine consumer needs	Process capability study using control charts
	Set quality levels and risks	Economic analysis and negotiations
	Determine plan	Use published procedures if possible
Initiation	Train inspector	Include plan, procedures, records, and action
	Apply plan properly	Ensure randomization
	Analyze results	Keep records and control charts
	Feedback information	Keep producer informed of results and trends
Operation	Assess protection	Check quality history against OC curves
	Adjust plan	Change severity to reflect quality history
	Decrease sample size if warranted	Switch to cumulative results plans with good history
Phase-out	Eliminate inspection effort where possible	Use check inspection procedures or control charts
Elimination	Spot check only	Remove all inspection when justified by extensive favorable history

SOURCE: E. G. Schilling, *Acceptance Sampling in Quality Control* (New York: Marcel Dekker, 1982).

In addition, traditional AQLs do not provide the level of quality demanded by most manufacturers today. A 1% AQL corresponds to 10,000 defectives per million. As we have discussed elsewhere in this book, many manufacturers are now looking toward much smaller rates of defects. To have a defect rate of 10 parts per million, an AQL of 0.001% is necessary. Traditional published sampling plans do not apply to such low levels of defect rates. Finally, acceptance sampling should be viewed not as an end in itself but as a means to a goal: the elimination of poor quality. The goal of quality assurance should be to reach a level of quality where inspection is not necessary. This is the ongoing focus of efforts in Japanese firms and the philosophy of W. Edwards Deming.

Schilling presents a life-cycle approach to sampling inspection, shown in Table 18.5.[4] The preparation stage begins with an analysis of the quality system to select the appropriate plan. This includes examining production capability, consumer needs, and past quality history. If extensive history of excellent quality is observed, for example, no inspection is necessary. If little history and poor quality are noted, 100% inspection is necessary. Between these extremes, a sampling procedure can usually be justified. Quality levels and risks must also be specified.

In the initiation stage, inspectors must be trained to implement the sampling procedures properly. Good records must be kept to analyze and monitor results. Once the system is established, it should be monitored closely and adjusted for severity of inspection. *Causes* of poor quality should be recognized and eliminated, enabling inspection to be phased out eventually.

---

[4]Edward G. Schilling, "An Overview of Acceptance Control," *Quality Progress*, Vol. 17, No. 4 (April 1984), pp. 22–25.

QUALITY IN PRACTICE

Sampling Patient Perceptions in a Multiple-Hospital System[5]

Maintaining uniform service quality is a problem that confronts administrators of multiple-hospital systems. One eight-hospital group in Southern California successfully inaugurated such a program by actively involving hospital staffs in questionnaire modification, survey feedback, and action planning based on survey results. Administrators found the results useful in problem diagnosis and management decisions.

Prior to this study, some hospitals had performed patient surveys on their own, but these questionnaires provided no basis for comparison between hospitals, since they varied widely in form, content, and administrative method. A consultant was used to help develop the survey and gain acceptance for the procedures. The consultant met with each administrator and assistants, including the director of nursing, at each medical center. Questionnaire content and survey procedures were reviewed, and support

[5]Adapted from K. M. Casarreal, J. I. Mills, and M. A. Plant, "Improving Service through Patient Surveys in a Multi-hospital Organization," *Hospital & Health Services Administration*, Health Administration Press, Ann Arbor, MI, March/April 1986, pp. 41–52. © 1986, Foundation of the American College of Health Care Executives.

was offered for any action planning indicated by survey results.

To ensure complete responses and a high return rate, interviewers questioned patients and filled out questionnaires. The survey lasted for two or three days at each hospital. A stratified random sample was used. The hospital's bed list was used to generate the sample; 10 beds or half the beds (whichever was smaller) were chosen at random in each unit. The nursing supervisors identified patients inappropriate for the sample due to grave illness, emotional instability, or recent surgery. The final overall sample of 972 patients demographically resembled patient census profiles both for each hospital and for the region as a whole. Table 18.6 shows the sample profile.

The questionnaire used included opportunities to rate observed staff behavior and to record subjective perceptions of staff attitudes. The questionnaire included demographic and hospital experience questions and made provisions to record patients' voluntary comments verbatim. The final questionnaire contained 90 to 144 items, depending on preferences of local administrators for adding questions. An example of some of the questions is shown in Figure 18.20.

TABLE 18.6 **Profile of Sample**

Variables		Percent of Total Sample (N = 972)	Percent of Total Hospital Patient Days, 1982–1983 (excluding newborns*)	Sample Range (Individual Hospitals) Low	High
Gender:	Female	58%	58%	53%	62%
	Male	42	42	38	47
Ethnicity:	Asian	3%	3%	0%	7%
	Black	16	15	1	44
	Hispanic	14	11	2	29
	White	65	69	43	92
	Other	2	2	1	4
Age:	Under 18	10%	10%	3%	15%
	18–35	30	23	22	43
	36–55	19	19	11	28
	Over 55	41	48	34	48

*Parents of newborns were almost never available to answer for their babies as survey respondents, effectively excluding them from the population available for sampling.

(continued)

FIGURE 18.20   **Sample Staff Behavior Questions**

ADMISSIONS

11. Altogether, how long did you have to wait to be admitted?
    More than 1 hour: ___ 1 hour: ___ 30 min. ___ 15 min. ___
               (1)   (2)   (3)   (4)

12. If you had to wait 30 minutes or longer before someone met with you, were you told why?
    YES: _____(1)   NO: _____(2)   Did not wait 30 minutes: _____(3)

NURSING STAFF

21. Did a nurse talk to you about the procedures for the day?
    Never: _____(1)   Sometimes: _____(2)   Often: _____(3)   Always: _____(4)

22. Were you on IV fluids?
    YES: _____(1)   NO: _____(2)
    A. If YES, did the IV fluids ever run out?
       YES: _____(1)   NO: _____(2)

MEDICAL STAFF

28. Did the doctor do what he/she told you he was going to do?
    Never: _____(1)   Sometimes: _____(2)   Often: _____(3)   Always: _____(4)

HOUSEKEEPING

36. Did the housekeeper come into your room at least once a day?
    YES: _____(1)   NO: _____(2)

39. Was the bathroom adequately supplied?
    Always: _____(1)   Often: _____(2)   Sometimes: _____(3)   Never: _____(4)

X-RAY

When you received services from the x-ray technician, were the procedures explained to you?
    Always: _____(1)   Often: _____(2)   Sometimes: _____(3)   Never: _____(4)

FOOD

34. Generally, were your meals served at the same time each day?
    Always: _____(1)   Often: _____(2)   Sometimes: _____(3)   Never: _____(4)

Using comparisons, the regional hospital administrator could tell local administrators which areas needed strengthening or correction. A typical area in need of further attention was food and food services: A lower proportion of patients responded as "very satisfied" for food and food services than in other parts of the questionnaire. A more detailed survey of food services was conducted and a new menu plan was eventually established.

Additional hospitals in the region were expected to be built, so several questions regarding patient preferences of room size, types of furniture, and furniture arrangements were included. Answers were used in design decisions.

Administrators and nursing supervisors studied problem units where patient opinion of one or more staff groups was lower than average. They found that some problems were due to temporarily abnormal conditions; in other cases, they worked with unit leaders to solve serious problems. In nursing situations, supervisors stressed shortening response time to patient calls. They also urged nurses to give patients reasons for delays in response and to inform patients about forthcoming daily routines.

As a result of the survey, a variety of short-term training programs was instituted, including a special communications module on the art of answering patients' questions for nurses, a short course in frequently used Spanish phrases, and explanations of particular technical procedures that stimulated patient comment, for example, intravenous procedures.

Key Issues for Discussion

1. Why do you believe that a stratified random sample was used as opposed to other types of sampling procedures?

2. Why was it important to compare the sample profile to the patient census?

3. How were the results of the survey used for quality improvement?

Eliminating Acceptance Inspection at Hewlett-Packard through Supplier Quality Improvement[6]

A supplier to Hewlett-Packard's Computer Division, in Cupertino, California, provided a unique assembly at a reasonable price but could not deliver the

[6]Adapted from John Flores and Constantine Pavsidis, "Help Your Supplier." Reprinted with permission from *Quality,* Vol. 23 (September 1984), pp. 42–43, a publication of Hitchcock Publishing, a Capital Cities/ABC, Inc., Company.

part without a high number of rejects. Management's first reaction was to consider a new supplier. However, the supplier had been difficult to find, and the decision was made to help the supplier do a better job.

A project team, headed by the procurement engineer and aided by the buyer and incoming inspection supervisor, was formed. Its goals were to

FIGURE 18.21 **Hewlett-Packard's Quality Improvement Plan**

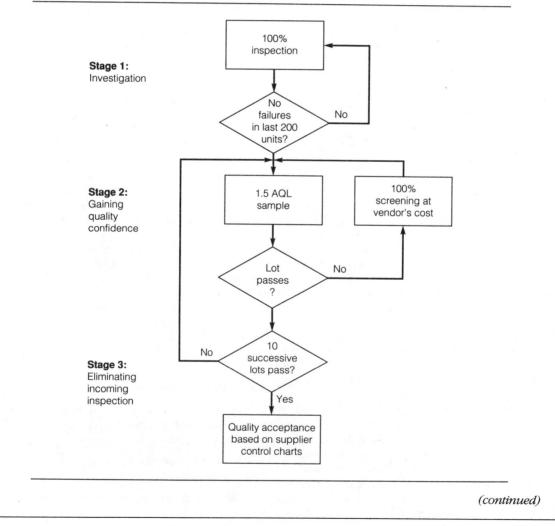

(continued)

eliminate incoming inspection and establish direct shipment of the supplier's assemblies into stock. The project team developed a three-stage plan to achieve these goals (illustrated in Figure 18.21). The plan consisted of a gradual relaxation of inspection requirements based on performance, with the ability to return to more stringent inspection if quality began to deteriorate.

The investigation in the first stage consisted of the following procedures:

- Analyzing the vendor's production and quality assurance capabilities.

- Communicating HP's product requirement specifications to the supplier.

- Assuring that the vendor's production and quality processes met requirements.

- Establishing the same quality measurement methods, materials, and equipment at the vendor and at the HP plant.

- Videotaping the supplier's process.

- Performing inspection on initial production runs before shipment.

To assure that corrective actions were working, HP data and vendor data were compared to ensure that the same quality method, materials, and equipment were used. The vendor was provided positive corrective feedback through control charts and Pareto analysis. Through such auditing practices, it was discovered that the supplier was simply misreading specifications on one part and that measuring equipment and adjustment instructions in the supplier's assembly stations were incompatible. These problems were easily corrected.

Hewlett-Packard benefited in several ways from this program. Supplier appraisal costs were reduced greatly, as was the average lead time from incoming inspection to finished goods inventory (from 14 days to 1 day). Regular 100% inspection was eliminated, as were rework returns.

Key Issues for Discussion

1. What aspects of total quality management are evident in this case?

2. What benefits did Hewlett-Packard accrue through this program?

Summary of Key Points

- Sampling is used to estimate population parameters and for acceptance inspection.

- The method of selecting a sample and the sample size are important factors that affect the amount of information contained in a sample.

- The most common types of sampling procedures are simple random sampling, stratified sampling, systematic sampling, cluster sampling, and judgment sampling. Each method has inherent advantages and disadvantages.

- Systematic errors in sampling such as bias can be reduced or eliminated through proper planning and design.

- A simple random sample is a sample of size n drawn from a population of size N in such a way that every possible sample of size n has an equal chance of being selected.

- An acceptance sampling plan is a description of the sample size and an associated acceptance or rejection number. Sampling plans may be single, double, multiple, or sequential.

- In selecting a sampling plan, one should consider the purpose, degree of risk, ease of administration, amount of inspection required, cost, and size of lots inspected.

- Producer's risk is the risk of rejecting a good quality lot; consumer's risk is the risk of accepting a poor quality lot.

- Operating characteristic curves give the probability of accepting a lot of a specified quality and are useful in comparing different sampling plans.

- Sampling plans are indexed by the degree of consumer or producer protection afforded by the plans. Common methods of indexing are indifference quality level, limiting quality/lot tolerance percent defective, acceptable quality level, and average outgoing quality limit.

- Published sampling plans such as MIL-STD-105 are widely used but are restricted in scope and applicability. Modern computer programs provide significantly more flexibility in designing sampling plans.

Questions for Review and Discussion

1. What two factors influence sampling procedures?

2. Discuss the basic questions that have to be addressed in a sampling study.

3. Describe the different methods of sample selection and provide an example in which each would be most appropriate.

4. What are the sources of systematic error in sampling? How can these be overcome?

5. Define a *sampling plan*.

6. Explain the differences between single, double, and multiple sampling plans.

7. What procedures should be followed in physically selecting a sample?

8. Discuss the important factors that need to be considered in selecting a specific sampling plan.

9. Explain the concepts of producer's and consumer's risk.

10. What is meant by severity of inspection? What levels of inspection are commonly used in practice?

11. Describe the basic methods for indexing sampling plans. How do they differ from each other in purpose?

12. What is an operating characteristic curve? Discuss how OC curves are used.

13. What is MIL-STD-105D? List the features included in this document.

14. Describe the sequence of operations that is typically followed in using MIL-STD-105D.

15. What are the economic issues involved in acceptance inspection? If sampling is never "optimal," why is it ever used?

16. Describe the life cycle of acceptance sampling.

Problems

1. You wish to obtain a simple random sample from your class in order to conduct a survey. Describe how to use the random numbers in Appendix C to obtain a sample of 50% of your class. Draw the sample and compare it to the class profile (male/female, academic major, etc.).

2. Refer to the control chart in Figure 16.9 and the calculations in Figure 16.20. Suppose that you wish to conduct a more detailed process capability study with a 99% confidence level to estimate the mean with a sampling error of at most 5.0. What is the appropriate sample size?

3. Determine the appropriate sample size to estimate the proportion of sorting errors in the post office example in Chapter 16 (Example 4) at a 95% confidence level. You wish to have an allowable error of 0.01.

4. Using Table 18.1, suppose that the population consists of 2,000 units. The critical rate of occurrence is 1%, and you wish to be 99% confident of finding at least one nonconformity. What sample size should you select?

5. For a single sampling plan with $n = 25$ and $c = 0$, find the probability of accepting a lot that has a fraction nonconforming of 2%. of 6%.

6. For a single sampling plan with $n = 50$ and $c = 4$, find the probability of accepting a lot that has a fraction nonconforming of 3%. of 7%.

7. Verify the OC curves in Figure 18.6 for $n = 10, c = 1; n = 15, c = 0$; and $n = 15$, $c = 1$ by computing the probability of acceptance for values of p between 0 and 0.25 in increments of 0.05.

8. Draw an OC curve for the Robertson Electronics example for a plan with $n = 15$ and $c = 2$. Show the effect of increasing n in increments of 5 up to 30. Show also the effect of increasing c in increments of 1 up to 6.

9. Draw the AOQ curve and estimate AOQL for the plans in Figure 18.6 by visually estimating P_a from the graphs.

10. In Problem 5, find the producer's and consumer's risk if AQL = 2% and LQL = 6%.

11. In Problem 6, find the producer's and consumer's risk if AQL = 3% and LQL = 8%.

12. Find the average outgoing quality for a plan with $n = 50, c = 4$, and $p = 4\%$. What is the average outgoing quality limit?

13. Find the average outgoing quality for a plan with $n = 40, c = 3$, and $p = 5\%$. What is the average outgoing quality limit?

14. Compute the average total inspection for various values of p and sketch the ATI curve for $N = 5,000, n = 50$, and $c = 4$. What effect does increasing N to 10,000 have?

15. Sketch the ATI curve for $N = 800, n = 40$, and $c = 3$. What effect does decreasing c to 0 have?

16. For $n = 50$ and $c = 3$, find the probability of acceptance if the lot quality is 1%, 3%, 5%, and 7%. Plot the OC curve.

17. Determine a sampling plan for a lot size of 1,000 and an AQL of 2.5% under normal inspection using MIL-STD-105D.

18. For the parameters given in Problem 17, determine the sampling plan under tightened and reduced inspection using MIL-STD-105D.

19. Determine sampling plans for a lot size of 20,000 and AQL of 1.5% for normal, tightened, and reduced inspection levels using MIL-STD-105D.

20. What are the acceptable quality level and sample size for normal inspection of a lot of size 5,000 and an acceptance number of 7?

21. What is the sampling plan for a lot size of 20 under tightened inspection and an AQL of 0.10?

Bibliography

Heyes, Gerald B. "Determining Sample Size and Error for Attribute Sampling," *Quality Progress,* November 1983, pp. 32–36.

Hunt, Robert O. "Quality from the Source," *Quality,* April 1982, pp. 54–56.

Montgomery, D. C. *Introduction to Statistical Quality Control,* 2nd ed., New York: John Wiley & Sons, 1991.

Papadakis, E. P. "Sampling Plans and 100% Nondestructive Inspection Compared," *Quality Progress,* April 1982, pp. 38–39.

Robbins, C. L., and Robbins, W. A. "What Nurse Managers Should Know about Sampling Techniques," *Nursing Management,* Vol. 20, No. 6, June 1989, pp. 46–48.

Appendixes

Areas for the Standard Normal Distribution

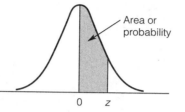

Area or probability

0   z

Entries in the table give the area under the curve between the mean and z standard deviations above the mean. For example, for $z = 1.25$ the area under the curve between the mean and z is 0.3944.

z	0.00	0.01	0.02	0.03	0.04	0.05	0.06	0.07	0.08	0.09
0.0	0.0000	0.0040	0.0080	0.0120	0.0160	0.0199	0.0239	0.0279	0.0319	0.0359
0.1	0.0398	0.0438	0.0478	0.0517	0.0557	0.0596	0.0636	0.0675	0.0714	0.0753
0.2	0.0793	0.0832	0.0871	0.0910	0.0948	0.0987	0.1026	0.1064	0.1103	0.1141
0.3	0.1179	0.1217	0.1255	0.1293	0.1331	0.1368	0.1406	0.1443	0.1480	0.1517
0.4	0.1554	0.1591	0.1628	0.1664	0.1700	0.1736	0.1772	0.1808	0.1844	0.1879
0.5	0.1915	0.1950	0.1985	0.2019	0.2054	0.2088	0.2123	0.2157	0.2190	0.2224
0.6	0.2257	0.2291	0.2324	0.2357	0.2389	0.2422	0.2454	0.2486	0.2518	0.2549
0.7	0.2580	0.2612	0.2642	0.2673	0.2704	0.2734	0.2764	0.2794	0.2823	0.2852
0.8	0.2881	0.2910	0.2939	0.2967	0.2995	0.3023	0.3051	0.3078	0.3106	0.3133
0.9	0.3159	0.3186	0.3212	0.3238	0.3264	0.3289	0.3315	0.3340	0.3365	0.3389
1.0	0.3413	0.3438	0.3461	0.3485	0.3508	0.3531	0.3554	0.3577	0.3599	0.3621
1.1	0.3643	0.3665	0.3686	0.3708	0.3729	0.3749	0.3770	0.3790	0.3810	0.3830
1.2	0.3849	0.3869	0.3888	0.3907	0.3925	0.3944	0.3962	0.3980	0.3997	0.4015
1.3	0.4032	0.4049	0.4066	0.4082	0.4099	0.4115	0.4131	0.4147	0.4162	0.4177
1.4	0.4192	0.4207	0.4222	0.4236	0.4251	0.4265	0.4279	0.4292	0.4306	0.4319
1.5	0.4332	0.4345	0.4357	0.4370	0.4382	0.4394	0.4406	0.4418	0.4429	0.4441
1.6	0.4452	0.4463	0.4474	0.4484	0.4495	0.4505	0.4515	0.4525	0.4535	0.4545
1.7	0.4554	0.4564	0.4573	0.4582	0.4591	0.4599	0.4608	0.4616	0.4625	0.4633
1.8	0.4641	0.4649	0.4656	0.4664	0.4671	0.4578	0.4686	0.4693	0.4699	0.4706
1.9	0.4713	0.4719	0.4726	0.4732	0.4738	0.4744	0.4750	0.4756	0.4761	0.4767
2.0	0.4772	0.4778	0.4783	0.4788	0.4793	0.4798	0.4803	0.4808	0.4812	0.4817
2.1	0.4821	0.4826	0.4830	0.4834	0.4838	0.4842	0.4846	0.4850	0.4854	0.4857
2.2	0.4861	0.4864	0.4868	0.4871	0.4875	0.4878	0.4881	0.4884	0.4887	0.4890
2.3	0.4893	0.4896	0.4898	0.4901	0.4094	0.4906	0.4909	0.4911	0.4913	0.4916
2.4	0.4918	0.4920	0.4922	0.4925	0.4927	0.4929	0.4931	0.4932	0.4934	0.4936
2.5	0.4938	0.4940	0.4941	0.4943	0.4945	0.4946	0.4948	0.4949	0.4951	0.4952
2.6	0.4953	0.4955	0.4956	0.4957	0.4959	0.4960	0.4961	0.4962	0.4963	0.4964
2.7	0.4965	0.4966	0.4967	0.4968	0.4969	0.4970	0.4971	0.4972	0.4973	0.4974
2.8	0.4974	0.4975	0.4976	0.4977	0.4977	0.4978	0.4979	0.4979	0.4980	0.4981
2.9	0.4981	0.4982	0.4982	0.4983	0.4984	0.4984	0.4985	0.4985	0.4986	0.4986
3.0	0.4986	0.4987	0.4987	0.4988	0.4988	0.4989	0.4989	0.4989	0.4990	0.4990

Factors for Control Charts

n	X-charts				s-Charts				R-charts					
	A	A_2	A_3	c_4	B_3	B_4	B_5	B_6	d_2	d_3	D_1	D_2	D_3	D_4
2	2.121	1.880	2.659	0.7979	0	3.267	0	2.606	1.128	0.853	0	3.686	0	3.267
3	1.732	1.023	1.954	0.8862	0	2.568	0	2.276	1.693	0.888	0	4.358	0	2.574
4	1.500	0.729	1.628	0.9213	0	2.266	0	2.088	2.059	0.880	0	4.698	0	2.282
5	1.342	0.577	1.427	0.9400	0	2.089	0	1.964	2.326	0.864	0	4.918	0	2.114
6	1.225	0.483	1.287	0.9515	0.030	1.970	0.029	1.874	2.534	0.848	0	5.078	0	2.004
7	1.134	0.419	1.182	0.9594	0.118	1.882	0.113	1.806	2.704	0.833	0.204	5.204	0.076	1.924
8	1.061	0.373	1.099	0.9650	0.185	1.815	0.179	1.751	2.847	0.820	0.388	5.306	0.136	1.864
9	1.000	0.337	1.032	0.9693	0.239	1.761	0.232	1.707	2.970	0.808	0.547	5.393	0.184	1.816
10	0.949	0.308	0.975	0.9727	0.284	1.716	0.276	1.669	3.078	0.797	0.687	5.469	0.223	1.777
11	0.905	0.285	0.927	0.9754	0.321	1.679	0.313	1.637	3.173	0.787	0.811	5.535	0.256	1.744
12	0.866	0.266	0.886	0.9776	0.354	1.646	0.346	1.610	3.258	0.778	0.922	5.594	0.283	1.717
13	0.832	0.249	0.850	0.9794	0.382	1.618	0.374	1.585	3.336	0.770	1.025	5.647	0.307	1.693
14	0.802	0.235	0.817	0.9810	0.406	1.594	0.399	1.563	3.407	0.763	1.118	5.696	0.328	1.672
15	0.775	0.223	0.789	0.9823	0.428	1.572	0.421	1.544	3.472	0.756	1.203	5.741	0.347	1.653
16	0.750	0.212	0.763	0.9835	0.448	1.552	0.440	1.526	3.532	0.750	1.282	5.782	0.363	1.637
17	0.728	0.203	0.739	0.9845	0.466	1.534	0.458	1.511	3.588	0.744	1.356	5.820	0.378	1.622
18	0.707	0.194	0.718	0.9854	0.482	1.518	0.475	1.496	3.640	0.739	1.424	5.856	0.391	1.608
19	0.688	0.187	0.698	0.9862	0.497	1.503	0.490	1.483	3.689	0.734	1.487	5.891	0.403	1.597
20	0.671	0.180	0.680	0.9869	0.510	1.490	0.504	1.470	3.735	0.729	1.549	5.921	0.415	1.585
21	0.655	0.173	0.663	0.9876	0.523	1.477	0.516	1.459	3.778	0.724	1.605	5.951	0.425	1.575
22	0.640	0.167	0.647	0.9882	0.534	1.466	0.528	1.448	3.819	0.720	1.659	5.979	0.434	1.566
23	0.626	0.162	0.633	0.9887	0.545	1.455	0.539	1.438	3.858	0.716	1.710	6.006	0.443	1.557
24	0.612	0.157	0.619	0.9892	0.555	1.445	0.549	1.429	3.895	0.712	1.759	6.031	0.451	1.548
25	0.600	0.153	0.606	0.9896	0.565	1.435	0.559	1.420	3.931	0.708	1.806	6.056	0.459	1.541

SOURCE: Adapted from Table 27 of ASTM STP 15D *ASTM Manual on Presentation of Data and Control Chart Analysis*. Copyright 1976 American Society for Testing and Materials, Philadelphia, PA.

APPENDIX C

Random Digits

63271	59986	71744	51102	15141	80714	58683	93108	13554	79945
88547	09896	95436	79115	08303	01041	20030	63754	08459	28364
55957	57243	83865	09911	19761	66535	40102	26646	60147	15702
46276	87453	44790	67122	45573	84358	21625	16999	13385	22782
55363	07449	34835	15290	76616	67191	12777	21861	68689	03263
69393	92785	49902	58447	42048	30378	87618	26933	40640	16281
13186	29431	88190	04588	38733	81290	89541	70290	40113	08243
17726	28652	56836	78351	47327	18518	92222	55201	27340	10493
36520	64465	05550	30157	82242	29520	69753	72602	23756	54935
81628	36100	39254	56835	37636	02421	98063	89641	64953	99337
84649	48968	75215	75498	49539	74240	03466	49292	36401	45525
63291	11618	12613	75055	43915	26488	41116	64531	56827	30825
70502	53225	03655	05915	37140	57051	48393	91322	25653	06543
06426	24771	59935	49801	11082	66762	94477	02494	88215	27191
20711	55609	29430	70165	45406	78484	31639	52009	18873	96927
41990	70538	77191	25860	55204	73417	83920	69468	74972	38712
72452	36618	76298	26678	89334	33938	95567	29380	75906	91807
37042	40318	57099	10528	09925	89773	41335	96244	29002	46453
53766	52875	15987	46962	67342	77592	57651	95508	80033	69828
90585	58955	53122	16025	84299	53310	67380	84249	25348	04332
32001	96293	37203	64516	51530	37069	40261	61374	05815	06714
62606	64324	46354	72157	67248	20135	49804	09226	64419	29457
10078	28073	85389	50324	14500	15562	64165	06125	71353	77669
91561	46145	24177	15294	10061	98124	75732	00815	83452	97355
13091	98112	53959	79607	52244	63303	10413	63839	74762	50289
73864	83014	72457	22682	03033	61714	88173	90835	00634	85169
66668	25467	48894	51043	02365	91726	09365	63167	95264	45643
84745	41042	29493	01836	09044	51926	43630	63470	76508	14194
48068	26805	94595	47907	13357	38412	33318	26098	82782	42851
54310	96175	97594	88616	42035	38093	36745	56702	40644	83514

14877	33095	10924	58013	61439	21882	42059	24177	58739	60170
78295	23179	02771	43464	59061	71411	05697	67194	30495	21157
67524	02865	39593	54278	04237	92441	26602	63835	38032	94770
58268	57219	68124	73455	83236	08710	04284	55005	84171	42596
97158	28672	50685	01181	24262	19427	52106	34308	73685	74246
04230	16831	69085	30802	65559	09205	71829	06489	85650	38707
94879	56606	30401	02602	57658	70091	54986	41394	60437	03195
71446	15232	66715	26385	91518	70566	02888	79941	39684	54315
32886	05644	79316	09819	00813	88407	17461	73925	53037	91904
62048	33711	25290	21526	02223	75947	66466	06232	10913	75336

SOURCE: Reprinted from Page 44 of *A Million Random Digits With 100,000 Normal Deviates,* by the Rand Corporation. New York: The Free Press, 1955. Copyright 1955 by The Rand Corporation. Used by permission.

APPENDIX D

Binomial Probabilities

Entries in the table give the probability of x successes in n trials of a binomial experiment, where p is the probability of a success on one trial. For example, with six trials and $p = 0.40$, the probability of two successes is 0.3110.

n	x	0.05	0.10	0.15	0.20	0.25	0.30	0.35	0.40	0.45	0.50
1	0	0.9500	0.9000	0.8500	0.8000	0.7500	0.7000	0.6500	0.6000	0.5500	0.5000
	1	0.0500	0.1000	0.1500	0.2000	0.2500	0.3000	0.3500	0.4000	0.4500	0.5000
2	0	0.9025	0.8100	0.7225	0.6400	0.5625	0.4900	0.4225	0.3600	0.3025	0.2500
	1	0.0950	0.1800	0.2550	0.3200	0.3750	0.4200	0.4550	0.4800	0.4950	0.5000
	2	0.0025	0.0100	0.0225	0.0400	0.0625	0.0900	0.1225	0.1600	0.2025	0.2500
3	0	0.8574	0.7290	0.6141	0.5120	0.4219	0.3430	0.2746	0.2160	0.1664	0.1250
	1	0.1354	0.2430	0.3251	0.3840	0.4219	0.4410	0.4436	0.4320	0.4084	0.3750
	2	0.0071	0.0270	0.0574	0.0960	0.1406	0.1890	0.2389	0.2880	0.3341	0.3750
	3	0.0001	0.0010	0.0034	0.0080	0.0156	0.0270	0.0429	0.0640	0.0911	0.1250
4	0	0.8145	0.6561	0.5220	0.4096	0.3164	0.2401	0.1785	0.1296	0.0915	0.0625
	1	0.1715	0.2916	0.3685	0.4096	0.4219	0.4116	0.3845	0.3456	0.2995	0.2500
	2	0.0135	0.0486	0.0975	0.1536	0.2109	0.2646	0.3105	0.3456	0.3675	0.3750
	3	0.0005	0.0036	0.0115	0.0256	0.0469	0.0756	0.1115	0.1536	0.2005	0.2500
	4	0.0000	0.0001	0.0005	0.0016	0.0039	0.0081	0.0150	0.0256	0.0410	0.0625
5	0	0.7738	0.5905	0.4437	0.3277	0.2373	0.1681	0.1160	0.0778	0.0503	0.0312
	1	0.2036	0.3280	0.3915	0.4096	0.3955	0.3602	0.3124	0.2592	0.2059	0.1562
	2	0.0214	0.0729	0.1382	0.2048	0.2637	0.3087	0.3364	0.3456	0.3369	0.3125
	3	0.0011	0.0081	0.0244	0.0512	0.0879	0.1323	0.1811	0.2304	0.2757	0.3125
	4	0.0000	0.0004	0.0022	0.0064	0.0146	0.0284	0.0488	0.0768	0.1128	0.1562
	5	0.0000	0.0000	0.0001	0.0003	0.0010	0.0024	0.0053	0.0102	0.0185	0.0312
6	0	0.7351	0.5314	0.3771	0.2621	0.1780	0.1176	0.0754	0.0467	0.0277	0.0156
	1	0.2321	0.3543	0.3993	0.3932	0.3560	0.3025	0.2437	0.1866	0.1359	0.0938
	2	0.0305	0.0984	0.1762	0.2458	0.2966	0.3241	0.3280	0.3110	0.2780	0.2344
	3	0.0021	0.0146	0.0415	0.0819	0.1318	0.1852	0.2355	0.2765	0.3032	0.3125
	4	0.0001	0.0012	0.0055	0.0154	0.0330	0.0595	0.0951	0.1382	0.1861	0.2344
	5	0.0000	0.0001	0.0004	0.0015	0.0044	0.0102	0.0205	0.0369	0.0609	0.0938
	6	0.0000	0.0000	0.0000	0.0001	0.0002	0.0007	0.0018	0.0041	0.0083	0.0156

n	x	0.05	0.10	0.15	0.20	0.25	0.30	0.35	0.40	0.45	0.50
						p					
7	0	0.6983	0.4783	0.3206	0.2097	0.1335	0.0824	0.0490	0.0280	0.0152	0.0078
	1	0.2573	0.3720	0.3960	0.3670	0.3115	0.2471	0.1848	0.1306	0.0872	0.0547
	2	0.0406	0.1240	0.2097	0.2753	0.3115	0.3177	0.2985	0.2613	0.2140	0.1641
	3	0.0036	0.0230	0.0617	0.1147	0.1730	0.2269	0.2679	0.2903	0.2918	0.2734
	4	0.0002	0.0026	0.0109	0.0287	0.0577	0.0972	0.1442	0.1935	0.2388	0.2734
	5	0.0000	0.0002	0.0012	0.0043	0.0115	0.0250	0.0466	0.0774	0.1172	0.1641
	6	0.0000	0.0000	0.0001	0.0004	0.0013	0.0036	0.0084	0.0172	0.0320	0.0547
	7	0.0000	0.0000	0.0000	0.0000	0.0001	0.0002	0.0006	0.0016	0.0037	0.0078
8	0	0.6634	0.4305	0.2725	0.1678	0.1001	0.0576	0.0319	0.0168	0.0084	0.0039
	1	0.2793	0.3826	0.3847	0.3355	0.2670	0.1977	0.1373	0.0896	0.0548	0.0312
	2	0.0515	0.1488	0.2376	0.2936	0.3115	0.2965	0.2587	0.2090	0.1569	0.1094
	3	0.0054	0.0331	0.0839	0.1468	0.2076	0.2541	0.2786	0.2787	0.2568	0.2188
	4	0.0004	0.0046	0.0185	0.0459	0.0865	0.1361	0.1875	0.2322	0.2627	0.2734
	5	0.0000	0.0004	0.0026	0.0092	0.0231	0.0467	0.0808	0.1239	0.1719	0.2188
	6	0.0000	0.0000	0.0002	0.0011	0.0038	0.0100	0.0217	0.0413	0.0703	0.1094
	7	0.0000	0.0000	0.0000	0.0001	0.0004	0.0012	0.0033	0.0079	0.0164	0.0312
	8	0.0000	0.0000	0.0000	0.0000	0.0000	0.0001	0.0002	0.0007	0.0017	0.0039
9	0	0.6302	0.3874	0.2316	0.1342	0.0751	0.0404	0.0207	0.0101	0.0046	0.0020
	1	0.2985	0.3874	0.3679	0.3020	0.2253	0.1556	0.1004	0.0605	0.0339	0.0176
	2	0.0629	0.1722	0.2597	0.3020	0.3003	0.2668	0.2162	0.1612	0.1110	0.0703
	3	0.0077	0.0446	0.1069	0.1762	0.2336	0.2668	0.2716	0.2508	0.2119	0.1641
	4	0.0006	0.0074	0.0283	0.0661	0.1168	0.1715	0.2194	0.2508	0.2600	0.2461
	5	0.0000	0.0008	0.0050	0.0165	0.0389	0.0735	0.1181	0.1672	0.2128	0.2461
	6	0.0000	0.0001	0.0006	0.0028	0.0087	0.0210	0.0424	0.0743	0.1160	0.1641
	7	0.0000	0.0000	0.0000	0.0003	0.0012	0.0039	0.0098	0.0212	0.0407	0.0703
	8	0.0000	0.0000	0.0000	0.0000	0.0001	0.0004	0.0013	0.0035	0.0083	0.0176
	9	0.0000	0.0000	0.0000	0.0000	0.0000	0.0000	0.0001	0.0003	0.0008	0.0020
10	0	0.5987	0.3487	0.1969	0.1074	0.0563	0.0282	0.0135	0.0060	0.0025	0.0010
	1	0.3151	0.3874	0.3474	0.2684	0.1877	0.1211	0.0725	0.0403	0.0207	0.0098
	2	0.0746	0.1937	0.2759	0.3020	0.2816	0.2335	0.1757	0.1209	0.0763	0.0439
	3	0.0105	0.0574	0.1298	0.2013	0.2503	0.2668	0.2522	0.2150	0.1665	0.1172
	4	0.0010	0.0112	0.0401	0.0881	0.1460	0.2001	0.2377	0.2508	0.2384	0.2051
	5	0.0001	0.0015	0.0085	0.0264	0.0584	0.1029	0.1536	0.2007	0.2340	0.2461
	6	0.0000	0.0001	0.0012	0.0055	0.0162	0.0368	0.0689	0.1115	0.1596	0.2051
	7	0.0000	0.0000	0.0001	0.0008	0.0031	0.0090	0.0212	0.0425	0.0746	0.1172
	8	0.0000	0.0000	0.0000	0.0001	0.0004	0.0014	0.0043	0.0106	0.0229	0.0439
	9	0.0000	0.0000	0.0000	0.0000	0.0000	0.0001	0.0005	0.0016	0.0042	0.0098
	10	0.0000	0.0000	0.0000	0.0000	0.0000	0.0000	0.0000	0.0001	0.0003	0.0010
11	0	0.5688	0.3138	0.1673	0.0859	0.0422	0.0198	0.0088	0.0036	0.0014	0.0005
	1	0.3293	0.3835	0.3248	0.2362	0.1549	0.0932	0.0518	0.0266	0.0125	0.0054
	2	0.0867	0.2131	0.2866	0.2953	0.2581	0.1998	0.1395	0.0887	0.0513	0.0269
	3	0.0137	0.0710	0.1517	0.2215	0.2581	0.2568	0.2254	0.1774	0.1259	0.0806
	4	0.0014	0.0158	0.0536	0.1107	0.1721	0.2201	0.2428	0.2365	0.2060	0.1611
	5	0.0001	0.0025	0.0132	0.0388	0.0803	0.1321	0.1830	0.2207	0.2360	0.2256
	6	0.0000	0.0003	0.0023	0.0097	0.0268	0.0566	0.0985	0.1471	0.1931	0.2256
	7	0.0000	0.0000	0.0003	0.0017	0.0064	0.0173	0.0379	0.0701	0.1128	0.1611
	8	0.0000	0.0000	0.0000	0.0002	0.0011	0.0037	0.0102	0.0234	0.0462	0.0806
	9	0.0000	0.0000	0.0000	0.0000	0.0001	0.0005	0.0018	0.0052	0.0126	0.0269

n	x	0.05	0.10	0.15	0.20	0.25	0.30	0.35	0.40	0.45	0.50
	10	0.0000	0.0000	0.0000	0.0000	0.0000	0.0000	0.0002	0.0007	0.0021	0.0054
	11	0.0000	0.0000	0.0000	0.0000	0.0000	0.0000	0.0000	0.0000	0.0002	0.0005
12	0	0.5404	0.2824	0.1422	0.0687	0.0317	0.0138	0.0057	0.0022	0.0008	0.0002
	1	0.3413	0.3766	0.3012	0.2062	0.1267	0.0712	0.0368	0.0174	0.0075	0.0029
	2	0.0988	0.2301	0.2924	0.2835	0.2323	0.1678	0.1088	0.0639	0.0339	0.0161
	3	0.0173	0.0853	0.1720	0.2362	0.2581	0.2397	0.1954	0.1419	0.0923	0.0537
	4	0.0021	0.0213	0.0683	0.1329	0.1936	0.2311	0.2367	0.2128	0.1700	0.1208
	5	0.0002	0.0038	0.0193	0.0532	0.1032	0.1585	0.2039	0.2270	0.2225	0.1934
	6	0.0000	0.0005	0.0040	0.0155	0.0401	0.0792	0.1281	0.1766	0.2124	0.2256
	7	0.0000	0.0000	0.0006	0.0033	0.0115	0.0291	0.0591	0.1009	0.1489	0.1934
	8	0.0000	0.0000	0.0001	0.0005	0.0024	0.0078	0.0199	0.0420	0.0762	0.1208
	9	0.0000	0.0000	0.0000	0.0001	0.0004	0.0015	0.0048	0.0125	0.0277	0.0537
	10	0.0000	0.0000	0.0000	0.0000	0.0000	0.0002	0.0008	0.0025	0.0068	0.0161
	11	0.0000	0.0000	0.0000	0.0000	0.0000	0.0000	0.0001	0.0003	0.0010	0.0029
	12	0.0000	0.0000	0.0000	0.0000	0.0000	0.0000	0.0000	0.0000	0.0001	0.0002
13	0	0.5133	0.2542	0.1209	0.0550	0.0238	0.0097	0.0037	0.0013	0.0004	0.0001
	1	0.3512	0.3672	0.2774	0.1787	0.1029	0.0540	0.0259	0.0113	0.0045	0.0016
	2	0.1109	0.2448	0.2937	0.2680	0.2059	0.1388	0.0836	0.0453	0.0220	0.0095
	3	0.0214	0.0997	0.1900	0.2457	0.2517	0.2181	0.1651	0.1107	0.0660	0.0349
	4	0.0028	0.0277	0.0838	0.1535	0.2097	0.2337	0.2222	0.1845	0.1350	0.0873
	5	0.0003	0.0055	0.0266	0.0691	0.1258	0.1803	0.2154	0.2214	0.1989	0.1571
	6	0.0000	0.0008	0.0063	0.0230	0.0559	0.1030	0.1546	0.1968	0.2169	0.2095
	7	0.0000	0.0001	0.0011	0.0058	0.0186	0.0442	0.0833	0.1312	0.1775	0.2095
	8	0.0000	0.0000	0.0001	0.0011	0.0047	0.0142	0.0336	0.0656	0.1089	0.1571
	9	0.0000	0.0000	0.0000	0.0001	0.0009	0.0034	0.0101	0.0243	0.0495	0.0873
	10	0.0000	0.0000	0.0000	0.0000	0.0001	0.0006	0.0022	0.0065	0.0162	0.0349
	11	0.0000	0.0000	0.0000	0.0000	0.0000	0.0001	0.0003	0.0012	0.0036	0.0095
	12	0.0000	0.0000	0.0000	0.0000	0.0000	0.0000	0.0000	0.0001	0.0005	0.0016
	13	0.0000	0.0000	0.0000	0.0000	0.0000	0.0000	0.0000	0.0000	0.0000	0.0001
14	0	0.4877	0.2288	0.1028	0.0440	0.0178	0.0068	0.0024	0.0008	0.0002	0.0001
	1	0.3593	0.3559	0.2539	0.1539	0.0832	0.0407	0.0181	0.0073	0.0027	0.0009
	2	0.1229	0.2570	0.2912	0.2501	0.1802	0.1134	0.0634	0.0317	0.0141	0.0056
	3	0.0259	0.1142	0.2056	0.2501	0.2402	0.1943	0.1366	0.0845	0.0462	0.0222
	4	0.0037	0.0349	0.0998	0.1720	0.2202	0.2290	0.2022	0.1549	0.1040	0.0611
	5	0.0004	0.0078	0.0352	0.0860	0.1468	0.1963	0.2178	0.2066	0.1701	0.1222
	6	0.0000	0.0013	0.0093	0.0322	0.0734	0.1262	0.1759	0.2066	0.2088	0.1833
	7	0.0000	0.0002	0.0019	0.0092	0.0280	0.0618	0.1082	0.1574	0.1952	0.2095
	8	0.0000	0.0000	0.0003	0.0020	0.0082	0.0232	0.0510	0.0918	0.1398	0.1833
	9	0.0000	0.0000	0.0000	0.0003	0.0018	0.0066	0.0183	0.0408	0.0762	0.1222
	10	0.0000	0.0000	0.0000	0.0000	0.0003	0.0014	0.0049	0.0136	0.0312	0.0611
	11	0.0000	0.0000	0.0000	0.0000	0.0000	0.0002	0.0010	0.0033	0.0093	0.0222
	12	0.0000	0.0000	0.0000	0.0000	0.0000	0.0000	0.0001	0.0005	0.0019	0.0056
	13	0.0000	0.0000	0.0000	0.0000	0.0000	0.0000	0.0000	0.0001	0.0002	0.0009
	14	0.0000	0.0000	0.0000	0.0000	0.0000	0.0000	0.0000	0.0000	0.0000	0.0001

n	x	0.05	0.10	0.15	0.20	*p* 0.25	0.30	0.35	0.40	0.45	0.50
15	0	0.4633	0.2059	0.0874	0.0352	0.0134	0.0047	0.0016	0.0005	0.0001	0.0000
	1	0.3658	0.3432	0.2312	0.1319	0.0668	0.0305	0.0126	0.0047	0.0016	0.0005
	2	0.1348	0.2669	0.2856	0.2309	0.1559	0.0916	0.0476	0.0219	0.0090	0.0032
	3	0.0307	0.1285	0.2184	0.2501	0.2252	0.1700	0.1110	0.0634	0.0318	0.0139
	4	0.0049	0.0428	0.1156	0.1876	0.2252	0.2186	0.1792	0.1268	0.0780	0.0417
	5	0.0006	0.0105	0.0449	0.1032	0.1651	0.2061	0.2123	0.1859	0.1404	0.0916
	6	0.0000	0.0019	0.0132	0.0430	0.0917	0.1472	0.1906	0.2066	0.1914	0.1527
	7	0.0000	0.0003	0.0030	0.0138	0.0393	0.0811	0.1319	0.1711	0.2013	0.1964
	8	0.0000	0.0000	0.0005	0.0035	0.0131	0.0348	0.0710	0.1181	0.1647	0.1964
	9	0.0000	0.0000	0.0001	0.0007	0.0034	0.0116	0.0298	0.0612	0.1048	0.1527
	10	0.0000	0.0000	0.0000	0.0001	0.0007	0.0030	0.0096	0.0245	0.0515	0.0916
	11	0.0000	0.0000	0.0000	0.0000	0.0001	0.0006	0.0024	0.0074	0.0191	0.0417
	12	0.0000	0.0000	0.0000	0.0000	0.0000	0.0001	0.0004	0.0016	0.0052	0.0139
	13	0.0000	0.0000	0.0000	0.0000	0.0000	0.0000	0.0001	0.0003	0.0010	0.0032
	14	0.0000	0.0000	0.0000	0.0000	0.0000	0.0000	0.0000	0.0000	0.0001	0.0005
	15	0.0000	0.0000	0.0000	0.0000	0.0000	0.0000	0.0000	0.0000	0.0000	0.0000
16	0	0.4401	0.1853	0.0743	0.0281	0.0100	0.0033	0.0010	0.0003	0.0001	0.0000
	1	0.3706	0.3294	0.2097	0.1126	0.0535	0.0228	0.0087	0.0030	0.0009	0.0002
	2	0.1463	0.2745	0.2775	0.2111	0.1336	0.0732	0.0353	0.0150	0.0056	0.0018
	3	0.0359	0.1423	0.2285	0.2463	0.2079	0.1465	0.0888	0.0468	0.0215	0.0085
	4	0.0061	0.0514	0.1311	0.2001	0.2252	0.2040	0.1553	0.1014	0.0572	0.0278
	5	0.0008	0.0137	0.0555	0.1201	0.1802	0.2099	0.2008	0.1623	0.1123	0.0667
	6	0.0001	0.0028	0.0180	0.0550	0.1101	0.1649	0.1982	0.1983	0.1684	0.1222
	7	0.0000	0.0004	0.0045	0.0197	0.0524	0.1010	0.1524	0.1889	0.1969	0.1746
	8	0.0000	0.0001	0.0009	0.0055	0.0197	0.0487	0.0923	0.1417	0.1812	0.1964
	9	0.0000	0.0000	0.0001	0.0012	0.0058	0.0185	0.0442	0.0840	0.1318	0.1746
	10	0.0000	0.0000	0.0000	0.0002	0.0014	0.0056	0.0167	0.0392	0.0755	0.1222
	11	0.0000	0.0000	0.0000	0.0000	0.0002	0.0013	0.0049	0.0142	0.0337	0.0667
	12	0.0000	0.0000	0.0000	0.0000	0.0000	0.0002	0.0011	0.0040	0.0115	0.0278
	13	0.0000	0.0000	0.0000	0.0000	0.0000	0.0000	0.0002	0.0008	0.0029	0.0085
	14	0.0000	0.0000	0.0000	0.0000	0.0000	0.0000	0.0000	0.0001	0.0005	0.0018
	15	0.0000	0.0000	0.0000	0.0000	0.0000	0.0000	0.0000	0.0000	0.0001	0.0002
	16	0.0000	0.0000	0.0000	0.0000	0.0000	0.0000	0.0000	0.0000	0.0000	0.0000
17	0	0.4181	0.1668	0.0631	0.0225	0.0075	0.0023	0.0007	0.0002	0.0000	0.0000
	1	0.3741	0.3150	0.1893	0.0957	0.0426	0.0169	0.0060	0.0019	0.0005	0.0001
	2	0.1575	0.2800	0.2673	0.1914	0.1136	0.0581	0.0260	0.0102	0.0035	0.0010
	3	0.0415	0.1556	0.2359	0.2393	0.1893	0.1245	0.0701	0.0341	0.0144	0.0052
	4	0.0076	0.0605	0.1457	0.2093	0.2209	0.1868	0.1320	0.0796	0.0411	0.0182
	5	0.0010	0.0175	0.0668	0.1361	0.1914	0.2081	0.1849	0.1379	0.0875	0.0472
	6	0.0001	0.0039	0.0236	0.0680	0.1276	0.1784	0.1991	0.1839	0.1432	0.0944
	7	0.0000	0.0007	0.0065	0.0267	0.0668	0.1201	0.1685	0.1927	0.1841	0.1484
	8	0.0000	0.0001	0.0014	0.0084	0.0279	0.0644	0.1134	0.1606	0.1883	0.1855
	9	0.0000	0.0000	0.0003	0.0021	0.0093	0.0276	0.0611	0.1070	0.1540	0.1855

						P					
n	x	0.05	0.10	0.15	0.20	0.25	0.30	0.35	0.40	0.45	0.50
17	10	0.0000	0.0000	0.0000	0.0004	0.0025	0.0095	0.0263	0.0571	0.1008	0.1484
	11	0.0000	0.0000	0.0000	0.0001	0.0005	0.0026	0.0090	0.0242	0.0525	0.0944
	12	0.0000	0.0000	0.0000	0.0000	0.0001	0.0006	0.0024	0.0081	0.0215	0.0472
	13	0.0000	0.0000	0.0000	0.0000	0.0000	0.0001	0.0005	0.0021	0.0068	0.0182
	14	0.0000	0.0000	0.0000	0.0000	0.0000	0.0000	0.0001	0.0004	0.0016	0.0052
	15	0.0000	0.0000	0.0000	0.0000	0.0000	0.0000	0.0000	0.0001	0.0003	0.0010
	16	0.0000	0.0000	0.0000	0.0000	0.0000	0.0000	0.0000	0.0000	0.0000	0.0001
	17	0.0000	0.0000	0.0000	0.0000	0.0000	0.0000	0.0000	0.0000	0.0000	0.0000
18	0	0.3972	0.1501	0.0536	0.0180	0.0056	0.0016	0.0004	0.0001	0.0000	0.0000
	1	0.3763	0.3002	0.1704	0.0811	0.0338	0.0126	0.0042	0.0012	0.0003	0.0001
	2	0.1683	0.2835	0.2556	0.1723	0.0958	0.0458	0.0190	0.0069	0.0022	0.0006
	3	0.0473	0.1680	0.2406	0.2297	0.1704	0.1046	0.0547	0.0246	0.0095	0.0031
	4	0.0093	0.0700	0.1592	0.2153	0.2130	0.1681	0.1104	0.0614	0.0291	0.0117
	5	0.0014	0.0218	0.0787	0.1507	0.1988	0.2017	0.1664	0.1146	0.0666	0.0327
	6	0.0002	0.0052	0.0301	0.0816	0.1436	0.1873	0.1941	0.1655	0.1181	0.0708
	7	0.0000	0.0010	0.0091	0.0350	0.0820	0.1376	0.1792	0.1892	0.1657	0.1214
	8	0.0000	0.0002	0.0022	0.0120	0.0376	0.0811	0.1327	0.1734	0.1864	0.1669
	9	0.0000	0.0000	0.0004	0.0033	0.0139	0.0386	0.0794	0.1284	0.1694	0.1855
	10	0.0000	0.0000	0.0001	0.0008	0.0042	0.0149	0.0385	0.0771	0.1248	0.1669
	11	0.0000	0.0000	0.0000	0.0001	0.0010	0.0046	0.0151	0.0374	0.0742	0.1214
	12	0.0000	0.0000	0.0000	0.0000	0.0002	0.0012	0.0047	0.0145	0.0354	0.0708
	13	0.0000	0.0000	0.0000	0.0000	0.0000	0.0002	0.0012	0.0045	0.0134	0.0327
	14	0.0000	0.0000	0.0000	0.0000	0.0000	0.0000	0.0002	0.0011	0.0039	0.0117
	15	0.0000	0.0000	0.0000	0.0000	0.0000	0.0000	0.0000	0.0002	0.0009	0.0031
	16	0.0000	0.0000	0.0000	0.0000	0.0000	0.0000	0.0000	0.0000	0.0001	0.0006
	17	0.0000	0.0000	0.0000	0.0000	0.0000	0.0000	0.0000	0.0000	0.0000	0.0001
	18	0.0000	0.0000	0.0000	0.0000	0.0000	0.0000	0.0000	0.0000	0.0000	0.0000
19	0	0.3774	0.1351	0.0456	0.0144	0.0042	0.0011	0.0003	0.0001	0.0002	0.0000
	1	0.3774	0.2852	0.1529	0.0685	0.0268	0.0093	0.0029	0.0008	0.0002	0.0000
	2	0.1787	0.2852	0.2428	0.1540	0.0803	0.0358	0.0138	0.0046	0.0013	0.0003
	3	0.0533	0.1796	0.2428	0.2182	0.1517	0.0869	0.0422	0.0175	0.0062	0.0018
	4	0.0112	0.0798	0.1714	0.2182	0.2023	0.1491	0.0909	0.0467	0.0203	0.0074
	5	0.0018	0.0266	0.0907	0.1636	0.2023	0.1916	0.1468	0.0933	0.0497	0.0222
	6	0.0002	0.0069	0.0374	0.0955	0.1574	0.1916	0.1844	0.1451	0.0949	0.0518
	7	0.0000	0.0014	0.0122	0.0443	0.0974	0.1525	0.1844	0.1797	0.1443	0.0961
	8	0.0000	0.0002	0.0032	0.0166	0.0487	0.0981	0.1489	0.1797	0.1771	0.1442
	9	0.0000	0.0000	0.0007	0.0051	0.0198	0.0514	0.0980	0.1464	0.1771	0.1762
	10	0.0000	0.0000	0.0001	0.0013	0.0066	0.0220	0.0528	0.0976	0.1449	0.1762
	11	0.0000	0.0000	0.0000	0.0003	0.0018	0.0077	0.0233	0.0532	0.0970	0.1442
	12	0.0000	0.0000	0.0000	0.0000	0.0004	0.0022	0.0083	0.0237	0.0529	0.0961
	13	0.0000	0.0000	0.0000	0.0000	0.0001	0.0005	0.0024	0.0085	0.0233	0.0518
	14	0.0000	0.0000	0.0000	0.0000	0.0000	0.0001	0.0006	0.0024	0.0082	0.0222

n	x	0.05	0.10	0.15	0.20	*p* 0.25	0.30	0.35	0.40	0.45	0.50
19	15	0.0000	0.0000	0.0000	0.0000	0.0000	0.0000	0.0001	0.0005	0.0022	0.0074
	16	0.0000	0.0000	0.0000	0.0000	0.0000	0.0000	0.0000	0.0001	0.0005	0.0018
	17	0.0000	0.0000	0.0000	0.0000	0.0000	0.0000	0.0000	0.0000	0.0001	0.0003
	18	0.0000	0.0000	0.0000	0.0000	0.0000	0.0000	0.0000	0.0000	0.0000	0.0000
	19	0.0000	0.0000	0.0000	0.0000	0.0000	0.0000	0.0000	0.0000	0.0000	0.0000
20	0	0.3585	0.1216	0.0388	0.0115	0.0032	0.0008	0.0002	0.0000	0.0000	0.0000
	1	0.3774	0.2702	0.1368	0.0576	0.0211	0.0068	0.0020	0.0005	0.0001	0.0000
	2	0.1887	0.2852	0.2293	0.1369	0.0669	0.0278	0.0100	0.0031	0.0008	0.0002
	3	0.0596	0.1901	0.2428	0.2054	0.1339	0.0716	0.0323	0.0123	0.0040	0.0011
	4	0.0133	0.0898	0.1821	0.2182	0.1897	0.1304	0.0738	0.0350	0.0139	0.0046
	5	0.0022	0.0319	0.1028	0.1746	0.2023	0.1789	0.1272	0.0746	0.0365	0.0148
	6	0.0003	0.0089	0.0454	0.1091	0.1686	0.1916	0.1712	0.1244	0.0746	0.0370
	7	0.0000	0.0020	0.0160	0.0545	0.1124	0.1643	0.1844	0.1659	0.1221	0.0739
	8	0.0000	0.0004	0.0046	0.0222	0.0609	0.1144	0.1614	0.1797	0.1623	0.1201
	9	0.0000	0.0001	0.0011	0.0074	0.0271	0.0654	0.1158	0.1597	0.1771	0.1602
	10	0.0000	0.0000	0.0002	0.0020	0.0099	0.0308	0.0686	0.1171	0.1593	0.1762
	11	0.0000	0.0000	0.0000	0.0005	0.0030	0.0120	0.0336	0.0710	0.1185	0.1602
	12	0.0000	0.0000	0.0000	0.0001	0.0008	0.0039	0.0136	0.0355	0.0727	0.1201
	13	0.0000	0.0000	0.0000	0.0000	0.0002	0.0010	0.0045	0.0146	0.0366	0.0739
	14	0.0000	0.0000	0.0000	0.0000	0.0000	0.0002	0.0012	0.0049	0.0150	0.0370
	15	0.0000	0.0000	0.0000	0.0000	0.0000	0.0000	0.0003	0.0013	0.0049	0.0148
	16	0.0000	0.0000	0.0000	0.0000	0.0000	0.0000	0.0000	0.0003	0.0013	0.0046
	17	0.0000	0.0000	0.0000	0.0000	0.0000	0.0000	0.0000	0.0000	0.0002	0.0011
	18	0.0000	0.0000	0.0000	0.0000	0.0000	0.0000	0.0000	0.0000	0.0000	0.0002
	19	0.0000	0.0000	0.0000	0.0000	0.0000	0.0000	0.0000	0.0000	0.0000	0.0000
	20	0.0000	0.0000	0.0000	0.0000	0.0000	0.0000	0.0000	0.0000	0.0000	0.0000

APPENDIX E

Poisson Probabilities

Entries in the table give the probability of x occurrences for a Poisson process with a mean μ. For example, when $\mu = 2.5$, the probability of four occurrences is 0.1336.

					μ					
x	0.1	0.2	0.3	0.4	0.5	0.6	0.7	0.8	0.9	1.0
0	0.9048	0.8187	0.7408	0.6703	0.6065	0.5488	0.4966	0.4493	0.4066	0.3679
1	0.0905	0.1637	0.2222	0.2681	0.3033	0.3293	0.3476	0.3595	0.3659	0.3679
2	0.0045	0.0164	0.0333	0.0536	0.0758	0.0988	0.1217	0.1438	0.1647	0.1839
3	0.0002	0.0011	0.0033	0.0072	0.0126	0.0198	0.0284	0.0383	0.0494	0.0613
4	0.0000	0.0001	0.0002	0.0007	0.0016	0.0030	0.0050	0.0077	0.0111	0.0153
5	0.0000	0.0000	0.0000	0.0001	0.0002	0.0004	0.0007	0.0012	0.0020	0.0031
6	0.0000	0.0000	0.0000	0.0000	0.0000	0.0000	0.0001	0.0002	0.0003	0.0005
7	0.0000	0.0000	0.0000	0.0000	0.0000	0.0000	0.0000	0.0000	0.0000	0.0001

					μ					
x	1.1	1.2	1.3	1.4	1.5	1.6	1.7	1.8	1.9	2.0
0	0.3329	0.3012	0.2725	0.2466	0.2231	0.2019	0.1827	0.1653	0.1496	0.1353
1	0.3662	0.3614	0.3543	0.3452	0.3347	0.3230	0.3106	0.2975	0.2842	0.2707
2	0.2014	0.2169	0.2303	0.2417	0.2510	0.2584	0.2640	0.2678	0.2700	0.2707
3	0.0738	0.0867	0.0998	0.1128	0.1255	0.1378	0.1496	0.1607	0.1710	0.1804
4	0.0203	0.0260	0.0324	0.0395	0.0471	0.0551	0.0636	0.0723	0.0812	0.0902
5	0.0045	0.0062	0.0084	0.0111	0.0141	0.0176	0.0216	0.0260	0.0309	0.0361
6	0.0008	0.0012	0.0018	0.0026	0.0035	0.0047	0.0061	0.0078	0.0098	0.0120
7	0.0001	0.0002	0.0003	0.0005	0.0008	0.0011	0.0015	0.0020	0.0027	0.0034
8	0.0000	0.0000	0.0001	0.0001	0.0001	0.0002	0.0003	0.0005	0.0006	0.0009
9	0.0000	0.0000	0.0000	0.0000	0.0000	0.0000	0.0001	0.0001	0.0001	0.0002

					μ					
x	2.1	2.2	2.3	2.4	2.5	2.6	2.7	2.8	2.9	3.0
0	0.1225	0.1108	0.1003	0.0907	0.0821	0.0743	0.0672	0.0608	0.0550	0.0498
1	0.2572	0.2438	0.2306	0.2177	0.2052	0.1931	0.1815	0.1703	0.1596	0.1494
2	0.2700	0.2681	0.2652	0.2613	0.2565	0.2510	0.2450	0.2384	0.2314	0.2240
3	0.1890	0.1966	0.2033	0.2090	0.2138	0.2176	0.2205	0.2225	0.2237	0.2240
4	0.0992	0.1082	0.1169	0.1254	0.1336	0.1414	0.1488	0.1557	0.1622	0.1680

					μ					
x	2.1	2.2	2.3	2.4	2.5	2.6	2.7	2.8	2.9	3.0
5	0.0417	0.0476	0.0538	0.0602	0.0668	0.0735	0.0804	0.0872	0.0940	0.1008
6	0.0146	0.0174	0.0206	0.0241	0.0278	0.0319	0.0362	0.0407	0.0455	0.0540
7	0.0044	0.0055	0.0068	0.0083	0.0099	0.0118	0.0139	0.0163	0.0188	0.0216
8	0.0011	0.0015	0.0019	0.0025	0.0031	0.0038	0.0047	0.0057	0.0068	0.0081
9	0.0003	0.0004	0.0005	0.0007	0.0009	0.0011	0.0014	0.0018	0.0022	0.0027
10	0.0001	0.0001	0.0001	0.0002	0.0002	0.0003	0.0004	0.0005	0.0006	0.0008
11	0.0000	0.0000	0.0000	0.0000	0.0000	0.0001	0.0001	0.0001	0.0002	0.0002
12	0.0000	0.0000	0.0000	0.0000	0.0000	0.0000	0.0000	0.0000	0.0000	0.0001

					μ					
x	3.1	3.2	3.3	3.4	3.5	3.6	3.7	3.8	3.9	4.0
0	0.0450	0.0408	0.0369	0.0344	0.0302	0.0273	0.0247	0.0224	0.0202	0.0183
1	0.1397	0.1304	0.1217	0.1135	0.1057	0.0984	0.0915	0.0850	0.0789	0.0733
2	0.2165	0.2087	0.2008	0.1929	0.1850	0.1771	0.1692	0.1615	0.1539	0.1465
3	0.2237	0.2226	0.2209	0.2186	0.2158	0.2125	0.2087	0.2046	0.2001	0.1954
4	0.1734	0.1781	0.1823	0.1858	0.1888	0.1912	0.1931	0.1944	0.1951	0.1954
5	0.1075	0.1140	0.1203	0.1264	0.1322	0.1377	0.1429	0.1477	0.1522	0.1563
6	0.0555	0.0608	0.0662	0.0716	0.0771	0.0826	0.0881	0.0936	0.0989	0.1042
7	0.0246	0.0278	0.0312	0.0348	0.0385	0.0425	0.0466	0.0508	0.0551	0.0595
8	0.0095	0.0111	0.0129	0.0148	0.0169	0.0191	0.0215	0.0241	0.0269	0.0298
9	0.0093	0.0040	0.0047	0.0056	0.0066	0.0076	0.0089	0.0102	0.0116	0.0132
10	0.0010	0.0013	0.0016	0.0019	0.0023	0.0028	0.0033	0.0039	0.0045	0.0053
11	0.0003	0.0004	0.0005	0.0006	0.0007	0.0009	0.0011	0.0013	0.0016	0.0019
12	0.0001	0.0001	0.0001	0.0002	0.0002	0.0003	0.0003	0.0004	0.0005	0.0006
13	0.0000	0.0000	0.0000	0.0000	0.0001	0.0001	0.0001	0.0001	0.0002	0.0002
14	0.0000	0.0000	0.0000	0.0000	0.0000	0.0000	0.0000	0.0000	0.0000	0.0001

					μ					
x	4.1	4.2	4.3	4.4	4.5	4.6	4.7	4.8	4.9	5.0
0	0.0166	0.0150	0.0136	0.0123	0.0111	0.0101	0.0091	0.0082	0.0074	0.0067
1	0.0679	0.0630	0.0583	0.0540	0.0500	0.0462	0.0427	0.0395	0.0365	0.0337
2	0.1393	0.1323	0.1254	0.1188	0.1125	0.1063	0.1005	0.0948	0.0894	0.0842
3	0.1904	0.1852	0.1798	0.1743	0.1687	0.1631	0.1574	0.1517	0.1460	0.1404
4	0.1951	0.1944	0.1933	0.1917	0.1898	0.1875	0.1849	0.1820	0.1789	0.1755
5	0.1600	0.1633	0.1662	0.1687	0.1708	0.1725	0.1738	0.1747	0.1753	0.1755
6	0.1093	0.1143	0.1191	0.1237	0.1281	0.1323	0.1362	0.1398	0.1432	0.1462
7	0.0640	0.0686	0.0732	0.0778	0.0824	0.0869	0.0914	0.0959	0.1002	0.1044
8	0.0328	0.0360	0.0393	0.0428	0.0463	0.0500	0.0537	0.0575	0.0614	0.0653
9	0.0150	0.0163	0.0188	0.0209	0.0232	0.0255	0.0280	0.0307	0.0334	0.0363
10	0.0061	0.0071	0.0081	0.0092	0.0104	0.0118	0.0132	0.0147	0.0164	0.0181
11	0.0023	0.0027	0.0032	0.0037	0.0043	0.0049	0.0056	0.0064	0.0073	0.0082
12	0.0008	0.0009	0.0011	0.0014	0.0016	0.0019	0.0022	0.0026	0.0030	0.0034
13	0.0002	0.0003	0.0004	0.0005	0.0006	0.0007	0.0008	0.0009	0.0011	0.0013
14	0.0001	0.0001	0.0001	0.0001	0.0002	0.0002	0.0003	0.0003	0.0004	0.0005
15	0.0000	0.0000	0.0000	0.0000	0.0001	0.0001	0.0001	0.0001	0.0001	0.0002

					μ					
x	5.1	5.2	5.3	5.4	5.5	5.6	5.7	5.8	5.9	6.0
0	0.0061	0.0055	0.0050	0.0045	0.0041	0.0037	0.0033	0.0030	0.0027	0.0025
1	0.0311	0.0287	0.0265	0.0244	0.0225	0.0207	0.0191	0.0176	0.0162	0.0149
2	0.0793	0.0746	0.0701	0.0659	0.0618	0.0580	0.0544	0.0509	0.0477	0.0446
3	0.1348	0.1293	0.1239	0.1185	0.1133	0.1082	0.1033	0.0985	0.0938	0.0892
4	0.1719	0.1681	0.1641	0.1600	0.1558	0.1515	0.1472	0.1428	0.1383	0.1339
5	0.1753	0.1748	0.1740	0.1728	0.1714	0.1697	0.1678	0.1656	0.1632	0.1606
6	0.1490	0.1515	0.1537	0.1555	0.1571	0.1584	0.1594	0.1601	0.1605	0.1606
7	0.1086	0.1125	0.1163	0.1200	0.1234	0.1267	0.1298	0.1326	0.1353	0.1377
8	0.0692	0.0731	0.0771	0.0810	0.0849	0.0887	0.0925	0.0962	0.0998	0.1033
9	0.0392	0.0423	0.0454	0.0486	0.0519	0.0552	0.0586	0.0620	0.0654	0.0688
10	0.0200	0.0220	0.0241	0.0262	0.0285	0.0309	0.0334	0.0359	0.0386	0.0413
11	0.0093	0.0104	0.0116	0.0129	0.0143	0.0157	0.0173	0.0190	0.0207	0.0225
12	0.0039	0.0045	0.0051	0.0058	0.0065	0.0073	0.0082	0.0092	0.0102	0.0113
13	0.0015	0.0018	0.0021	0.0024	0.0028	0.0032	0.0036	0.0041	0.0046	0.0052
14	0.0006	0.0007	0.0008	0.0009	0.0011	0.0013	0.0015	0.0017	0.0019	0.0022
15	0.0002	0.0002	0.0003	0.0003	0.0004	0.0005	0.0006	0.0007	0.0008	0.0009
16	0.0001	0.0001	0.0001	0.0001	0.0001	0.0002	0.0002	0.0002	0.0003	0.0003
17	0.0000	0.0000	0.0000	0.0000	0.0000	0.0001	0.0001	0.0001	0.0001	0.0001

					μ					
x	6.1	6.2	6.3	6.4	6.5	6.6	6.7	6.8	6.9	7.0
0	0.0022	0.0020	0.0018	0.0017	0.0015	0.0014	0.0012	0.0011	0.0010	0.0009
1	0.0137	0.0126	0.0116	0.0106	0.0098	0.0090	0.0082	0.0076	0.0070	0.0064
2	0.0417	0.0390	0.0364	0.0340	0.0318	0.0296	0.0276	0.0258	0.0240	0.0223
3	0.0848	0.0806	0.0765	0.0726	0.0688	0.0652	0.0617	0.0584	0.0552	0.0521
4	0.1294	0.1249	0.1205	0.1162	0.1118	0.1076	0.1034	0.0992	0.0952	0.0912
5	0.1579	0.1549	0.1519	0.1487	0.1454	0.1420	0.1385	0.1349	0.1314	0.1277
6	0.1605	0.1601	0.1595	0.1586	0.1575	0.1562	0.1546	0.1529	0.1511	0.1490
7	0.1399	0.1418	0.1435	0.1450	0.1462	0.1472	0.1480	0.1486	0.1489	0.1490
8	0.1066	0.1099	0.1130	0.1160	0.1188	0.1215	0.1240	0.1263	0.1284	0.1304
9	0.0723	0.0757	0.0791	0.0825	0.0858	0.0891	0.0923	0.0954	0.0985	0.1014
10	0.0441	0.0469	0.0498	0.0528	0.0558	0.0588	0.0618	0.0649	0.0679	0.0710
11	0.0245	0.0265	0.0285	0.0307	0.0330	0.0353	0.0377	0.0401	0.0426	0.0452
12	0.0124	0.0137	0.0150	0.0164	0.0179	0.0194	0.0210	0.0227	0.0245	0.0264
13	0.0058	0.0065	0.0073	0.0081	0.0089	0.0098	0.0108	0.0119	0.0130	0.0142
14	0.0025	0.0029	0.0033	0.0037	0.0041	0.0046	0.0052	0.0058	0.0064	0.0071
15	0.0010	0.0012	0.0014	0.0016	0.0018	0.0020	0.0023	0.0026	0.0029	0.0033
16	0.0004	0.0005	0.0005	0.0006	0.0007	0.0008	0.0010	0.0011	0.0013	0.0014
17	0.0001	0.0002	0.0002	0.0002	0.0003	0.0003	0.0004	0.0004	0.0005	0.0006
18	0.0000	0.0001	0.0001	0.0001	0.0001	0.0001	0.0001	0.0002	0.0002	0.0002
19	0.0000	0.0000	0.0000	0.0000	0.0000	0.0000	0.0000	0.0001	0.0001	0.0001

					μ					
x	7.1	7.2	7.3	7.4	7.5	7.6	7.7	7.8	7.9	8.0
0	0.0008	0.0007	0.0007	0.0006	0.0006	0.0005	0.0005	0.0004	0.0004	0.0003
1	0.0059	0.0054	0.0049	0.0045	0.0041	0.0038	0.0035	0.0032	0.0029	0.0027
2	0.0208	0.0194	0.0180	0.0167	0.0156	0.0145	0.0134	0.0125	0.0116	0.0107
3	0.0492	0.0464	0.0438	0.0413	0.0389	0.0366	0.0345	0.0324	0.0305	0.0286
4	0.0874	0.0836	0.0799	0.0764	0.0729	0.0696	0.0663	0.0632	0.0602	0.0573

					μ					
x	7.1	7.2	7.3	7.4	7.5	7.6	7.7	7.8	7.9	8.0
5	0.1241	0.1204	0.1167	0.1130	0.1094	0.1057	0.1021	0.0986	0.0951	0.0916
6	0.1468	0.1445	0.1420	0.1394	0.1367	0.1339	0.1311	0.1282	0.1252	0.1221
7	0.1489	0.1486	0.1481	0.1474	0.1465	0.1454	0.1442	0.1428	0.1413	0.1396
8	0.1321	0.1337	0.1351	0.1363	0.1373	0.1382	0.1388	0.1392	0.1395	0.1396
9	0.1042	0.1070	0.1096	0.1121	0.1144	0.1167	0.1187	0.1207	0.1224	0.1241
10	0.0740	0.0770	0.0800	0.0829	0.0858	0.0887	0.0914	0.0941	0.0967	0.0993
11	0.0478	0.0504	0.0531	0.0558	0.0585	0.0613	0.0640	0.0667	0.0695	0.0722
12	0.0283	0.0303	0.0323	0.0344	0.0366	0.0388	0.0411	0.0434	0.0457	0.0481
13	0.0154	0.0168	0.0181	0.0196	0.0211	0.0227	0.0243	0.0260	0.0278	0.0296
14	0.0078	0.0086	0.0095	0.0104	0.0113	0.0123	0.0134	0.0145	0.0157	0.0169
15	0.0037	0.0041	0.0046	0.0051	0.0057	0.0062	0.0069	0.0075	0.0083	0.0090
16	0.0016	0.0019	0.0021	0.0024	0.0026	0.0030	0.0033	0.0037	0.0041	0.0045
17	0.0007	0.0008	0.0009	0.0010	0.0012	0.0013	0.0015	0.0017	0.0019	0.0021
18	0.0003	0.0003	0.0004	0.0004	0.0005	0.0006	0.0006	0.0007	0.0008	0.0009
19	0.0001	0.0001	0.0001	0.0002	0.0002	0.0002	0.0003	0.0003	0.0003	0.0004
20	0.0000	0.0000	0.0001	0.0001	0.0001	0.0001	0.0001	0.0001	0.0001	0.0002
21	0.0000	0.0000	0.0000	0.0000	0.0000	0.0000	0.0000	0.0000	0.0001	0.0001

					μ					
x	8.1	8.2	8.3	8.4	8.5	8.6	8.7	8.8	8.9	9.0
0	0.0003	0.0003	0.0002	0.0002	0.0002	0.0002	0.0002	0.0002	0.0001	0.0001
1	0.0025	0.0023	0.0021	0.0019	0.0017	0.0016	0.0014	0.0013	0.0012	0.0011
2	0.0100	0.0092	0.0086	0.0079	0.0074	0.0068	0.0063	0.0058	0.0054	0.0050
3	0.0269	0.0252	0.0237	0.0222	0.0208	0.0195	0.0183	0.0171	0.1060	0.0150
4	0.0544	0.0517	0.0491	0.0466	0.0443	0.0420	0.0398	0.0377	0.0357	0.0337
5	0.0882	0.0849	0.0816	0.0784	0.0752	0.0722	0.0692	0.0663	0.0635	0.0607
6	0.1191	0.1160	0.1128	0.1097	0.1066	0.1034	0.1003	0.0972	0.0941	0.0911
7	0.1378	0.1358	0.1338	0.1317	0.1294	0.1271	0.1247	0.1222	0.1197	0.1171
8	0.1395	0.1392	0.1388	0.1382	0.1375	0.1366	0.1356	0.1344	0.1332	0.1318
9	0.1256	0.1269	0.1280	0.1290	0.1299	0.1306	0.1311	0.1315	0.1317	0.1318
10	0.1017	0.1040	0.1063	0.1084	0.1104	0.1123	0.1140	0.1157	0.1172	0.1186
11	0.0749	0.0776	0.0802	0.0828	0.0853	0.0878	0.0902	0.0925	0.0948	0.0970
12	0.0505	0.0530	0.0555	0.0579	0.0604	0.0629	0.0654	0.0679	0.0703	0.0728
13	0.0315	0.0334	0.0354	0.0374	0.0395	0.0416	0.0438	0.0459	0.0481	0.0504
14	0.0182	0.0196	0.0210	0.0225	0.0240	0.0256	0.0272	0.0289	0.0306	0.0324
15	0.0098	0.0107	0.0116	0.0126	0.0136	0.0147	0.0158	0.0169	0.0182	0.0194
16	0.0050	0.0055	0.0060	0.0066	0.0072	0.0079	0.0086	0.0093	0.0101	0.0109
17	0.0024	0.0026	0.0029	0.0033	0.0036	0.0040	0.0044	0.0048	0.0053	0.0058
18	0.0011	0.0012	0.0014	0.0015	0.0017	0.0019	0.0021	0.0024	0.0026	0.0029
19	0.0005	0.0005	0.0006	0.0007	0.0008	0.0009	0.0010	0.0011	0.0012	0.0014
20	0.0002	0.0002	0.0002	0.0003	0.0003	0.0004	0.0004	0.0005	0.0005	0.0006
21	0.0001	0.0001	0.0001	0.0001	0.0001	0.0002	0.0002	0.0002	0.0002	0.0003
22	0.0000	0.0000	0.0000	0.0000	0.0001	0.0001	0.0001	0.0001	0.0001	0.0001

					μ					
x	9.1	9.2	9.3	9.4	9.5	9.6	9.7	9.8	9.9	10
0	0.0001	0.0001	0.0001	0.0001	0.0001	0.0001	0.0001	0.0001	0.0001	0.0000
1	0.0010	0.0009	0.0009	0.0008	0.0007	0.0007	0.0006	0.0005	0.0005	0.0005
2	0.0046	0.0043	0.0040	0.0037	0.0034	0.0031	0.0029	0.0027	0.0025	0.0023
3	0.0140	0.0131	0.0123	0.0115	0.0107	0.0100	0.0093	0.0087	0.0081	0.0076
4	0.0319	0.0302	0.0285	0.0269	0.0254	0.0240	0.0226	0.0213	0.0201	0.0189
5	0.0581	0.0555	0.0530	0.0506	0.0483	0.0460	0.0439	0.0418	0.0398	0.0378
6	0.0881	0.0851	0.0822	0.0793	0.0764	0.0736	0.0709	0.0682	0.0656	0.0631
7	0.1145	0.1118	0.1091	0.1064	0.1037	0.1010	0.0982	0.0955	0.0928	0.0901
8	0.1302	0.1286	0.1269	0.1251	0.1232	0.1212	0.1191	0.1170	0.1148	0.1126
9	0.1317	0.1315	0.1311	0.1306	0.1300	0.1293	0.1284	0.1274	0.1263	0.1251
10	0.1198	0.1210	0.1219	0.1228	0.1235	0.1241	0.1245	0.1249	0.1250	0.1251
11	0.0991	0.1012	0.1031	0.1049	0.1067	0.1083	0.1098	0.1112	0.1125	0.1137
12	0.0752	0.0776	0.0799	0.0822	0.0844	0.0866	0.0888	0.0908	0.0928	0.0948
13	0.0526	0.0549	0.0572	0.0594	0.0617	0.0640	0.0662	0.0685	0.0707	0.0729
14	0.0342	0.0361	0.0380	0.0399	0.0419	0.0439	0.0459	0.0479	0.0500	0.0521
15	0.0208	0.0221	0.0235	0.0250	0.0265	0.0281	0.0297	0.0313	0.0330	0.0347
16	0.0118	0.0127	0.0137	0.0147	0.0157	0.0168	0.0180	0.0192	0.0204	0.0217
17	0.0063	0.0069	0.0075	0.0081	0.0088	0.0095	0.0103	0.0111	0.0119	0.0128
18	0.0032	0.0035	0.0039	0.0042	0.0046	0.0051	0.0055	0.0060	0.0065	0.0071
19	0.0015	0.0017	0.0019	0.0021	0.0023	0.0026	0.0028	0.0031	0.0034	0.0037
20	0.0007	0.0008	0.0009	0.0010	0.0011	0.0012	0.0014	0.0015	0.0017	0.0019
21	0.0003	0.0003	0.0004	0.0004	0.0005	0.0006	0.0006	0.0007	0.0008	0.0009
22	0.0001	0.0001	0.0002	0.0002	0.0002	0.0002	0.0003	0.0003	0.0004	0.0004
23	0.0000	0.0001	0.0001	0.0001	0.0001	0.0001	0.0001	0.0001	0.0002	0.0002
24	0.0000	0.0000	0.0000	0.0000	0.0000	0.0000	0.0000	0.0001	0.0001	0.0001

					μ					
x	11	12	13	14	15	16	17	18	19	20
0	0.0000	0.0000	0.0000	0.0000	0.0000	0.0000	0.0000	0.0000	0.0000	0.0000
1	0.0002	0.0001	0.0000	0.0000	0.0000	0.0000	0.0000	0.0000	0.0000	0.0000
2	0.0010	0.0004	0.0002	0.0001	0.0000	0.0000	0.0000	0.0000	0.0000	0.0000
3	0.0037	0.0018	0.0008	0.0004	0.0002	0.0001	0.0000	0.0000	0.0000	0.0000
4	0.0102	0.0053	0.0027	0.0013	0.0006	0.0003	0.0001	0.0001	0.0000	0.0000
5	0.0224	0.0127	0.0070	0.0037	0.0019	0.0010	0.0005	0.0002	0.0001	0.0001
6	0.0411	0.0255	0.0152	0.0087	0.0048	0.0026	0.0014	0.0007	0.0004	0.0002
7	0.0646	0.0437	0.0281	0.0174	0.0104	0.0060	0.0034	0.0018	0.0010	0.0005
8	0.0888	0.0655	0.0457	0.0304	0.0194	0.0120	0.0072	0.0042	0.0024	0.0013
9	0.1085	0.0874	0.0661	0.0473	0.0324	0.0213	0.0135	0.0083	0.0050	0.0029
10	0.1194	0.1048	0.0859	0.0663	0.0486	0.0341	0.0230	0.0150	0.0095	0.0058
11	0.1194	0.1144	0.1015	0.0844	0.0663	0.0496	0.0355	0.0245	0.0164	0.0106
12	0.1094	0.1144	0.1099	0.0984	0.0829	0.0661	0.0504	0.0368	0.0259	0.0176
13	0.0926	0.1056	0.1099	0.1060	0.0956	0.0814	0.0658	0.0509	0.0378	0.0271
14	0.0728	0.0905	0.1021	0.1060	0.1024	0.0930	0.0800	0.0655	0.0514	0.0387

					μ					
x	11	12	13	14	15	16	17	18	19	20
15	0.0534	0.0724	0.0885	0.0989	0.1024	0.0992	0.0906	0.0786	0.0650	0.0516
16	0.0367	0.0543	0.0719	0.0866	0.0960	0.0992	0.0963	0.0884	0.0772	0.0646
17	0.0237	0.0383	0.0550	0.0713	0.0847	0.0934	0.0963	0.0936	0.0863	0.0760
18	0.0145	0.0256	0.0397	0.0554	0.0706	0.0830	0.0909	0.0936	0.0911	0.0844
19	0.0084	0.0161	0.0272	0.0409	0.0557	0.0699	0.0814	0.0887	0.0911	0.0888
20	0.0046	0.0097	0.0177	0.0286	0.0418	0.0559	0.0692	0.0798	0.0866	0.0888
21	0.0024	0.0055	0.0109	0.0191	0.0299	0.0426	0.0560	0.0684	0.0783	0.0846
22	0.0012	0.0030	0.0065	0.0121	0.0204	0.0310	0.0433	0.0560	0.0676	0.0769
23	0.0006	0.0016	0.0037	0.0074	0.0133	0.0216	0.0320	0.0438	0.0559	0.0669
24	0.0003	0.0008	0.0020	0.0043	0.0083	0.0144	0.0226	0.0328	0.0442	0.0557
25	0.0001	0.0004	0.0010	0.0024	0.0050	0.0092	0.0154	0.0237	0.0336	0.0446
26	0.0000	0.0002	0.0005	0.0013	0.0029	0.0057	0.0101	0.0164	0.0246	0.0343
27	0.0000	0.0001	0.0002	0.0007	0.0016	0.0034	0.0063	0.0109	0.0173	0.0254
28	0.0000	0.0000	0.0001	0.0003	0.0009	0.0019	0.0038	0.0070	0.0117	0.0181
29	0.0000	0.0000	0.0001	0.0002	0.0004	0.0011	0.0023	0.0044	0.0077	0.0125
30	0.0000	0.0000	0.0000	0.0001	0.0002	0.0006	0.0013	0.0026	0.0049	0.0083
31	0.0000	0.0000	0.0000	0.0000	0.0001	0.0003	0.0007	0.0015	0.0030	0.0054
32	0.0000	0.0000	0.0000	0.0000	0.0001	0.0001	0.0004	0.0009	0.0018	0.0034
33	0.0000	0.0000	0.0000	0.0000	0.0000	0.0001	0.0002	0.0005	0.0010	0.0020
34	0.0000	0.0000	0.0000	0.0000	0.0000	0.0000	0.0001	0.0002	0.0006	0.0012
35	0.0000	0.0000	0.0000	0.0000	0.0000	0.0000	0.0000	0.0001	0.0003	0.0007
36	0.0000	0.0000	0.0000	0.0000	0.0000	0.0000	0.0000	0.0001	0.0002	0.0004
37	0.0000	0.0000	0.0000	0.0000	0.0000	0.0000	0.0000	0.0000	0.0001	0.0002
38	0.0000	0.0000	0.0000	0.0000	0.0000	0.0000	0.0000	0.0000	0.0000	0.0001
39	0.0000	0.0000	0.0000	0.0000	0.0000	0.0000	0.0000	0.0000	0.0000	0.0001

Values of e^{-iN}

To find $e^{-1.5}$, choose $N = 15$ and $i = .10$.

N	.01	.02	.03	.04	.05	.06	.07	.08	.09	.10	.11	.12
1	0.990	0.980	0.970	0.961	0.951	0.942	0.932	0.923	0.914	0.905	0.896	0.887
2	0.980	0.961	0.942	0.923	0.905	0.887	0.869	0.852	0.835	0.819	0.803	0.787
3	0.970	0.942	0.914	0.887	0.861	0.835	0.811	0.787	0.763	0.741	0.719	0.698
4	0.961	0.923	0.887	0.852	0.819	0.787	0.756	0.726	0.698	0.670	0.644	0.619
5	0.951	0.905	0.861	0.819	0.779	0.741	0.705	0.670	0.638	0.607	0.577	0.549
6	0.942	0.887	0.835	0.787	0.741	0.698	0.657	0.619	0.583	0.549	0.517	0.487
7	0.932	0.869	0.811	0.756	0.705	0.657	0.613	0.571	0.533	0.497	0.463	0.432
8	0.923	0.852	0.787	0.726	0.670	0.619	0.571	0.527	0.487	0.449	0.415	0.383
9	0.914	0.835	0.763	0.698	0.638	0.583	0.533	0.487	0.445	0.407	0.372	0.340
10	0.905	0.819	0.741	0.670	0.607	0.549	0.497	0.449	0.407	0.368	0.333	0.301
11	0.896	0.803	0.719	0.644	0.577	0.517	0.463	0.415	0.372	0.333	0.298	0.267
12	0.887	0.787	0.698	0.619	0.549	0.487	0.432	0.383	0.340	0.301	0.267	0.237
13	0.878	0.771	0.677	0.595	0.522	0.458	0.403	0.353	0.310	0.273	0.239	0.210
14	0.869	0.756	0.657	0.571	0.497	0.432	0.375	0.326	0.284	0.247	0.214	0.186
15	0.861	0.741	0.638	0.549	0.472	0.407	0.350	0.301	0.259	0.223	0.192	0.165
16	0.852	0.726	0.619	0.527	0.449	0.383	0.326	0.278	0.237	0.202	0.172	0.147
17	0.844	0.712	0.600	0.507	0.427	0.361	0.304	0.257	0.217	0.183	0.154	0.130
18	0.835	0.698	0.583	0.487	0.407	0.340	0.284	0.237	0.198	0.165	0.138	0.115
19	0.827	0.684	0.566	0.468	0.387	0.320	0.264	0.219	0.181	0.150	0.124	0.102
20	0.819	0.670	0.549	0.449	0.368	0.301	0.247	0.202	0.165	0.135	0.111	0.091
21	0.811	0.657	0.533	0.432	0.350	0.284	0.230	0.186	0.151	0.122	0.099	0.080
22	0.803	0.644	0.517	0.415	0.333	0.267	0.214	0.172	0.138	0.111	0.089	0.071
23	0.795	0.631	0.502	0.399	0.317	0.252	0.200	0.159	0.126	0.100	0.080	0.063
24	0.787	0.619	0.487	0.383	0.301	0.237	0.186	0.147	0.115	0.091	0.071	0.056
25	0.779	0.607	0.472	0.368	0.287	0.223	0.174	0.135	0.105	0.082	0.064	0.050
26	0.771	0.595	0.458	0.353	0.273	0.210	0.162	0.125	0.096	0.074	0.057	0.044
27	0.763	0.583	0.445	0.340	0.259	0.198	0.151	0.115	0.088	0.067	0.051	0.039
28	0.756	0.571	0.432	0.326	0.247	0.186	0.141	0.106	0.080	0.061	0.046	0.035
29	0.748	0.560	0.419	0.313	0.235	0.176	0.131	0.098	0.074	0.055	0.041	0.031
30	0.741	0.549	0.407	0.301	0.223	0.165	0.122	0.091	0.067	0.050	0.037	0.027

N	.13	.14	.15	.16	.17	.18	.19	.20	.21	.22	.23	.24
1	0.878	0.869	0.861	0.852	0.844	0.835	0.827	0.819	0.811	0.803	0.795	0.787
2	0.771	0.756	0.741	0.726	0.712	0.698	0.684	0.670	0.657	0.644	0.631	0.619
3	0.677	0.657	0.638	0.619	0.600	0.583	0.566	0.549	0.533	0.517	0.502	0.487
4	0.595	0.571	0.549	0.527	0.507	0.487	0.468	0.499	0.432	0.415	0.399	0.383
5	0.522	0.497	0.472	0.449	0.427	0.407	0.387	0.368	0.350	0.333	0.317	0.301
6	0.458	0.432	0.407	0.383	0.361	0.340	0.320	0.301	0.284	0.267	0.252	0.237
7	0.403	0.375	0.350	0.326	0.304	0.284	0.264	0.247	0.230	0.214	0.200	0.186
8	0.353	0.326	0.301	0.278	0.257	0.237	0.219	0.202	0.186	0.172	0.159	0.147
9	0.310	0.284	0.259	0.237	0.217	0.198	0.181	0.165	0.151	0.138	0.126	0.115
10	0.273	0.247	0.223	0.202	0.183	0.165	0.150	0.135	0.122	0.111	0.100	0.091
11	0.239	0.214	0.192	0.172	0.154	0.138	0.124	0.111	0.099	0.089	0.080	0.071
12	0.210	0.186	0.165	0.147	0.130	0.115	0.102	0.091	0.080	0.071	0.063	0.056
13	0.185	0.162	0.142	0.125	0.110	0.096	0.085	0.074	0.065	0.057	0.050	0.044
14	0.162	0.141	0.122	0.106	0.093	0.080	0.070	0.061	0.053	0.046	0.040	0.035
15	0.142	0.122	0.105	0.091	0.078	0.067	0.058	0.050	0.043	0.037	0.032	0.027
16	0.125	0.106	0.091	0.077	0.066	0.056	0.048	0.041	0.035	0.030	0.025	0.021
17	0.110	0.093	0.078	0.066	0.056	0.047	0.040	0.033	0.028	0.024	0.020	0.017
18	0.096	0.080	0.067	0.056	0.047	0.039	0.033	0.027	0.023	0.019	0.016	0.013
19	0.085	0.070	0.058	0.048	0.040	0.033	0.027	0.022	0.018	0.015	0.013	0.010
20	0.074	0.061	0.050	0.041	0.033	0.027	0.022	0.018	0.015	0.012	0.010	0.008
21	0.065	0.053	0.043	0.035	0.028	0.023	0.018	0.015	0.012	0.010	0.008	0.006
22	0.057	0.046	0.037	0.030	0.024	0.019	0.015	0.012	0.010	0.008	0.006	0.005
23	0.050	0.040	0.032	0.025	0.020	0.016	0.013	0.010	0.008	0.006	0.005	0.004
24	0.044	0.035	0.027	0.021	0.017	0.013	0.010	0.008	0.006	0.005	0.004	0.003
25	0.039	0.030	0.024	0.018	0.014	0.011	0.009	0.007	0.005	0.004	0.003	0.002
26	0.034	0.026	0.020	0.016	0.012	0.009	0.007	0.006	0.004	0.003	0.003	0.002
27	0.030	0.023	0.017	0.013	0.010	0.008	0.006	0.005	0.003	0.003	0.002	0.002
28	0.026	0.020	0.015	0.011	0.009	0.006	0.005	0.004	0.003	0.002	0.002	0.001
29	0.023	0.017	0.013	0.010	0.007	0.005	0.004	0.003	0.002	0.002	0.001	0.001
30	0.020	0.015	0.011	0.008	0.006	0.005	0.003	0.002	0.002	0.001	0.001	0.001

APPENDIX G

Chi-Square Distribution

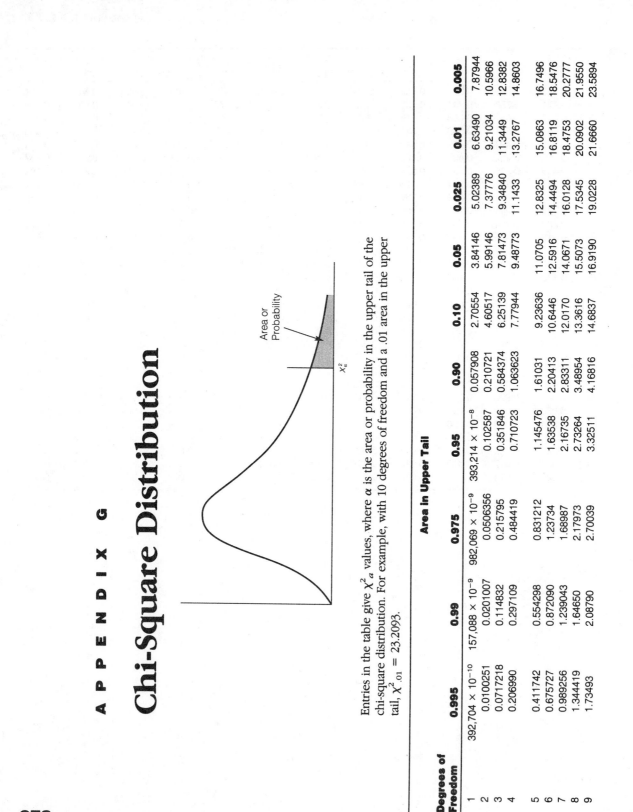

Area or Probability

χ_α^2

Entries in the table give χ_α^2 values, where α is the area or probability in the upper tail of the chi-square distribution. For example, with 10 degrees of freedom and a .01 area in the upper tail, $\chi_{.01}^2 = 23.2093$.

	Area in Upper Tail										
Degrees of Freedom	0.995	0.99	0.975	0.95	0.90	0.10	0.05	0.025	0.01	0.005
1	$392{,}704 \times 10^{-10}$	$157{,}088 \times 10^{-9}$	$982{,}069 \times 10^{-9}$	$393{,}214 \times 10^{-8}$	0.057908	2.70554	3.84146	5.02389	6.63490	7.87944
2	0.0100251	0.0201007	0.0506356	0.102587	0.210721	4.60517	5.99146	7.37776	9.21034	10.5966
3	0.0717218	0.114832	0.215795	0.351846	0.584374	6.25139	7.81473	9.34840	11.3449	12.8382
4	0.206990	0.297109	0.484419	0.710723	1.063623	7.77944	9.48773	11.1433	13.2767	14.8603
5	0.411742	0.554298	0.831212	1.145476	1.61031	9.23636	11.0705	12.8325	15.0863	16.7496
6	0.675727	0.872090	1.23734	1.63538	2.20413	10.6446	12.5916	14.4494	16.8119	18.5476
7	0.989256	1.239043	1.68987	2.16735	2.83311	12.0170	14.0671	16.0128	18.4753	20.2777
8	1.344419	1.64650	2.17973	2.73264	3.48954	13.3616	15.5073	17.5345	20.0902	21.9550
9	1.73493	2.08790	2.70039	3.32511	4.16816	14.6837	16.9190	19.0228	21.6660	23.5894

Area in Upper Tail

Degrees of Freedom	0.995	0.99	0.975	0.95	0.90	0.10	0.05	0.025	0.01	0.005
10	2.15586	2.55821	3.24697	3.94030	4.86518	15.9872	18.3070	20.4832	23.2093	25.1882
11	2.60322	3.05348	3.81575	4.57481	5.57778	17.2750	19.6751	21.9200	24.7250	26.7568
12	3.07382	3.57057	4.40379	5.22603	6.30380	18.5493	21.0261	23.3367	26.2170	28.2995
13	3.56503	4.10692	5.00875	5.89186	7.04150	19.8119	22.3620	24.7356	27.6882	29.8195
14	4.07467	4.66043	5.62873	6.57063	7.78953	21.0641	23.6848	26.1189	29.1412	31.3194
15	4.60092	5.22935	6.26214	7.26094	8.54676	22.3071	24.9958	27.4884	30.5779	32.8013
16	5.14221	5.81221	6.90766	7.96165	9.31224	23.5418	26.2962	28.8454	31.9999	34.2672
17	5.69722	6.40776	7.56419	8.67176	10.0852	24.7690	27.5871	30.1910	33.4087	35.7185
18	6.26480	7.01491	8.23075	9.39046	10.8649	25.9894	28.8693	31.5264	34.8053	37.1565
19	6.84397	7.63273	8.90652	10.1170	11.6509	27.2036	30.1435	32.8523	36.1909	38.5823
20	7.43384	8.26040	9.59078	10.8508	12.4426	28.4120	31.4104	34.1696	37.5662	39.9968
21	8.03365	8.89720	10.28293	11.5913	13.2396	29.6151	32.6706	35.4789	38.9322	41.4011
22	8.64272	9.54249	10.9823	12.3380	14.0415	30.8133	33.9244	36.7807	40.2894	42.7957
23	9.26043	10.19567	11.6886	13.0905	14.8479	32.0069	35.1725	38.0756	41.6384	44.1813
24	9.88623	10.8564	12.4012	13.8484	15.6587	33.1962	36.4150	39.3641	42.9798	45.5585
25	10.5197	11.5240	13.1197	14.6114	16.4734	34.3816	37.6525	40.6465	44.3141	46.9279
26	11.1602	12.1981	13.8439	15.3792	17.2919	35.5632	38.8851	41.9232	45.6417	48.2899
27	11.8076	12.8785	14.5734	16.1514	18.1138	36.7412	40.1133	43.1945	46.9629	49.6449
28	12.4613	13.5647	15.3079	16.9279	18.9392	37.9159	41.3371	44.4608	48.2782	50.9934
29	13.1211	14.2565	16.0471	17.7084	19.7677	39.0875	42.5570	45.7223	49.5879	52.3356
30	13.7867	14.9535	16.7908	18.4927	20.5992	40.2560	43.7730	46.9792	50.8922	53.6720
40	20.7065	22.1643	24.4330	26.5093	29.0505	51.8051	55.7585	59.3417	63.6907	66.7660
50	27.9907	29.7067	32.3574	34.7643	37.6886	63.1671	67.5048	71.4202	76.1539	79.4900
60	35.5345	37.4849	40.4817	43.1880	46.4589	74.3970	79.0819	83.2977	88.3794	91.9517
70	43.2752	45.4417	48.7576	51.7393	55.3290	85.5270	90.5312	95.0232	100.425	104.215
80	51.1719	53.5401	57.1532	60.3915	64.2778	96.5782	101.879	106.629	112.329	116.321
90	59.1963	61.7541	65.6466	69.1260	73.2912	107.565	113.145	118.136	124.116	128.299
100	67.3276	70.0649	74.2219	77.9295	82.3581	118.498	124.342	129.561	135.807	140.169

Reprinted by permission of Biometrika Trustees from Table 8, Percentage Points of the χ^2 Distribution, by E. S. Pearson and H. O. Hartley, *Biometrika Tables for Statisticians*, Vol. I, 3rd Edition, 1966.

Solutions to Even-Numbered Problems

Chapter 3

2. The Taguchi Loss Function is: $L(x) = k(x - T)^2$
The calculated $k = 37,037$. $\therefore$ for $(x - T) = 0.0045$, $L(x) = 37,037(0.0045)^2$
$= \$0.75$

4. For a specification of $2.000 \pm .002$ mm:

a. $k = 1,000,000$

b. $EL(x) = k(\sigma^2 + D^2) = \$1.082$

6. The composite index for quality costs shows that total quality cost has been stable at \$.07/total sales \$. Internal failure rates have been reduced substantially, from \$168.20 in the first quarter to \$66.40 in the fourth quarter. External failure rates have shown improvement in the fourth quarter, dropping from \$42.80 in the third quarter to \$28.60 in the fourth. Increases in prevention and appraisal expenditures have apparently led to improvements in failure costs. The overall index has fallen slightly. Management should maintain or increase the level of prevention and appraisal in an effort to reduce quality costs, especially failure costs.

8. The largest costs are internal failure (56.6%) and appraisal (27.1%). It appears that more can and must be done in the area of quality training, a component of prevention (currently 7.8%), if failure, appraisal, and overall quality costs are to be brought under control. External failure costs only represent 8.6% of quality costs, so it appears that screening methods are working fairly well. Note that the above proportions are fractions of the total quality costs of \$247,450.

10. (This problem requires the use of concepts of calculus.)

$I = [p - C(q) - m] D(q)$

Therefore: $dI/dq = [p - C(q) - m]D'(q) - D(q)C'(q) = 0$

For the firm to remain in business, $p - C(q) - m$ must be greater than 0. Given this, at the point where $dI/dq = 0$, we must have $C'(q) > 0$, in order for a solution to exist. This point may be called q^*. The value of q, called q_0 that minimizes $c(q)$ must satisfy $C'(q_0) = 0$. Therefore, $q_0 < q^*$.

Chapter 8

2. For $C_1 = \$0.25$ and $C_2 = \$500.00$

$p = \dfrac{C_1}{C_2} = \dfrac{0.25}{500} = 0.0005 \ or \ 0.5$ errors/1000 transactions

Chapter 12

2. a. Instructions on setup are in the chapter.

  b. $\bar{x} = 22.86$; $s = 4.6887$ using 8 groups, $i = 3$, with group 1 as $12 - 14.99$, group 2 as $15 - 17.99$, etc.

  Answers may vary, depending on how the groups are formed.

  c. From the Quality Management Analyst (QMA) software:

  $\bar{x} = 22.748$; $s = 4.6985$; $Md = 22.5$

4. For $p = 0.20$, $n = 6$, $x = 4$; $f(x = 4) = 0.01536$

6. For $p \doteq 0.10$, $n = 5$, we have:

Number of successes	Probability	Cumulative probability
0	0.5905	0.5905
1	0.3280	0.9185
2	0.0729	0.9914
3	0.0081	0.9995
4	0.0005	1.0000
5	Negligible	1.0000

8. Use the Poisson distribution because of the large N.

  a. $f(0) = 0.1353$; Therefore, $f(>0) = 0.8647$ that all have received the book.

  b. $f(2) = 0.2707$

  c. $f(5 \text{ or fewer}) = 0.9834$

10. Use the Poisson approximation to the binomial, with $p = 0.025$, $\mu = np = 2.5$.

  $P(1 \le x \le 4) = 0.8091$

12. $P(3 < x) = 0.8413$; $P(2 < x < 3.25) = 0.3072$

14. If mean time between failures (MTBF), $\mu = 1400$ hours, $P(x < 700 \text{ hrs.}) = 1 - 0.3935 = 0.6065$

16. For $\mu = 3$, $\sigma = 3$

  a. If $n = 9$, then $\sigma_{\bar{x}} = 0.133$; if $n = 25$, then $\sigma_{\bar{x}} = 0.08$

  b. $z_9 = 7.5$, so $P(z_9 \ge 7.5) = 0$
  $z_{25} = 12.5$, so $P(z_{25} \ge 12.5) = 0$

18. $H_0 : \mu < 2.5$ With $\alpha = .05$; $\mu = 2.5$; $\sigma = 0.6$; $\bar{x} = 2.75$
  $H_1 : \mu > 2.5$

  Test statistic $z = 2.5$ must be compared to $z_\alpha = 1.645$

  Since $z > z_\alpha$, the null hypothesis, $H_0 : \mu < 2.5$ is rejected.

20. The data from the drying oven example in Table 12.1 can be ploted on normal probability plotting paper to show a mean of 49 (versus 48.91 in the text) and a standard deviation of 7.0 (versus 6.52 in the text). The normality hypothesis must be *rejected* if the probability of a Type I (α) error is set at 0.05. The test shows a $\chi^2 = 5.70$, and $P(\chi^2 > 5.70) = 0.06$.

22. $r = 0.890113$; $r^2 = 0.792302$

Chapter 13

2. a. Variables   **d.** Variables

   b. Attributes   **e.** Attributes

   c. Attributes

4. $\bar{x}_1 = 0.9907$; $\bar{R}_1 = 0.028$
$\bar{x}_2 = 0.9967$; $\bar{R}_2 = 0.038$

$\bar{x}_D = 0.0060$; $\bar{\bar{R}} = 0.033$

$D_4 = 2.574$; $UCL_R = 0.0849$, all ranges below

$K_1 = 3.05$; $K_2 = 3.65$

$OV = 0.0119$; $RR = 0.1014$; $EV = 0.10065$

Equipment variation $= 83.9\%$, Operator variation $= 9.92\%$
R & R variation $= 84.5\%$
Concentrate on reducing equipment variation

6. z -1.88; $\mu = 21.316$

8. $\bar{x} = 38.649$; s $= 0.443$

10. $c_p = 1.36$; not satisfactory
New $\sigma = 0.3$ for $c_p = 2.0$

12. $\bar{x} = 0.5750$; $\sigma = 0.0065$
$c_p = 0.359$; not satisfactory

14. a. Data set 1: $\bar{x} = 1.7446$; s $= 0.0163$; 3s $= 0.0489$
Data set 2: $\bar{x} = 1.9999$; s $= 0.0078$; 3s $= 0.0234$
Data set 3: $\bar{x} = 1.2485$; s $= 0.0052$; 3s $= 0.0156$

   b. $\bar{x}_T = 4.9930$; $\sigma_{Process} = 0.0187$
Process limits: $4.9930 \pm 3(0.0187)$ *or*
4.9369 to 5.0491 vs. specification limits of
4.919 to 5.081 for a confidence level of 0.9973.

16. $\bar{x} = 24.0014$; s $= 0.0097$
$c_p = 1.031$; within limits
$c_{pl} = 1.079$; within limits
$c_{pu} = 0.993$; out of limits

18. $\bar{x} = 50.25$; $\sigma = 1.5$

a. $c_p = 0.889$
$c_{pl} = 0.889$
$c_{pu} = 0.889$

Conclusion: the process does not have adequate capability.

b. $c_p = 0.889$
$c_{pl} = 0.944$
$c_{pu} = 0.833$

Conclusion: the process *still* does not have adequate capability.

c. $\sigma_{new} = 1.35$
$c_p = 0.988$
$c_{pl} = 0.741$
$c_{pu} = 0.988$

Conclusion: the process *still* does not have adequate capability, although the c_p and c_{pu} are very close to minimum acceptable level.

20. $\bar{x} = 0.2085$; $s = 0.0039$; $\bar{\bar{x}} \pm 3s = 0.1968$ to 0.2202

22. $c_p = 0.439$
$c_{pl} = 0.561$
$c_{pu} = 0.302$

The Min $(c_{pu}, c_{pl}) = 0.302$

Conclusion: the process does not have adequate capability.

Chapter 14

Only one problem appears in Chapter 14.

Chapter 15

2. From $0 - 50$, slope $= 0.6$
From $50 - 100$, slope $= 1.2$
From $0 - 100$, slope $= 0.9$

4. $\lambda = \dfrac{2}{1760}$

6. $\lambda = 0.001$; $P(x < 800) = 0.55$

8. For $\theta = \dfrac{1760}{2} = 880$ hours; For $\theta = \dfrac{1624}{3} = 541.3$ hours

10. $\lambda = \dfrac{1}{1000}$

12. For no preventive maintenance, MTBF $= 34$ hours. Expect 61.2 failures/yr.

Cost $= \$1,836$, therefore, do no maintenance.

14. $R_{cc} = 0.99$
System $R = 0.9125$

16. a. 0.315

  b. 0.717

18. a. 0.90

  b. 0.99 for parallel systems

Chapter 16

2. For $\bar{\bar{x}} = 480; \bar{R} = 34$

  $UCL_{\bar{x}} = 496.422; LCL_{\bar{x}} = 463.578$
  $UCL_R = 68.136; LCL_R = 0$

  Estimated $\sigma = 13.418$

4. $\bar{\bar{x}} = 95.398; \bar{R} = 0.665$
  $UCL_{\bar{x}} = 95.882; LCL_{\bar{x}} = 94.913$
  $UCL_R = 1.518; LCL_R = 0$

6. $\bar{\bar{x}} = -1.0349; \bar{R} = 3.0337$
  $UCL_{\bar{x}} = 0.7155; LCL_{\bar{x}} = -2.7854$
  $UCL_R = 6.4132; LCL_R = 0$

  Conclusion: the process appears to be out of control, with points "hugging" the center line.

8. a. Two points outside upper control limit.

  b. Process is in control

  c. Mean shift upward in second half of control chart.

  d. Points hugging upper and lower control limits.

10. $\bar{\bar{x}} = 0.0756; \bar{R} = 0.0046$
  $UCL_{\bar{x}} = 0.0783; LCL_{\bar{x}} = 0.0729$
  $UCL_R = 0.0097; LCL_R = 0$

  Estimated $\sigma = 0.0020$

  Limits on individual values $= \bar{\bar{x}} \pm 3\,\sigma_{est} = .0816$ to $.0696$

12. $\bar{\bar{x}} = 46.175; \bar{R} = 5.45$
  $UCL_{\bar{x}} = 49.320; LCL_{\bar{x}} = 43.030$
  $UCL_R = 11.521; LCL_R = 0$
  Estimated $\sigma = 2.343$

  Limits on individual values $= \bar{\bar{x}} \pm 3\,\sigma_{est} = 39.15$ to 53.20

  % below LSL = 1.74%
  % above USL = 1.97%
  Total % outside = 3.71%

14. With data from problem 5 and USL = 500, LSL = 300:

  a. $c_p = 1.772$
    $c_{pl} = 1.778$

$c_{pu} = 1.767$
$c_{pk} = 1.767$

% outside = 0% indicating that the process is well within specification limits.

b. $URL_X = 476.813$
$LRL_X = 323.187$

16. Initially, $\bar{p} = 0.13$, $s_p = 0.0453$

Revised $\bar{p} = 0.1247$ (after sample 12 was removed), $s_p = 0.0234$

$UCL_p = 0.1948$
$LCL_p = 0.0546$

18. Initially, $\bar{p} = 0.2888$, $s_p = 0.0453$

Throw out all 39 and over, revise, throw out all over 30, revise again.

Revised $\bar{p} = 0.1856$, $s_p = 0.0389$

$UCL_p = 0.0689$
$LCL_p = 0.3023$

Chapter 17

2. The data obtained from Chapter 16, Table 16.1, and the s-chart from Chapter 17 show the following:
$\bar{R} = 0.1680$; $UCL_R = 0.3551$; $LCL_R = 0$
$\bar{s} = 0.0717$; $UCL_s = 0.1497$; $LCL_s = 0$

The patterns of an R-chart would be similar, but the s-chart shows tighter limits.

4. The data from Chapter 16, problem 6 on the $\bar{x}$–s chart shows: $\bar{s} = 1.2409$; $UCL_s = 2.437$; $LCL_s = 0$

6. Using data from Chapter 16, problem 10, as individual measures, with 5 sample moving ranges, the $\bar{x} - R$ chart shows:
$\bar{R} = 0.0049$; $UCL_R = 0.0010$; $LCL_R = 0$
$\bar{\bar{x}} = 0.0756$; $UCL_{\bar{x}} = 0.0819$; $LCL_{\bar{x}} = 0.0693$

All points appear to be in control.

8. Using data from Chapter 16, problem 5 the median chart shows:
$\tilde{\tilde{x}} = 400$; $\tilde{R} = 26$
$UCL_{\tilde{x}} = 432.89$; $LCL_{\tilde{x}} = 367.11$
$UCL_R = 71.37$; $LCL_R = 0$

Point 23 on the $\tilde{x} -$ chart is out of control.
Point 16 on the R $-$ chart is out of control.
These findings are identical to those of problem 16–5.

10. For the np chart control limits: $28.88 \pm 3\sqrt{28.88(0.712)} = 28.88 \pm 13.60 = 15.28$ to 42.48

After identifying and correcting the assignable causes, outside the range ± 13.60, the revised range is:

$$20.67 \pm 3\sqrt{20.67(0.793)} = 20.67 \pm 12.15 = 8.52 \text{ to } 32.82$$

12. For the c-chart: number defective = 176, number of samples = 10
$\bar{c} = 176/10 = 17.6$
$\bar{c} \pm 3\sqrt{\bar{c}} = 17.6 \pm 3\sqrt{17.6} = 17.6 \pm 12.59 = 5.01 \text{ to } 30.19$

14. For the u-chart conditions: 4 total samples, with a total of 9 defective items
$\bar{u} = 9/4 = 2.25$
$\bar{u} \pm 3\sqrt{\bar{u}/n} = 2.25 \pm 3\sqrt{2.25/4} = 2.25 \pm 2.25 = 0 \text{ to } 4.50$

16. Using data from Chapter 16, problem 5, the zone control chart shows:

Zone

D	> 431.958 [UCL]	
C	421.402 − 431.958	
B	410.846 − 421.402	
A	389.734 − 410.846	(Center line = 400.290)
B	379.178 − 389.734	
C	368.621 − 379.174	
D	< 368.621 [LCL]	

All points are in control.

18. For z = ± 2.75, P(z > 2.75) = P(z < −2.75)
Percent outside = 2(0.003) = 0.006 *or* 0.6%

20. This problem is an exercise for advanced, computer-literate students.

Chapter 18

2. Referring to the control chart, Figure 16.9 and the calculation on Figure 16.20, for a 99% confidence level, and a sampling error of 5, we get:
$n = (z_{\alpha/2})^2 \, \sigma^2/E^2 = (2.57)^2 (16.302)^2/5^2 = 70.21$, use 71

Based on $\sigma = \bar{R}/d_2 = 27.6/1.693 = 16.302$

4. Using Table 18.1, for a population of 2,000 the sample size required for a critical 1% rate, with a 99% confidence level is *approximately:* 400 (use 98.9% confidence, critical rate of 1%).

6. a. For n = 50, c = 4, fraction non-conforming of 3%:
$$\sum_{x=0}^{4} f(x) = 0.9832$$

b. For n = 50, c = 4, fraction non-conforming of 7%:
$$\sum_{x=0}^{4} f(x) = 0.7290$$

8. Two typical examples of this "family" of curves would be where:

a. For n = 15, c = 2, fraction non-conforming, p = 0.05:

$$\sum_{x=0}^{2} f(x) = 0.964$$

p	P_a
0.05	0.9638
0.10	0.8159
0.15	0.6042
0.20	0.3980
0.25	0.2361

b. For n = 15, c = 3, p = 0.05:

$$\sum_{x=0}^{3} f(x) = 0.9945$$

p	P_a
0.05	0.9945
0.10	0.9444
0.15	0.8227
0.20	0.6482
0.25	0.4613

10. Producer's risk = 1 − 0.603 = 0.397
Consumer's risk = 0.213

12. For AOQ conditions of: n = 50, c = 4, p = 0.04 (Poisson approximation):
AOQ = $P_a p$

p	P_a	$P_a p$	
0.01	0.999	0.0100	
0.02	0.997	0.0198	
0.03	0.983	0.0295	
0.04	0.951	0.0380	AOQ
0.05	0.896	0.0448	
0.06	0.821	0.0493	
0.07	0.729	0.0510	AOQL
0.08	0.629	0.0503	

14. For ATI conditions of: n = 50, c = 4, N = 5000:
ATI = n + (1 − $P_a p$)(N − n)

p	(1 − P_a)	P_a	ATI
0.01	0.001	0.999	55
0.02	0.003	0.997	65
0.03	0.017	0.983	135
0.04	0.049	0.951	293
0.05	0.104	0.896	565
0.06	0.179	0.821	936

16. For points on the OC curve:

p	P_a
0.01	0.998
0.03	0.937
0.05	0.760
0.07	0.533

18. Data from the tables show:

Reduced inspection, code G, AC = 3, Re = 4, n = 32
Tightened inspection, code K, AC = 7, Re = 8, n = 125

20. From the tables:

N = 5000, code L, Ac = 7, AQL = 1.5%, n = 200

Index